Applied Social Psychology

Edited by

Stanley W. Sadava
Donald R. McCreary
Brock University

Prentice Hall, Upper Saddle River, New Jersey 07458

Library of Congress Cataloging-in-Publication Data

Sadava, Stanley W.
    Applied social psychology / Stanley W. Sadava, Donald R. McCreary.
        p.   cm.
    Includes bibliographical references (p.   ) and indexes.
    ISBN 0-13-533175-7
    1. Social psychology.   I. McCreary, Donald R.   II. Title.
HM251.S197   1997
302—dc20   96-32439
                           CIP

Editorial Director: Peter Janzow
Acquisition Editor: Heidi Freund
Editorial Assistant: Emsal Hasan
Director of Production and Manufacturing: Barbara Kittle
Managing Editor: Bonnie Biller/Fran Russello
Project Manager: Linda Pawelchak
Manufacturing Manager: Nick Sklitsis
Prepress and Manufacturing Buyer: Tricia Kenney
Cover Director: Jayne Conte
Cover Design: Kiwi Design
Electronic Art Creation: Asterisk Group
Proofreading: Maine Proofreading Services

This book was set in 10/12 Times Ten by Americomp
and was printed and bound by RR Donnelley & Sons Company.
The cover was printed by The Lehigh Press, Inc.

Printed in the United States of America
10 9 8 7 6 5 4 3 2 1

ISBN 0-13-533175-7

Prentice-Hall International (UK) Limited, *London*
Prentice-Hall of Australia Pty. Limited, *Sydney*
Prentice-Hall Canada Inc., *Toronto*
Prentice-Hall Hispanoamericana, S. A., *Mexico*
Prentice-Hall of India Private Limited, *New Delhi*
Prentice-Hall of Japan, Inc., *Tokyo*
Simon & Schuster Asia Pte. Ltd , *Singapore*
Editora Prentice-Hall do Brasil, Ltda., *Rio de Janeiro*

SWS: To honor the memory of my parents
and grandparents

DRM: To my mother, for teaching me to value
excellence; to my father, for teaching me
patience and honesty; and to my grandmother,
for teaching me the importance
of independence and responsibility

Contents

3 The Contribution of Surveys to Applied Social Psychology   28

Michael King

4 Program Evaluation   47

S. Mark Pancer

8 Social Psychology and the Forensic Interview 136
Stephen Moston

9 Social Psychology in the Courtroom 157
Jeffrey E. Pfeifer

Preface

We have been teaching basic courses in social psychology for many years. Over this period of time, it became obvious to us that many of our students were interested in the more practical side of social psychology; they wanted an in-depth understanding of the ways in which it has been applied in the real world. Their appetite had been whetted by coverage of some areas of application in *basic* textbooks (usually health, law, the environment, and, often, business and politics). It was their interest that compelled us to put together this textbook because, when we looked at the field, we saw an anomaly. On the one hand, applied social psychology has burgeoned over the past decade; it has an excellent journal, with others in more specialized areas, and there are increasing numbers of social psychologists working in nonacademic settings or doing contract research on applied projects. On the other hand, there was only one textbook in print, and that one had become dated and its methodology was too esoteric for students who may have had only a few psychology courses. It became apparent to us that if we were to have the textbook we needed, we would have to do it ourselves.

Instead of writing the entire textbook, however, we chose to invite applied social psychologists who were expert in their fields to write the chapter they wanted to see written. The advantages of using invited chapters in this field are compelling. Applied social psychology has become increasingly specialized, necessitating knowledge of both social psychology and the applied field itself. To apply social psychology to business, health, or the law, you must have a sophisticated understanding of business, health, or the law, as well as social psychological theories and methods of conducting research. We also wanted to have these chapters written by social psychologists who are out there, doing social psychology in these applied areas. We wanted to capture the firsthand excitement and satisfaction—as well as the frustrations—of applying social psychology, and only those actually engaged in doing this work can convey these feelings. Students are taken into actual work settings to see how a social psychologist conducts a survey for a client, evaluates a social program, improves the communication skills of medical students, consults for the courts, designs a marketing campaign or a program to reduce pollution, and resolves conflicts in an organization. After reading these chapters, we hope that students can begin to understand why there is nothing so practical as a good theory!

Of course, an edited book will never have the consistency in style that a single-authored or collaborative book will have. Our authors, however, have been conscious of this problem and have been most cooperative in implementing our editorial guidelines. We believe that the book is consistent and engaging and hope that both instructors and students will enjoy reading and using it.

When anyone plans to write a textbook, he or she must first decide what to include—and what to omit. It would be impossible to be comprehensive or encyclopaedic in this textbook—and it would be undesirable. We believe it is better to sacrifice some breadth for some depth if students are to understand what is involved in applying social psychology. To this end, we surveyed several applied journals, as well as many of our colleagues. What we found was that there was a small core of social psychological topics most people considered to be applied. As a result, we chose to include chapters in the core areas we identified and then we added chapters from some of the emerging areas of contemporary interest (e.g., aging, conflict resolution, the media). Of course, space limitations compelled us to omit some worthy and relevant topics, such as education, sports, primary prevention of AIDS and other illnesses, politics, and the design of the built environment. Perhaps these could be included in *Applied Social Psychology: The Sequel.*

We wanted this book to be accessible to students with a broad range of interests and ambitions. We assume that the student will have some background in psychology, although he or she may not necessarily be completing a major in the field. This permits us to develop our topics in some depth and sophistication.

The first chapter introduces the field and provides some historical background that shows that social psychology has always had one foot in the lab and the other outside in real life. The next three chapters introduce the student to the methods that are the stock-in-trade of the applied social psychologist, such as designing research, conducting surveys, and evaluating social programs. In preparing these chapters, we are not assuming that the student has any course background in research methods. We then turn to a topical approach of the areas of applied social psychology. Most chapters include an opening vignette and case materials that will bring the relevant research and major issues to life.

We would like to express our appreciation to many colleagues and friends who have encouraged us in this project. In particular, we want to express our appreciation to those colleagues who readily accepted our invitation to contribute to this volume. Your willingness to accept our constraints and our deadlines, and your enthusiasm for your particular area of specialization, as well as for the book as a whole, took us through some dark moments. We also want to express our great appreciation to Stuart Oskamp for his concluding chapter, which gives us all some perspective on where we are going.

We thank Karen Clark, who assisted us with the indices with her usual skill and good humor, Rosa Ferraro for her help in tracking down references, and John Lavery for his comments on Chapter 5. We are also grateful to the following reviewers: Joseph G. Marrone, Siena College; John W. Reich, Arizona State University; and Wesley Schultz, St. Lawrence University. Our families and friends encouraged us, tolerated us, and humored us, as appropriate.

We are excited about this book because we believe that social psychology has much to offer our society in terms of solutions to many of its social problems. We hope students will find that this excitement and realistic optimism are contagious. Let us know what you think!

Stanley W. Sadava
Donald R. McCreary
Department of Psychology
Brock University
St. Catharines, Ontario
CANADA L2S 3A1

1 Applied Social Psychology: An Introduction

Stanley W. Sadava
Brock University

> I often wish that this phrase "applied science" had never been invented. For it suggests that there is a sort of scientific knowledge of direct practical use, which can be studied apart from another sort of scientific knowledge, which is of no practical utility and which is termed "pure science." But there is no more complete fallacy than this.
>
> Thomas Huxley (*Science and Culture*)

Why should science be considered important? When most people are asked this question, they respond that it can be applied to solve problems or provide new inventions. Indeed, science has given us the means to diagnose and cure diseases, travel beyond the bounds of our planet, communicate instantaneously and effortlessly across the world, and purchase an astonishing array of consumer products. In this era of constrained public finances and cutbacks, public support for continued funding of science rests on expectations of its "technological fruits" (Kidd & Saks, 1980).

Within all disciplines, a distinction is drawn between *pure and applied science.* Pure science seeks understanding for its own sake (science as an end in itself) in the context of academic freedom, sheer curiosity, and the "free market" of ideas. Applied science seeks to utilize the ideas and discoveries of research for some explicit, concrete, real-life purpose. Thus, the pure scientist may study the structure and interaction of proteins in the cell, and the applied scientist may use this knowledge to search for the causes and cures of cancer. It is implied that the value of pure science lies entirely in demonstrable applications.

However, as Huxley observes in the quotation cited, the distinction between pure and applied science may be more apparent than real. History shows many examples of ways in which theoretical, curiosity-driven research can eventually yield unanticipated real-world benefits. For example, "pure" research on the neurophysiology of the brain is having significant impact on the diagnosis and treatment of mental illnesses. Einstein's early, highly theoretical work on the nature of light led eventually to the invention of lasers. On the other hand, research driven by practical considerations may yield more basic understanding. For example, research on AIDS has provided great advances in our understanding of the immune system. It may well be possible and desirable to blur the distinction that research dedicated to knowledge and driven by curiosity also belongs to the application side, and that knowledge can be presumed to be useful at some point, if not immediately.

Certainly, social psychology is characterized by a blurring of boundaries between the basic and applied. Basic textbooks in social psychology invariably treat topics that pertain to the real world: prejudice, close relationships, violence, and leadership, along with others that have obvious real-world application, such as attitude change applied to advertising, game theory to conflict, or social modeling to the effects of television violence (e.g., Alcock, Carment, & Sadava, 1994; Aronson, Wilson, & Akert, 1994; Sabini, 1992). Indeed, to many social psychologists, this very blurring of boundaries between pure and applied is one of the discipline's most compelling and attractive features.

Given this consideration, applied social psychology is defined by Oskamp (1984) as follows: "applications of social psychological methods, theories, principles or research findings to understanding or solution of social problems" (p. 12). The reader will note that the field is defined both in terms of its contribution to an understanding of problems and to their solution, a theme that is discussed more fully later. Note also that social problems are being defined in their broadest sense. For example, one may apply the principles of persuasion to sell cigarettes (a marketing problem) or to prevent adolescents from smoking (a health problem). The findings regarding courtroom testimony may be applied to improve courtroom procedures or simply to develop legal strategies in a high-profile case.

We must remember that applying social psychology does not necessarily mean improving our quality of life (Kipnis, 1994). Indeed, any applied science may be used for good or ill. Salvadorean social psychologist Martín-Baro (1990), who was subsequently murdered by government-sponsored death squads, warned against a facile scientific neutrality that "quickly becomes a form of collaboration with the established powers, masking the conflict of interest that comes into play" (p. 104). Science has consequences, and scientists cannot avoid responsibility for the consequences of their work. If our goal is to promote human welfare, applied science cannot be divorced from social values.

HISTORICAL BACKGROUND

From its early development, social psychology has always been a hybrid, at once theory/research-based and problem-driven. In particular, the profound influence of *Kurt Lewin,* the "practical theorist" (Marrow, 1969), resonates to the present time. Much of his influence in his own time was said to be due to his charismatic personality. Consider that he actually convinced people of the intellectually daring proposition that one could use the methods of science to attack complex social problems. For example, in the decade of the 1930s, many people in democratic nations were attracted to the fascist form of government, as practiced in the dictatorships of Hitler, Mussolini, and Franco. Many Europeans of that era overlooked the ethical shortcomings inherent in the fascist regimes. These governments were decisive and efficient, and they could make the trains run on time. In contrast, democracy seemed ineffectual. Lewin and his students sought to challenge their assumptions about democracy. They brought the problem of leadership style into the laboratory in the famous boys clubs experiments with autocratic, democratic, and laissez-faire leadership. These experiments showed, in a preliminary way, that autocratic leadership depended on the immediate power exerted by the leader, that aggressive behavior within the group was often precipitated by autocratic leadership, and that democratic leadership can indeed be efficient (Lippitt & White, 1943).

During World War II, a time of severe food shortages, nutritionists in the United States tried to convince people to use organ meats, such as beef hearts and kidneys. Despite the fact that these meats were readily available at lower prices, and that they were accepted in other cultures, these efforts were unsuccessful. Lewin (1958) reasoned that attitudes toward what is acceptable food are acquired and maintained in a social context, and so trying to change them purely by attempts at individual persuasion would fail. His solution was to organize small discussion groups of homemakers, both to introduce a new social norm with regard to organ meats and to have the homemakers engage in mutual self-help (the forerunners of many such self-help groups). Those who had participated in group discussions in which they could see that others were willing to try the new meats were much more likely to serve these meats at home than were those who simply heard a persuasive talk (and would tell their friends and relatives about it).

In another project, Lewin's students (Coch & French, 1948) tackled the problem of how to get workers to accept changes in production methods without loss in productivity or morale. In a pajama factory owned by the family of one of his students, Lewin's group arranged to have these changes explained clearly to the workers and, further, to have them participate in how the changes were to be implemented. The results were greater productivity and higher morale than was usually the case when such changes occurred in factories. It is interesting that Lewin visited Japan during the decade before World War II, where his ideas on worker participation and industrial productivity apparently had more of an impact than in his native (Germany) or adopted (United States) homelands.

Action Research

Lewin (1946) called his approach *action research,* in which the acquisition of knowledge was seen as inseparable from the application of such knowledge to social change. He specified that social research should lead to social action and thus proposed a model that includes both science and social action (Aguinis, 1993). Action research was seen as a cyclical process of planning, action, and evaluation, with continuous feedback of the results of research to all parties involved. At the same time, social action, and the research that evaluated this action, would feed back to modify theory; the society and life itself would become an extension of the laboratory. In short, action research was to be used concurrently to solve a problem and to generate new knowledge (Bargal, Gold, & Lewin, 1992). For example, Lewin was especially intrigued with majority-minority group relations, particularly in democratic and pluralistic societies. Based on work that he and others had done involving group processes, Lewin devised and conducted intergroup workshops, in which members of two conflicting groups would come to know each other and, perhaps, to accept the other group. The early work with this format showed that difficulties arose as a result of the different interpersonal styles of communication used in the two groups, as well as from the disadvantaged situation of the minority group, which tended to be related to the "notorious lack of confidence and self-esteem of most minority groups" (Lewin, 1946, p. 214). From these investigations came the important insight that intergroup conflict would be reduced, not only by changing the prejudiced attitudes of the majority or advantaged group, but also by increasing the self-esteem and group solidarity of the minority group. This insight had an important impact on later civil rights and feminist movements.

Lewin was a founding member of the Society for the Psychological Study of Social Issues, an organization made up primarily of social psychologists that "seeks to bring theory and practice into focus on human problems of the group, the community and the nation, as well as the increasingly important ones that have no national boundaries" (statement of purpose of the *Journal of Social Issues*). This group has continued the tradition of action research in many cases.

Post-Lewin Action and Reaction

The activist vision of social psychology was not sustained in the decades following Lewin's death in 1947 (Kidd & Saks, 1980). Growing aspirations of social psychology for scientific respectability meant abandoning large-scale, often uncontrolled field research in favor of the small-scale, tightly controlled, elegant laboratory experiment with compelling internal validity (albeit limited external validity). Indeed, a series of small-scale experimental studies, each built on the preceding ones, became the dominant research paradigm. Impressive methodological progress was accomplished in research on social perception, conformity, dissonance, cooperation, aggression, altruism, and interpersonal attraction. It was a time for development and testing of basic theory rather than practicing social psychology in the external world. In the late 1960s, a new Zeitgeist emerged in Western societies, a concern with relevance and social change. This brought with it a new era of reexamining what we were up to in psychology. A sense of crisis generated debate as to whether social psychology, with its tendency to engage in clever laboratory experiments on often abstruse problems, had sacrificed relevance for rigor and was described as "fun and games" in the lab (Elms, 1975; Gergen, 1973; Ring, 1967). Researching fine points in dissonance theory, attributions, or non-zero-sum games seemed divorced from the compelling realities of war and social inequities.

One response by some social psychologists was to venture out of the laboratory, in order to test theories in real-world settings. The *field experiment* responded to a concern with external validity, the extent to which findings could be generalized beyond the experimental situation. Clearly, the dissemination of findings from such studies would be more convincing. In this way, social psychology moved closer to seeking an understanding of pressing social issues, although this did not necessarily include application of such knowledge to advance social change. Indeed, many other researchers *retreated* further into the lab, where they focused on the evolution of more complex methodologies and the development of the more esoteric theories of social cognition and other phenomena.

This schism between social psychologists engaged in a laboratory science and those engaged in field research was a challenge to the viability of social psychology as an enterprise. The crisis in social relevance did not cause us to abandon the lab; indeed, research on social cognition, for example, has been applied productively to understand how individuals who have been victims of rape, incest, or disabling illnesses or accidents make some sense of their situation and come to terms with it (Silver, Boon, & Stones, 1983). However, it also led social psychologists to new areas of research: the law, health, environment, communication media, business, and gerontology.

APPLYING SOCIAL PSYCHOLOGY

Recall that applied social psychology is defined as "applications of social psychological methods, theories, principles or research findings to understanding or solution of social problems" (Oskamp, 1984, p. 12) . In his presidential address to the American Psychological Association, Miller (1969) described two ways in which psychology may have an impact on social change. One of them would be to apply knowledge directly to social problems, such as utilizing our knowledge of persuasion to induce people to conserve energy, or employing our research on perception and memory to change certain courtroom procedures regarding eyewitness testimony. Miller referred to this approach as *psychotechnology*.

Such methodological advances can also be applied to test and evaluate the effects of social change. Indeed, Campbell (1969) advocated a society in which reforms themselves are seen as experiments, always subject to appraisal, evaluation, and alteration. How might an *experimenting society* work? There is a great deal of discussion today about welfare reform, much of it based on assumptions about how welfare affects the motivation to work and ability to plan for the future. In other words, much of the political discussion is based on psychological assumptions. An experimenting society might design and test out alternatives, perhaps based on altering monetary amounts, limiting periods of eligibility, or instituting guaranteed incomes (negative income tax). Such programs can be tested, for example, in terms of how the incentive for work is affected (Rossi & Lyall, 1976).

Miller also pointed out that psychology can influence a society by disseminating our concepts and the results of our research, thus changing our conception of what is humanly possible or desirable. He called on us to "give psychology away," to promote beneficial change by challenging people's general assumptions about human nature itself. For example, one can easily see how research on gender has profoundly altered societal stereotypes and has changed gender roles. Social psychology has informed us that women can be effective leaders and that men can be nurturant parents. Clearly Oskamp's (1984) definition of applied social psychology, by including both understanding and resolution of social problems, reflects Miller's earlier vision.

Miller's (1969) notion of giving psychology away encapsulated the idea that psychological knowledge, as communicated to the masses, can change a culture and a society. More narrowly, social psychological knowledge might be applied to provide us with important insights on an issue or event. For example, Colman (1991) described a case in which eight railway workers were convicted of murdering four strikebreakers during a tense labor-management conflict in South Africa. In such cases at that time in South Africa, the death penalty was mandatory unless "extenuating circumstances" were demonstrated. The testimony of a social psychologist concerning the role of conformity, obedience, and deindividuation in these circumstances was crucial to reducing some of the sentences. Perhaps most significantly, the social psychologist warned the juries of the fundamental attribution error, our tendency to explain the behavior of individuals (including defendants) only in terms of individual differences in personality, motivation, and emotional state, ignoring the power of the situation. Although this testimony had limited impact on the sentencing of defendants, the fact that it was accepted and taken seriously indicates that social psychology can indeed be "given away" with some consequence.

Lewin's ideal is one in which social psychological knowledge is applied to real-life problems. Equally important is Lewin's belief that what we learn from our attempts to ameliorate real-life problems may provide feedback to enhance fundamental theory. For example, we may apply basic knowledge on social cognition to understand the processes and biases in eyewitness testimony (perhaps altering the criteria by which eyewitness accuracy has historically been assessed by the courts), and what we have learned in that context can support or alter theories of social cognition. Deutsch (1969) has argued that his basic laboratory research on cooperation and competition may well have greater social relevance and impact than his earlier applied research on interracial housing.

Others have argued that the term *applied social psychology* is itself divisive to the discipline and that it misrepresents the field itself (Mayo & LaFrance, 1980). These people advocate replacing the two adjectives, *basic* and *applied,* with one, *applicable,* that would describe a social psychology that is, at the same time, concerned with building knowledge, improving the quality of life, and being engaged in real-life intervention toward those ends.

One crucial consideration is how such problems are defined. For example, defining the problem of crime purely in terms of personality or genetic factors will dictate the kind of research (and knowledge) that will follow, all of it focused on individual differences between those who do and do not engage in criminal activity. Conversely, research that looks at situational and social system factors related to crime, such as family, community, and poverty, will lead inexorably to a different knowledge base. Indeed, some have argued that the dominance of social psychology by individuals within the individualistic culture of the United States has led to an understanding of social problems in terms of the malign influence of groups upon the individual (Sampson, 1977). For example, excessive conformity and obedience to authority, as well as the reluctance of bystanders to intervene in emergencies, have been studied in terms of the inability of individuals to resist social pressures or influence. Other, more communitarian cultures may well consider an absence of a sense of community or solidarity with others as the problem of greater concern.

PRACTICAL THEORY

Lewin (1944) said the following:

> Many psychologists working in an applied field are keenly aware of the need for close cooperation between theoretical and applied psychology. This can be accomplished in psychology, as it has in physics, if the theorist does not look towards applied problems with high-brow aversion or with a fear of social problems, and if the applied psychologist realizes that there is nothing so practical as a good theory. (p. 169)

Note that Lewin presents both an eloquent defense of good theory and an argument that theorists be concerned with real-life problems outside the laboratory.

Many examples of practical theories can be cited (Oskamp, 1984). Cognitive dissonance may offer some ways of dealing with organizational problems such as salary inequities, conflicts, and lack of cooperation (Varela, 1971). Indeed, it is interesting to note that Festinger and his colleagues developed this highly influential theory as a result of a participant field study, in which the social psychologists joined a doomsday cult (Festinger, Riecken, & Schachter, 1956). What struck them as particularly fascinating and unexpected was that the group members began to proselytize for their cause only after the prophecy of world destruction failed. Cognitive dissonance theory grew out of this observation. Note that a study of a real-life problem, that of cults, contributed to the development of a theory and a body of laboratory research based on that theory. It should also be noted that Festinger had been a student and colleague of Kurt Lewin.

Other practical theories merit attention. *Attribution theory* may be applied to problems such as classroom behavior, mental and physical health, and spousal abuse (Frieze, Bar-Tal, & Carroll, 1979). Fiedler's (1967) *contingency theory of leadership effectiveness,* in which the style of the leader (task or maintenance) should fit with the circumstances of the group itself, has been applied in numerous settings including business and other organizations, military units, and sports teams. Theory and research on *mixed-motive games* have been applied to labor-management and other conflict situations. All chapters in this book contain examples of practical theories.

APPLIED SOCIAL PSYCHOLOGY TODAY

The social psychologist may adopt many different roles in intervention, such as activist, mediator, planner, organizer, evaluator, advocate, expert witness, or consultant. These different roles imply different definitions of "the problem." Fisher (1982) suggests that the applied social psychologist must have both research and practical skills, whereas others suggest that this combination better describes the field than each participant in it. Certainly Oskamp's (1984) definition of applied social psychology considers both to be equally valid and important. Social psychology today shows the influence of both trends: the development of rigorous, lab-based scientific discipline—particularly reflecting the influence of social cognition—and the extension of social psychology to understand and, perhaps, solve contemporary social problems. The *Journal of Social Issues* and the *Journal of Applied Social Psychology* best represent the range and rigor of contemporary applied social psychol-

TABLE 1-1 Frequency of Articles Published in *Journal of Applied Social Psychology* and *Journal of Social Issues*, January 1980–April 1995

Health	26
Gerontology	26
Mental health	128
Communication	83
Race or racism	58
Gender issues	138
Sexual assault	45
Abortion	15
Family or parenting	20
Attitudes or public opinion	164
Law enforcement	85
Law and the courtroom	81
Marketing, advertising	47
Industrial/organizational	143
Conflict management	67
International relations	62
Environment	91
Methodology	68
Program evaluation	45
Social policy or social change	32

ogy. Table 1–1 shows the primary topics that form the basis of our applied discipline today. It must be noted that many other relevant applied social psychology papers are published in specialty interdisciplinary journals pertaining to health, law, environment, management, gerontology, and so on.

In this textbook, the initial chapters deal primarily with methods. These are the tools of the trade for the applied social psychologist in conducting research, measuring public opinion, and evaluating the effectiveness of social programs. We then turn to a consideration of how social psychology has been applied to a consideration of health-related issues (physical health, aging, and mental health) and to the law (the forensic interview and courtroom situations). Subsequently, we address areas of current interest with regard to social issues. These include consumer behavior, media influences, the environment, conflict, and leadership. The final chapters (a) concern our evolving understanding of gender issues and (b) provide a perspective on where applied social psychology has been and where it is going. In all of these areas, the reader should focus on the ways in which social psychological theory and research have illuminated our understanding of important issues, and how social psychological principles can be applied to solving, or at least ameliorating, social problems.

Social psychology began with almost unbounded optimism regarding the solution of social ills. Science, which gave us jet travel, mass media, modern medicine, and other wonders of modern life, was also going to help us solve problems of war and peace, racism and sexism, and the effects of technology itself. How have we fared? A cursory glance at a newspaper or TV news show indicates that the old problems persist (e.g., war and violence, prejudice and intergroup tension) and new problems—or a new awareness of problems—have arisen (e.g., crises in health care, environment, and economic productivity). Indeed, Sarason (1978) argues that some social problems, such as poverty, violence, and mental illness, are so persistent and intractable as to defy solution. The best that can be hoped for is continued effort and gradual improvement.

Further, as noted earlier, social problems often involve personal values and political ideology, and therefore apparent solutions to social problems may be rejected. For example, even though a more humane rehabilitative approach to imprisonment may be demonstrably superior in reducing recidivism among convicted criminals, such treatment may conflict with a conviction shared by many that the punishment should fit the crime, and therefore the proposal may be rejected.

Perhaps the pioneers in social psychology were rather naive in their optimism. On the other hand, social psychology has made, and continues to make, significant contributions to the improvement of societies and the betterment of the human condition. Although they don't have all the answers, social psychologists can provide us with useful information, important insights, and fresh approaches. The readers of the subsequent chapters in this book are invited to judge for themselves.

2 Research Methods in Applied Social Psychology

Donald R. McCreary

Brock University

Research is a multistep process. Before actually performing a scientifically based study, however, a researcher must first address seven issues (1) identifying the research goals, (2) defining the variables, (3) selecting a research method, (4) identifying the ethical considerations of the study, (5) identifying the practical considerations of the study, (6) analyzing the data, and (7) determining the limitations of the study.

The goal for this chapter is to consider each of these seven points in order. To make this process more meaningful, a specific research study is used to illustrate the processes involved in each issue. This research (Cooper & Mackie, 1986) was designed initially to study the impact that playing aggressive video games can have on the aggressive nature of children's play. Because this study used a specific set of methodologies to achieve their expressed research goal, however, there will be some cases when Cooper and Mackie's work will not be applicable. In these instances, hypothetical extensions of this study will be proposed. The original experiment is described more thoroughly in Box 2–1, and it is strongly recommended that it be read before proceeding to the next section.

One assumption has been made in writing this chapter: that the reader has had some exposure to research methods and statistics. Because most introductory psychology and social psychology texts present an overview of these two topics, little time will be spent defining terms. If the reader feels lost at first, it might help to re-

**Box
2–1**

*Overview of Cooper and Mackie (1986): Video Games
and Aggression in Children*

For years, social scientists have been studying the possible harmful effects that watching violent television can have on children's social development. More recently, however, concern has developed over the violent nature of a related form of children's entertainment: video games. The supposition is that playing with video games that require the player to instigate violent acts as a means of winning may lead that individual to act more violently in his or her day-to-day social interactions. Although television and video games are similar, the main difference between the two is that watching televised aggression is passive while playing with aggressive video games is interactive. With these kinds of video games, aggressive actions (which are under the direct control of the player) have obvious and positive consequences on the outcome of the game. In other words, when playing with violent video games, the player is both the aggressor and the victim, and the ultimate reward comes from being the former more often than the latter.

Cooper and Mackie (1986) sought to determine the effect of playing aggressive video games on the level of aggressivity in children's free play. Based on the literature addressing the relationship between viewing televised aggression and acting aggressively afterward, Cooper and Mackie designed an experiment to test the following hypotheses. First, they believed that playing an aggressive video game (e.g., one that requires a lot of shooting at a computer-generated "enemy") would lead to a significantly higher level of postexperimental aggression than would playing an equally active, but less aggressive, video game or a pencil-and-paper (i.e., nonvideo) game. Second, they believed that these effects would be more pronounced for girls because of their relative lack of exposure to this entertainment medium. Their third hypothesis addressed the active versus passive distinction between television and video games. They proposed that playing an aggressive video game would lead to significantly more postexperimental aggression than if someone simply observed another person playing the game.

Their participants were 84 fourth- and fifth-grade children, approximately half male. These children were tested in same-sex pairs. Upon entering the experimental laboratory, they were randomly assigned to be either a player or an observer. Next, they were randomly assigned to play either an aggressive (Missile Command) or nonaggressive (Pac Man) video game, or a control game (maze-solving). After playing with one of these games for 8 minutes, the pairs were separated and asked to play with a group of four toys. Each one of these toys was selected because it was rated by another group of children as either aggressive (a 3-foot-high plastic warrior with spring-released fists for hitting and darts for shooting), active (a basketball set), skill-testing (pinball), or quiet (building blocks). The amount of time the children spent playing with the aggressive toy during the 8-minute session was recorded.

The results showed that, overall, playing with an aggressive video game did have a significant impact on the amount of time the participants spent playing with the aggressive toy (hypothesis 1), and that this effect was stronger for girls than for boys (hypothesis 2). As can be seen in Table 2–1, the average amount of time spent playing with the aggressive toy was highest in the condition in which the children played with the aggressive video game. However, whereas boys spent large amounts of time playing with the aggressive toy irrespective of the game they played, the girls differed greatly in this respect. Girls who played Pac Man or did maze puzzles spent very little time playing with the aggressive toy, whereas girls who played with the Missile Command video game spent almost 6 times longer playing with this toy af-

TABLE 2–1 Amount of Time Spent Playing with an Aggressive Toy as a Function of Video Game Condition (in seconds)

	Missiles	Pac Man	Control
Boys	84.62	78.69	62.33
Girls	79.63	13.75	15.88
Average[a]	82.13	46.22	39.11

[a] This indicates the mean of the boys' and girls' aggressive toy play in each of the three video game conditions.

Source: Adapted from Cooper & Mackie, 1986.

terward. Cooper and Mackie's third hypothesis, that being a player is different from being an observer, was not supported. Thus, it did not seem to matter if someone watched or played with the aggressive or nonaggressive game; watchers and players spent the same amount of time with the aggressive toys afterward.

view the appropriate sections of other textbooks. However, if the reader is comfortable with the material covered here and wants to learn more about research methodology in applied contexts, a series of suggested readings appears at the end of the chapter. Also, many of the chapters in this book will deal with methodological issues specific to their area.

IDENTIFYING RESEARCH GOALS

Research must be well thought out in advance, taking care to consider all possible problems that may arise. One way that problems can be averted is by clearly defining the *research question* (i.e., the goal of the study). A clearly stated purpose tells the researcher exactly what he or she is attempting to do. It also identifies the main variables of interest and the expected relationship between them.

Often, the research purpose is stated as a formal *hypothesis*. For example, Cooper and Mackie (1986) might have started out with a desire to study "the effect of interactive video games on children's aggression." As it is presently written, however, this statement is too vague and does not clearly tell the researcher why or how the study was performed; the research goal needs to be stated much more clearly. An explicitly stated goal might be something like the following: "The purpose of this study is to determine whether playing with interactive video games of an aggressive nature causes an increased level of aggression in children." This version of the research goal tells the investigator (and the reader as well) three key points about the study. First, it identifies the main variables of interest: aggressive video games and aggression in children. Second, it states that the goal of the study is to show the *causal* effect these video games have on children's aggression levels (as opposed to a *correlation* between the two). Third, it states a *direction* for the effect, in that playing with aggressive video games is expected to cause an increase in children's aggression levels.

DEFINING VARIABLES

After the goal is established, a researcher needs to define his or her variables more clearly. For instance, in the example used here, an investigator wants to find out if playing with aggressive video games causes children to become more aggressive. What does it mean to "play with video games" and what does the researcher consider "aggression" to be? Thus, the first step is to provide a *conceptual definition* of one's variables. For example, what is it about aggression that is of interest? Is it anger, frustration, hostility, physical violence, or emotional battering? Each of these concepts is related to aggression so the researcher needs to be clear on which one (or combination) of these he or she is using in the conceptual definition of aggression. Stating how one conceives of the variables is an important step.

Once the researcher has conceptualized the variables, an *operational definition* must be formulated for each. Each variable must be defined in a way that is both observable and measurable, as well as consistently applicable to all participants. For example, having children play with a video game is not an appropriate operational definition. In what way must the children play with it? For how long will each of the children play? For example, Cooper and Mackie (1986) determined that each child should play with his or her assigned game for 8 minutes. Presumably, they believed that this timespan allowed the child to become adequately involved with the game and to master its components.

However, many constructs that applied social psychologists are interested in studying are not directly observable. For example, how does one measure aggression? In these instances, the researcher must find one or more *behavioral indices* or representations of the variable under examination. Several possibilities exist for measuring a child's aggressivity: One can ask participants to rate their own level of aggression (e.g., ask them to rate how aggressive they feel on a 7-point Likert scale), ask parents or teachers to rate the child's aggressivity, or have trained observers watch the child in a structured environment and make a determination based on the participant's own behavior. Each of these ways of measuring aggression is an example of how one can operationally define an abstract construct such as aggression. Cooper and Mackie (1986) chose the third way to measure aggression. They believed that the amount of time a child spent playing with an aggressive toy (to the exclusion of other, nonaggressive toys) was an indication of the amount of aggression the child was experiencing. Thus, Cooper and Mackie had trained observers record the amount of time the children spent playing with each of the four toys in the playroom.

SELECTING A RESEARCH METHOD

Like those studying basic social psychological issues, applied social psychologists have a wide variety of research methods available to them. Because of the diverse contexts and goals in which applied social psychological research is conducted, determining which method (or methods) to use is often the most important point researchers need to address once they have determined the nature of the problem to be studied.

The research designs most commonly used by applied social psychologists fall into three basic groups: experimental, correlational, and quasi-experimental. Each of these is considered to be an example of *quantitative* research. In other words, researchers often use one or more of these methods to attain numerical indices of, for example, differences between groups, relationships between variables, or differences across time. Increasingly, however, a fourth general research method is used. *Qualitative* research tends to be nonnumerical in form and often involves looking at similarities and differences in ideas or comments. These are variables that cannot be reduced easily to numbers. The four research methods will be outlined next.

Experimental Designs

When a researcher wants to infer that one factor causes another to change (either in a specific direction or just as a general change), then he or she will most likely want to employ an experimental methodology. In fact, this is one of the most powerful research tools used for exploring causal relationships. This method cannot prove the existence of a causal relationship. Assuming the procedures described here are followed correctly, however, it does allow one to make a *causal inference.*

Using an experimental design first involves making a distinction between the independent and dependent variables. The *independent variable,* or the grouping factor, is the experimental manipulation. This is the variable that is under the direct control of the experimenter, and it is the variable that is expected to cause the hypothesized outcome. The independent variable (e.g., level of video game violence) can usually be broken down into two or more mutually exclusive groups to which participants are randomly assigned. One or more of these groups represent the *experimental* condition because subjects receive, or are exposed to, the cause the researcher is hoping to link to a particular outcome. To help in determining if the manipulation causes the desired result, those in the experimental group often are compared to a group of people who did not receive, or were not exposed to, this factor. Those in this latter condition are called the *control* group. For instance, in Cooper and Mackie's (1986) study of video games and aggressivity, the independent variable is the aggressive nature of the video game. Here, Cooper and Mackie have randomly assigned children to play with either Missile Command (the experimental group) or a nonviolent game involving marker pens and finding one's way through mazes (the control group). In this way, a comparison can be made of how aggressive participants from the two groups are after playing with the games. If those in the experimental condition are more aggressive than those in the control group after playing with their video games, it can be *inferred* that playing with the aggressive video game causes children to become more aggressive in their play behavior.

There may be other possible explanations for an observed difference between the experimental and control groups, however. In Cooper and Mackie's study, an increased level of aggression in the experimental group may have been a result of playing with video games in general, and not just playing with aggressive ones. In other words, playing with any video game may be exciting (irrespective of how aggressive or violent its content may be), which might be creating a heightened level of arousal in children. This, in turn, may be what is causing the children to act in more aggressive ways. Thus, it becomes necessary to tease out this possible confounding factor. This is often done by using one or more *comparison groups*. As an illustration, remember that Cooper and Mackie believed it was the violent nature of video games that caused aggressive behavior, and not the games' level of excitement. Thus, they wanted to vary the aggressive nature of the video games while controlling for the degree to which the video game was considered to be exciting. To do this, they included a comparison group: one in which the children played with an equally exciting but nonviolent video game.

Once a participant is randomly assigned to an experimental, comparison, or control group and is exposed to whatever manipulation is under investigation, the researcher measures the impact of that manipulation by studying its effect on the *dependent variable*. The dependent variable is that which is expected to change as a function of exposure to the independent variable. In other words, it is the outcome measure. In Cooper and Mackie's study, the dependent variable is the amount of time the child spends playing with the aggressive toy (i.e., one of four possible toys) in a free-play setting after playing with a video or maze game. If the dependent variable is significantly higher in the experimental group than in the comparison and control groups, the inference is that playing with aggressive video games causes children to be more aggressive.

There are several strengths and weaknesses of the experimental method. Its main strength is that it enables us to make causal inferences based on the observed differences. Because subjects are randomly assigned to the various experimental, comparison, and control groups, there should be few systematic differences in the background characteristics of the participants in each group. Thus, random assignment helps to eliminate differences between participants in experimental and control groups as a possible reason for between-group differences. As such, the factor most likely to cause the outcome is the one thing in which the groups differed: the experimental manipulation.

Even if there are differences, however, one cannot be absolutely certain that the effect will still be observable when tested in the "real world," as opposed to the artificial environment created and controlled by the experimenter. In fact, this is the main weakness of the experimental design (as it is performed in the social psychological laboratory): its relative lack of *external validity* or *situational generalizability*. The extent to which behaviors produced in an unfamiliar and overcontrolled lab setting will be reproduced in more natural environments is always in question. For

Cooper and Mackie's study, the question of external validity can be posed in the following way: Will children interact aggressively with others after playing with an aggressive video game in either a familiar arcade setting or their own home (as opposed to rooms at school containing unfamiliar people and toys)? In each of these contexts they have access to the game, but there are situational constraints that may inhibit the display of aggressive behavior, or at least some forms of it.

A third weakness of the experimental design lies in the difficulty of adapting it to field research. The degree of control obtained in the lab often is unattainable in a field setting, which may reduce a researcher's ability to make causal inferences. In the field, however, the key issues surrounding application of an experimental method remain the degree of control the investigator has in (a) defining the independent variable; (b) randomly assigning participants to experimental, comparison, and control groups; and (c) defining when the dependent variable will be assessed. As long as sufficient control is maintained in these three areas, any outcome differences between those in the experimental and control groups should be directly attributable to the presence or absence of the independent variable. In fact, the use of an experimental method in a field setting may increase the external validity of the research and enhance the power of the findings.

Correlational Designs

When a researcher wants to study how the presence (or absence) of one *naturally occurring* variable is related to the presence of another naturally occurring variable, a correlational methodology is used. A correlational approach can also be used when it is either impractical or unethical to use an experimental method. The correlational approach is a passive procedure, compared to the active manipulations of the experimental approach. There are no independent or dependent variables, no experimental or control groups, and assumptions that the presence of one variable causes the other to increase or decrease cannot be made.

Questions of a correlational nature typically ask how strongly two variables are related to one another (i.e., the *magnitude* of the relationship) and whether variable A is related to the presence or the absence of variable B (i.e., the *direction* of the relationship). For example, Cooper and Mackie (1986) found that for both boys and girls, there was a moderately positive correlation between liking the Missile Command video game and how much action was involved in the game. The more action the game contained, the more the boys and girls liked it. However, this was the only relationship shared between the two groups of children. For boys, there was no relationship between (a) how successful they were at the game and how much they liked it, (b) their success and their desire to play the game more, or (c) how violent they rated the game and their wish to play more of the game. Girls, on the other hand, liked the aggressive game more if they were successful at it. The more points they made, the more they wanted to play it. Still, the more violent the girls rated the game, the less they wanted to play it (i.e., a negative correlation).

Typically, correlations are calculated between two variables only, such as between how successful a child is at playing Missile Command and the length of time he or she spends playing with the aggressive toy. However, researchers can use more than two variables when describing this kind of relationship. This is called "controlling" for a third variable and it uses a statistical technique known as a *partial correlation*. This procedure mathematically removes the relationship between the third variable and the first, and between the third variable and the second, leaving the correlation between the first two variables free of any influence from the third. For example, the relationship between success at Missile Command and how long a child spends playing with the aggressive toy may vary depending on a third variable: how much he or she likes Missile Command. To determine whether the relationship between the first two variables is significant irrespective of how much children like or dislike the video game, a partial correlation is calculated controlling for their degree of liking. Thus, a correlational design can employ many variables and is not limited to an understanding only of the relationships between two variables.

The main strength of the correlational design is its practicality. Because there are no experimental manipulations involved, it is much easier to conduct a correlational study. This issue is important when one is doing field research and observing people in their natural environments. The main weakness of this design, however, lies in the area of causal inferences. If a correlation between two variables is significant, and one wants to interpret the relationship in a causal way, then there are five possible causal interpretations: (1) Variable *X* caused variable *Y*; (2) variable *Y* caused variable *X*; (3) a third variable (*Z*) caused the relationship between *X* and *Y*; (4) a reciprocal relationship exists between *X* and *Y* such that *X* may cause *Y*, which, in turn, causes *X*, etc.; and (5) the correlation may just be a fluke, in which case it makes no sense to try and make causal inferences. Each of these causal inferences is just as valid as any other and, because one can never be sure which of the five is the correct one, no inference of causation is usually made.

Quasi-Experimental Designs

In some instances, an applied social psychologist will have some control over an independent variable but not enough to allow for a true experimental manipulation. In other cases, he or she will have control over when a dependent variable is assessed but will not have an experimental and control group to determine its causal effectiveness. In situations such as these, a quasi-experimental approach is necessary.

There are several different kinds of quasi-experimental methods, many more than can be described in the space allotted to this chapter (see Cook & Campbell, 1979, for a more comprehensive review of the quasi-experimental methodologies). The two most relevant approaches for applied social psychology are the *nonequivalent control groups* and *time-series* designs. These are discussed in turn.

Like the experimental approach, the nonequivalent control groups design involves a comparison between two or more groups on the same dependent variable. Unlike the experimental approach, the participants in these groups are not randomly assigned to the experimental, comparison, or control conditions; rather, when they come to the researcher, they are already members of a group. The group a participant belongs to is based on extraneous factors that the psychologist cannot control, and, in most cases, the groups have been formed for some other purpose (e.g., school classes, work groups, sports teams, neighborhoods).

For example, if Cooper and Mackie (1986) had wanted to study the impact of playing aggressive video games using a nonequivalent control groups method, one approach they might have taken would have involved finding children who often played with violent video games (the experimental group) and children who had never played with this type of video game (the control group). They would then have observed the children playing with the four kinds of toys in the same manner as in their experimental approach. What makes this a nonequivalent control groups design is that the children's assignment to experimental or control group was not randomly determined; they were selected on the basis of their previous game-playing behavior.

A second form of quasi-experimental research is the group of methods commonly referred to as time-series designs. The time-series method involves following either the same group of participants (i.e., a *panel* study) or a series of different groups of participants (i.e., a time-lag study) over time. The differences between the two time-series approaches lie in the samples they use. The panel study approach follows one group of participants over time and observes changes in the outcome measure; this is similar to the longitudinal approach used by developmental psychologists but typically involves a greater number of observations. The time-lag approach looks at differences in the same outcome variable, but in separate groups of people measured at different points in time; this is a variation on the cross-sectional approach used by developmental psychologists.

A variation of the panel design can also look at changes in the *correlations* between two variables across time and can be used to help overcome one of the main problems of correlational research: its lack of power when inferring causation. This method is called the *cross-lagged panel technique* (Campbell & Stanley, 1966) and involves correlating variables *A* and *B* at two time periods. Once this is done, variables *A* and *B* at Time 1 are correlated with variables *B* and *A,* respectively, at Time 2. This kind of method helps eliminate the problem of whether variable *A* causes variable *B,* or vice versa, as well as whether a reciprocal relationship exists between the two, because one of these two pairings often will be statistically nonsignificant (see the section on analyzing data for a further discussion of statistical significance). However, the cross-lagged panel technique is only a partial solution to the correlational causality problem because it does not rule out the possibility of a third variable causing the relationship between *A* and *B* or whether the relationship is a random error.

A vivid example of the cross-lagged panel technique comes from the literature on the relationship between watching television violence and acting in aggressive ways. For the most part, research in this area has been correlational in nature; and even though the literature contains many studies showing a direct relationship between the amount of violent television a person watches and his or her level of aggression, the methodology puts limitations on any causal inference made. One way around this problem was devised by Lefkowitz, Eron, Walder, and Huesmann (1972), using a cross-lagged panel method. Lefkowitz et al. examined the correlation between the aggressive content of a group of Grade 3 children's favorite television shows and their aggressiveness in the classroom. This initial study found a significantly positive correlation between the two variables, which suggested that the more violent the child's favorite television shows, the more aggressive the child tends to be. Because this was a correlational study, it could not be stated for certain that watching these violent television shows caused children to act more aggressively. Thus, 10 years after their initial investigation, Lefkowitz et al. (1972) tested the same children again. They found that although the correlation between the amount of violence in their favorite Grade 13 TV shows did not correlate with their Grade 3 levels of aggression (suggesting that aggressive people watch aggressive TV shows), there was a significant positive correlation between the level of aggressivity in their favorite childhood TV shows and how aggressive they acted 10 years later in adolescence (see Table 2–2). This suggests that watching aggressive TV shows at Time 1 can lead a child to become aggressive in later life.

Whereas the previous two examples showed how a time-series design can be used when following the same group of people on a longitudinal basis, a time-series design can also follow different groups of people, looking for changes in group averages over time. All a researcher has to do is gather a random sample of participants according to a clearly defined set of criteria, follow the same sampling procedures at all future testings, and always measure the dependent variable in the same way. If this is done, then any differences in the outcome measure across samples should be attributable to changes in the population over time.

To demonstrate the most popular versions of these time-series designs, variations on Cooper and Mackie's (1986) study will be proposed. In a panel study, the same group of participants is followed over time. Adapting Cooper and Mackie's

TABLE 2–2 **Correlations Between Grade 3 and Grade 13 TV Violence and Aggression Ratings Using a Cross-Lag Panel Technique**[a]

	TV-3	TV-13	AGG-3
TV-13	.05		
AGG-3	.21	.01[b]	
AGG-13	.31[c]	-.05	.38

[a] TV-3 = aggressivity of favorite television shows while in Grade 3; TV-13 = aggressivity of favorite television shows while in Grade 13; AGG-3 = classroom aggression levels in Grade 3; AGG-13 = classroom aggression levels in Grade 13.

[b] Aggression levels at Time 1 are not correlated with the amount of aggression in their favorite TV shows at Time 2.

[c] The amount of aggression in their favorite TV shows at Time 1 is significantly correlated with their aggression levels at Time 2.

Source: Adapted from Lefkowitz et al., 1972.

study to this method might take the form of following a group of boys and girls for one or more years and monitoring their video game usage and their level of aggressive play at frequent intervals. To maximize the effectiveness of any causal inference made from this design, one possibility is to select participants who initially had not had any exposure to video games; this would control for the degree of prior experience with aggressive games. A time-lag approach can examine (e.g., on a yearly basis) changes in the percentages of boys and girls who play with video games, changes in the percentages of those games that are violent, changes in the violence rating children make regarding specific games, and changes in the degree of aggressive play in which children engage after playing these video games.

Of specific interest to applied social psychologists is the *interrupted* time-series design. What this implies is that, at some specific point in a time-series study, an event occurs that has a significant impact on the group (or groups) under investigation; for example, a social calamity (e.g., AIDS) can change people's behavior or a change in managerial practices can lead to changes in worker productivity. These interruptions can be planned (e.g., as in most program evaluation research) or unplanned (e.g., as in many social calamities). In this way, a group's performance on a dependent variable is measured both before and after the occurrence of a significant event, and differences between the preevent and postevent scores are determined. For example, legislation addressing the violent content of video game material aimed at children may be introduced. A researcher may, or may not, be aware of this legislation in advance. If he or she is conducting a panel or a time-lag study at the time the legislation is adopted, then it will be possible to examine the impact of that legislation on children's video game playing and their aggression levels. In other words, they would be in a position to evaluate the effectiveness of the legislation (e.g., Smith et al., 1984; Whitehead, Craig, Langford, MacArthur, Stanton, & Ferrence, 1975).

As with the other research methods discussed here, there are strengths and weaknesses to both the nonequivalent control groups and time-series designs. The main strength of these quasi-experimental methods lies in their increased degree of control, compared to the correlational method. The experimenter's ability to gather two nonequivalent groups together or determine the starting point and spacing between testings in a time-series design represents choices made by the researcher, and these choices represent control. Because of this increased control, causal inferences are more plausible.

On the downside, there are limitations to both. Cook and Campbell (1979) have identified several factors that may impinge on the validity of any significant differences between nonequivalent groups. Because of the lack of random assignment to experimental and control groups, the equivalency between groups that is normally achieved by a random assignment procedure is missing in this method. As a result, groups tend to come to the researcher preformed and have different histories and experiences with the dependent variable (e.g., aggressive play). One group may do better than the other not because it lacks or possesses the independent variable (e.g., playing with violent video games) but because, over time, it may have worked out different strategies to cope with the independent variable. This is the kind of extraneous variable that may have an unknown effect on the dependent variable, thereby limiting the validity of causal inferences.

There are also problems with time-series designs, especially the interrupted time-series methods. Cook and Campbell (1979) describe two of the more frequent issues. First, the interrupting factor may not be implemented rapidly. As a result, it often becomes unclear exactly when the treatment factor actually began to have an effect on the participants. For example, legislation concerning violent video games for children may take 2 or 3 years to formulate and pass. In that time, there may be a lot of media attention as the industry tries to regulate itself before the government steps in to control the problem. Because of this media exposure, children's behavior may be affected by the legislation even before it is passed. Even after it is passed, it may not be known when children are first affected by it because they already own many violent games with which they play on a regular basis.

The second point made by Cook and Campbell (1979) is that the treatment's implementation may proceed at differing rates in differing populations and that this may affect how people react to it. If this is the case, then to what extent is information about a treatment's effect in one group comparable to other groups if *how* that treatment is initiated varies from group to group? Thus, if legislation dealing with violent video games proceeds at one speed in one country and another speed in a second country, will it have the same effect on the relationship between video game playing and children's aggressive behaviors?

Qualitative Methods

Qualitative research methods were first developed in the 1920s and 1930s by those in sociology and anthropology as a way of addressing the influences that customs and cultures have on individual and group behavior (Denzin & Lincoln, 1994b). Since then, this heterogenous group of methodologies has been adopted by many other disciplines, including psychology, education, and the allied health fields. Whereas quantitative methods provide ways to show the *degree* to which groups differ or variables are related, qualitative research stresses

> the socially constructed nature of reality, the intimate relationship between the researcher and what is studied, and the situational constraints that shape inquiry. Such [research emphasizes] the value-laden nature of inquiry. [It seeks] answers to questions that stress how social experience is created and given meaning. In contrast, quantitative studies emphasize the measurement and analysis of causal relationships between variables, not processes. (Denzin & Lincoln, 1994b, p. 4)

Unlike the three main quantitative procedures described earlier, there are no major groupings of qualitative methods. In the recent *Handbook of Qualitative Methods* (Denzin & Lincoln, 1994a), 24 different chapters testify to the diverse nature of this set of methods. Two of these are discussed briefly here: case studies and participant observation.

Case studies are in-depth analyses of individual experiences. Depending on one's research goal, Stake (1994) notes that case studies can fall into three different categories. The *intrinsic* case study is designed to study a particular individual (e.g., a historical figure). The findings from these kinds of case studies are not meant to be generalized to other people, nor are they planned to test specific theories. *Instrumental* case studies, however, are used to examine the influence of specific treatments or effects and to test theories. The individual is examined in depth, and he or she is thought to be representative of others undergoing the treatment or exposure to a specific independent variable. As such, the findings from an instrumental case study are thought to be generalizable to the public. The third type of case study described by Stake (1994) is the *collective* approach. This method is an extension of the instrumental case study to include more than one person in a treatment or control condition. In this way, redundancy and variety across participants are highlighted, giving the researcher a richer set of data upon which to draw generalizable speculations and conclusions.

Instrumental and collective case studies are more commonly used by applied social psychologists than are intrinsic case studies. For example, if Cooper and Mackie had chosen the case study approach, they might have interviewed a small group of children who were known to be violent, as well as another group of children who were known to be nonviolent. They then might have asked these children questions about their use of video games in general, and violent video games in particular, as well as how these games make them feel, how they know they have had enough of a game, and how they feel their behavior has changed as a result of playing with these games, and so on.

A second form of qualitative research commonly used in applied social psychology is *participant observation*. Using this method involves becoming an active observer. The observer makes no attempt to hide behind one-way mirrors or to use other forms of video monitoring; he or she joins the group under observation. Burgess (1984) and Atkinson and Hammersley (1994) describe four different forms of participant observation, each varying in the degree to which the observer makes his or her research intentions known and becomes involved with the group. In the *complete participant* version of this method, the observer participates in the group's activities but remains distant and watches others covertly, not divulging his or her research agenda or the fact that the participants are being monitored. In the *participant-as-observer* role, the observer develops relationships with group members, using them as informers in attempts to understand the reasons for the group's behavior. There is no attempt to hide the research goal and the observer does not conceal the fact that research is the primary purpose. The latter two forms of participant observation are not used very often. The *observer-as-participant* role involves a brief, open contact with participants whereas the *complete observer* role involves passive observation (e.g., video monitoring). The people being studied are unaware that they are being observed; the research goal is not discussed with them.

Applying participant observation methods to studying the effect of playing violent video games on children's aggressive behavior can use any of these four methods. For example, in the complete participant role, researchers could take over supervisory roles in a video arcade, which would enable them to observe boys' and girls' behavior as the children play selected games. The participant-as-observer role would require a different tactic. These researchers might simply be observers in the arcade. They would not have to masquerade as employees, and they could openly discuss the research goal with those playing the games.

The main strength of the qualitative approaches described here is the novel approach to the gathering of information that would not be gathered in a quantitative study. These kinds of data can have as important an impact on the understanding of social problems and the implementation of changes to address them as quantitative research has. However, qualitative research tends to be frowned upon by many quantitative researchers because of its uncontrolled and nonnumerical format.

Avoiding Monomethod Bias

In many instances, both basic and applied scientists tend to find a good method for testing a theory or examining an effect and then use only that method. In these cases, and after repeated use, it becomes unclear whether the observed findings are a result of the independent variable (e.g., exposure to violent video games) or the method used to study its effect. This is called monomethod bias (Campbell & Fiske, 1959). To avoid monomethod bias, it is always advisable to develop a research program that (a) combines quantitative and qualitative research or (b) uses more than one quantitative method or more than one qualitative method. The goal is not just to use correlative methods or a case history approach, but to combine methods in order to achieve a richer set of data and a more enhanced understanding of a social problem.

ETHICAL CONSIDERATIONS

All universities, major psychology associations, granting agencies, and scientific journals have adopted ethical guidelines for the treatment of human participants (e.g., American Psychological Association, 1992; British Psychological Society, 1995; Canadian Psychological Association, 1986). This is done to ensure that participants are treated fairly and in as humane a manner as possible. These guidelines must be met before the research is conducted (i.e., they must be built into the design of the study). They describe issues pertaining to the need for participants to be informed about the nature of the study in which they are participating, the extent to which they can be deceived about the study, and the maintenance of participant anonymity. In some cases, however, participants are not informed about the exact nature of a study or they are put into stressful situations. In these instances, the cost to the participant is always compared to the scientific benefit of the findings. Groups of professionals will weigh the cost/benefit balance and, before giving their approval for the study to proceed, must be assured that the participants are at no risk.

PRACTICAL CONSIDERATIONS

Once all the ethical considerations have been dealt with, the researcher needs to determine the practicality of the project he or she has designed to that point. The main considerations usually involve access to appropriate participants and the testing procedures they will undergo. Whether children or adults are being slated for participation, the experimenter needs to know about several factors. They must determine how the participants will be recruited, whether there are permissions other than the participants' own that need to be secured (e.g., parental approval is necessary when children are participating), whether participants will be paid for their time and effort, and where the testing or observation will take place.

DATA ANALYSIS

A complete discussion of statistical methods is beyond the scope of this chapter. There is one point, though, that is central and needs further elaboration. This involves the distinction between descriptive and inferential statistics. Depending on the research method (or methods) chosen, the experimenter will be relying primarily on one or the other set of statistics.

Descriptive Statistics

Descriptive statistics seek to do just that: describe a sample's general characteristics and responses to the dependent variable. The kinds of variables one is seeking to describe are important in determining the exact statistical procedures used. If a variable is *categorical* (i.e., if membership in one category precludes membership in another category, such as biological gender), then one would want to note the frequencies, percentages, or percentage of frequencies of participants (or their responses) in each category.

Continuous variables (i.e., variables such as 7-point Likert scales that have a minimum, a maximum, and a distribution of scores in between) are amenable to several different kinds of descriptive statistics. One can determine a variable's mean (i.e., its arithmetic average), median (i.e., the point in the distribution at which half the people scored higher and half scored lower), and mode (i.e., the most common response). Another way of describing continuous variables is by discussing their *variability*. Because all participants in a study will not score the same on the dependent variable (e.g., they may not exhibit the same degree of aggression, even if they played only with a nonviolent video game), it becomes desirable to describe the range of scores (i.e., the maximum minus the minimum), as well as the standard deviation of scores. This latter statistic describes the average degree of variability around the variable's mean. The higher the standard deviation, the larger the range.

Inferential Statistics

In research, it is often observed that two groups of people will rarely have the exact same score on a dependent variable. When researchers compare experimental and control groups, however, they expect to find group differences. Therefore, one needs to know whether the differences observed between these two groups are caused by the experimental manipulation, or whether they are just further examples of the random differences one normally finds. Thus, the goal of inferential statistics is to determine whether the differences between experimental and control groups on the dependent variable are a result of the independent variable, in other words, whether the differences are *statistically significant*.

For example, Cooper and Mackie (1986) observed that the amount of time boys spent playing with the aggressive toys differed depending on whether the boy played with the violent or nonviolent video game or with the control game (see Box 2–1). But are these differences the result of the games the children played or just random differences? In order to determine whether a statistic (e.g., one measuring a mean difference) is meaningful, researchers use a test for statistical significance that employs the concept of probability to determine the odds that the observed effect may have occurred by chance alone. Most experimenters adopt 5% ($p < .05$) as the minimum likelihood of a chance occurrence, which means that a researcher should be confident that 95 times out of 100 the effect observed is caused by the independent variable. All statistical analyses that examine group differences (e.g., *t*-tests, analyses of variance, chi-square) or the relationships between two or more variables (e.g., correlation, regression) have tests for statistical significance. Only if a test meets the $p < .05$ criterion can it be said that the differences between groups are a result of the independent variable, or that two variables are significantly correlated.

RESEARCH LIMITATIONS

All researchers need to examine the limitations of their findings. The two most common limitations concern the size or magnitude of the observed findings and the generalizability of the results to other populations.

Practical Significance

Researchers routinely determine the *statistical significance* of differences between their experimental and control groups, or relationships among two or more variables of interest (often using statistics described earlier in this chapter). These statistical tests assess the probability that any differences between the groups are more than just random variation or that the correlation between two variables is significantly different from zero. Tests of statistical significance, however, do not determine the strength of those associations, otherwise known as the *practical signifi-cance* of the findings. It is important for researchers to assess the strength of associ-ations in their findings so that they do not place undue weight on a statistically sig-nificant finding that has no practical utility (Tabachnick & Fidell, 1989).

Practical significance is most often an issue in studies with large samples. Tests of the strength of association in experimental designs typically examine the percent-age of variance in the dependent variable that is associated with the independent variable. In correlational studies, the size of the squared correlation coefficient (r^2) typically gives an estimate of the percentage of shared variance between the two variables. In both cases, the more shared variance between the dependent and inde-pendent variables, the greater the strength of association and the more meaningful the findings. There are no specific guidelines for how strong these tests of associa-tion need to be, and, once reported, they should be a point for discussion in the aca-demic field.

Generalizability

Researchers must also question whether their findings are specific to the group of people they studied or whether the results can be generalized to the population as a whole. This is a problem especially for psychology, which has used data gathered from university undergraduates to build up a knowledge base of human behavior. Sears (1986) has criticized this fact, noting that university students represent a very small subset of the general population. Whether or not this kind of sample homo-geneity is found in applied social psychological research is unknown. Certainly, ap-plied research is more varied in terms of the contexts in which it is performed. With increasing pressures on funding sources for external research, however, applied so-cial psychologists might start turning more regularly to the most available source of research participants: introductory psychology students.

SUGGESTED READINGS

Bryant, F. B., Edwards, J., Tindale, R. S., Posavac, E. J., Heath, L., Henderson, E., & Suarez-Balcazar, Y. (Eds.). (1992). *Methodological issues in applied social psychology*. New York: Plenum.

> This book was written for advanced students and professionals in applied social psy-chology. It provides exceptional chapters on all phases in applied research, from finding and planning for adequate financial resources to identifying social problems, conduct-ing several kinds of applied social research, understanding data analysis issues, and preparing project reports. This latter chapter is especially interesting because profes-sors teach their students to write for an academic audience; the goal is to teach students to write in a way that will get them published in scientific journals. However, most ap-plied social research is funded by nonacademic agencies and writing for these audi-ences requires a completely different approach.

Cook, T. D., & Campbell, D. T. (1979). *Quasi-experimentation: Design and analysis issues for field settings*. Boston: Houghton Mifflin.

This is a very informative book for both students and professionals. It describes how to perform several types of quasi-experimental research, as well as providing strategies for analysis. It details possible problems in generalizing the findings beyond the samples in the experiment. This book has become a benchmark in applied social research.

Denzin, N. K., & Lincoln, Y. S. (Eds.). (1994). *Handbook of qualitative research*. Thousand Oaks, CA: Sage.

This is an advanced book, written for a professional audience, but it is accessible to motivated students. It is a necessary reference tool for anyone serious about conducting qualitative research. It has breadth of coverage, offering chapters on the history and traditions in the field, the politics of doing qualitative research, as well as several chapters on the various qualitative methods and ways of interpreting this kind of research.

Oskamp, S. (1984). *Applied social psychology*. Englewood Cliffs, NJ: Prentice Hall.

This book was written for advanced undergraduates and has been, for over 10 years, the most thorough textbook in the area. Although some of its examples and topical coverage are rather dated, it contains five chapters on applied social research methods. Each chapter is very informative and offers extensive examples.

3 The Contribution of Surveys to Applied Social Psychology

Michael King
California State University, Chico

By the late 1980s the spread of AIDS had become a critical concern for public health officials in North America. Would the disease become epidemic among the heterosexual population as it had among male homosexuals? On which behaviors and attitudes should education efforts be focused? The answers to those questions required an accurate knowledge of current sexual practices and attitudes in the general population, the kind of picture that is provided only by a survey. Yet there had been very few general population surveys of sexual behavior since the ground-breaking Kinsey studies in the 1940s (Kinsey, Pomeroy, & Martin, 1948; Kinsey et al., 1953).

Fortunately a large-scale general population survey of sexual attitudes and behavior in the adult U.S. population was conducted in 1990 (Leigh, Temple, & Trocki, 1993). According to that survey, a high level of risk was found among those with multiple sex partners, mostly the unmarried, who represented 14% of the sample. Fewer than one in ten of those having more than one partner in the previous year reported using a condom every time they had sex. Those having multiple partners expressed concern about AIDS but indicated that they felt little risk of contracting the human immunodeficiency virus (HIV). The survey also showed that only 3.6% of married respondents reported having sex with someone other than a spouse in the past year, indicating a low level of risk for that group. A more controversial finding in the 1990 survey is that only 2% reported primary homosexual or bisexual orientation, about the same as that found in a 1970 Kinsey Institute survey (Fay, Turner, Klassen, & Gagnon, 1989) but far lower than reports from less careful studies, which have estimated that up to 10% of the population has a primary homosexual orientation. The finding that many who engage in high-risk sex deny or minimize their risk has led to mass media educational messages that emphasize the risk and the methods by which it can be reduced.

These 1990 survey findings were supported in a later nationwide survey by the National Opinion Research Center (Laumann, Gagnon, Michael, & Michaels, 1994). The 1994 survey also demonstrated the effectiveness of education programs aimed at high-risk adults (e.g., those with multiple sex partners); high-risk respondents in 1994 reported using condoms more frequently and were more concerned about AIDS and HIV than in 1990. These findings have encouraged the development of even stronger public health efforts to promote condom use among heterosexual adults with multiple sexual partners.

This brief episode in the battle against AIDS illustrates the power of the survey to inform public policy and initiatives. What follows is an examination of the basic features of the survey method that have made it such an important tool in applying social psychology to many difficult and important human problems. As indicated in Chapter 2 of this book, the survey is not the only method used by social psychologists. It is, however, the most frequently used and, when it is based on a sample from a large population, it often produces powerful findings that can be applied to human concerns (King, 1987).

CHARACTERISTICS OF A SURVEY

A survey is broadly defined as the process of collecting information from a sample of people who have been selected to represent a larger population. The information resulting from the survey sample is then generalized back to the larger population. In this way, three types of knowledge can be gained from surveys: (a) accurate *description* of how attitudes and behaviors are distributed in the population, (b) analysis of the *associations* among attitudes and behaviors, and (c) clues to *cause and effect* relationships.

The surveys with which we are most familiar are the descriptive political polls that tell us, for example, about the U.S. president's popularity or whether Canadians support a referendum on constitutional changes. Yet the power of the survey goes beyond these descriptive functions by examining associations among the psychological characteristics of individuals and their social environment. In so doing, surveys have become the primary methodological link between social psychology and many other disciplines that have a strong applied orientation (Sudman, 1976). A survey can combine information on perceptions, attitudes, feelings, and behaviors with information on the cultural and social context in which those who are surveyed function. Thus, political scientists have used surveys to identify broad political ideologies (liberalism versus conservatism), political party identification, specific issue orientation, and candidate image as psychological factors that influence voting. They have also discovered that the relative influence of these factors differs depending on the cultural and social status of the individual. For example, the adult sexuality survey described in the vignette provided public health practitioners with a realistic descriptive picture of HIV risk. That survey went beyond description and examined the associations between high-risk behaviors and attitudes. The discovery of a dissonant set of attitudes among those at high risk suggested new approaches to public education.

Economists use surveys to better understand how people's confidence in the economy can influence their decision to spend money and such data are widely used along with social and economic status factors to forecast future economic cycles. Surveys are used extensively in the development and testing of advertising effectiveness and in evaluating consumers' satisfaction with products. Market researchers have become alarmingly effective at combining social and psychological characteristics to target potential customers for their products. Their approach has been called *psychographics* because it provides a social psychological lifestyle profile that can guide the packaging and promotion of a product. It is interesting to note that surveys have also guided the packaging and marketing of politicians, treating them much like other goods (McGinnis, 1969). Surveys have been used in the legal system to determine if public sentiment in the community where a defendant is to be tried will allow for selection of an unbiased jury (Wrightsman, Nietzel, & Fortune, 1994). Jury consultants in high-profile cases such as the O.J. Simpson murder trial also use surveys to identify the social and psychological characteristics of potential jurors who may be sympathetic toward their client.

In the last 20 years, survey data have been increasingly used to build causal models that go beyond a description of populations and an examination of the association among psychological and social characteristics to identify cause and effect relationships (Asher, 1976). Causal modeling combines the correlational data that are produced by surveys with logic, and sometimes repeated surveys, to estimate the direction and strength of causal relationships among variables. This use is well illustrated by a longitudinal study of cigarette smoking in a group of 461 Los Angeles residents who were surveyed four times over a 13-year period from early adolescence to adulthood (Stein, Newcomb, & Bentler, 1996). The surveys collected data on cigarette smoking, cheerfulness and depression, extroversion, quality of social relations, and peer cigarette use. The data were considered together using a sophisticated type of causal model called *path analysis* to determine which factors predicted smoking at which ages. Early adolescent initiation of smoking was associated with cheerfulness, extroversion, high sociability, and peer use; continued smoking was associated with depression and poor social relations. The correlation between smoking in early and late adolescence was weak, indicating that many teens experiment with, but do not continue using, cigarettes. The resulting causal model suggests that intervention strategies designed to help inoculate seventh graders from peer pressure to experiment may not be useful with adults or even late adolescents who have continued smoking. Strengthening social relationships and teaching coping and stress reduction skills are suggested by the causal model as potentially helpful approaches for longer-term smokers.

These brief examples are a reminder that, somewhat like atomic energy, surveys have been widely used for both good and ill. As in the case of the sexual attitude and behavior survey cited earlier, a number of surveys have figured prominently in guiding public policy and programs. Surveys have also been used to sell us products that we do not want and political candidates who do not represent our interests, and the use of such surveys may even compromise justice in the legal system. This chapter is designed to help the reader better understand why the survey has been such a widely applied tool, to provide some basic guidelines with which to evaluate the scientific credibility of the many surveys that are encountered, and to address the ethical dilemmas raised by the diverse use of surveys.

A BRIEF HISTORY OF THE SURVEY METHOD

General population surveys had their beginnings in the popular-magazine readership surveys of the 1920s and 1930s. Those surveys were used as the basis of news stories in much the same way that the news network polls are used today. There is an important difference, however. The early surveys included only readers of the magazines who were interested enough to send in their views and thus were biased. The current media polls are usually based on scientifically selected samples of the general population and more accurately reflect the population's views. The flaws of the early magazine polls were dramatically revealed in the failure of the Literary Digest Poll to predict the 1936 American presidential election between Roosevelt and Langdon. That failure led to greater dependence on fledgling polling organizations such as Gallup, which used more scientifically chosen samples and were able to predict correctly Roosevelt's victory.

After World War II, academic survey research centers were established to enable social scientists to apply survey methods to the rapidly emerging fields of social psychology, sociology, political science, and economics. Prominent among those centers, which now number in the dozens, is the Survey Research Center in the Institute of Social Research (ISR) at the University of Michigan. The ISR Center for Political Studies initiated the most significant general population surveys of political behavior (Campbell, Converse, Miller, & Stokes, 1960), and its Center for Economic Research produces the familiar consumer confidence data. The ISR pioneered a uniquely social psychological approach to understanding factors that affect the psychological quality of people's lives (Campbell, 1981), which has also been applied by the York University Institute of Behavioural Research to the Canadian population (King, Atkinson, & Murray, 1982).

Although the primary interest of academic social scientists has been in testing theories and in adding to the knowledge base of their disciplines, the presence of survey research centers at academic institutions encouraged the spread of an emerging survey methodology into nonacademic fields. The potential uses of the new methodology were quickly recognized by students who entered business and began using surveys to identify markets and to evaluate advertising and other business activity. As schools of business began to appear on university campuses, the survey method became a prominent fixture in their marketing courses. Other applied disciplines, such as communications and education, followed suit; by the 1970s survey research had become a staple in most university business and social science curricula, exposing students to survey methods and their practical uses. This vast exposure has contributed to a dramatic increase in the applications of surveys over the past 40 years, to the point that they now are deemed indispensable in business, politics, and education and are widely used in other fields.

An extremely important arena in which surveys have become prominent is the development and implementation of public policy. The survey is an ideal tool to provide information efficiently about large populations; this information is critical to forging policies and programs that best serve the needs of that population. The example with which this chapter begins is only one of the many ways in which surveys have guided government efforts to enhance the quality of people's lives. The study described in Box 3–1, "Parks for People," further illustrates how a survey can inform decisions about how to expend public resources.

Even a brief history of the survey method must note the contribution of the American Association of Public Opinion Research (AAPOR). Since 1946, AAPOR has provided a forum in its publication, the *Public Opinion Quarterly,* for scientific improvements in surveys and has consistently promoted high standards and ethical behavior among all those who conduct and use survey research (Sheatsley & Mitofsky, 1992). AAPOR has also served as a meeting ground outside the universities for academic researchers and those in the applied arenas of business and public policy.

This history has led to at least three constituencies for surveys and the information that surveys produce: (a) academic social scientists, whose principal interest is development and testing of theory; (b) practitioners in business and other strictly applied fields; and (c) social scientists, who use surveys to increase the effectiveness of policies and programs designed to address human needs. To these we may add a fourth group of survey users. This category is comprised of students in the social and behavioral sciences who will encounter many surveys both as a basis for knowledge in their field and as an element in the mass media interpretation of everyday events.

WHAT MAKES A GOOD SURVEY?

Most surveys, including many that appear in the published journals, have shortcomings that call for caution in interpreting or applying their results. Conducting a valid survey presents the researcher with many choices and requires skills that must be developed with time and experience. Principles of good survey practice, covered in detail in the annotated sources referenced at end of this chapter, are briefly ad-

Box 3–1   *Parks for People: The East Bay Regional Park Study*

The tax revolt of the late 1970s and 1980s severely limited funds available for purchase and development of park facilities by local governments. In 1987, the East Bay Regional Park District (in the San Francisco East Bay area of California) was facing a crisis in its ability to develop new park lands while it continued to maintain current park facilities. East Bay Regional Parks is the largest municipal park district in the United States. It manages park lands for an area ranging from inner-city Oakland to Berkeley Hills to wilderness areas adjacent to some of the most affluent suburbs in the Bay Area. The population it serves has social and economic diversity equal to that found in most metropolitan areas.

The district wanted to better understand the attitudes, concerns, and interests of its constituents so that it could structure a public financing bond measure that would be successful and would meet residents' needs. To this end, the district contracted in early 1987 with the author and a colleague to conduct a survey of residents served by the district.

The survey used a sample of 1,515 randomly selected residents in the area served by the park to estimate the views of all residents about the following specific issues: (a) the desire for more regional parks; (b) the preference for more undeveloped open-space land versus more urban recreational-use facilities such as ball fields, recreation centers, and picnic areas; and (c) the level of support for funding measures at various costs. The survey also collected information about the respondents' social and economic characteristics and their general attitudes about recreation, wildlife, and preserving the natural environment. These questions provided a social psychological context for respondents' views on the specific issues. Respondents in the survey were contacted during February 1987, using a random-digit dialing procedure and were interviewed by telephone. Random-digit dialing (RDD) is a commonly used sampling approach in which a list of phone numbers is generated by computer so that all possible assigned numbers have equal probability of being chosen for the list. Thus, unlisted numbers are included and a truly representative sample may be chosen. A check of the demographic characteristics of the sample against U.S. Census data for the larger population in the East Bay area verified that the sample closely mirrored that population.

The survey identified four preferred uses for any new parks funding: (a) the protection of shorelines; (b) the maintenance of existing park facilities; (c) the purchase and protection of open-space ridge lands; and (d) the development of new park and recreational facilities. Analysis indicated that the population in the district tended to cluster into two distinct constituencies with different priorities: (a) urban middle- and working-class residents, who were most concerned about further development of urban recreational facilities; and (b) more affluent suburban residents, whose strongest concern was the preservation of shoreline habitat and undeveloped open space. The former group tended to be inner-city dwellers in Oakland, Berkeley, Richmond, and Alameda and were most concerned about urban parks and playgrounds, provide needed recreational opportunities. The latter were more likely to live in affluent suburbs such as Orinda, Walnut Creek, and Pleasanton and were more concerned about preserving remaining undeveloped habitat for wildlife and greenbelt respite from urbanization.

The survey showed that a general bond-financing measure did not have support from the two-thirds necessary for passage. Survey results also indicated clearly that a measure focusing on only one or the other of the constituencies would fail dramatically. On the positive side, the survey found a greater than two-thirds support for a funding measure that would be used just for parks and facilities in the respondent's immediate home area. These results led the park district to delay a bond election and to plan a yearlong campaign designed to present a bond-financing measure that would combine enough of the diverse interests to gain passage.

Utilizing these survey results, the park district developed a "package" of benefits that reflected the concerns of the two diverse constituencies and earmarked funds for use by local agencies. The measure, which was put on the ballot in the fall of 1988, provided $126 million for regional park land and trails acquisition, $42.25 million for regional park land maintenance, and $56.25 million to be used by city and county park agencies for local improvements. The measure was passed by 67.5% of voters in November 1988. It was the first public park finance measure to be passed in California since the 1978 tax-limiting Proposition 13.

The survey played a critical role in providing a clear picture of the desires and preferences of a heterogeneous population served by the park district. It allowed the park district to develop a funding package that was responsive to the concerns and needs of a large and diverse metropolitan population. The cynical, or politically conservative, person might question whether social psychology should use its survey methods to aid organizations such as the park district in their efforts to raise taxes. Cynicism and political persuasion aside, there are certainly ethical issues raised by any foray into the world of applied social psychology. My colleague and I believed that our survey served the people of the East Bay area as much as it did the park district. It communicated the varied concerns and desires of the population in a manner that is far more objective than the representations of politically or economically influential individuals or pressure groups. In a very real sense, the survey served the *needs assessment* function discussed in the program evaluation chapter of this book. After receiving the results of the survey, it was difficult for the district to fail to respond to the diverse needs of its constituents. Those interested in more detailed information on the methods in this survey and its use by the park district may find a detailed account in Fletcher and King (1993).

dressed here in the hope that the reader will become a discerning consumer of the multitude of survey studies that he or she will encounter as a student.

The first choice faced by the survey researcher is the method or *mode* to use in selecting and collecting information from a sample. Next, the researcher must select or create the questions to be asked. A sample will then be selected. Finally, the actual survey must be conducted. Each of these phases, to be discussed in turn, is crucial to producing valid knowledge and each must follow scientific principles regardless of whether the survey is designed to test a theory, to gain a business advantage, or to provide data for a human needs application.

SURVEY MODE

Information in large-scale surveys is generally collected using one of three methods, or modes. These include (a) *mail surveys,* in which standardized printed questionnaires are sent to respondents by mail to be completed and then returned by mail; (b) *face-to-face personal interviews* in which respondents are selected, approached, and interviewed in person by trained interviewers using a predesigned set of questions; and (c) *telephone interviews,* in which respondents are contacted and interviewed over the phone using scripted questions. Each of these methods has advantages and disadvantages, so no method is best for all survey purposes. Factors to be considered in choosing a method include cost and other resources required, the extent to which the sample will represent the larger population of concern, and the expected quality of the resulting information. Table 3–1 contrasts these three methods. A more complete comparison may be found in Frey (1989), from whose work this table was adapted.

A quick look at the table reveals why telephone surveys have become so prominent in recent years. They are relatively inexpensive; provide representative samples; may be completed quickly; and, for straightforward, nonsensitive issues, provide adequate data quality. These advantages are illustrated in a typical nationwide phone survey of 1,500 respondents, such as the Gallup Poll or news media polls that can be completed and analyzed for reporting within a 2- or 3-day period. Such quick turnaround is especially important when polls are used to gauge the impact of a current event, such as public reaction to U.S. military involvement in Bosnia in late 1995.

The East Bay Parks survey (Fletcher & King, 1993) highlighted in Box 3–1 further illustrates why the telephone mode is often chosen. A first consideration in that survey was that the park district needed information quickly to help decide whether to pursue a bond measure that would generate much needed capital immediately or to wait. Mail or face-to-face surveys would have taken longer to complete and would have prolonged that decision. Fortunately, the issues at hand were not sensitive or particularly complex because the cost of the survey was a factor, eliminating the face-to-face mode. There was concern that a mail survey might not provide enough

TABLE 3–1 Comparison of Survey Modes

	Survey Mode		
Factor	Mail	Face-to-Face	Telephone
Resources			
Cost	low	high	low/med
Personnel needs	low	high	high/med
Time to complete	long	long	short
Representation			
Sample coverage	poor	very good	very good
Response rate	low	very high	high
Refusal rate	high	low	moderate
Data Quality			
Control over interview	poor	good	moderate
Social desirability potential	low	high	moderate
Potential for sensitive questions	moderate	high	moderate
Potential for complex questions	low	high	moderate
Use of open-ended questions	poor	good	moderate
Ability to probe answers	poor	good	good
Confidentiality	poor	poor	moderate

sample coverage to represent accurately the views of all members of the area population. The phone survey emerged as the best method for obtaining the needed information.

Even with their considerable advantages, telephone surveys require carefully worded scripts, training and supervision of interviewers, and organized and persistent follow-up to ensure that a high percentage of those sampled respond to the survey. Therefore, a telephone survey cannot usually be conducted adequately without a professional survey organization.

Face-to-face interviews are still the method of choice when the research topic is sensitive and complex, when in-depth probing and clarification of responses are desired, and when resources are available to cover the higher costs of interviewer time and travel, as well as the logistics of the overall management of interviewers in the field. The major drawback of face-to-face surveys is their high cost, which is at least $150 per completed interview, compared with a per interview cost of $25 to $50 for phone surveys and a per interview cost of $15 to $25 for mail surveys. Complex topics and issues can be communicated effectively face to face with the use of visual aids. This is illustrated by the ISR National Election studies in which positive or negative feelings toward a candidate are measured using a card depicting a thermometer marked in degrees (Campbell, Converse, Miller, & Stokes, 1960). The respondent is asked to use the visual scale on the card to indicate how warmly he or she feels about each of the candidates. Even with its inherent advantage in dealing with sophisticated and sensitive topics, the face-to-face method must be administered carefully because the presence of an interviewer may enhance the human tendency to provide socially desirable answers.

The mail survey mode, although least desirable on many counts, is frequently used when cost is an overriding factor or information is desired from a particular population. The wide availability of mailing lists makes targeting in mail surveys relatively easy. If one wished to survey only people who are registered to vote, surveys could be mailed to a sample selected from public voter registration rolls, which include addresses. Other special interest populations can be targeted through use of magazine subscription or organizational mailing lists, which are generally available for a nominal cost. For example, a computer software company interested in features desired in new computer programs might survey a sample selected from the subscription lists of the leading personal computer magazines. Despite their widespread use, mail surveys often have participation rates below 20% of those contacted. Low participation rates should raise serious questions about whether the resulting survey data are a valid representation of the population under study because those who do not respond in a survey almost always differ in their opinions and social characteristics from those who do respond (Groves, 1987).

Recently, researchers have begun to use combinations of these methods to capitalize on their respective strengths. This is illustrated in the combination of an initial phone contact with mailing of descriptive materials and a follow-up phone interview to assess the economic value attached to preservation of a complex natural ecosystem. The resource in question was a wetlands area in California's central valley, and the survey addressed the willingness of residents throughout the state to bear the expense of several possible programs designed to restore and preserve this natural habitat. An initial phone contact was used to ensure representative sample coverage. Then a booklet was mailed to respondents to portray visually and explain the complex habitat and restoration issues. Finally, an interview was conducted by phone in which questions were asked about the material in the booklet. Comparison of the sample and data in this survey with that from a parallel mail-only survey showed the combined mail/phone survey to have produced a much more representative sample and more realistic estimates of the economic value of those wetlands (Loomis & King, 1994). For example, the mail-only survey estimated that the average California household was willing to pay $366 per year to maintain wetlands, whereas the combination phone/mail/phone survey yielded an estimate of $206 per year.

The U.S. government-sponsored survey of sexual attitudes and behavior described at the beginning of this chapter (Leigh et al., 1993) is an example in which sensitive questions were to be asked and adequate funding was available. That survey combined face-to-face initial contact to maximize sample coverage with a written questionnaire to ensure confidentiality and to minimize the tendency of respondents to provide socially desirable responses. The survey included responses from 2,058 individuals who were chosen through a sampling of all households in the United States. Those who completed the survey represented 70.3% of the households that were originally selected. They were contacted in person and asked to complete a questionnaire booklet that was later collected by the interviewer in a sealed envelope to guarantee anonymity. The large number of people in the survey, the use of sealed questionnaires to ensure anonymity, and a high participation rate produced the most accurate reading to that time of adult sexual behavior and attitudes in the United States.

WORDING, FORMAT, AND CONTEXT

Surveys, like statistics, can lie if the questions asked are designed to produce a desired response or if they are thoughtlessly crafted. Because of the pervasive use of self-report surveys, a considerable stock of questions covering many topics of interest to applied social psychology has been developed through trial and revision. Use of already tested questions, which may be found in the Gallup Opinion Index, the Roper Center Archive of Surveys and Polls, and the invaluable volume by Robinson, Shaver, and Wrightsman (1991), as well as in published research reports, is advisable to ensure validity and comparability of survey findings with other surveys that have used the same questions. Another excellent source of effective questions is the General Social Survey (GSS), which includes hundreds of questions that have been administered by the National Opinion Research Center in annual surveys of the adult U.S. population since 1972 (Davis & Smith, 1993). The GSS questions have the added advantage of possessing historical normative data. For example, since 1972, the GSS has asked the following question about attitudes concerning gun control: "Would you favor or oppose a law which would require a person to obtain a police permit before he or she could buy a gun?" Examination of the GSS data on this question shows that gun control was endorsed by more than two-thirds of the respondents in 1972, rising to 76% in the years 1988-1991 and to 81% in 1993. This national trend toward greater support for gun control will provide an important context for interpreting the results of new surveys in which the GSS question is used to gauge support or opposition for government policies.

When established measures are not available, the survey researcher's task is considerably more difficult. Before they can be used in a survey, new questions must be carefully developed and pretested to ensure that they meet conventional standards of reliability and validity (i.e., that they measure what they purport to measure and do so consistently). Even in simple opinion polls, a professional organization will pretest and refine new questions before using them in a survey that is to be released to the media. Such pretesting examines at minimum the distribution of responses, degree of nonresponse, and internal consistency among responses to several questions designed to measure the same construct. Thereby it may be determined that a question successfully identifies individual differences among respondents, as opposed to eliciting the same response from everyone, that it is clear and relevant enough for the majority to respond, and that it elicits responses similar to those elicited by other comparable questions. For more complex research projects, the pretest measurement development phase may involve combining multiple questions into additive scales or indices using psychometric techniques, such as Likert scaling. As a result, the development phase may demand a larger investment of time and resources than the actual survey data collection.

Although the development and evaluation of valid and reliable measures are complex processes, three aspects are so fundamental that they bear noting here. These are the wording, format, and context of questions. Interested readers may pursue the topic further in the introductory treatment by Converse and Presser (1986) or the more advanced exposition of Sudman and Bradburn (1982).

Question Wording

When evaluating previously used questions or when constructing new questions, the basic principle is to keep the language simple and direct. Avoid negatives and questions that address more than one attitude or issue. The latter are called *double-barreled* questions and are often a clue to surveys or polls that are designed to produce a desired result rather than objective data. Double-barreled questions often appear on the pseudosurveys sent to constituents by members of the U.S. Congress. The following hypothetical example is relevant to the U.S. Pacific Northwest, where controversy rages over forest management practices: "Do you favor putting hard-working forest products workers out of work by passing more laws that limit timber production?" Such a question taps into attitudes on both unemployment and forest preservation. Its emphasis on unemployment seems designed to underestimate the level of support for protection of forest habitats and would thus present a biased picture of general population attitudes. Although such biased questions are often used deliberately to produce a desired result, they are sometimes inadvertently used by researchers who genuinely want an accurate understanding of public attitudes. If one wished to assess overall attitudes about restricting timber harvesting to protect an endangered species habitat, a question such as the following would be more objective: "Some people have proposed new laws that would restrict harvesting timber in forests to protect a critical habitat for certain animals and plants. From what you know about the possible effects of such laws, would you say you support them or oppose them?" This question asks for a general opinion and does not encourage the respondent to focus on any particular facet of this complex issue.

Question Format

Most surveys use closed-ended questions, or those that present the respondent with a set of alternatives from which to choose. It has been shown how such questions may be constructed to bias the results. To avoid putting words into the respondents' mouths, some researchers use open-ended questions that allow respondents to express their views in their own words. For example, a survey researcher might let the respondent know that passing laws to protect forests is a controversial issue on which there are many differing opinions and that he or she would like to hear the respondent's opinion in his or her own words. Such open-ended questions have their pitfalls as well, because they require that the researcher categorize, summarize, and interpret a large number of unique responses. Different researchers may categorize and interpret the responses differently, leading to results that are unreliable or difficult to repeat. Consider the following response to an open-ended question. Would *you* categorize it as generally favoring or opposing more restrictive timber harvesting laws?

> Well, I enjoy the outdoors and would like to protect wildlife. The lumber companies have made a mess in some places. People need to work, though, and I'd hate to see them lose their jobs. I wish we could do something about this situation without hurting people. It's tough to know what to do.

This example illustrates why open-ended questions are best administered by experienced interviewers who have been trained to elicit *elaboration* so that the responses can be more useful in research. One would clearly need further elaboration from this respondent to make a judgment about the general support or opposition. Because of the problem of reliability and the interviewing skills required, open-ended questions are used primarily by experienced researchers and typically in the exploratory stages of a research study to better understand how the topic under study is conceived by respondents.

When using closed-ended questions, the fixed-response alternatives may be constructed to represent any of several scales of measurement common in psychology. They may be (a) *nominally scaled* questions, such as the state or province of residence, with mutually exclusive categories that do not represent degree along some dimension; (b) *ordinally scaled* questions, such as the degree of support or opposition to the death penalty (with the alternatives representing degrees but not equal intervals on a dimension); or (c) *intervally scaled* questions, such as age or income (items within these categories differ by equal degrees). Any of these scale types may be used in survey research. The decision regarding which type of questions to use is dictated by the statistical treatment to which the data will be subjected and the ease with which respondents can use the categories. The more sophisticated statistical treatments that are important in applied social psychology, such as correlation, multiple regression, factor analysis, and analysis of variance, require intervally scaled measures, whereas the percentages and modes that characterize public opinion polls may be applied to nominally scaled measures.

The mode of the survey discussed earlier may also limit the kinds of categories that may be used. Telephone surveys, in particular, are not suitable for use of large sets of categories because the categories must be read over the phone. In general, it is difficult to ask a phone respondent to consider thoughtfully more than four or five alternative responses to a question. Thus, most phone surveys are limited to nominal and ordinal questions. Mail or other paper-and-pencil questionnaire surveys have the advantage that the respondent may consider a large number of categories. It is even possible in mail and face-to-face surveys to represent a dimension graphically so that the response may be recorded without reference to discrete categories. The previously noted ISR political survey candidate *feeling thermometer* illustrates use of a visual aid for an intervally scaled measure in a face-to-face interview.

Question Context

Another important factor affecting the validity of survey questions is the order of their presentation. As social psychologists know, the context of a question will influence how people respond. Consider this commonly asked question about abortion: "Please tell me whether or not you think it should be possible for a pregnant woman to obtain a legal abortion if the woman wants it for any reason" (Davis & Smith, 1993). If this question were asked immediately following a question about women's rights, it would probably elicit a somewhat different response than if it were asked immediately following a question about euthanasia or a question about cruelty to infants and children. The question about timber harvesting restrictions posed earlier would elicit a biased response if it immediately followed general questions about protection of the environment or questions about the economic situation and unemployment. Preceding environmental protection questions would frame the timber harvest question as an environmental issue, whereas questions about the economy would frame it as an economic issue. It is important to be aware of the context in which questions are asked in order to evaluate potential bias.

SAMPLE SELECTION PROCEDURES

The principal strength of surveys, use of a small sample to estimate the larger population, is often their greatest weakness. Sampling is a complex and technical topic that is well introduced to the novice by Kalton (1983). For our purposes here, two basic principles are important: (a) *random selection* of people to the survey and

(b) making *all possible efforts* to gain a response from each of those who are sampled. An ideal sample would be one in which all people in the population are thrown into a single pool so that each has an equal opportunity to be selected for the sample. A subset would be randomly selected and all of those selected would then be surveyed. In practice, there is seldom an easily accessed *pool* of people to study. The survey researcher must start with telephone numbers, or households on a city map, or voting registration lists, or organizational membership lists, none of which is complete or accurate. Even the U.S. government's 1990 Census was challenged by those who believed that many homeless and minority people were not counted because they were more difficult to locate and interview.

In practice, most surveys of large populations use a multistage sampling approach in which larger units, called *clusters,* are sampled randomly and further random samples are chosen within those chosen clusters. Telephone surveys such as the East Bay Parks study described in Box 3–1 use random digit dialing (RDD) to contact a representative sample. In that technique, a computer generates random phone numbers having the same proportional representation of area codes and dialing prefixes as the numbers that are assigned to residences. Although over 95% of persons in the United States live in households that have a phone, and the percentage is higher in Canada and most European countries, many of those phone numbers are not publicly listed. Thus, by calling numbers created by a computer, people not having listed numbers have the same likelihood of being called as those with listed numbers.

The most common sampling deficiency is to use a sample of opportunity that does not represent the population that the researcher wishes to understand. The sexual attitudes and behavior survey cited earlier was particularly needed in the effort to limit the spread of AIDS because a 30-year void of valid scientific information had been filled to overflowing with studies of sexuality based on limited groups such as college students (King & Sobel, 1975), samples of opportunity in which only those willing to discuss their sex lives came forward (Hite, 1976), or readers of particular magazines (Tavris & Sadd, 1977). Such limited studies tended to overestimate the levels of infidelity, promiscuity, and homosexuality and would have misled, rather than informed, in an area that is particularly subject to myth and moral judgment in the absence of sound and comprehensive scientific data.

The principle that those who have strong interest in a survey topic usually have different views and experiences from those whose interest is not strong enough to come forward is further illustrated by the ubiquitous talk radio programs found throughout North America. One would hope that the level of frustration, cynicism, intolerance, and anger evidenced by callers, present in some members of society, is not as prevalent in the general population as these programs would indicate. As you read about surveys in the mass media or your academic textbooks, note carefully the way in which the survey sample was chosen. If the report you read does not describe the sampling procedure, you cannot be certain that it was chosen scientifically.

The sample that *is* chosen is seldom the sample that completes the survey. Many of those chosen cannot be contacted; still others refuse to participate or do not have sufficient proficiency in the language of the survey to participate. If the number in the original sample who do not participate is high, serious questions should be raised about whether the sample that remains is representative of the population under study. The participation rates in a survey should be reported. When they are low, the researcher should check the characteristics of the sample against those of the larger population to verify that the sample is representative. This was done in the case of the East Bay Parks survey by comparing the demographic characteristics of the sample against those from U.S. Census data for the area. In the sexual behavior survey described at the beginning of this chapter, interviews were completed with 70.3% of the sample chosen so there was less concern about respondents being unrepresentative of the population. Based on the author's experience, properly managed mail surveys should be expected to achieve a participation rate of at least 50%. Phone surveys should achieve a 60% to 70% rate, and face-to-face surveys should achieve participation from at least 70% of those chosen. During the 1970s, the U.S. government established 70% as a minimum participation rate for government-sponsored surveys.

SURVEY IMPLEMENTATION

Participation rates in a survey can be maximized by proper survey implementation. This includes everything from how those in the sample are initially contacted to the degree of polish or professionalism shown by the interviewers or questionnaire, to the amount of effort expended in follow-up in order to gain participation from those who are reluctant or difficult to contact. A very effective implementation program is presented by Dillman (1978) in his *total design method*. Dillman's approach begins with an initial contact by letter or phone call to introduce the purpose and sponsorship of the survey so that the respondent will understand that it is a legitimate information-gathering activity. Next comes the information-gathering contact, which may be conducted by phone or mail. In the case of mail surveys, Dillman suggests that a follow-up postcard be mailed about 4 days after the questionnaire so that the respondent will be reminded while the questionnaire is still at hand. At least two additional follow-ups are suggested for mail surveys that are not returned, and a new copy of the questionnaire should be included if the second follow-up is several weeks after the initial questionnaire mailing. In the case of phone surveys, it is common practice to make five or more calls to reach persons who have been sampled. Although not common, it is sometimes necessary to call up to 20 times to achieve the level of participation desired. When a phone survey refusal rate is high, the survey organization may even need to call back those refusals using especially skilled interviewers, to ensure that the results are not biased in favor of those who are more cooperative.

This brief discussion of implementation should explain why surveys, even mailed questionnaires, are so costly. Unfortunately, it also explains why many surveys often do not meet scientific standards. The researchers do not have the economic or personnel resources to conduct a proper survey. Because of sampling or implementation deficiencies, surveys may underrepresent those having low income and education, those who move frequently, those not speaking the language of the survey, and those with lower interest in the survey topic, resulting in a biased picture of the views of the overall population.

ESTIMATING SURVEY ACCURACY

One of the most difficult to understand but critical survey concepts is *sampling tolerance,* sometimes called *sampling error.* This phenomenon is usually reported as a plus or minus value range within which the results of a survey are alleged to be accurate (e.g., ± 3 percentage points). Sampling tolerance, then, is an estimate of the range of variation in response that might be expected as a result of the probability that any randomly drawn sample might not accurately reflect the population from which it was drawn. Obviously, that probability is greater if the sample is small and less if the sample is large. If a researcher were to sample all members of a population, there would be no sampling tolerance. If he or she were to sample only a dozen persons, the sampling tolerance would be very large. A properly selected and implemented sample of only 500 persons can yield reasonably accurate estimates for large populations such as the adult population of the United States.

A particular sample size is chosen to achieve a desired sampling tolerance with a given level of confidence, usually the familiar ± 5% *at the 95% confidence level.* Determining the sample size required for a desired level of accuracy is somewhat complex, as it takes into account the sampling design (e.g., simple random, cluster) and the degree of variability expected in the survey estimates. Formulas for calculating sample size and sample tolerance may be found in any basic survey sampling text such as Kalton (1983). In the East Bay Parks survey described in Box 3–1, a larger than usual sample was chosen to provide for a sampling tolerance of ± 2.5% so support for a funding measure could be closely estimated. That meant that the park district could assume with 95% confidence that the level of support for a bond measure in the general population was within 2.5 percentage points of the 58.5% who indicated support in the survey. Another way of thinking about sampling tolerance is that if 100 such surveys were conducted using the same sample sizes and random selection, the resulting estimates of support for a bond would be expected to be between 56 and 61% in 95 of those surveys. Social scientists will often select a sample larger than needed to estimate the larger population so that subgroups of the sample may be examined with acceptable accuracy. The sexual-practices survey cited earlier sampled 2,058 adults so that behavior and attitudes of the smaller subsample of those who reported multiple partners, $n = 271$, could be examined with confidence. It is important to know the sampling tolerance of a survey and of subgroups analyzed in the survey to evaluate the likely accuracy of results. In addition, it is important to keep in mind that sampling tolerance is the *upper limit* of accuracy. Other factors such as question wording and context, method of sampling, and implementation can further diminish accuracy.

ETHICAL ISSUES IN THE USE OF SURVEYS

In recent years survey researchers have come under fire for engaging in unethical practices. Most of that criticism is a response to a dramatic increase in "selling under the guise" of a survey, a practice dubbed *sugging,* in which a telephone salesperson introduces his or her pitch with the statement, "we are conducting a survey." These blatant abuses, along with ethical concerns in legitimate surveys, led the American Association of Public Opinion Research to establish a code of ethics and practices that is now subscribed to by most academic and private sector survey research organizations (Sheatsely & Mitofsky, 1992). This code calls for honesty and integrity in all dealings with respondents, the clients for whom they work, and the public. For respondents, this means clearly identifying the content, sponsorship, and purpose of the survey so that they may make an informed judgment about whether they wish to participate. If assurances are made that responses will be held confidential or anonymous, those assurances must be honored. Respondents should be treated with respect during all phases of the information-collecting process.

The code of ethics calls for the researcher to disclose fully to those who sponsor surveys the limitations and shortcomings of the survey and to avoid use of methods that deliberately introduce bias into the results. A survey report should include information on who sponsored it, who conducted it, exact wording and sequencing of questions, description of the population and how a sample was selected, sample sizes and sampling tolerance, and the method place and dates of data collection. All of this information is seldom available in published research reports or media summaries, but it should be obtainable with a phone call or letter to the sponsor of the survey. You might test this with a follow-up request for information on a survey about which you have read.

AAPOR encourages survey researchers and others knowledgeable about survey methods to assume some responsibility for preventing public misuse or distortions of survey data. Because surveys have become so prominent in our culture, their misuse is considerable. Misuse can include innocent overgeneralization of results to a population not represented by the survey sample; citation of selective survey results out of context; uncritical use of results from biased questions; or even misappropriation of the term *scientific* to describe the results from unscientific surveys such as media "call-in polls," which are not based on randomly selected samples. During several years when the author of this chapter provided a brief weekly commentary on polls on his local public radio station, every opportunity was taken to alert the public to the more obvious distortions and misuses of surveys.

A controversial ethical issue that has not been resolved in the United States is the potential of polls to influence the outcome of an election. Of particular concern are media-sponsored exit polls that are conducted on election day and released before voting is completed. Predictions about the election outcome, which are a prominent feature of this type of media presentation, may influence the vote of those who have not yet cast their ballots. They may even decide not to vote if the polls indicate that their candidate or issue has little chance of winning. If such fears are valid, then political polls near the end of an election campaign will have done the democratic process a disservice. Canada, the United Kingdom, Australia, and other countries have acknowledged this possibility and banned the release of poll results in the period immediately preceding and during the election.

Another interesting ethical issue that often confronts social psychologists who conduct surveys that bear on public policy is the all-too-frequent political opposition. Such opposition may limit or even prevent the conduct of the survey that is designed to inform public policy. For example, carefully planned surveys of sexual practices in the United States and Britain have had previously committed government funding withdrawn after moral objections from the political right (Miller, 1995). Those surveys were eventually conducted but on a dramatically reduced scale and with nongovernment funding. Such political interference is perhaps a testament to the powerful potential of surveys to influence public policy.

SUMMARY

With the basic ideas presented in this chapter you are now equipped to take a more careful look at surveys and to help your fellow students and friends distinguish legitimate surveys from those that are self-serving or blatantly unscientific. This method's greatest strength, efficiency in representing the attitudes and behaviors of a large population, can be realized when survey researchers adhere to good scientific practice. Strong traditions and standards that have forged this method into one of the key tools of applied social psychology have evolved within the survey research community.

Surveys have tremendous potential for providing an important information base that can inform and guide efforts to enhance and expand the human experiences described in other chapters of this book. The most common type of knowledge to be gained from surveys is a description of how attitudes and behaviors are distributed in the population. Descriptive knowledge, reflected in the dozens of polls and surveys reported weekly in the mass media, is only a starting point in the social psychologist's use of surveys. Successful applications of surveys such as those cited in this chapter go beyond description; they examine the associations among the social and psychological factors assessed in the survey. The uniquely social psychological contribution is to look at the associations among attitudes and behaviors in the social context in which those factors interact. Use of surveys by social psychologists to evaluate cause and effect relationships is less common but is expected to play a greater role in the future.

Although surveys have been applied to promote narrowly defined interests, as in the case of candidate polls, marketing of products, and generating entertainment, they have also been instrumental in helping address human and societal problems. One of the greatest contributions of social psychology has been the use of surveys to inform and guide public policy by providing an accurate picture of the attitudes and behaviors of the public and how those attitudes and behaviors are affected by the social context in which the individual functions. Future applications of social psychology will be enhanced significantly to the extent that we will be able to design and conduct scientifically sound surveys and can convince those who make public policy of the surveys' relevance.

SUGGESTED READINGS

Converse, J. M., & Presser, S. (1986). *Survey questions: Handcrafting the standardized questionnaire.* Beverly Hills: Sage.

This excellent introductory guide discusses basic principles of question construction with numerous examples from different types of surveys. It identifies most of the common mistakes made in survey wording and presents effective alternatives. A more complete and advanced treatment of issues in survey wording may be found in Sudman and Bradburn (1982).

Dillman, D. A. (1978). *Mail and telephone surveys: The total design method.* New York: John Wiley & Sons.

This volume has become the bible for students who are beginning seriously to conduct surveys. It covers basic ideas on sampling, design, and questionnaire development clearly, but its greatest contribution is the conceptualization of the *total design* method, a series of activities designed to produce high-quality, valid data from surveys.

Ferber, R., Sheatsley, P., Turner, A., & Waksburg, J. (1980). *What is a survey?* Washington, DC: American Statistical Association.

If it is not available in your library, this very brief volume may be obtained from the American Statistical Association, 806 Fifteenth Street, Washington, DC. It is an excellent introductory overview of the steps necessary in conducting a scientific survey. It is written by experts for nonexperts.

Frey, J. H. (1989). *Survey research by telephone.* Newbury Park, CA: Sage.

Chapter 2 of this book is the clearest and most complete discussion of the advantages and disadvantages of the commonly used methods of collecting survey data. It is also a good introductory reference for learning the nuts and bolts of conducting telephone surveys. A more advanced treatment of telephone survey methodology may be found in Groves et al. (1988).

Kalton, G. (1983). *Introduction to survey sampling.* Beverly Hills, CA: Sage.

This concise volume provides an excellent brief introduction to sampling, including the mathematical basis for determining sample size and estimating sampling tolerance. Common simple and complex sampling designs are discussed with detailed descriptions of the sampling procedures used in national face-to-face and telephone surveys.

Robinson, J. P., Shaver, P. R., & Wrightsman, L. S. (1991). *Measures of personality and social psychology attitudes.* San Diego: Academic Press.

Robinson et al. have done survey researchers a great service by bringing together in one volume many of the survey measures that have been widely used by social psychologists. Measures of constructs such as sex roles, life satisfaction, locus of control, shyness, authoritarianism, as well as many others are presented in topical chapters. The actual wording of questions is given, along with discussion of each measure's reliability, validity, and history of use. This volume should be a first stop in the search for previously developed social psychological measures.

4 Program Evaluation

S. Mark Pancer
Wilfrid Laurier University

Lakeview School is like many schools in cities across the Western world. The students range from 12 to 15 years of age. Some of them come from very wealthy homes, while others live in housing developments and are supported by government assistance. Over the last few years, there has been a substantial increase in the number of immigrant families who have moved into the school district. Walking along the school hallways, one now sees students with many variations of skin color, head coverings, and clothing, a number of them speaking with accents that clearly distinguish their origins as being from outside the country.

In its long history, Lakeview School has had few discipline problems of any note. There has been the occasional fight on the school premises, and some incidents of bullying. Within the last few years, however, the amount of fighting has increased substantially. Some of the students are afraid to go to school, for fear of being harassed and beaten. There are even reports that students are coming to school with weapons—pieces of metal pipe, knives, and the like.

These incidents and reports are of concern to everyone involved in the school—the principal, the teachers, the students, their parents, and local school officials. Members of the school's parents association have approached the school principal about their concerns, and it has been decided to form a committee to look into the problem and see what can be done about it. The school board has heard about the initiative that the Lakeview group is undertaking and has promised some funding to establish a program in the school to deal with school violence. If the Lakeview program proves to be successful, the board will consider the possibility of putting the program in place in other district schools that are experiencing similar problems.

When the committee holds its first meeting, it is confronted with a number of questions. How much violence is there in the school? Is the violence being experienced in other schools in the district? What kind of program should it develop? How will it know that the program, once it is developed, will be implemented as planned? How will it know whether it is successful? How much will the program cost, and will the benefits that are derived from the program be worth the costs incurred in operating the program?

PROGRAMS AND PROGRAM EVALUATION

The people at Lakeview School are not the only ones who struggle with these kinds of questions. Individuals who deal with a wide range of social problems, from poverty, to crime, to health problems such as AIDS or cardiovascular disease, must answer the same kinds of questions if they are to develop programs that are effective in dealing with these serious social issues. It was the need to find answers to questions such as these that gave rise to the science of program evaluation.

Before we can understand what is meant by the term *program evaluation,* it is useful to consider what is meant by a *program*. The key function of a social program is social change; using this as a basis, a *program* can be defined as an organized set of activities having as its main objective the production of some kind of change in the program's recipients or their environment.

Table 4–1 lists a number of different social programs and the kinds of changes that these programs are designed to effect. Some of these programs are designed to reduce problems such as crime, traffic fatalities, or behavior problems in school-children. Others are intended to increase or enhance factors that are associated with well-being, such as salary levels, job satisfaction, life skills, and self-esteem. Evaluators often refer to such changes as *outcomes* of the program.

Given that social programs can be defined in terms of social change, *program evaluation,* or the more current and comprehensive term, *evaluation research,* can be defined as the application of a broad range of social research methods to answer questions about the need for social programs, the way in which such programs are

TABLE 4–1 Program Change Goals

Program	Desired Change
Drinking and driving	Reduction in alcohol-related traffic offenses and deaths
Corrections (e.g., neighborhood watch)	Reduction in crime, recidivism
Job retraining	Reduction in unemployment; increase in salary levels, job satisfaction
Heart disease prevention	Reduction in incidence of cardiovascular disease; reduction in health care costs
Literacy programs	Increase in language skills such as reading and writing
Exercise, fitness programs	Improvement in physical health; reduction in absenteeism (for workplace fitness programs)

designed and implemented, and their effectiveness in producing desired changes or outcomes at a reasonable cost.

PURPOSES OF EVALUATION

Program evaluation is a relatively new discipline in the social sciences. It emerged in the 1960s, at about the same time that governments were embarking on a wide range of large-scale social programs in housing, income maintenance, health, education, criminal justice, and other areas (Shadish, Cook, & Leviton, 1991). The establishment of these programs required a massive increase in expenditures on the part of government. With these increases in spending came an increase in the need for accountability. Evaluation research promised to provide program managers with a means of proving that their programs were achieving the intended outcomes at a reasonable cost.

Another purpose of evaluation research is to aid in program improvement and decision making. Evaluation research can provide information that can help decision makers make adjustments to the program that will enhance its efficiency and effectiveness. Evaluation results can also be used in making decisions about whether to maintain funding for a program.

Program evaluation results can also be useful in terms of program advocacy and public relations. Results indicating that a program is having a significant impact on program participants provide a powerful base from which to advocate for a continuation of funding or an expansion of program services. Evaluation information can also be useful in informing the public about the nature of the program and the kinds of results the program has been achieving.

It is often the case that programs must evaluate their services in order to meet legislative or funding requirements. This is particularly true for new programs. In order to receive funding, new programs almost invariably must demonstrate that they have considered how they will evaluate their services by submitting a detailed evaluation plan.

APPROACHES TO EVALUATION

Evaluation research offers a wide range of different approaches to answering questions that concern those involved in social programs. These different approaches can often be combined when conducting a comprehensive evaluation of a program.

The Stakeholder Approach

There are many individuals and groups who have a stake in the outcome of any program evaluation. These "stakeholders" include the program's staff and managers, those who receive the program's services, members of the community in which the program operates, those who fund the program, and those responsible for evaluating the program. Each of these individuals and groups has a unique perspective on what the program is all about. The *stakeholder approach* to evaluation involves bringing together representatives of all the different groups that have a stake in the evaluation process to make decisions about how the program is to be evaluated (Weiss, 1983). By involving key stakeholders in the evaluation process, the needs of all those whose lives are affected by the program and its evaluation can be addressed, and there will be a better likelihood that the evaluation results will be used.

Utilization-Focused Evaluation

When program evaluation began to develop as both a social science and a profession, it was thought that evaluation results would have substantial and immediate effects on program operations. It came as somewhat of a shock, then, when a number of reviews of program evaluation studies indicated that, in general, evaluation results had had little impact on program decision making (e.g., Weiss, 1977). This discovery led to a search for a more *utilization-focused evaluation* approach, to ensure that evaluation results would be more relevant and useful in making program decisions. Patton (1986) suggested several ways in which evaluations could be made more utilization-focused: by considering the needs and interests of those who were in a position to use the evaluation results; by involving those intended users in the evaluation process; and by changing the evaluator's role from that of a "social scientist," who merely reports the results and then leaves, to a "change consultant," who continues to work with program stakeholders to help them plan their response to the evaluation results. This approach to program evaluation is similar to, and compatible with, a stakeholder approach to evaluation.

Quantitative versus Qualitative Approaches

Quantitative approaches to evaluation utilize objective measures (which produce quantitative or numerical scores) to gauge the extent to which a program is achieving its intended effects. This often involves administering standardized measures to program recipients at the beginning and end of their involvement in the program, and comparing their results to those from a group of individuals not involved in the program. For example, a program designed to enhance the academic achievement of school children might be evaluated by administering a standardized achievement test to the children before and after their involvement in the program and comparing their scores to a group of children who were not given the opportunity to participate in the program. If the children in the program achieve significantly higher scores than children in the comparison group, the program is considered to have been successful.

The purpose of *qualitative* or *naturalistic* approaches to program evaluation is to achieve an understanding of how the program is experienced by those who are involved in it. This usually requires the use of methods different from those employed in a quantitative evaluation. The evaluator using this kind of approach would most likely interview program stakeholders about their experience with, and perceptions of, the program. He or she would then make extensive observations of the program as it is in operation. These interviews and observations would then be analyzed to yield a description of the key elements of the program and the way it affects those involved, from the stakeholders' perspective. Rather than containing tables and numbers, a report based on a qualitative evaluation would likely include many quotes and descriptions of observations to help give the reader a sense of what it was like to be involved in the program, and how it affected those who were involved (Lincoln & Guba, 1985; Patton, 1990).

Formative and Summative Evaluation

One way of classifying or categorizing evaluations is in terms of the functions or purposes they serve. Scriven (1967), one of the pioneers in the theory of program evaluation, suggested that evaluations could be classified into those that were primarily formative or summative in their intent. *Formative* evaluations are designed primarily to provide information that can be used in helping to form, develop, or improve the program. *Summative* evaluations, on the other hand, are intended to provide information that can be used in "summing up" the program's worth or value. Summative evaluations typically occur at a later stage in the program's development, and they are designed to provide a kind of report card for the program, indicating the extent to which the program has achieved its major objectives.

The Developmental Stage Approach to Evaluation

Programs can be seen as progressing through a number of stages as they move from initial design to the point when staff have been hired and services are being provided on a stable, ongoing basis. Each stage in this process can be characterized by a major issue or question that needs to be resolved before proceeding to the next stage. For example, one of the first questions to be addressed in planning a program is how many people would be in need of such a program. A "needs assessment" would be the most appropriate type of evaluation research procedure for answering this question. Much later in the program's development, after the program has been in operation for some time, the key question to address is whether the program is having the desired impact on participants. An "outcome evaluation" would be the most appropriate evaluation procedure to employ at this stage of the program's development.

According to the *developmental stage* approach, the type of evaluation that is utilized should be closely related to the program's stage of development and the key issues that need to be addressed at that stage (Pancer & Westhues, 1989; Suchman, 1973). Table 4–2 lists the major stages that programs move through in the course of their development. It also details the key issue or question associated with each stage and the type of evaluation that is used to address the questions associated with

TABLE 4–2 Matching Evaluation With the Stage of Program Development

Stage of Program Development	Major Question Addressed	Type of Evaluation
Assessment of community needs	To what extent are community members achieving at least a minimal standard of health, education, literacy, etc.?	Needs Assessment
Design of program to meet community needs	What kind of program is needed to achieve at least a minimum standard of health and well-being?	Evaluability Assessment
Program implementation and operation	How can the program be put into operation, and once it is in operation, how do we determine whether it is operating as planned?	Process Evaluation
Producing program outcomes	Is the program having the intended effects?	Outcome Evaluation
	At the desired level of cost?	Cost-Benefit or Cost-Effectiveness Evaluation

that stage. Each of the major types of evaluation listed in the table is discussed in subsequent sections of this chapter.

ASSESSING THE NEED FOR PROGRAMS

Programs often come into being to deal with significant economic, social, health, and mental health problems. The more serious the problem, the more crucial it is to put a program into place to deal with it. But how can the severity of these problems be determined? The first step in doing this is to establish minimal standards of economic, social, physical, and emotional well-being. The "poverty line" is an example of such a standard. Many communities have agreed upon a level of income that is considered the minimum necessary for an individual or family to live without experiencing significant hardship. Families whose incomes fall below this level are likely to experience serious difficulties in terms of having adequate living accommodations, food, and other necessities. With the availability of such a standard, and a knowledge of the income levels of families within a particular community, one can determine how many "poor" people there are in a community simply by counting the number, or percentage, of families whose incomes fall below the minimum income level.

A *needs assessment* involves the identification of areas in which there is a gap between what is viewed as a necessary level and what actually exists. A comprehensive needs assessment involves not only identifying the kinds of needs experienced by a given population or community, but also the extent to which there are existing program resources already available in the community to address those needs (Siegel, Attkisson, & Carson, 1978). For example, a community that has a high number of poor families and few programs to assist those families is likely to be in greater need than a community with similar numbers of poor families but several programs already in place to address the needs of those families.

Three major kinds of approaches have been identified to assess needs: indicator approaches, survey approaches, and community impressions approaches (Milord, 1976).

Indicator Approaches

Indicator approaches to assessing the needs of a group or community involve the examination of "indicators" or information that is already available from a variety of sources (e.g., hospital and school records, census data, crime statistics). One type of indicator approach involves examining records of the extent to which presently available services are utilized. Consider the example of Lakeview School described at the beginning of this chapter. School officials in the Lakeview School district are considering putting programs to reduce violence into other schools in the district. One way of deciding which schools are most in need of such programs is to examine existing records from each school in the district to determine the number of incidents of violence (e.g., fights, bullying incidents) that have been reported at each of the schools over a specified period. One of the obvious limitations of such approaches is that they are dependent on the accuracy and validity of the records available. It may well be the case that many incidents of bullying or aggression are not reported to school officials because the victims fear reprisals from the perpetrators.

Another indicator approach involves using available statistics in a more inferential or indirect manner. This approach usually entails defining a "population-at-risk." In other words, a particular segment of the population may have a significantly greater likelihood of developing a problem or condition. It has been clearly established, for example, that there is a relationship between poverty and both physical and mental health problems (Wilkinson, 1986). The poor, then, would constitute a population-at-risk for mental health problems. In deciding where to establish a mental health program, one could use census data to identify those neighborhoods that contain a high proportion of individuals with low incomes and would therefore be more likely to experience mental health problems. Although such approaches are relatively easy and inexpensive to use, their indirect nature and reliance on inference caution against using them as the only indication of need.

Survey Approaches

Surveys provide a much more direct indication of need in a given population. In conducting a needs assessment by means of a survey, one would administer a measure designed to identify problems or conditions to a random sample of individuals from the group or population of concern. To determine the extent to which violence is a problem at each of the schools in the Lakeview School district, for example, a random sample of students at each of the schools may be asked to complete a survey that asks them how often they have been involved in violent episodes (e.g., threats, fights, bullying). This approach was used by Olweus (1991) to determine the incidence of bullying in Norwegian schools (see Box 4–1). Surveys represent an improvement over indicator approaches in that they provide a more direct and valid indication of need. Their major drawback is that they typically require a large expenditure of time and money.

Community Impressions Approaches

Community impressions approaches involve asking for people's impressions of what the most prevalent needs are by means of key informant interviews, focus groups, and community forums. In gathering impressions of need by means of *key informant interviews*, one would generate a list of 10 to 15 individuals who are particularly knowledgeable about the needs of the group being assessed. For example, if one were considering a program to deal with school violence, the list of key informants might include school counselors, school officials, or student representatives from

Box
4–1 **An Example of a Program Evaluation:**
The Norwegian Antibullying Program

It is an unfortunate truism that those who fall victim to social evils such as crime and violence are often those with the least power in society. This kind of victimization can begin at a very young age, as research on bullying and child aggression shows us. Bullying can range from indirect behaviors such as teasing, gossip, and the subtle exclusion of victimized children from group activities, to more direct behaviors involving extortion, verbal attacks, and physical abuse. Studies in Norway, the United Kingdom, and Canada tell us that large numbers of school children are harassed and bullied by their peers. A nationwide survey conducted in Norway indicated that some 83,000 students—about one student in seven—were involved in bullying incidents "now and then" or more frequently (Olweus, 1991). A recent survey in Toronto, Canada, revealed even higher rates of bullying, with 15% of students indicating that they had bullied others more than once or twice during the previous term at school, and 20% indicating that they had been the victims of bullying more than once or twice during the term (Ziegler & Rosenstein-Manner, 1991).

The consequences of bullying are harmful to both the victim and the perpetrator. Victims of bullying experience considerable emotional and physical pain. They often blame themselves for the attacks and come to see themselves as worthless and unattractive. These feelings can have a devastating impact; in 1982, three Norwegian boys aged 10 to 14 committed suicide as a consequence of severe bullying by their peers. The outcomes for the bullies themselves can also be quite negative. Olweus (1991) found that 60% of the boys who had been characterized as bullies in grades 6 to 9 had been convicted of a crime by the time they reached the age of 24.

The suicides of the three Norwegian boys in 1982 triggered a number of reactions, culminating in the initiation of a nationwide antibullying program in Norwegian schools in the fall of 1983. The main elements of the program included the circulation of a publication that informed schools about bullying and provided strategies that teachers could use to deal with the problem, parent-teacher meetings to inform parents about the problem, and the establishment of rules in each classroom concerning bullying and how such behavior would be dealt with. In addition, a four-page booklet containing information and advice on bullying was distributed through the schools to all families with school-age children, and a video showing episodes from the lives of two bullied children was shown widely throughout the country.

The evaluation of the program involved collecting information from approximately 2,500 students from grades 4 to 7 over a period of several years. In the spring term of 1983, 4 months prior to the beginning of the intervention in the fall, each student was asked to respond to two key questions concerning bullying over the previous term: (a) How often have you been bullied in school?; and (b) How often have you taken part in bullying other students in school? Responses were made on a scale that ranged from "it hasn't happened this spring" (scored 0) to "about once a week" (scored 3) to "several times a day" (scored 6). These questions were asked again the following spring, 8 months after the intervention began, and in the spring term after that, 20 months after the intervention began.

The fact that the program was adopted in all schools in the country presented a challenge to developing a suitable evaluation design. How could the evaluators find a group of children not involved in the program to compare with children who were involved if all children in the country participated in the program? The solution that they decided upon was to utilize a "quasi-experimental design" in which children's postintervention scores were compared with the preintervention scores of children who had been the same age a year earlier and had not yet, at that time, been involved in the intervention. For example, the outcome scores of children in grade 5 who had just completed 8 months of the program were compared to the previous year's scores of children who had been in grade 5 that year and had not yet been exposed to the program.

The results of the evaluation indicated marked differences between the children who had been involved in the program compared with children of the same age before their involvement in the program, with a reduction of approximately 50% in students' reports of being bullied or of bullying others. Evaluation research played an important role in the initiation and development of the antibullying program, and its use in other countries. Olweus's needs assessment research on the prevalence of bullying in Norwegian schools helped convince government authorities to mount the program in the first place. The evaluation of the program's outcomes told those in government and the school system that the program was working and helped convince people in several other countries that policies and programs like those developed in Norway merited serious consideration.

groups that are frequent targets of such violence. Each of these individuals would likely be familiar with many students who had been involved in violent incidents in the school and would therefore be knowledgeable about the prevalence and seriousness of the problem.

In a typical *focus group,* 8 to 12 individuals convene to discuss a particular topic under the direction of a facilitator or a moderator (Stewart & Shamdasani, 1990). The moderator is present to ensure that everyone has a chance to express an opinion on the issues at hand, and to keep the discussion on topic. The group is "focused" in that it is usually asked to address a small number of key questions. In a focus group concerned with school violence, for example, focus groups consisting of 8 to 10 students might be asked to discuss questions such as "To what extent is school violence a problem at this school?"

In a *community forum,* the entire community is invited to a meeting to discuss the issue of concern. As in a focus group, the discussion is focused on a particular question or issue, and a moderator or panel is present to facilitate the discussion. Each person is given a limited amount of time to speak, and the major purpose is to elicit as many perspectives as possible on the needs of the community.

The major advantage of community impressions approaches such as key informant interviews, focus groups, and community forums is that they allow stakeholders a direct involvement in identifying their needs. The major disadvantage of such procedures is that relatively few individuals—those key informants who are interviewed, or those who attend the focus groups or community forums—are the ones involved in identifying the needs of the entire community. This can be problematic if a significant proportion of the individuals who are not interviewed, or who do not attend the group interviews or forums, have different ideas about what their community needs.

ASSESSING A PROGRAM'S EVALUABILITY

After it is decided that a program is needed, many other questions arise. What kinds of goals should that program be trying to accomplish? What kind of program should be put into place? How likely is it that the program that is being planned will achieve its objectives? These questions apply not only to programs in the design stage; they are also relevant for programs that have been in operation for some time. *Evaluability assessment* (Rutman, 1977, 1980; Wholey, 1987) is a procedure that is designed to answer these kinds of questions.

Evaluability assessment focuses on three features of a program: its goals or intended effects, the program activities or services that are used to achieve those goals or effects, and the rationale or logic that links the goals and program activities. In order for a program to be considered "evaluable," that is, ready for a formal evaluation of its services, the following conditions should apply:

- The program goals must be clear, specific, and measurable
- Its major activities should be coherent and clearly articulated
- There should be a convincing rationale as to why the program's activities should be expected to achieve the program's major goals

In the following sections, each of these elements of evaluability is considered in turn.

Program Goals

There is perhaps nothing more crucial to the development of a sound program than a set of clearly articulated, concrete, and measurable program goals. It is the goals of a program that justify its reason for existence, for they express the essence of what the program is attempting to accomplish. In general, two different kinds of goals can be specified for a particular program. *Service or activity goals* (Pancer, 1989; Patton, 1986; Rush & Ogborne, 1991) relate to the kinds of services that the program provides, or the kinds of activities in which the program engages. They refer to what the program does and describe a desired level of program services or activities over a specified period of time. Consider the example of Lakeview School. In order to reduce the incidence of violence in the school, Lakeview School has initiated an antiviolence program. This plan involves the distribution of printed educational material about school violence to parents, teachers, and students and calls for a series of classroom discussions about fighting and bullying in an attempt to provide the students with nonviolent ways of resolving their difficulties. The service or activity goals for such a program specify the amount of service or activity the program undertakes. The antiviolence program might, for example, set itself the following goals:

- To distribute educational materials to all children from the school, as well as to their parents
- To have at least two discussions concerning school violence with each class in the school

Often, programs will include only service or activity goals in documents that describe what they are trying to accomplish. Although these kinds of goals are important, if only service goals are provided to indicate what a program is attempting to achieve, a critical element of the program's purpose is missing. As defined earlier, the major objective of a program is to bring about some kind of change in the program participants or their environment. This suggests that a comprehensive description of a program's purposes should include goals that describe the kinds of changes that will occur in program participants or their environments as a result of the program's operations. Goals relating to these changes are referred to as *change or outcome goals* (Pancer, 1989; Patton, 1986; Rush & Ogborne, 1991). In the Lakeview antiviolence program, the key change goal would likely be to reduce the number of violent incidents (e.g., threats, fights, bullying) involving students at Lakeview School.

In order to ensure that they are concrete and measurable, a program's goals should specify not only what the program is attempting to change (e.g., participants' knowledge, skills, attitudes, behavior, health status), but also how large a change is expected, over what time the changes are expected to occur, and how long the changes are expected to last.

Program Activities

Often, programs receive funding even though very little information is provided about the activities they will include. This poses serious difficulties for individuals who are attempting to evaluate the program. Suppose there is evidence that students who have participated in an antiviolence program are less likely to be involved in violent incidents. What produced this outcome? How would someone go about replicating the program in other schools? Suppose the program has proved unsuccessful. How would one determine why the program failed? Was it because the educational materials provided insufficient information to help students, parents, and teachers deal with the problem, or were the classroom discussions not engaging or sufficiently relevant to capture students' interest? Without a detailed knowledge of what constitutes the major program activities, these questions are difficult to answer.

A comprehensive description of a program's activities requires a detailed account of what happens to individuals who participate in the program. How do they first come to participate in the program? Who provides the program services or activities? Who participates in the program? What do the service providers say to or do with participants? For example, a comprehensive description of the antiviolence program at Lakeview School would include a detailed account of what was contained in the educational materials, how lengthy they were, and how and to whom they were distributed. For the classroom discussions, the program description would include information on the number of discussions held with each class, the length of each discussion, who led the discussion, and the topics and questions that were addressed in the discussion.

Program Logic or Theory

It takes a great deal of effort and expense to develop and implement a program. If the program fails, this effort and expense has gone to waste. Unfortunately, this kind of result occurs much too frequently. Why does this happen? In many instances, program developers have not given enough attention to the *logic* or *theory* that underlies their program (Bickman, 1987; Pancer & Westhues, 1989). The logic of the program provides a link between the program's activities and its intended effects. It provides a justification for expecting that the program's activities will produce the desired changes in program participants or their environments. This kind of linking rationale can come from sources such as evaluations of programs designed to deal with similar needs or problems or from theories or research about the causes of the problems to be dealt with. An illustration of the latter can be seen in the development of a program to help children who were having difficulty getting along with their peers. Shure and Spivack (1988) had found, in earlier research, that adolescents who were having difficulty relating to their peers seemed to be "stuck" on one way of handling conflicts. When the investigators incorporated training in how to think about different ways of dealing with conflicts into their problem-solving skills program, they were able to help children improve their ability to get along with their peers. The earlier research, in this instance, provided a reason for expecting a program that included such activities to produce better interpersonal skills.

ASSESSING A PROGRAM'S PROCESSES AND SERVICES

When a program is planned, a great deal of consideration is given to the kinds of services that will be provided and whom those services are meant to benefit. For a program to be successful, services of reasonable quality should be provided in sufficient quantities to individuals who are truly in need. Unfortunately, there are many instances in which program services aren't provided in sufficient quantities (Rossi, 1978), or the quality of those services is so poor that it is unlikely that anyone would ever benefit from them. Sometimes, high-quality programs are provided in sufficient quantities, but they are provided to individuals who don't really need them.

How can one ensure that programs are provided in sufficient quantity and quality to the right people? The first step, as indicated in the previous section on program evaluability, would be to establish service or activity goals that specify the kinds of activities that should be occurring, and their extent or amount. Once these are specified, however, how is one to determine whether the goals have been achieved? One means of doing this is through a management information system.

Management Information Systems

A management information system is a way of collecting information about program participants and the program activities in which they are involved, in order to aid in program management. Information about program participants is often collected when individuals first come into contact with a program, by means of an "intake" form. At this time, each individual who is going to be involved in the program can be asked about age, educational level, marital status, income level, and the reason for becoming involved in the program. By aggregating the information from the intake forms of all individuals who become involved in the program over a specified period (usually a month, quarter, or year), one can obtain a detailed picture of the people who are participating in the program. Consider, for example, a program of fitness classes that is designed to improve the cardiovascular health of people who don't get regular exercise. It would be important to ask participants how much exercise they have been getting on a weekly basis. If it turns out that most of the people who have signed up for the program are already getting regular exercise, the program may not be attracting the individuals it was originally designed to help. This information would be useful to the program managers. They might decide to advertise their program in a different way in order to appeal to more individuals who really need the program.

In order to monitor the nature and amount of services that a program provides, information is often collected each time an individual participates. In a fitness program, this could involve keeping a record for each individual, noting the kinds of exercises that individual has participated in, as well as the length of each exercise session. This information can be aggregated to obtain information such as how many people participate in the program over a given period of time, and how much exercise each participant gets over that time period. This kind of information can be useful in making decisions about the program. If it is determined, for example, that most participants are coming to exercise classes only once a week (a frequency that is considered insufficient to produce any cardiovascular benefit), the program has to find a way to increase the frequency of attendance.

Process Evaluation and Quality Assurance

Process evaluation and quality assurance techniques are used to assess the nature of the services or activities provided by the program, and the extent to which these services achieve a reasonable standard of quality. The focus of *process evaluation* is on how the program operates, as opposed to what it produces in the way of outcomes. Such evaluation typically involves observation of the program while it is in operation as well as interviews with program managers, staff, and participants. The purpose of these observations and interviews is to determine what elements of the program are helpful in allowing it to achieve its intended outcomes, and what elements are not helpful. Pancer, McKenzie-Mohr, and Orr (1995) utilized a process evaluation approach as part of their assessment of a group therapy program for men who had assaulted their female partners. By observing several of the weekly group sessions and interviewing men who had participated in the program, the evaluators were able to determine what some of the more useful elements of the program were. One of the elements that appeared to be crucial in helping the men change their abusive attitudes and behaviors was the fact that each of the groups had a female co-leader who could provide a woman's perspective on the issues that were discussed.

Quality assurance procedures are used to ensure that the quality of the services provided by the program meets a reasonable standard (Frankel & Sinclair, 1982; Sinclair & Frankel, 1984). The first step in such a procedure is the development of the standards or criteria against which program processes or services will be gauged. The standards that are used may concern items such as the qualifications of the program staff who are providing the services, the nature of the services provided, or the physical environment in which the program takes place. One type of program for which there has been considerable development of these kinds of quality standards is early childhood or day-care programs. The Early Childhood Environment Rating Scale (ECERS) (Harms & Clifford, 1980), for example, is an instrument that is widely used across North America to assess the quality of day-care programs for children. In completing the ECERS, an assessor rates several different features of the day-care environment, such as the extent to which stimulating toys are available for the children's use.

ASSESSING PROGRAM OUTCOMES

The ultimate, and arguably most important, basis on which to evaluate a program is the extent to which it has achieved its change or outcome goals. The most common way of evaluating a program's outcomes or impact involves the use of quantitative methods. A more recent approach, which has received growing recognition from evaluators and program personnel, has involved the use of qualitative or naturalistic methods.

The Quantitative Approach

Earlier, a program was defined as an organized set of activities designed to produce certain specified changes in the program participants or their environments. In conducting a quantitative outcome evaluation, one of the first steps is to find a suitable measure of those behaviors that are supposed to change as a result of the program. To evaluate a program designed to reduce school violence, for example, one would want to find some way of measuring the amount of violent or aggressive behavior in the school. This could be accomplished in a number of ways. Successful approaches might include: observing the students and recording the number of incidents involving threat and fighting that occur during the observation period; having students keep a daily log in which they make note of any threats or fights in which they are involved; or having students estimate retrospectively how many aggressive incidents they have experienced over a given period of time.

Once a suitable measure is found, the next step in conducting a quantitative outcome evaluation is to specify an evaluation design. The key objective of this design is to answer two major questions:

1. To what extent have the desired changes (specified in the program goals) occurred?
2. Can these changes be attributed to the program?

An evaluation design is simply a plan that specifies when and to whom the selected outcome measure will be administered. These two key elements determine the confidence with which one can say that the program participants changed in the desired way and that any changes were the result of involvement in the program. Table 4–3 presents two possible designs for an outcome evaluation of a program designed to help reduce violence in school.

In the first design, the one group, pretest posttest design, 50 students who have volunteered for the antiviolence program are observed during free-play periods for a period of 1 month. Let us suppose that, in total, these children are involved in 73 aggressive incidents over that 1-month period. They then participate in a 3-month program that is designed to change their attitudes toward aggressive behavior and provide them with some skills that will help them solve their problems without resorting to violence. When the program ends, the students are again observed for a 1-month period, during which time the number of aggressive incidents drops to 16. What does this tell us? It indicates that the kinds of changes the program was de-

TABLE 4–3 Two Evaluation Designs

One Group Pretest Posttest Design			
Participants	Pretest	Program	Posttest
50 program participants	number of aggressive incidents in month before program (73 incidents)	3-month antiviolence program	number of aggressive incidents in month after program (16 incidents)

Pretest Posttest Design With a Comparison Group			
Participants	Pretest	Program	Posttest
Program Group: 50 program participants	number of aggressive incidents in month before program (73 incidents)	3-month antiviolence program	number of aggressive incidents in month after program (16 incidents)
Comparison Group: 50 students who were not involved in program	number of aggressive incidents in month before program (70 incidents)	no program	number of aggressive incidents in month after program (72 incidents)

signed to produce have actually occurred. We can therefore answer the first question, which asks whether the desired change has occurred, in the affirmative.

Can these changes be attributed to the program? Unfortunately, the one group pretest posttest design does not give us much confidence in saying that it was participation in the program that produced the change that occurred. Many things might have occurred during the 3 months that the program was operating that could have produced the reduction in the number of aggressive incidents observed. For example, new, nonviolent games or activities could have become popular during the 3-month program period, and children's involvement in these games during their free playtime may have kept them so busy that they didn't have time to get involved in fights and bullying. Thus, it may have been the games, and not the program, that produced the reduction in violent behavior. By adding a comparison group to the pretest posttest design (see Table 4–3), we can determine with much greater confidence whether any changes that we observed were the result of the program. In the comparison group design, the number of aggressive incidents involving individuals who have not participated in the program are recorded during the same month-long periods during which program participants were observed. If comparison group individuals do not show a reduction in aggressive episodes, and program participants do, then we can be more confident that it was the program that produced the reduction in violence for program participants. The more similar comparison group individuals are to those in the program group, the more certain we can be that it was the program, and not some other factor, that produced any changes we see. The best way of ensuring equivalence between the comparison group and the program group is to assign individuals who have volunteered for the program randomly to one or the other of the two groups.

Qualitative Approaches

Qualitative or naturalistic approaches to program evaluation make some fundamentally different assumptions about the impact that a program has on those who are involved. These approaches assume that programs are complex entities that are unique to the social, historical, and temporal context in which they are embedded. They assume further that each person involved in the program will have an experience that is to some extent unique and cannot be adequately described by looking at numerical scores on a few standardized measures. In order to develop a more complete and meaningful understanding of people's experiences with a program, a naturalistic evaluator would argue that different, more qualitative methods must be employed.

Three major data collection methods are used in qualitative evaluation research: (a) in-depth, open-ended interviews; (b) direct observation; and (c) review of program documents and records (Patton, 1990). The interviews, observations, and documents are the sources of the quotes and descriptions that make up the "data" contained in a qualitative evaluation report. The major purpose of a qualitative evaluation report is to give the reader a sense of what it was like to be involved in the program, and how the program affected those who participated. The following quote was taken from a report on an evaluation of a program designed to reduce social, emotional, physical, and school problems in young children from families living in low-income neighborhoods (Pancer & Cameron, 1995). One of the program's distinguishing features was that the children's parents were involved in developing the programs that would be offered in their communities. In the following quote, a project mother talks about how she became involved in the program, and what this involvement meant to her:

> At the beginning, I was not hoping to get anything. It was just an outlet. I didn't think about getting a job out of it or anything like that. It was just a place to go that I didn't have to take a bus. But then, sitting on various committees and actually having people seeming like they were listening to me [gave me] confidence 'cause I thought, I always knew I had a brain but it was dormant there for a while . . . and I started getting respect for the first time in a long time. People were actually listening to me.

Quantitative or Qualitative?

How does one decide whether to use a quantitative or qualitative approach to a particular evaluation? If the purpose is to gain a holistic, in-depth understanding of the program's impact from the perspective of those involved in the program, a qualitative approach would be the method of choice. If, on the other hand, the purpose of the evaluation is to determine the extent to which all program participants have achieved the goals established by the program, a quantitative approach would be preferable. However, a number of evaluation researchers have argued that the best approach is one of "methodological pluralism," in which both qualitative and quantitative methods are employed in any evaluation (Patton, 1990; Sechrest & Sidani, 1995).

ASSESSING PROGRAM COSTS IN RELATION TO PROGRAM OUTCOMES

One of the most important decisions faced by policymakers, governments, and human service organizations is how to allocate the limited resources at their disposal. With limited resources, not every program can be funded. How is one to decide which programs should be supported and which should not? One basis on which to make these decisions is the effectiveness of the program. Another is the cost of the program. *Cost-benefit* and *cost-effectiveness* analysis are methods that allow one to look at program outcomes or effects in relation to the costs required to produce them.

The first step in each of these analytic approaches is to determine the costs of the program. The typical procedure in assessing costs is the "ingredients" approach (Levin, 1975). This involves listing all the "ingredients" or inputs that are required to operate the program; these ingredients would include the staff or personnel needed to provide program services, the facilities in which the program operates, and any materials or equipment required. Once the ingredients have been specified, a cost can be determined for each, and a total program cost can be calculated by totaling the costs of the individual ingredients. This total cost can then be converted to a cost per program participant (by dividing by the total number of participants), or a cost per hour of service (by dividing by the total number of hours of service provided).

Cost-Benefit Analysis

One way of looking at program outcomes in relation to program costs is to put both outcomes and costs in dollar amounts. Such an approach was used in the evaluation of the Perry Preschool Program in Ypsilanti, Michigan (Schweinhart & Weikart, 1988). This program was designed to provide high-quality early childhood education to poor children in an attempt to counteract some of the educational deficiencies that might otherwise impede their progress in later life. Three- and four-year-old children from families of low socioeconomic status were randomly assigned to the specialized preschool program or to a control group. Those in the preschool group attended classes 5 mornings a week for 7 months of the year, and their parents received a home visit from a teacher once a week, at a cost of approximately $5,000 per child for a year in the program. The children who had been in the preschool program and the control group were then followed for several years. By the age of 19, those who attended the preschool, when compared to control children, were less likely to have needed special education services (for an average savings of $5,000 per child), to have been arrested (a savings of $3,000), or to have received welfare assistance (a savings of $16,000). The total benefits, in terms of reduced costs, were approximately $28,000, over five times the annual program operation costs for each child in the program.

Cost-Effectiveness Analysis

Not all programs produce outcomes that can be measured in dollars and cents. Mental health or literacy programs, for example, yield outcomes that would be difficult to put into monetary terms. This means that one can no longer talk about whether a program's benefits are greater than its costs, because the benefits are measured in different units than the costs. One is monetary; the other is not. Program outcomes can still be looked at, however, in relation to program costs through the use of cost-effectiveness analysis.

Consider a case in which there are two different programs designed to improve the reading skills of young children. One program has children working with a professional tutor on a twice-weekly basis, and the other involves assigning children to volunteer "reading buddies" who read with them each day. Both programs are proven effective in improving children's reading skills, but the tutoring program is slightly more effective, producing an increase of 2 grade levels in reading, compared to a 1.5 grade level increase for children in the buddy program. However, the tutorial program is also more expensive, costing $800 for each child, compared to the buddy program's costs of $300 for each child. How does one decide which program to support? In employing cost-effectiveness analysis, a cost-effectiveness ratio is calculated for each program, that ratio being an indication of how much it costs to produce a unit of change or outcome. This would show that it costs $400 for each grade-level increase in reading using the tutorial program, and only $200 for each grade-level increase using the buddy program. In other words, the cost-per-unit increase is lower for the reading buddy program than for the tutorial program.

SUMMARY

Social programs are complex and expensive undertakings. Every stage in the development of a program poses challenges and questions that must be carefully considered in order to maximize the program's ultimate likelihood of success. Evaluation research can play a crucial role in helping to answer the questions that arise in the process of developing and implementing programs, and in assessing a program's impact.

Although evaluation research employs many of the techniques and methods used in other kinds of applied social research, it is different from them in a number of ways. Much applied social research is designed to help us understand important social issues or problems, or to provide us with ideas about what kinds of policies or programs might be effective in addressing these issues or problems. Evaluation research can be used to achieve these same ends, but its major purpose is more immediate. Its mission is to guide the ongoing development and day-to-day operation of programs, so that those programs can achieve maximum effect at a reasonable cost.

Another key difference between other kinds of applied social research and evaluation research concerns the role of the researcher. Evaluation researchers play a much more active role than other kinds of researchers in the ongoing decision-making process that occurs in the development and implementation of social programs. Today's evaluation researcher must be knowledgeable about the politics and dynamics of organizations and skilled in working with stakeholder groups, in addition to being familiar with the tools and techniques of applied research. The modern role of the evaluation researcher has been described as that of a change consultant or change agent, working hand-in-hand with program stakeholders to conduct research that will help shape programs that will achieve maximum benefit to society (Guba & Lincoln, 1989; Patton, 1986).

SUGGESTED READINGS

Evaluation and Program Planning. Tarrytown, NY: Pergamon.

> This major journal publishes articles based on evaluations of a wide range of social programs. The focus is on program planning as well as evaluation, and how evaluation research can contribute to the process of planning programs.

Evaluation Review. Thousand Oaks, CA: Sage.

This is one of the major journals in the evaluation research field. It publishes results of evaluation studies in areas such as child development, health, education, and social welfare. It also contains a number of articles on various evaluation methodologies and on the present "state of the art" in evaluation research.

Patton, M. Q. (1986). *Utilization-focused evaluation* (2nd ed.). Newbury Park, CA: Sage.

This practical and readable book provides guidelines for conducting evaluation research. The focus is on how to ensure that evaluation results are actually used to improve the effectiveness and impact of programs.

Patton, M. Q. (1990). *Qualitative evaluation and research methods*. Newbury Park, CA: Sage.

Evaluation researchers looking for a comprehensive guide to the use of qualitative methods in program evaluation will find this volume most useful.

Posavac, E. J., & Carey, R. G. (1992). *Program evaluation: Methods and case studies* (4th ed.). Englewood Cliffs, NJ: Prentice Hall.

One of the major texts in the evaluation research field, this book provides information on the planning of evaluations, the use of evaluation in planning and monitoring programs, quantitative and qualitative approaches to outcome evaluation, and the analysis of costs in relation to outcomes. It also deals with a number of issues relating to the practice of evaluation, such as ethical standards in conducting evaluation research, and how to write an evaluation report.

Rossi, P. H., & Freeman, H. E. (1993). *Evaluation: A systematic approach* (5th ed.). Thousand Oaks, CA: Sage.

One of the first major texts in evaluation research, this book is now in its fifth edition. It provides a thorough review of how evaluation research can be used to assess the need for programs, assist in planning and monitoring programs, and examine program outcomes.

5 Social Psychology of Health Care

Stanley W. Sadava

Brock University

Dr. Ed Rosenbaum had a long and distinguished career as a specialist in internal medicine and rheumatology, and as chief of staff at a major medical center. Medicine was a family obsession: A brother, three sons, and two daughters-in-law had all taken on medical careers.

For some time, he had experienced a persistent sore throat and hoarseness. After a period of denial, he described his symptoms to a colleague over coffee (a "curbstone consultation"). His colleague took a quick look and assured him that this was nothing to worry about. Over the next few years, several "quick and dirty" diagnoses were offered, including allergies and "something psychological." Reassured, he carried on. Eventually, a colleague looked at his case more carefully and sent him off for a biopsy. Suddenly, he had switched roles: Now, he was Ed Rosenbaum, a "helpless patient," transported about in a wheelchair, wearing skimpy hospital gowns, given the usual consent forms to sign. One day he was told that he would have to go to another building for a new ID card to suit the new computer system. After another hour of waiting, he was given his new card, which had his correct name but omitted the MD. "They have completely reduced me to the status of a patient" (Rosenbaum, 1988, p. 116).

Above all was the waiting, waiting with increasing anxiety about the possible results of the biopsy. Finally came the diagnosis that he feared: cancer of the larynx. He was assured that it was quite treatable, and treatment was begun quickly. He was required to undergo more examinations and further tests, including CAT scans. When one resident estimated an 85% success rate with radiation treatment for this type of cancer, Rosenbaum observed that prescribing is different from receiving. Despite the fact that, as Ed the doctor, he understood outcome research, Ed the patient was increasingly apprehensive.

On one occasion, after a treatment, he was ready to leave but was instructed to stay, as it was Tuesday, "Doctor's Day." As he had important questions to ask his physicians, he remained for some hours, after which he was told that the physician was too busy to see him now, and he would have to wait until next week. Next week, he enjoyed a short and perfunctory visit with his radiologist. On his last treatment, he was allowed to talk only to the assistant of his physician who, he was assured, was "as good as Dr. R."

At last, the moment of truth had arrived: assessing the results of treatment. The physician entered the room, anaesthetized the throat for an examination, then exited without comment. On his return, he examined the throat and simply said "so far, so good." Then he left the room, leaving his patient in a state of limbo, alone with his fears. Eventually the positive results of treatment became evident, and he returned to practice and a full life.

Dr. Ed Rosenbaum's book became, in altered form, a motion picture, *The Doctor* (Randa Haines, 1991), starring William Hurt. It is recommended as a fine illustration of the roles of patient and physician.

Psychology has become deeply involved in promoting good health, preventing and treating illness, and improving the health care system (Matarazzo, 1980). Social psychology has been defined as the discipline that sets out to understand how the thoughts, feelings, and behaviors of individuals are influenced by the actual, imagined, or implied presence of others (Allport, 1935). This chapter sets out to explore the interface between health and social psychology, and to examine the ways in which social psychology can be applied to understand or solve health-related issues (Oskamp, 1984). Examples of the social psychology of health include applying the principles of persuasion to influence people to quit smoking and begin an exercise program, studying how physicians and patients communicate, and investigating how interpersonal relationships can affect health or recovery from illness.

Much of the research in social psychology has been devoted to the study of primary prevention, promoting healthier lifestyles, safe sex, and so on. Other research has explored factors that contribute to illness, such as the role of stress. Each of these productive research areas would easily constitute a chapter in itself. In the present chapter, health care—the treatment of illness within medicine and the allied professions—is the focus.

First, two social psychological factors related to the etiology (i.e., causes) of illnesses and recovery from illness are examined: gender and the relationship between stress and social support. Then discussion turns to what it means to be sick. Sickness as a social role, the importance of a sense of control, and the impact of medical technology are discussed. Next, the relationship between physicians and their patients, as well as the problem of patient noncompliance with the recommendations of their physicians, is examined. The chapter concludes with some recommendations for change.

ETIOLOGY AND RECOVERY

Life Expectancy, Health, and Gender

Everyone hopes for a long and healthy life. Life expectancy, however, is not distributed evenly in society; for example, in 1988 the life expectancy in the United States was 75.6 years for whites but only 69.4 years for African Americans. Socioeconomic status also is a powerful determinant of health and illness, and these differences appear at all levels of social class; that is, those who are the wealthiest enjoy better health than those who are somewhat less affluent, and those in poverty have the lowest life expectancies (Adler et al., 1994). In this section, two apparently contradictory facts are discussed: Women tend to have longer life expectancies than men but experience more illness during their lives.

Women in the developed world live an average of about 7 years longer than men (Wingard, 1984). Indeed, the survival advantage for women has increased dramatically since 1900 (Wingard & Cohn, 1990). Since deaths due to pregnancy and childbirth have declined spectacularly (Waldron, 1983), women's advantage in life expectancy exists at every stage in the life cycle, from conception to death (Strickland, 1988).

Why would this be true? In part, it relates to behavior. Men are at least twice as likely as women to die from lung cancer, cirrhosis of the liver, heart disease, violence, suicide, or accidents. Other data show that males tend to engage more frequently in high-risk behaviors, such as smoking, excessive drinking, and various forms of acting-out (Harrison, 1978). Indeed, the female advantage has declined somewhat in recent years, accompanied by increases in female smoking and other substance use (Rodin & Ickovics, 1990). Beyond these social and behavioral differences, the very real possibility that biological factors play a protective role for women must be considered. For example, the role of estrogen as a protective factor in cardiovascular disease is well established.

However, despite their greater life expectancy, women tend to have higher rates of physical illness, more days in which they are disabled or unable to work, and more visits to a physician; and they use both prescription and nonprescription drugs more frequently (Verbrugge, 1989). At least five reasons have been suggested to explain the apparent tendency for women to experience more illness: (a) *biological differences* based on hormones or genes that render women more vulnerable to certain illnesses; (b) *acquired risks* of illness and injury encountered in work and leisure activities, lifestyle, and health habits, such as smoking and driving habits (although some of these risks may be more characteristic of the male role, others may be more typical among women); (c) *psychosocial* aspects of health, in particular how men and women react differently to the perception of symptoms and decisions regarding medical care (e.g., sick role behavior); (d) *health-reporting behavior,* including the fact that women are more likely to talk about their symptoms to family, friends, physicians, and interviewers; and (e) women use medical care more consistently than men, and the effects of taking better care of themselves may be more evident in later life. Note that in the United States for example, 70% of all tranquilizers and antidepressant medications are prescribed to women, and 66% of surgical proce-dures are performed on women (Rodin & Ickovics, 1990).

It is generally believed that sick role behavior, health reporting, and prior health care largely account for these male-female differences, although one urban Canadian study suggests that the differences are relatively modest (Kandrack, Grant, & Segall, 1991). Will these factors account for the greater morbidity (i.e., ill-ness) rates in women? An important study by Verbrugge (1989) utilized survey data from a metropolitan area in the United States. After an extensive initial interview, participants kept a daily *health diary* in which they recorded symptoms, health-related actions, mood, and events of the day. Included in the data are measures of acquired risks (e.g., lifestyle, stress, socioeconomic factors), psychosocial factors of health (e.g., how individuals value health, their attitudes toward their own health, feelings of vulnerability to illness), and health-reporting behavior. In general, their results indicated that men reported more satisfying and less stressful lives but more exposure to lifestyle risks such as smoking, alcohol consumption, and obesity. Men also tended to be somewhat less likely to seek medical care because of time con-straints and a lack of established ties to their physicians; there were no consistent sex differences in health-reporting behavior. When sex differences in these factors were statistically controlled, the differences in illness rates between men and women nar-rowed to the vanishing point. Again, one must consider the possibility that being male is a biological risk (Harrison, 1978).

Stress and Social Support

Over 90 years ago, the pioneering sociologist Durkeim (1897–1951) described how the emergence of an industrialized, technological society was leading to the loss of a sense of social integration, as the ties between individuals and their extended fami-lies, religious institutions, and communities were strained or dissolved. He argued that the resulting loss of supportive relationships was antithetical to well-being, leading to outcomes such as suicide.

More recently, an extensive literature has linked resistance to stress to the ex-istence of a network of people on whom we can rely, whom we know value us and care for us. As always, measurement of social support is an important consideration. Some research focuses on the network of social support, whereas other studies focus on feelings of belonging and satisfaction with the support that people can derive from their relationships (Sarason, Levine, Basham, & Sarason, 1983). Of course, so-cial support may be restricted in *domain,* such as the solid support received from a superior or fellow worker on the job, because this relationship does not extend beyond the work environment.

Social support is clearly related to both morbidity (illness) and mortality (death) (e.g., Haynes & Feinleib, 1980). It seems that there is a threshold effect, however, in that only those at the extremely low end of the social support continuum are at risk (Scheonbach, Kaplan, Fredman, & Kleinbaum, 1986). Moreover, it seems that it is the specific combination of high stress and very low social support that is a strong predictor of negative health outcomes (Ruberman, Weinblatt, Goldberg, & Chaudhary, 1984).

Several studies suggest that the level of social support predicts recovery from serious illness. Married patients tend to take less medication and recover more rapidly from surgery (Kulik & Mahler, 1989), and social isolation is associated with higher death rates and poor recovery from heart disease (Ruberman et al., 1984). Another study found that recovery from coronary heart disease was facilitated by support, which was defined in this case by low scores on a measure of loneliness (Fontana, Kerns, Rosenberg, & Colonese, 1989). Other data have linked loneliness to unpleasant emotional states and poor subjective health (Sadava & Pak, 1991).

Models of Social Support and Health. A more interesting question is how social support may have an impact on health and recovery from illness. It is important to differentiate between *main-effects models* of how social support affects reactions to stress and models in which social support *moderates* the effects of stress (Cohen & Syme, 1985) . The main-effects model is one in which social support has a direct effect on health. Individuals with strong social support may have *models* and *reinforcement* for health-enhancing behaviors. Social support also boosts the person's self-esteem and thus will have an impact on general feelings of well-being that are so important when suffering illness (Ward et al., 1991). Although such explanations would seem to be compelling, the evidence is rather mixed (Kaplan & Toshima, 1990).

A *moderator variable* is one that influences relationships between other variables. For instance, the relationship between the temperature outside and how warm or cold it feels would be moderated by the time of year: The same temperature could be experienced as being cold in summer but unusually warm in winter. A moderating-variable model of social support is one in which social support buffers or ameliorates the impact of stress, assisting the person to cope (e.g., Thoits, 1986). Supportive others may help the person to reinterpret the stressful event (e.g., "it's not so bad after all"). Supportive others may also encourage the person to adapt, such as by complying with medical recommendations; seeking help and advice from appropriate others (such as lawyers, accountants, counselors); or simply by taking care of himself or herself.

Consider that what seems stressful to some may be experienced as challenging to others. Several studies indicate that a *negative emotional state* (e.g., anxiety, fear, depression), rather than stress itself, may be crucial to the experience of illness (Carver et al., 1993; Watson & Pennebaker, 1989). Further, individuals may have other effective coping resources besides seeking support from others. These coping mechanisms may include effective problem solving, well-timed escape or distraction from such problems (after all, everyone agrees on the value of vacations), and even a sense of humor, all of which help buffer the impact of stress (e.g., Trice & Price-Greathouse, 1986).

Consider, as well, the possibility that being ill causes a disruption in social support. People may feel uncomfortable when interacting with someone who is physically impaired or who is critically ill, perhaps because their usual notions of how to behave in typical social contexts (i.e., *role schemas*) do not tell them how to act appropriately in such unusual and stressful situations (Wortman & Dunkel-Schetter, 1979). Marital and other relationships may suffer if the healthy individual is excessively concerned with caretaking, or if he or she withdraws from emotional involvement with someone who seems unlikely to recover. It has been argued that people with strong social support also tend to be people more likely to have good health habits. They are more likely to comply with medical recommendations and therefore may be the kinds of people most likely to recover from illness. In one study, however, a lack of support from family members was related to higher 5-year mortality rates among kidney dialysis patients, but those with and without strong support did not differ in their compliance to the medicinal and dietary regimens necessary for their condition (Christensen, Wiebe, Smith, & Turner, 1995).

Cancer patients often lack social support just at the time when it is most needed (Dakof & Taylor, 1990; Wortman & Dunkel-Schetter, 1979; Zemore & Shepel, 1989). Whereas casual friends and acquaintances may withdraw from the cancer patient, patients generally reported that they were more able to confide in close family members than were those in a control group (where the diagnosis was benign). These patients differentiated between social support that was helpful and that which was unhelpful, albeit well-meaning. In the latter category were both avoidance by friends and efforts by close family members to minimize the problem or criticize how the patient was dealing with it. Most helpful to them was social support that was directed toward building their emotional resources, such as self-esteem. On the other hand, patients suffering from chronic but non–life threatening illnesses (e.g., irritable bowel syndrome, headaches) reported that tangible forms of social support were more helpful to them than more emotional support (Martin, Davis, Baron, Suls, & Blanchard, 1994). Another study that differentiated among types of social support found that only the kind of support that aided the individual's self-esteem predicted postoperative recovery, whereas feelings of closeness, belongingness, and the more tangible types of support were not related to recovery (King, Reis, Porter, & Norsen, 1993). Indeed, one study of breast cancer patients found that while significant others (usually the patient's husband or her daughter) responded supportively to the physical impairments of the patients, emotional distress tended to erode support: The significant other withdrew and the relationship seemed less intimate than it had been previously (Bolger, Foster, Vinokur, & Ng, 1996). Thus, at least with regard to this particular illness, social support may be ineffective when it is most needed.

Implications. Support groups, in which patients can gain assistance in coping with both their illnesses and treatments such as chemotherapy and hemodialysis, have become a common component of treatment for many illnesses, including kidney diseases, scoliosis, heart disease, and cancer. Some groups are designed for mutual emotional and practical support; others focus more specifically on training patients in coping skills such as relaxation, assertiveness, problem solving, and simply planning pleasant activities (Telch & Telch, 1986).

Support groups are most likely to be utilized by white, middle-class females. Even though these individuals may have had negative experiences with medical personnel, they do not report an unusual lack of support from their families and friends (Taylor, Helgeson, Reed, & Skokan, 1991). In a sense, those who would most benefit from social support—those who lack family or other stable and intimate social ties—are least equipped to benefit from it. If support groups are generally beneficial, then they must be designed to be attractive and accessible to males and other ethnic groups.

Although many people benefit from the support of others, those who are ill find themselves in a unique situation with regard to their relationships with others. This will be examined in more detail later.

THE SICK ROLE

> Dr. Rosenbaum, a physician from a family of physicians, learned much about his profession when he became a patient. Suddenly, his role had changed drastically from physician in control to "helpless patient." Often students performed some of the procedures. Even though Rosenbaum understood the need for training new physicians, he wondered "why on me?" While fitting him to the table, the two technicians talked to each other about what to do, as though he weren't there. Then Dr. R entered the room, didn't say a word to him, felt his neck, looked at the X-Ray , said OK, and walked out. Rosenbaum was "stupefied" by his behavior.

Despite having years of experience in dealing with patients, Dr. Rosenbaum's insights came uniquely by personal experience as a patient. This section focuses on what it means to be sick; subsequent discussion turns to how health care professionals behave toward those defined as patients.

What does it mean to *be sick*? Psychologists have proposed that "being sick" involves a role schema, a set of expectations and images associated with this state. To most people, and for most illnesses, it begins with the recognition of symptoms, the sense that something is not quite right (or is very wrong) with how they are feeling. When these symptoms are sufficiently noticeable (e.g., debilitating or distressing), people tend to search for an explanation for them. That is, people generate *attributions* or explanations for why they are feeling as they do. Often the symptoms are ambiguous and misattributions may occur. For example, unusual weight gain may be attributed to gluttony when it might be due to depression, a side effect of medication, or a metabolic problem. Members of various cultures vary in how they both experience and report symptoms such as pain (Lipton & Marbach, 1984). If the symptoms are more severe or more unusual, people tend to seek medical assessment, to confirm in their own minds that they are sick.

Individuals who are sick occupy a distinct social role, which is accompanied by its own prescribed pattern of illness behavior (Parsons, 1951). Consider that adults are expected to be self-sustaining, independent, and both able and willing to meet their social responsibilities. However, when they are sick, people are temporarily allowed to be dependent on others and are excused from performing other roles and tasks. In fact, Parsons specifies two *rights* and two *duties* that make up the prescription for the sick role. The sick person has (a) a right to be excused from normal social roles, (b) a right not to be held responsible for the condition, (c) a duty to try to get well, and (d) a duty to cooperate with competent medical care. The duties are designed to ensure that the privileges of being sick are only temporary and that the person will eventually resume his or her normal roles and responsibilities.

Although being sick is usually not a pleasant condition, consider some of the benefits of being sick: avoiding responsibilities ("sick leave"); receiving care, sympathy, and even chicken soup from others; and allowing oneself to be dependent on others. Adults who report frequently using illness to avoid school or work tend to have had childhood experiences of being reinforced for being sick and in having parents as models for such behavior (Moss, 1986).

The concept of a sick role, however, fails to describe the experience of those who suffer from *chronic* or *terminal* illnesses (Cogswell & Weir, 1964). People who suffer from illnesses such as severe arthritis may resist being treated as "different" specifically because they are unlikely to recover. They may believe it imperative to cover up or minimize their condition in order to avoid the stigma of malingering and to maintain their relationships with others. They may even blame themselves for their condition, in an attempt to find some meaning in their predicament (Elder, 1973). Individuals who cannot expect to recover will often abandon medical care or refuse to follow the recommended diet, exercise, or medication. On the other hand, they may seek solace and hope in unproved remedies or outright quackery.

It is important to understand that chronically ill patients who receive overprotective care tend to be more depressed and less involved in their own recovery (Thompson, Sobolew-Shubin, Graham, & Janagian, 1989). Being overprotected involves not being allowed to do what they can do for themselves, having others make decisions for them, being treated as a child, and generally experiencing a loss of control over their own lives (Thompson & Sobolew-Shubin, 1993). Indeed, one study of patients hospitalized after experiencing a heart attack indicated that those who perceived that their health was under their own control were more likely to make a better adjustment, unless surgical intervention was deemed necessary. In cases where surgery was required, a perception that their health was indeed determined by factors outside themselves was realistic and adaptive. The issue of perceived control is discussed more fully elsewhere in this chapter.

Now consider two life-threatening illnesses that pose problems for the individual in the sick role: cancer and AIDS.

Life-Threatening Illness

Cancer. Five patterns of coping with cancer are identified (Dunkel-Schetter, Feinstein, Taylor, & Falke, 1992): (a) *cognitive escape-avoidance* (e.g., hope for a miracle), (b) *behavioral escape-avoidance* (e.g., try to feel better by eating, drinking, smoking, or drug use), (c) *distancing* (e.g., make light of it, don't let it get to you), (d) *focus on the positive* (e.g., find new faith, rediscover what's important in life), and (e) *seek and use social support* (e.g., talk to someone for information or about feelings). Although seeking social support is an important coping strategy for people in this situation, a person with cancer may be avoided—even stigmatized—by others (as noted earlier in this chapter). The word "cancer" arouses strong feelings of anxiety and personal vulnerability. There may also be reactions of physical aversion if the physical appearance of the person has deteriorated as a result of the disease or treatment.

More important, family, friends, and even medical personnel are uncertain about how to behave toward a person who is ill. Out of genuine concern for the person, they may feel obligated to be optimistic, cheerful, and "positive." This is a difficult task, indeed, given the situation. People may avoid the patient entirely, and visits by friends, family, nurses, and physicians tend to become fewer and shorter. Their positive words may be inconsistent with nonverbal cues such as fewer smiles, greater interpersonal distance, and the sadness or nervousness in their voice. In addition, they tend to avoid open communication about the important topic: cancer. Interviews with women who had radical mastectomies for breast cancer revealed that the vast majority had not discussed it with their husbands before or while in the hospital, and only 50% had discussed it afterward (Krantz & Johnson, 1978).

Terminal cancer patients find themselves in a terrible dilemma. Although they are understandably fearful about both their health and their capacity to meet family responsibilities, and need to discuss these matters, they find it difficult to talk and others find it difficult to listen to them. Desperately, patients may try various tactics to gain attention and support. For example, they may exaggerate their illness and discomfort, or they may tell others what they want to hear, being as "positive" as possible and becoming a player in the death-bed drama.

A patient recalls, "I got congratulations for being so brave and cheerful. I liked that, so I got more brave and cheerful. And, the more brave and cheerful I was, the more everyone seemed to love me, so I kept it up. I became positively euphoric" (Rollins, 1976, p. 70). This behavior is based on assumptions that cancer can be beaten if one has the "right" attitudes. Indeed, the model of the "heroic" cancer patient implies that the person can halt or retard the progress of the illness by becoming more effective, expressive, positive, and courageous (Doan & Gray, 1992).

Of course, relatively few people have much experience in coping with serious illness. In a situation of intense uncertainty, most people tend to fall back on stereotyped roles and schema-driven reactions, or they avoid the issue as much as possible. The result is often isolation and a loss of intimacy at a time when it is most needed. As noted earlier, contemporary cancer treatment increasingly recognizes the social role implications of having cancer, and supportive programs have been developed to overcome this dilemma.

Acquired Immune Deficiency Syndrome. Throughout history, public reactions to epidemics have not always been characterized by either rationality or empathy (Conrad, 1986). People suffering from AIDS often find themselves isolated and deprived of social support because of people's fear of the disease. Those identified as AIDS patients may be evicted by landlords, fired from a wide variety of jobs, and refused baptism by church elders. Parents of school-age children have even tried to bar children who have contracted AIDS from public schools. Pryor, Reeder, and Vinacco (1989) conducted a series of studies in which subjects were asked to imagine having their child in a class with a hemophiliac child who was diagnosed as having contracted AIDS through a blood transfusion. As one would expect, subjects who believed AIDS to be highly contagious were resistant to having their child in school with an AIDS patient.

There are several reasons why individuals with AIDS are socially rejected and stigmatized. Clearly, one factor is homophobia, an unreasonable fear of and rejection of homosexuals. People who have an inordinate fear of contracting AIDS from casual contact sources (e.g., contaminated dishes, shared soap, proximity to sneezes) and who favor compulsory quarantine for AIDS victims also hold negative attitudes toward homosexuals (Winslow, Rumbault, & Hwang, 1989). In one illustrative study (Triplet & Sugarman, 1987), subjects were presented with eight "case histories" of persons suffering from AIDS, serum hepatitis, Legionnaire's disease, or genital herpes who were described as either heterosexual or homosexual. Subjects attributed the greatest degree of personal responsibility for their illness to persons described as homosexual and indicated that they would be unwilling to share a hospital room with an AIDS patient or have a close family member do so.

In contrast with these findings are those of another study, in which female subjects were told that they were to interview someone with AIDS (versus someone with cancer or who was homosexual or who was simply another student). They were asked to set up two chairs in a manner that would enable them to conduct a comfortable interview. These subjects set the chairs for the interview with the person with AIDS at a farther distance than they did in the other three cases. In this situation, the stigma and accompanying social distance were specific to AIDS, not to homosexuality (Cohn & Swift, 1992).

Clearly, being ill because of AIDS does not carry with it the same sick role benefits accorded to most people who are seriously ill. Thus, improving the quality of life becomes a major challenge for health professionals. Support groups, as described earlier in this chapter, are particularly crucial to those who are stigmatized and often isolated, even from their own families in some cases. At a societal level, it is incumbent on health professionals to combat stigmas and stereotypes and to stress that everyone is subject to human weaknesses. As medication succeeds in lengthening the life expectancy of those who are HIV-positive, the social implications of this epidemic loom ever larger.

PERSONAL CONTROL AND HEALTH CARE

> Dr. Rosenbaum described one memorable scene in which he asked his physician why this illness had happened to him. This is a common and reasonable question among those in this situation who seek to understand and thus to gain some sense of control.

The physician informed him that cancer of the larynx occurs in heavy smokers and heavy drinkers. Dr. Rosenbaum informed his physician that he neither smoked nor drank to any significant extent. The attending physician didn't reply, only turned on his heel and walked out. " 'A typical doctor,' he thought: It's impossible for him to say, 'I don't know.' " (Rosenbaum, 1988, p. 212)

When people are sick they experience firsthand the frailty of the human condition. It is a vulnerable state, with feelings of uncertainty, distress, and helplessness. An abundant research literature has linked good health to a sense of personal control, the perception that one's outcomes in life, including health, are determined by one's own actions. Indeed, there is some evidence that perceived control may be linked to *killer cells,* a component of the immune system (Kiecolt-Glaser & Glaser, 1990). It can also be reasoned that a sense of personal control will involve patients in making better choices regarding their health care and other aspects of their lives (Kaplan, 1991).

Clearly, feelings of control are related to adjustment and recovery from physical illnesses such as breast cancer (Taylor, Lichtman, & Wood, 1984), arthritis (Nicassio, Wallston, Callahan, Herbert, & Pincus, 1985), and heart disease (Michela, 1986). However, because these studies are conducted only at one point in time, it is not possible to infer that a sense of personal control will cause a better prognosis (Pearlin, Meaghan, Lieberman, & Mullen, 1981). It is possible that feelings of control will result from an improved state of health, or that some third variable will cause both perceived personal control and recovery. Perhaps people with a strong sense of control are also more adept at obtaining support from health care workers and their own families, which would lead to a better prognosis.

Most people want to be "good patients" and try to be as cooperative, unquestioning of medical authority or hospital rules, passive, and cheerful (or at least uncomplaining) as they can manage in the circumstances (Taylor, 1979). Indeed, Taylor (1979) points out that being a good patient may be good for the staff, but not for the patient. Physicians like their patients when they are in better physical and emotional health and when they are more satisfied with their care (Hall, Epstein, DeCiantis, & McNeil, 1993). Well-liked patients may pay a price: (a) *loss of control,* a sense that they must sacrifice the freedom normally expected by adults to a set of institutional rules and professional decisions; (b) *depersonalization,* a loss of personal identity (e.g., they now assume the identity of a medical insurance number or become the "hernia repair in 214A"); and (c) *ignorance* of matters about which a normal adult would feel a right to know (e.g., the reasons to take a certain medication).

Reality and Beliefs in Control

In a classic study of the postoperative recovery of college students, it was found that those who reported moderate levels of preoperative fear and who had prior information about what to expect experienced the smoothest recovery. Those who were most relaxed and nonchalant about their impending surgery reported the most postoperative difficulty and those with high preoperative fear fared somewhat worse. It was suggested that the "work of worrying," based on *realistic expectations,* was important in facilitating postoperative recovery (Janis, 1958).

Unfortunately, realistic perception may have its costs (Taylor & Brown, 1988). An extensive body of research leads to the conclusion that three *positive illusions* are linked to better health: (a) having an unrealistically positive evaluation of oneself; (b) having an exaggerated sense of control over the events and outcomes of one's life; and (c) being unrealistically optimistic. There obviously must be limits to how far one can or should bend reality. Otherwise, someone with a sense of absolute control and unreservedly positive expectations for the future will inevitably have a rude awakening. Nonetheless, a positive and resilient mental outlook is linked to the probability of survival from cancer (Scheier & Carver, 1993). In another study, HIV-positive individuals who were not ill tended to be more optimistic about their chances of not contracting AIDS (Taylor et al., 1991). Thus, positive illusions may have benefits for physical and mental well-being (Taylor, 1989).

Why might this be true? In part, one would logically expect that someone who is optimistic would take a more active role in treatment and recovery, such as complying with treatment. However, this proposition has not been consistently supported by research (Colvin & Block, 1994). Further research is needed to specify the personal and situational factors that will mediate the effects of realistic and even unrealistic levels of control. For example, maintaining a sense of personal control in the face of chronic or terminal illness may well be maladaptive because the patient is, indeed, helpless to influence the course and outcome of the disease (Burish et al., 1984). In such cases, personal control means deciding when to terminate treatment and how to face death. Increasingly, society has become aware of the imperative of self-determination at this stage of life (Clarke, 1986).

Technology and Control

Modern medical practice utilizes breathtaking advances in medical technology, such as computer-assisted diagnostic devices, microsurgery, transplantation, an ever-increasing array of psychiatric medications, in vitro fertilization, constant monitoring of vital functions, and less invasive procedures such as laser surgery and angioplasty. The costs and benefits (social, personal, and financial) of this rapidly advancing technology are under active consideration and debate (see Box 5–1). Social psychology can inform people about some of the costs. For instance, medical technology can widen the distance between physician and patient (e.g., having a CAT scan is a different experience from direct patient-doctor interaction). In addition, the fact that technology enables doctors and patients to accomplish what they could not accomplish before can raise new issues. For example, the impact of the reproductive technologies may be felt on parents, children, and the relationship between them (Colpin, 1994).

Public opinion surveys in Australia, China, Europe, Japan, the United Kingdom, and the United States show an interesting ambivalence concerning biotechnology, an appreciation of possible benefits balanced by a concern over "playing

Box
5–1

Mistakes in Aviation and Medicine

Airline pilots are carefully selected, highly trained professionals working in the complicated, high-technology environment of modern aviation. Despite the high volume of traffic and the complexity of the machinery today and the catastrophic consequences of errors, flying is relatively safer than it was in the earlier, more simple days of aviation. Clearly, the airplanes of today are vastly superior in terms of safety, but equally important is the system of safety that has developed throughout the world. Training, regulation, airplane maintenance, and air traffic control are all part of that system of safety.

Most important, the system has been designed on the assumption that even highly trained professionals are subject to human error. Monitoring instruments and interpersonal communication provide extensive and consistent feedback to pilots, crew, and ground personnel. In many cases, the same information is provided from several different sources. Procedures are standardized for trip plans, navigation, and airplane maintenance. Pilots and other crew undergo rigidly enforced training, certification, and repeated competency examinations, which are administered every 6 months. Finally, governmental and international agencies regulate safety standards and investigate all accidents and near-accidents, all with the goal of learning from them and thus increasing safety.

The contrast with medicine, also a high-technology profession, is stunning. In hospital settings, physicians are often critical and demanding of each other (Konner, 1987). Many physicians work alone in private practice, where professional backup and consultation are less likely than in the hospital or clinic. Professional colleges and hospital review committees are concerned with errors. However, responsibility is attributed exclusively to an individual, rather than to the system in which the individual physician, nurse, or technician is working. The result is increased risk to the patient, an exponential growth in complaints and lawsuits, increased costs to the system, and stress to the health care professional (Bogner, 1994).

Two types of errors occur. One type is the mistake: The wrong medication is administered to the wrong patient, a necessary or prescribed treatment is forgotten, a necessary test was not ordered, or the results of a test were misinterpreted. Glaring, even spectacular, examples occasionally reach the mass media, in which the wrong baby is given to a happy couple or the wrong leg has been amputated. The other type of error may be characterized as a knowledge-based error: This may be an unanticipated drug interaction, failure to utilize a new procedure, or employment of an outdated procedure. Contemporary medical care is complicated and is growing in complexity because of the increasing technological nature of treatment and the explosive growth of knowledge as represented by reports in the many medical journals and computer databases: "Physicians and nurses need to accept the notion that error is an inevitable accompaniment of the human condition, even among conscientious professionals with high standards. Errors must be accepted as evidence of system flaws, not character flaws" (Leape, 1994, p. 1857). Therefore, health care systems must be redesigned. It is time for changes in the milieu in which medicine is practiced.

God" (Kapp, 1993; Macer, 1994). Indeed, some have suggested that an implicit *triage* exists in hospitals to allocate intensive treatment in terms of the anticipated need and benefits of the procedure. Further, in an age of scarce resources, how much should be devoted to expensive technologies? For example, computerized tomography (C-T) scans provide a powerful and safe diagnostic tool that may be overused for rather trivial problems, or for results that could be obtained a bit less rapidly, and a lot less expensively, by other means (Rachlis & Kushner, 1989). Similarly, patients who have suffered a mild heart attack may fare just as well at home after a few days of observation in a hospital as they would in a high-tech, high-cost coronary care unit (Eggerton & Berg, 1984).

Another important issue pertains to the treatment of the terminally ill. At what point should resuscitation be abandoned and when should artificial life supports cease? Several studies have surveyed health care workers regarding the choices in treatment of the critically ill (Christakis & Asch, 1995; Cook et al., 1995). Continued efforts are more likely to be endorsed when the patient is relatively young, when cognitive functioning is at a relatively high level, and when the patient is seen as relatively likely to survive in the long term. Perhaps more surprisingly, withdrawal of treatment is more likely to be endorsed by younger physicians, specialists more often than primary care physicians, those who are in more contact with intensive care patients, and those who are neither Roman Catholic nor Jewish. Thus, both the characteristics of the patient and the characteristics of the physician influence these life-or-death decisions.

Clearly, continued discussion is needed, and it must be informed by well-designed research. Social psychological perspectives can contribute significantly to an understanding of the impact of medical technology on medical practice, the experience of being a patient, and the relative costs and benefits of various procedures. Even Dr. Rosenbaum, who understood much of what was going on, felt overwhelmed and alienated by the procedures to which he was subjected.

COMMUNICATION AND ADHERENCE TO MEDICAL RECOMMENDATIONS

Physician-Patient Interaction

The average primary care medical visit lasts less than 20 minutes (Nelson & McLemore, 1988). Much is expected in a relatively brief period of communication; the physician should establish or renew rapport with the patient, gain information about medical history and current symptoms, conduct whatever physical examinations are appropriate, order diagnostic tests, and discuss alternatives for further assessment and treatment. Research shows clearly that effective communication, such as inviting and answering questions, and *partnership building,* which involves attempts by the physician to boost the status of the patient and to enlist his or her cooperation, are related to greater patient satisfaction, better understanding and recall of information, and greater compliance to the recommendations of the physician (Hall, Roter, & Katz, 1986).

Do physicians communicate clearly and do their patients understand? *Interpersonal speech accommodation theory* enables social psychologists to study how people of different speaking styles interact and communicate (Giles, Bourhis, & Taylor, 1977). *Speech maintenance* occurs when the two parties continue to talk as they always have, oblivious to the speaking pattern or style of the other. *Speech divergence* serves to accentuate those differences, and the resultant social gap between them, whereas *speech convergence* occurs when one or both participants attempt to adopt the speech pattern of the others (e.g., by adopting the vocabulary, accent, or language itself, as in a bilingual situation). Speech convergence tends to promote social harmony by minimizing status differences, thereby increasing mutual understanding and liking.

A study of physicians, nurses, and patients in a hospital examined the use of medical language and ordinary language in that setting (Bourhis, Roth, & MacQueen, 1989). As expected, the physicians communicated with each other primarily in medical language. The physicians believed that they were using ordinary language with their patients; however, neither the patients nor the nurses agreed with this perception of convergence on the part of physicians. Both patients and physicians believed that it was inappropriate of patients to converge by using medical language with their physicians. That is, physicians should use ordinary speech, but patients, even those who are well informed, are not invited to use technical language.

Perhaps the crucial distinction is between *doctor-centered* and *patient-centered* communication. Doctor-centered communication consists of structured questions with simple answers and is intended to arrive rapidly at an accurate diagnosis. In patient-centered communication, the physician attempts to clarify the presenting problem and eventual diagnosis through more open-ended types of questions. Patients are encouraged to describe their problems in their own words. They are also encouraged to ask questions about the causes of their illness, treatment alternatives, and prognosis, to which the physician responds in clear, comprehensible language. It is apparent that the latter approach, although more time-consuming, could be even more successful in enabling the physician to arrive at the accurate diagnosis and having the patient feel better about the process.

The relationship between physician and patient can also promote positive expectations about the treatment. The well-documented *placebo effect* is not restricted to medication but also extends to many medical procedures (Shapiro & Morris, 1978). Indeed, in retrospect, much of the history of medicine concerns apparently effective procedures that proved to have placebo foundations. Although the placebo effect has been explained as the mobilization of hope, the power of suggestion, or a self-fulfilling prophecy, it is evident that it all rests on communication between the patient and the physician. Indeed, if the physician and patient believe in neither the treatment nor each other, the treatment is unlikely to be effective.

Gender. Even in childhood, girls are more likely to visit the school nurse than are boys (Lewis, Lewis, Lorimer, & Palmer 1977). Female patients tend to be given more information than do male patients, and technical information tends to be presented to women more clearly (Waitzkin, 1985). Further, physicians are more likely to ask female patients their opinions or feelings, and female patients are more likely to express tension and ask for help (Stewart, 1983). In general, women tend to be more adept in communication skills—including nonverbal skills—and in eliciting support from others (Sarason, Sarason, Hacker, & Basham, 1985). Thus it is not surprising that female patients tend to have more positive experiences with their physicians than do male patients.

On the other hand, female physicians tend to spend more time with their patients, particularly female patients (Roter, Lipkin, & Korsgaard, 1991). Much of the difference is attributed to the early history-taking phase of the visit. Female physicians tend both to talk more than their male counterparts and to elicit more talking on the part of their patients. They tend to conduct longer visits, ask more questions, smile and nod more to the patient, and make more back-channel responses—those indicators of agreement and approval displayed while the patient is speaking (e.g., "mm-hmm," "OK," "right"). Patients are more willing to give information and make more partnership types of statements to female physicians (Hall, Irish, Roter, Ehrlich, & Miller, 1994). Indeed, female physicians tend to like their patients more, particularly when the patients are less seriously ill, when patients are satisfied with their care, and, perhaps surprisingly, when patients are males (Hall, Epstein, De-Ciantis, & McNeil, 1993).

Finally, physicians have another purpose in talking with their patients—that is, to elicit the cooperation and collaboration of the patients in their own recovery. Medicines are useless unless they are taken, and treatment for coronary illnesses will not usually enhance the quantity or quality of life unless lifestyle changes also occur. Thus, patient adherence has become recognized as a crucial issue in medical care.

Compliance With Medical Regimens

Dr. Rosenbaum found that "prescribing is different from receiving." As a patient, he was expected to comply with what was recommended. Basic to the physician-patient relationship is that the physician, as the expert, recommends a certain course of action, and the patient complies with these recommendations. This is scripted in the sick-role schema. Of course, persuasion and compliance are social psychological processes that are readily applied to the medical setting.

Many patients fail to adhere to specific treatment recommendations (Becker, 1985; DiMatteo & DiNicola, 1982). Moreover, physicians tend to underestimate the noncompliance problem among their own patients (DiMatteo & DiNicola, 1982; Norell, 1981). Indeed, noncompliance rates are estimated to be at least 30%, depending on the patient population and the behavior in question. Estimates of noncompliance range from about 20% to 30% for short-term regimens for acute problems (such as following a prescribed course of antibiotics), to more than 40% for preventive regimens, and more than 50% for changes in lifestyle (DiMatteo & DiNicola, 1982). Noncompliance rates are higher among patients with chronic conditions and with regimens involving lifestyle changes such as diet, exercise, and smoking. Other recommendations include taking a medication as directed, changing a dressing, scheduling another appointment, monitoring a symptom, and simply reporting accurately to the physician about failure to comply.

Why do patients fail to comply? Although some physicians may attribute noncompliance to a rebellious attitude by patients or to their inability to think beyond the moment, research has failed to identify a noncompliant personality type (Kaplan & Simon, 1990). Indeed, compliance or noncompliance is not a consistent pattern of behavior. Studies of diabetics show that they often comply with some parts of their regimens but not others (Glasgow, McCaul, & Schafer, 1987). Although some may fail to comply because they did not understand the instructions, to attribute this lack of understanding to the patients is to commit the *fundamental attribution error* of ignoring factors such as the clarity of the physicians' instructions and explanations.

Noncompliance is much more complex than simply an ignorant, deviant, or oppositional behavior. Patients make judgments about the utility of any medical intervention, judgments about how they are feeling, and judgments about their own independence and their own need for personal control (Liang, 1989; Roberson, 1992). The medical practitioner must understand these decisions from the patient's point of view if there is to be any hope of altering those decisions.

Much of the research on patient noncompliance has concerned hypertension. High blood pressure poses grave risks to those afflicted. However, because it is usually undetectable to the person, many patients are reluctant to take antihypertensive medication. To complicate the matter, the medication tends to cause several unpleasant side effects, including drowsiness and sexual dysfunctions. Refusal to take such medication may be referred to as *rational noncompliance,* in that the apparent long-term rewards are outweighed by the obvious short-term costs (Becker, 1985; Donovan & Blake, 1992).

One important study assessed compliance to recommended medication, exercise, and diet regimens among 1,828 patients (with diabetes, hypertension, or heart disease) and their physicians ($N = 186$) over 2 years (DiMatteo et al., 1993; Sherbourne, Hays, Ordway, DiMatteo, & Kravitz, 1992). This study indicated that certain characteristics of the physician enhanced compliance. These traits included the extent to which the physician was satisfied with his or her job, the number of patients seen per week, the number of tests ordered, and the tendency to answer the patients' questions. Physician satisfaction has been shown elsewhere to promote the well-being of the patient (Weisman & Nathanson, 1985). Although one might expect that the busier physicians had less time for their patients, they also seemed to be more popular and more successful in eliciting compliance and tended to schedule follow-up appointments for patients to check on medication use. Patient characteristics were also important: Compliance was more common among patients who were older, who tended to use avoidance coping strategies, who were distressed with their own state of health, and who were satisfied with their medical care. Thus, characteristics of both the physician and the patient combine to influence compliance.

Finally, as suggested earlier, patients are less likely to comply if they have not been given clear explanations for the recommended action, and if they have not been provided appropriate support and encouragement (Hall, Roter, & Katz, 1986). Indeed, physicians who are sensitive to the nonverbal, vocal tone of their patients, such as emphasis, intonation, and pitch of the voice, are more successful (DiMatteo,

Hays, & Prince, 1986). Note that there is no consistent evidence that the sheer amount of time spent with the patient will predict compliance, but rather what happens during that time.

Strategies for Compliance. Social psychological principles can help people better understand the processes involved in compliance (Cialdini, 1993). Moreover, these principles can be applied in a concrete manner to the practice of medicine. Consider these examples.

   1. People exhibit a strong need to be consistent in their attitudes and their actions. In particular, one action tends to engender a sense of commitment to future actions that are consistent with the first. Thus, Freedman and Fraser (1966) found that people who complied to a small request, that of displaying a small, neatly lettered sign for safe driving, subsequently were more likely to agree to erect a massive, ugly sign on their lawns than were those who had not been approached previously. Freedman and Fraser called this the *foot-in-the-door technique,* identified decades ago by salespeople. Health professionals can apply this technique by first eliciting a commitment to a small lifestyle change before progressing to larger changes.

   2. People tend to validate the correctness of their attitudes and their actions by comparing themselves to others in the same situation, particularly if it is a relatively ambiguous situation. Health professionals may apply these *social comparison processes* by publicizing desirable changes in behavior, such as the decrease in smoking among certain groups in society, or a decrease in eating red meat.

   3. Recommendations are more likely to elicit compliance when they come from a respected, credible source. Physicians are generally seen as credible sources, particularly when they are experienced. While *expert power* in itself cannot assure compliance, it can be used effectively.

CHANGING MEDICAL PRACTICE

In an era of various public and private health insurance schemes, the individual physician no longer has absolute independence and authority to practice as he or she sees fit. Increasingly assertive patients, nurses, and other health professionals have further eroded this authoritarian role. The complexity of contemporary medicine has made cooperation and collaboration almost imperative in many situations. The entry into the profession of significant numbers of women and minorities has also helped to change the image and reality of the "typical" physician. For all of these reasons, medical practice is undergoing significant changes.

The Physician-Patient Interaction

Roter and Hall (1992) suggest seven principles of physician-patient interaction that, in their words, can transform the way medicine is practiced. See Box 5–2 for an example of how these principles have been implemented.

1. Communication should allow the patients to tell the story of their illness, and the physician to hear it. Of course, this means that physicians must appear to the patients to be taking a personal interest in them, and to be committed to doing a good job for them. But telling their story is not always easy; even Dr. Ed Rosenbaum was given superficial attention and glib reassurance. Patients may believe that their complaints do not justify medical attention, or they may fear that they are appearing foolish or ignorant about the nature or causes of their illness. Often, the doorway question—"By the way, doctor, I have chest tightness" (or a lump in my breast, problems in remembering things)—necessitates extending the medical appointment beyond what was expected by either party.

2. Communication should reflect the special "expertise" that each patient brings to his or her illness. The patient does have the day-to-day experience of living with a given level of health or illness. Indeed, one study of over 23,000 elderly people revealed that simply asking the patient, "At the present time, how would you rate your health?" predicted their health and even survival over the next 17 years (Idler & Kasl, 1991). It is also interesting to note that although medical personnel rate the health of patients solely in terms of the *biomedical* data, patients tend to rate their health in terms of their own *functioning* (e.g., ability to walk without a cane, days off work) and their *emotional state* (Hall, Epstein, & McNeil, 1989).

3. Communication should reflect the relationship between the patient's mental state and physical illness. Many symptoms reported to physicians may not be linked directly to identifiable organic problems. These symptoms may include headaches, insomnia, fatigue, diarrhea, weight fluctuations, assorted aches and pains, and dizziness. Physicians must take the possibility of organic illness seriously, but they must also consider the impact of stressful life circumstances or psychiatric disorders in producing these very real and debilitating symptoms.

4. Communication should maximize the usefulness of the physician's expertise. Indeed, the research literature shows consistently that most patients want information that is clear, relevant, and useful to them. Sharing information and expertise can also help induce the patient to comply with the recommendations. However, both physicians and patients must accept the limits to this expertise—it is not omniscience. Recall that Dr. Rosenbaum asked his physician why this cancer of the larynx had happened to him. When the physician realized that the patient neither

Box
5–2

Training Physicians to Communicate

A well-recognized anthropologist at Harvard University decided to enter medical school at the age of 33. In an account of his training in various services of a medical school hospital, Konner (1987) has interesting insights about the triumphs, tragedies, and stresses of medical training; his fellow medical students; patients; and the teaching styles of various instructors and clinical supervisors. Perhaps most important, he observes how the stress, time demands, and reliance on technology result in an attitude of detachment, thereby alienating physicians from their patients. The physicians' objective is to spend the least amount of time possible to obtain the desired results. They tend to talk rather than to listen. Note also that, at least according to one earlier study, medical students in their first year ask fewer leading questions and obtain more relevant interpersonal information from their patients than do students in their final year of medical school. Thus, medical students *learn* not to know the patient, nor do they allow the patient to tell his or her personal story.

Given the importance of physician-patient communication in eliciting patient compliance, reducing stress, and promoting recovery, it would seem obvious that such skills should be an intrinsic component of clinical training. Increasing attention to communication skills has become evident in many training programs, both for medical students and practicing physicians. One such program (Inui, Youirtee, & Williamson, 1976) was a two-hour session for internal medicine residents that dealt with increasing compliance of patients with prescriptions for alleviating high blood pressure. During the session, the noncompliance problem was documented, and the need to understand the patient's history and beliefs about his or her medical problem was emphasized. Strategies for improving compliance were reviewed, including correcting patients' misconceptions about high blood pressure, the complications and risks of untreated hypertension, and the efficacy of therapy. Physicians who went through this program subsequently spent more time educating their patients than did the control group, resulting in much improved compliance. These improvements were still in effect 6 months later.

Roter and Hall (1992) devised an extensive program for community-based primary care physicians designed to improve their interviewing skill and their recognition of patients' psychosocial problems. The physicians were assigned to 8-hour interviewing skills groups that included the following:

- Using open-ended questions and having patients set priorities to establish their own concerns
- Asking for the patients' opinions, experience, and interpretations
- Eliciting and responding to the emotions of the patient, including the expression of empathy and supporting the patient's own efforts

The results were assessed by taping and coding actual patient interviews in the physicians' own offices (with prior consent of all parties, of course). Compared to the control groups, the physicians actually did use their training effectively. Six months later, their patients showed significantly greater improvement in well-being and mental health than did those of the control group.

The objective is not to supplant solid diagnostic skills, sophisticated technology, and advanced means of treatment. Rather, it is to pay more attention to the state of mind of the patients, their need to communicate in this vulnerable state of illness, and their sense of well-being. This, too, is good medical practice, and social psychologists can contribute significantly. Perhaps today or tomorrow, physicians may not have to deal with such a shock when, as happened with Dr. Ed Rosenbaum and with most human beings, they experience illness firsthand.

smoked nor drank to any excess, he turned on his heels and left the room, rather than admit to both of them that he did not know.

5. Communication should attend to the emotional content of the situation as well as to factual information. That is, in addition to the factual information that patients want about their illness—prognosis, side effects of medications, etc.—they also want to know that the physician cares about them and their recovery. Although most of the verbal interaction, at least from the physician, tends to be factual in nature, nonverbal communication can help alleviate anxiety and convey a positive attitude to the patient. Sensitivity to the nonverbal cues of patients can reveal valuable information about their emotional and physical state.

6. Communication should be *reciprocal*. Consider that the relationship between physician and patient is rather one sided: The physician can help the patient but the patient cannot usually help the physician. However, the patient can comply or not comply with the recommendations of the physician, may or may not express appreciation or gratitude, may or may not pay bills (under a direct-payment system). It must also be recognized that patients are not usually swayed by the incompetent physician with the affable bedside manner. In one experiment in which subjects viewed taped episodes of doctor-patient interactions, a competent physician was viewed as courteous (unless outright rude), but a courteous, friendly physician was not rated as competent unless cues of competence were present (Willson & McNamara, 1982).

7. Communication should enable both participants to overcome stereotyped roles. Clearly, both patients and physicians have learned role schemas, and their interactions tend to be schema-driven—almost automatic or scripted in nature. Neither party wishes to behave in ways that may be perceived as unprofessional or presumptuous. Thus, for example, the physician may be reluctant to ask questions of a personal nature (such as those dealing with sexuality or alcohol consumption) and patients will not insist on seeing their medical charts.

Models of Physician-Patient Interaction

Consider four prototypes of the doctor-patient relationship (Roter & Hall, 1992), which are based on a definition of the extent of control exerted by each of the two parties: physicians and patients. The *traditional* or *paternalistic form* is characterized by high physician control and low patient control, in which the dominant physician and passive patient play their assigned roles. Recall Dr. Rosenbaum's experience: "I am used to commanding but now I have no power. . . . No one asks me what to do. Instead they tell me what to do and I must submit" (Rosenbaum, 1988, p. 77). Indeed, patients generally prefer that their physicians assume the dominant role (and responsibility) in decision making. This is particularly true of patients who are elderly or low income, and those who are most seriously ill (Ende, Kazis, Ash, & Moscowitz, 1989).

The inverse would be when patient control is high and physician control is low, a model described as *consumerist*. In a society in which one is bombarded with encouragement to buy, tempered by the warning "caveat emptor," a consumer orientation to medical practice is almost inevitable. Of course, when the patient pays the physician directly or indirectly through subscription to an insurance plan, cost-consciousness plays a major role. However, even when financial cost is not at issue, patients often read health-related articles and books and increasingly avail themselves of professional complaint mechanisms and the legal system to press a grievance against their physician.

If a total lack of control by either party exists, the relationship is characterized by *default*. Neither party has assumed nor relinquished responsibility, and nothing has been negotiated between them. Often the patient drops out of treatment, goes to a different physician, or presses a legal or professional complaint against the physician. Indeed, much of the medical malpractice phenomenon can be attributed to a lack of communication (Shapiro, Simpson, & Lawrence, 1989).

Finally, consider the relationship characterized by *mutuality,* one in which control is shared. In such relationships, the expertise and experience of both parties are respected, and decisions involving both the goals and means of treatment are collaborative. For example, decisions regarding treatment for cancer may involve chemotherapy or radiation, with their unpleasant and often debilitating side effects, or surgery that may be disfiguring or risky. The physician must work out, with the patient, the goals, probabilities (both of survival and of maintaining an acceptable quality of life), self-image, issues of personal relationships, and so on.

A classic instance of this kind of relationship was that between Norman Cousins, a well-known author and magazine editor, and his physician. Cousins was faced with a virulent form of ankylosing spondylitis, a serious and degenerative illness, and found that medications were both ineffective and toxic. Together, Cousins and his physician decided that Cousins would move from the demoralizing environment of a hospital. He would find a more pleasant environment (a hotel room), cease most medication, and promote positive emotional experiences, such as laughter, which he enjoyed while watching Marx Brothers movies. This worked well—it was a collaborative effort in mobilizing the body's own resources (Cousins, 1979).

It may appear to the reader that the optimal pattern for medical encounters would be mutuality, and indeed, the research supports such a conclusion in general. Certainly Dr. Ed Rosenbaum was both shocked and discouraged when even he was not treated in this way. However, a note of caution must be introduced. Old schemas die hard, and many patients may both expect and prefer a more one-sided relationship, in which the physician assumes control and responsibility. The sense of vulnerability that one feels when one is sick often influences what is expected of the physician at that time. Factors such as previous experience, cultural background, and the nature of the illness must be considered in arriving at a balance appropriate to the particular patient and the particular situation. Research can help to illuminate situations in which various models of health care will be appropriate.

Financial Incentives

Does the fee-for-service payment system that characterizes much of medical care today discourage the physician from taking the time to communicate with the patient (Rachlis & Kushner, 1989)? Here, it can be observed how the economics of medicine affect the social psychology of medical practice. Spending time talking with the patient is not usually defined as a billable service. Thus, many physicians tend to limit the time that they spend in such activity. However, the system may provide incentives for scheduling extra visits to the office, which, in turn, increase health care costs to society.

On the other hand, alternative payment systems can alter physician behavior. Renaud et al. (1980) rehearsed students to simulate patients with muscle tension headaches and then sent them to physicians, some of whom were paid on a fee-for-service basis and others of whom were paid on a salary basis. They told each physician that they had previously been prescribed a benzodiazapine tranquilizer and needed a new prescription. Strikingly, the fee-for-service physicians spent only a fraction of the time with the patient as did the salaried physicians—an average of 8 minutes, as opposed to 21 minutes for the salaried physicians. The fee-for-service physicians took less complete medical histories, were more likely to prescribe medication for a longer period of time without appraisal, were less likely to give explicit warnings about side effects, and were less likely to give advice about alternatives to medication. Overall, researchers rated 50% of the encounters with salaried physicians as "adequate" (not impressive according to their standard), a rating that was given to only 17% of the encounters with fee-for-service physicians.

An important study by Davidson, Molloy, and Bédard (1995) focused on general practitioners who had ordered at least 200 prescriptions for elderly patients under a governmental drug plan in the province of New Brunswick. The researchers compared those physicians whose patients had relatively lower and higher rates of morbidity (days in hospital) and mortality. Those whose patients fared relatively worse tended to have seen more patients per day and billed more per year. It is possible that the busier physicians were better diagnosticians and therefore more in demand, particularly among those who were more seriously ill. More likely, however, they tended to spend less time per patient in an office visit and would therefore be less likely to spend time talking with the patient and more likely to accord with patient expectations for a prescription. Indeed, the physicians with larger patient volume tended to prescribe more drugs overall (including antidepressants, anticholesterol medications, neuroleptics, and nonsteroidal anti-inflammatory medications). Clearly, the incentives in the fee-for-service system have implications not only for physician-patient communication but also for patient outcomes.

SUMMARY

In this chapter, it has been shown how social psychology intersects with medical practice. Social psychology is fundamental to an understanding of the importance of gender in the etiology of illness, the importance of social support to both vulnerability to illness and prospects for recovery, the social experience and schemas associated with being sick, the importance of a sense of personal control, and the crucial impact of physician-patient communication in accurate diagnosis, recovery, and compliance with physician recommendations. Some real-life applications of what psychology has learned have been presented.

Important changes in the practice of medicine are taking place. The rapid development of new technologies, alternative models of payment for medical services, increasing sensitivity in medical training to the importance of effective communication and the impact of cultural differences, all have had, and will have, a significant impact on health care. Social psychology has an important role to play, both in illuminating the processes and outcomes of how medicine is practiced and in developing solutions.

SUGGESTED READINGS

DiMatteo, M. R., & DiNicola, D. D. (1982). *Achieving patient compliance.* New York: Pergamon.

> Somewhat dated but still indispensable, this is a systematic consideration of a problem that had been largely ignored up to that time—but not afterward. It contains solid foundations in social psychological theory and research.

Eiser, J. R. (Ed.). (1982). *Social psychology and behavioral medicine.* New York: Wiley.

> This is a set of theoretical and empirical papers on health behaviors and the influence of psychosocial factors on illness and recovery.

Rachlis, M., & Kushner, C. (1989). *Second opinion. What's wrong with Canada's health care system and how to fix it.* Toronto: Harper & Collins.

> This well-informed critique presents a health care system based on fee-for-service in which government is the single insurer. The alternative proposed is decidedly not a privately run system but is based on greater use of other health-care personnel. This alternative would emphasize primary prevention and would pay more attention to individual patients.

Radley, A. (1994). *Making sense of illness: The social psychology of health and disease.* London: Sage.

> This book provides an illuminating step-by-step review of the process of becoming ill, seeking professional help, and dealing with chronic illness. An illuminating set of social psychological studies of physician-patient verbal communications, this book includes a consideration of the influence of both physician and patient characteristics, an exami-

nation of the processes of communication in typical medical encounters, and some well-considered suggestions for improvement.

Roter, D. L., & Hall, J. A. (1992). *Doctors talking with patients/Patients talking with doctors.* Westport, CT: Auburn House.

This book contains an illuminating set of social-psychological studies of physician-patient verbal communications. It includes a consideration of the influence of both physician and patient characteristics, an examination of the processess of communication in typical medical encounters, and some well-considered suggestions for improvement.

Shumaker, S. A., & Czajkowski, S. M. (Eds.). (1994). *Social support and cardiovascular disease.* New York: Plenum Press.

A collection of papers that present various conceptions of what social support is, the book presents evidence linking support to the causes, development, and treatment of CVD.

Spacapan, S., & Oskamp , S. (1988). *The social psychology of health.* The Claremont Symposium on Applied Social Psychology. Beverly Hills, CA: Sage.

This is a compilation of advanced-level papers by well-known researchers on psychosocial factors in health (e.g., social support, perceived control) and health promotion.

Spiro, H. M. (1986). *Doctors, patients and placebos.* New Haven: Yale University Press.

A fascinating and provocative review and discussion of the placebo effect in medical treatment, in the context of the relationship between physician and patient, is the focus of this book.

Taylor, S. E. (1989). *Positive illusions: Creative self-deception and the health mind.* New York: Basic Books.

This well-supported argument by a social psychologist opines that a somewhat unrealistic optimism about one's self, one's health, and the future can enhance physical and mental well-being.

6 Social Psychology and Aging

Michael Ziegler
York University

The Canadian National Health and Research Development Program (NHRDP) recently announced a competition for research into the impact of substance abuse or misuse by elderly persons on themselves, their families, and their communities. (*Substance* refers to alcohol and prescription and nonprescription drugs.) A major interest of the agency is the impact of drugs on the independence of the elderly. The investigation is carried out in the community by researchers employing a variety of techniques and approaches. The grant is designated as a "Community Researcher Award," an ideal opportunity for an applied social psychologist interested in the elderly.

Health issues are of central concern for both applied social psychologists and gerontologists. A concern with health combined with the special vulnerability of the elderly leads to a focus on drug use among some elderly persons. Although the elderly are less likely abusers of illegal drugs (in part because addicts to hard drugs may not survive to old age; in part because such addicts often quit), they are often abusers of legal prescriptive drugs and over-the-counter analgesics, laxatives, and alcohol. The elderly ingest a larger quantity and a wider variety of drugs (the consumption of multiple drugs is called *polypharmacy*) as treatment for health problems. These drugs may interact and lead to tragic consequences. Excessive medication often results from *ageist* attitudes (e.g., when a physician automatically prescribes drugs instead of examining the underlying cause of a problem). One in four prescriptions is wrongfully given, which contributes to problems such as amnesia and heart and respiratory failure (Willcox, Himmelstein, & Woodhandler, 1994).

Zimberg (1974) found that about one-third of problem drinkers become alcoholic late in life. This reflects problems with isolation, boredom, and feelings of abandonment (all of which indicate an impoverished *environment*). Of particular interest are gender differences. Women are greater consumers of both prescription and nonprescription drugs and are more frequently alcohol abusers for the first time late in life (perhaps reflecting widowhood and stress). Women are also at greater risk for institutionalization.

The issue of drug abuse by the elderly illustrates four important concerns of applied social psychologists: (a) health enhancement (e.g., finding means of reducing unwarranted drug dependence); (b) ageism (demonstrating how prejudice against the elderly contributes to drug abuse); (c) sexism (critically examining the gender gap in the late life circumstances of the elderly); and (d) the role of the environment (in contributing to depression and self-destructive behavior).

APPLYING SOCIAL PSYCHOLOGY TO GERONTOLOGY

Gerontology is an interdisciplinary field that includes biology, physiology, psychology, sociology, anthropology, and related subjects. It is the study of the aging process with a focus on the elderly of all species but especially humankind. Old age is a social construct, a period of life that is differently defined in various cultures (although all cultures have some category corresponding to old age). The quality of late life is greatly affected by attitudes, beliefs, practices, and circumstances in society at large. The role of applied social psychologists is to recognize, document, and demonstrate how these factors limit or enhance well-being. This, in turn, allows them to design effective intervention programs to enhance well-being among the elderly.

Natural Experiments

George Maddox (1990) has examined how aging is affected by social and political policies. Maddox strongly argues that the concept of *biological necessity* in human development is an illusion. As important as biological changes are, the allocation of resources (including education, income, and social position) determines the experience of growing old. Chronological age as a marker of physical, psychological, and social status has little meaning because the circumstances of people's lives contribute substantially to these variables. Two basic principles of social psychology are closely connected to Maddox's view of aging: the importance of the *situation* (in contrast to biology or the passage of time) and the understanding of *aging as a social construct* (i.e., a life stage in which social attitudes and expectations can limit or enhance individual potential).

Maddox suggests that societies are large-scale "experiments" testing the effects of differential distribution of resources over the life span. We know, for example, that social policy regarding public welfare greatly affects life expectancy. Most of the increase in life expectancy over the last century came from improved sanitation and stabilization of food supplies. In the poorest countries today, life expectancy is only 60% of that of North Americans. In Afghanistan, for example, males' and females' life expectancy at birth is 44 and 43 years, respectively (U.S. Bureau of Census, 1991). The corresponding figures in Canada are 74 and 81 years; for the United States, 72 and 79 years (U.S. Bureau of Census, 1991). The difference is not due to biological differences between populations; it results from differences in living conditions (see Table 6–1 for a sample of figures on the proportions of elderly as of 1991 and as projected for 2020). Successive cohorts in North America, Maddox notes, have been wealthier, better educated, and healthier. As a result, they have lived longer. And in North America, lower socioeconomic status is associated with lower life expectancy, greater risk of disability, and greater likelihood of institutionalization. The poor, in this society, have a shorter life by 6 to 10 years.

The difference in resources also affects gender differences, an important matter in late life. Maddox examined the prevalence of disability in males and females. He found that, as has been indicated in all related studies, females have a higher

TABLE 6–1   Proportion of Persons Over 60 and 75 Years of Age (and indication of survival beyond 75 by gender) as of 1991 and as Projected for 2020[a]

Country	Percentage age 60 and over		Percentage age 75 and over		Percentage female age 75 and over	
	1991	2020	1991	2020	1991	2020
Canada	16.0	26.3	4.7	8.3	62.5	60.3
Mexico	5.8	10.6	1.5	3.0	55.5	60.9
United States	16.9	24.6	5.3	7.2	64.4	62.4
Germany	20.6	29.6	7.1	11.6	70.2	61.0
Sweden	22.8	28.9	8.2	11.1	61.8	59.5
United Kingdom	20.7	26.6	6.9	9.6	65.9	60.9
China	8.9	16.5	1.9	4.1	59.7	57.1
India	6.1	10.4	1.0	2.1	48.2	53.8
Japan	17.2	30.2	4.3	11.0	63.0	59.9
Ethiopia	4.5	4.9	0.6	0.9	58.8	58.7
Nigeria	4.0	5.1	0.4	0.9	44.9	52.0
Tunisia	7.4	12.3	1.5	3.3	45.3	58.5
Brazil	6.6	12.1	1.4	2.8	61.7	62.7
Chile	9.3	16.6	2.2	4.6	63.2	62.0
Ecuador	5.7	9.9	1.3	2.1	55.4	55.9

[a] These statistics and projections are taken from a report published by the U.S. Bureau of Census (September 1991). The report, in chart form, contains data for 100 countries.

level of disability (although they have a greater life expectancy by more than 7 years). However, when Maddox controlled for differences in education and income (i.e., indices of the allocation of resources), the disability difference disappeared. Rodin and Ickovics (1990) also note a relationship between illness and poverty among women.

The implication of Maddox's findings and observations for the applied social psychologist is extensive and strong. As the natural societal experiments have shown, sufficient income, combined with education and opportunity, can enhance aging. Persons who are disadvantaged will age poorly; redressing their problem will positively affect their aging. Social intervention provides an alternative to institutional care in many cases. The applied social psychologist has a role to play in documenting the relationship between disadvantages and aging as well as advocating and implementing programs for alleviating liabilities (see Box 6–1).

THE ISSUES OF BIAS ARE ISSUES OF AGING

Prejudice and discrimination are important areas of application of social psychology. Just as racism and sexism have wide currency in discussing prejudice, the term *ageism* (coined in 1969 by Robert Butler) has been recognized as describing prejudice against persons based on age. Ageism is a "profound psychosocial disorder characterized by institutionalized and individual prejudice against the elderly, stereotyping, myth-making, distaste, and/or avoidance" (Butler, 1978, p. 14). According to Butler (1980),

> There are three distinguishable yet interrelated aspects to the problem of aging: (a) *Prejudicial attitudes* toward the aged, toward old age, and toward the aging process, including attitudes held by the elderly themselves; (b) *discriminatory practices* against the elderly, particularly in employment, but in other social roles as well; and (c) *institutional practices and policies* which, often without malice, perpetuate stereotypical beliefs about the elderly, reduce their opportunities for a satisfactory life and undermine their personal dignity. The attitudes and beliefs, the discriminatory behaviors, and the institutional norms and policies are related and mutually reinforcing to one another. (p. 8)

In a broader sense, ageism includes prejudice and discrimination against any age group, including the young (Kimmel, 1988). Social psychological theory, research, and application have broad relevance to ageism. Ageist practices limit opportunities for the elderly and distort programs and aids for the elderly. For example, the unwarranted expectation that the elderly are incompetent leads to unnecessary institutionalization of many old persons.

Ageism is widespread in our society and discrimination, particularly in the workplace, is commonplace. Prejudice against the elderly has been found in 6- to 8-year-old children (Isaacs & Bearison, 1986). Recently, researchers have examined the presence of ageism in the field of psychology and have amassed evidence of the extent of age-based discrimination. These issues are discussed in the following sections.

Applications of Psychology to Issues of Aging

B.F. Skinner and K. Warner Schaie are both distinguished psychologists who have written on themes central to social psychological theory.

B.F. Skinner, although not a social psychologist, championed a basic viewpoint that is highly compatible with social psychology. Like most social psychologists, he viewed the social context as a major factor in affecting behavior. (Unlike most social psychologists, Skinner vehemently denied the relevance of cognition.) He argued that many problems of the elderly resulted from environmental deficiencies (Skinner, 1983). Focusing, as he did so consistently, on reinforcers, he wrote "In a world in which our behavior is not generously reinforced we [the elderly] are said to lack zest, joie de vivre, interest, aspirations, and a hundred other desirable states of mind and feelings" (p. 242). He attributed the boredom and depression of many elderly to sparse reinforcement.

K. Warner Schaie has pioneered research on age changes in intellectual skills and methods for studying aging. He has also written persuasively on ageism in psychology (1988, 1993). Psychologists, he notes, are products of the society in which they live. As such, their work, including the language they use in writing about the elderly, reflects their social background and setting. Schaie suggests that ageism permeates psychology.

Schaie (1993) documents ageism in psychologists' use of language in the following examples:

a. Describing a research topic as concerning a "problem of aging," rather than focusing on building or extending an explanatory model
b. Relying on biological models of decrement or decline
c. Ignoring research participants' health status
d. Assuming age is the cause of differences or changes in behavior with slight consideration of alternate explanations
e. Using inappropriate or offensive research instruments
f. Confusing age differences with age changes
g. Overlooking individual differences (Schaie, 1993, pp. 49–51)

Research has revealed the ageist bias of these common practices in psychological reports. These practices are not just offensive: They distort research findings and bias theory. In turn, the effective application of research is reduced.

Ageism in Psychology

As described in Box 6–1, ageist language is replete in psychological reports and concepts. Language is not the only manifestation of ageism; ageist views explicitly and implicitly reside in our textbooks and also in the provision of services. In an analysis of a sample of 139 introductory and advanced psychology textbooks published over a 40-year time span, Whitbourne and Hulicka (1990) found evidence of continuing ageism despite frequent attempts by authors to present a positive view of aging. Ageism in these texts occurs in the continuing neglect of the elderly, limited representation of research on relevant topics (with noteworthy disregard of methodological issues), frequent or excessive emphasis on the plight of the elderly, and representation of old age as a period of decline. Childhood and adolescence are present about five times as frequently as adulthood and old age in the sample of texts. Although there was increased attention over time to various positive aspects of aging, some texts also had a "condescending tone" and emphasized physical and social loss, biological decline, diminishing psychological functions (with a disproportionate emphasis on Alzheimer's disease), and social isolation. The focus on the distressed elderly, the minority who have severe problems, inevitably reinforces a negative view of aging. The "emphasis on older adults as vulnerable and helpless heightens the perception that they are desperately in need of experts to solve their problems" (Whitbourne & Hulicka, 1990, p. 1135). See Box 6–2 for an example of the misconceptions that help promote these beliefs.

One consequence of the relative absence of the elderly in psychological texts, research, and clinical training is the neglect of this population in the provision of psychological services. Kimmel (1988) cites studies indicating that 41% of clinical staff of community mental health centers had no training in geriatric services and 45% of the centers had no programs specifically for the elderly. Drugs are more frequently recommended for treatment of depression of elderly patients than for other age groups (Rodin & Langer, 1980), although psychotherapy has been found to be as effective with the old as with the young (Thompson, Gallagher, & Breckenridge, 1987).

How Serious Is Ageism?

Levin and Levin (1980) assert that ageism is a widespread cultural phenomenon whose longstanding acceptance bridges regional and social differences. Kenyon (1992) writes that ageism often manifests itself in subtle ways: "For many people, it can be a source of lowered self-respect and loss of personal meaning" (p. 2). Further, he notes that many older people internalize the negative *metaphors of aging,* consequently limiting their activities and reducing their contribution to society. According to a meta-analysis by Kite and Johnson (cited in Levy & Langer, 1994), attitudes toward the elderly are about one-third of a standard deviation more negative than toward the young.

The negative stereotypes may not be conscious. Perdue and Gurtman (1990) suggest that ageism is so entrenched in our culture that it may occur unintentionally, automatically, and routinely, influencing social judgment below the level of conscious awareness. They report the results of two studies that support the occurrence of *automatic ageism.* In the first study, 30 undergraduates were asked to recall trait adjectives that they had previously judged as applicable or inapplicable to a young person and to an old person. Significantly more negative than positive adjectives presented in the task with the old target were recalled; more positive than negative adjectives were recalled with the young target: "When individuals process information related to individuals designated as 'old,' evaluatively negative information appears to be encoded in such a manner as to render it relatively more accessible in

**Box
6–2**

The Facts on Aging Quiz (FAQ)

In 1977, Erdman B. Palmore published a multipurpose quiz assessing knowledge about the elderly. Respondents indicated if each item was a true or false statement. Reflecting the popularity of this quiz, a second version was published in 1981. The following items are examples selected from these two quizzes:

1. The majority of old people (past age 65) are senile (i.e., have defective memory, are disoriented or demented).
2. All five senses tend to decline in old age.
3. Most old people have no interest in, or capacity for, sexual relations.
4. The majority of old people feel miserable most of the time.
5. Most older workers cannot work as effectively as younger workers.
6. About 80% of the aged are healthy enough to carry out their normal activities.
7. The reaction time of most old people tends to be slower than the reaction time of younger people.
8. In general, most old people are socially isolated and lonely.
9. Older workers have fewer accidents than younger workers.
10. The aged have higher rates of criminal victimization than persons under 65.
11. There are two widows for each widower among the aged.
12. The majority of aged live alone.
13. When the last child leaves home, the majority of parents have serious problems adjusting to their "empty nest."
14. The life expectancy of men at age 65 is about the same as women's.

In his two articles, Palmore documents the accuracy of his scoring key (see Palmore, 1977, 1981). By 1981, Palmore reports that over 40 studies have been published using the initial FAQ. The quiz has been used to assess general level of information about the elderly, identify major misconceptions, and compare knowledge of different groups. It has also been used extensively to explore and counter bias against the elderly as well as to stimulate discussion in workshops directed at training workers with the elderly. Total score on the FAQ correlates with measures of ageism; greater ageism is associated with more misconceptions (cf. Fraboni, Saltstone, & Hughes, 1990). In general, respondents indicate more negative than positive age bias.

Our attitudes and beliefs about aging and the value we assign to the elderly will contribute to the social policies we implement. For the applied social psychologist, a clear understanding of the characteristics and circumstances, as well as the potentials and problems of aging, is essential. Misinformation regarding the elderly is biased information usually implying that old people are a "problem." The elderly and the aging process in the latter half of life have been poorly understood and frequently misrepresented in both the professional and popular media. Misinformation supports negative stereotypes and bias toward the elderly, which, in turn, has led to discrimination, neglect, and excessive institutionalization.

(*Answers:* Items 2, 6, 7, and 9 are true; 1, 3, 4, 5, 8, 10, 11, 12, 13, and 14 are false.)

Source: Palmore, 1977, 1981. Copyright The Gerontological Society of America. Reprinted with permission.

memory; the reverse seems to be true for those targets labelled as 'young' " (p. 204). In the second study, students made judgments regarding the evaluative significance of traits following brief "priming" with the word *old* or *young*. The presentation of the priming terms was subliminal, that is, beneath the level of conscious awareness. Students made connections more quickly with negative traits when primed with *old* than when primed with *young*. The opposite pattern was found with positive traits. These results suggest that the widespread ageist attitudes prevalent in our society are learned so early and so completely that their expression is automatic with intentionally positive expression of attitudes requiring suppression of the unintended negative tendency (see Devine, 1989, for a discussion of automaticity and stereotypes).

Other research supports the view that ageism is endemic. First, Rodin and Langer (1980) demonstrated that altering attribution for behavior from aging to environmental faults led to higher activity and greater sociability for residents of a nursing home. Second, Sigelman and Sigelman (1982) report that regarding voting behavior, ageism is a more potent variable than either sexism or racism. Third, the fact that discrimination is faced by older people in the workplace well before retirement age has been clearly documented: A Department of Labor investigation found that employment was limited in 60% of unskilled industrial jobs to the 35–49 age range (cf. Bessey & Ananda, 1991).

The Impact of Negative Stereotypes on Memory

The common expectation that the elderly have poorer (long-term) memory has been accepted as a truism in gerontology. However, a recent study by Levy and Langer (1994) questions its validity. They studied memory in the young (age 15 to 30) and old (age 59 to 91) in three cultures: Chinese hearing, American hearing, and American deaf. In the American hearing culture, there is a strong expectation that as one gets old, memory declines. This can set up a self-fulfilling prophecy that may lead to "decreased effort, less use of adaptive strategies, avoidance of challenging situations, and failure to seek medical attention for disease-related symptoms of forgetfulness" (quoted by Levy & Langer, 1994, p. 990). In contrast to the American hearing, the Chinese hearing and the American deaf have a substantially more positive view of aging. The negative expectations are less likely acquired by the deaf because they are excluded from much of mainstream American culture. Respect for the elderly is an integral part of Chinese culture.

Levy and Langer found that both the Chinese and the deaf had a significantly more positive view than the hearing Americans (with the Chinese most positive). Among the young, there were no differences in memory between cultures. Among the old, the Chinese scored significantly better than the American hearing and deaf (who, in turn, outscored the hearing Americans). In fact, the scores for the elderly Chinese did not differ significantly from the young Chinese. The correlation between positive view of aging and memory scores among the elderly subjects was .49 ($p < .01$). These results suggest that a negative view of aging contributes to lower performance on a memory task. The Levy and Langer study suggests that negative stereotypes can result in substantial harm to many elderly persons.

Dementia (most commonly caused by Alzheimer's disease) is a problem associated with advancing age. However, most elderly will never suffer profound memory loss. A major accomplishment of researchers has been the demonstration that severe memory loss is the result of disease, not aging. Although there is no certainty regarding the frequency of occurrence, estimates suggest that moderate to severe dementia is found in 4% to 6% of persons over age 65. Clearly, overestimation of dementia (including Alzheimer's disease) is a form of ageism.

Discrimination

The primary focus of attention on discrimination against the elderly has been in the work domain, particularly in cases forcing retirement or firing older workers while retaining or hiring young workers. Legislative changes have greatly limited mandatory retirement on the basis of age in Canada and the United States. The U.S. Congress passed the Age Discrimination in Employment Act (ADEA) in 1967, outlawing arbitrary discrimination based on age (Bessey & Ananda, 1991). The original act protected private industry workers aged 40 to 65 against discrimination. In 1974, the act was extended to protect state, local, and most federal government workers. In 1978, amendments extended the protection to age 70 and, in 1986, the 70-year-old upper age limit was eliminated for most professions (excluding firefighters, police, college and university professors, and high-level executives). Consequently, age-based discrimination is illegal for nearly all (joining the protected status of race and gender).

As with the other protected statuses, discrimination must be proved in court, which is not easy (as documented by Bessey & Ananda, 1991). As Riley and Riley (1991) point out, the case must continually be remade that older workers are "able to perform far better than expected" and that "the strength and capacities of older people have been grossly underestimated" (p. 460). Under the ADEA, jury trials are available. Discrimination can be established in two ways: by proving that the individual's dismissal reflected disparate treatment (the most common approach) and demonstration of adverse impact, that is, "the plaintiff must show that the defendant's employment policy has a disproportionately negative effect on the protected age group" (Bessey & Ananda, 1991, p. 434). The first approach relies on proof of motive to discriminate. It must be established, for example, that an older worker was fired (despite good job qualifications and successful job performance) and was replaced by a younger worker. The second case relies on proving that the employer's policy has a disproportionately negative effect on older workers. This may be achieved by demonstrating that the selection criteria, such as a measure of reaction time, is irrelevant to successful job performance. This approach relies on research evidence regarding the characteristics of the elderly and the impact of aging. Refuting the myths regarding age provides a basis for a successful suit. Successful use of this tactic has been elusive (Bessey et al., 1991), suggesting that more convincing research is required. The applied social psychologist can contribute by documenting evidence of discrimination, assisting in reevaluation of hiring policies, advising on public policy, developing programs in opposition to discrimination, and assisting organizations that represent the interests of the elderly in their pursuit of fairness.

Overall Attitudes Toward the Elderly

Despite ample evidence of misinformation concerning aging, prejudice, and discrimination against the elderly, people do not hold a uniformly negative view of the aged. The general response appears to be more positive than negative, with a mixture of both (cf., Braithwaite, Lynd-Stevenson, & Pigram, 1993; Hickey, Hickey, & Kalish, 1968; Lutsky, 1980; Schmidt & Boland, 1986; Schonfield, 1982). Some ambivalence in emotional response is likely, given the association of old age with ill health, cognitive decline, death, impoverishment, and social loss (especially death of a spouse). These associations are accompanied simultaneously with positive responses of empathy, concern, and affection (particularly for specific old persons), which in turn provides a foundation for developing programs to enhance the well-being of the elderly.

GENDER ISSUES ARE ALSO ISSUES OF AGING

Kimmel (1988) writes that "Vulnerability to ageism in old age is associated demographically with being a woman, living alone, and having a poor health status" (p. 175). The elderly are more likely female, reflecting their 7- to 8-year life expectancy advantage. After age 80, there is a ratio of two females for every male. Strikingly, there is a ratio of five widows for every widower (see Palmore, 1981). Consequently, many of the very old are widowed and living alone. Though women live longer, they have higher disability rates. Given historical circumstances that reflect substantial generational differences, women have been comparatively poorly educated and lack substantial, consistent, and financially rewarding work histories.

The status of aged females reflects the cumulative disadvantage of their earlier lives. Although women are now in the work force in unprecedented numbers and proportions, they earn only about two-thirds of men's earnings. This means that elderly women's financial status is low; they have little in personal resources to draw on. In turn, they are financially dependent on others (husband, family, or public welfare). Not surprisingly, the impoverished elderly are overwhelmingly female and widows. Aged couples are relatively financially secure because they are a couple. The death of the husband commonly exhausts savings (due to illness-related expenses) and reduces pension payments to the survivor. Women's health issues also require attention. Some illnesses are primarily or solely restricted to women (e.g., breast and uterine cancer). Others are substantially more common in women, including osteoporosis, rheumatoid arthritis, lupus, diabetes, anemia, respiratory disorders, and gastrointestinal problems (Rodin & Ickovics, 1990).

In summary, the very old include many women who are poor, disabled, and alone. This group is at greatest risk for depression, physical illness, and institutionalization. They should be targeted for intervention services.

ISSUES OF HEALTH PSYCHOLOGY ARE ISSUES OF AGING

Although less afflicted by acute disorders such as the common cold and some major categories of mental illness (e.g., schizophrenia and substance abuse), the elderly, disproportionately, are unhealthy. They are particularly vulnerable to chronic ills such as heart and circulatory diseases, cancers, and arthritis. As a rough rule, 20% of persons over age 65 are significantly impaired; they require assistance from others to maintain an adequate independent lifestyle. It should be emphasized that 80% are independent and generally unimpaired. Of course, if you focus on the sick, you get a very different view of the elderly than if you attend to the healthy. Too easily, when thinking about the elderly, the ill, the isolated, the neglected, and the impoverished come to mind (reflecting the availability heuristic).

The lifestyle factors that impact on health, such as inactivity, smoking, poor nutrition, and inadequate housing, yield a cumulative effect in old age since ill health is the outcome of a lifetime of habits and practices: "As much as 50% of mortality from the 10 leading causes of death in the United States today can be traced to aspects of life-style" (Rodin & Ickovics, 1990, p. 1018). Nevertheless, altered lifestyle may lead to improved health even in later life. Substantial data support the view that smoking cessation has benefits at all ages (especially on respiratory disorders and heart disease); exercise programs (e.g., stretching, weightlifting, and walking) have produced dramatic improvements in 80- and 90-year-old participants. In a recent study, after 10 weeks of strength training, 80- and 90-year olds' strength improved over 100% while their walking speed increased by 12% and their stair-climbing ability improved 28% (Brody, 1994).

It is clear that health intervention programs aimed at lifestyle changes among the elderly are extremely valuable. As an example, consider the domain of sexual activity. AIDS is not only a concern for the young. Although it is less common, AIDS among the elderly is increasing proportionally and the elderly are particularly vulnerable for HIV infection due to both social and physical changes. A postmenopausal change that increases risk of infection in women is the accompanying thinning and associated fragility of the vaginal wall combined with decreased secretion and diminishing lubrication. Consequently, the risk of vaginal bleeding as a result of intercourse is greater and transmission of the retrovirus from an infected partner is greater. The change in social circumstances because of death of the spouse means that new sexual partners will often be sought and their sexual history and

HIV status are uncertain. Further, many men, following the loss of their wives, may use the services of prostitutes who may be conduits of infection. Heterosexual transmission of HIV accounts for a greater proportion of cases among the elderly than for the general population and the trend is upward (*New York Times,* 1994). Elderly homosexuals also share the same risk factors as their younger peers. AIDS is more virulent in older patients; AIDS prevention among the elderly is an important area of primary prevention.

Vulnerability and Control

Old age is a period of life during which many losses occur. These may include loss of health; reduced income following retirement; sensory impairment—especially hearing loss; decreasing mobility; and loss of companions, including family members. The sense of control that has been shown to be so important for happiness and health is severely threatened in late life.

The sense that one has control over desired outcomes (i.e., that a person attributes his or her behavior to an internal locus rather than to an external agency) is as crucial to the elderly as it is to the young (cf. Mercer & Kane, 1979; Reid & Ziegler, 1981; Ziegler & Reid, 1983). A strong sense that one controls desired outcomes is associated with better health (both physical and mental), higher morale, more effective behavior, and even survival. Conversely, psychological well-being is diminished by a sense that external factors control one's life. Some negative changes popularly associated with advancing age may result from loss of a sense of control due to environmental changes (Slivinske & Fitch, 1987). For a discussion of the empirical demonstration of the value of enhanced responsibility and control, see Box 6–3.

Achieving or maintaining a sense of control may have particular importance for health even though control maintenance may be difficult in the health domain. Expert opinion and direction are considered vital in the treatment of chronic illness. The individual often has little choice but to follow the regime set out by the medical authority, especially when the illness is severe and the person is in an institution (an acute- or chronic-care hospital or nursing home). Even with severe restraints on choice, some sense of efficacy can be retained with positive consequences.

"Studies have shown that changes in options for control may profoundly affect emotional and physical health . . . possibly by influencing stress resistance, physiological responses, and behavior relevant to health" (Allen, 1986, p. 1271). A sense of control has a moderating effect on stress, thereby diminishing its perceived intensity. Being able to predict the onset of aversive events reduces distress. The physiological reaction to stress reduction includes decreased autonomic reactivity, lower blood pressure and pulse rate, and lower concentration of blood lipids and corticosteroids. Enhanced stress, however, increases all these factors with a concomitant negative impact on health. Increased sense of control, which may be achieved through infor-

Box
6–3 ## Responsibility, Predictability, and Control

The most striking contribution that applied social psychology has made to gerontology has been based on the work of Langer and Rodin on the effects of enhanced responsibility (1976) and Schulz (1976) on predictability and control. Both studies were published in the same year in the *Journal of Personality and Social Psychology*.

The Schulz study is less well known but methodologically more elegant. Participants in the study, volunteers from a church-affiliated old age home, were randomly assigned to one of four conditions. In three of the four conditions, they were visited by college undergraduate volunteers. In one condition, participants determined the frequency and duration of the volunteers' visits; in a second situation, participants were informed of the scheduled visit and its duration in advance; and, in a third instance, the visits took place at random and without prior warning. These three conditions were yoked together so that the frequency and duration of the visits were set by the first condition for the other two groups. Visits took place an average of 1.3 times per week and lasted for approximately 50 minutes. The participants reported enjoying these visits equally in all groups. Two months into the study, participants' health status, psychological status, and activity level were evaluated. Both predictability and control had powerful effects on the participants. Those in both the control and predictability groups were healthier (as rated by the home's activity director) and took fewer medications. They were happier (self-rated as more hopeful and other-rated as having more "zest for life") and more active (activity level was higher and more future commitments were made). Schulz summarizes the results as follows: "Predict and control groups were consistently and significantly superior on indicators of physical and psychological status, as well as physical activity" (p. 571).

This study supports the conclusion, based on correlational studies, that enhanced control has positive consequences on the well-being of the elderly. The failure to show differences in the effect of control and predictability is puzzling; it may be that predictability is particularly important in an institutional environment. The effects of predictability and control were strong despite their minimal duration; the visits once or twice a week by pleasant young strangers were embedded in the institutional routine. This small imputation produced a powerful outcome. This consequence suggests the great vulnerability of the institutionalized aged.

Langer and Rodin's study was carried out in a nursing home. The experimental group consisted of the residents of one floor of the home; the comparison group resided on another floor. Although the floors were randomly selected for the experimental or comparison treatments, the individual residents were not randomly assigned to conditions. The experimental manipulation consisted of a talk by the home director to all participants both in a group and individually, along with a presentation of specific events and options. For the experimental group, efforts were made to enhance personal responsibility; the message to the contrasting group emphasized the responsibility of the staff for residents' well-being (i.e., encouraging an internal and external locus of perceived control, respectively). One feature of this study is particularly memorable. In the responsibility enhancement group, each resident was offered the choice of a present—a plant; if the resident accepted the gift, he or she could choose a particular plant. In the comparison group, individuals were presented with the plant as a present without any options.

The results of this brief manipulation were remarkable. One to 3 weeks later, the responsibility-enhanced group described themselves as happier and more active; they were rated by an interviewer as more alert; nurses described them as more sociable and generally improved; and several behavioral measures indicated greater participation in program activities. In sum, a seemingly trivial manipulation had substantial effects, indicating the importance of a sense of responsibility (or control). These results have been replicated in other studies (cf. Banziger & Roush, 1983; Mercer & Kane, 1979; Slivinske & Fitch, 1987).

Most striking are the long-term consequences of these studies. Both groups of participants were evaluated at a later date. Eighteen months following the intervention, Rodin and Langer (1977) reported that responsibility induction continued to show substantial positive effects. Participants in this condition were more actively interested in their environment, more sociable, self-initiating, increasingly vigorous, and healthier. Although the results were not statistically significant, the mortality rate among the responsibility-enhanced group was half (15%) that of the comparison group (30%). These differences occurred despite the fact that the groups did not remain intact; residential mobility was high due to remodeling in the home. Apparently, the talk by the administrator and the simple accompanying gestures (e.g., the plant gift) induced a change that had profound and enduring effects.

The Schulz study participants were also reassessed 24, 30, and 42 months after the end of the initial study: "Both the number of persons exhibiting declines [in health and zest for life] and the magnitude of the declines were significantly greater for predict and control-enhanced groups when compared to the no-treatment and random groups" (Schulz & Hanusa, 1978, p. 1196). Most troubling, the mortality rate was marginally but significantly higher in the control-enhanced and predictability groups combined, in contrast with the no-treatment and random groups.

It seems that in one instance, enhanced control has a long-term positive outcome and in the other a negative one. What might account for the different results? One important differentiating factor is that in the Schulz study, the control enhancement came to a relatively abrupt end (a limited experience of control encouraging an external, unstable, and limited self-view); the Langer and Rodin study was open-ended with the essential change directed at an enduring (internal, stable, global) self-attribution (Schulz & Hanusa, 1978).

The lessons of these two studies are very important for the applied social psychologist. First, it is essential to recognize that the institutionalized elderly are a population at risk; they are vulnerable to any intervention—even seemingly minor ones. Second, the outcome at the conclusion of the intervention may not be the long-term effect: What is positive in the short term may be very negative in the long term. Third, the issue of perceived control may be particularly important in institutional contexts. Fourth, as programmers and researchers, we are ethically bound to consider the long-term effects of interventions, including the consequence of ending an intervention. This applies to pilot programs, as well as to settings in which long-term funding may be insecure.

mation seeking, self-care, and effective interaction with physicians, may, in turn, lead to stronger adherence to recommendations (Allen, 1986).

Stress

The elderly are also affected by major life stressors such as loss of a spouse. The research literature has long focused on the importance of social support for stress management. The presence of social support is seen as crucial although the specific source of support may have different meaning and impact. At least one person—one confidant—is crucial for well-being. Shanas (1979, 1980) and other investigators have conclusively proved that the family remains a primary source of social support and companionship. Daughters have traditionally been helpful with personal care and assistance. Sons are more likely to help their elderly parents economically. Developing programs to better enable family members to care for their elders will become increasingly important as a means of avoiding institutional care. Stress reduction, enhanced control, and changes of lifestyle are potential domains for the applied social psychologist.

ISSUES OF ENVIRONMENTAL PSYCHOLOGY ARE ISSUES OF AGING

In 1980, Lawton optimistically observed that "Environmentally oriented gerontologists are currently in great demand as consultants in housing design, urban planning, institutional planning, and similar areas" (p. 162). The applied social psychologist can be such a consultant.

Lawton (1990), a leader in the field of environmental psychology of late life, emphasizes the importance of control achieved through enhanced environments: "By learning to apply choice and self-direction in the everyday uses of their housing, occupants of any level of intactness or impairment can actively affect their overall quality of life" (p. 640). For the immobilized, this points to the need for a well-organized "control center" that allows effective monitoring of the setting. A vantage point that faces a window; table surfaces that hold enriching personal objects such as food, photos, and reading material; and easy access to communication devices that extend psychological space (TV, radio, and telephone), enhance psychological health. Toileting facilities with convenient, safe pathways, which are equipped with effective supports, grab bars, and railings, are essential for independent living.

The built environment impacts strongly on the elderly; the environmental psychologist can make a substantial contribution to the health, mobility, and security of the elderly. According to Lawton, environmental psychology of late life began with the publication of O. R. Lindsley's article on geriatric behavioral prosthetics in 1964. The precepts of the field emphasize mobility, safety, control, privacy (especially in institutions), sociability, and legibility. These factors are increasingly considered in construction of purpose-built housing for the elderly and nursing homes. With the impaired elderly, a supportive environment is crucial (Table 6–2). This idea is contained in the "environmental docility hypothesis": "The less competent the individual, the greater the impact of environmental factors on that individual" (Lawton, 1980, p. 14).

Sensory loss is inevitable in late life, although there is considerable variability in extent. Greater susceptibility to glare, differential losses of color receptors, lessened visual acuity, loss of hearing (especially high-pitched sounds), and impaired balance all have environmental design implications (Rule, Milke, & Dobbs, 1992).

TABLE 6–2 Twelve Environmental Interventions for Cognitively Impaired Older Persons

1. Provide privacy to enhance sense of self and separateness from others.
2. Provide opportunities for social interaction.
3. Promote a sense of control and autonomy.
4. Supply strong cues for location and orientation so that residents can find their way from one place to another.
5. Ensure a safe and secure environment.
6. Compensate for physical and cognitive limits on ability to function in the environment.
7. Furnish a stimulating, challenging environment.
8. Compensate for sensory losses (e.g., loss of hearing and vision).
9. Give a sense of familiarity and continuity (e.g., by including personal objects and possessions in the new residence).
10. Provide an attractive, noninstitutional design.
11. Allow for personalizing the environment so that it appears unique and individualized.
12. Provide an environment that has the capability to change over time to meet the changing needs of the resident.

Source: Adapted from Regnier & Pynoos, 1992.

For example, reduced surface glare, color design that recognizes diminished sensitivity to the blue-green color range, clear demarcation of boundaries, use of acoustical tile to absorb background noise, and floor surfaces that provide ample traction should be incorporated into the design of buildings for the elderly (or anyone with similar problems or who is expected to develop these problems). Many of these design improvements are clearly low-tech. (The area of high-tech, computer-based apparatus designed to enhance functioning is developing rapidly, although it is still in an early stage.)

Increasingly, public buildings are designed for access of persons with sensory or mobility difficulties. Ease of access is of general importance for the elderly because falling is a serious problem, especially for those with osteoporosis. A fall may result in a broken hip, which may have fatal consequences. The elderly account for 69% of deaths from falls (Harootyan, 1988). Many of these falls occur on stairs. The 7/11 stairway (a safer stairway with a 7-inch riser and 11-inch tread depth) is often used in public buildings and is often required by building codes. In private buildings, however, an 8- or 9-inch riser combined with a 9- or 10-inch tread depth is common. Carpeting softens the surface, reduces the tread depth, and creates a less safe stairway for the elderly. Changing building codes to require accessibility for everyone may increase construction cost but has value in enhancing individual mobility and personal dignity.

Bathrooms can be hazardrous places for the elderly. Design improvements would include softer, nonglare surfaces. Easy access to facilities, a stall shower, accessible cabinets, and secure railings are also advantageous. An alarm device is highly useful in case of an emergency. Some progress has been made in designing "soft" bathtubs and improved toilets. These kinds of changes increase security, a sense of control, and, consequently, independence.

Physical safety and mobility are definitely affected by the environment; opportunities for social interaction may also be influenced. In a classic study, Sommer and Ross (1958) showed that arrangement of furniture in a geriatric residence altered social interaction: Simply positioning chairs in groups of four around tables, instead of around the room's periphery, increased human contact.

The careful consideration of psychological needs, behavior, age changes, and the interface between the elderly individual and the environment is a rich field for exploration by social psychologists with applied interests.

THE METHODOLOGICAL ISSUES OF DEVELOPMENTAL PSYCHOLOGY ARE THE METHODOLOGICAL ISSUES OF AGING

Studying the aging process per se requires tolerance for ambiguity. Aging, itself, cannot be manipulated. The effects of age can only be observed. Consequently, the essential method of developmental psychology is correlational. There are two main approaches: the *cross-sectional method* and the *longitudinal method*. In the cross-sectional method, separate groups of people of different ages are studied all at once. For example, in 1996, an experimenter might study 40-year-olds' memory for word lists compared to 60-year-olds' memory for the same words. To do this, he or she would recruit one group of 40-year-olds and another group of 60-year-olds, then give them the memory tests. Any differences between the two groups would be attributed to their difference in age and, hence, a process of aging. The longitudinal method, on the other hand, follows the same people over time. In this way, an experimenter would recruit a group of 40-year-old people, test their memory for word lists, and then follow them for 20 more years so he or she could test their memories when they were 60 years of age. If people perform differently at 60 (compared to their performance at 40), then the changes are thought to be caused by the aging process.

There are problems with these two methods, however. The problem with the cross-sectional method is that people born at different times in history (e.g., 1936 versus 1956) will not differ only due to their age but also because they are members of different *age cohorts*. People of different cohorts can grow up in very different worlds. Consider the group of 40- and 60-year-olds waiting to do the memory test. Those who were born in 1956 were raised in a period of economic boon, while those who were born in 1936 were well into adulthood before these economic good times appeared. The Great Depression and World War II probably played a large part in the growing up of these older people but were not experienced by the younger group. Still, there are also problems with the longitudinal method. That is, as people age, they become more experienced, or adapted to their lifestyle. Consequently, if they differ over time in their ability to remember word lists, is it because they have aged or because they have adapted to different needs in their environment?

The methods developed in gerontology are aimed at eliminating these alternate interpretations. For example, in addressing the question of cognitive ability as related to age, one major confound is the generational difference in education level. Early studies in psychology failed to take this into account, which led to an exaggeration of the extent of cognitive loss in late life. By combining the cross-sectional and longitudinal approaches systematically (for a study of *sequential* strategies, see, for example, Schaie, 1965), along with critical analysis of sources of influence, alternative explanations can be evaluated and minimized.

Many applied problems do not concern aging; the action researcher is more interested in showing the impact of programmatic intervention (although there may be an interaction between age and intervention). Questions such as the impact of increasing control on health or the effectiveness of psychotherapy with 80-year-olds are answered using experimental, not correlational, methods. Two issues are germane to the use of experimental methods with the aged. The first is a familiar problem: the artificiality of laboratory studies. The laboratory is an alien place for the elderly; the props of the laboratory, such as nonsense syllables, event recorders, and computers, may result in findings of limited generalizability. The second issue, related to the first, is the high level of anxiety many elderly persons experience when they are aware they are being assessed by psychologists. This reaction seems to reflect a fear that the tests will show cognitive decline (approaching senility, incipient Alzheimer's disease). The elderly have come to expect accelerating memory loss and general decline in thinking prowess, and they interpret minor memory slips as evidence of their own frailty. Consequently, the elderly experimental subjects are anxious, and their frame of mind may lead to poor performance. Test results, then, are misleading. From a research design perspective, it is important that both the experimental and control group experience equivalent degrees of anxiety! A more humane tactic is to provide a reassuring atmosphere for all participants.

Another problem concerns the operational definition of variables (the measures employed). Too frequently, measures are developed and evaluated (in terms of reliability and validity) on young persons (particularly university psychology students). These measures are then assumed to be universally valid even when items may refer to school and career choices. A simple recommendation, then, is that the reliability and validity must be established for the targeted age group.

Still another common problem (particularly in studies in applied settings) is an overrepresentation of the infirm, institutionalized, or organized elderly. It is not surprising that researchers seek out participants who are easily identified and whose cooperation is readily obtained. Old age homes, nursing homes, and senior recreation centers provide convenient sources of subjects (just as the institutionalized young, such as university students, provide a convenient source of young adult subjects). Even the noninstitutionalized community dwellers are frequently identified as the result of negative features; for example, psychologists may recruit research participants at community centers where they are enrolled in day-care programs. Senior citizen center members are not representative of the elderly; many centers specialize in services to the needy elderly. Such samples of convenience are too often extrapolated to the population as a whole, with the unintended consequence that the researchers perpetuate negative images of aging.

A strong case could be made that ethical issues should be carefully considered in designing and conducting research with elderly persons. The very old, in particular, are a vulnerable population. The short- and long-term consequences of any intervention should be evaluated. For example, failure to continue a program can have a negative impact that may lead to increased illness and mortality (see Box 6–3). Another concern is with obtaining informed consent from cognitively impaired persons.

For too long, the elderly have been ignored by researchers and professionals alike. Both basic and applied research on the character and problems of aging have been increasing exponentially. This represents movement in a positive direction by psychologists and related professionals, and it will certainly provide benefits for the elderly in the future.

SUMMARY

What does this change in attitude toward the elderly mean for the applied social psychologist? Applied social psychologists can play a variety of roles from advisor to advocate and from program planner to evaluator. They can work with designers and architects to enhance the social and psychological well-being of the frail or impaired elderly. New and existing programs for the elderly from day care to elder hostels will benefit from program evaluation. Applied psychologists can utilize research findings, such as the strong impact that increased control has on well-being, to improve the lives of the institutionalized elderly. The role of advocate is another part that can be effectively played, for example, in helping to eliminate ageism and discriminatory practices. Out of these roles will come new insights and, potentially, new theory.

Barring personal or collective catastrophe, everyone will become old. The elderly differ from other minority groups in that everyone gets a turn. What that turn will be like for us depends to a great extent on what we as a culture do now to increase our understanding of the aging process and the basis for successful aging. We already know a great deal about aging well: We know that adequate income, personal control, education, sense of purpose, and a healthy lifestyle all contribute to a "golden age." But a great deal remains unknown. So far, investigators have been pleasantly surprised by their findings. Although physically slower, the elderly are cognitively, mentally, socially, and even physically better off than we had previously thought. The elderly are much more varied than any other age group; many respond extremely well to effective intervention.

Basic research, program evaluation, intervention, and social change all intermix to form a fascinating problem domain for the applied scientist interested in the final years of life. The complexities of the problems are only exceeded by the fascination of the endeavor and the potential for contribution to human welfare. Application of psychological theory and practice has potential in all the areas discussed.

SUGGESTED READINGS

Binstock, R., & George, L. (Eds.). (1990). *Handbook of aging and the social sciences* (3rd ed.). San Diego, CA: Academic Press.

Part of the same series as the *Handbook of the Psychology of Aging,* this book provides excellent literature reviews on topics of interest to the applied social psychologist, including articles on family life and social support.

Birren, J. E., & Schaie, K. W. (Eds.). (1990). *Handbook of the Psychology of Aging* (3rd ed.). San Diego, CA: Academic Press.

This excellent collection of review chapters deals with topics that are essential for a broad understanding of the psychological dimensions of aging. These areas include biological and social influences, generational differences, and methodological issues.

Langer, E. J., & Rodin, J. (1976). The effects of choice and enhanced personal responsibility for the aged: A field experiment in an institutional setting. *Journal of Personality and Social Psychology, 34,* 191–198.

This is the classic article in the area of applied social psychology; it is well worth reading as a model of design in an applied setting. The ingenuity of the investigators is particularly noteworthy.

Peterson, D. A. (1987). *Career paths in the field of aging: Professional gerontology.* Lexington, MA: Lexington Books.

This book provides a guide to education in the field of gerontology as well as an overview of career opportunities.

Regnier, V., & Pynoos, J. (1992). Environmental intervention for cognitively impaired older persons. In J. E. Birren, R. B. Sloane, & G. D. Cohen (Eds.), *Handbook of Mental Health and Aging* (2nd ed.). San Diego, CA: Academic Press.

This chapter will be of particular interest to anyone concerned with the ways in which the environment can be altered to enhance the quality of life of the cognitively impaired elderly.

7 Social Psychology and Mental Health

James E. Alcock

Glendon College, York University

A clinical psychologist is appointed director of a new clinic to counsel troubled teenagers. In her first three months on the job, she discovers that many of the problems brought to her clinic revolve around feelings of not "fitting in" with peers. Clients report feeling particularly uncomfortable when interacting with members of the other sex and tell her that they have been rebuffed in their approaches to potential dates because they "said stupid things" or acted in an inappropriate manner. Yet, they are not sure of just how they should present themselves, and despite the plethora of self-help and pop psychology books available, they can find nothing that teaches them how to avoid looking foolish when asking someone out.

The psychologist's problem is that despite her own success at dating before she was married, she does not know what to tell her clients about "how" to date. It just came naturally to her to ask someone out or to graciously accept or decline an invitation. In speaking with associates, she discovers that there is very little that has been published regarding such social interactions. Fortunately, she has a colleague who is an applied social psychologist, and whose interest is whetted by her concern. He undertakes to study the "social psychology of dating" in order to understand better the key factors that contribute to a sense of competence and appropriateness in this social situation. He discovers that there is indeed a "script" that applies (i.e., there is a general set of procedures that are typically followed and expected) and that nonverbal communication plays an important role in that script. Factors such as tone of voice, eye contact, physical proximity, and facial expression prove to be as important as what is actually said.

Using the information produced by this applied empirical research, the clinician establishes a social skills training workshop devoted to teaching her clients how to approach people for dates. She finds that with such training, and with practice through role-playing, the clients' anxiety levels go down as their social skill levels go up. She then monitors them as they begin to transfer these newly acquired skills to their own social world. Ultimately, as they experience more success in this social situation, their self-esteem increases, promoting even more self-confidence in social situations and greatly reducing the emotional distress that originally led them to seek help.

This fictitious example illustrates the benefits of bringing social and clinical psychology jointly to bear on problems that individuals face in their social lives. Because human beings are social animals, and unsatisfying or disruptive social relationships can be either cause or consequence of psychological distress, it is not surprising that the subject matter of clinical psychology is in many ways closely related to issues and research in the field of social psychology, as reflected in the scientific literature. Social psychological research is well represented in journals such as the *Journal of Consulting and Clinical Psychology* and the *Journal of Abnormal Psychology,* and the titles of other journals such as the *Journal of Social and Clinical Psychology* and the former *Journal of Abnormal and Social Psychology* bear clear witness to the overlap of the two fields.

Yet, despite these close links in subject matter and the publication of some applied social psychological research in clinical journals, the two areas remain more isolated from one another than their common interests would dictate. Moreover, at the level of actual application, little social psychological research has had a direct impact on clinical psychology (Strong, 1987). This is in part because social psychologists have been more concerned with basic research, typically through experimentation involving university students, and have not focused their efforts on clinical problems or on the development of techniques that would assist the clinical psychologist. Social psychology's relative lack of influence in the clinical domain is also, to a substantial degree, due to the clinician's unfamiliarity with, or lack of interest in, mainstream social psychology. Clinicians are, of course, aware of the importance of social factors in the lives of their clients, yet it is rare for a clinician to turn to social psychology for assistance in understanding or dealing with a client's problems.

There is much that clinicians could learn from social psychology. As described in the opening vignette, individuals who have not acquired appropriate social skills may experience significant failures in their social lives. Such failure can lead to emotional distress (e.g., anxiety, depression, lowered self-esteem), as well as destructive behaviors, including aggression, substance abuse, and even suicide. Moreover, it should be virtually self-evident that when individuals are in serious interpersonal conflict, the lessons learned by social psychologists about the nature of conflict and conflict resolution are vitally relevant. Social psychological knowledge about interpersonal attraction, social perception, impression management, and communication is also essential to a thorough understanding of individual and interpersonal problems. By becoming knowledgeable about social psychology, the clinician is in a much better position to teach clients to change and to improve their lives than were he or she simply to take a narrow approach based on the traditional disease model, which involves treating a "disorder." Theory and basic research in social psychology provide a gold mine of information for the clinician.

In this chapter, various areas of social psychology that have direct relevance to the provision of clinical psychological services are discussed. The discussion ranges from abstract issues such as the sociocultural definitions of mental health and mental illness, to consideration of the therapy process as a social psychological event, and the ways in which social psychological knowledge can be applied to some specific clinical problems.

DEFINITION OF MENTAL ILLNESS

Before turning to a discussion of the relevance of social psychological knowledge to clinical psychology and the field of mental health, it is important to consider briefly how "mental illness" is defined and diagnosed. In the eyes of some members of the public, anyone who is distressed enough to seek out psychiatric or psychological help is "mentally ill." Yet, most clients seen in private practice by psychiatrists and psychologists are rather ordinary people with a particular problem that overwhelms them. For example, recall the troubled teenagers described in the opening vignette. They felt they did not fit in and were emotionally distressed as a result. This problem falls well within the purview of clinical psychology but is hardly a matter of "mental illness."

The term *mental illness* is vague in its meaning, and its definition is very much related to social and cultural factors. An important element in the diagnosis of mental illness is the degree to which an individual's behavior corresponds to norms of appropriate behavior in a variety of social and occupational roles (Freeman & Giovannoni, 1969). Whereas mental illness is generally defined in terms of maladaptive, deviant, or personally distressing behavior (Nevid, Rathus, & Greene, 1994), it is in fact a deviation from social norms that is often the major basis for such a definition (Ullmann & Krasner, 1975). This is because behavior is not usually considered clinically abnormal if society at large believes it to be within the realm of normalcy. For example, playing Russian roulette is clearly maladaptive and self-destructive, and so is cigarette smoking, given its strong links to cancer and heart disease. Yet it is the Russian roulette player, and not the smoker, who is likely to be viewed as having mental or emotional problems. The reason for this is that most societies accept smoking as normal behavior even though it is hazardous.

Even the diagnosis of schizophrenia and other psychotic problems (which may ultimately prove to have a biochemical basis) is made on the basis of behavior that deviates from what is taken to be normal in a particular society. Having visions of angels or visitations by Jesus Christ may not be considered at all abnormal in a fundamentalist Christian community and, indeed, may be cause for admiration, but people outside that community may well interpret such visions as hallucinatory and indicative of psychosis.

MENTAL HEALTH PROBLEMS AND CROSS-CULTURAL FACTORS

The social psychological investigation of cross-cultural differences in what is viewed as mental illness can aid considerably in helping to define psychological abnormality in one's own culture, and help to distinguish it from simple deviance from societal norms. By stripping away elements that vary as a result of culture, and examining common elements that are found across all cultures, one is in a better position to discover the actual contribution of biochemical and genetic factors. For example, is anorexia nervosa a psychological disorder? Certainly it is viewed as such, but it is a disorder that rarely occurs outside of developed and affluent Western countries, and it is very much linked to socially defined models of what it means to be physically attractive. Is it not then appropriate to consider anorexia nervosa to be, at least in part, a social psychological problem? Even depression varies in its presentation in different cultures. Unlike in Europe or North America, feelings of guilt, inadequacy, and sinfulness are not associated with depression in Asian cultures (Argyle, 1992). It has even been suggested that people need to have acquired Judeo-Christian ideas of sin and guilt before they can be depressed in the Western manner (Marsella, 1980). Unless one is reared in a culture in which childhood transgressions result in parental efforts to induce guilt, it is not likely that a depressed mood will elicit feelings of guilt in adulthood. In this vein, thoughts such as "I am no good, I never do anything right" are thought to reflect childhood experiences with guilt by parental induction.

As mentioned earlier, attitudes toward mental illness, even toward serious disorders such as schizophrenia, strongly influence the degree to which a society accepts or rejects someone behaving in a deviant fashion (Szasz, 1961). For example, Jenkins and Karno (1992) point out that the term *schizophrenia* is associated in mainstream American society not only with a certain stigma, but also with the expectation that the disorder is of long-term duration. However, their research shows that many Mexican Americans attribute symptoms of schizophrenia to *nervios* (nerves), a label that is also applied to a wide range of symptoms, including those manifested in anxiety and depression. Hence, there is less stigma associated with the label and a greater expectation of recuperation, for *nervios* is taken to be a rather common condition that may touch everyone from time to time. Labeling schizophrenic symptoms in terms of *nervios,* rather than in terms of *loco* (i.e., insane), a much more serious condition, leads to the person being treated in an encouraging and supportive manner. (However, even though such labeling leads to destigmatization of schizophrenia, more research is needed to determine the effects this may have on the course of the symptoms. It may well be that there are positive effects, but on the other hand, it is also possible that this may lead to less effective treatment of the schizophrenia.)

Basic research aside, the understanding of cultural factors obviously has direct value to clinical service delivery. An awareness of cultural variations better prepares the therapist whose clientele includes people from other cultures. For example, a male reared in a culture in which all marriages are arranged and dating never occurs may experience considerable emotional distress and even depression if, upon emigrating to the West, he is unable to make female friends. A therapist unaware of sociocultural differences may attribute the problem to some emotional conflict or personality trait, but, as in the opening vignette, perhaps all the client really needs is to learn how to go about dating. The applied social psychologist can help the clinician understand the role that cultural factors play in mental distress (Kagitcibasi & Berry, 1989).

PSYCHOSOCIAL STRESS AND MENTAL HEALTH

Further evidence that the study of social behavior plays an important role in understanding and dealing with psychological disorders derives from the fact that stress resulting from social interactions (or from a paucity of desired social interactions) can contribute mightily to the development of psychological disorders. By understanding societal stresses, one is better able to develop methods to help individuals deal with them. Major life changes can be very stressful and can lead both to physical and emotional deterioration.

Holmes and Rahe (1967) developed a "social adjustment scale," which, based on their research, was intended to reflect the relative amounts of disruption caused by various life events. Many of the major stressors listed on their scale are wholly or partly related to social relationships (e.g., death of a spouse, divorce, loss of job, retirement, and even marriage). Because such research is, by necessity, correlational in nature, one cannot be certain that it is the social relationship that promotes well-being. It could be that emotionally healthy people are more likely to succeed in relationships. Nonetheless, interruptions in desired interactions with others produce great difficulty for most people, sometimes leading to the need for clinical intervention.

Social psychologists have studied the extent to which social support can help protect an individual from some of the consequences of stress. Research has found, for example, that married people enjoy greater levels of both psychological and physical health (Burman & Margolin, 1992; Lee, Seccombe, & Shehan, 1991), and rates of depression and other mental disorders are higher for people who are divorced, separated, or bereaved. Social support provided by marital relationships, as well as by both the extended family and friends, helps to buffer an individual against the various stressors that might otherwise take a more serious toll (Cohen & Wills,

1985). Social support can reduce distress through increasing self-confidence and self-esteem, generating positive feelings, suppressing anxiety and depression, and leading the individual to perceive external stressors as less burdensome (Argyle, 1988). Talking to family and friends not only serves to provide a more realistic interpretation of stressful events, but the sense of sharing one's problems, the feeling that one is not all alone in dealing with a stressor, and the sense of well-being that derives from the caring that others show may all contribute to a lessening of the impact of a stressor. The effects are not just psychological. There is accumulating evidence that physiological reactions to stress are also attenuated by the presence of a solid social support network (Uchino, Kiecolt-Glaser, & Cacioppo, 1992), and that this contributes to a lower risk of illness and death (Blazer, 1982; Monroe & Steiner, 1986).

PSYCHOTHERAPY AS A SOCIAL PSYCHOLOGICAL EVENT

Psychotherapy is itself a social event. It involves the exchange of ideas between therapist and client, with the therapist usually making the deliberate effort to influence the attitudes, beliefs, and behaviors of the client in order to improve his or her psychological well-being. All that social psychologists have learned about social influence has relevance to the therapeutic interaction. And because therapeutic events involve attitude and behavior change, the wise therapist will make the effort to become informed about the social psychological principles that relate to attitude change.

There are various ways in which a social psychologist might approach the study of the therapeutic interchange. Two such approaches, the *interpersonal influence model* (Yesenosky & Dowd, 1990) and the *social exchange model* (Derlega, Hendrick, Winstead, & Berg, 1992), are outlined in the following section. By studying the psychotherapeutic interaction in terms of the structure provided by such models, the social psychologist can help the clinician to improve therapeutic methods and increase clinical effectiveness.

Interpersonal Influence Model

The interpersonal influence model of psychotherapy involves concepts familiar to the social psychologist, such as impression management, cognitive dissonance, and the kinds of power that the therapist possesses vis-à-vis the client. The broad outline of this model is as follows. The power of the counselor or therapist (as perceived by the client) underlies the therapeutic relationship and allows the influence process to occur. Social psychologists have delineated several different types of power (Alcock, Carment, & Sadava, 1994; Stephan & Stephan, 1990), and counselors and therapists possess and employ all of them to one degree or another. They possess *expert power* in that they are presumed by the client to be skilled in dealing with psychological problems. They possess *referent power* to the extent that they are seen as attractive role models to their clients. They possess *legitimate power* in that they are generally licensed or authorized in some manner to provide psychological services. They possess *informational power* in that they are presumed to have great knowledge and insight regarding the problem that brings the client to the therapist's office. They also possess *reward* and *coercive power* to some extent, particularly as the therapeutic relationship develops, in that their reactions can have either a reinforcing or punitive effect upon the client.

According to this model, the therapist knowingly or unknowingly employs his or her power through two social psychological influence mechanisms. First, the therapist introduces a view of the client, or of the client's problem, that is psychologically discrepant with the client's own view. The discrepancy between these two views produces cognitive dissonance, which serves as an agent of change, pushing the individual to modify behaviors or beliefs in order to minimize the dissonance. If, for example, the client insists that his father is a loving man whose judgment is beyond reproach, and if the therapist interprets the father's behavior as controlling and condescending, the client is confronted by a strong discrepancy in the resulting cognitions. One cognition may be "I respect and admire my therapist's insight and ability," whereas another might be that "The therapist's interpretation of events is very different from my own." Dissonance between these two cognitions may be reduced either by coming to doubt the ability of the therapist or by modifying one's own beliefs, bringing them into line with those of the therapist. To the extent that a good relationship has been established between therapist and client, it may be difficult to reject what the therapist says without creating even greater dissonance (now between this rejection and the prevailing belief in the therapist's wisdom). Moreover, there is generally a desire on the part of a client to create a good impression in the therapist's eyes, and such impression management involves, in part, giving serious consideration to the therapist's viewpoint, rather than disagreeing with or challenging the therapist. Thus, dissonance can be most readily reduced, while impression management is also served, by coming to share the therapist's interpretation of the father's behavior. This will then provide the therapist with good grounds for promoting change in the way the client deals with his father and the manner in which he interprets future interactions with him.

Similarly, in the situation described in the opening vignette, the therapist may indirectly produce dissonance between a client's presenting cognition that "I am not very likeable" and the contrary positive cognition produced by the therapist's words and actions. The easiest way to reduce this dissonance is to move toward the therapist's viewpoint.

The second mechanism in the interpersonal influence model is related to the effects of behavior change on attitude change. The relationship between attitudes and behavior is a complex one, but there is abundant evidence that acting in a manner inconsistent with an attitude often leads to change in the attitude to bring it more into line with the behavior; in other words, attitude change follows behavioral change (Zimbardo & Leippe, 1991). Therapists often recommend new ways of dealing behaviorally with situations in the client's life, and to the extent that the client changes his or her behavior in order to follow the therapist's advice, there will be an impetus toward change in the associated attitudes and beliefs. Going back again to the opening vignette, the client who is low in self-confidence and who explains un-successful dating in terms of lack of personal worth is likely to experience improved self-worth as his or her behavior—modified by the role-playing and the coaching of the therapist—begins to produce results. Successful behavior in the dating arena leads to changes in the cognition that "no one wants to go out with me. I'm not like-able or attractive."

SOCIAL EXCHANGE THEORY

Another approach to understanding the social dynamics of the therapeutic relation-ship is in terms of social exchange theory (Derlega et al., 1992). The social exchange model of social interaction assumes that, just as in commercial interactions, individ-uals seek to maximize profits and minimize losses (Thibaut & Kelley, 1959). In social interactions, what is exchanged is not money or goods, but such things as approval, interest, friendship, love, and understanding. Costs include such things as the amount of time and energy one needs to invest in the relationship, as well as possi-ble negative feelings generated by the exchange. The basic premise of this theory is that relationships are more likely to endure when the rewards are high and when the costs are low. However, people sometimes stay involved even in "unprofitable" re-lationships (i.e., in which costs exceed rewards) because there is no better deal, such as a more attractive relationship elsewhere. If one needs companionship, then even a companion who is constantly undermining one's self-esteem may be preferable to having no friend at all.

This model is applicable to the relationship between therapist and client. Whether a client continues in the interaction is strongly influenced by the percep-tion that what is gained is worth the time and effort involved in attending sessions and in putting the therapist's suggestions into practice. Rewards for the client in-clude attention, compassion, the therapist's interest, and ultimately, improvement in the problem area that brought about the therapeutic relationship. Costs include out-lays of money and time, as well as the emotional pressure brought about by the ther-apeutic process. The therapist's rewards involve not only financial remuneration, but also the satisfaction that results from helping someone overcome his or her problems, and the sense of worth and competence that is bolstered by the client's improvement and gratitude. The costs to the therapist include time and energy ex-pended in trying to help the client, as well as possible frustration and disappoint-ment if the client does not respond in the intended manner. A therapeutic relation-ship can go into decline if either the therapist or the client begins to suffer excessive costs relative to the actual or expected rewards.

Consider, for example, the troubled teenagers described in the opening vi-gnette. Why should they continue to attend therapy sessions? If they do not get something out of it, they are unlikely to continue to participate. Why does the psy-chologist make such efforts to help them? She, too, gets something out of it, quite apart from financial recompense. Both client and therapist are involved in a mutu-ally beneficial exchange. The therapist benefits from feelings of success and well-being as the clients improve in attitude, behavior, and contentment, whereas the clients benefit not only from whatever improvements they are able to effect in their social lives as a result of the social skills training, but also from the interest and approbation provided by the therapist.

Through the study of psychotherapy as a relationship between two people that is similar in many ways to other personal relationships, and by the analysis of how commitment to the relationship develops as a function of the perception of a worthwhile exchange, applied social psychological research can potentially lead to better understanding of, and improvement in, the therapeutic relationship.

SOCIAL PSYCHOLOGICAL FACTORS RELEVANT TO AN UNDERSTANDING OF PSYCHOLOGICAL PROBLEMS

Much emotional distress and maladaptive behavior—at the level of the individual, the couple, or the family—involve factors and processes familiar to the social psychologist. In the section that follows, several domains of social psychological research and theory, including social perception and cognition, attribution theory, communication, and conflict resolution, are briefly examined in terms of their relevance to understanding and ameliorating mental health problems. Their specific applications are addressed later in this chapter.

Social Perception and Social Cognition

The manner in which one perceives the social world, and the way in which we perceive ourselves in that world, bears an important influence on self-esteem and feelings of "fitting in." A person's knowledge of the world is organized in terms of categories, or *schemas*. A schema is simply a set of interconnected facts, beliefs, and opinions that a person possesses, with respect to a particular social object. Individuals possess schemas with regard to all manner of social objects, including people, events, roles, and even themselves. These schemas influence both the perception of social events and the memories of past experiences. If the schemas are in some way faulty, they will skew and distort the interpretation of reality.

The clients in the opening vignette appear to have developed a schema about themselves that included a belief in their own social inadequacy. Each time a potential dating situation arises, such a person is likely to approach it with little confidence and the expectation of defeat. Such an approach, of course, makes defeat more likely, thus strengthening the sense of social inadequacy and unattractiveness as part of the self-schema. Part of what the therapist accomplishes through teaching the clients about how to date is to change their self-schema: "I'm a loser—no one would want to go out with me" is gradually transformed into "I am likeable; I am capable of successful dating; I just need to learn how." The schemas one holds with respect to others are equally important. If Harry's schema for his father is one that elevates the man to virtual sainthood, then Harry may always feel inadequate and may view himself as a failure and a disappointment to his father. By working to change this schema, the therapist can help Harry to gain a more appropriate perception of his father, and this in turn will influence Harry's self-schema. He will be less likely to interpret his own life in terms of inadequacy and failure.

Similarly, people lacking confidence may have constructed inappropriate schemas for certain events. An *event schema* refers to all that a person knows regarding what to expect and how to act in a particular kind of situation. For example, in the opening vignette a male client's event schema for asking someone out on a date may lead him to alienate the women he asks, and he then feels rejected when they refuse his invitation. He may view this rejection in terms of his own inadequacy instead of in terms of inappropriate behavior based on an incorrect event schema. The therapist, through coaching and the use of role-playing, helps the client develop a more appropriate event schema for asking someone out on a date.

Attribution Theory

The student of social psychology is well aware of the importance of attributional processes to both individual and interpersonal well-being. People constantly look for causes of events that occur around them. As they give interpretations to these events, they make judgments about the motivations of the other people involved in them. For example, if Martha is not invited to a party, she may attribute this to the snobbery of the host, to the fact that the party revolves around a football game and the host knows that she does not like football, or to her own lack of attractiveness to others. The attribution that she makes will have an important impact on her self-schema and ultimately her self-esteem, as well as on the way in which she treats the party's host in the future.

Attribution theory has stimulated a great deal of research in social psychology and, when this research is focused on distressed individuals or couples, it can provide considerable insight into psychological problems and may point to solutions. By studying how individuals assign causes to events, and by helping them modify this process when it appears deficient, the therapist can often make great strides in helping the client attain not only a better level of self-understanding and self-esteem, but also an improved level of social functioning, which in turn enhances emotional well-being.

Communication

Communication is vital to a good relationship, and poor communication makes it much more likely that minor conflicts of interest will lead to major disputes. This is true not only in relationships between marital partners, families, and friends, but also between individuals and their coworkers and other people with whom they must interact. It is just as true in the relationship between therapist and client. The social psychological study of communication, both verbal and nonverbal, has a great deal to offer the therapist in terms of teaching individuals to interact better with one another and to make more appropriate attributions about each other's actions, as well as aiding the therapist in the practice of the therapy itself. Tone of voice or facial gesture can undermine or reverse the meaning of a verbal communication. Often, individuals are unaware of the double message they send; sometimes what was intended as a positive verbal message is taken by the listener to be inflammatory or demeaning because of the tone of voice or the facial expression or some accompanying gesture.

Conflict and Conflict Resolution

Considerable social psychological research has been devoted to the study of interpersonal and intergroup conflict, and there is much in the resulting literature that can find successful application in the clinician's office. Many individuals and couples experience serious emotional distress as a result of interpersonal conflict. When a couple presents for "marriage therapy," the problem almost always involves conflict to some degree. Such couples usually have inappropriate power-sharing arrangements (e.g., deciding on where to go on vacation) and inadequate conflict management skills (e.g., how to negotiate solutions). A counselor or therapist familiar with the social psychology of conflict resolution will be much better prepared to understand the factors contributing to the conflict, and to propose methods of reducing it.

APPLICATION OF SOCIAL PSYCHOLOGICAL KNOWLEDGE TO SPECIFIC CLINICAL PROBLEMS

The social psychological knowledge gained from the study of schemas, attributions, communication, and interpersonal conflict has important applications to a wide range of individual emotional problems. These include, among others, low self-esteem, panic disorder, depression, shyness, loneliness, anger, and relationship problems.

Low Self-Esteem

One's self-schema is greatly influenced by the attributions that one makes. People who suffer from low self-esteem, some of whom go on to become chronically depressed, tend to blame negative events either on their own inadequacy or on the vicissitudes of a cold, unloving world (Sweeney, Anderson, & Bailey, 1986). Such faulty attributions increase distress. By systematically observing an individual through careful review and analysis of ongoing experiences, the therapist can often clearly demonstrate to the client the role of his or her inappropriate attributions. Then the therapist can coach the client in methods of supplanting the faulty attributions with more appropriate ones. As the attributional process changes, the client begins to take on a clearer view of himself or herself and of the social world and gradually comes to believe that he or she can influence this social world in an important and positive way. For example, recall the opening vignette. Suppose a young man, already harboring a negative schema about himself with regard to his attractiveness and desirability in the eyes of women, approaches a student in his class and asks her to accompany him to a movie. The classmate declines, saying that she has too much work. If the young man attributes the refusal to his own unattractiveness, then this response constitutes rejection and will produce more distress and erode his self-esteem. If, on the other hand, he has learned to be careful about attributions, he might instead think to himself, "I have no information that indicates that I am the reason why she did not want to go to a movie tonight. She said she has work to do and I have no good reason to think she is being untruthful." Such a simple change in the attribution process can, over time, produce dramatic changes in the individual's well-being, promoting behavior that is likely (at least from time to time) to result in dates, which may, in turn, produce even more confidence. As more appropriate attributions and more effective behavior begin to take over, increases in self-esteem tend to follow.

Depression

Depressed individuals typically have negative self-schemas, characterized by beliefs such as "I am mediocre at everything" or "No one respects me." The research literature demonstrates that negative cognitions are associated with vulnerability to depression in both adults and children (Hilsman & Garber, 1995). Viewing the world through a depressive schema sets up self-fulfilling prophesies. If individuals believe that no one respects them, then they are likely to misinterpret all sorts of situations in those terms. For example, they may turn down invitations to parties on the ground that the offer is probably made only out of politeness. Then, when people stop inviting them because they never accept, this confirms that the people making the invitations never really wanted them to attend their parties anyway.

Some people tend toward an attributional style that leads them to be vulnerable to depression. Three types of attribution produce a vulnerability to depression (Pyszczynski & Greenberg, 1985; Seligman, Peterson, Kaslow, Tanenbaum, Alloy, & Abramson, 1984). These attributions include (a) *internal* attributions for negative experiences (i.e., the interpretation of such events as the consequence of personal inadequacies rather than situational factors); (b) *stable* attributions for negative experiences (i.e., the interpretation of such events as the consequence of rather permanent features of the person's personality); and (c) *global* attributions for negative experiences (i.e., the interpretation of such events as being due to general aspects of one's personality rather than to particular character weaknesses that might be readily corrected).

A number of studies have confirmed that depressed people have a greater tendency to attribute their failures to internal, stable, and global factors. In one such study, Metalsky and Joiner (1992) found that when people with this tendency were faced with a high level of a naturally occurring life stressor, they reacted with symptoms of depression rather than showing more appropriate anxiety symptoms. For them, the stress led to a focus on their own sense of inadequacy and low self-worth. Thus, the effect of even a high level of stress depends greatly upon the attributions one makes about oneself and the events one faces.

The major difference between nondepressed and mildly depressed individuals is that the former are biased in the direction of positive thinking. They overestimate their ability to influence events, they take for granted that successful outcomes are in large part the result of their own efforts and abilities, and they attribute negative outcomes not to their own characters, but to the situation (Beck, 1976). Among depressed people, on the other hand, there is what amounts to a kind of *depressive realism* (Alloy, Albright, Abramson, & Dykman, 1990). Depressed individuals often show fewer biases in their attributions than do nondepressed persons. Nondepressed people tend mistakenly to see positive events as happening more often to themselves than to others, and negative events as occurring more often to others than to themselves. In contrast, depressed people more accurately see no difference between themselves and others with regard to the frequency of occurrence of positive and negative events (Crocker, Alloy, & Kayne, 1988).

Social psychologists have studied the role of *coping styles* in depression. For example, Pyszczynski and Greenberg (1987) have presented a *self-focus* model of depression, which suggests that, in order to cope effectively, healthy individuals are able to "write off" certain discrepancies between what they would like to be and would like to have with what they really are and what they actually have, and then move on with their lives. However, individuals who cannot do this, and who continually focus on some irreversible loss, continue to experience intensely negative emotional reactions that, in time, produce a negative self-image that maintains or worsens the depressed emotional state.

Panic Attacks

Individuals who suffer panic attacks are generally extremely distressed by this type of occurrence. They may report that they believed that they were having a heart attack, that they were going to pass out, or even die. After one such attack, fear builds about the possibility of further attacks, and this fear indeed makes further attacks more likely. Such a client usually attributes the panic attack either to some undiscovered physical disorder, which again creates more anxiety or to some mental deterioration (e.g., "I am going crazy"). Part of the therapy for such panic involves work on the faulty *attribution* process that is almost always present. Through teaching the client about arousal in the autonomic nervous system, and by explaining that the symptoms that he or she feels (e.g., heart pounding, shortness of breath, possible chest pains, dizziness, feelings of losing control) are exactly those of extreme autonomic arousal, the client learns to interpret these reactions in a manner that does not suggest extreme peril (Beck, Sokol, Clark, & Berchick, 1992). Then, by teaching breathing techniques to help diminish the autonomic arousal, the therapist can make great strides in helping the client to overcome the anxiety when it occurs (Ley, 1991). It is much easier at this point to help the client explore, come to understand,

and ultimately deal with whatever stressors are responsible for the anxiety in the first place. These stressors are very often social in nature, involving unrecognized problems in close personal relationships.

Shyness

Although few social psychologists have focused on the direct application of social psychology to clinical problems, the area of shyness provides an important contrast. The most important research into shyness, as well as the most significant attempts to "treat" it, have been carried out by Zimbardo, a social psychologist. That a social psychologist has tackled the problem of shyness should not be surprising, for shyness is first and foremost a difficulty in social interaction.

Zimbardo and his collaborators set up a shyness clinic in a university setting. Using applied social psychological research, they developed techniques for helping people to overcome shyness. These techniques involved altering attributions that people made about themselves, as well as *social skills training* (Brodt & Zimbardo, 1983; Zimbardo, 1977). Box 7–1 describes more clearly how social skills can improve one's social functioning.

Shy people often attribute the anxiety feelings that they experience in a social situation to their shyness, which makes them feel even more inadequate and uncomfortable. By teaching the individual to attribute these symptoms to something else (e.g., the hustle and bustle at the cocktail party), Zimbardo found that shy individuals perform in a less shy manner and begin to break out of the negative feedback loop that ties anxiety in one social situation to expectations of anxiety in the next. Undoubtedly, the psychologist in the opening vignette would find among her clients some cases of extreme shyness and would have to pay particular attention to helping those individuals surmount the shyness problem before beginning to deal with the problem of dating.

Loneliness

Loneliness is a major source of psychological distress for many people and can promote serious depressive reactions. The therapist who knows little about the social psychological study of loneliness may fail to deal with the problem adequately, sometimes failing even to recognize the role that loneliness plays in other disorders. For example, if a client who has only recently been married seeks help for emotional distress, loneliness may not even be considered as a possible problem by either therapist or client. And yet, research has revealed a significant incidence of loneliness in a sample of recently married people, reflecting problems with the quality of the relationship, rather than with being alone (Sadava & Matejcic, 1987). Loneliness can lead to other serious problems such as male aggressiveness toward women (Check, Perlman, & Malamuth, 1985) and alcohol problems (Sadava & Thompson, 1986).

In part, loneliness can be understood in terms of attributions that people make (Peplau, Russell, & Heim, 1979). If people interpret their feelings of loneliness in

**Box
7–1**

Social Skills Training

Mental health depends in part on an individual's ability to cope within a given sociocultural context. If he or she lacks the necessary social skills, then he or she will be less able to cope with stress and more prone to mental distress. Argyle (1992) reported that 27% of a sample of neurotic outpatients suffered difficulties in social interactions and had only one-quarter as many friends as control subjects. He also found that their nonverbal communication was less positive than that of controls—less gaze at others, less proximity with others, and less smiling. Also present were more drooping posture, gloomy facial expressions, sad voice tone, and self-touching rather than communication with others. Again, a negative feedback loop is set up whereby such negative aspects of nonverbal communication may push others away, leading to greater feelings of rejection or unworthiness, and so on.

The situation in which a child is reared plays a vital role in subsequent adjustment or maladjustment. Not only are some children brought up in conditions that are much more stressful, the adults and peers around them are also more likely to be experiencing this same stress and perhaps coping in maladaptive, ineffectual ways. Consequently, the child is likely to acquire, both through modeling and inappropriate reinforcement, similar maladaptive patterns of behavior (Eron & Peterson, 1982).

The social skills model is based on the notion that some forms of mental disorder are either the result of, or are aggravated by, incompetence with regard to social skills and can be alleviated or removed through training in social skills (Trower, Bryant, Argyle, & Marziller, 1978). Trower et al. (1978) point out that there are two possible sequences of events: Either (a) the lack of social competence is the primary problem and leads to rejection, social isolation, and resultant emotional problems; or (b) other kinds of mental disorders produce interference in the ability to relate socially to others, and this in turn leads to social isolation, increased distress, and deterioration in the condition.

By training distressed individuals in the necessary social skills for maintaining appropriate social relationships, the therapist can help the individual to reverse the negative feedback loop resulting from his or her actions. Better social interactions will result, leading to increases in self-esteem and enjoyment of life.

Of course, before one can train others in the appropriate use of social skills, it is necessary to appreciate fully just what those skills are. It is in this context that the social psychologist has a great deal to offer. Argyle and colleagues, through careful research into various aspects of social interaction that are beyond the capacity of individuals themselves to describe, were able to show the importance of various roles and social rules of nonverbal behaviors (Argyle, Furnham, & Graham, 1981). They developed a social-skills training approach involving modeling of appropriate social skills in a particular relevant situation. The approach involves having the "trainee" role-play, following the modeled behavior, videotaping the trainee, and reviewing the tape with him or her in order to facilitate understanding and improvement. (Assertiveness training, as carried out by many therapists, is the application of a similar approach to one specific type of problem.)

Controlled studies have found the social skills approach to be as effective as cognitive therapy (Argyle, 1992). A major problem for the approach is to produce generalization from the modeling situation to real life. This is attempted through the assignment of homework between sessions, in which the trainee attempts to model the behavior in a real-life setting and then subsequently reviews the outcome with the trainer.

terms of being socially rejected or in terms of personal inadequacy, they are likely to feel much more distress than if they interpret the same feelings in terms of a lack of appropriate people in the social environment. The latter attribution may lead people to seek out other social situations, whereas the former may lead them toward a depressive reaction.

Cutrona (1982) carried out research into factors that are related to chronic loneliness. First-year college students were tested for loneliness in the fall and then again the following spring. Cutrona compared students who were less lonely in the spring than in the fall with students who continued to be just as lonely. Initial causal attributions proved to play a crucial role in ongoing loneliness. Those students whose loneliness did not remit made internal, stable attributions about their loneliness more often. That is, they attributed the problem to their personality, and they viewed being lonely as a stable, unchanging situation. Moreover, these same students tended to believe that only a satisfying romantic relationship could cure their loneliness, whereas students who had become less lonely in the course of the school year emphasized the satisfaction that comes from nonromantic friendship.

Cutrona's research indicates the importance of initial attributions about the cause of loneliness. In the opening vignette, the teenagers who did not "fit in" were taught through social skills training that the cause of their social difficulties was not tied to stable aspects of their personalities, but rather, to aspects of their behavior that they could learn to change.

Hostility and Aggression

Social psychologists have invested considerable effort in the study of aggressive behavior. The clinical psychologist, too, is sometimes faced with a client whose anger and aggressiveness are a substantial part of the referring problem. What can the social psychologist teach the clinician? First of all, *catharsis* research has clearly shown that imagining or viewing violence does not decrease violent tendencies and may actually increase them (Baron, 1983). For example, research shows that viewers of hockey, football, or wrestling violence are more hostile after viewing the violence (Arms, Russell, & Sandilands, 1979; Quanty, 1976). Another example comes from Ebbesen, Duncan, and Konecni (1975). They conducted a field experiment with a group of engineers and technicians who had just received layoff notices that had left them feeling angry. In the first part of the experiment, some of the subjects were asked questions that encouraged the venting of hostility. For example, they were asked to come up with examples of ways in which the company had mistreated them in the past. The rest of the subjects were not given such questions. Subsequently, all subjects responded to a questionnaire that evaluated their attitudes and feelings toward the employer and the supervisor. Those who had had the opportunity to express their hostility in the first instance would be expected to show a decrease in hostility if the catharsis hypothesis is correct. They did *not* show a decrease in hostility. Rather, their hostile feelings were actually intensified. This is important information for the therapist who is tempted to treat anger and aggression by having clients imagine venting their spleen against targets that have frustrated or angered them.

The rich social psychological literature on aggression can also help the child psychologist faced with an aggressive child. Children model their behaviors on those they observe around them, and this is as true of aggressive behavior as anything else (Bandura, 1973). The literature clearly shows that controlling children's aggressive behavior through the use of physical force, although capable of temporarily suppressing the behavior, is likely actually to promote aggression in the future. Not only does the child come to recognize the effectiveness of aggression, but physically punitive parents provide excellent examples of aggressive discipline that the child can subsequently model to bend other people to his or her wishes.

Another area of social psychology that is of particular relevance to a clinician dealing with aggressive behavior is *excitation-transfer theory* (Zillman, 1971, 1984). This theory posits that excitation in the nervous system is more or less the same, regardless of whether the accompanying emotion is frustration, anger, fear, sexual arousal, or some other feeling. According to the theory, the excitatory component of the emotion does not disappear immediately after the stimulus that elicited it has ceased. It lingers on for a while. This residual excitation can augment and intensify an emotional state that is elicited by other stimuli a short time later. Zillman's (1971) research has demonstrated that subjects who experienced either sexual or aggressive arousal subsequently produced more aggressive behavior toward a confederate who had irritated them. Indeed, watching a sexually arousing film led to more subsequent aggression toward the confederate than did watching an aggressive film.

The implications of this and other related research are important for understanding and treating anger and aggression problems. For example, an individual may return home from a frustrating day at work, after having experienced a heightened level of physiological arousal as a result of a confrontation with a colleague when leaving the workplace. This arousal state can linger and make an outburst of anger more likely if, for example, the person's child subsequently spills milk on the floor. Individuals and couples are generally unaware of the role of previous arousal states in producing feelings of anger and aggressiveness. Coming to understand this transfer of excitation is an important step in learning to deal with anger more appropriately.

Chronic Pain and Disability

Accidents and resulting injury or disability represent tremendous stressors for the individual and his or her family. Not only is there often chronic, unremitting pain to deal with, but individuals may lose much of their social and recreational lives. Also, their status and power (real and perceived), both within and outside the family, may drastically change.

Applied social psychological research can contribute significantly to the understanding and treatment of accident and trauma victims. For example, Frey and Rogner (1987) emphasized the importance of social psychological research into the convalescence of accident patients as a means toward understanding the postaccident adaptation process. In this context, perceived control over stressors has been demonstrated by social psychologists to be important in terms of coping effectively

(Glass & Singer, 1972). Attribution of self-efficacy in terms of being able to live with disability or pain, or even recover from it, has an important effect on the employment of coping behavior and the undertaking of actions necessary to facilitate recovery. In one relevant study (Bulman & Wortman, 1977), it was found that paralyzed accident victims who believed that their accidents had been unavoidable handled their disabilities better than those who thought that they could have avoided the accident. Frey and Rogner (1987) also found that the less an accident is later viewed as avoidable, the better the convalescence. Conversely, they observed that high self-blame for an accident is associated with a poorer recuperation process. Frey and Rogner also found that the perception of control over, and responsibility for, recovery is associated with a better recuperation process. Potentially, they point out, such findings could lead to therapeutic measures directed at reducing self-blame for an accident and increasing perceived control over the rehabilitation process.

Most people think of pain as a purely physical phenomenon requiring physical remedies. In recent years, however, pain researchers have begun to view pain as a psychological experience. Even though all pain does have physical correlates, these correlates are sometimes related to something outside the brain that is causing the pain, sometimes to pathological brain discharges, and sometimes to brain events triggered by thoughts (Merskey, 1978). Social psychological factors often play a significant role in the pain experience.

For example, when people are sick or in pain, they take on a particular role that is relatively well defined within a given society. In mainstream North American society, the sick individual is excused from work and whatever other obligations he or she may have had when not sick, but the individual is expected to take measures aimed at returning to a state of health. In addition, it is expected that the individual will not act as though being ill is an enjoyable state. Thus, society allows people to drop their normal duties and obligations, provided that they appear to be ill and are acting responsibly—caring for themselves in order to promote a recuperation.

However, chronic pain and disability are another matter. When pain becomes chronic, it leads to serious changes in the individual's lifestyle, and social psychological factors take on a greater and greater role in the course of the disability (Alcock, 1986). When an individual is unable to resume his or her normal role for a considerable period of time, a number of important social changes ensue. If the person was formerly the head of the household, his or her spouse will probably take on a greater and greater level of responsibility and exercise greater power. This leads to changes in the relationship that often promote both individual distress and interpersonal conflict.

Consequently, family dynamics may be significantly transformed. If the pain sufferer is the father in a traditional household, his incapacitation may produce considerable insecurity among family members. If the wife takes over more and more of the traditional male role because the husband is unable to perform that role, resentment on both sides may result. If, because of financial difficulties, the wife has to seek work outside the home, the sick husband may find himself being more and more drawn into the traditional female role, making school lunches, taking the children to the bus stop, and so on. Now, the wife, with new-found independence, may be unwilling to submit any longer to the authority of the husband. She may find that she enjoys the new-found leadership role and the power and independence that go with it.

Chronic pain and disability almost always present themselves within a social context. As the foregoing examples suggest, applied social psychology can make an important contribution to rehabilitation through the careful study of relevant social psychological factors and influences.

Relationship Problems

The subject of intimate relationships has received growing attention from social psychologists in recent years. As mentioned earlier, marriage and other close relationships have a strong bearing on mental health (Burman & Margolin, 1992), and deficiencies or breakdowns in such relationships can lead to a host of problems, including severe depression, anxiety, and alcoholism. Indeed, marital problems are the single most common reason for seeking psychological counseling (Veroff, Kulka, & Douvan, 1981). Social psychologists have contributed greatly to the understanding of marital contentment and dysfunction through the study of the affective and cognitive aspects of marital interaction (Bradbury & Fincham, 1990), as well as the application of social psychological knowledge pertaining to romantic love and jealousy, attributions, communication, and conflict resolution.

By understanding the nature of romantic love, for example, in terms of Berscheid and Walster's (1974) two-factor theory, the therapist may be able to help an individual sort out the reasons for being attracted to another individual who, on the basis of a rational analysis, seems quite inappropriate or undesirable. According to this theory, romantic love involves both physiological arousal and situational cues that lead to the arousal being interpreted as romantic love. Thus, physiological arousal, whether produced by excitement, fear, or whatever else, can be interpreted by the individual in terms of romantic love, provided situational cues make such an interpretation salient.

Other emotions, too, are involved in relationship issues, and sometimes it is difficult to distinguish among them. For example, Fitness and Fletcher (1993) studied the extent to which married couples can discriminate between love, hate, anger, and jealousy. They found that each of these four emotions develops like a script, and that each is set off by a particular type of event that generates a particular pattern of cognitive appraisal, followed by a series of interrelated behaviors and partner reactions. Through such research, the applied social psychologist can provide the clinical psychologist with a framework for understanding dysfunctional relationships and for helping people improve their relationships by changing their patterns ("scripts") of interaction.

The study of attributions in marriage has been a particularly fruitful field. Attributions for events within a marriage play a major role in determining the behaviors of partners in the marriage; and by teaching couples to change the attributions they make, the therapist can help the couple improve their relationship. The attribution process, however, is vulnerable to cognitive bias. For example, the actor-observer bias (Jones & Nisbett, 1971) often contributes to relationship problems: individuals tend to interpret the causes of their own actions as *situational,* and the causes of the other person's actions as *dispositional;* that is, "I yelled because you just won't listen" (situational) versus "I know you yelled because you're irrational and cannot control your temper" (dispositional).

People in happy relationships tend to interpret their partner's positive behaviors as reflections of the partner's personality; whereas with distressed couples, it is the negative behaviors that are taken to reflect the underlying personality (Jacobson, McDonald, & Follette, 1982). Further, Bradbury and Fincham (1990) found that spouses in distressed marriages overemphasize the importance of negative events within the marriage and interpret them as being representative of an ongoing, global problem. On the other hand, these same spouses interpret positive events as nonrepresentative and relatively unimportant (e.g., "Sure, John takes me dancing—big deal, I wish he'd just learn to take off his muddy boots before he comes into the house"). This is not just a matter of unhappy people making inappropriate attributions. The attributions go sour first. Research shows that negative attributions predict decreases in marital satisfaction a year later (Fincham & Bradbury, 1993).

Where relationship conflicts usually develop with reference to specific behaviors, they often turn into attributional conflicts, with the parties arguing over why one or the other acted in a particular way (Orvis, Kelley, & Butler, 1976). Both parties usually believe that they understand their own motives, which are viewed as proper and as justifying their actions; therefore, they end up at loggerheads. The other person is seen as being the cause of the problem. Indeed, people in distressed relationships become more and more likely to blame their marital partner for the conflict (Madden & Janoff-Bulman, 1981).

Apart from faulty attributions, distressed relationships often reflect a poor grasp of conflict management techniques. Conflicts are commonly misunderstood by protagonists, and the people involved in the relationship may not even share a common perception of what the conflict is about. Worse, often the apparent conflict is not the real conflict at all (Alcock et al., 1994). Then, as with conflicts in general, destructive threats may emerge, producing a threat-counterthreat spiral, turning the conflict into one in which "winning" and saving face become the major goals. Thus, distressed couples often state that they generally cannot remember what started the latest battle, but they end up threatening divorce or violence anyway.

Drawing on the extensive social psychological literature of conflict resolution, the therapist dealing with a relationship conflict should take pains to establish a clear and common perception by the two parties as to just what is the real conflict. Next, the process by which the couple deals with this conflict (and conflicts in general) must be explored with steps being taken to teach and promote techniques of constructive conflict resolution. Often, the subject matter (i.e., the *content*) of a conflict is less important than the *process:* The couple is drawn into rancorous and destructive conflict over all sorts of issues, big and small, and the dynamics of these conflicts prove to be very similar. Establishing as a mutual goal the development of positive conflict management techniques often helps a distressed couple begin to work together. Then, by showing how small concessions can be used to signal a readiness to cooperate to end a dispute, the therapist can teach the couple that each individual can initiate unilaterally a constructive conflict resolution approach, rather than waiting for the other party to make the first conciliatory move.

The clinician confronted with relationship conflicts must also be sensitive to the important role both verbal and nonverbal communication plays in creating and maintaining conflicts. Misperception of an intended message fosters faulty attributions that then serve to increase the conflict. By helping the parties to communicate more clearly, the clinician is in a better position to help them understand the true nature of their conflict, and to promote constructive resolution of it.

The therapist also needs to pay attention to the somewhat different ways in which men and women are socialized with regard to communication, because such differences can often produce serious misunderstandings (Wiemann & Giles, 1988). Within male-female couples, much miscommunication comes about, in part, because women are more likely to use indirect language to signal their wishes, whereas men more typically make direct requests (Tannen, 1990). Moreover, women tend to use a conversational style that is associated with low social power (Wiemann & Giles, 1988), and feminine speech qualities such as higher pitch and softer volume have been found to be associated, in and of themselves, with perceptions of lower social power (Montepare & Vega, 1988). Thus, a woman may unknowingly send signals that can trigger perceptions of weakness, uncertainty, or low power, and these perceptions can exacerbate an ongoing conflict if her male partner, perceiving weakness, reacts in an exploitative manner.

Thus, through teaching a distressed couple about the dynamics of conflict, and training them in constructive conflict resolution techniques, the social psychologically astute clinician can make a significant contribution to promoting relationship harmony. Just as important, by carrying out research into conflict in troubled relationships, the applied social psychologist can contribute greatly to the development of better counseling techniques.

SUMMARY

Social psychology deals with social behavior and social relationships and how they are affected by various personal and situational factors. The eminent social psychologist Michael Argyle (1992) expresses regret that social psychology, having developed sophisticated research techniques and ingenious experimental manipulations in order to study social behavior and social relationships, transformed itself into a research discipline focused on "other-worldly situations in which subjects sat in little rooms in total isolation and pressed buttons, or sat in little rooms and answered strange questions" (p. 1). In the pursuit of underlying basic principles of social behavior, social psychologists, he says, have eliminated the actual contents of social interactions, dropping the most interesting material and focusing only on the highly abstract and supposedly fundamental components.

It is the applied social psychologist who can bring the fruits of basic research to bear on the original subject matter of social psychology—the real-life interactions among people. As this chapter attests, this is no less an important quest when problems relating to mental health and well-being are concerned. The clinical psychologist who learns about and applies social psychological knowledge will undoubtedly be a better and more successful clinician, and the social psychologist who makes an effort to study and apply social psychological principles in the context of clinical psychological problems can make a substantial and meaningful contribution toward reducing emotional distress and improving mental health.

SUGGESTED READINGS

Abramson, L.Y. (Ed.). (1988). *Social cognition and clinical psychology: A synthesis*. New York: Guilford.

> This is a collection of chapters written by a number of different authorities, relating research in social cognition to psychotherapeutic issues. It provides a good starting point for the examination of the literature relating the social psychological study of cognitive factors to the understanding and treatment of psychological problems.

Argyle, M. (1992). *The social psychology of everyday life*. London, England: Routledge.

> Argyle argues that social psychology is far too often focused on situations that have little to do with everyday life. In this highly readable and important book, he turns social psychological inquiry toward important subjects such as work, leisure, conversation, social relationships, and mental health, marshaling an impressive array of social psychological studies to help him in this quest.

Brehm, S. (1985). *Intimate relationships*. New York: Random House.

> This is an excellent overview of recent social psychological research and theory relating to intimate relationships. Many of the subjects discussed in this chapter, including conflict, communication, love, and loneliness, are given extensive coverage. Other topics include sexuality, jealousy, commitment, and therapeutic interventions. Considerable emphasis is placed on the way that intimate relationships typically evolve and sometimes dissolve.

Peplau, L. A., & Perlman, D. (Eds.). (1982). *Loneliness: A sourcebook of current theory, research and therapy*. New York: Wiley Interscience.

> This collection of papers brings together theoretical and empirical literature relating to loneliness. As the title suggests, it is a sourcebook; and it provides an excellent summary of literature pertaining to social psychological theory and research with regard to loneliness. It also provides a good overview of the application of social psychological knowledge to the clinical treatment of loneliness.

Snyder, C. R., & Forsyth, D. F. (Eds.). (1991). *Handbook of social and clinical psychology: The health perspective*. New York: Pergamon.

> This handbook provides a compendium of research and theory concerning the ways in which social psychological knowledge is relevant to the diagnosis and treatment of various medical and physical disorders.

Zimbardo, P. G. (1977). *Shyness: What it is and what to do about it.* Reading, MA: Addison-Wesley.

The student of applied social psychology will be interested in this book not just for what it says about shyness, but for what it indicates about the applicability of social psychological research to problems that in the past have been considered to be purely in the domain of the clinician.

8 Social Psychology and the Forensic Interview

Stephen Moston

Essex, England

In 1982, a 22-year-old London woman made an allegation that she had been sexually assaulted by a group of young men and women. What made this case problematic for the court was that the woman, named Mary, was classified as "mentally handicapped" (she had a full scale IQ of 47 on the Wechsler Adult Intelligence Scale) and the prosecution was based largely on her testimony. In order to determine the reliability of Mary's testimony, the Director of Public Prosecutions asked two psychologists to conduct an evaluation of Mary. Gudjonsson and Gunn (1982) devised a number of tests to assess the extent to which Mary would answer questions with information that an interviewer suggested. They began their examination in the morning by testing her intellectual functioning and then in the afternoon by asking her to recall what had happened during the earlier test. Her recall was fairly accurate and she even remembered several of the questions she had been asked. Mary was then asked a series of leading questions, her answers were challenged, and she was told to provide more accurate ones. Her responses showed a clear pattern. For abstract or complicated ideas, she was particularly suggestible. When she was sure about events, however, she was highly resistant to suggestion. The process of cross-examination was recommended as a means of verifying Mary's testimony. If she was sure something had happened, then her story would be consistent. Mary's testimony was subsequently tested in court and the jury returned guilty verdicts for five of the six defendants.

Mary's case highlights a common finding in research on suggestibility. A person can be identified as being highly suggestible in one situation, yet highly resistant in another. Given this apparent paradox, researchers have generally rejected the notion that there is such a thing as a "suggestible" person. Suggestibility is perhaps best thought of as being largely determined by situational influences, whereby it is possible for almost any person to be classified as suggestible depending on the circumstances.

Issues of suggestibility are important in a number of different areas of psychological research, including the study of testimony in criminal investigations. For example, although children's testimony is attacked on several grounds, including their apparently poor ability to describe witnessed events spontaneously (free recall), it is their alleged suggestibility that is most frequently cited as grounds for distrusting their testimony.

Although concerns over the suggestibility of *witnesses* have been extensively studied by psychologists, it is now being increasingly recognized as an equally relevant topic when studying the statements of *suspects* (e.g., cases in which suspects may make false confessions in the absence of any obvious coercive pressure). Recent cases of recovered memories are yet another area in which issues of suggestibility have been raised. A *recovered memory* is one in which a person recalls an incident that he or she had hitherto been unable to recall. A key mechanism believed to be important in such cases is *repression*—the person represses memories too painful to bear. In recent years the issue of recovered memory has focused on clinical settings in which patients recall childhood abuse, and it is difficult to determine whether the memories are real or are the result of suggestions made by therapists. What makes both false confessions and false memories intriguing is that the individuals concerned may come to believe that they have committed or experienced crimes, even to the point of testifying in court and implicating themselves or family members.

In the case of children as witnesses, patients in therapy, and suspects in police custody, there are a number of similarities in the way in which interviews are conducted. In each situation the result is the same: The person being interviewed may provide information that is inaccurate, or information that originated with the interviewer, rather than the interviewee. This is not to say that all interviews are flawed. The end result of questioning may well be an accurate account of past events and erroneous suggestions resisted by the interviewees, possibly more so than those cases in which suggestions are accepted. However, the emphasis here is on how problems in interviewing can arise. Consequently, this chapter highlights flaws in interviewing procedures rather than trying to establish what might constitute "best practice." The focus is on how the social dynamics of the interview can shape the outcome of questioning and how suggestibility is influenced by a series of social psychological processes.

DEFINING SUGGESTIBILITY

Suggestibility is a term that is widely used in psychological research, yet it lacks a single unifying definition. This is because the process of suggestibility is seen as incorporating a diverse range of behaviors, from the effects of placebo treatments and hypnosis to forensic issues such as false confessions, false memories, and eyewitness testimony. Given such a diverse range of phenomena, Gudjonsson (1992) suggests that there is a vast collection of clever experimental and applied studies demonstrating suggestibility, but lacking a coherent framework to interpret such a diverse pattern of results.

Within the context of interviewing, suggestibility may be defined as "the tendency of the individual to *accept* uncritically information during questioning" (Gudjonsson & MacKeith, 1988, p. 190, emphasis in original). Suggestibility differs from *compliance,* which is defined as "the tendency of the individual to go along with requests or demands made by people perceived to be in authority, even though the person does not necessarily agree with them" (Gudjonsson & MacKeith, 1988, p. 190). The main difference between the two concepts is that suggestibility implies personal acceptance of a proposition. No such acceptance is required in situations of compliance, in which the person accepts the communication either to avoid conflict or confrontation, not because of personal acceptance of the request. Although it is theoretically possible to distinguish between these two concepts, in practice it is often difficult to make such a distinction. The recalling of suggested information might imply that an individual has accepted the information and incorporated it into memory, yet the subject may be merely compliant and providing the answer he or she believes the interviewer wants to hear. This point was illustrated by King and Yuille (1987), who found that children would accept misleading suggestions that contradicted their earlier free recall, and furthermore that they would subsequently admit to simply having "gone along" with misleading suggestions. This behavior clearly derives from *social* rather than *cognitive* malleability, that is, compliance rather than suggestibility.

Within criminal investigations, issues pertaining to the suggestibility of those being interviewed have been raised on a number of occasions. Thus, the aim of this chapter is to demonstrate how a knowledge of social psychological research helps to develop an understanding of some of the most controversial aspects of contemporary criminal investigations. Three contemporary issues in forensic interviewing are briefly introduced. These are the testimony of children, false memories, and false confessions. As will be shown, each of the topics shares a number of common features, which center on the social dynamics during questioning.

THE TESTIMONY OF CHILDREN

Attitudes toward the competencies of children as witnesses in criminal trials have changed dramatically over the last century. These attitudes have ranged from an initially hostile view, in which children were categorized as inherently unreliable, to an unquestioning faith in their abilities, to a more cautious acceptance that children may be prone to errors on certain occasions but are also quite capable of providing accurate and detailed testimony.

The position that children's testimony cannot be trusted can be traced back over the centuries, but it was not until this century that experimental research confirmed popular opinion. Probably the most influential study was that reported by Varendonck (1911, cited in Whipple, 1913; and also in Goodman, 1984, the latter includes a translation of the original article). Working on a murder case in Belgium, Varendonck was asked to evaluate the information obtained from two young girls, aged 8 and 10. The victim in this case had been a third young girl who had been playing with these two shortly before her disappearance. The authorities investigating the case assumed that the two girls would have seen the abduction of their friend and would thus be able to identify the killer. The two children had initially claimed to know nothing about the murder, but after several days, and some highly suggestive questioning, they had given investigators a description of the murderer (in fact, they described the father of one of the girls).

Varendonck believed that the testimony obtained from the two girls was unreliable. In order to demonstrate how children could be swayed by leading questions he devised a series of experiments in which he incorporated questions similar to those asked of the young girls. For example, some 7-year-olds were asked the color of the beard of one of the teachers in their building. The majority answered "black" and two children did not answer. In fact, the teacher had no beard. The majority of 8-year-olds (19 out of 20) offered a color to the same question. Only one said he had no beard. In another experiment a teacher visited a class and stood talking to them for five minutes. All the time he kept his hat on. Immediately after he had left, the children were asked "In which hand did he hold his hat?" Seventeen children answered "Right"; seven said "Left"; and only three gave the correct answer. These responses enabled Varendonck to convince the court that the young girls' testimony may have resulted from suggestive questioning.

Over the following years, the testimony of children was treated skeptically, in part influenced by the Freudian notion that children fantasize about sexual encounters with adults. With a growing awareness that the sexual abuse of children is relatively prevalent (incidence figures differ depending on how abuse is defined), attitudes changed dramatically. Perhaps as part of a desire to offset years of ignoring children's calls for help, and buoyed up by psychological research suggesting that children's free recall testimony (i.e., their ability to recall a witnessed event with little or no prompting) was highly accurate (e.g., Marin, Holmes, Guth, & Kovac, 1979), clinicians and therapists quickly assumed a position stating that the testimony of children was inherently *accurate.*

Although free recall may be largely accurate, its limited scope necessitates the asking of additional questions to further prompt the child, and it is these kinds of questions that tend to be the source of concern. This situation is well illustrated in the study by Saywitz, Goodman, Nicholas, and Moan (1991), in which girls aged 5 and 7 years underwent a medical examination. For half of the girls, the examination involved a vaginal and anal examination that required ethical clearance to be performed. In free recall many did not mention the genital examination until directly questioned about it. Studies such as this also attempt to address the basic question of how children react when they are asked leading questions (e.g., the girls who did not receive the vaginal and anal examination were also asked if they had experienced such an event, to which the vast majority replied that they had not). Will they try to answer in the way they believe the interviewer wants them to, even to the extent of fabricating an accusation of sexual abuse? These are the types of questions that social workers and police officers ask of psychologists, and they are not easily answered. Before considering such issues, one must first appreciate the complexity inherent in carrying out psychological research on such topics.

Issues of Validity in Eyewitness Research

To a certain extent, the psychological research on suggestibility during the 1980s served to muddle issues rather than clarify them. The general pattern of results from studies suggested that most children are highly resistant to suggestion (see Ceci & Bruck, 1993a, for a review). However, these studies suffered from a number of methodological limitations that make it hard to interpret the findings (Ceci & Bruck, 1993b). Suggestibility was assessed in a rather cavalier fashion, often without any theoretical rationale. In some cases an applied rationale is equally absent. Most psychologists are unfamiliar with police investigative procedures and devise studies based on what they *presume* to be of applied relevance. For example, a typical study assessing suggestibility would involve groups of school children witnessing a staged event or film, such as a stranger entering the classroom. The children would not be involved in this event in any way. This event would be "emotionally neutral" and the children would be interviewed only once about the event by a university researcher. The reason for this interview would often be obscure and of minimal significance to the children concerned. Also, the number of suggestions put to the children differed in number (some studies featured a single suggestive question whereas others posed more) and style, with many centering on trivial or peripheral details.

Such studies differ from child abuse cases on a number of critical dimensions, including the stress involved in being abused, as well as the emotional distress in discussing it with an adult. Other differences include that the staged events occurred only once, but most abuse cases feature multiple (often similar) incidents; the adult stranger was unknown to the children, but abuse cases usually involve known adults; experimental questioning occurred only once, whereas multiple interviews are typical in abuse cases; the university researchers were of lower perceived status than police officers; and the university interviewers often knew full details of the incident involved, whereas interviewers in abuse cases do not. These, and a number of other factors, are important considerations that psychologists have only recently begun to address. The danger is that, as Ceci and Bruck (1993a) point out, experimental work may have resulted in a possible *underestimation* of children's suggestibility.

In recent years, researchers have modified the standard eyewitness paradigm considerably in a quest to achieve greater levels of *ecological validity*. For example, delays in questioning of up to 2 years are being studied (e.g., Poole & White, 1993), children are likely to be interviewed on several occasions (e.g., Poole & White, 1991), events may be stressful (e.g., Goodman, Hirschman, Hepps, & Rudy, 1991), and the interviewer may be introduced as a police officer (e.g., Tobey & Goodman, 1992). The events have also changed, with a greater tendency toward studies in which children are active participants rather than bystanders (e.g., Rudy & Goodman, 1991) and isolated rather than in groups. Some studies have also featured real witnesses (e.g., Yuille & Cutshall, 1986). These steps have helped to increase the face validity of experimental research, which is a necessary step in convincing a skeptical judicial system of the value of psychological work. The need to develop stringent research methodologies that accurately reflect the complexities of real eyewitness cases is an issue that has been addressed in several papers by Yuille (e.g., Yuille, 1986, 1993). For example, Yuille (1986, p. 230) writes:

> In short, it is an interesting and challenging game which psychologists play in their laboratories but it is often irrelevant. The only way we can learn about eyewitness behavior is to study real witnesses to real crimes. Of course we may learn as a result that some of the laboratory findings were applicable to the real world. But only real world data will tell us this. I suggest that this is a general conclusion that all people involved in the criminal justice system should draw. Laboratory research should be ignored unless there exists strong evidence to show its applicability outside of the context in which it was collected. The researcher is obliged to show the value of his/her work by direct evidence before any attention should be given to it.

The importance of this point can be illustrated by comparing the types of leading questions that children are asked in experimental studies. Typically, the questions are nonhostile and reasonably clear, at least in terms of the construction of the sentence. If such studies lead to the conclusion that children are no more suggestible than adults, it may be that, as Ceci and Bruck (1993a) suggested, research is seriously underestimating the power of suggestive questioning in real cases.

Apart from the differences in interviewers' nonverbal behavior, tone of voice, and other characteristics, the questions asked in these two situations are markedly different. Research by Brennan and Brennan (1988) on the interviewing of children in courts in Australia identifies a number of types of suggestive questioning that are unlikely to appear in many psychological studies. They found that the problems that children face include multifaceted questions, the use of unnecessary negatives in questions (e.g., "Now you had a bruise, did you not, near one of your breasts, do you remember that?") as well as confused or ambiguous questions. One such example is the following:

> *Q.* "Well I know, I understand what you say you have been talking to her today but you see what I am asking you is this, that statement suggests that you said those things that you now say are wrong to the police. Now did you say it to the police or did you not?"
> *A.* "I don't know." (Brennan & Brennan, 1988, p. 68)

The types of strategies described by Brennan and Brennan are far more hostile and confusing than those seen in psychological research (what researcher would deliberately include such a confusing question?). These questions would seem more likely to influence testimony than the straightforward misleading suggestions employed in experimental work. Unclear questions promote uncertainty, making the listener more reliant on the context of questioning, whereas hostile, accusatory questions are likely to increase anxiety. Other strategies identified by Brennan and Brennan include the use of earlier statements as the basis for questioning—where discrepancies between statements at each time are put to the child as proof of confused recall, or possibly deceit.

FALSE MEMORIES

In the United States in 1990, George Franklin was charged with the murder (11 years previously) of an 8-year-old girl, Susan Nason. The major evidence against Franklin was provided by his daughter Eileen, who had also been 8 at the time and a friend of the girl who was killed. What makes this case so unusual is that, in the intervening years, Eileen had been unaware of her father's actions. Her memory of the murder came to light only after Eileen experienced a flashback, prompted by a question from her own young son, during which she recalled the look of betrayal on Susan's face just before the murder. Shortly afterward, Eileen entered therapy. Over the course of treatment she recalled more details of Susan's murder and her subsequent testimony helped to convict her father (Loftus, 1993), although this conviction was subsequently overturned in April 1995.

The issue of recovered memories has become increasingly controversial, with two opposing positions. One is that the recovered memories are real and that therapeutic devices such as hypnosis and dream interpretation are necessary in uncovering past experiences that many adults find too painful to bear and to articulate. Such a view is often reinforced by figures on the widespread incidence of child sexual abuse. Given that, until recently, children's claims of sexual abuse were routinely dismissed as childish fantasy, it becomes plausible to believe that victims might repress memories of abuse or reinterpret them to make them less threatening.

The alternative position is that the memories are not real, that they are a result of suggestions made to vulnerable individuals in therapy. A concern that is expressed here is that it is often the case that some therapists, many of whom have had inadequate training (i.e., they may not be fully qualified psychiatrists, psychologists, or counselors), are using techniques that they do not fully understand and are influencing patients to falsely remember abuse. As will become clearer later in this chapter, the two opposing views are entrenched and the debate involving the accuracy of recovered memories is highly contentious.

The topic of false memories has now attained the status of a "moral panic." Large numbers of cases are coming to light in which patients undergoing therapy recall past experiences of sexual abuse, even though they had no recollection of any such abuse prior to entering therapy. The chief concern here is whether the memories are real, in which case abuse really did occur, or whether they are false, the result of suggestions put to patients during therapy. The arguments for the validity of such memories center on the notion of repressed memories, a key concept in psychoanalytic work, in which an individual represses a memory that is too painful to bear. Given the requirement that the incident be highly distressing, it is perhaps unsurprising to discover that experimental research has failed to find support for such a phenomenon (see Loftus, 1993, for a review). It is, however, a widely held belief that people are capable of holding false memories; that is, they can recall, often in great detail, events that never actually occurred. One of the most telling examples of this ability is given by Jean Piaget (1962), in which he describes how, as a child, he was nearly kidnapped by a stranger in a park but was saved by the bravery of his nanny. Many years after the incident, Piaget learned that it had never actually occurred and was a fiction devised by the nanny to ingratiate herself with Piaget's parents.

Cases featuring repressed memories often share a number of similarities, including a lack of any recovered information that could unambiguously authenticate the story, such as the location of a missing murder weapon. Instead, the information recalled goes beyond public knowledge and is simply uncheckable. For example, in the case of Eileen Franklin, she recalled which side of the door Susie had used when she allegedly entered George Franklin's car (Loftus, 1993), a fact with no real forensic relevance.

The decision of whether to believe a person who recovers a repressed memory is typically decided on a case-by-case basis, with some juries accepting such statements as facts, whereas other trials end with the condemnation of the therapist concerned and, in some cases, the therapists are sued for damages (e.g., the case of Holly Ramona; see Bagnall, 1994). Reasoned calls for corroboration (e.g., Slovenko, 1993) have largely gone unheeded.

The debate over false memories has also spilled over into other domains, in which patients undergoing therapy recall past lives or remember being kidnapped by aliens (Bagnall, 1994). In such cases, short of accepting a solution that could become an episode of *The X-Files,* researchers have tended to concentrate on demonstrating the ways in which false ideas can be implanted into memory. The types of therapy that patients are receiving have become the subject of attention, with some researchers focusing on the role that hypnosis plays in eliciting false memories (e.g., McConkey, 1995). However, although hypnosis is often implicated in cases of false memories, it is not an essential prerequisite; as discussed later in this chapter, false confessions to an involvement in a crime can occur without hypnosis. The key question to be addressed here is how can false memories be implanted? Do the dynamics of the interview situation allow psychologists to put forward an alternative explanation for the origins of recovered memories? These issues are discussed shortly.

As a final comment on the issue of false memories, it is important to note that the evidence in this debate centers on a number of *case studies*. These cases vary considerably, making it almost impossible to integrate them, let alone to produce *group data*. Ordinarily, psychological research features groups of subjects so that individual differences are less likely to influence findings. Because it is difficult experimentally to create situations in which false memories can be implanted into groups of subjects, psychologists cannot easily rely on conventional experimental procedures to study such phenomena. Nevertheless, with some careful thought and planning, appropriate research paradigms may be developed. However, a problem that researchers will face is the extent to which subjects have truly incorporated information into memory—forgotten it and then recalled it—rather than merely claiming to have done so. In other words, research psychologists must distinguish between suggestibility and compliance, as discussed earlier. Such concerns are equally as important in understanding the next issue, that of false confessions.

FALSE CONFESSIONS

In recent years, the legal system in the United Kingdom has been severely attacked over the way in which innocent suspects have been convicted on the basis of coerced confessions. An example of this is the case of the Guildford Four, in which Gerald Conlon and others were threatened and tortured in order to elicit confessions following a bombing campaign carried out by the Irish Republican Army (IRA; see Conlon, 1990, for a personal account of the coercive interrogation dramatized in the film *In the Name of the Father*). Although violence, real or implied, is undoubtedly likely to persuade many innocent suspects to confess, not all false confessions can be so easily understood. On occasion, false confessions may occur voluntarily or in the absence of any obvious threats. Kassin and Wrightsman (1985) make a distinction among three different types of false confessions.

1. *The Voluntary Confession.* This is offered in the absence of any form of external pressure. That is, a person volunteers an unsolicited confession to a police officer, even though that person has not committed any offense. This form of confession often occurs in highly publicized investigations when a desire for notoriety prompts many people to confess spontaneously. For example, in the Lindbergh kidnapping in the United States, some 200 people voluntarily confessed.

2. *The Coerced-Compliant Confession.* This form of admission is seen as resulting from coercion (real or imagined) during the questioning of a suspect. An individual may make a false confession during questioning because he or she perceives that this will bring some *immediate* instrumental gain. Perceived gains may include the cessation of questioning or the possibility of being released.

3. *The Coerced-Internalized Confession.* There are occasions when, through fatigue, pressure, or suggestion, an innocent suspect actually comes to believe that he or she has committed an offense. Suspects may accept that they did commit an offense typically because they do not trust their own memory, and they begin to accept (at least temporarily) the suggestions made by the interviewing officers (e.g., Gudjonsson & LeBegue, 1989).

Gudjonsson and MacKeith (1988) suggest that coerced-compliant confessions are most likely to result from aggressive interviewing techniques, whereas internalized confessions are produced by more gentle and subtle forms of questioning. Internalized confessions are most likely to result with individuals who have a tendency to become easily confused, lack confidence in their memory, and show a marked susceptibility to suggestion. Within those convicted in court, both voluntary and coerced-internalized confessions are seen as relatively rare; coerced-compliant false confessions are believed to be the most prevalent. Incidence figures on false confessions, by their very nature, are almost impossible to estimate. The closest indications have come from a recent study by Gudjonsson and Sigurdsson (1994), in which the entire sample of convicted offenders in Iceland in a 1-year period was questioned. Some 12% of the sample claimed to have made a false confession at some time in the past (not to the offense for which they were currently imprisoned) and, in most cases, there was no attempt to retract the confession as it was typically made to protect another person.

Although psychologists have carried out an extensive range of studies on the questioning of witnesses, there is an apparent dearth of literature on the questioning of suspects. This is almost certainly due to the complexities of designing research studies that mimic real-life interrogations (for an interesting exception, see Kassin & McNall, 1991). It is relatively straightforward to ask a subject to play the role of an eyewitness, but it is not so easy to ask him or her to assume the role of a suspect. Nevertheless, the number of psychological studies on police interrogation has increased in recent years (see Gudjonsson, 1992, for a review), and this trend looks set to continue as police forces around the world look to psychologists for advice on training.

Contrary to popular opinion, police officers are not usually skilled interrogators. Empirical research in England (e.g., Baldwin, 1992; Moston & Engelberg, 1993; Moston and Stephenson, 1993) reveals that suspects are rarely ever "persuaded" to confess (see Moston, Stephenson, & Williamson, 1992) and that most confessions are made at the very outset of questioning. Cases in which a denial is retracted and a confession made are extremely rare (less than 3% of cases according to Baldwin, 1992). However, differences in legal regulations governing the detention and questioning of suspects vary considerably between countries. Questioning strategies endorsed in the United States (e.g., Inbau, Reid, & Buckley, 1986) would be outlawed in other countries, such as the United Kingdom, making international comparisons difficult. For example, in the United States, lying to suspects may be permitted—an officer may directly state (or suggest) that a witness has identified the suspect, when no such identification has been made. In the UK, any deception by interviewers would not be tolerated by the courts, and all resulting evidence would be ruled as inadmissible.

Coerced-internalized confessions can be considered a type of false memory, with the main difference being that instead of recalling the experiencing of a crime that never occurred, the suspect recalls committing a crime that he or she did not commit. As unlikely as it may seem, there may well be occasions in which both types of false memory can come together in a single case. Box 8–1 discusses a case in which an accusation based on recovered memories was confirmed by the accused, even though his guilt seems unlikely.

THE PROCESS OF SUGGESTION

The following section addresses the issue of how suggestive information is conveyed to interviewees. It focuses on the social dynamics of the interview setting, emphasizing the way in which social psychologists have contributed to an understanding of suggestibility that can be used in a forensic setting. It should be noted here that alternative approaches to this topic can also be taken, including focusing on the characteristics of those categorized as suggestible, for example, by trying to identify personality characteristics that correlate with suggestibility. For reviews of alternative ways of conceptualizing and researching suggestibility, see Gheorghiu, Netter, Eysenck, and Rosenthal (1989) and Schumaker (1991). It should also be noted that each of the factors discussed here is examined in isolation, whereas in reality they are strongly interrelated. The four issues to be discussed here are (a) the credibility of interviewers, (b) the role of expectations in interviews, (c) social isolation, and (d) interviewing techniques.

The Credibility of the Interviewer

Research suggests that an interviewer who is high in credibility, because of either social status or apparent expertise, is more likely to influence the responses of an interviewee than a person low in perceived credibility. In the case featured in Box 8–1, the interviewers were former colleagues of the accused, together with a religious minister, all of whom would have been high in credibility for the suspect. Ceci, Ross, and Toglia (1987) showed how suggestions put to 4-year-old children (concerning a story that had been read to them the day before) were more likely to be accepted when put forward by an adult than another child. Such a finding tells researchers that it is not the misleading information per se that results in a suggestible response, but rather that the identity of the person proposing this information is crucial. In other words, it is the characteristics of the sender that determine when someone will take on the suggested message, more than the characteristics of the message itself. Similar findings have been reported in other studies, including Kwock and Winer (1986). They found that children aged 9 and 12 would give the correct answer "Both" to questions such as "Is this black or a square?" when the object shown was a black square more often to a peer interviewer than to an adult interviewer.

**Box
8–1**

The Perfect Crime?

In 1988 Paul Ingram, a chief civil deputy in the Thurston County, Washington, Sheriff's Department, was accused of repeatedly raping his two daughters over a period of 17 years. Although he initially denied involvement in any crimes, over a five-month period during which he was socially isolated and repeatedly interrogated by his former colleagues and psychologists, he came to make a series of admissions that eventually resulted in his being sentenced to a 20-year prison sentence.

The accusations against Ingram were made by two of his daughters, Julie and Ericka. The initial accusation was made after Ericka had attended a church-sponsored retreat intended to encourage young women to reveal abuse. Ericka began by claiming that her father had raped her, an accusation that soon expanded as she also accused all of the men (i.e., Ingram's law enforcement colleagues) who attended Saturday night poker parties at her home. After this revelation, Ericka wanted to tell her mother about the rapes, but her sister expressed concern that the accusation might distress their mother. When subsequently asked by detectives how the mother could not have known about the 17-year ordeal, the girls changed their story and accused their mother of also having participated in the sexual assaults. The girls' stories were to change a number of times as the investigation proceeded, eventually culminating in accusations that a satanic cult had been involved in the abuse. This cult was supposedly responsible for a number of crimes, including physical torture of the girls, a coat-hanger abortion for Ericka, and the murder of 25 infants (the number of infants allegedly killed was eventually to reach 250). No physical evidence existed to support any of these accusations. Sites where bodies were supposedly buried revealed no corpses; the girls were found to have no physical marks that would suggest torture, and all the accused, save only Ingram himself, denied the accusations. Another curious aspect of the girls' stories was that even though they supposedly had each attended hundreds of satanic rituals, neither could remember any details of the group's basic rituals. Ericka recalled scenes of torture and murder, but when pressed to describe the mundane rituals of the group, she claimed that recalling such details was too stressful.

With the current awareness of the possibility of false memories, the testimony of Julie and Ericka appears to be of dubious validity. Even prosecutors seemed unsure of how to deal with many aspects of the case and confined their charges against Ingram to the sexual assaults on his daughters, despite the fact that his daughters reported his alleged involvement in the serial killings of dozens or possibly hundreds of infants.

The case would almost certainly not have resulted in a conviction were it not for the confessions that Ingram made. How he came to make these admissions is the focus of a paper by psychologist Richard Ofshe, who was asked to evaluate Ingram's testimony by the state prosecutors. Ofshe (1992) reports what is perhaps one of the strangest cases in recent forensic research, in which false memories and false confessions came together in a single investigation.

Ingram's initial denial was not accepted by the officers investigating the case. The investigators believed the girls' testimony, even though, since 1985, the girls had made a series of accusations of rape or attempted sexual abuse against a number of men, none of which ever resulted in trials. During the prolonged period over which Ingram was questioned, he was socially isolated, even from other prisoners. He was questioned by authority figures who were high in credibility; they were, after all, former colleagues whom Ingram trusted, who strongly asserted a belief in his guilt. Other interrogators came to include a pastor and two clinical psychologists, who suggested to Ingram that his failure to remember his involvement in the abuse of his daughters was the result of "programming" by the satanic cult and that his memory would return only if he made a confession. In order to help him to overcome this programming, Ingram was advised to empty his mind and to "pray on" his crimes. Ofshe argues that this procedure resulted in a dissociative state in which Ingram was able to produce highly detailed admissions, following from the suggestions made by his interrogators. Ingram was able to recall events in such detail that when asked to state the times at which incidents occurred, he would be able to visualize the scene, seeking out a clock or watch that was present, and then being able to read the time. Recollections of shadowy figures that were present at the rituals gradually came to be identified as colleagues and friends.

The basic pattern to the confessions was that after an initial denial, Ingram would be instructed to "pray on" what had happened, after which he would be able to recall information to substantiate the assertions of his interrogators. Ingram showed a complete acceptance of the idea that he was repressing all recollection of the abuse, something he attributed to the possession of his body by Satan. Ingram, like his interrogators, was a fundamentalist Christian who believed in the literal presence of Satan on earth and that Satan had the ability to possess a person and to render him or her unaware of personal actions. This belief laid the foundation for Ingram to begin to distrust his own memory, which, coupled with a belief that his daughters would not lie about such things, opened him to the possibility that he could have committed actions for which he had no memory.

Skeptical of the confessions given by Ingram, Ofshe devised a test to see if Ingram would make confessions to crimes that had not occurred. Ofshe suggested to Ingram that he had forced his son and daughter to have sex while he watched, something that was strongly denied by the daughter when Ofshe questioned her. Initially Ingram could not recall any such incident, but a day later he was able to remember every detail of the incident, even though it had never taken place. When confronted over this recollection and told that it was not real, Ingram asserted that it was real, at least as real as all the other crimes to which he had confessed.

Ofshe concludes that Ingram is probably innocent of the crimes for which he was convicted, an unfortunate victim of hysteria over ritual child abuse and the self-fulfilling prophecies of investigators who, influenced by personal beliefs, ignored the evidence in the case. The case of Paul Ingram is a truly bizarre one. There is an accusation and a confession; all that is missing is a crime.

This pattern of responding is not exclusive to children. Other studies have found that adults are also influenced by the status of the interviewer. In these studies, it has been found that those designated as experts, as opposed to apparent novices, are more likely to influence responses. Smith and Ellsworth (1987) found that when adults were questioned about a filmed bank robbery, they would be more likely to accept suggestions put to them by an interviewer who had supposedly studied the film very carefully, as compared to a person who had limited knowledge of the film. Similarly, McDevitt and Carroll (1988) showed children videotaped messages in which the speaker was either consistent or inconsistent in making arguments. If the children were warned that the speaker was trying to trick them, they were more likely to report the inconsistencies in their messages.

These findings help to explain why children may appear to be excessively suggestible in comparison to adults. When children are interviewed, the interviewer (an adult) is perceived as powerful and of high status. When a child is interviewed by an adult who is also a police officer, this appears to contribute slightly to suggestibility (e.g., Tobey & Goodman, 1992), although other findings are equivocal. Brigham, Van Verst, and Bothwell (1986) found that an adult interviewer dressed as a security guard did not influence the testimony of children (on several measures, including suggestibility) as compared to a casually dressed interviewer. They suggested that children may perceive all adults as authority figures, although a possible confound here was that the casually dressed interviewer introduced himself as a student working for the Florida State University Police Department. The children may have misinterpreted this as meaning that the interviewer was a police officer.

For adult subjects, the interviewer is more likely to be a peer, particularly if the adult subjects are university students being questioned by university researchers. Such a pattern of results might change somewhat if adult subjects were to be interviewed by a police officer, especially if that officer wore a uniform (see Bushman, 1988). A police officer is likely to be one of the most powerful figures of source credibility in Western society. Consequently, the suggestions put to suspects in police custody are originating from a strong, credible source. Not only does the officer have social authority, but expert authority too, by virtue of having investigated a crime scene, examined the evidence, and talked to witnesses.

In a similar way, counselors and therapists may also be viewed as high in credibility, something that many therapists will reinforce in their clients, perhaps by reminding them of their vast experience in dealing with people in similar circumstances (Loftus, 1994). They are helped here by their training, which confers on them the status of "expert," and by the fact that their methods are also used by many other therapists. The widespread media coverage of recovered memories also enhances therapists' credibility and counterarguments are seemingly ignored (Ofshe & Watters, 1993).

Expectations and Self-Fulfilling Prophecies

Probably the single most important criticism that has been made of interviews throughout the criminal justice system is that interviewers have a marked tendency toward adopting self-fulfilling prophecies (e.g., McConville, Sanders, & Leng, 1991). In interviews with children and adults, witnesses and suspects, police officers have been observed to carry out questioning that results in flawed statements. Clinicians, counselors, and other interviewers are often similarly flawed in their interviewing procedures.

Case construction begins with the creation of a hypothesis that interviewers seek to verify. They do so by asking questions that will elicit information that meets this hypothesis. Information that contradicts the hypothesis tends to be ignored. The British legal system has recently been severely criticized following revelations concerning the convictions of innocent suspects, such as the Guildford Four (see Conlon, 1990; Gudjonsson, 1992). In these cases, a recurring feature was the way in which investigating officers selectively filtered the evidence in the case, concentrating on information that supported their views about the suspects' guilt and ignoring statements from witnesses that suggested innocence. In interviews with children, similar errors of judgment can be observed when interviewers seek to establish that a child has been abused.

A study by Ceci, Leichtman, and White (in press) shows that when interviewers were given misleading information about an incident involving children, their subsequent interviews with those children became distorted. When interviewers were provided with accurate information about what had happened (i.e., the children had played a game), one interviewer was able to elicit highly accurate statements from children. However, when provided with erroneous information, the same interviewer elicited incorrect information from about one-third of the preschoolers questioned and one-fifth of the children aged 5 to 6.

In subsequent studies described by Ceci and Bruck (1993a), the statements from such interviews were shown (on video) to researchers and clinicians who were asked to evaluate the children's statements. This showed that the incorrect statements were generally viewed as credible, with the assessors believing the children's statements, even expressing confidence in their judgments. In fact, the children who were least accurate received the highest credibility ratings.

In interviews with suspects, police officers often begin their questioning with the presumption that the person being interrogated is guilty. Stephenson and Moston (1993) found that from a sample of over 1,000 cases in which officers were asked to record their views about an interview shortly before it took place, about three-quarters of interviewers were sure of the suspects' guilt. For them, the stated aim of the interview was to obtain a confession.

Therapists have also been observed to adopt a stance in interviewing that conveys their strong personal expectations about the causes of a client's current problems. For example, Loftus (1993) reports that in initial consultations, therapists who suspected their clients had been sexually abused would categorically state to their clients that their current problems were a direct result of prior sexual abuse. The ways in which this was done ranged from the relatively open-minded, "You know, in my experience, a lot of people who are struggling with many of the same problems you are have often had some kind of really painful things happen to them as kids—maybe you were beaten or molested and I wonder if anything like that ever happened to you?," through to, "You sound to me like the sort of person who must have been sexually abused. Tell me what that bastard did to you." The effects of such strong assertions are discussed later in this chapter.

Social Isolation

One common characteristic of interviews with witnesses, suspects, and patients in therapy is that at the time of the interview, the interviewee is socially isolated (for an example, see Box 8–1). Either attempting to ensure privacy, or to guard against contamination, the interviewer will ensure that contact between the interviewee and others is minimized.

In the case of children as witnesses, Moston and Engelberg (1992) argue that the social isolation of young children could be considered as a possible stressor in interviews. It is certainly the case that when asked if they would like to be interviewed in the presence of a friend or relative, children show a clear preference for being allowed to do so (e.g., Goodman et al., 1988). The desire to be with others in stressful situations has been called the *affiliative desire* (Schachter, 1959) and has been observed in a number of settings in which subjects have been left to wait prior to stressful situations. For example, Schachter found that adults waiting for what they believed would be an electric shock showed a preference toward waiting with others in the same situation.

For children, the isolation that occurs during questioning may inhibit their free recall. Moston (1992) found that children aged 7 and 10 years who had witnessed a staged event (an adult stranger entering a classroom) would recall more information (such as what the person looked like, and what he or she said and did), if interviewed in the presence of a peer who had not seen the event, but with whom the witness had discussed the incident prior to questioning. There was no effect of the presence of another person on suggestibility, and there was no contamination in testimony. It has since been argued (e.g., Morgan & Williams, 1993) that a support person may assist children during the investigative process, although this is an issue that warrants further empirical study, as there are a variety of ways in which support can be provided.

Similar arguments also exist concerning the interrogation of suspects in criminal investigations. Manuals on interrogation strategies (e.g., Inbau et al., 1986) have long recognized the value of isolating suspects as part of an attempt to induce a confession. Although such isolation may well increase the chances of a confession, it does not necessarily ensure that it is the truth. In several cases in England, the social isolation of juveniles while in police custody appears to be directly linked to their decision to make false confessions of the coerced-compliant type (see Gudjonsson, 1992, for examples). Consequently, juveniles and those suspected of being "vulnerable" to suggestion (a term that also includes those with mental illnesses or intellectual disabilities) must be interviewed in the presence of an "appropriate adult." This appropriate adult will typically be a lawyer, parent, or social worker whose task it is to oversee the interrogation of the vulnerable suspect. Whether parents or social workers are capable of guarding a person against inappropriate police questioning is a hotly debated point, with many researchers concerned that these people are unfamiliar with the laws on interrogation and thus are unsuited to the role assigned to them. There is a further complication in that it is widely observed that parents can become extremely ruthless interrogators, demanding that their children confess, threatening them, and, on occasion, using violence to elicit the "right" answer (Evans, 1993). The use of a lawyer as a support person appears to be a more promising procedure, yet false confessions have been coerced in the presence of lawyers who failed to act to protect their clients. In part, this may be due to the use of unqualified "agents," instead of trained lawyers, to attend interviews.

After a period of coercive questioning has resulted in a confession, the suspect may then be allowed contact with family members or a lawyer, at which time he or she will retract the confession. However, the earlier confession will almost certainly have been recorded on audio or video and will be used as evidence in court, leaving the suspect to explain it.

In therapy that uncovers (or ostensibly recovers) repressed memories of abuse, it is common to find that the patient has been told to cut off ties with the abuser, and possibly even from all other family members. In effect, because these other people deny that abuse has occurred, the patient is told not to discuss the matter with these people. This social isolation cuts the patient off from dissenting voices. Anyone who could possibly contradict the memory that abuse has occurred is removed from contact with the patient, making that person even more reliant on the therapist as a source of social support. Whereas retractions of sexual abuse allegations may occur in children following pressure from family members (Summit, 1983), the social isolation of the patient may well contribute to the fostering of a false memory. This situation is further complicated by the introduction of a new support network in the form of a victim-support group, the members of which can assert to the newcomer the value of the therapist's methods and conclusions (Ofshe & Watters, 1993), which is likely to enhance the credibility of the therapist even further.

Interviewing Techniques

The range of persuasive interviewing techniques available to interviewers is considerable. Topics that have been studied within this aspect of suggestibility include the wording of questions (e.g., Loftus & Palmer, 1974), the use of the definite article (Dale, Loftus, & Rathbun, 1978), and repeated questioning (e.g., Moston, 1987). Here, two aspects of interviewing are discussed: the way in which the interviewer asserts a belief about the interviewee's past and the use of spurious technology, or other equally dubious means, to lend credibility to an argument.

Assertions Made by the Interviewer. Interviewers can convey their expectations about the information they believe they are going to elicit from a person in a number of different ways. The police officer may directly confront a suspect with an accusation that he or she has committed a crime, or the therapist may state that a patient shows the "signs" of sexual abuse. In each case, the interviewer will assert his or her belief in the interviewee's guilt or past experiences. For example, in police interrogations, officers are often advised to state their conviction that the suspect is guilty at the outset of questioning (e.g., Inbau et al., 1986).

Irving and Hilgendorf (1980) describe a range of strategies or tactics used by police officers that they believe are influential in eliciting confessions from suspects. This work centers on the techniques police use to persuade suspects that the benefits of a confession outweigh the disadvantages. They suggest that four primary strategies are open to interviewers: (a) reduce the apparent advantages of denial; (b) increase the apparent disadvantages of denial; (c) increase the advantages of confession; and (d) reduce the disadvantages of confession. Tactically, an interviewer could tell the suspect that the evidence against him or her is overwhelming and that there is no point in denying (i.e., reduce advantages of denial) or that a confession will make them feel better by allowing them to "get things off their chest" (i.e., accentuate the advantages of confession).

One problem with asserting that a suspect is guilty is that officers will support their accusation by listing some, or all, of the evidence against the suspect. The problem that then arises is how to validate the confession, given that the suspect can now make a full and detailed confession, even though the suspect initially knew nothing about the crime (Moston & Engelberg, 1993). Rather than using evidence to refute something that a suspect has said, such as a denial, evidence is used as a persuasive device in order to ensure that the suspect does not try to deny the accusation.

In the case of the patient in therapy, the therapist will also assert his or her views about the person's condition. Here the "evidence" will consist of checklists of behaviors displayed by incest survivors (Loftus, 1993), books on sexual abuse, and so forth. The patient is advised to read such books because they will confirm the therapist's conclusions. As with the innocent suspect who picks up enough information in questioning to be able to fabricate a confession, such books contain sufficient information for the client to be able to reproduce a seemingly authentic accusation of sexual abuse (see Ofshe & Watters, 1993). The danger here is that the interviewer is creating a self-fulfilling prophecy by providing the interviewee with information. When this information is duly echoed back, the interviewer concludes that his or her initial expectations were correct. In courts in England, where taped records of interviews have been analyzed in detail and shown to display such flawed interviewing, confessions have been ruled as unreliable and convictions overturned on appeal. This has forced interviewers to concentrate on open-ended, information-gathering styles of questioning with minimal prompting. In sharp contrast, therapists will argue that such procedures are essential for uncovering the truth and that they produce valid information. Public stereotypes about the ways in which these groups conduct interviews, involving a coercive police officer and an open-minded therapist, would thus appear to be the opposite of reality.

The Use of Technology/Skills to Support an Assertion.   When confronted with an accusation that they have either committed, or been the victim of, a criminal act, an interviewee's initial reaction is likely to be denial that anything has occurred. The task of the interviewer is to show why he or she has made such an assertion, or at least to back it up with some independent evidence. One popular strategy is to persuade the interviewee that his or her faulty memory cannot be trusted. Police officers will often use the polygraph (or "lie detector") to support their assertions. The suspect will be tested and, often regardless of the outcome of the test, be told that deceit has been detected. It is not actually necessary for a real polygraph to be used, provided that the suspect believes a sophisticated device has somehow discovered some deception. For example, interviewers have been known to use ploys such as wiring suspects to photocopiers in which a piece of paper saying "You are lying" has been placed. As the suspect answers, the interviewer pushes the copy button and out comes the machine's verdict on the suspect's answer. The polygraph is central to a number of false confessions (e.g., Gudjonsson & LeBegue, 1989), when suspects are convinced that they can no longer trust their own memory. Science, in the shape of flashing lights and noisy machinery, is thought to have uncovered the "truth."

In the absence of technology the interviewer or therapist can resort to other ploys, such as "It's written all over your face," or "I can tell what you are thinking; your body language gives it away" (Moston & Stephenson, 1993). Although the detection of deception through nonverbal cues is inherently unreliable (e.g., Ekman & O'Sullivan, 1989), most interviewees are likely to be unaware of this fact. The suspect or client is then likely to start questioning his or her confidence in the recollection of past events, looking to the interviewer for guidance in clarifying what has happened.

One major problem with the ability to detect deception is that assessments are affected by a person's initial assumptions. In other words, if an interviewer believes that the person being questioned is deceptive, then he or she will interpret that person's behavior accordingly. Similarly, if the interviewer is certain of a person's innocence, then behavioral cues will be interpreted in ways that verify that belief (Kraut, 1980). This can be illustrated with a simple example. If an interviewer believes that a person is guilty, a pause before answering a question will be interpreted as a sign of deceit, in that the suspect needs time to fabricate a lie. However, if the interviewer assumes that the suspect is innocent, that same pause will be interpreted as a sign of honesty, in that the suspect is taking time to think carefully in order to give the right answer. This situation is mirrored in the logic of therapists when a patient denies having been abused; therapists say "of course they deny it, they are repressing it." With such clarity of logic, the patient cannot possibly convince the therapist the abuse did not occur. In police interrogation, and now in therapy, a denial is a starting point in negotiations, something to be ignored as an obvious deception. The obvious has once again been ignored. The guilty may protest their innocence, but so, too, will the innocent.

SUMMARY

A number of social psychological factors influence the responses that interviewees provide during investigative interviews. Factors such as the credibility of the speaker, expectations, and social isolation, coupled with assertive, though not necessarily coercive, interviewing techniques have each been shown to influence levels of suggestibility. Using such information, psychologists have offered advice to police officers and the courts concerning appropriate interviewing techniques. They have also helped to dispel some widely held myths about the ability of interviewers and interviewees.

Probably the greatest recent success that psychologists have had in the field of investigative interviewing has been to dispel the notion of the excessively unreliable child witness. Psychological research during the 1970s, and especially the 1980s, challenged legal systems around the world. Studies showed that children were capable of providing high-quality testimony, even in extreme circumstances (e.g., Jones

& Krugman, 1986). In both North America and Europe, the laws governing the questioning of children underwent a number of dramatic revisions, including changes to rules regarding the need for corroborative evidence (see Spencer & Flin, 1990). Other changes included the introduction of video links and, in some countries, the ability to present videotaped evidence in order to spare the child the stress of testifying in court. It is currently recognized that children will generally be highly resistant to false suggestions concerning sexual abuse, although there may be occasions when testimony can become distorted. However, when certain safeguards are in place, the scope for contamination appears relatively limited.

Psychologists have also achieved some measure of success in modifying police interviewing procedures (at least in the United Kingdom), although there the need for change was largely recognized in the absence of any research. Before public outcry over mishandled cases involving false confessions, the police had been reluctant to allow psychologists into the interview room, maintaining an air of secrecy about what went on in interviews. The introduction of tape and video recording made it possible for independent observers to examine interrogation practices. Gudjonsson's pioneering research on suggestibility (e.g., Gudjonsson, 1992) has highlighted ways in which empirical research can be carried out in areas that many had previously considered to be beyond the scope of experimental inquiry.

With regard to false memories, a rather muddled situation still remains. As Ofshe and Watters (1993) point out, reasoned argument holds little sway against a determined opponent. They compare the current outbreak of false memory cases to past examples of mass hysteria that society now looks back on in bewilderment: How could anyone hold views we now know to be patently absurd? The conditions under which false memories can be implanted and the very real scope for creating elaborate fantasies with no grounding in reality (other than that shared by the therapist and unfortunate patient) are considerable. Comparing this to the evidence for repressed memory, for which the detailed elaborations of patients on past events are held up as "proof" (even though such memories are totally unlike conventional memories), is obviously an uneven contest. Psychology societies around the world issue guidelines on interviewing practice to safeguard against false memories, but if therapists choose to ignore them, then the current situation looks as though it will continue. Despite the success of psychologists in challenging commonly held notions about concepts such as suggestibility in witnesses and suspects, the profession still has a long way to go when attacking ideas that rely more on belief than empirical evidence.

SUGGESTED READINGS

Ceci, S. J., & Bruck, M. (1993). Child witnesses: Translating research into policy. *Social policy report: Society for Research in Child Development* (Vol. 7, No. 3). Ann Arbor: University of Michigan Press.

This is an excellent, well-written discussion of children's testimony. It describes a number of innovative research studies and considers some of the difficulties in applying psychological research.

Gudjonsson, G. (1992). *The psychology of interrogations, confessions and testimony.* Chichester, England: John Wiley.

A comprehensive review of the author's research on police interrogation, this book includes a large number of case studies. It also contains details of the *Gudjonsson Suggestibility Scale,* a tool for assessing interrogative suggestibility.

King M. A., & Yuille, J. C. (1987). Suggestibility and the child witness. In S. J. Ceci, M. P. Toglia, & D. F. Ross (Eds.), *Children's eyewitness testimony.* New York: Springer-Verlag.

This is a very good discussion of how the social dynamics of the interview situation can influence children's testimony. It complements the article by Ceci and Bruck listed earlier.

Loftus, E. F. (1993). The reality of repressed memories. *American Psychologist, 48,* 518–537.

This useful summary of the main issues surrounding recovered memories contains a number of informative examples and summarizes a number of recent controversial cases.

Ofshe, R., & Watters, E. (1993, March/April). Making monsters. *Society,* pp. 4–16.

In the essay on the topic of false memories (no references), the authors present a damning critique of therapists, their logic, and the methods used in recovering memories.

Schumaker, J. F. (Ed.). (1991). *Human suggestibility: Advances in theory, research and application.* London: Routledge.

One of the few books to discuss suggestibility in a number of different areas of psychological research, including hypnosis, religious experiences, and placebos, this work also delves into forensic areas such as eyewitness testimony and police interrogation.

9 Social Psychology in the Courtroom

Jeffrey E. Pfeifer[1]

University of Regina

Although social psychologists have long been interested in studying various factors related to the legal system, the recent increase in highly publicized cases such as those involving O.J. Simpson and Rodney King in the United States and Paul Bernardo and his wife Karla Homolka in Canada has served to focus this interest on issues concerning the fairness of the trial process. (Bernardo and Homolka were tried in connection with one of the most gruesome cases in Canadian history involving the abduction, assault, and murder of two teenage schoolgirls.) This social psychological interest in courtroom dynamics is augmented by the fact that the courtroom itself represents a microcosm of the world of social psychology in which one may witness the animation of numerous theories and models, including those representing attraction, attributions, attitudes and behaviors, conflict resolution, prejudice and discrimination, social influence, communication, and collective behavior.

In an attempt to identify some of the areas in which social psychologists have played an active role in the courtroom, this chapter has been divided into a number of sections representing the various events that occur from the time a defendant enters a courtroom until the presentation of evidence is completed and the jurors are instructed as to their duty. Specifically, after reviewing the historical antecedents regarding the integration of law and psychology, this chapter discusses the social

[1] The author wishes to thank Kate Scarmalis and Nicole Weber for their comments on earlier drafts of this chapter.

psychological contributions to various issues, such as change of venue (attitude formation), jury size (conformity and group decision making), jury composition and selection (attitudes and paralanguage), extra-evidential factors and juror decision making (prejudice and discrimination), the use of expert testimony (attitude change/persuasion), and jury instructions (communication).

Each of the sections begins with a description of an actual case that illustrates the application of social psychology to courtroom procedures. Although the cases are from U.S. courts, they represent a number of general scientific concepts that can be equally applied to other legal systems such as those in Canada and Great Britain. In addition, each section ends by describing possible future avenues of social psychological investigation. It is hoped that the research and materials presented throughout this chapter will not only illustrate the numerous areas in which social psychologists have contributed to our knowledge of courtroom dynamics, but will also illustrate the vast areas that have yet to be tapped.

THE INTEGRATION OF LAW AND PSYCHOLOGY

It may be argued that the integration of law and psychology resulted from an early philosophical belief that the sciences should not be viewed as separate and distinct entities, but rather as interrelated segments. Descartes, for example, suggested that the sciences were so interconnected that it would be easier to study them as a whole rather than in isolation (Cairns, 1935). It was not until the early 1900s, however, that his philosophical belief in scientific integration was specifically addressed by the sciences of law and psychology.

In the introduction to his historic work, *On the Witness Stand: Essays on Psychology and Crime,* Hugo Munsterberg (1908) argued that there was a need to create an independent experimental science that would address issues of practical life in areas such as education, medicine, economics, and the law. According to Munsterberg, the time had arrived for psychologists to supplement the *traditional psychological approach* of engaging in secluded research with an *applied psychological approach* that was directly relevant to the problems of real life. As an example of the usefulness of this independent science, Munsterberg then dedicated the remainder of his book to reviewing specific areas in which "psychology and law come in contact," such as eyewitness memory, detection of deception, and crime prevention.

Psychologists like Munsterberg, however, were not the only individuals who recognized the need for a more interactive relationship between the law and other sciences. For example, Munsterberg's call to move beyond traditional psychology was echoed by a number of legal scholars, such as Louis Brandeis and Roscoe Pound, who argued that *classical jurisprudence* (the belief that the law was a logical tool that could be rationally applied to cases to reach a correct legal solution) should be replaced by *realistic jurisprudence* (the belief that the law should be supplemented with additional contextual material, such as social science evidence, in order to reach a solution to a case). As in the case of Munsterberg, these legal scholars argued that the law should no longer operate within a vacuum but should be receptive to the contributions that other sciences might have to offer (for a review of this movement see Monahan & Walker, 1994). The legal movement toward realistic jurisprudence was illustrated in a 1907 U.S. Supreme Court case in which Louis Brandeis filed a brief that described medical, statistical, and social scientific evidence regarding the need to restrict the number of hours women may be required to work per day (Lief, 1930). Although there is no direct evidence that the Court relied on the scientific information provided by Brandeis, the mere fact that it was presented represented a significant step toward scientific integration between law and other sciences.

Although significant progress toward the integration of law and psychology had been made by the late 1920s, both psychologists and legal scholars were still seeking to define the role that would be played by each of the disciplines. Legal scholars who now accepted the idea of increased scientific integration were struggling with the issue of defining the roles that psychology and the law would play. For example, 9 years before being appointed a U.S. Supreme Court Justice, Felix Frankfurter suggested, "[w]e are still largely in the social stage of the social sciences. We are mostly only talking about collaboration, and have as yet hardly begun to experiment on the processes by which to 'integrate' or 'co-ordinate' or 'collaborate' with one another. We have hardly got over the discovery that we are members of the same family; we have not yet required family habits with one another" (MacLeish & Prichard, 1939, pp. 290–291).

A possible solution to Justice Frankfurter's comments regarding scientific collaboration, however, may be found in the early work of Slesinger and Pilpel (1929). These two social scientists reviewed the relatively short history of legal psychology and, in an attempt to provide a framework for the integration of these sciences, suggested that, "in the rough and ready generality of legal research and the greater precision of psychological investigation, we may have a solution to the problem under discussion [i.e., defining legal psychology]. A science requires a subject-matter and a method; perhaps legal scholarship will supply the one, psychological research the other" (p. 680).

In the 60 years since the comments of Slesinger and Pilpel, it may be argued that their model has represented the integration of law and psychology, especially in regard to applied social psychological research. Social psychologists interested in applying their knowledge to the legal arena, for the most part, continue to examine legal concepts and procedures empirically in order to increase our understanding of the trial process. A number of these concepts and procedures are reviewed in the following section.

CHANGE OF VENUE: CAN A DEFENDANT GET A FAIR TRIAL WHEN THERE IS EXTENSIVE MEDIA COVERAGE ABOUT THE CRIME?

On August 27, 1974, an elderly white jailer named Clarence Alligood was found dead in a locked cell in the women's section of the Beaufort County jail in Washington, North Carolina. Although Alligood was found in the cell, his pants and shoes were located outside the cell. A 20-year-old black female named Joan Little who had been occupying the cell was missing and presumed to have been responsible for the death of the jailer. Days later, Joan Little, accompanied by her attorney, turned herself in to the local authorities and stated that she had killed Alligood in self-defense as he attempted to rape her. Due to the extensive media coverage of the death of Alligood, and the subsequent disappearance and reemergence of Joan Little, the defense team attempted to have the trial moved to another district. In support of its claim, the defense team submitted a study conducted by a number of social psychologists that indicated that the extensive media coverage of the death of Alligood had led to prejudicial attitudes toward Joan Little in Beaufort County. These attitudes, they argued, would lead to an unfair trial. After hearing the evidence, the judge granted a change of venue and ordered the trial to be held in Wake County rather than Beaufort County where the incident had occurred. After a 5-week trial, Joan Little was acquitted of all charges.

As illustrated in this case, a *change of venue* refers to situations in which a request is made to move a trial to a different location because the level of prejudice against the defendant is so high that he or she would not be able to get a fair trial in the current location (Monahan & Walker, 1994). In order to convince a judge that a trial should be relocated to a community other than the one in which the alleged crime occurred, counsel must present evidence that suggests that "prejudicial pretrial publicity or local knowledge and continuing passions must be so inflamed to make it nearly impossible to select an impartial jury" (Hans & Vidmar, 1986, p. 58). In other words, attorneys must present tangible evidence that the pretrial publicity surrounding a specific case has led to a level of community prejudice against the defendant that is so pervasive that an impartial hearing is all but impossible (see e.g., *Pennsylvania v. Cohen,* 1980). For the most part, the tangible evidence that is presented by attorneys in support of their claim consists of valid and reliable public opinion surveys conducted by qualified individuals such as social psychologists.

Although the trial of Joan Little was important for many reasons, it is perhaps best known as one of the most well-documented cases in which social scientists actively played a role in establishing the groundwork for a change of venue motion. In the case of Ms. Little, the defense team presented the results of a random poll that indicated that the extensive pretrial publicity about the case had resulted in a community belief that Joan Little did not kill Clarence Alligood in self-defense (McConahay, Mullin, & Frederick, 1977). In effect, the social scientists argued that pretrial publicity had culminated in prejudicial attitudes toward Joan Little in the community. Because the jurors for the trial would be selected from the community, Joan Little would not receive a fair trial unless it was moved to a more attitudinally neutral community.

The claims of the social scientists in the Joan Little case have been bolstered by a number of more recent empirical studies that indicate that prejudicial pretrial publicity about a specific defendant tends to have a negative effect on the dispositional decisions of mock jurors. Ogloff and Vidmar (1994), for example, divided subjects into four groups and supplied each group with a differing level of pretrial publicity regarding a case of a priest accused of sexually abusing young boys at an orphanage (based on the Mount Cashel Case in St. John's, Newfoundland). Subjects in group 1 were supplied with the case facts regarding the incident. Subjects in group 2, however, were also supplied with prejudicial newspaper articles describing the case. Subjects in group 3 were supplied with prejudicial video footage of the case, whereas subjects in group 4 were supplied with the newspaper and video information. As hypothesized, subjects who were presented with pretrial publicity (i.e., groups 2, 3, and 4) were significantly more likely to rate the priest as guilty than subjects who did not receive the information (i.e., group 1). Although the authors suggest that the results clearly indicate a relationship between specific pretrial publicity and mock juror decision making, Greene (1990) cautions that application of this type of research to actual juries is at best "rudimentary and speculative."

In addition to the investigation of mock juror decision making and pretrial publicity, a number of social psychologists have also attempted to define how a properly conducted survey should be carried out in a change-of-venue application. For example, while describing the first successful use of survey evidence for a change of venue in Canada, Vidmar and Judson (1981) reviewed the techniques they had employed in a criminal fraud trial. According to these authors, the success of the survey techniques employed in this case was attributable to a number of elements, such as (a) sampling subjects who were eligible for jury duty, (b) asking subjects questions that are similar to those likely to be asked in the courtroom, and (c) introducing the results to the court through expert testimony as opposed to a written report. Similarly, according to Frederick (1987), the most reliable methodology available to a social scientist to illustrate the level of pretrial prejudice against a defendant is a sound survey that includes (a) a random sample of jury-eligible persons from the community of interest, (b) a random sample of jury-eligible persons from a second community to serve as a baseline or comparison group, and (c) a questionnaire that includes questions about the perceived level of publicity regarding the case in question, specific attitudes regarding the guilt of the defendant, and general attitudes (e.g., racial attitudes, attitudes toward crime).

Since the Joan Little trial, a number of other highly publicized cases have been tried in alternative communities because of extensive prejudicial pretrial publicity and/or inflamed community bias against a defendant. Most notably, the trials of the officers involved in the Rodney King case in California and the trial of Paul Bernardo in Ontario were moved in order to help negate the bias created by negative and extensive pretrial media coverage. Social psychologists continue to investigate empirically the effects of pretrial publicity on community attitudes as well as juror decision making in order to establish grounds for a change of venue.

Future Research

There are a number of issues that future research may investigate regarding the issue of change of venue. First, social psychologists are likely to be faced with the question of whether it is possible, in the technologically advanced world in which we live today, to find a community that has not been affected by media coverage of a sensational trial. For example, even though the Canadian judiciary placed a national media ban on many of the facts in the Karla Homolka case (in order to diminish the possible prejudicial impact on potential jurors in the subsequent trial of her husband Paul Bernardo), it would have been difficult, indeed, to find a community in Canada that had not heard the grisly details through various means such as electronic mail and international media. With the increased usage of electronic media and other outlets for information distribution, future research may tend more toward examining whether an alternative to the change of venue may be more appropriate to deal with pretrial publicity. Although initial research indicates that procedures such as jury selection and judicial instruction do not effectively control for specific pretrial publicity (Carroll et al., 1986), further research in this area may reveal potentially effective procedures.

Second, researchers have begun to examine whether pretrial publicity may adversely affect the fairness of a trial, even if the publicity is not directly linked to the specific case at hand. For example, is it possible that a defendant who is accused of killing someone during a drug deal might apply for a change of venue because there has recently been a large amount of prejudicial pretrial publicity regarding the general issue of drugs and violence? In order to shed some light on this question, Greene and Wade (1987) conducted a study in which they found that subjects were more likely to judge a defendant as guilty if they had previously been exposed to pretrial publicity regarding a comparable case in which the defendant was correctly found guilty than if exposed to a similar case in which the defendant was incorrectly found guilty. Although these results are interesting, Greene (1990, p. 440), herself, suggests that a "review [of] the topic of general media effects raises more questions than it resolves." Future research in this area may lead to answers to some of these questions.

Finally, social psychologists have yet to examine rumor transmission thoroughly as a form of prejudicial pretrial publicity. Although it is not currently perceived as a traditional form of pretrial publicity, it may be argued that rumor transmission leads to prejudicial attitudes that are just as strong as those created by pretrial media reports. The effect of rumor transmission as a form of pretrial prejudice may be exacerbated in situations such as the Karla Homolka trial in Canada. In such cases, the public may satiate its thirst for knowledge by resorting to rumors that may be even more damaging than the actual trial facts. Future research, therefore, may investigate the degree to which these rumors affect the prejudicial attitudes of potential jurors.

JURY SIZE:
HOW MANY PEOPLE SHOULD SIT ON THE JURY
TO ENSURE A FAIR TRIAL FOR A DEFENDANT?

On July 3, 1968, a defendant named Williams was on trial for robbery in a Florida courtroom. Although a trial for robbery was not an uncommon occurrence, what made the Williams case notable was the fact that the defendant was being tried by a 6-member jury rather than the customary 12-member jury. This reduction in jury size was due to a recently enacted Florida law that allowed for the use of 6-member juries in noncapital criminal cases (i.e., cases that do not involve the possibility of capital punishment). After being found guilty, Williams appealed to the U.S. Supreme Court on the basis that his Sixth Amendment right to be tried by a jury had been violated. In essence, Williams argued that the Sixth Amendment guaranteed him the constitutional right to be tried by an impartial jury of 12—*not 6*. However, after reviewing the case, the Court declared that the use of 6-member juries in non-capital criminal cases does not violate a defendant's Sixth Amendment rights (*Williams v. Florida*, 1970). In support of its decision, the Court referred to a number of social psychological studies on conformity and group decision making, which it (the Court) suggested showed no significant difference between the decision-making capabilities of groups of 12 and groups of 6. Although the *Williams* decision was confined to noncapital criminal trials, it was quickly expanded to include civil cases as well (*Colgrave v. Battin*, 1973).

Taken together, the *Williams* and *Colgrave* decisions not only represented a fundamental shift in the constitutional definition of a jury but also represented one of the most glaring examples of judicial ignorance of social scientific evidence. According to Saks (1974, p. 18), "[t]he briefs presented by opposing counsel [in the *Williams* and *Colgrave* cases] were oblivious to well-established social science findings and/or methodological principles which would have supported the appellant [i.e., Williams and Colgrave]. In short, the law's confrontation with some relatively simple empirical questions was simply an embarrassment." In essence, Saks argued that the empirical data on which the Court relied in the two cases regarding group decision making was questionable for a number of reasons. These reasons are reviewed next.

Empirical Evidence Cited in *Williams*

In *Williams,* the U.S. Supreme Court stated that the issue at hand involved the question of whether a 6-member jury, in comparison to a 12-member jury, would be less likely to successfully fulfill the "purpose of the jury" as stated in *Duncan v. Louisiana* (1968; i.e., to act as a safeguard against prosecutorial and judicial bias or corruption). In deciding that no difference existed, the Court specifically referred to a number of empirical studies, including the early research on conformity conducted by Asch (1951). Specifically, the Court argued that the limited number of experiments that had been conducted indicated that there was no significant difference between a 6-member jury and a 12-member jury (*Williams v. Florida*, 1970). In particular, the Court stressed the fact that research indicates that a defendant is no less likely to find a juror who will vote to acquit in a 6-member jury than in a 12-member jury.

Although the Court employed research to bolster its decision, Saks (1974) argued that the studies were misinterpreted on a number of counts. First, the Court failed to recognize an important aspect of the social psychological research on conformity and group decision making. Specifically, the Court did not address the significant impact on conformity that results when an individual perceives that he or she has an ally. For example, even though a 5–1 jury is proportionally equal to a 10–2 jury (i.e., 83%–17% split), research on conformity suggests that the single person in the 6-member jury is much more likely to change his or her vote and conform to the other members of the jury than are the two people in the 12-member jury—because of the perceived presence of an ally. As such, a defendant stands a greater chance of acquittal in a 12-member jury than a 6-member jury, even though the proportion of members voting to acquit is similar. In addition to this, the Court failed to address the fact that 6-member juries would be significantly less likely than 12-member juries to provide a representational cross-section of the community. Finally, the Court failed to make a distinction between the civil cases that the studies had examined and the criminal case represented by *Williams.* That is, the Court simply took the findings of empirical studies of civil cases and generalized their findings to criminal cases.

Empirical Evidence Cited in *Colgrave*

Although there was relatively little empirical research to guide the Court in *Williams,* by the time the *Colgrave* decision was reached, at least four studies had been conducted that specifically examined the effects of group size on jury behavior (see, e.g., Bermant & Coppock, 1973; Institute of Judicial Administration, 1972; Kessler, 1973; Mills, 1973). Although the Court argued that these four studies provided convincing empirical support for the *Williams* decision, Saks (1974) argued that their usefulness was limited by faulty methodologies and confounding variables. For example, although the Bermant and Coppock (1973) and Institute of Judicial Administration (1972) studies did not find a significant difference between 6- and 12-member juries in civil cases, they failed to control for at least two other important variables: case complexity and amount of damages sought. Specifically, according to Saks (1974), these two studies are not as informative as the Court suggests because the lack of a significant difference in findings based on jury size may be due to the confounds created by the complexity of a case or the amount of damages. A similar confound is found in the Mills (1973) study, which failed to account for the effect of a mediation board that might have been employed to settle more complex or expensive cases. Finally, Saks (1974) argued that the results of the only study to be conducted in a controlled environment (Kessler, 1973) were also suspect because of their lack of external validity. That is, the fact that the study was conducted in a tightly controlled laboratory environment with mock jurors suggests that the direct generalization of results to the functioning of an actual jury is, at best, tenuous.

Cases Since *Williams* and *Colgrave*

In deciding that 6-member juries were just as likely to safeguard the constitutional rights of defendants as were 12-member juries, the Court did not address at least one important question—is a jury of fewer than 6 members also constitutional? The answer to this question, however, was soon to be found in *Ballew v. Georgia* (1978). Ballew, a manager of an adult theater in Georgia, was arrested for distributing obscene materials. At trial, Ballew was found guilty by a 5-member jury and subsequently appealed the decision on the grounds that a 5-member jury violated his constitutional right to a fair trial. The U.S. Supreme Court decided that Ballew was correct and at the same time put a definite lower limit on the question of jury size: 6-member juries are acceptable, 5-member juries are not.

From the viewpoint of social psychologists, what is most interesting, and confusing, about the Ballew decision is that the Court referred to five specific research-related reasons for its belief that a 5-member jury is too small to protect a defendant's constitutional rights under the Sixth Amendment. Specifically, the Court referred to (a) a number of studies and articles that indicated that smaller juries are less likely than larger juries to provide a context for effective group deliberations (interestingly, a number of the references cited by the Court were published before the *Williams* decision); (b) a study that indicated that an innocent person was significantly more likely to be convicted in a smaller jury than by a larger jury; (c) research indicating that smaller juries are detrimental to the defendant because a jury member who initially votes to acquit will be more likely to change his or her decision without an ally and an ally is more likely to be present in a 12-member jury than in a 6-member jury; (d) research indicating that smaller juries are less likely to have minority representation and, as such, are less likely to represent a cross-section of the community; and (e) a number of methodological problems that may "mask" differences in the findings of 6-member juries compared to 12-member juries.

Not surprisingly, the U.S. Supreme Court's decisions regarding the issue of jury size are confusing to social psychologists for a number of reasons. First, it appears that the Court is inconsistent in its reliance on research concerning group decision making. That is, the Court seemed to be unconvinced by research on conformity and group size in the *Williams* and *Colgrave* cases, yet it found the research compelling in the *Ballew* case. Second, it appears that the Court has made a psychological delineation with regard to the issue of conformity without regard for the empirical findings of social psychologists. In other words, although the Court has decided that there is a definite psychological difference between a 5-member jury and a 6-member jury, there is very little social psychological research to support this contention. Finally, it appears that the Court does not see a difference between the decision-making abilities of 6-member and 12-member juries, except in capital cases, in which a defendant must be tried by a 12-member jury. Again, this inconsistency is confusing to social psychologists who investigate issues of conformity and group decision making.

Future Research

Unlike other issues discussed in this chapter, future questions regarding the issue of jury size do not appear to be of great concern. Social scientists may continue to investigate areas such as group processes and conformity in an attempt to further bolster their belief that 6-member juries are significantly different from 12-member juries. It is unlikely, however, that this additional evidence will sway the Court. As Saks (1974, p. 20) states, "[t]he Court currently believes the matter of equality of performance for different-size juries is now well established, when in truth there is still no evidence to support such a conclusion."

Although it is doubtful whether additional social psychological evidence will serve to alter the belief of the U.S. Supreme Court on this issue, researchers may continue to examine the question of jury size in order to influence a number of state courts that continue to empanel 12-member juries, and possibly the court systems of other countries such as Canada, which have yet to address this question. As such, there are a number of possible areas of future research. For example, social psychologists may attempt to examine whether the seriousness of a crime is related to group decision making in juries of different sizes. As stated earlier, the U.S. Supreme Court currently believes that capital cases are different enough from noncapital cases to warrant a 12-member jury. Future research may indicate whether there is a psychological difference to support this differentiation.

JURY COMPOSITION AND SELECTION: CAN SOCIAL PSYCHOLOGISTS HELP SELECT IMPARTIAL JURORS?

In 1971, eight individuals were arrested and charged with conspiring to engage in a number of federal offenses involving antiwar activities. Because the government opted to hold the court proceedings in Harrisburg, Pennsylvania, the case soon came to be known as the Harrisburg Seven trial. The defense attorneys in this case were joined by a team of social scientists who were quick to point out that the pool of prospective jurors assembled by the court was not demographically representative of the local community. In response to this discrepancy, the presiding judge ordered a second, more representative pool of prospective jurors to be drawn. The social scientists then conducted a number of interviews with people in the Harrisburg area in an attempt to identify the demographic and attitudinal characteristics related to conviction or acquittal proneness. (For a review of this study see Schulman, Shaver, Colman, Emrich, & Christie, 1973.) Results of the interviews indicated that the ideal juror (for the defense) would be "a female Democrat with no religious preferences who held a white-collar job or a skilled-laborer position" (Wrightsman, Nietzel, & Fortune, 1994, p. 37). Armed with the findings of the social scientists, the defense team proceeded to select jurors who most closely matched that template. After listening to, and deliberating over, the evidence in the case, the jury members reported that they were unable to come to a unanimous decision. Ten jurors opted for a verdict of not guilty and two jurors opted for a verdict of guilty. Faced with a hung jury, the government decided not to pursue a second trial and the defendants were released.

The trial of the Harrisburg Seven is a significant one in psycholegal history because it represents one of the best-documented cases in which social scientists were actively engaged in the process of jury selection. In addition to this notoriety, the trial of the Harrisburg Seven also illustrates the two basic areas of jury selection and composition in which social psychologists may play a role: the *venire* and *voir dire*. A *venire* is the pool of potential jurors that are assembled before a trial. *Voir dire* refers to the process of selecting jurors from the venire.

The Venire

According to the United States Jury Selection and Service Act (1968), the goal of the venire is to assemble a pool of potential jurors who represent a fair cross-section of the community. In order to accomplish this goal, the act provides the court with a model for the process of selecting a pool of potential jurors. Specifically, the model indicates that potential jurors are first identified through the use of voters' lists from the relevant jurisdiction. Once individuals have been identified they are sent a questionnaire, which they are legally obligated to return. Questionnaire responses are then examined in order to identify individuals who should be removed from the list of potential jurors due to disqualification or exemption. In order not to be disqualified, an individual must (a) be a citizen of the United States who is at least 18 years of age and has resided in the judicial district for at least one year; (b) be able to read, write, speak, or understand the English language; (c) be physically and mentally capable to render satisfactory jury service; and (4) not be currently charged, or have been convicted of, a federal or state offense. Similarly, an individual is exempt from jury service if he or she is a member of the armed services or the police or fire department or a public officer who has been elected to his or her post. In addition, other potential jurors may request to be removed from service for a number of reasons, including age (over 70 years old), profession (e.g., members of the clergy, registered health care workers, attorneys, university professors), or undue hardship or inconvenience (e.g., a person living more than 80 miles from the court, a person who has served on a jury within the last 2 years). Finally, the venire is selected from the remaining pool of potential jurors.

Although the intent of the Jury Selection and Service Act is to create a model for the selection of potential jurors who are representative of the community, a number of individuals have argued that this has not occurred. Hans and Vidmar (1986), for example, suggest that voters' lists are often inadequate because they fail to identify many young people, minorities, and the poor and homeless. The nonrepresentativeness issue was addressed in a study by Alker, Hosticka, and Mitchell (1976), who reviewed the jury selection model as applied in the Massachusetts district of the Eastern Division of the U.S. District Court and found that the selection process discriminates against the poor, the young, minorities, women, and persons with low and high educational attainment. Despite these criticisms, the jury selection model continues to be employed as a template for selection of the venire.

Voir Dire and the Role of Scientific Jury Selection

After the venire is assembled, a process known as voir dire occurs in which attorneys may ask potential jurors a number of questions in order to determine whether they are acceptable to both the court and the parties involved in the trial (Frederick,

1984). After asking questions of potential jurors, attorneys may attempt to remove a juror through a *challenge for cause* or a *peremptory challenge*. A challenge for cause involves asking the judge to dismiss a potential juror because of obvious bias or prejudice that may affect decision making. For example, in the United States, a potential juror may be dismissed from a capital case jury during the voir dire if he or she does not believe in the death penalty (see Box 9–1). A peremptory challenge, on the other hand, occurs when an attorney moves to dismiss a potential juror based solely on his or her discretion.

Given the discretionary use of peremptory challenges, it is not surprising that social scientists have developed a number of techniques for aiding attorneys in selecting acceptable jurors. According to Frederick (1984), social scientists have developed three basic jury selection techniques that are related to social psychology: the *survey approach, in-court attitude ratings,* and *in-court nonverbal communication ratings.* The survey approach consists of providing individuals in the community with the case facts and asking them how they would respond if they were a juror. In addition, basic demographic and personality information is collected. This information is then analyzed in order to create a profile of a favorable juror. Aside from the Harrisburg Seven trial, this technique has been employed in a number of other prominent cases such as the Wounded Knee trial (Christie, 1976) and the Black Panther trial of Huey Newton (Blauner, 1972).

In-court attitude ratings, in contrast, involve asking potential jurors questions during voir dire that seek to identify their personality type or their current attitudes toward the case at hand. For example, during the voir dire in the Joan Little trial, the psychologists prompted defense attorneys to ask questions that would indicate whether a potential juror was an extreme authoritarian, on the basis that authoritarians tend to be rigid, conservative, and racist, and, as such, would certainly represent a less than ideal choice for the defense of a black woman accused of killing a white man in the southern United States. Finally, in-court nonverbal communication ratings are employed to examine a potential juror. The social scientists involved in the Joan Little trial attempted to evaluate the truthfulness of potential jurors by observing their body language during the voir dire (McConahay, Mullin, & Frederick, 1977). Since the Joan Little trial, social psychologists have conducted numerous studies on specific aspects of nonverbal communication such as facial expressions, eye contact, body language, and paralanguage (i.e., tone of voice, volume, pitch) (Rime, 1983). The results of these studies have been employed by both psychologists and lawyers to guide their evaluations of potential jurors during the voir dire. For example, while questioning a potential juror, a lawyer may attribute a lack of eye contact as a signal of deception. Similarly, a potential juror who employs powerless speech may be viewed as a person who might be easily swayed by other jurors during the deliberation process. Although the relationship between nonverbal communication cues and actual juror behavior has been critically questioned by a number of social scientists, lawyers continue to employ this technique during the voir dire (see, e.g., Blinder, 1978).

Faced with continual criticisms regarding the effectiveness of scientific jury selection, however, social scientists have increasingly begun to refocus their energies

**Box
9–1** *Challenge for Cause and the Death-Qualified Juror*

One of the more controversial "challenge for cause" issues in the United States involves the concept of death-qualified juries. The controversy revolves around the fact that a number of states that currently allow capital punishment (i.e., the death penalty) as a sentencing option require that the jury serve two functions during the trial process. First, the jury is asked to determine the guilt of the defendant (i.e., guilt phase), and, if the defendant is found guilty, the same jury is then asked to decide whether to impose the death penalty (i.e., sentence phase). Not surprisingly, the controversy surrounding this issue involves the role that a potential juror's death-penalty attitudes should play in the jury selection process. Specifically, social scientists are interested in whether death-penalty attitudes of potential jurors would affect the guilt phase of a trial in a capital case.

This issue was first addressed in 1968 when William Witherspoon appealed his death sentence to the U.S. Supreme Court on the basis that a number of potential jurors had been removed for cause during voir dire because of their attitudes toward the death penalty (*Witherspoon v. Illinois*, 1968). Specifically, jurors who said that they would not impose the death penalty under any circumstances were removed from the jury. As a result of these removals for cause, Witherspoon argued that the jury was more likely to vote to convict. In support of his claim, Witherspoon presented the Court with three unpublished studies that indicated that individuals who held negative attitudes toward the death penalty were less likely to convict a defendant than individuals who did not hold negative attitudes toward the death penalty. The Court, however, ruled that it was not unconstitutional for potential jurors to be removed for cause in a capital case if their attitudes toward the death penalty would lead them to automatically vote against imposing the death penalty regardless of the trial evidence, or would not allow them to make an unbiased decision regarding the guilt of the defendant (these jurors subsequently became known as "Witherspoon Excludables" or WEs). The Court's decision, however, was quickly challenged by a number of social scientists who argued that death-qualified juries (i.e., those that did not include WEs) were more likely to convict a defendant than non–death-qualified juries (i.e., those that did include WEs).

Although the Court in *Witherspoon* was supplied with only three unpublished studies regarding the conviction proneness of death-qualified juries, by 1986 the American Psychological Association (APA) believed that the evidence regarding conviction proneness was so strong that it submitted an amicus curiae brief in *Lockhart v. McCree* (1986). In this brief, the APA reviewed nearly 30 years of research that indicated a relationship between death-qualified juries and conviction proneness (Bersoff & Ogden, 1987). As in *Witherspoon*, however, the Court concluded that, despite the apparent social scientific evidence, the use of death-qualified juries was not unconstitutional. The APA brief and the Court's subsequent decision are interesting on at least two accounts. First, this issue is a marked illustration of the potential conflict that can occur between empirical findings and the law. Second, the submission of the brief itself ignited a social scientific controversy regarding the proper role of empirical evidence in the legal arena (see Elliot, 1991; Ellsworth, 1991).

from the general principles of investigation listed earlier (i.e., demographics, body language, and personality characteristics) to a more *case-specific approach* (Smith & Malandro, 1986). In the case-specific approach, emphasis is placed on the use of focus groups and jury simulation studies in which subjects are presented with an abbreviated form of the evidence from an upcoming trial and asked to make individual and group decisions based on their interpretations. In addition, emphasis is placed on trying to understand how subjects create their personal narrative, or script, of the evidence that is presented to them. (For a review of this concept, see Pennington & Hastie, 1988.)

Future Research

Future research on jury composition and selection may be directed toward a number of areas. First, in terms of the venire, it is clear that the current model, although a marked improvement over previous techniques of jury selection, is discriminatory in regard to certain groups. As cited earlier, empirical analyses indicate that the use of voter lists, combined with removals due to disqualifications, exemptions, and excuses, has led to the empaneling of jury pools that tend to underrepresent minorities, women, and the poor. Although a number of alternatives have been employed in an attempt to remedy this underrepresentation (i.e., supplementing voters lists with driving permit registrations and welfare rolls), the problem remains. Perhaps future research in this area may yield a more successful technique for gathering a pool of potential jurors that represents a fair cross-section of the community.

Second, a number of psychologists, as well as legal scholars, have recently begun to question the extent to which lawyers should be allowed to question potential jurors during the voir dire. Historically, courts in the United States have allowed lawyers to ask lengthy and wide-ranging questions in order to probe a potential juror's attitudes, beliefs, and behaviors (see, e.g., Moran, Cutler, & Loftus, 1990), whereas the Canadian courts tend to restrict the number and types of questions that a lawyer may ask a potential juror (Vidmar & Melnitzer, 1984). Given that the goal of the voir dire is to create a fair and impartial jury, psychologists as well as lawyers have begun to argue that the Canadian model may be too restrictive (see, e.g., Cooper, 1994; Vidmar & Melnitzer, 1984), whereas the U.S. model may be too excessive and lead to the use of peremptory challenges to dismiss jurors improperly on the basis of race, religion, or political ideologies (see, e.g., Gordon, 1985). Future research in this area may be directed toward examining whether the conservative Canadian prototype is more likely to yield an unbiased jury than the more liberal model employed by courts in the United States.

Finally, although scientific jury selection has become a major business in the United States, social scientists have remained largely unimpressed by its results (see, e.g., Fulero & Penrod, 1990; Penrod, 1990). Accordingly, it has been argued that increased empirical analysis of this concept should be conducted. One possible avenue for empirical investigation of jury selection may lie in the direction of research on the cognitive processing of potential jurors (see, e.g., Graziano, Panter, & Tanaka, 1990).

EXTRA-EVIDENTIAL FACTORS AND JUROR BIAS: ARE JURY VERDICTS AFFECTED BY FACTORS SUCH AS RACE AND SOCIOECONOMIC STATUS?

On October 12, 1978, a jury in Fulton County, Georgia, convicted a black man named Warren McCleskey of murder and sentenced him to death. According to trial testimony, McCleskey allegedly shot and killed a white police officer during a furniture store robbery. McCleskey appealed his conviction to the United States Supreme Court on the grounds that the death penalty in Georgia was administered in a racially discriminatory manner (*McCleskey v. Kemp,* 1987). In support of his claim, McCleskey referred to a study conducted by Baldus, Woodworth, and Pulaski (1985), which reviewed over 2,000 murder trials in Georgia and concluded that there was a significant racial discrepancy in the imposition of the death penalty. Specifically, after controlling for over 230 variables, the Baldus et al. study found that black defendants were significantly more likely than white defendants to receive the death penalty, especially when the victim was white. For example, results indicated that the death penalty was imposed in 22% of the cases in which the defendant was black and the victim was white but in only 3 percent of the cases in which the defendant was white and the victim was black. Although the Court examined the Baldus et al. study in detail, it nonetheless concluded that McCleskey had not offered any evidence that indicated that *he* had personally been discriminated against (*McCleskey v. Kemp,* 1987). In other words, the Court decided that even though there may be a relationship between race and the imposition of the death penalty in Georgia, the evidence offered by McCleskey did not prove that he was a victim of racism specifically. McCleskey's death sentence was, therefore, upheld (for an extensive review of the *McCleskey* case, see Baldus, Woodworth, & Pulaski, 1991).

According to the law, a jury's verdict should be based on an impartial review of legally relevant (or evidential) factors that are presented throughout the trial process (Hester & Smith, 1973). As the McCleskey case illustrates, however, it has been argued that certain extra-evidential factors, such as race and socioeconomic status, may play a role in these decisions (for a review of these studies, see Mazzella & Feingold, 1994; Pfeifer, 1990).

Defendant and Victim Race

Although researchers are interested in a variety of extra-evidential factors that may affect juror decision making, it has been argued that no single factor has received as much empirical attention as that of race and its effect on juror decisions (Hagan, 1974). As early as 1941, Johnson (p. 103) argued that, "[t]he administration of justice itself is from beginning to end so much a part of the whole system of Negro-white social relations that it must be viewed not only as a process which discriminates against Negroes ... but also as a direct and indirect causative factor in the production of Negro crime." In essence, Johnson was suggesting that because the courtroom was no different from other aspects of American society in which black individuals are treated differently from white individuals, researchers should not ignore the discriminatory potential of the judicial system (including the jury) when investigating the issue of "black crime." It was not until after the extensive jury study conducted by Kalven and Zeisel (1966), however, that researchers took up the challenge offered by Johnson and began in earnest to examine empirically the role of racism on juror decision making.

Throughout the 1970s and 1980s, a number of studies were conducted that indicated that mock jurors were more likely to treat black defendants differentially in cases ranging from embezzlement to rape and murder (see, e.g., Bernard, 1979; Foley & Chamblin, 1982; Gray & Ashmore, 1976; Ugwuegbu, 1979). Field (1979), for example, found that white mock jurors were significantly more likely to assign a lengthier sentence to a black defendant (in comparison to a white defendant) in a rape trial, especially if the victim was described as white. Similarly, Stephan and Stephan (1986) attempted to examine the effect of defendant race on mock juror decision making by asking Hispanic and non-Hispanic subjects to listen to audiotaped segments of an assault trial and decide on the guilt of a defendant who spoke either English or Spanish. Results indicated that non-Hispanic subjects rated the Spanish-speaking defendant significantly guiltier than Hispanic subjects. Interestingly, this bias in ratings was eliminated when a judge's instruction advised subjects to ignore the fact that the defendant's testimony was translated (for a review of the importance of instructions in jury decision-making studies, see Pfeifer, 1991). The relationship between defendant ethnicity and mock juror decision making was also examined by Pfeifer and Ogloff (1988), who provided English Canadian subjects with a trial transcript (relating sexual assault) in which the defendant was portrayed as either English Canadian, French Canadian, or Native Canadian. Although subjects rated the Native Canadian and French Canadian defendants significantly guiltier than the English Canadian defendant, like the Stephan and Stephan study, this differential disappeared when subjects were provided with jury instructions that outlined their duties and responsibilities.

Although a number of studies such as those described previously appear to indicate a relationship between race and mock juror decision making, a recent article that reviewed over 40 studies conducted between 1972 and 1994 concluded that black defendants were no more likely to be found guilty of committing crimes (Mazzella & Feingold, 1994). A number of social psychologists, however, continue to argue that juror decision making can be adversely affected by a defendant's race because of psychological phenomena such as stereotyping and cognitive representations. Klein and Creech (1982), for example, argue that racially based differences in the decisions of white mock jurors may be due to the fact that subjects tend to distort their evaluation of neutral evidence in favor of white victims when a defendant is black. When the defendant is portrayed as white, however, this distortion does not occur and the result is that mock jurors tend to rate black defendants guiltier than the white defendants.

Ten years later, Dane (1992, p. 33) has expanded on the work of Klein and Creech by suggesting that "when jurors discover that a defendant, victim, or some trial participant is . . . black or white . . . such discovery often results in jurors using stereotypes as filters. . . . That is, jurors' stereotypes about the characteristics of members of a certain group are used to evaluate whether a member of that group could have engaged in the criminal activity in question." In other words, it may be argued that white mock jurors tend to rate black and white defendants differentially because they are employing their stereotypes regarding the relationship between race and crime.

Socioeconomic Status (SES)

As with race, the issue of socioeconomic status has also received a fair amount of empirical attention. Reed (1965), for example, administered self-report question-naires to a sample of Louisiana jurors and found that low-status defendants tended to be treated more harshly than high-status defendants. In an attempt to verify em-pirically the findings of Reed and others, Gleason and Harris (1975), asked 84 white mock jurors to evaluate the guilt of a high- or low-socioeconomic-status defendant charged with armed robbery. Results indicated that subjects rated the lower-SES de-fendant significantly guiltier than the higher-SES defendant. Finally, a review of 20 studies examining the relationship between SES and mock juror decision making in-dicated that defendants portrayed as having a lower SES were rated guiltier than de-fendants portrayed as having a high SES (Mazzella & Feingold, 1994).

According to social psychologists, this differential treatment is linked to stereotypes that individuals hold with regard to lower SES people. For example, while studying actual witnesses in trials, researchers found that lower-SES witnesses were more likely to engage in powerless speech and higher-SES witnesses were more likely to engage in powerful speech (Conley, O'Barr, & Lind, 1978). Based on these observations, Lind, Erikson, and O'Barr (1978) conducted a study in which mock jurors were asked to view videotaped testimony delivered in either a powerful or powerless style and rate the honesty of the testimony. As expected, results indi-cated that testimony delivered in a powerless style was rated more negatively than testimony delivered in a powerful style. Based on these results, the authors suggest that jurors are likely to treat lower-SES defendants differently from high-SES de-fendants because the lower-SES defendants are more likely to employ a powerless speech style.

Future Research

Although it appears that there is an abundance of empirical research that suggests that mock jurors tend to be biased decision makers, the issue is far from resolved. A number of recently published articles have begun to question the external validity of mock juror studies (see, e.g., Bermant, McGuire, McKinley, & Salo, 1974; Pfeifer, 1990; Weiten & Diamond, 1979; Wilson & Donnerstein, 1977). It has been argued that these studies employ a similar methodological procedure in which white college students (mock jurors) are asked either to view a videotape or to read transcript seg-ments of a trial in which the race of the defendant and victim is varied. They are subsequently asked to rate the guilt of the defendant and/or recommend a sentence (Pfeifer, 1990). According to Pfeifer (1990), this standardized experimental procedure detracts from the external validity of results because of a number of factors, including: (a) the primary use of college students as subjects; (b) concentration on aspects of the juror as opposed to the jury; (c) the realism of the situation (subjects in these studies are always aware that their decisions will not have real consequences); (d) the use of measures that do not reflect actual trials (i.e., using scales of guilt or sentencing as a measure of prejudice); and (e) the lack of some important aspect of the trial situation (i.e., instructions opening statements, deliberations).

In an attempt to respond to some of these external validity limitations, researchers have begun to study juror decision making in situations that more readily replicate actual trial situations. For example, in order to more closely examine the role of situational realism on juror decision making, Wilson and Donnerstein (1977) convinced subjects that their decisions would have actual consequences. Subjects were led to believe that a fellow student (described as either attractive or unattractive) had been accused of stealing an examination and that, after reading the facts of the case, their decision would either be used as a basis for dealing with the accused student or would have no effect on the student. Results of this study indicated that the attractiveness level of the student did not play a role in the subjects' decisions for the real conditions but did play a role in the hypothetical conditions. Based on these results, Wilson and Donnerstein (1977, p. 188) suggest that,

> It is clear that we still have not attained the ideal goal of working with real life juries. We have only gone one step closer by including real consequences in the decision-making process. Future research should attempt to move even closer to a true jury setting by establishing the conditions of a true jury simulation with courtroom proceedings etc. while at the same time including real consequences in the decision-making process.

A second possible area of future investigation revolves around the suggestion that research indicating juror bias may simply reflect an experimental illustration of prejudice as opposed to actual discrimination. In other words, it has been suggested that although the previously mentioned studies appear to indicate that mock jurors hold prejudicial attitudes toward certain groups, there is little evidence to suggest that these attitudes are directly related to the discriminatory behaviors of actual jurors (Pfeifer, 1990). Specifically, it has been argued that subjects in laboratory studies are being assessed on their attitudes (or prejudices) as opposed to their behaviors, and as such, it is a large and perilous leap to assume that discriminatory behaviors will naturally follow. In support of this contention, a number of recent studies have reported that mock jurors who are supplied with instructions to guide their decision making do not appear to rate black defendants guiltier than white defendants (Hill & Pfeifer, 1992; Pfeifer, 1991; Pfeifer & Ogloff, 1991). Future research may aid us in better understanding the connection between a prejudicial attitude held by a juror and the discriminatory behavior (i.e., rendering an actual verdict) that may or may not follow.

EXPERT EVIDENCE:
SHOULD A SOCIAL PSYCHOLOGIST PROVIDE EXPERT
TESTIMONY AT A TRIAL?

In 1977, 15-year-old Ronney Zamora was put on trial for killing an 82-year-old woman who returned unexpectedly and caught him in the process of burglarizing her home. At trial Zamora plead not guilty by reason of insanity, explaining that his actions were caused by the fact that he was a "television addict" who had watched so much violent television that he suffered from "involuntary subliminal television intoxication" and was, therefore, unable to distinguish between right and wrong. In an attempt to support his client's plea, Zamora's lawyer requested that the judge allow a local psychologist to describe the scientific literature dealing with the association between television violence and aggression in children (see *Florida v. Zamora*, 1977). After questioning the psychologist, however, the judge decided that her testimony should not be presented to the jury because "she would have been . . . unable to testify that watching television programs to excess affects an individual to the extent that said individual would not be able to distinguish between right and wrong" (*Zamora v. State*, 1978, p. 779). In other words, the judge decided that, regardless of the current social psychological evidence regarding the association between television violence and aggression, the expert would not be unable to testify as to whether excessive television watching caused Zamora to enter into a state of mind in which he could not delineate between right and wrong. Ronney Zamora was ultimately found guilty on all counts and subsequently appealed to the District Court of Appeal of Florida, arguing that the trial judge improperly excluded the psychologist from testifying on the issue of the effect of television violence on adolescent viewers. The District Court, however, found that the testimony was properly excluded and upheld the jury's guilty verdicts (*Zamora v. State*, 1978).

Aside from the obvious social psychological interest (i.e., the relationship between aggression and television violence), the trial of Ronney Zamora is an important one because it illustrates a number of elements that are of current interest to social psychologists who offer expert testimony. Specifically, although social psychologists have taken on the role of expert witness at a rapidly increasing pace, there remain a number of important issues with regard to this role, such as (a) when is it appropriate for social psychologists to give expert testimony; (b) what role should a social psychologist play when giving testimony; and (c) what are the ethical and moral questions involved in giving expert testimony.

The Appropriateness of Expert Testimony

During a trial, witnesses are called to describe any relevant firsthand knowledge (i.e., events they have personally seen or heard) in order to aid the jury in a better understanding of the case. In some trials, however, lawyers may argue that an expert witness is needed in order to explain technical or scientific information to the jury.

Social psychologists have been called upon to testify in areas such as discrimination, conformity, compliance, group dynamics, prison crowding, religious cults, and trademark infringement (Pfeifer & Brigham, 1993). Before testifying, however, an expert witness must be accepted by the court because, unlike other witnesses, an expert may be asked for his or her opinion or inferences regarding the case (Schwitzgebel & Schwitzgebel, 1980).

Over the years, courts have adopted various tests for evaluating whether an expert witness should be allowed to testify. In *Dyas v. United States* (1977), the court suggested a threefold test for deciding whether a jury should hear expert evidence on any given topic, including psychology. According to *Dyas,* an expert may testify if (a) the subject matter to be discussed is so complex or technical that it is beyond the ken of the average person, (b) the witness must be qualified to speak to the issue at hand, and (c) there must be scientific acceptance of the information presented by the witness in his or her field. In other words, a court would be likely to allow a social psychologist to testify about scientific or technical phenomena (i.e., research on aggression, discrimination) if the concepts to be discussed are more than mere common sense, the expert is qualified to speak about the issues, and the testimony is supported by the field of psychology.

In most cases, psychologists are easily able to demonstrate the first two prongs of the test to the court. It was quickly recognized, however, that the important, and controversial, part of the *Dyas* test is found in the ability to illustrate that the testimony given by an expert was "accepted" by the scientific world. The difficulty of proving scientific acceptance of psychological testimony is by no means novel to the courts. In 1923, the D.C. Circuit Court was asked to evaluate whether expert testimony regarding the polygraph was at such a level that it was scientifically accepted (*Frye v. United States,* 1923). In ruling on the issue, the court imposed the now famous Frye test, which stated that, "while courts will go a long way in admitting expert testimony deduced from a well-recognized scientific principle or discovery, the thing from which the deduction is made must be sufficiently established to have gained general acceptance in the particular field in which it belongs" (p. 1014). Although various courts have gone on to suggest that the scientific acceptance of testimony may be established through avenues such as scientific writings or previous judicial opinions (see, e.g., *New Jersey v. Cavallo,* 1982), a number of other courts have begun to abandon the Frye test in favor of evaluating expert testimony in terms of its probative value (i.e., will the testimony aid the jury in making the appropriate decision?) as documented by Rules 401–403 and 702–704 of the U.S. Federal Rules of Evidence (Bureau of National Affairs, 1975).

Regardless of the legal standard that is employed by any given court to evaluate expert testimony, there remain numerous controversies within the field of psychology itself regarding whether a scientific foundation exists for psychologists to testify. Konecni and Ebbesen (1986) suggest that even though courts have often allowed psychologists to testify in trials involving eyewitness testimony, the scientific understanding of actual eyewitnesses is still relatively low. Similarly, Morse (1990) argues that recent attempts to introduce testimony suggesting a psychological self-defense for homicide in cases involving battered spouses employs unacceptably soft science and contains core concepts that are vague and lack rigorous empirical support. Interestingly, the court in *Zamora* did not comment on the scientific reliability of the psychologist's claim that there is a relationship between violent television viewing and aggression in children, but rather it suggested that the expert would be unable to testify to the central question in an insanity plea (i.e., does excessive violent television viewing lead to an inability to distinguish between right and wrong?).

The Role of Expert Witnesses

Once an expert has been accepted by a court, however, there remain a number of other issues that relate to the actual testimony that occur. Chief among these is the decision that each expert makes regarding his or her role in the courtroom. According to a number of psychologists, there are at least two major issues that surround the role of an expert: advocacy versus education and ultimate issue testimony.

The first issue is whether an expert witness perceives him- or herself as either an *educator* who has been asked to objectively explain psychological phenomena to the jury in an impartial fashion or as an *advocate* who has been retained to present psychological information in a fashion that may involve "clever editing, selecting, shading, exaggerating, or glossing over" (Saks, 1990, p. 296). One of the major questions regarding this issue is whether experts such as social psychologists have a duty or obligation to inform the judge and jury about possible limitations of their studies when testifying in court. The confusion over this issue is illustrated by the results of a survey of nonclinical psychologists who engage in expert testimony. Specifically, the results of this survey indicate that,

> [L]ike most psychologists, [the] respondents appear to agree in principle that psychologists have a responsibility to point out research limitations when presenting limitations to the court. What is less clear, however, is how far that responsibility extends and to whom it extends. . . . That is, does the psychologist have a responsibility to present the possible limitations of his or her work to only the attorney who has retained them, or does that responsibility extend to the judge/jury and opposing counsel? (Pfeifer & Brigham, 1993, p. 340)

Regardless of whether an expert serves as an educator or advocate, he or she must also decide whether to provide *ultimate issue testimony*. Ultimate issue testimony occurs when an expert not only presents a psychological model or theory to the court, but also testifies as to whether a specific individual represents an example of the phenomenon. In the *Zamora* case, the psychologist was retained by the defense to describe the social psychological literature on media and aggression. However, had the psychologist gone on to testify that Ronney Zamora was legally insane because of his excessive viewing of violent television, she would have been engaging in ultimate testimony.

According to Slobogin (1989), the ultimate issue question is a particularly thorny one for psychologists because the courts are often looking for ultimate issue testimony from experts. For example, in the *McCleskey* case (described earlier), even though the U.S. Supreme Court referred to the fact that the study conducted by Baldus et al. (1985) indicated a discrepancy that appeared to correlate with race, it was quick to point out that McCleskey did not offer any evidence to suggest that he, personally, was a victim of racial discrimination. This desire on the part of the courts to encourage ultimate issue testimony is often supplemented by the fact that some psychologists may view themselves as "imperial experts" who may ignore or disregard scientific evidence in favor of their own best guess (Saks, 1990).

Therefore, once a social psychologist decides to testify as an expert witness, he or she must be prepared to decide whether to take on the role of an educator or an advocate. In addition, the social psychologist must be prepared to deal with pressure from attorneys as well as judges to comment on ultimate issue testimony. These decisions are not easy ones to make and may lead to a number of ethical or moral dilemmas (see Box 9–2).

Future Research

The issues surrounding the ethical dilemmas that social psychologists may face as expert witnesses will only continue to grow as courts increasingly seek their input about research, models, and theories. As such, it is highly probable that this issue will continue to attract increased attention in the future. One area that appears to be increasingly researched revolves around the impact of an expert witness who is court appointed, as opposed to being retained by one party in the case. This issue is an important one because psychologists are increasingly being encouraged to play the role of an educator rather than an advocate when testifying in court. However, a number of legal scholars are concerned that a court-appointed expert may hold more sway with jurors and may therefore cause an imbalance in the traditional adversarial system. In order to address this question, a number of studies have recently been conducted to investigate the effect that adversarial versus nonadversarial testimony has on the decision making of mock jurors. For example, one study indicated that the testimony of court-appointed experts (i.e., nonadversarial) did not negatively impact the decision making of mock jurors in comparison to the traditional adversarial testimony employed by the courts (Brekke, Enko, Clavet, & Seelau, 1991). The authors are quick to point out, however, that although their results indicate that court-appointed experts do not appear to unduly affect mock juror decision making, "[f]uture research should examine other types of non-adversarial expert evidence . . . that might exert a different influence on jury decision making" (p. 473).

In addition to this line of research, psychologists are also examining the effect that specific expert testimony may have on mock juror decision making. Schuller (1992) asked mock jurors to read a trial transcript of a homicide in which a wife was accused of killing her abusive husband. In order to examine the impact of Battered Spouse Syndrome (BSS) testimony on decision making, subjects were presented with no expert testimony, general expert testimony regarding BSS, or specific expert

| Box 9–2 | **Ethical Dilemmas and the Expert Witness** |

Social psychologists who appear as expert witnesses may face a multitude of additional ethical and moral dilemmas. For example, the results of a recent survey of nonclinical forensic witnesses found that psychologists who testified in court were concerned with ethical issues. These included (a) the possibility that the legal system may misuse expert testimony to suit its own needs; (b) the dilemma one faces when one is retained to represent a client who he or she believes is guilty or at least morally culpable; and (c) ethical considerations associated with being remunerated for one's testimony (Pfeifer & Brigham, 1993).

One area of ethical concern for social psychologists who act as expert witnesses is the psychologist's ability or desire to testify to "the truth, *the whole truth,* and nothing but the truth" when on the witness stand. Given that the courtroom is an adversarial arena, lawyers do not ordinarily allow an expert witness to testify about everything they may know regarding a theory or model. In other words, expert witnesses are not simply asked to present their entire knowledge regarding a psychological phenomenon (i.e., supporting research as well as refuting research) but are generally constrained by the questions the lawyers ask. For example, had the psychologist been allowed to testify in the *Zamora* case, the defense lawyer would have questioned her about research indicating a connection between television violence and aggressive behavior. The defense lawyer would not have questioned the psychologist about research that does not support this connection or weaknesses in the model, even though the expert is certainly aware of this information. Therefore, unless the prosecuting attorney asks questions regarding these issues, the psychologist would not be able to tell the court "the whole truth" about the violent television/aggression theory, even if she wanted to.

A number of suggestions have been offered for dealing with the ethical dilemmas a social psychologist may face when engaging in expert testimony. To begin with, psychologists may turn to the ethical guidelines provided by various professional associations such as the American Psychological Association (1992) and the Canadian Psychological Association (1991) for general principles of conduct. Because these formal guidelines do not address specific concerns of expert witnesses, however, a set of "Specialty Guidelines for Forensic Psychologists" (Committee on Ethical Guidelines for Forensic Psychologists, 1991) was created. Although these guidelines provide additional information regarding ethical dilemmas faced by expert witnesses, research indicates that a large percentage of individuals who engage in expert testimony are either unaware of the guidelines or find them inapplicable to many situations (Pfeifer & Brigham, 1993). Therefore, because the individual psychologist is often left on his or her own to resolve the ethical dilemmas that occur within the context of testifying as an expert witness, a number of individuals have suggested alternative resources, such as using moral reasoning (Goldman, 1986) and providing lawyers with a clear understanding of one's position before being retained (Hollien, 1990).

testimony in which the witness supplemented the general testimony with an opinion that the defendant was representative of an individual who was suffering from BSS. Results of this study suggest that mock jurors are more likely to incorporate the BSS testimony into their decision making if it is specifically related to the defendant by the expert.

These findings illustrate at least two important points for future research on expert testimony. First, there is a possibility that the use of specific expert testimony may lead to prejudice against some defendants (Gabora, Spanos, & Joab, 1993). For example, although mock jurors appeared to have been more lenient toward a defendant if she was identified as suffering from BSS in the Schuller study, one wonders whether subjects would be similarly inclined to be lenient if the defendant were a male on trial for sexual assault who claimed that he was suffering from post-traumatic stress disorder. Future research may illustrate whether mock juror decision making is equally affected by specific expert testimony for all cases or for only select cases. Second, the use of specific expert testimony may be viewed as an illustration of ultimate issue testimony (see previous discussion). That is, psychologists may have to decide when and if the criticisms levied against the use of ultimate issue testimony are outweighed by the value of specifically indicating how a defendant fits a psychological category such as BSS or post-traumatic stress syndrome.

JURY INSTRUCTIONS:
WHAT ROLE DOES THE JUDGE'S INSTRUCTION
PLAY IN A JURY'S VERDICT?

In 1985, 75-year-old Roswell Gilbert was arrested and charged with murdering his 73-year-old wife, Emily. During trial testimony, the jury learned that Emily was suffering from osteoporosis (an incurable degenerative bone disease) and had pleaded with her husband on a number of occasions to put an end to her suffering. As a result of her unbearable pain and constant pleading for relief, Gilbert loaded his gun and shot his wife twice in the back of the head. Pleading not guilty at trial, Gilbert stated that he was simply doing what was best for his wife. The jury returned a verdict of guilty of first-degree murder. Later interviews with jurors indicated that even though there may have been extenuating circumstances, they were constrained by the law as described to them in the jury instructions.

The trial of Roswell Gilbert, at least anecdotally, represents the importance jury instructions may play in the trial process. As in the Gilbert trial, after the presentation of evidence and closing arguments, jurors are provided with *charging instructions,* which traditionally contain four segments (Tanford, 1990). First, jurors are provided with introductory instructions, which describe their role as the fact-finders (e.g., they evaluate witness credibility, act impartially). Second, jurors are informed of the basic procedures that should guide their decision making (e.g., presumption of innocence, burden of proof, and defining reasonable doubt). Third, jurors are provided with the substantive law relevant to the case at hand (e.g., the definition of first-degree murder or fraud). Finally, jurors are provided with a set of cautionary instructions that attempt to clarify how certain types of testimony can be reliably evaluated (e.g., eyewitness testimony, testimony based on hypnosis). Interestingly, although a trial always contains a jury instruction, or charge, many studies examining mock juror decision making omit this element (Pfeifer, 1990). Recently, however, psychologists and others have begun to take more of an interest in the role that instructions might play in the trial process. Three areas that have attracted considerable attention recently are *jury nullification, instruction comprehension,* and the *timing of instructions.*

Jury Nullification

Although jurors are generally faced with the job of trying to apply a legal principle with which they agree (e.g., robbery, murder), in some cases jurors may be asked to deliberate on a trial in which they are unsure about whether the application of the law in the specific case best serves the public interest. For example, few jurors would have trouble applying the law regarding murder (as explained to them in the judge's charge) to a case in which a young man walks up to someone he does not like and shoots that person in the head. The direct application of the laws regarding murder, however, may not be as easily applied in cases of euthanasia, such as that in the Gilbert case described earlier. In essence, although jurors believe in the spirit of the law, there are cases (i.e., abortion, euthanasia) in which the simple application of the law may go against perceived community standards. In such cases, juries have an inherent right to nullify, or ignore, the law and find a defendant not guilty even though he or she may be blatantly guilty according to the letter of the law.

Although a jury has a right to nullification, courts have historically been reluctant to inform a jury of this right on the basis that it is common knowledge and, as such, there is no need to convey the information during the instructions (see, e.g., *United States v. Dougherty,* 1972). (The exceptions to this position are juries in Indiana and Maryland, which receive the nullification instruction.) A number of legal scholars and social psychologists disagree with this position, however, and argue that the right of nullification is not common knowledge and should be told to a jury because it might significantly impact juror decision making. In order to test this hypothesis, Horowitz (1988) conducted a study in which subjects were presented with trial information about a murder case, a euthanasia case, or a case in which a drunk driver hit and killed an individual. In addition, subjects were provided with a set of standard instructions, nullification instructions (similar to those employed in Maryland), or radical nullification instructions (proposed by Van Dyke, 1970). Results indicated that the radical instruction appeared to significantly impact subjects. Specifically, subjects who received the radical instruction were more likely than subjects who received the standard instruction to vote for acquittal in the euthanasia case. This finding has recently been replicated by Pfeifer, Brigham, and Robinson (in press), who found that a nullification instruction significantly decreased the guilt rating of a defendant in a euthanasia case similar to the Gilbert case.

Although the Horowitz study indicates that the inclusion of a nullification instruction significantly impacts mock juror decision making in certain cases such as euthanasia, it may also provide us with an illustration of the importance of instruction comprehension. Specifically, it may be argued that the radical nullification instruction employed by Horowitz was more effective because it clearly informed jurors about the right of nullification, whereas the standard nullification instruction informed jurors of this right in a less clear fashion. This issue is discussed in more detail next.

Instruction Comprehension

In addition to the insight regarding mock juror decision making, the nullification research discussed earlier raises a point of interest in terms of a juror's ability to understand the instructions that are given to him or her by the judge. Specifically, research in this area has traditionally employed either a standard nullification instruction or a radical nullification. The major distinction between the two sets of instructions revolves around the explicitness with which the nullification right is explained. The standard nullification instruction informs jurors of their right to accept or reject the judge's instructions and apply the law as they understand it; the radical instruction explicitly informs subjects that they have the right to disregard the law in this case if they believe that it would be inappropriate to apply it. One might argue that the effectiveness of the radical nullification instruction found in the Horowitz (1988) study may be attributed to the simple fact that subjects can understand or comprehend this type of instruction.

Unlike the radical nullification instruction, however, it appears that a substantial number of jurors find pattern jury instructions difficult to understand. Specifically, research indicates that jurors have a difficult time understanding specific instructions regarding reasonable doubt (e.g., Severence & Loftus, 1982), presumption of innocence (e.g., Strawn & Buchanan, 1976), and elements of substantive law (e.g., Borgida & Park, 1988). According to Tanford (1990), juror confusion is caused by lawyers who are attempting to draft instructions that are "legally precise." This legal precision, however, leads to terminology and phrasing that is incomprehensible to the average juror. In order to rectify this situation, Tanford (1990) lists 10 guidelines suggested by psycholinguists to increase juror comprehension of instructions by eliminating many of the grammatically confusing elements. This grammatical confusion is illustrated by the typical instruction that is currently given to jurors to help them determine proximate cause, "[w]hen I use the words 'proximate cause' I mean, first, that there must have been a connection between the conduct of the defendant which the plaintiff claims was negligent, and the injury complained of by the plaintiff, and second, that the occurrence which is claimed to have produced the injury was a natural and probable result of such conduct of the defendant" (Kassin & Wrightsman, 1988, p. 150). In addition, Tanford (1990) suggests that juror confusion might also be decreased through the use of concrete examples of legal concepts that could be specifically applied to the case at hand.

Timing of Instructions

Another area of direct interest to social psychologists involves the issue of when instructions should be given to the jury. Although social psychologists have long been interested in the effect of serial positioning on the formation of attitudes, researchers are only now beginning to look at the effect of the timing of instructions on juror decision making. Traditionally, U.S. and Canadian courts instruct the jury as to its duty at the conclusion of the trial. However, researchers interested in human cognitive processing have begun to argue that jurors would be more efficient and effective decision makers if they were supplied with instructions to guide their decisions at the beginning of the trial as well as at the end (Tanford, 1990). Specifically, it has been argued that providing jurors with preliminary instructions allows them to create a cognitive schema or framework to process the subsequent evidence presented to them (Kassin & Wrightsman, 1988).

Although the argument for preliminary instructions has received empirical support (see, e.g., Elwork, Sales, & Alfini, 1977; Kassin & Wrightsman, 1979), other studies have found that preliminary instructions do not significantly affect the decision making of mock jurors (see, e.g., Cruse & Brown, 1987). Given this discrepancy in results, as well as the current penchant of social psychologists to investigate the cognitive processes involved in social decision making, it is likely that this area of investigation will continue to provide a fertile ground for future research.

Future Research

Future research may be aimed toward a number of areas. First, in terms of the research on the nullification instruction, one study suggests that this may be a double-edged sword. Although it appears that informing the jury of its right to nullify may lead to a more just verdict, it also appears that knowledge of the right to nullify may lead to increases in discriminatory decision making (Hill & Pfeifer, 1992). Specifically, these authors found that mock jurors were more likely to rate a black defendant guilty than a white defendant if they were provided with a nullification instruction that allowed them to resort to their prejudicial attitudes. Given this result, future research may investigate how a nullification instruction may be implemented effectively without allowing for prejudicial decision making.

In addition, Tanford (1990) suggests that future research on juror comprehension of instructions should examine whether supplying jurors with written instructions would be more effective than simply providing oral instructions. Research on the social psychology of communication indicates that individuals are more able to comprehend complex information when it is written as opposed to verbalized. Given that jury instructions often involve complex information, future research might investigate whether supplying jurors with a written copy of the instructions would increase their effectiveness.

SUMMARY

It is clear that the movement toward integrating law and psychology that began early in this century will continue into the next century. Social psychologists, in particular, are increasingly being invited to enter into the world of law and psychology because our discipline, by its very nature, addresses a large number of issues that are of interest to judges and lawyers. This chapter has attempted to review some of the areas to which social psychologists have traditionally contributed as well as areas that future research might address. The reader will note that each of the sections in this chapter clearly begin with a question that might be answered by social psychological models, theories, and research. The reader will also note, however, that no clear answer is provided for those questions. This omission should not be taken as an indication that social psychologists have not taken up the call to answer these questions. Rather, the lack of an answer to these questions represents the fact that social psychology, like the law, is a continually evolving science that requires continual reexamination and refinement in order to fully understand human behavior. This process of continual evolution was recognized by Slesinger and Pilpel (1929, p. 683) in their article on the newly emerging field of legal psychology: "[S]ystematic analysis of the gross behavior of people in legal situations is the important first step. The testing of hypotheses, uncovered by this analysis either in the field of judicial behavior or any other, is the next indicated step. This unpopular, unspectacular research needs encouragement because it is fundamental but exceedingly slow in coming to fruition." The journey toward a complete understanding of human behavior in legal situations, begun almost 65 years ago, may not be complete, but social psychologists have certainly made significant strides in our comprehension of courtroom dynamics.

SUGGESTED READINGS

Anderson, P. R., & Winfree, L. T. (Eds.). (1987). *Expert witnesses*. New York: University of New York Press.

> This book contains a number of chapters that discuss various elements related to the use of social science experts in trials. In addition to reviewing a number of potential ethical and moral dilemmas that an expert witness might face, the authors discuss the possible misuses of scientific knowledge by the courts as well as the scholarly obligations of the witnesses.

Hans, V. P., & Vidmar, N. (1986). *Judging the jury*. New York: Plenum Press.

> This book critically examines a number of social psychological processes related to jury decision making. In addition to reviewing research on issues such as jury composition and jury biases, the authors briefly present psychological and legal histories that relate to their discussions.

Kalven, H., & Zeisal, H. (1966). *The American jury*. Chicago: University of Chicago Press.

> This book is considered by many to represent one of the premier psychological analyses of juries and their verdicts. In addition to reviewing past research on various aspects of jury decision making, this book also includes a number of original studies conducted by the authors that continue to be cited today.

Saks, M. J., & Hastie, R. (1978). *Social psychology in court*. New York: Van Nostrand Reinhold.

> This book reviews much of the early work investigating the various social psychological phenomena that occur within the confines of the courtroom. Aside from describing a number of elements related to juries, the authors review other important aspects of the courtroom, such as the social psychological impact of lawyer presentation styles.

10 Consumer Behavior

Nancy D. Rhodes
Texas A&M University

Three weeks before graduation, Eileen's parents announced that they were giving her a wonderful graduation present: a new car! Eileen was thrilled, and in spite of a heavy load of finals, immediately began trying to decide what car she wanted to buy. Eileen vaguely remembered seeing a car ad recently that featured a good-looking football player. The car in the ad looked sporty and fun, so she decided to take one for a test drive. She liked the car but thought she should get more information about other models in her price range. She visited a number of car dealerships, picked up information packets, and test-drove a number of vehicles. When car ads came on TV, Eileen dropped everything and listened carefully to the claims made in the ads.

As time for graduation got closer, Eileen spent more time talking to her friends and parents about the cars she was interested in. Her parents were especially concerned that she find a car with advanced safety features. Her friends wanted her to get something really sporty. Eileen began to feel a bit overwhelmed by all the information she had gathered. She also found it kind of frustrating to try to make sense of all the technical jargon, especially since she was also extremely busy studying for finals. The day she needed to make her decision, she took her boyfriend with her to see her two favorite cars. He didn't like the model she had at the top of her list—the one from the TV ad with the foot-

> ball player. He had a number of good reasons for thinking it was not as good as the other model. After considering the points he made, Eileen decided to go with his recommendation.

The situation described here illustrates the intersection of marketing and social psychology. Attention to ads, memory for ads, evaluation of product choices, and even consideration of the opinions of significant others all have been shown to affect consumers' behavior in the marketplace. Over the last three decades, researchers in the areas of social psychology and consumer behavior have studied the effects of persuasive appeals (in this context, advertisements) on attitudes toward products and on subsequent purchase of those products. Social psychology has contributed a great deal to the study of consumer behavior, particularly in understanding how consumers process information in advertisements and how the processing of that information affects purchase decisions.

This chapter reviews the research on consumer behavior that draws on social psychological theories of persuasion and social influence. As a starting point, the chapter reviews some of the important social psychological theories of attitude change. The early theories placed a heavy emphasis on *processing* the content of the ad. Later modifications to this line of research placed a greater emphasis on the amount of *thinking* an ad generated. The chapter next considers whether attitude change is really the basis for purchase behavior. Other goals to behavior—for example, an intention to purchase something or prior purchasing behavior—may be more important than attitudes. Additionally, the chapter examines the social context in which purchase decisions are made. The opinions of people important to a purchaser may affect the purchase decision. The chapter reviews work that describes how this social influence occurs. Finally, the chapter touches briefly on the social policy implications of consumer research and reviews the major methodological concerns of both academic and applied researchers in consumer psychology.

THE EMPHASIS ON PERSUASION

At the heart of marketing techniques is the desire to change consumers' attitudes about a product. Going back to the opening vignette, marketers assume that if Eileen has a positive attitude toward a particular car, she will purchase it. (Later sections of the chapter discuss whether advertising really produces attitude change, and whether attitudes really do influence purchasing behavior.) Indeed, research indicates that the persuasiveness of an advertisement is the key to increased sales (Blair & Rosenberg, 1994; Rosenberg & Blair, 1994). Much of advertising, therefore, is directed toward establishing a favorable attitude toward a particular brand name. Marketing research has drawn heavily from the rich history of attitude change research in social psychology (Maloney, 1994). The attitude change theories that are currently generating the greatest interest in consumer research are concerned with how consumers process information in a persuasive appeal.

In the most general sense, persuasion theories are concerned with *"who* says *what* . . . to *whom* [emphasis added] with what effect?" (Lasswell, 1948, p. 37). In persuasion research, the "who" is generally the *source* of the communication, the "what" is the *content* of the message, and the "whom" is the message recipient, or the *target* of the persuasive appeal. The types of persuasion situations that have been considered in social psychology are quite broad. For example, a newspaper editorial, an argument with one's spouse, and a child's whining can all be defined as persuasive messages. In the more narrow context of this chapter, the source is generally a salesperson or a spokesperson in an advertisement, the message is the sales pitch or the advertisement, and the recipient is the consumer.

THE MESSAGE-PROCESSING APPROACH

In the 1950s and 1960s, a great deal of work was conducted on how learning affects attitudes and persuasion (Hovland, Janis, & Kelley, 1953; Janis et al., 1959; McGuire, 1968, 1985). These ideas were also applied to advertising. The dominant model in the 1960s assumed that consumers must *attend to, comprehend,* and then *yield* to the claims in an ad for attitude change to occur (Alwitt & Mitchell, 1985; Maloney, 1994). Furthermore, if attitude change is to affect purchase behavior, the ad must be remembered and acted upon (e.g., Bettman, 1986; Keller, 1993). Each step must be completed in turn, or the ad will not result in increased sales.

The Role of Attention

What if an advertiser were to broadcast an ad, and no one listened? Advertisers have been aware of the obviously important role of *attention* in persuasion for a long time (e.g., Bettman, 1979; Rossiter & Percy, 1987; Wright & Bostio, 1983). Researchers in advertising and consumer psychology have identified a number of features of ads that make them more likely to be attended to. Attention is more likely when the intensity of the stimulus is high. For example, bright colors and loud sounds generate greater attention than ads having less intense features (Solomon, 1992). Distinctive ads are most likely to attract attention. To the extent that an ad's intensity, color, and size differ greatly from other ads, it will get attention (Andrews, Akhter, Durvasula, & Muehling, 1992). Visually complex stimuli attract attention, particularly in print advertisements for which the consumer controls the exposure time (Solomon, 1992). The relevance of the ad is also important. If an ad or product is personally relevant, consumers are more likely to attend (Engel, Blackwell, & Miniard, 1986). Finally, magazine ads that contain sexually suggestive pictures of attractive women have been shown to increase men's attention (Reid & Soley, 1983).

If advertisers are to be successful in attracting attention to their ads, they must overcome *advertising clutter* (Cobb, 1985; Ray & Webb, 1986). Consumers are continuously bombarded with a tremendous amount of advertising. One recent analysis indicated that television viewers encounter more than 20 commercials in an hour of viewing prime-time TV, and approximately 37 ads per hour in daytime (American Association of Advertising Agencies and the Association of National Advertisers, 1991). As an advertiser, getting your message across in such a cluttered environment poses significant challenges. Consumers are capable of processing only so much information before experiencing sensory overload. Studies have demonstrated a clear reduction in attention, recall for ad claims, and persuasion when consumers have been exposed to greater numbers of ads (Mord & Gilson, 1985; Webb & Ray, 1979).

How do you get your ads noticed in an environment that is already saturated with ads? One strategy is to purchase a large block of advertising in a medium to dominate the consumer's attention. Advertisers using this strategy might place ads on consecutive pages in a magazine or have a number of consecutive billboards along the highway devoted to their messages (Solomon, 1992). Another strategy is to place ads in unusual places. Possibly the most unusual example to date is that a well-known canned soup company placed ads in church bulletins (Foltz, 1985).

In negotiating for advertising time and space, advertisers must concern themselves with more than just the total number of ads being presented. They must also worry specifically about what else is being advertised. One study demonstrated that the effects of other ads are made worse when the clutter is made up of the ads for competing products; this is known as *competitive clutter* (Kent, 1993). When many ads for similar products are aired, consumers seem to have difficulty differentiating the ad claims (Burke & Srull, 1988; Keller, 1991). In television advertising, whether the ad airs on one of the major networks or on a cable channel can be a strong determinant of the amount of clutter the ad encounters. A recent analysis indicated that the largest source of competitive clutter was on cable channels where advertisers of specialized products compete for the attention of a select group of consumers (Mandese, 1993).

Recent technological innovations have presented new challenges to advertisers. Widespread use of remote control devices for televisions has created the problem of *zapping* commercials, that is, changing the channel during commercial breaks (Kaplan, 1985). Furthermore, the use of videotape recorders has made possible the practice of *zipping,* or applying the fast-forward function on the remote control to zip past ads. Although it seems obvious that both zipping and zapping would reduce the effectiveness of ads, recent studies have indicated that the overall effects are not as bad as initially feared. Zufryden, Pedrick, and Sankaralingam (1993) demonstrated that zapped ads may actually be more effective than nonzapped ads. Apparently, the act of zapping draws enought attention to the TV that consumers are able to process ad claims. Similarly, Gilmore and Secunda (1993) have demonstrated that zipping of ads that have been seen previously can actually enhance brand recall. It appears that viewers actually have to pay closer attention to the ad while zipping, so that they will not miss the point at which the program begins again. This level of attention to the fast-forwarded images translates to processing of some brand-related information, particularly if the ad features a static image (Harvey & Rothe, 1985; Reiss, 1986).

The Role of Comprehension

If advertisers are going to get consumers to buy their products, they must craft messages that can be understood and remembered. So, all things being equal, *comprehension* should be an important part of persuasion. Certainly, early models of persuasion placed a great deal of importance on the comprehension of persuasive messages (e.g., McGuire, 1985) . But the evidence in support of comprehension as a vital process in persuasion is not so clear. Typically, comprehension has been measured by a person's *memory* for a given ad. If learning and understanding the content of a message are important parts of persuasion, then logically one would expect that people who demonstrate strong memory for an advertisement would also be the most influenced by it. However, efforts to link memory for a persuasive appeal to attitude change have resulted in mixed support for the message-learning position (see Cook & Flay, 1978; Eagly & Chaiken, 1993, for reviews).

One reason for this lack of support has to do with the quality of the arguments that a person might be able to call to mind, both at the time of attitude formation and, later, at the time of recall. When a recipient processes product-relevant claims in an ad, it is likely that only the strong arguments result in attitude change. However, when asked to remember the ad claims at a later time, the person is likely to recall both strong and weak arguments. Therefore, even if you recall a large number of product claims, you might not be persuaded if most of the claims you remember are weak (see Petty, Unnava, & Strathman, 1991), and this would attenuate the recall-attitude change relationship. Chattopadhyay and Alba (1988) improved on the ability to predict attitude change from memory for message content by taking into account both the number of messages recalled and the strength of the recalled arguments. Recall of more relatively strong than weak arguments results in greater persuasion than recall of more relatively weak than strong arguments.

Support for the memory-persuasion relation was obtained in a recent study of ad recall (Unnava, Burnkrant, & Erevelles, 1994). Subjects read or listened to ads containing both strong and weak arguments. The order of arguments was varied so that some subjects received the strong arguments first and others received weak arguments first. Overall, recall of more strong than weak arguments led to more positive attitudes toward the product (in this case, a book bag). Also, the arguments that were recalled first had the strongest relation to attitude. It was found that the order of presentation of the arguments was important in the messages presented auditorily, but not in written format: For auditory messages, the arguments presented first were remembered better than arguments presented later. Thus, when strong arguments are presented first in an auditory message, attitudes are more positive than when weak arguments are presented first.

Thus, there is some recent evidence that message comprehension, as measured by recall of message arguments, is related to persuasion. A major shortcoming of most of the work evaluating message comprehension is that the settings in which many persuasion studies have taken place are constructed to obtain unusually high levels of comprehension. Because most persuasion researchers want to ensure good comprehension of the information, most such studies are conducted in laboratory settings with college students as subjects, with simplistic messages, and with few distractions. Therefore, virtually all subjects demonstrate nearly perfect comprehension of the material, making it impossible to find a relation between comprehension and persuasion. In the real world, however, attention is not constrained, messages are not uniformly simple, and people are not uniformly able to process them. When material is presented in a real-world setting, such as a shopping mall, comprehension is dramatically reduced (Jacoby & Hoyer, 1987). One study estimated that approximately 30% of televised communication (program content as well as advertising) is miscomprehended by the general public (Jacoby & Hoyer, 1982). There is clearly a need to investigate persuasion effects in contexts that more closely mimic real-world settings if the true effects of attention and comprehension are to be understood (see Eagly & Chaiken, 1993).

The message-learning perspective provided an important step in understanding how processing of persuasive messages affects persuasion. Work based on this perspective has focused primarily on the early part of the process of persuasion, especially those factors that facilitate or inhibit attention and comprehension. A basic assumption of this work is that consumers are active and rational processors of ad claims. The Elaboration Likelihood Model focuses on the thought processes underlying attitude change, with a greater emphasis on the consumer as a cognitive miser. The model acknowledges that there are some circumstances when careful processing of ad claims is unlikely and provides a framework for understanding the consequences of both careful and careless processing in persuasion.

THE ELABORATION LIKELIHOOD MODEL

The *elaboration likelihood model,* or ELM, is concerned with predicting the conditions under which message recipients are likely to think about, or cognitively elaborate on, persuasive arguments presented to them (Petty & Cacioppo, 1986; see also the *heuristic/systematic model,* Chaiken, 1987). There are two processing routes that recipients can take when they are exposed to a persuasive appeal: the central route and the peripheral route. According to this model, the likelihood that a recipient will evaluate persuasive arguments carefully depends on his or her motivation and ability to do so at that moment.

When people use the *central route* to persuasion, they carefully evaluate the content of the message. They think about the statements that the advertisement makes about the product and generate thoughts that reflect the careful processing. When using the central route, people are good at picking out the strong arguments and they quickly dismiss the weak ones. If asked to report on their thoughts while processing the message, recipients using central processing generate thoughts that are favorable to the message if the message is strong, and they generate thoughts unfavorable to the message if the message is weak. Because of this message-relevant elaboration, recipients processing centrally are persuaded by strong messages, but not by weak messages.

What prompts people to process a message centrally? People typically use the central route when they are *highly motivated* to evaluate a message, for example when they anticipate making a large purchase in the near future. For example, in the vignette at the beginning of the chapter, Eileen did not process car ads centrally until her parents told her they would buy her one. Prior to knowing that a car was in her near future, Eileen had processed the ads only to the extent of noticing the good-looking football player. Once Eileen knew that she was about to purchase a car, she thought more carefully about the television commercials. For example, she became more concerned with claims that the car has advanced safety features and a quiet ride. In central processing, consumers evaluate the statements according to information they already possess and decide whether the statements are convincing.

Consumers also must have the *ability* to process the message in order to do so using the central route. That is, they must have enough time, few distractions, and the basic intelligence required to read, understand, and think about the ad. Recall from the vignette that Eileen began to feel unable to process the information about the cars because of pressures related to studying for finals. This lack of ability to evaluate carefully all of the features of the cars resulted in Eileen basing her decision on the recommendation of her boyfriend—an example of persuasion through the *peripheral route.*

If a recipient lacks sufficient motivation or ability to process the message carefully, the recipient will rely on peripheral cues or heuristics to make a judgment as to whether the message position is valid. *Peripheral cues* typically found in ads are anything other than substantive arguments that might generate a favorable impression. In the earlier example, the advertiser used a popular sport figure to present the information about a car. Alternatively, an ad might have happy music playing in the background, or a well-known expert might be the spokesperson. A somewhat different type of peripheral processing occurs when recipients rely on *heuristics* in memory, such as "experts are generally correct" (Chaiken, 1980; Eagly & Chaiken, 1993). Heuristics are simple decision rules that message recipients rely on to simplify the process of making judgments. Thus, if a television viewer watches an ad in which an expert is extolling the virtues of a particular diet product, the viewer can make a quick judgment that the product is probably good, without having to carefully evaluate the information.

Peripheral processing is likely when people are rushed, uninvolved, or otherwise not interested in paying careful attention to advertising. Recipients processing peripherally tend to evaluate the message in general terms, do not process the quality of the arguments, and make an overall judgment based on their reaction to the strongest peripheral cues. Attitude change resulting from peripheral processing tends to be less long-lasting and does not predict behavior as well as attitude change produced through central processing.

An example of research testing this model was conducted by Andrews and Shimp (1990) using mock beer ads as the persuasive stimuli. The researchers manipulated the subjects' level of involvement in the message by promising half the subjects a sample of the beer (high involvement), whereas the other half of the subjects were not promised a gift (low involvement). The attractiveness of the source was also manipulated. Half of the subjects saw an ad with an attractively dressed couple enjoying the beer; the other half of the subjects saw an ad with the same couple dressed unattractively. Finally, the quality of the arguments was varied. Some subjects read strong reasons to drink the new reduced-alcohol beer (e.g., "Break is a smart choice for those times when you want to relax without becoming intoxicated"), and some subjects read weak reasons (e.g., "Break has been designed with the beer drinker in mind"). Subjects in the high-involvement condition generated more thoughts about the message content than low-involvement subjects and were more persuaded by strong than weak arguments. Furthermore, the low-involvement subjects generated more thoughts relative to the source than high-involvement subjects and were more persuaded by the attractive than the unattractive source. The results of the study are highly supportive of the ELM: High involvement in the product resulted in central processing and persuasion based on careful consideration of the message content; low involvement resulted in peripheral processing and persuasion based on the peripheral cue of source attractiveness.

Many features of the persuasion context have been tested to evaluate their effects on processing of persuasive messages. Of greatest concern are the characteristics of the source, message, or recipient. Because these variables have been demonstrated to affect processing and persuasion, they deserve careful consideration.

Source Effects

Sports heroes and celebrities are in high demand to endorse products in advertising. Clearly, advertisers believe that associating a successful and well-liked person with their product will boost sales. A positive impression of a celebrity endorser can affect the image consumers form of the product (Walker, Langmeyer, & Langmeyer, 1993). According to persuasion theories such as the ELM, an attractive spokesperson should serve as a peripheral cue when processing motivation is low and should enhance product evaluation. As processing motivation and ability increase, source characteristics can serve as central cues. That is, an attractive or credible source can prompt the recipient to believe that the message has value and should be processed (Petty & Cacioppo, 1984, 1986).

Recent work has demonstrated that recipients sometimes rely on source characteristics, even when processing centrally. Heath, McCarthy, and Mothersbaugh (1994) had subjects process information about two competing products. In carefully evaluating the information about the product attributes, subjects were led to the conclusion that there was no substantive difference between the products. Under those conditions, the celebrity status of the source determined the final evaluation of the product. It should be noted that the investigators assumed that subjects were engaging in central processing of the attributes. Unfortunately, no direct measures of processing were taken.

Given the lucrative endorsement contracts that are common for popular celebrities, advertisers clearly believe that celebrity endorsements can enhance consumers' evaluations of a product. But what happens when a single celebrity appears in a number of ads for a variety of products? In spite of the fact that multiple contracts are becoming more common (Elliot, 1991), celebrities (and the marketing firms that hire them) risk losing credibility and persuasive impact as the number of different product endorsements increases. Once a source has endorsed more than two products, consumers' liking for the source, belief in the source's expertise and trustworthiness, and attitude toward the ad all drop off sharply. It is thought that this drop in liking for the source is a result of changes in our attributions for the source's behavior (Tripp, Jensen, & Carlson, 1994). Once consumers have come to the conclusion that the source is endorsing numerous products for monetary gain, it is difficult to believe that the source really uses, and believes in, the products. Celebrity endorsement is most effective when the product is related to the celebrity's area of expertise. That is, Michael Jordan is probably an effective spokesperson for basketball shoes, but probably not for underwear (Lynch & Schuler, 1994; Tripp et al., 1994).

Recipient Characteristics

Of particular interest to researchers are the characteristics of consumers that predispose them to process an advertisement carefully or not. Variables that have generated a great deal of interest are the recipient's involvement with the product and the recipient's general level of interest in thinking about things.

Product-Relevant Involvement. The ELM is clear on its predictions for product involvement. Involvement should enhance motivation to evaluate message content. Someone who is highly involved in an issue or product should use the central route in processing relevant information, should carefully evaluate the appeal, and should be persuaded more readily by strong than weak arguments, as was shown in the study of beer ads described earlier (Andrews & Shimp, 1990).

Research has demonstrated that under conditions of high product involvement, attitude change is indeed a function of the quality of the arguments presented (Burnkrandt & Unnava, 1989). Similarly, Schumann, Petty, and Clemons (1990) demonstrated that with high levels of involvement, additional repetitions of an ad were more persuasive if they contained additional product-relevant claims. Under low involvement, repetitions were more persuasive if they presented additional peripheral cues.

One problem with work in this area is that the term *involvement* has a wide variety of meanings attached to it in the research. A meta-analytic review of work on involvement and persuasion was conducted, drawing exclusively on the consumer research literature (Costley, 1988). This review, which utilized statistical methods of combining the results of a large number of studies, demonstrated that, overall, higher levels of involvement are associated with greater attitude change and greater brand recall. Unfortunately, the meta-analysis also revealed a high degree of variation of findings across the studies evaluated, making it difficult to draw general conclusions. This is probably an effect (in part, at least) of the variety of operational definitions of involvement that have been used in research in this area. Involvement has variously been defined as prior experience with the product class, self-relevance of the message, task instructions given by the experimenter (e.g., it is considered more involving for the experimenter to request that the subject carefully evaluate the message content than to proofread the test), and the number of thoughts generated during ad exposure, among others. Greater precision in the definition of *involvement* is clearly needed.

Need for Cognition. Another recipient characteristic that has been studied in the context of the ELM is *need for cognition*. The construct of need for cognition differentiates people on their natural motivation to think about persuasive messages (among other things). People with high need for cognition enjoy thinking carefully about abstract problems, enjoy solving puzzles, and seek out complexity in their everyday interactions with people and objects. People with low need for cognition do not enjoy the process of thinking and avoid thinking about complex issues. For individuals who are high in need for cognition, strong arguments have been demonstrated to be more persuasive than weak ones. In contrast, people who have a low need for cognition are less motivated to process and thus are persuaded more by positive than negative peripheral cues. People low in need for cognition are unlikely to differentiate strong from weak arguments (Haugtvedt, Petty, Cacioppo, & Steidley, 1988). Thus, the effects for need for cognition support the ELM's claim that when individuals are motivated to carefully evaluate a message's claims, they will be sensitive to the quality of the arguments presented. In contrast, when motivation to process is low, peripheral cues become more relevant than argument quality.

These information-processing theories of attitude change have generated a tremendous amount of research activity and have provided guidance to marketers working in applied settings. It is certainly important to know how advertising affects consumers' attitudes toward advertisements and products. This information has no utility, however, if attitudes do not predict the behavior of interest: buying. The following section describes some of the issues involved in predicting behavior from attitudes.

DO ATTITUDES PREDICT BEHAVIOR?

Everyone is familiar with the concept of attitude, and many readers would agree that it is important to understand attitudes so that people's behavior can be better predicted. Underlying this belief is the intuitively reasonable assumption that how you feel about something will determine how you act toward it. This assumption is also at the heart of much research in social and consumer psychology (Petty, Unnava, & Strathman, 1991). However, in the late 1960s, some researchers in social psychology began to question whether attitudes really do relate to behavior. An influential review of 47 studies (Wicker, 1969) strongly criticized the work on attitudes, arguing that there was little evidence that attitudes underlie actions. This critique prompted other researchers to defend the concept of attitudes. Even so, many people still believed that attitudes were important and worthy of study and began to research the relationship between attitudes and behavior.

Levels of Specificity

One problem with attempting to find a relationship between attitudes and behavior is that measures are being taken at different *levels of specificity* (Ajzen & Fishbein, 1977). As an example, think about your attitude toward the use of animals in research. Are you highly favorable, moderately favorable, moderately unfavorable, or highly unfavorable toward the use of animals in research? Now, think about the last time you bought shampoo. Did you buy a product that explicitly stated that no animals were used in testing the product? If attitudes predict behavior, you should find that people who are highly opposed to animal testing would always buy products that used no animals in their development, and those who are not opposed to the use of animals in research would buy products that used animals in their research. In thinking about your own experience, was your behavior consistent with your attitude?

You may realize by now that your purchase of any specific product depends upon a number of factors in addition to your attitude. Any given situation may contain impediments to acting in accordance with attitudes. For example, you may have had a discount coupon for a new brand of shampoo. If you happened to be low on money, the discounted price may have been more important at that moment than your opposition to animal research. So, you may have purchased the shampoo, in spite of a highly unfavorable attitude toward animal testing, because of short-term economic pressures.

Another variable influencing your behavior in a specific situation is the *modeling* of behavior appropriate to the situation (e.g., Cialdini, Reno, & Kallgren, 1990). You use other people's behavior as a guide to what the norm is. Suppose you went to the store with a friend who is a vocal opponent of animal testing, and she made a point of checking the labels of all products she was purchasing to be sure no animals were used. You also probably would have bought a product with the "cruelty free" label, regardless of a moderately favorable attitude toward the use of animals in research.

As is clear from this discussion, any specific opportunity to behave can be affected by a wide range of factors, which may or may not be related to your attitude. Much research in this area has measured attitude, which is a general evaluation, and tried to predict a single act. By trying to relate attitudes to specific behaviors, researchers have confused two different levels of specificity and have limited their ability to detect a relationship. By evaluating both attitudes and behaviors at common levels of specificity, relationships should become clearer (Ajzen & Fishbein, 1977). One strategy for measuring attitudes and behavior at a common level of specificity is to average across a large number of behaviors (Weigel & Newman, 1976). For instance, if you were to calculate the percentage of all personal care products you have purchased over the last year with the "cruelty free" label, it would likely be closely related to your attitude about the use of animals in research.

Another approach to coping with the problem of different levels of specificity is to measure attitudes at a more specific level. This approach is described in the next section.

The Theory of Reasoned Action

The *theory of reasoned action* (Fishbein & Ajzen, 1975, 1980) provides a framework for understanding the complex manner in which attitudes and behavior are related. In contrast to a simple relationship between attitudes and behavior, as had previously been assumed, this model proposed a number of mediating variables in the attitude-behavior relationship. The best predictor of a specific behavior is the *intention* to perform that behavior at a specific time (Ajzen & Fishbein, 1972, 1973). So, if a researcher discovers in a phone survey that a consumer intends to purchase a particular brand of laundry soap the next time he or she goes to the store, you can be pretty sure that the consumer will indeed make that purchase.

What determines the intention to perform the behavior? Two factors combine to form the behavioral intention. These are the attitude toward the act and the subjective norm. The *attitude toward the act* simply refers to the individual's evaluation of performing the behavior. The evaluation is formed from beliefs the individual has about the positive or negative outcomes associated with performing the behavior. The consumer might consider a number of beliefs about buying a house in the next 6 months, such as, "I can get more living space for the money," "I will start building equity," "I could get a good interest rate," and "I would waste a lot of time packing all my stuff." The attitude toward buying a house in the next 6 months is a function of the consumer's evaluation of how positive or negative each of the outcomes is, and how likely the outcome is to occur if the consumer engages in the behavior.

The *subjective norm* refers to the individual's perception of the "appropriate" behavior in the situation, that is, what the significant people in the individual's social world would think of the individual engaging in this act. Just as in the opening vignette, when Eileen considered what her friends and parents thought she should buy, the subjective norm is formed of a consumer's beliefs about what significant others want the consumer to do. For different people, and at different times, relatively more importance may be placed on the attitudinal or the normative determinants of behavioral intention (Bagozzi, Baumgartner, & Yi, 1992).

The Fishbein and Ajzen model generated a great deal of research interest in the consumer behavior literature (e.g., Netemeyer & Bearden, 1992; Sheppard, Hartwick, & Warshaw, 1983; Taylor & Todd, 1995). Because of the nature of consumer behavior, the model has intuitive appeal to marketers. Specifically, it is more useful to marketers to know how a consumer feels about buying a car in the next year than to know the consumer's general attitude toward cars. The model has been supported in studies predicting the purchase of consumer products (Beatty & Kahle, 1988; Brinberg & Cummings, 1983; Warshaw, 1980) and other behaviors such as one's intention to donate blood (Bagozzi, 1981) or vote (Singh, Leong, Tan, & Wong, 1995). In one meta-analysis of 87 studies that investigated the theory of reasoned action in consumer behavior settings, strong support for the model was obtained (Sheppard et al., 1983).

Evidence in support of the theory of reasoned action has not been unanimous. Bentler and Speckart (1979) examined the structure of the model to determine whether attitudes are necessarily mediated by intention. Respondents' intentions to use drugs in the following 2 weeks were measured, in addition to their attitude, subjective norm, and an additional variable, *past behavior*. Actual drug-taking behavior was measured 2 weeks later. Consistent with the model, attitudes and subjective norm predicted intention, which, in turn, predicted behavior. Contrary to the model's predictions, however, attitudes exerted an independent influence on behavior that was not mediated by intention. Furthermore, past behavior also proved to be a significant predictor of behavior, a finding pointing to the importance of habit (see next section).

Some tests of the theory of reasoned action have questioned the role of the subjective norm. For example, in a study by Thompson, Haziris, and Alekos (1994), attitudes based on beliefs about the flavor-enhancing value of using olive oil in cooking strongly predicted purchase of olive oil. They found no effect of subjective norm on purchase of olive oil. This lack of evidence for the subjective norm has been demonstrated in other studies of food choice (Sapp & Harrod, 1989; Tourila, 1987). Another study found that the subjective norm may have a direct effect on the formation of attitudes rather than on behavioral intention (Oliver & Bearden, 1985). Thus, the model has received mixed support in empirical tests.

Other researchers have attempted to deal with the problem of low attitude-behavior relations by examining some of the factors that affect whether a person will act in accordance with his or her attitudes. One approach in particular has led to findings that are highly applicable to marketing contexts. According to this approach, in order for an attitude to predict behavior, the attitude must be highly *accessible* (Fazio, 1986). Accessibility in this context refers to being able to quickly retrieve the attitude from memory. Attitudes are more accessible, and therefore more predictive of behavior, when they are based on direct experience and are repeatedly expressed. Extensions of this work into consumer research have demonstrated that consumers' purchase behavior is more closely related to their attitudes for products with which they have had direct experience, as compared with products for which they have only seen advertisements (Fazio, Powell, & Williams, 1989; Smith & Swinyard, 1983).

Habits

The previous section described how attitudes predict behaviors that are carefully reasoned. Many behaviors that occur in purchase settings, however, may not be carefully considered. Think, for example, of the last time you bought laundry detergent. Did you think carefully about the many claims you have heard about the performance of each of the myriad brands of laundry detergent? Did you select on the basis of the lowest cost, or the brand you happened to have a coupon for? Or, did you simply recognize the packaging for the brand you purchased most recently and thoughtlessly grabbed that one? If you engaged in the latter behavior, you were responding out of *habit*. It is likely that much repeat purchase behavior is conducted out of habit, if for no other reason than that consumers simply cannot consider the important features of every item they place in their shopping carts. As long as you have experienced no great dissatisfaction with the soap you purchased last, for example, you are likely to purchase the same brand next time.

According to Triandis (1977), habit, or prior behavior, may be the best predictor of future behavior in situations that are highly familiar. In contrast, in unfamiliar situations, intentions to perform the behavior are probably the best predictor. A meta-analytic review was recently conducted that evaluated the situations in which prior behavior predicts later behavior (Ouellette & Wood, 1995). For behaviors that occur frequently, prior behavior is the best predictor of future behavior. For example, someone who buys milk at least once a week will probably buy the same brand of milk each week. Prior behavior also predicts future behavior when there are no impediments to action. That is, someone who picks up a breakfast meal at a particular fast-food restaurant every morning will continue to do so as long as nothing gets in the way of the normal routine. But what happens if an unusual event prevents a consumer from engaging in habitual behavior? In the case of impediments, attitudes become a better predictor than past behavior. If the fast-food restaurant is closed, for example, the person's attitudes toward a variety of breakfast foods will predict what the person will do.

Impulse Purchases

This chapter has focused on the full range of processes a consumer can engage in, from careful processing of ad claims and product features to less effortful decisions based on peripheral cues and habits. A specific type of consumer behavior that is possibly the least relevant to theories of persuasion is impulse buying. Nonetheless, social psychological approaches can help in understanding this behavior as well.

Rook and Gardner (1993) examined impulse buying in relation to the consumer's mood at the time of the purchase. They found that impulse purchases were likely in a variety of mood states; however, it appeared that purchases in different types of moods served different functions. In positive moods, impulse purchases appeared to be geared toward maintaining the positive mood. Furthermore, they were characterized by little deliberation. In contrast, purchases made in negative moods were somewhat more deliberate. For example, someone who had just done poorly on an exam reported purposefully shopping for compact discs as a way to forget the negative event.

These results mesh nicely with work in social psychology that has demonstrated that people are much more thoughtful about a variety of things, including processing persuasive messages and information-rich ads (e.g., Gardner, 1994; Schwarz, Bless, & Bohner, 1991; Worth & Mackie, 1987), when they are in neutral or negative moods than when they are in happy moods. A clearer understanding of how mood and product-relevant thought combine in purchase decisions can help marketers in choosing the most appropriate in-store display to capitalize on impulse buying. Furthermore, advertisers can better select the mood-inducing stimuli for their product or ad (Gardner, 1985, 1994), or in choosing the appropriate context for their ad (Gardner, 1994; Goldberg & Gorn, 1987). For example, it might make a difference in ad processing if viewers are watching a happy movie or a sad movie just prior to viewing the ad.

SOCIAL INFLUENCES ON CONSUMER BEHAVIOR

The previous sections considered many of the factors leading to an individual's purchase choice. These have taken into account the many pieces of information an individual must process in making a purchase. Attention to, and comprehension of, the contents of advertising; generation of favorable or unfavorable thoughts as a result; and past behavior have all been demonstrated to be important processes in consumer research. What has largely been missing from the models discussed so far is the influence of other people on the process. Social psychology has a rich history in the study of how people are influenced by their social environment. This work is highly relevant to consumer decisions and deserves more detailed consideration.

Asch's classic work on conformity forms the basis for the study of how the behavior of a group can affect an individual (Asch, 1951). In the prototypical study, a naive subject arrives at the lab for what the subject believes is a study of perception but is really a test of his or her tendency to conform to the views of others. There are already seven other subjects there, and the subject takes the only empty seat available. What the subject does not know is that all the other people in the room are actually confederates of the experimenter. The experimental task is to judge which of three lines is the same length as a standard line. In the experimental procedure, the stimulus for each trial is presented, and the "subjects" answer out loud, in turn, what they believe the correct answer to be. Of course, the situation is rigged so that the naive subject just happens to be among the last group members to respond. On a specified set of trials, the confederates are instructed to answer incorrectly, that is, to report that a line obviously different in length from the standard is the correct one. The important issue is whether the subject will endorse an obviously incorrect answer simply because the other group members have. The findings indicate that on about one-third of the trials in which the other group members endorsed an incorrect answer, the subject also endorsed the incorrect response. Approximately 75% of all subjects gave the incorrect answer at least once. Although Asch's original work was conducted using perceptual judgments, further work demonstrated that conformity occurs whether the judgments are based on objective, perceptual stimuli or more subjective, attitudinal stimuli (Hardy, 1957).

Later considerations of conformity proposed two mechanisms through which influence could occur in situations such as this (Deutsch & Gerard, 1955). The first mechanism, *normative influence,* refers to the subjects' fear of social sanctions if they deviate from the group. Someone might fear being laughed at or ostracized by the other group members for not knowing the answer. In general, normative influence is operating when people do something because it will help them fit in with a reference group. The second mechanism, *informational influence,* is a result of wanting to hold correct attitudes. People gather information about the attitudes and behaviors of others as evidence about reality. For example, in the Asch paradigm, a subject might go along with the group because the subject reasons that the other group members may see the stimulus from a different angle, so they are probably correct.

Conformity pressures are common in purchasing situations. On any given Saturday afternoon at a shopping mall, you can see many groups of women shopping together. What happens if one woman picks up an outfit for the approval of others, but her friends unanimously dislike it? According to Asch's findings, she is unlikely to take this particular outfit into the fitting room.

A study was recently conducted to examine just such influence processes (Rhodes, 1995). In a modified Asch paradigm, female subjects came to the lab for a study of "focus groups." They were told they would be discussing photos of women's fashions with other group members (all female). They received written ratings of the photos. These ratings were ostensibly made by the women in the group. In a high social influence condition, they were told their written ratings would be shown to the other group members and would form the basis for the discussion. In a low social influence condition, they were told that their written ratings would never be seen by the other people. The amount of persuasive information was also varied: Some subjects received statements, again supposedly written by the other group members, describing why they liked or disliked the clothing; other subjects were given only the ratings made on a rating scale. The results indicated that negative ratings by the other group members were highly influential. Subjects' ratings were much lower than those of a control group if they thought the others disliked the clothing. Only when there was no information provided and no social pressure were the ratings similar to those of the control group. Positive ratings by the other group members were less influential: Only when there were both informational and social pressures to conform were the subjects' ratings higher than those of the control group. Thus, it appears that negative social pressure is more influential than positive. This study has implications for sales staff in retail stores, as well. It is clear from these data that a salesperson should have strong reasons why a particular outfit would be a good clothing purchase for a customer who appears to be wavering.

Similar findings have been found in investigations of *word-of-mouth* effects. Word-of-mouth can be a significant source of information for consumers. Analyses of the content of word-of-mouth communications have demonstrated that the information contained in these situations is generally positive (Arndt, 1967). However, when negative information is communicated, it appears to be highly persuasive (Richins, 1983). It could be that because word-of-mouth information is generally positive, any negative information is highly salient because it is relatively rare and thus generates greater attention (Mizerski, 1982).

METHODOLOGICAL CONCERNS

What methods do consumer researchers use to understand the processes of persuasion? The methods used in consumer research are highly varied and are difficult to characterize briefly. Many of the research methods used currently have been borrowed and adapted from other fields. These diverse methods all have their strengths and weaknesses. Additionally, researchers in consumer psychology work in diverse areas, each with specific goals. Thus, in order to comment on the methods used, the setting that the researcher is working in must also be considered.

Research in Academic Settings

Many consumer researchers work in *academic settings;* that is, they conduct research and teach at universities. Their goal in conducting research is generally to understand the theoretical basis for consumer choice. Their intention is to advance the field by conducting experiments that clarify an aspect of consumer research and then publishing the results in academic journals. This type of research tends to be *predictive* in nature. That is, if the researcher has information about all of the relevant variables, he or she should be able to predict how a consumer will act. Much of the work that has been considered in this chapter is of this type.

As with all types of experimental research, laboratory studies in consumer behavior must be carefully planned and executed in order to address adequately the research questions. Every possible aspect of the experiment must be carefully controlled so that the effects of the manipulated variables will be clear. For example, a researcher might want to know whether public service ads presenting fear-arousing messages would be more effective than unemotional, factual messages in reducing attitudes toward smoking. In creating the ads to be used in the study, the researcher must consider a number of features of the ads that have nothing to do with the emotional content. For example, the researcher would want to make sure both ads were equally understandable, interesting, of equal length, and so on, so that differences in smoking attitudes after exposure to the ads would clearly be caused by the emotional content of the messages.

Academic research in consumer psychology has been criticized because it is so strongly based on laboratory experiments (Lauden, 1983; Peter, 1991). Furthermore, the focus of these experiments is on ever more minute processes. In general, as experiments become more focused on these types of processes, they also become less relevant to actual purchase behavior. For example, much of the persuasion research focuses on how a specific feature of an ad will affect processing of the message in certain situations. That is, if it is determined that well-reasoned arguments are more persuasive in high-involvement situations than in low-involvement ones, an important piece of information for understanding the process of persuasion has been added to the body of knowledge. However, because experiments tend to be conducted in carefully controlled laboratory settings, the information gained may not tell the researcher much about how people actually process product-related messages in natural contexts. In a lab experiment, research participants typically have nothing else to do but read or watch the ads in question. Furthermore, it is generally clear that the experimenter expects them to pay attention to the ad. This structured laboratory situation bears little resemblance to ad exposure in real life, when many stimuli compete for a recipient's attention. For example, a busy father with cranky kids may not have the motivation or the ability (because of demands on his attention) to engage in central processing of an advertisement describing the wonderful features of a new disposable diaper, even if he is frequently involved in the activity of changing diapers.

The type of people selected for use as research participants is another important feature of research that differentiates academic researchers from other researchers. Academic researchers frequently make use of *convenience samples*. Many studies are conducted on college students enrolled in introductory marketing or psychology courses. This is done because the subjects are easy to recruit and require no monetary payment, although course credit is usually offered. A criticism of using such samples is that the results of the research may not *generalize* to other samples. That is, will the findings obtained from a sample of participants with certain characteristics (e.g., age, ethnicity, family status) be relevant for other samples? Academic researchers respond that their results are generalizable because of the nature of the variables they are studying. They are tracking internal processes that are thought not to vary greatly from individual to individual. For example, if it can be demonstrated that a highly involving message increases processing and subsequent ad recall among 20-year-old college sophomores, the effects should be the same among 40-year-old female executives.

Research in Applied Settings

In contrast to academic researchers, researchers employed in *applied marketing research* settings are far more concerned with real-world applications. A researcher in this setting is less interested in testing the theoretical processes leading to consumer choice; of much greater concern is whether a particular ad will boost sales. A good researcher in an applied setting will keep abreast of theoretical developments and incorporate them in the applied work, but the central focus is on gaining information from and about consumers that will enable a company to sell more of its product.

Applied researchers make heavy use of *survey research* methods to evaluate consumers' needs and their perceptions of how various products will meet those needs. Whereas academic researchers are concerned with the cognitive underpinnings of consumer choice, the applied researcher is concerned with finding out what percentage of the population is likely to purchase a product. Or, as in the example in the research box (see Box 10–1), applied researchers may try to evaluate consumers' likely acceptance of modified products. Therefore, applied researchers are much

Box
10–1

When Market Research Fails,
or Why They Don't Sell "New Coke" Anymore

In the early 1980s, the makers of Coca-Cola were concerned. Coca-Cola's market share was slipping, and Pepsi's was on the rise. In spite of expensive and extensive ad campaigns, and successfully launching Diet Coke, Coke still dropped 1 percentage point in market share in 1984. Although 1 percentage point doesn't sound like a lot, it accounts for millions of dollars in lost sales—most of the loss going to Pepsi. Furthermore, this was a trend that had started in the mid-1960s and showed no signs of stopping.

This was not very long after Pepsi's highly successful "Pepsi Challenge" ad campaign. In the challenge, ads showed candid shots of regular Coke drinkers amazing themselves by their preference for Pepsi in a blind taste test. Coke's own taste tests showed a very disturbing preference for the taste of Pepsi, by a 58–42 margin. There was a crisis climate at Coke. Confidence in the product was low. The company believed there was only one explanation for Coke's continual slide: The taste simply wasn't as good as Pepsi's. Consumers preferred a sweeter drink.

The research and development team took over. Under orders of great secrecy, they were charged with the task of changing the formula for Coke. They were to try to make it taste "smoother," and give it less bite. In short, they were to make it taste more like Pepsi. They eventually came up with an altered formulation that beat the classic formula by 6 percentage points in blind taste tests.

While the formula was being altered, market researchers asked long-time Coca-Cola drinkers how they would feel if Coke "added a new ingredient" to make the drink "smoother." Results indicated that only about 11 percent of confirmed Coca-Cola drinkers would be angry. Notice, the question did not specifically ask the consumers how they would feel if Coca-Cola was replaced with a drink that tasted different. The Coke executives, confident that people would be thrilled with the new formula, went ahead with plans for a new ad campaign and launched the new formula.

The first negative reaction encountered was at the news conference announcing the new formula. Reporters at the conference challenged the Coke executives with the assumption that the reformulation had been a defensive response to the Pepsi challenge. The Coke people denied that assertion, of course, but unconvincingly.

The next negative reaction came when long-time Coke drinkers realized that Coke was actually replacing their favorite drink with a Pepsi clone. Many devoted Coke drinkers became extremely upset. People complained and wrote letters in droves. Some people poured New Coke into sewers. Thousands of people each day called the company. In short, the Coca-Cola manufacturers had created a huge mess.

How could the Coca-Cola people have been so wrong about the reaction of their loyal customers to a change in the formula? The easy answer is that they simply asked the wrong questions. They did the taste tests, and they asked about adding a new ingredient to the old formula, but in all of the market research conducted prior to the distribution of the new formula, they never asked customers how they would feel if the makers of Coca-Cola changed Coke. Coke was more than a soft drink to many people. An example of the comments the company received from the thousands of letters written sums up the sentiment: "Changing Coke is just like breaking the American dream, like not selling hot dogs at a ball game" (Pendergrast, 1993, p. 363). People identified with Coke; they had memories of significant times in their lives with Coke. To them, changing Coke was blasphemy.

After 3 months of bad publicity and complaints, Coke reintroduced the original formula as "Classic Coke," much to the delight of many consumers. New Coke stayed on the market for 5 years and never received more than a 7% market share. The company officials were accused of planning the whole New Coke debacle simply to improve sales of Classic Coke. However, in the words of Coke CEO Roberto Goizueta, "We are not that dumb and we are not that smart" (Pendergrast, 1993).

Could the Coca-Cola executives have avoided these problems with New Coke? It is difficult to say with certainty. Because they were concerned with developing the product secretly, it would have been impossible to survey a few thousand consumers and ask them how they would react if Coca-Cola changed its formula. The Coca-Cola experience certainly points to the importance of asking the relevant questions. In defense of the marketing researchers who conducted the work for Coca-Cola, it is easy to see after the fact what questions they should have asked. Much more difficult is anticipating what issues are important to consumers in advance of a marketing campaign.

Perhaps the most important lesson that can be taken from the failure of New Coke is that it is important for marketers to consider not just market share and net profits, but also what their products mean in the lives of their customers. According to McKracken (1986), consumer goods become invested with cultural meaning. It is a tribute to the success of early marketing of Coca-Cola that its customers have invested so much meaning in their product. Many of the letters written to Coke to protest the new drink touched on just this sort of feeling: that the makers of Coke were destroying their memories, their identity, and their culture by tampering with "their" Coca-Cola. If market research in the development of New Coke had been sensitive to the values associated with Coca-Cola, they might have been able to circumvent the difficulties in changing the formula. Perhaps they might have decided to abandon entirely the attempt to change the formula.

A final point that Coca-Cola's experience clearly illustrates is that there are limits to what marketers and social psychologists can persuade consumers to accept. In spite of decades of research on persuasion, and in spite of millions of dollars spent on the ad campaign, the majority of cola drinkers chose not to purchase the product. Consumers do not mindlessly act in accordance with the whims of advertisers. Consumers can have a powerful effect on huge corporations such as Coca-Cola simply by refusing to buy a product that clashes with their own values.

more likely than academic researchers to be concerned with the sample of respondents they obtain. That is, the researchers must ensure that the sample of people who respond are similar to the greater population in terms of characteristics believed to be important to their responses. That way, researchers can be sure that the responses of the sample are representative of the target population.

The idea that people with different characteristics will have different attitudes about consumer products is inherent in the concept of market segmentation. *Market segmentation* refers to the process of dividing a population into groups or segments with similar characteristics (Wind, Rao, & Green, 1991). Because different groups of people have needs and desires for different products, as well as different levels of income, a goal among researchers is to find meaningful ways to identify those segments of the population most likely to be influenced by a particular marketing strategy. Segments can be created using *demographic variables* such as age, sex, ethnicity, and family size; geographic variables such as region, city size, and climate; *psychographic variables* such as personality, motives, and lifestyles; or *behavioristic variables* such as benefit expectations, brand loyalty, and price sensitivity (Pride & Ferrell, 1992). Further developments in market segmentation have demonstrated that consumers can be in *overlapping clusters;* that is, they can belong in multiple segments at the same time (Arabie, Carroll, DeSarbo, & Wind, 1981).

An example of how important market segmenting can be is illustrated by a recent market failure. In 1987, Colgate-Palmolive introduced a new product that was a combination laundry detergent and fabric softener. Because it was in a hurry to beat the competition to the stores, C-P neglected to conduct careful market research. The product was targeted to large families. Yet, the product was perceived by members of large families as too costly; large families tend to have tight budgets. Thus, the product failed largely because the company marketed it to the wrong segment. The product would likely have been more successful if marketing efforts had been targeted toward single people, apartment dwellers, and college students. These groups are typically more willing to pay extra for convenience. Thus, an error in market segmentation can be quite costly (Applebaum, 1990).

In the past decade there has been a significant narrowing of the focus of marketing research to more and more molecular processes (e.g., the focus on information processing) among academic consumer researchers. This development has recently been countered by a surge in interest in motivation and interpretive research (Hirshman, 1986; Holbrook & O'Shaughnessy, 1988; Wind et al., 1991). This shift includes a focus on a more realistic unit of analysis, that is, a focus not on the individual consumer but on the family unit. Market researchers should also look more closely at the situational nature of purchase decisions. Additionally, examining cross-cultural variations and determinants of consumer behavior is an important step in understanding the general principles that underlie consumer behavior. Furthermore, greater communication with researchers in other fields will help enrich and strengthen the base of knowledge in consumer research.

CONSUMER RESEARCH AND SOCIAL POLICY

What effect does advertising have on society? Is our society improved by the vast number of commercial messages our citizens are exposed to, or is it somehow detrimental to be continually bombarded with inducements to buy? In general, people have negative attitudes toward advertising. Advertising was viewed by one panel of consumers as misleading, boring, irritating, offensive, silly, and trivial (Mittal, 1994).

A need for social policy arises in situations in which it is to society's benefit to intervene in the exchange between a marketer and its consumers. Two important areas of concern are guaranteeing fairness in advertising and ensuring that children are not exploited (Andreasen, 1990).

Fairness in Advertising

Of greatest concern in evaluating fairness in the marketplace is advertising. Does advertising mislead consumers? Social policymakers must address whether to regulate advertising to minimize miscomprehension and to avoid deception. So far, in our society, regulatory agencies have evaluated complaints of deception on a case-by-case basis. However, some researchers believe efforts in consumer research should focus on the types of statements in ads that are especially likely to mislead, so that general regulations can be developed (Grunert & Dedler, 1985). Three types of deceptive statements have been identified. The first is the *unconscionable lie*, specifically, making a blatantly false statement. The second type of deception is the *claim-fact discrepancy*. This type of deception leads the consumer to make an inference that is not true. An example would be leading the consumer to believe that if one item is on sale, all similar items are also on sale. The third type of deception is a *claim-belief discrepancy*. This type of deceptive practice takes advantage of common beliefs held by consumers in an effort to mislead them. For example, an advertiser might advertise a price per square foot for carpet, with the expectation that consumers will assume the price is really the more common price per square yard (Gardner, 1975). An automobile dealership may advertise what appears to be a low monthly payment for a new car, which might mislead consumers who do not realize the quoted payment reflects the monthly cost to lease, rather than to buy, the car. Unfortunately, it is difficult to evaluate empirically the extent of the impact of unfair advertising on purchase behavior, so the degree of intervention necessary is unclear.

Protection of Children

The protection of children from the exploitation of marketers is also an important issue for social policy researchers. Because of their age and lack of experience, children may be particularly vulnerable to marketing tactics. The greatest concern is that children may not understand the persuasive intent of advertising and thus may trust the claims made in advertisements (Ward, Reale, & Levinson, 1972). One solution is to air announcements aimed at teaching children about the persuasive nature of advertising so that they can learn to become more discriminating consumers.

An additional concern is the marketing of harmful products to children. The tobacco industry in general, and R. J. Reynolds in particular, has been criticized for generating cigarette ads that are appealing to children. The Joe Camel cartoon character is perhaps the most widely known and the most controversial of the cigarette ads. Critics of the ad claim that it is a ploy to attract children to cigarettes. The Joe

Camel character certainly attracts the attention of children. One study demonstrated that over 90% of high school students recognize the character (as compared with fewer than 75% of adults). A similarly large proportion of high schoolers are also aware that Joe Camel cartoons are cigarette ads and can identify Camel cigarettes as the brand of cigarettes the ad is selling (DiFranza et al., 1991). What is less clear is whether the Joe Camel ads are truly enticing young children to smoke cigarettes. After the Joe Camel ad campaign began, Camel cigarettes captured a greater percentage of the cigarettes sold to young people than previously (Pierce et al., 1991). However, a point of controversy is whether the Joe Camel ads have actually increased the percentage of all teenagers who smoke (Males, 1992). Executives from the tobacco industry say "no." They claim that a certain percentage of teens are going to smoke anyway. Health professionals believe that the advertising directed at children entices young people to smoke at an early age.

At the heart of the issue is the question of whether the government has the right to regulate advertising of legal products. There is certainly precedent for doing so. Alcohol (except wine and beer) and cigarettes are no longer advertised on television in the United States. In 1995, President Clinton requested that the Food and Drug Administration (FDA) regulate cigarettes in the same way it regulates addictive medications. If the FDA follows through on that recommendation, advertising of cigarettes could be limited to text-only, black-and-white presentations. Obviously, the tobacco industry is motivated to prevent such a change.

The proposed changes in advertising for cigarettes have sparked controversy among advertising professionals. In one view, the government is unfairly punishing the advertising industry for marketing a legal product (Garfield, 1995). According to this view, it would be far more effective to actively enforce existing laws preventing the sale of cigarettes to minors than to impose regulations on advertising (Rotfield, 1994). A contrasting view is that the ad industry should voluntarily stop promoting dangerous products to children. The public image of the ad industry is severely damaged by continuing to actively pursue accounts for cigarette ads (DesRoches, 1994). This particular social policy issue promises to be a point of controversy for the foreseeable future.

SUMMARY

The work reviewed in this chapter demonstrates the value of applying social psychological theories and research methods to the applied area of consumer behavior. Many of the theories that were developed in social psychology to explain persuasion and social influence are applicable to consumer choice as well. Future areas for continued collaboration between social psychologists and consumer researchers include further developing models predicting behavior, examining the motivations of consumers, and further elaborating on the influence of the social environment in consumer decisions.

SUGGESTED READINGS

Advertising Age

This is a weekly industry newspaper that focuses on innovations in advertising and market research. Specifically geared for professionals in the field, the articles tend to be short and easily comprehended. Reading *Advertising Age* is an excellent way to keep abreast of developments and debates in the field of advertising.

Eagly, A. H., & Chaiken, S. (1993). *The psychology of attitudes*. Fort Worth: Harcourt Brace Jovanovich.

This is a highly technical book pitched at academic researchers and graduate students in social psychology. It is, however, the most complete treatment of the theory and research in attitudes available at the current time. It contains the answer to virtually any question that might be posed about attitudes. It is an essential resource for anyone interested in pursuing work in attitudes or persuasion, whether in academic or applied settings.

Foxall, G. R., & Goldsmith, R. E. (1994). *Consumer psychology for marketing*. London: Routledge.

This book provides an excellent application of consumer behavior research to marketing decisions. Targeted at marketing professionals, its main theme is that good consumer research can benefit marketing by helping marketers know the people who make up the market.

Pendergrast, M. (1993). *For God, country, and Coca-Cola: The unauthorized history of the great American soft drink and the company that makes it*. New York: Charles Scribner's Sons.

This highly readable book is not specifically about consumer behavior. It is, however, a fascinating account of the history of Coca-Cola. In telling the story of Coke, Pendergrast gives many insights into the market research and advertising campaigns that helped Coke become, well, Coke.

Waldrop, J., & Mogelonsky, M. (1992). *The seasons of business: A marketer's guide to consumer behavior*. Ithaca, NY: American Demographics.

This highly innovative book examines the influences on consumer behavior over the course of a year. It describes, for example, the patterns of purchasing surrounding the holidays or during summer vacations. The authors consider all sources of influence on consumers, from weather patterns to the types of products that are most likely to be on sale in a given time of the year.

11 Media Influences

Donald R. McCreary

Brock University

The Russell family is like most others in their neighborhood, especially with regard to the ways they use the several forms of communication media available to people these days. For example, consider Linda and Tim Russell. They are both professionals and have worked hard to provide well for their family. Because their jobs require a lot of individual work at a computer, both Linda and Tim have arranged their schedules so that they work at home one day per week. There are two computers in their home, one for them and one for their two children, and each computer has a modem. Because of this, Tim and Linda are able to bring their work from the office and complete it on their home computers. If they need to contact the office (or if the office needs to contact them), they either telephone or leave an electronic mail message. Moreover, computers are not the only type of communications media in the Russell household. Both Linda and Tim read newspapers and watch TV news programs to keep in touch with local and world affairs; they encourage their twin, 13-year-old-children (Ethan and Emily) to do the same.

Their son, Ethan, is a sports fanatic and (as his family often jokes) a TV addict. In fact, he often combines his two loves and spends much of his spare time watching all kinds of sporting events on television. When not watching sports, Ethan plays video games and watches music videos and horror movies. Because his family has a satellite dish, he has access to numerous sports, music, and movie channels that broadcast 24 hours a day. In between classes at school, he reads *Sports Illustrated* and discusses the latest player trades in baseball, football, and hockey with his friends.

Emily also uses several forms of media. Emily, however, hates sports. She and her friends spend their spare time watching the numerous soap operas on both daytime and evening television, going to the movies (they prefer romantic comedies), and reading about fashion in magazines such as *Vogue* and *Elle*. During her spare time, Emily likes to "surf" the Internet, looking for information on books, movies, and her favorite musicians, as well as material for her book reports and projects at school.

INTRODUCTION

Several forms of communication media have infused Western culture. People watch television, go to the movies, read magazines and books, listen to the radio, and communicate via the telephone and international computer networks (e.g., the Internet and online services such as CompuServe and America Online). The purpose of these media is mainly twofold. One aim is to inform and educate. To this end, people often read newspapers and magazines to keep apprised of the most recent social and political events, or they watch specialty television channels (e.g., the History Channel, the Discovery Channel, or CNN) that have been designed to educate people on specific topics. Schools and universities use textbooks, computers, and other forms of audio-visual aids to assist in educating their students. Finally, businesses use several types of media to train their employees (e.g., video and books) and to advertise their products to consumers; in other words, they want to inform and educate people about what their products do, where they can be bought, and when they are on sale.

The media's second major purpose is to entertain. In fact, this function pervades all types of media. The medium used most frequently for entertainment is television. This is evidenced by the strong presence of entertainment-based programming, which provides a mixture of situation comedies, dramatic serials, made-for-TV movies, and several forms of reality-based TV (e.g., talk shows, crime and rescue re-creations). Recent American statistics show that one or more household TV sets are turned on for an average of 7 hours per day, and the average person in the United States spends more than 21 hours per week watching television (Gerbner, Gross, Morgan, & Signorielli, 1994).

As for other forms of media, there are an astounding number of fiction and nonfiction books published every year. The interest in comic books, among both the young and old, is quite high. Telephones are often used for entertainment purposes, especially when people call specialty services that provide the listener with everything from horoscopes and psychic readings to multiperson chat lines, on which a caller can talk to a number of different people at once. Computers have certainly entered the entertainment realm. The increased popularity of program- or CD-ROM-driven games is only one aspect of how people use computers for entertainment. There has also been an increase in the popularity of online computer services that provide users with access to the Internet, the World Wide Web, and interactive bulletin boards, on which like-minded people can discuss their favorite music, read reviews of movies and CDs, and even write a collective novel.

If the media's primary purpose is to entertain and educate, then why are applied social psychologists interested in studying their impact on people? That is, applied social psychology is interested in developing an understanding of *social problems* and finding solutions to them (Oskamp, 1984). The implication is that items most people consider to be innocuous (e.g., magazines, books, television, and computers) may be causing social problems. If so, then these problems need to be better understood and eventually solved.

This chapter discusses the ways in which the media have been shown to contribute to social problems. When discussing media effects, Williams (1986a) suggests that they can be grouped into two distinct categories, what she terms *displacement effects* and *content effects*. Displacement effects are concerned with the fact that watching television detracts from the time available to perform other, more important tasks. Content effects, on the other hand, are more concerned with *what* children and adults inadvertently learn from the media.

Before proceeding, however, it is important to address three drawbacks, or biases, that can be found within media theories and research. The first is that most of the thinking and research on media influences is concerned only with the effects of television. In fact, relatively little attention is paid to other forms of media (e.g., books, newspapers, movies, computers, and computer games). The belief appears to have been that, because it is so salient and omnipresent in our culture, TV is the medium that has the most potential to have a negative impact on people. So, with regard to the hypothetical Russell family described in the opening vignette, researchers would be more concerned with the amount of television each family member watches, as well as the programming content they are exposed to. Even though the Russells use several other forms of media, the assumption is that television will have the most significant influence on them.

Second, most researchers study the harm (or benefits) that media have on children, with little parallel research conducted with adults. This research is motivated by the assumption that children are more strongly influenced by both the displacement effects and the content of the media. Wartella and Reeves (1985), as well as Williams, Rice, and Rogers (1988), describe how media research has been driven by the study of their effects on our culture's youth. Williams et al. note that prior to 1970, there were only 300 English publications examining the impact of television on children, but by 1980 there were over 1,670 publications addressing this relationship (i.e., a 557% increase in only 10 years). Wartella and Reeves describe how similar rates of increase were evidenced during the proliferation of radio and movies. Unlike television research, however, once the diffusion rate of radio and motion pictures peaked (i.e., when most people had a radio or went to the movies regularly), the research interest in their influence declined sharply. This pattern has not been found with television research; even though most families have had at least one television for the past 20 years, research interest on the influence of television has grown substantially instead of dissipating.

This point leads to the third issue to be raised, and that is that media research most often studies the *unintended* effects of media. That is, those interested in media influences tend to be more intrigued by effects that a medium did not intend (e.g., aggression, stereotypes) rather than its overt attempts to teach others (e.g., the popular American children's show *Sesame Street* that was produced to teach children to count and read). The notion that the Russell children might be inadvertently affected by the violent content of cartoons or the gender-typed portrayal of men and women in music videos tends to create a larger volume of research than that attempting to determine whether prosocial content is effective. One reason cited for this special interest in unintended effects is that a medium's content may reflect social unrealities or stereotypes (Gerbner et al., 1994). As a result, children may inadvertently adopt unrealistic social beliefs and expectations from television and other media. For example, until very recently, North American situation comedies portrayed the family in a middle-class, "white-collar" manner, in which both the mother and father work in highly esteemed jobs. Many North American families come from strong blue-collar environments in which parents perform lower status manual labor, or they belong to families that live at or below the poverty line because one or both parents are unemployed. By watching situation comedies, the Russell children may have seen only a one-sided portrayal of the North American family, and they may come to believe that what they see on television is an accurate depiction of the way the majority of people live. The phenomenal popularity of such shows as *Roseanne* indicates that the blue-color segment of the population may be more fairly represented in the future.

In the following discussion of displacement and content effects, the reader should be forewarned that the theories and much of the research are based on the *unintended* impact that *television* has on *children*. Wherever possible, research showing similar findings in other forms of media, and with adults, will be given.

DISPLACEMENT THEORY

One of the physical laws people have to live with is that there are only 24 hours in each day. As if this were not bad enough, the way people portion out their activities on any given day is done in a zero-sum manner; spending time doing one activity means there is less time to devote to other pursuits. For example, after subtracting sleep time and time spent in work or school, there is very little time left for recreation and (for students) homework.

This has important implications for children. During childhood there are several important developmental milestones that must be attained. These milestones include cognitive growth (e.g., creativity, imagination, intelligence), as well as the development of language and reading skills. Displacement theory states that, when children watch television, they are taking important time away from activities geared toward meeting these developmental goals. As a result, the more television children watch, the poorer they are expected to do in tests of these milestones (e.g., psychological tests of creativity or academic tests of reading ability) because they have had less time to spend learning the necessary skills.

In this way, displacement theory is specifically directed toward describing the impact that television has on children's cognitive growth, their educational attainment, as well as other activities that cannot be time-shared with TV (e.g., many leisure pursuits). For example, consider cognitive growth. The pre–high school era is one of the most important points in children's intellectual development (Harrison & Williams, 1986). Many of the skills children learn in school that help to foster cognitive growth need to be reinforced with practice at home. As a result, children need to spend a certain number of hours outside of school practicing their math skills and mastering their cognitive abilities through play and other exercises. Because children tend to spend so much of their out-of-school time watching television, however, they are displacing time that might be better spent mastering these skills and abilities.

Because displacement theory predicts a *causal* relationship between TV viewing and academic and cognitive outcomes, the most direct way to examine this inference is by using an experimental design. An experimental approach would necessitate finding a large sample of children who had *never* been exposed to TV and then randomly assign them to either a TV-viewing condition or a non-TV-viewing condition. Once this has been done, their performance on variables such as cognitive growth and academic performance can be measured both before and after the experimental group is exposed to television. If the children in the experimental group (i.e., those who watched TV) reduced their scores on the outcome measures while the control group (i.e., those who still had no TV exposure) remained the same, then displacement effects would be the cause. Similar assumptions would be made if the control group improved its abilities whereas the experimental group went unchanged. An even greater experimental test of this hypothesis would involve comparing the control group to two comparison groups: a high-TV-viewing group (e.g., 3–4 hours per day) and a low-TV-viewing group (e.g., 1–2 hours per day).

However, this kind of experiment is unrealistic in the 1990s. Given that most homes in North America have at least one television, it would be an impossible task to locate enough children who have not had extensive exposure to TV and who are otherwise representative of the general population. Still, there are two viable alternatives for studying displacement effects: (a) *correlational* studies that examine the relationship between the amount of time children spend watching TV and their cognitive and academic achievements; and (b) *quasi-experimental* designs that have taken advantage of the introduction of television to one or more communities and monitored the effects it had on people's behavior. Both kinds of studies have demonstrated significant displacement effects and will be discussed next.

Correlational Studies

Correlational research examines the relationship between two naturally occurring events; there are no experimental or control groups in this research design. Studies of this nature assess the amount of television children watch and then correlate that with variables such as their academic achievement, cognitive development, and degree of physical fitness. Displacement theory would predict a negative correlation between TV viewing and these outcomes. In other words, as TV viewing increases, factors such as school grades, creativity, and fitness should decrease.

Several studies have examined the relationship between the amount of television children watch and their reading and academic abilities. In a study of over 28,000 American high school seniors, Keith, Reimers, Fehrmann, Pottebaum, and Aubey (1986) found that the more TV these adolescents watched, the less time they spent doing their homework and the lower their reading and mathematics ability scores on nationwide standardized tests. Neuman (1988) and Potter (1987), however, have observed that for those children and adolescents who watch fewer than 4 hours of TV per day, there appears to be little impact on their reading abilities; it is only when TV viewing exceeds 4 hours per day that reading abilities are observed to be seriously impaired. This suggests that the relationship between TV viewing and academics/reading is not necessarily as linear as the displacement hypothesis would predict. That is, there appears to be a plateau effect whereby children who watch TV at levels at or beyond the plateau tend to be most adversely affected (Beentjes & Van der Voort, 1988).

A child's cognitive growth (e.g., daydreaming and creativity) might also be affected adversely by watching too much television. However, some would suggest that because of its varied nature, watching television often may actually stimulate cognitive growth instead of impairing it. Valkenburg and Van der Voort (1994) reviewed the scientific literature examining the evidence for the *cognitive stimulation* and *cognitive reduction* hypotheses. Their overview examined the impact of TV viewing separately for two measures of cognitive growth: daydreaming and creativity. They showed that the vast majority of research has found a positive relationship between TV viewing and the frequency of children's daydreaming. However, when Valkenburg and Van der Voort reviewed the relationship between the amount of time children spent watching TV and their degree of creativity, a negative relationship emerged. Thus, children who watch a lot of TV tend to daydream more often but are less creative than children who watch TV less frequently. These results show the mixed influence that TV has on cognitive development.

Because television tends not to be time-shared with physical fitness activities (especially in children), there should be a negative relationship between amount of TV viewing and level of physical fitness or obesity. Tucker (1986) examined this relationship in a sample of adolescent boys. He observed no effect of time spent watching TV on obesity levels. However, Tucker did find that children who watched TV less than 2 hours per day were significantly more physically fit than both moderate viewers (i.e., between 2 and 4 hours per day) and heavy viewers (i.e., more than 4 hours per day). The relationship between TV viewing and physical fitness and obesity in adolescent girls is still not known.

Even though the studies reported here illustrate the relationship predicted by displacement theory, correlational analyses *cannot* be used to make the causal inferences the theory wants to make; it is just as likely that children who do not do well in school, who have poorer cognitive abilities, or who are not as physically fit spend more time watching television *because* of these deficits rather than as a *result* of them. This point has been argued by Ritchie, Price, and Roberts (1987), whose 3-year panel study examined the amount of time a group of children spent watching TV, how well the children read, and how much time they spent reading. Ritchie et al. noticed that, over time, children who read well and read a lot continued to do so. They also observed that the amount of time children spent watching TV and both their reading ability and time spent reading were highly intercorrelated at all three testing points. When, over the course of their study, there were changes in reading time and abilities, the change was not necessarily correlated with the amount of TV viewing the child did. Thus, Ritchie et al. argue that it is impossible to determine if changes in reading are a *direct* result of increased time watching television or whether there are other intervening variables that need to be identified and tested in future research (e.g., peer support for reading activities).

Quasi-Experimental Studies

More powerful research methods are needed in order to determine if the causal relationship predicted by displacement theory can be supported. To this end, several studies have employed a quasi-experimental method known as the *interrupted time-series design*. Researchers who have utilized this method have taken advantage of a naturally occurring event (e.g., the introduction of television to one or more communities) in order to examine the impact that displacement caused by TV viewing has on children. In this way, they can use a pre-post design (i.e., taking measures of the dependent variables both before and after a special event has occurred), looking for changes in a group of people after TV has been introduced to their lifestyle.

However, unlike the correlational studies reported earlier, these studies do not correlate time spent watching TV with the outcome variables; it is only *assumed* that the introduction of TV causes children to spend less time developing their cognitive and reading abilities. Thus, quasi-experimental research first needs to determine that children living in communities without TV spend more time doing activities geared to stimulating cognitive development and reading. One of the first quasi-experimental studies to address this issue was conducted by Parker (1963; see also Cook & Campbell, 1979). Parker examined the impact of displacement on people's reading during the introduction of television in the United States. Between 1951 and 1953, there was a moratorium in the granting of new licenses to operate television stations. Parker identified 55 Illinois communities that had TV prior to this ban and then matched them with demographically similar communities that did not receive television until after the ban was lifted. Parker operationalized a community's involvement in reading by calculating the ratio of each community's public library book circulation to its population. This per capita statistic was calculated for all of the matched communities. Parker's data showed that the introduction of TV to a community (irrespective of whether it came prior to 1951 or after 1953) caused its per capita library circulation to drop significantly. For both the early and late TV communities, the decrease following the introduction of TV was statistically significant.

Whereas Parker's study aggregated children's and adult's reading into a per

capita circulation statistic, similar studies have examined the impact of TV's introduction specifically on the time children spend reading. Historically, the first of these
studies was conducted around the time of TV's introduction in the United Kingdom
(Himmelweit, Oppenheim, & Vince, 1958), followed by the United States and
Canada (Schramm, Lyle, & Parker, 1961), Japan (Furu, 1962), Australia (Murray &
Kippax, 1978), and South Africa (Mutz, Roberts, & van Vuuren, 1993). For example, Furu (1962) used a before-after design in order to determine whether the introduction of television had displacement effects on reading in Japanese children.
Furu's study was especially strong in that he also included a matched control group
of children who had no exposure to TV at any time during the study. He found that
once television had been introduced, those children who were exposed to TV reduced the amount of time they spent reading books, magazines, comic books, and
newspapers, compared to children in the control group.

Thus, television viewing does appear to displace time that would otherwise be
spent on tasks geared to helping children attain cognitive developmental and reading milestones. There are two reasons, however, why quasi-experimental studies addressing whether there are *actual* declines in children's cognitive growth and reading
abilities after the introduction of television are fairly uncommon. First, the earlier
studies of displacement did not adequately determine the cognitive and academic
effects of displacement. These studies tended to be more concerned with the impact
that the new medium of television had on people's use of the preexisting media (e.g.,
whether they read newspapers or books as frequently as before). In these studies, issues such as changes in reading abilities and time spent doing homework and other
cognitive tasks were only inferred from changes in the time the children spent utilizing the older media. A second reason these kinds of studies are uncommon is that,
with the advent of satellite communications and cable television, there are few (if
any) communities left in the Western world that do not have access to television. Because of this, it is not feasible to conduct a newer, more controlled, and psychologically focused pre-post, quasi-experimental study so that displacement effects can be
more thoroughly examined.

Still, even with these past and present limitations, there is one well-
documented case that provides important insights into the social psychological implications of displacement theory (Williams, 1986b). Unlike many of the previous
studies of this kind, the NOTEL study conducted by Williams and her colleagues
(see Box 11–1 for an overview) was not concerned with changes in media use. Their
goal was to study the social psychological impact that the introduction of television
had on members of the NOTEL community (albeit mostly the children).

Corteen and Williams (1986) studied TV's displacement effects on children's
reading. Because they believed that displacing reading activities might have a more
negative impact in younger children, Corteen and Williams tested boys and girls
who were in Grades 2, 3, and 8 before TV was introduced in NOTEL. Two years
later, they retested those same children (they were now in Grades 4, 5, and 10) in addition to testing a new group of children in Grades 2, 3, and 8. With regard to the
longitudinal data, Corteen and Williams found no evidence that children's reading
competencies declined after the arrival of television in NOTEL; however, by the

**Box
11-1**

Assessing the Impact of Television: A Naturalistic Study

In the summer of 1973, Tannis MacBeth Williams learned of a community in the interior of British Columbia, Canada, that did not receive, and had never received, any television broadcasts (the town was nicknamed NOTEL). This town was located in a geographic blind spot and was not particularly isolated from the rest of the province's population. However, what made this community special was that, within a year, a new signal repeater was to have been put into operation. This would give the people who lived there access to one television channel: the Canadian Broadcasting Corporation (CBC).

Williams's goal was to study the impact that the introduction of television had on that community. In order to study its many possible effects, she recruited a number of colleagues. In collaboration with Williams, they studied the ways in which the introduction of TV affected factors such as reading skills, cognitive development, aggression, gender role attitudes, and leisure activities, among others.

Williams and her colleagues used the arrival of television to do a naturalistic *pre-post* field study. In other words, she and her team went into the NOTEL community, collected their first pieces of data before TV's introduction there, and then returned after TV had established itself; at this point, they collected the same type of data a second time. They did this in two ways. Part of the data they collected was *longitudinal* in nature. This meant examining the same participants at both Phase 1 and, 2 years later, at Phase 2. In this manner, any changes in the participants between the two phases could be attributed to the introduction of television. However, some or all of those changes might be maturational in origin; this would suggest that changes over the 2 years might be due to natural cognitive and physical growth. To help control for this problem, Williams and her colleagues also collected *cross-sectional* data. If they tested children in Grades 2 and 4 at Phase 1, they then tested children in the same grades at Phase 2. This procedure helps identify increases or decreases in the average abilities of same-aged children after TV's introduction to NOTEL.

Using these two methods, Williams would have had an excellent understanding of how the NOTEL community was affected by the introduction of television. However, this type of pre-post design lacks a control group in which changes in society at large can be monitored. This deficiency would limit any cause-and-effect types of statements that Williams et al. would want to make. For example, they could not say that the introduction of TV *caused* children's reading scores to change. Other factors unrelated to TV might just as easily have caused the changes they observed (e.g., changes to the educational curriculum or differences in the children's maturational growth rates). Thus, Williams and her team went looking for comparison groups (i.e., towns that were similar in demographic makeup to the NOTEL community, but differed only in that they already had access to television). They found two such communities: one that had access only to a CBC channel (UNITEL), and one that had access to the CBC and the main three U.S. networks of the time: ABC, CBS, and NBC (this town was nicknamed MULTITEL).

Finding these comparison groups was important for making inferences about the cause of any changes they observed in the NOTEL group after TV was introduced. If changes occurred in NOTEL but not in UNITEL or MULTITEL, then the main culprit had to be the only major difference between the three groups: the introduction of TV to NOTEL during the intervening time period.

same token, their abilities did not increase either. Cross-sectionally, the data tell a very different story. At Phase 1 of the study, Grade 2 and Grade 3 girls and boys in NOTEL had significantly better reading abilities than same-grade children in UNITEL or MULTITEL. However, the introduction of TV to NOTEL saw a significant *decline* in the average NOTEL children's reading scores that was not matched in the other two towns. Thus, two years after TV's introduction, Grade 2 and 3 children in NOTEL appeared to give up their superior reading abilities; they developed the same (lower) reading abilities as children who had grown up with TV. The reading abilities of children in Grade 8 appeared to be unaffected by the introduction of TV to their community.

Harrison and Williams (1986) examined creativity changes in Grade 4 and 7 NOTEL children. The longitudinal data show that at Phase 1, NOTEL children were significantly more creative than same-grade children in the two comparison towns. However, after 2 years of watching television, the NOTEL children's creativity scores decreased and were similar to UNITEL and MULTITEL children's scores. This pattern was even more profound in the cross-sectional data. Before NOTEL had TV, children in Grades 4 and 7 had staggeringly higher creativity scores when compared to the children in UNITEL and MULTITEL. By Phase 2, the average level of creativity in Grade 4 and Grade 7 NOTEL children was approximately 40% less than it had been before TV was introduced, equalling the children in the other towns.

In summary, correlational research shows that children who watch a lot of television (especially more than 4 hours per day) tend to be most adversely affected. Their reading and math abilities are less than those children who watch less TV, and they also score lower on measures of creativity. Quasi-experimental evidence also suggests that reading ability and creativity decline as a result of displacement effects from watching television. This suggests that Tim and Linda Russell should be concerned about the amount of time their two children spend watching television; it is clear that time spent doing homework should take precedence. Whether or not Ethan and Emily Russell are too old to be adversely affected by displacement effects is unknown. The correlational data show negative relationships into adulthood, whereas the NOTEL data suggest that younger children are the most at risk for displacement effects.

CONTENT EFFECTS

Television programs carry more information than their producers typically intend, as do other kinds of media, such as magazines, books, comics, and music. For example, the way characters behave on TV tells us not only about the story's plot but also about what kinds of behavior are acceptable and expected by our culture. Content effects measure the extent to which these peripheral cues influence the viewer. Furthermore, they are the most studied aspect of the media's influence over people (especially that of television). Researchers studying content effects want to know how people using a medium such as television learn behaviors or attitudes that were not *intended* to be taught.

Several theories have been proposed to explain the how the mass media's content can influence people. The theories described next are the ones used most commonly by social psychologists to explain these effects. In order to emphasize the wide variety of content effects that can be studied, however, each section will be prefaced by an overview of a different media-related social problem. Once the problem has been described, the ways in which the highlighted theories are used to account for the social problem are discussed.

Social Learning Theory and Priming: The Case of Violence

Background. That television contains violent images is beyond debate. As Gunter (1994) describes, attempts to delineate the extent of mass media violence began as early as 1920 in the United States. At that time, the medium of interest was motion pictures, but the assumptions were the same: that watching violent images causes people to act violently. Since then, violence on television has become the main source of concern. Several studies have attempted to describe the level of televised violence and which kinds of programs might put children at greater risk for developing an aggressive behavioral repertoire (Tan, 1986).

There is a wide variety of research examining the impact that viewing violent actions and images on television has on the incidence of aggressive and violent behavior in both children and adults. Centerwall (1989) showed how the introduction of television in the United States, Canada, and South Africa was related to a substantial increase in the murder rates of white citizens in each of those countries (the data were limited to this group because the social-political situation in South Africa made it difficult to compare the lifestyles of blacks in North America and South Africa). Centerwall's data showed that between 1945 (when TV was first introduced in North America) and 1974 (just before TV's introduction in South Africa), per capita–based homicide deaths rose in both the United States and Canada by 93%, but actually decreased 7% in South Africa. Following the introduction of TV to South Africa, however, the per capita white homicide rate increased 56% (between 1975 to 1983), while the rates in Canada and the United States remained stable.

Other, more direct, evidence for the relationship between television viewing and aggressive behavior continues to show that the more violent TV children watch, the more aggressive they are. As part of a 3-year, multinational study of aggression rates and violent TV viewing, Wiegman, Kuttschreuter, and Baarda (1992) have shown that the amount of violent TV children watched in the first year of the study was significantly correlated with the peer-nominated rates of aggression in the third year. However, Wiegman et al. also show that this effect seems to be affected by the country in which an individual lives. The relationship between TV viewing and aggression levels tends to be strongest in children and adolescents living in the United

States and in Israeli cities. Similar findings were observed by Wood, Wong, and Chachere (1991). Their meta-analytic review of the experimental research, which examined the impact that watching violent television has on children's free play, found a moderate effect size (in other words, the impact was consistent across studies and fairly robust). Some have argued that TV viewing leads to aggression only in the laboratory and that it does not occur to the same degree in natural settings (e.g., schoolyards, playgrounds). However, Wood et al. also showed that viewing TV violence tended to induce aggressive play irrespective of whether the study was performed in a laboratory or in a natural setting.

Social Learning Theory (Bandura, 1977, 1994). Social learning theory has often been used by social psychologists to explain the ways in which people (especially children) model the aggression and violence they see portrayed in the media. Bandura (1977) has proposed that a person's observations of how others behave provide him or her with information about behavioral possibilities that are not already included in his or her own behavioral repertoire. Once an individual observes a new behavior being modeled, Bandura (1977) believes that he or she enters a four-stage process that culminates in the internalization of the observed behavior. First, the person must be paying *attention* to the behavior being modeled. Bandura has divided this feature into two components: (a) aspects of the stimulus that either can enhance or inhibit the likelihood of people paying attention to it (e.g., how distinctive or complex the stimulus is); and (b) characteristics of the observer that limit his or her experience of the stimuli (e.g., the person's present level of arousal or the existence of a perceptual set may increase or decrease the chances of the person attending to the modeled behavior).

Once the individual has paid attention to a modeled behavior, she or he must then *retain* that information. This often involves using a set of cognitive processes to encode and organize the observed information into an appropriate mental structure (i.e., a schema). With the information properly retained, the person next must *reproduce* the observed behavior. In order for this to occur, he or she must be physically capable of performing the action. Finally, if that action is to be retained in the individual's behavioral repertoire (as opposed to being just a one-time display), then he or she must be *motivated* to perform that behavior again. In other words, the behavior must be reinforced. This might involve a person being rewarded by others for his or her actions or the person rewarding himself or herself. Once these four conditions have been met, the individual has used social learning to add a new behavior to his or her repertoire.

To show that social learning processes play a causal role in the relationship between viewing violent television shows and acting in aggressive ways requires evidence that people do indeed model the violent actions they see portrayed in the media. Much of Bandura's initial research has shown ways in which children will repeat novel aggressive behaviors presented to them by televised models. The famous "Bobo Doll" experiments conducted by Bandura and his colleagues in the 1960s demonstrate this effect (e.g., Bandura, Ross & Ross, 1961). These studies use videotape produced specifically for the experiment. In these videos, models either perform aggressive actions toward a blow-up doll or act in a nonviolent way. After watching one of the two tapes, children are allowed to play in a room that, among its many toys, contains replicas of the blow-up doll and the tools used to hit it. In studies like this, children who watched the model hit the Bobo doll often mimicked the violent behavior they observed on the videotape.

Archival research into so-called "copycat crimes" also demonstrates how people model aggressive behavior. Berkowitz (1993) describes several incidences of people modeling suicide and other forms of aggression. For example, after highly publicized prize fights, the national homicide rate in the United States tends to increase; similar findings have been observed after highly publicized suicides.

Some argue that parental mediation is the most important way to reduce the negative impact of social learning (e.g., Singer, Singer, Desmond, Hirsch, & Nicol, 1988). However, Bandura (1994) notes that "modeling influences can strengthen *or weaken* restraints over behavior that have been *previously* learned" (p. 71, emphasis added). This point emphasizes the notion that social learning is a *dynamic* process. Parents may teach children not to act in an aggressive manner, thus instilling a sense of restraint; however, media influences can work either to erode or enhance these already learned behaviors and motivations. Although this may sound overly pessimistic, it is not. Bandura's belief that social learning theory can be used to get rid of unwanted behaviors means that television's undesirable influences can be combatted using the same modeling processes.

Priming. A second social psychological theory that can be used to explain the effects of violent television content on people's behavior is known as the *priming hypothesis*. This concept suggests that televised aggression tends to give people ideas about acting aggressively. They might be watching the aftermath of a violent event on the news, or they might be watching a violent movie. Either way, the priming hypothesis predicts that this kind of stimulus prepares people to think about acting in an aggressive way.

The priming hypothesis also suggests that people learn to associate stimuli with the commitment of violent acts. The presence of these associative stimuli (also known as *cues*) may enhance the likelihood of people acting aggressively. The *weapons effect,* described by Berkowitz and LePage (1967), is an excellent example of how cues can become associated with aggression and then can be used to trigger aggressive actions. Objects that are present when violence occurs (but are *not used* as weapons themselves) often become associated with violence and their presence in future situations is more likely to lead to violence. Research examining the weapons effect typically involves showing participants a video of an aggressive situation. Somewhere in that video will be an object that is not used in an aggressive way but stands out visually so that it gets people's attention. In this way, the object becomes associated with the violence. Other participants watch a violent video without the object being there. After viewing the violent video, subjects are brought into a laboratory where, among all the other furnishings in the room, the associated object is prominently placed. Research has shown that the likelihood of violence occurring increases significantly for those who associated violence with these cues (Berkowitz, 1993).

A study by Josephson (1987) provides an interesting demonstration of how an object as innocuous as a walkie-talkie can become associated with aggression and can prime people exposed to that cue to act more aggressively in a naturalistic game situation. Josephson randomly assigned a group of boys to watch either an aggressive or nonaggressive video. Those watching the aggressive video saw one of two videos: the one with the associative cue involved a violent police assault on a heavily armed group of criminals; the order to begin the assault came by walkie-talkie. The other aggressive video did not contain this associative cue. Later, all the boys were given the task of playing a game of floor hockey. While playing this game, their behavior was monitored for levels of aggression. Aggression levels were significantly higher in boys who had seen the aggressive video clip with the cue when the hockey game's referee used a walkie-talkie to confer with officials.

To summarize, social learning and priming are two theories that have been used to explain how violent content in the media can adversely influence users of those media. These theories predict that people are directly affected by violent content and that those who are exposed more frequently should be at greater risk than those who experience little exposure to that content. For example, Ethan Russell, the 13-year-old boy described in the opening vignette, is more likely to be affected by violent media than his twin sister Emily because he has surrounded himself with it. Ethan spends much of his spare time watching sporting events and horror movies; the level of interpersonal aggression in both types of programming is high. This can provide Ethan with several models of aggressive, antisocial behavior. Furthermore, Ethan enjoys playing video games, which, as studies have shown, can prime later aggression in its players (e.g., Anderson & Ford, 1987; Cooper & Mackie, 1986; Silvern & Williamson, 1987). Being exposed to one risk factor may not pose a significant threat, but exposure to several may be harmful.

Cultivation Hypothesis: The Case of Gender Stereotypes

Background. Television and most of the other types of media are full of gender stereotypic images of men and women. In fact, the media have become influential agents in the socialization of gender-related stereotypes (Durkin, 1985a). The media's influence often can begin at birth. Bridges (1993) has shown that cards congratulating parents on the birth of their child offer several gender-typed messages: Boy's cards and envelopes are never pink whereas girl's cards are never blue; action is more often a theme in boy's cards whereas gentleness is more commonly associated with girl's cards. Gender role bias in children's stories also provides a way for gender-typed messages to be passed on to children. Older story books often portray more male than female characters and the females in these stories are often relegated to passive roles or roles that require them to be dependent on the more active male characters. Current research suggests that although there have been changes in the ratio of male to female characters, females in newer children's stories are still represented in a passive and dependent way (Kortenhaus & Demarest, 1993).

Men and women are also portrayed differently in a wide range of print advertisements. Evidence from medical journals shows that advertisements depicting female characters most often present these women in gender stereotypic occupations (e.g., secretaries, waitresses) and portray women as the most frequent consumers of medication. This latter finding is in direct contradiction to reality, because men have been shown to use the medications being advertised much more frequently than women (Hawkins & Aber, 1993). The most striking gender stereotypic image in magazines comes from the way men's and women's physical appearance is portrayed. First, studies of the curvaceousness of women used to model or advertise products in magazines such as *Vogue* and *Ladies Home Journal* have shown a consistently positive correlation between trends to use thinner models and the rate of disordered eating among women (Silverstein, Perdue, Peterson, & Kelly, 1986). Also, magazines subject women to more implicit and explicit messages that they should diet, whereas men are told they need to become physically bigger by improving their muscle mass (Andersen & DiDomenico, 1992; Mishkind, Rodin, Silberstein, & Striegel-Moore, 1986; Silverstein et al., 1986; Wiseman, Gray, Mosimann, & Ahrens, 1992).

In addition to the print media, there are many ways in which television presents gender-biased images of men and women. Research shows that TV overrepresents men (McCauley, Thangavelu, & Rozin, 1988) and presents men's lives in ways that suggest they are more interesting and more powerful than women's lives (Durkin, 1986). When women are shown, they are mostly young (under 30), whereas men's ages tend to cross the life span (Durkin, 1985b, 1986). This presents the idea that it is culturally more acceptable for men to show their age but that women should always look young. Research examining the way men and women are portrayed in television commercials shows that women are more often used for food advertisements, in ads highlighting that a product is cheaper than similar items, and when a product will enhance the degree to which one can gain approval from others (e.g., breath mints). Men are more often used in voice-overs and are used to advertise practical products (Furnham & Bitar, 1993; Mazella, Durkin, Cerini, & Buralli, 1992).

Cultivation Hypothesis. What effects might the presentation of gender stereotypic images in the mass media have on children and adults? The *cultivation hypothesis* (Gerbner et al., 1994) suggests that people use television and the other forms of mass media to learn (either directly or indirectly) about the culture they live in and how it works. As described earlier, however, the media often portray a distorted view of that reality. This can result in people developing one of two distinct images of the "real world": *social reality* or *TV reality*. According to the cultivation hypothesis, those who watch the most TV should have a perception of reality that corresponds more with television's portrayal than with the actual social reality.

With regard to gender stereotypes in the media (especially television), the cultivation hypothesis would predict that people who watch a lot of TV should have more gender stereotypic attitudes and should act in more gender stereotypic ways than those who watch little TV. This assumption was supported by Signorielli and Lears (1992), whose study showed that the more time children in Grades 1, 3, 5, and 7 spent watching TV, the more likely they were to have stereotypic beliefs about which gender should be performing various household chores. However, a longitudinal study conducted by Morgan (1982) showed that TV viewing contributed to the development of sexist attitudes only for girls. In the NOTEL study, Kimball (1986) also observed a differential impact of TV viewing on boys and girls. She measured children's (Grades 6 and 9) gender stereotypic perceptions of their peers and their parents. Data were collected at two points in time: just before TV's introduction to NOTEL and 2 years afterward. Also, for this study in the NOTEL series, only cross-sectional data were collected. Kimball's results showed that for perceptions of their peers, the boys in NOTEL tended to be less gender-typed than boys in UNITEL and MULTITEL before TV's introduction to their community. However, 2 years after TV arrived in NOTEL, these boys were just as gender-typed as those in the other towns. A similar pattern emerged for girls' perceptions of their parents (Kimball, 1986).

Durkin (1985c) and Potter (1991) suggest that the assumption of linearity built into the cultivation hypothesis may not be accurate. In his review of the correlational evidence linking the amount of TV viewing with gender role beliefs, Durkin (1985c) notes that, in most of this research, the correlations are low, not significant, and even contradictory. Because the assumption of linearity is the underlying premise of correlation coefficients, the lack of a correlation (or its small size) could be a result of a *curvilinear* relationship similar to the plateau effect described in the discussion of displacement theory.

In summary, the cultivation hypothesis suggests that those with greater exposure to one or more media should be more inclined to adopt the media's distorted perceptions of the world (i.e., to view the media's notion of reality as *the* reality). To give an example, the kinds of media Emily Russell uses might predispose her to adopt more gender-stereotypic attitudes than her twin brother. Emily and her friends watch soap operas that often portray men and women in gender-typed roles; the commercials they see while watching TV also portray gender stereotypic images; the magazines Emily reads send her images about what women should look like, which may predispose her to believe she is overweight (when she really is not) because the models in the magazines are well below the national average for body fat. The more Emily is exposed to these messages, the more cultivation theory predicts she will come to believe that they tell the *real* story about how life is.

FUTURE DIRECTIONS
FOR MEDIA INFLUENCE RESEARCH

Where will applied social psychological research into the influence of the media go next? There are several directions it may take, but two are discussed here: intervention research and broadening the study of media influences to include the "new media" (Rice, 1984).

It was mentioned earlier that correlational analyses of displacement and content effects are difficult to interpret causally and, because almost everyone in the latter part of the 20th century has grown up with TV, quasi-experimental studies with proper control groups are now unrealistic. With this in mind, one might ask oneself where applied social psychology can make an impact in the study of displacement and content effects. One promising area is that of *intervention*. Research of this nature would concern itself with studying the impact of *restricting* the amount or type of television a child watches and observing its effects. For example, Gadberry (1980) studied the impact of decreased TV viewing in a sample of 6-year-olds who were randomly assigned to either a restricted (i.e., half their normal viewing time per day) or unrestricted viewing group. After 6 weeks, children whose TV viewing was restricted had higher performance IQ scores and were less impulsive. Parental reports showed that children in the restricted group used this extra time to do more reading. This intervention demonstrated the causal relationship between displacement effects and cognitive outcomes in a way that is essentially a backward approach compared to the previous research in this area.

Similar kinds of research can address content effects. Durkin (1985b) describes the "Freestyle" project, in which 9- and 12-year-olds were presented with a 13-part television series in which they were exposed to counter-gender-stereotypic role portrayals. When the children were given the opportunity to discuss each episode after viewing it, they became more open to people crossing gender-role boundaries and their gender-typed notions were lessened. Other research shows how intervening can influence modeled or primed behaviors. Waite, Hillbrand, and Foster (1992) studied the impact of a psychiatric hospital's decision to remove a TV channel carrying music videos from its televisions. Its removal resulted in significant decreases in the frequency of aggressive behaviors made by patients. Thus, even though one cannot study the impact of television's introduction, one can study the effects of its removal, restriction, or changes in its contents.

Finally, mention should be made about the introduction of the *new media* into our culture and the role that social psychology can play in studying its impact. With the advent of portable telephones, computers, modems, FAXes, CD-ROMs, and other forms of portable and digital media, new avenues open up for people, and new patterns of media use appear. How people use these new forms of media determine, in part, the problems that may arise out of their use. However, even though Kiesler, Siegel, and McGuire (1984) first brought this issue to psychology's attention more than a decade ago, social psychology has practically ignored the impact of the new media.

These new forms of communication can create several kinds of social problems. Kiesler et al. note that electronic mail can produce a social context in which social norms disintegrate. Because people cannot see or hear the person they are communicating with, nonverbal and paraverbal feedback is absent. This can result in people misinterpreting what others say (Rice & Love, 1987). Also, because social status cues are missing and there is a great degree of social anonymity, electronic communicating can be depersonalizing. This can lead to a sense of deindividuation, which may cause people to interact in more socially aggressive and socially inappropriate ways (i.e., the so-called "flaming" that occurs on computer bulletin boards is an example of this; it entails sending scathing and vulgar replies to people who disagree with your opinion on a subject). Although these factors can lead to many negative outcomes, they can also help others communicate more effectively by erasing barriers based on prejudice (e.g., a physical disability or deformity).

Another area of the new media whose impact is understudied is that of *telecommuting*. People who telecommute spend one or two days a week working at home either because of the distance they must travel to work or because of difficulties in arranging child care. These people have jobs that give them the freedom to make this arrangement; they usually do most of their work at a computer and can easily perform their work at home. Tim and Linda Russell (from the vignette) are examples of telecommuters.

Even though it appears to be an advantageous situation, there are some disadvantages to telecommuting that may leave the individual feeling more stressed than he or she would normally feel in a traditional office setting. First, the type of job an individual performs can have a significant impact on the telecommuting experience. Those in low autonomy positions have the least positive experiences, whereas highly skilled professionals who are accustomed to high levels of autonomy are the most satisfied (Olson & Primps, 1984). Second, because telecommuters tend to be isolated from the office, they lack a social support network to deal with work-related stress. Norman, Collins, Conner, Martin, and Rance (1995) showed that telecommuters who were able to cope with stress in a problem-focused manner had higher levels of job satisfaction. Even though there appear to be problems associated with telecommuting, an evaluation of a recent telecommuting program at Statistics Canada showed that working one day a week at home had significantly more benefits than harmful effects: Reduced role overload, reduced number of problems resulting from the interference between work and family, increased ability of the teleworker to manage personal and family time, and a positive effect on their family members were among the benefits (Statistics Canada, 1995).

SUGGESTED READINGS

Bryant, J., & Zillmann, D. (Eds.). (1994). *Media effects: Advances in theory and research.* Hillsdale, NJ: Lawrence Erlbaum.

This edited volume provides an excellent summary of social psychological research in the area of mass media. Topics range from an overview of research looking into the impact of the news on our perceptions of the world to how people have used the media to mount successful political campaigns.

Durkin, K. (1985). *Television, sex roles, and children.* Milton Keynes, U.K.: Open University Press.

This book documents the role that television plays in the socialization of gender roles in children. It is based on a series of three papers published in 1985 and 1986 in the *British Journal of Social Psychology*. It examines the gender-typed content of television and the effects it has on children and summarizes research geared to counter these outcomes.

Kiesler, S., Siegel, J., & McGuire, T. W. (1984). Social psychological aspects of computer-mediated communication. *American Psychologist, 39,* 1123–1134.

This paper is fairly old by new technology standards, it is its age that highlights social psychology's failure to study the impact of the new media. Kiesler and her colleagues discuss how social psychological processes such as deindividuation, the lack of social status cues, and the role of computing-specific norms can influence the way people use this increasingly popular form of communication. What is striking is that since its 1984 publication, social psychology has virtually ignored this whole issue.

Oskamp, S. (Ed.). (1988). *Television as a social issue.* Newbury Park, CA: Sage.

This book comprises Volume 8 in the Applied Social Psychology Annual series. Oskamp has collected a wide array of papers examining television from an applied social psychological viewpoint. Chapters are grouped according to theme: content, role portrayals, violence, prosocial values, and the future.

Williams, T. M. (Ed.). (1986). *The impact of television: A natural experiment in three communities.* New York: Academic Press.

This book summarizes the research from the NOTEL study Williams and her colleagues conducted before and after the introduction of television in that community. Its chapters cover topics as diverse as reading abilities, cognitive development, gender stereotyping, leisure activities, and aggression.

12 Environmental Social Psychology

William O. Dwyer
Bryan E. Porter
Frank C. Leeming
Diana P. Oliver
The University of Memphis

The assumption underlying environmental law is that it provides the threat of negative consequences for environmentally destructive behavior, thus serving to preserve environmental quality. To be effective, of course, these consequences must be applied; in Memphis, Tennessee, they were not being effectively applied, with the result that environmental code violations were becoming a significant and chronic problem. One source of this difficulty was that code inspectors in the four city and county agencies responsible for enforcement (the fire, health, housing, and building codes departments) were not making effective use of the environmental court, a special court that hears all environmental code cases in Memphis and Shelby County. Inspectors were reticent to bring cases before the court, and often the cases that were brought were not well prepared nor, in situations where more than one agency was involved, were they well coordinated. From a behavioral perspective, better environmental quality meant that this contingency system had to be improved.

To achieve this goal, the judge solicited the aid of environmental psychologists at the local university. They conducted a thorough needs analysis that resulted in the recommendation that a pilot project be implemented to increase interagency cooperation and use of the court through the formation of a relatively independent team of four inspectors, one from each agency, who could investigate environmental code violations together. Known as the E-Team, its task was (a) to investigate all code violations at selected addresses that received complaints, and (b) if compliance could not be obtained, to summon the violators so that, when warranted, the environmental court could bring to bear its contingency powers of fines and/or injunctions.

It took over a year of political maneuvering to make the E-Team a reality, and during its evolution, the team went through the anticipated "growing pains" and met with predictable resistance from peers and supervisors. Nevertheless, over a two-year period, the team has become a major part of a more efficient contingency-management system to control environmentally destructive behavior. It is definitely superior to the traditional system of individual inspectors working alone in four independent agencies, in which turf protection has significant influence.

Specifically, a 2-year evaluation of the E-Team's progress compared the average team member's activity (measured in terms of cases brought to court) to the average non–E-Team inspector working in the four agencies. It was found that the average E-Team member brought more than seven times the number of cases as the average non–E-Team inspector. Also, compared to non–E-Team inspectors, members of the E-team were better able to identify and prosecute cases involving multiple code violations across the jurisdictions of several agencies.

In spite of its success, the E-Team still struggles with being a subsystem organized by work process and having to exist in a more traditional, functionally organized, command-and-control bureaucracy. There is the predictable "them-and-us" culture separating the team from others in the system, and issues of communication still need to be addressed. But these are the kinds of issues familiar to applied social psychologists and amenable to remediation.[1]

Since the 1940s, there has been a subdiscipline in psychology known as "environmental psychology," but if the casual observer thumbs through the typical text in this area (and there are not many), he or she will discover that the emphasis is not on the environment as an environmentalist would construe the term, but rather on human attitudes about environment. Movements toward and movements away from various kinds of environments, with the emphasis on built environments, are promi-

[1] For more information about the E-Team, see Porter, B. E., Leeming, F. C., Dwyer, W. O., & LeBaron, L. (1995, November). *The environmental team (E-Team): Evaluation changes the face of code enforcement.* Paper presented at the Evaluation '95 International Conference, Vancouver, British Columbia, Canada.

nently featured. The typical text in environmental psychology devotes only one chapter (if that) to issues of environmental protection and preservation. It typically does not focus on planet earth and the potential ecological disasters that it faces. Generally, what will be included are topics such as personal space and privacy, territoriality, crowding, environmental perception and spatial cognition, environmental design and architecture, noise pollution, environmental stress, environmental attitudes, work environments, leisure environments, and, finally, conservation. Examples of recent texts of the traditional kind include Bell, Fisher, Baum, and Greene (1990); Gifford (1987); Holahan (1982); and McAndrew (1993).

A more recent text by Veitch and Arkkelin (1995) reflects the beginning of what could be a shift in the discipline's emphasis toward addressing a different set of environmental issues. These authors define environmental psychology as "a multidisciplinary behavioral science, both basic and applied in orientation, whose foci are the systematic interrelationships between physical and social environments and individual human behavior and experience" (p. 5). The first sentence of the preface to this book states "Humans have only recently, yet painfully, become aware of the ways in which they misuse and abuse the natural environment" (p. xi). Examination of the remainder of the book reveals a recurring emphasis on the theme of environmental protection—the growing focus of a new "environmental psychology."

THE NEW ENVIRONMENTAL PSYCHOLOGY

This chapter is about the environmental psychology recognized by Veitch and Arkkelin (1995). Specifically, it deals with humankind's adverse impact on the environment and what solutions psychology may have to offer. There is no doubt that there are serious environmental problems and that it will take behavior change—sometimes drastic behavior change—if earth's environmental quality is to be protected.

It is probably safe to say that most people over the age of 10 have at least some vague notion that our environment is in trouble, and yet our society is not effectively acting on this knowledge to make significant improvements in our situation. It goes without saying that the degradation of the earth's environment is caused largely by behavior, and the solutions to the problems of environmental quality must come primarily from behavioral change.

There is a lot of rhetoric about technical solutions to the problems of deteriorating environmental quality. Surely "they" will develop an inexpensive and efficient system for harnessing solar energy. Surely "they" will find more oil. Surely "they" will plant trees to combat the greenhouse effect. Surely "they" will find a way to feed the earth's burgeoning population of 5.6 billion. It is an undeniable fact, however, that there has been a strong relationship between technological development and environmental problems, a relationship that will probably continue to exist. No matter how effective the technological change, what is ultimately needed to preserve environmental quality is *behavioral change*. It is behavior that got us into this state of affairs, and it will be behavior change that will help to get us out if, indeed, the state of affairs can be changed.

WHAT APPLIED SOCIAL PSYCHOLOGY BRINGS TO SAVING THE ENVIRONMENT

The effort to accumulate scientific information about the environment and threats to its health spans a wide array of disciplines and people. Any text on environmental science will contain information from biology and ecology, physics and chemistry, geology and geography, climatology and economics. Sprinkled throughout these texts is also the underlying assertion that the preservation of environmental quality will necessitate a massive change in people's behavior.

Psychology brings two assets to the struggle to preserve environmental quality. First, it brings a sophisticated *methodology* for systematically uncovering functional relationships between behavioral and other variables. Psychologists know how to couch problems in answerable terms; they are good at experimental design and methodology, data collection, and evaluation. Second, over the last 120 years psychologists have uncovered a considerable knowledge base regarding the *determinants of behavior*, a host of functional relationships that allow them to predict and modify behavior. Many of these functional relationships have a direct bearing on the kinds of behaviors that impact environmental quality. Three content domains of psychology are particularly salient in influencing environmentally relevant behaviors, and all merit special attention: (a) attitude measurement and change; (b) the social psychology of "movements"; and (c) applied behavior analysis.

Attitude measurement, attitude change, and the relationships between attitude change and behavior change are topics studied extensively by social psychologists. They have learned much about attitudes, the components of attitudes, and what it takes to change them (Aronson, Wilson, & Akert, 1994; Worchel, Cooper, & Goethals, 1991). Social psychologists have learned that there is not necessarily a relationship between a person's attitude about a subject and his or her behaviors relevant to that subject. In other words, people often say or believe one thing, yet do another. Under what conditions do attitudes and behavior match? Clearly the environmental movement has to be aware of such information if it is to pursue the task of changing environmental attitudes and engaging in environmental education with the hope of improving the condition of the environment. It may not be enough merely to ask people to "think globally, act locally."

The social psychology of movements is a second and related area in which social psychology has much to offer (Stewart, Smith, & Denton, 1984). It is clear from the history of the environmental movement that society cannot rely solely on government to look out for the environment's best interests. Those in political power have interests of their own that will usually take precedence over the needs of the environment. It is not that governments are totally uncaring; since the early 1970s, nations have passed many laws (although not always stringently enforced) to protect the environment. But it is also true that much of what has been accomplished in the realm of environmental protection has been initiated through citizen activism. How do these movements get started? What motivates people to join them, contribute to them, and labor tirelessly for them? What makes people push for recycling, preserving the wilderness, preventing the Grand Canyon from being dammed, or pressuring the authorities to stop the killing of fur seals or slaughtering of great whales? Certainly there is something to be learned here that will be of value to environmental preservation.

Applied behavior analysts and behaviorally oriented social psychologists working with environmentally relevant behavior change represent another important approach. To the extent that behavior is determined by its consequences, and to the extent that the relevant consequences can be controlled, perhaps environmentally destructive behaviors can be punished and environmentally protective behaviors can be reinforced. The study of both *antecedent strategies* (i.e., events occurring before the behavior) and *consequence strategies* (i.e., events occurring after the behavior) for controlling environmentally relevant behaviors needs to be emphasized. Furthermore, environmental researchers need to extend their applications of learning principles to those discovered by the social learning theorists, and look at the possibilities for modeling appropriate environmentally relevant attitudes and behaviors throughout earth's population.

Although each of these three areas is valuable for understanding behavior and environmental quality, the applied behavior analysis approach was chosen for most of this chapter for two reasons. First, other chapters in this text have touched on the literature relevant to attitude change and social movements. Second, more than any other area of psychology, applied behavior analysis concentrates on observable behavior change in individuals and communities. How the environment is treated (i.e., how people actually behave toward it, not merely how people feel or think about preserving ecosystems) needs to be changed. Further, applied behavior analysis has developed a track record of successes in its capacity to produce environmental behavior change with the application of antecedents and consequences designed to promote that change.

OVERVIEW OF THE BEHAVIORAL APPROACH
TO ENVIRONMENTAL PROBLEMS

How does a behaviorist construe the problem of identifying and altering environmentally destructive behaviors? Simply put, *behaviorism* is the philosophy that there can be a science of behavior; it is possible to uncover functional relationships between behavioral variables and other variables that, in turn, can be used to describe, explain, predict, and, in some cases, control behavior (see Baum, 1994; Skinner, 1953). The experimental analysis of behavior is the name given to that science, and applied behavior analysis represents the application of that science to "real world" problems requiring behavior change. The underlying assumption of this science is that an individual's (or group's) behavior, including behavior relevant to the environment, is determined by a combination of evolutionary forces and the context in which the behavior occurs. Because controlling genetic factors is impractical, behaviorists have concentrated on contextual influences, that is, the pattern of consequences contingent upon behavior and the stimuli that signal the various contingencies. This pattern of past and present rewards and penalties is considered to be the proximal determinant of behavior (Baum, 1994).

The basic principles guiding the work of behavior analysts are summarized by Grant and Evans (1994), but two of these principles are particularly important. First is the premise that natural behavior is the primary focus of the scientist. Explanations of behavior in terms of hidden processes or "mental fictions" are to be avoided. The second principle, and the one that is discussed here in considerable detail, is that behavior analysts use scientific methods to study behavior. The following sections describe five basic stages involved in mounting a systematic attack on *any* problem: diagnosis, development of causal hypotheses, development of intervention, implementation of intervention, and evaluation of effects. These stages are those also found in the program evaluation literature (Rossi & Freeman, 1993). Because this chapter focuses on the domain of environmentally relevant behavior, activities associated with each stage are illustrated using examples drawn from that arena.

Stage 1: Diagnosis of Environmental Problems

Although the specific threats to environmental quality are too numerous to list, they generally fall within three main categories: overpopulation, loss of earth's resources, and pollution. Each of these is discussed briefly in the following sections.

Overpopulation. Certainly the underlying problem of humanity's assault on the environment has to be overpopulation—the existence of more people than can be comfortably supported by available resources. People (95 million more each year!) require space, food, energy, and other resources, but there are not enough of any of these. For example, more people starve today than ever before; each day 40,000 children under the age of five die of malnutrition or related diseases in poor countries (Miller, 1993).

Our population is growing at a frightening rate. It took 2 million years for the earth's population to reach 1 billion (1800); it took 130 more years to double to 2 billion (1930), 45 years to double again to 4 billion (1975). It has now reached the 5.5 billion level and, in fact, it is rising at such a rapid rate that the growth curve is almost vertical (Veitch & Arkkelin, 1995). Note that authors have been concerned about overpopulation for more than 200 years. In 1789, Thomas Malthus predicted problems caused by overpopulation in his famous *Essay on the Principles of Population*. He said population would increase at a geometric rate and that food production would not be able to keep up with it. He was fundamentally correct, as the grim statistics on those 40,000 children who die of starvation-related conditions every day would attest.

One of the greatest ironies associated with our efforts to preserve the environment is the general taboo that exists regarding discussions of the need to control population growth. In the Ehrlichs' book *The Population Explosion* (1990), the first chapter is entitled "Why Isn't Everyone as Scared as We Are?" They point out that our reticence to control procreation, or even to suggest that it be controlled, is exacerbating our greatest environmental problem. This reticence was clearly demonstrated by the omission of overpopulation as a theme at the 1992 Earth Summit held in Rio de Janeiro.

Loss of Resources. A second environmental problem is our abuse and depletion of natural resources. Because they are either destroyed, diluted, or displaced, many of our resources are becoming less available for use. In this category go such losses as water (e.g., aquifers being pumped dry), fuel (e.g., oil reserves being depleted), topsoil (e.g., erosion and desertification), and gene pools from extinct species (e.g., desecration of tropical rain forests). People live in a closed system; there are only so many resources and when they are gone, they are gone. The carrier pigeon's genes are lost forever, along with the genes of the thousands of other plants and animals that join the list of extinct species each year.

Pollution. The introduction of impurities into the environment is what most people think of when they hear the phrase "environmental quality." Certainly the quality of the environment is reduced by unnatural concentrations of both natural wastes and synthetic chemicals pumped into the air, earth, and water. According to Turk and Turk (1988), the United States annually produces over 80 billion kg of synthetic chemicals in more than 70,000 forms. For many of these chemicals, nature has no "kidneys" capable of breaking them down and treating their negative effects.

One of the scarier subjects in this arena is global warming. The pollution of carbon dioxide, methane, and other chemicals is contributing to the potential for the greenhouse effect, a problem that has received much attention in recent years. As McKibbon (1989) pointed out in *The End of Nature,* global warming is unique in that it will affect everybody everywhere; there will be no escaping it, and there will be no fixing it.

Stage 2: Development of Causal Hypotheses

After the serious problems with the environment have been identified, the next step is to attempt to understand why they exist. Although the specifics of this challenge require the talents of an array of scientific disciplines, the environmental problems mentioned earlier are, to a great extent, the result of human behavior: Overpopulation is caused by people's reproductive behavior, loss of resources is caused by people's consumatory behavior, and pollution is caused by people's careless behavior. Formulating causal hypotheses involves focusing on the question, "Why do people behave this way?"

Of course, the behaviorally oriented environmental psychologist would point to the context and respond that behavior is a product of past and present rewards and penalties. Psychologists with other orientations may choose to focus more on

Box 12–1

Borden's Themes Behind Ecological Commitment

Based upon his extensive research, Borden identified the following eight characteristics commonly associated with people who become committed to preserving environmental quality:

1. They have witnessed a sense of unfulfillment in others who are economically "successful." These others often, but not always, are the person's parents or relatives.
2. They experienced an introspective childhood that involved significant early (and often private) experiences with nature, even though they were not raised in any one particular environment (e.g., rural, suburban, or urban).
3. They were influenced by role models with some ecological or natural history interests—both familial and nonfamilial. (The two types were of apparently equal importance.)
4. They had an intense emotional experience involving the death (and occasionally the birth) of animals.
5. They returned to a "magical" play-place in the out-of-doors and discovered a drastic alteration (e.g., the cutting of a favorite tree, "development" of a woodland, pollution of a stream or beach).
6. They have romantic fantasies deriving from specific books, films, or television programs.
7. Early outdoor experiences such as backpacking, camping, birdwatching, or hunting and fishing, made a deep impression, although these were usually accompanied by the kinds of reactions noted in #4 above.
8. They have had dreams or daydreams of being a victim of nuclear catastrophe.

Source: Borden, 1986 (see also Borden, 1985). Used with permission from Richard Borden.

the person in the context, rather than strictly on the antecedents and consequences themselves. In trying to determine why people behave so badly with regard to the environment, it is important to point out that not everyone does. Box 12-1, describing "The Ecological Person," presents some work by Borden concerning how ecologically responsible people got to be that way. His work suggests some interesting possibilities for the development of intervention strategies.

In trying to understand the complex determinants of environmentally destructive behavior, two explanatory models are especially useful, one presented by a biologist, and one by a social psychologist. These models, both of which involve behavioral variables, provide some direction to people involved in attempting to foster behavior change in this arena. One is referred to as the *tragedy of the commons* and the other, the *social trap*. Each of these is described briefly in the following sections.

Tragedy of the Commons. In a now classic article that appeared in *Science* in 1968, called "The Tragedy of the Commons," Hardin characterized humankind's assault on the environment in terms of colonial New England's tradition of allowing farmers to graze their animals on the public village green or commons. The commons could support only so many grazing animals (its carrying capacity). Any given farmer, however, was tempted to put more animals on the green to increase his personal income even though it would mean that the entire group would eventually suffer. Thus, the farmer would pursue his own short-term welfare because he was able to pass the eventual negative consequences (i.e., the cost) of his irresponsible act on to the other farmers. Of course, the ultimate effect of his uncontrolled consumption was that everyone lost when the village green was destroyed. And so it is happening with spaceship Earth. In abusing our environment, people are acting like the farmer, hoping that others will pay for the consequences of our own selfish behavior. And like the farmer, our "pastures" are being overgrazed and our flocks are beginning to starve.

The question Hardin addresses is why humans tend to abuse the resources they share in common. Hardin also asks what it will take to alter this behavioral predisposition. Along the same lines, Aristotle once wrote, "For that which is common to the greatest number has the least care bestowed upon it. Everyone thinks chiefly of his own, hardly at all of the common interest" (Jowett, 1943, p. 83). The great thinkers have been aware of the commons problem for a long time.

Social Traps. One way of conceptualizing the "commons problem" is in terms of what social psychologists refer to as a social dilemma. Briefly, a social dilemma exists when a person is placed in the position of having to choose between his or her own self-interest or acting for the "common good." Generally, if the person acts in his or her self-interest (i.e., becomes a *defector*), and there are not many other defectors in the group, then the person benefits, at least in the short run. If, on the other hand, the person acts to foster the common good of the group (i.e., becomes a *cooperator*), and there are enough other cooperators in the group, then everyone in the group benefits, at least to a certain extent. One of the most commonly used analogs for studying social dilemmas is the famous "Prisoner's Dilemma game" (Aronson et al., 1994; Worchel et al., 1991).

In developing his social trap theory, Platt (1973) approached social dilemmas from a behavioral perspective, with emphasis on the relative effectiveness of immediate and delayed consequences. He pointed out that the immediate consequences of acting in the public interest are often negative. Extending his conceptualization to environmentally relevant behavior, it is apparent that sorting trash into separate recyclables, for example, requires additional work and recycled paper is more expensive to buy. Any positive effects of such proenvironmental behaviors would occur only in the distant future, if at all, and even then they may not affect the person who performed the behavior. Further, such positive consequences would often be in the form of the nonoccurrence of a condition rather than a material reward. On the other hand, behavior ultimately harmful to the environment is often followed immediately by tangible positive consequences. The immediate rewards associated with behaviors leading to overpopulation, resource depletion, and pollution are certainly apparent to everyone. It is well established that behavior is more strongly influenced by immediate, small rewards than it is by large penalties occurring at a later time. Such is the predicament of the smoker, the overeater, or anyone who is abusing the commons. It is difficult to overestimate the power of the immediate reinforcer. As the Ehrlichs pointed out (1990), human beings have evolved to respond to events and not trends.

For the behaviorally minded environmental psychologist, both Hardin and Platt offer paradigms for understanding some of the underlying causes of environmentally destructive behaviors, and both provide some insight into what kinds of interventions may help to mitigate the problem.

Stage 3: Development of Intervention Strategies

The next stage involves a consideration of what strategies offer the greatest potential for ameliorating specific target problems. In the following sections, several broad generalizations that have arisen from causal hypotheses involving the environment as a "commons" and social traps are first considered, followed by a more specific approach that might be advocated by a behavior analyst.

General Strategies. Hardin's essay certainly does not promote a sense of optimism. He believes that the solution to our tragedy of the commons is for people to undergo a fundamental change in their morality. How do psychologists interpret that mandate? From the behavioral perspective, such a fundamental change would require the manipulation of antecedents and consequences to obtain the desired behavior.

Platt (1973) suggested several techniques for manipulating the dysfunctional arrangement of consequences associated with beneficial and detrimental behaviors. These strategies include: (a) increasing the rewards for beneficial behaviors, (b) increasing the penalties for the detrimental behaviors and reducing the delay between behavior and penalty, (c) reducing the time between the initial rewards and the ultimate penalties, and (d) creating more government control over the unwanted behaviors. Of course, such control implies the need for strong central government, with the attendant loss of personal freedom.

More recently, Edney (1980) reviewed the social trap approach, as well as several other explanations of the tragedy of the commons. He granted that social trap theory is appealing because of its simplicity, but he also criticized it for minimizing the importance of cognitive processes, individual differences, and "reason." Based on research in real-world situations, as well as laboratory analogs (e.g., the Prisoner's Dilemma game), he proposed several generalizations regarding the conditions under which people will be more likely to act in the public interest rather than in their own self-interest. He divided these conditions into two major categories: (a) characteristics of the commons (i.e., the *resource*), and (b) characteristics of the commons consumers (i.e., the *participants*).

Characteristics of the Commons. Cooperation is increased when:

1. the commons (resource) is of lesser value,
2. the commons has not suffered very much depletion, and
3. the commons has been divided among participants so it has lost some of its "commons" characteristics.

Characteristics of the Participants. Cooperation is increased when:

1. there are fewer participants,
2. there is more friendship within the group,
3. group members have personalities that predispose them to act in the communal interest,
4. there is a higher level of "morality" within the group,
5. participants have prior experience in commons-management situations,
6. level of communication within the group is high,
7. there is a greater amount of public disclosure regarding the consumption levels of the group members, and
8. there is a greater level of, or probability of, retribution for abuse of the commons.

Edney (1980) concluded his review of the commons problem with the suggestion that some combination of dividing up the commons and encouraging trust will hold the key to mitigating the tragedy. To the extent that these generalizations reflect reality, they offer some cause for optimism about strategies for reducing the abuse of the commons. Clearly, they offer a wealth of environmentally related research opportunities, not only with laboratory analogs, but also in real-life, environmentally relevant situations.

The Behavior Analytic Approach. As pointed out earlier, the behavior analyst would contend that behavior harmful to the environment occurs because such behavior has been reinforced in the past. Proenvironmental behavior does not occur as often as it should because either such behavior has not yielded sufficient positive consequences, or such behavior has been actively suppressed by aversive consequences. The steps necessary to reverse this trend are obvious; environmental researchers need to find methods to maximize the positive consequences for behaving in ways that protect and preserve the environment, and to minimize positive consequences for behavior that threatens the environment. Such techniques have been described by, for example, Baum (1994), Grant and Evans (1994), and Kazdin (1994). A more detailed discussion of how these techniques have been applied to our environmental problems is presented in the following sections.

Stages 4 and 5: Implementation and Evaluation of Interventions

Implementation of the intervention strategy refers to the delivery of the selected program to a specified target group. An important consideration is ensuring that all targets that are expected to receive the program actually do, and that they continue to receive the program in the planned way throughout the course of the project. This important aspect of evaluation is known as "process evaluation" and is discussed in detail by Rossi and Freeman (1993). Another important consideration in planning the implementation of a new program is to ensure that it will be possible to evaluate the degree to which it is effective at altering the context and the behavior in question. This type of evaluation is known as "impact evaluation" and is the point at which expertise in research design and methodology come in—another asset of the environmental social psychologist.

After the intervention has been applied, or even during the intervention, evaluation of its effectiveness may show that it has been less effective than expected. In this case, the cycle of behavior-change attempts may begin anew with different interpretations of the problem, causal hypotheses, and intervention hypotheses. When the intervention is effective, the researcher may focus on another environmentally destructive behavior. This continuing five-step cycle can be illustrated in Figure 12–1.

USING THE BEHAVIORAL APPROACH TO ADDRESS ENVIRONMENTAL PROBLEMS

Historically, applied behavior analysis has centered on issues of individual behavior change such as reducing aggression levels in children, stopping nail biting and other habits, increasing study time, and reducing smoking. During the late 1970s, some of these researchers saw the value in focusing the techniques of applied behavior analysis on a larger scale to community problems that were much more significant in scope. In the environmental arena, applied behavior analysis techniques were directed at issues such as energy conservation, recycling, littering, water conservation,

FIGURE 12–1 Five-step process for identifying and remediating behavioral problems.

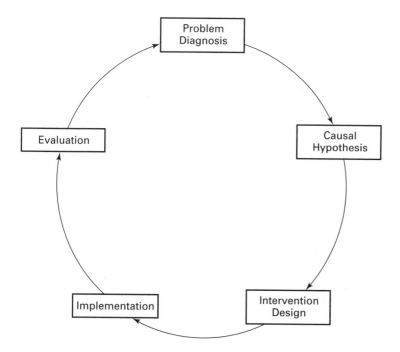

and bicycling as an alternative to driving (see Cone & Hayes, 1980; Geller, Winett, & Everett, 1982). Geller et al. (1982), especially, saw the future of behavioral techniques to be bright in preserving the environment.

Taxonomy of Behavior-Change Strategies

In attempting to modify environmentally relevant behaviors, what are the alternatives available to environmental psychologists for manipulating antecedents and consequences? Geller et al. (1990) reviewed the array of strategies used by applied behavior analysts and developed a taxonomy of 24 antecedent and consequence techniques and an intuitive method for assessing the degree to which they are effective as behavior-change devices. In a subsequent article reviewing behavioral interventions to preserve the environment since 1980, Dwyer, Leeming, Cobern, Porter, and Jackson (1993) simplified Geller et al.'s taxonomy to create a list of 18 techniques, 10 of which are antecedents and 8 of which are consequences. This revised taxonomy is presented in Table 12–1.

As Table 12–1 suggests, the 10 antecedent interventions can be further broken down into "passive" versus "active" and "individual" versus "group" dichotomies. The difference between individual and group interventions is self-explanatory, but the passive-active dichotomy warrants some explanation. Passive interventions present people (targets) with the materials or the means necessary to begin acting for the environment. Unlike active interventions, passive interventions do not engage targets in the decisions or methods to act. An example of a passive intervention is a written prompt such as a "no littering" sign. The decision to pass an antilittering law and the decision to post the sign were not made by the targets of the prompt.

Active interventions, on the other hand, *involve* targets in the decisions behind interventions. Targets have the ability to decide what types of behavior will be required. Further, these targets are given choices as to whether they will change their behavior in response to the intervention. For example, individuals may be given opportunities to commit to changing their behavior. Or groups may be given opportunities to set goals for changing the group's behavior as a whole.

Relative Effectiveness of Techniques

In reviews of 54 and 27 environmental studies, respectively, both Dwyer et al. (1993) and Porter, Leeming, and Dwyer (1995) provided information concerning the relative effectiveness of these antecedent and consequence interventions. Both reviews reported that active antecedents such as commitment—especially written commitment—led to more proenvironmental behavior (e.g., Pardini & Katzev, 1983–1984; Wang & Katzev, 1990). Both acknowledged that goal-setting was important (e.g., Hamad, Bettinger, Cooper, & Semb, 1980–1981; McCaul & Kopp, 1982). Dwyer et al. noted that modeling appropriate proenvironmental behaviors led to greater behavior changes (e.g., Winett, Leckliter, Chinn, & Stahl, 1984; Winett, Leckliter, Chinn, Stahl, & Love, 1985). Porter et al. specifically mentioned that the use of intervention agents (as models or promoters) was effective in encouraging others to

TABLE 12–1   Dwyer et al.'s (1993) Revised Taxonomy of Behavior-Change Interventions for the Environment

Antecedent Conditions

Passive-Individual
1. An individual can be exposed to *written information* that provides knowledge intended to encourage (i.e., prompt) target behaviors.
2. An individual can be exposed to *oral information* that provides knowledge intended to encourage target behaviors.
3. A person can be *assigned an individual goal* for engaging in some target behavior.
4. *Environmental alteration* refers to designing a part of the environment in a way that forces or encourages a target behavior (e.g., a low-flow shower head or a brightly painted trash barrel with a cover shaped like some animal or cartoon character to encourage litter disposal).

Passive-Group
5. *Assigned goal* for a group to engage in some target behavior.

Active-Individual
6. *Commitment from the individual* to engage in some target behavior.
7. A *personal goal selected by the individual* to engage in some target behavior.
8. *Competition between individuals* to foster some target behavior.

Active-Group
9. *Team goal* established by group consensus.
10. *Competition* between groups regarding level of some target behavior.

Consequence Conditions

Individual
11. *Feedback signaling direct, explicit, and reliable rewards or penalties.*
12. *Feedback signaling only indirect, uncertain, and distant rewards or penalties.*
13. *Reward* to the individual.
14. *Penalty* to the individual.

Group
15. *Feedback signaling direct, explicit, and reliable rewards or penalties.*
16. *Feedback signaling only indirect, uncertain, and distant rewards or penalties.*
17. *Reward* to the group.
18. *Reward* to the group.

Source: Dwyer, W. O., Leeming, F .C., Cobern, M. K., Porter, B. E., & Jackson, J. M. (1993). Critical review of behavior interventions to preserve the environment: Research since 1980. *Environment and Behavior, 25*(3), pp. 275–321. Copyright © 1993 by Sage Publications. Reprinted by permission of Sage Publications.

recycle (e.g., Burn, 1991; Hopper & Nielson, 1991). However, antecedents, such as written prompts, did not lead to much behavior change (as can be attested by asking someone if he or she *always* follows the posted speed limit).

With respect to consequences, both groups of authors found evidence that reinforcers and punishers of various types worked to increase proenvironmental behavior. Adding a bottle law was an instigator of more glass recycling in New York versus New Jersey, where there was no such law (Levitt & Leventhal, 1986). Giving lottery tickets to those who recycled paper increased recycling (e.g., Diamond & Loewy, 1991; Geller, Chaffee, & Ingram, 1975; Jacobs & Bailey, 1982–1983; Witmer & Geller, 1976). Providing feedback also led to increased proenvironmental activity (McClelland & Cooke, 1979–1980; Midden, Meter, Weening, & Zieverink, 1983; Katzev & Mishima, 1992). In fact, no matter what the intervention—antecedent or consequence—researchers reported increased *short-term* changes toward proenvironmental behavior.

There are at least two important limitations to the research involving behavioral interventions to increase proenvironmental behavior. The first limitation to the behavioral approach is one that continues to frustrate many researchers; it centers on the problem of behavior maintenance. The behavior change effected by most interventions is often short-lived once the interventions are discontinued. In the work reviewed by Dwyer et al., the studies reporting follow-up measures were virtually unanimous in this regard. Future research should be directed at discovering which interventions (or combinations of interventions) have longer lasting effects. A few studies have already shown promise for interventions involving written commitment (e.g., Cobern, Porter, Leeming, & Dwyer, 1995; Pardini & Katzev, 1983–1984) and "agenting" (e.g., Burn, 1991; Cobern et al., 1995; Hopper & Nielson, 1991).

Second, Dwyer et al. (1993) reported that many of the studies reviewed compared only one type of intervention versus a control, or a group of interventions combined in such a way that disentanglement of individual intervention effectiveness was impossible. Direct, intervention-to-intervention comparisons were not common in the literature. There has been little effort to compare systematically different interventions and combinations of interventions, a situation presenting a clear opportunity for future research.

Research Trends
in Environmental Behavioral Interventions

Both Geller et al. (1982) and Dwyer et al. (1993) concluded that the behavioral approach has merit in changing environmentally relevant behavior. However, Dwyer et al. reported a disconcerting trend in that, as the 1980s progressed, research investigating the merits of behavioral interventions for environmental problems waned (see Figure 12–2). This was not because researchers in the area were not finding successes. Rather, other forces were at work, forces that were not encouraging behavior scientists to pursue this line of study.

This trend was also noted by Geller (1990), who wrote an insightful analysis of the problem. He surveyed 10 behavioral scientists who were among the "main players" in ecologically relevant research of the late 1970s and early 1980s. He simply asked them what happened to the movement. Uppermost on their list was a general lack of academic, community, and governmental support for their work and findings. In other words, the psychologists did not perceive adequate reinforcements for their work. There was the additional problem that some of the behavioral solutions these researchers developed would have involved changing large systems, public policies, and cultural practices, an endeavor that was foreign to the thinking of many psy-

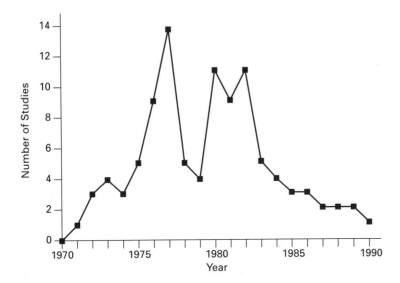

FIGURE 12–2 Frequency of published investigations studying behavioral interventions to preserve environmental quality, 1970–1990. (*Source*: Dwyer et al., 1993. Reprinted by permission of Sage Publications.)

chologists, especially those without a community or organizational orientation. The opening vignette describing the formation of the E-Team is one example of an attempt to intervene at a higher and more general level. Indeed, lowering the operant level of a child's temper tantrums seems much more manageable than getting cities to restructure their bureaucracies to promote environmental preservation.

On the other hand, environmental problems are not going away and, in our judgment, it is only a matter of time before the modification of environmentally relevant behavior will represent a significant proportion of the effort in applied psychological research. The past track record in this arena is a good one, and it is clear that such behaviors can be managed. Much more work needs to be done in the domain of targeting behavior change in large systems. However, any approach to understanding and effecting proenvironmental behavior change must exist with the social and political climate of the times.

Beating the Social Traps

Understanding how different antecedent and consequence strategies affect behavior change may help control the effects of social traps on environmentally relevant behavior. Recall that social traps result from the power of immediate reinforcers to overshadow the motivation to delay gratification for the group's benefit. Further, social traps occur when the future benefit is perceived to be distant and uncertain. Applying various interventions in the taxonomy given here may increase the motivation to delay and the perception that the benefit of future gains is not so distant.

Based on what is known about intervention effectiveness, using commitments or intervention agents could bring future consequences of our actions into the forefront. For example, being asked to commit to engaging in proenvironmental behavior today may improve the likelihood that one will actually change his or her behaviors to meet a commitment. This strategy has worked for improving fire safety behaviors such as keeping fire materials away from children, even though chances of fire injury/death are remote for most people (McConnell, Dwyer, & Leeming, in press). Thus, it is possible that such a strategy would encourage proenvironmental behavior change as well.

To decrease the potency of immediate benefits associated with abusing the environment, consequence interventions involving penalties could be used to remove the attractiveness of such behavior. For example, more bottle laws could be passed to encourage the return of recyclable materials. This approach was successful in increasing recycling in New York (Levitt & Leventhal, 1986). In addition, gasoline prices could be raised to discourage the purchase of energy-inefficient vehicles and encourage more carpooling. More laws could be passed regulating the use of toxic materials. In today's climate of government deregulation of environmental laws, however, some of these options are less likely to come to fruition.

As an alternative, the immediate benefits associated with proenvironmental behavior could be increased. Rewards (e.g., coupons for merchandise, lottery tickets for larger prizes) could be given to those who recycle the most materials in their neighborhood (Geller, Chaffee, & Ingram, 1975; Luyben & Bailey, 1979; Witmer & Geller, 1976). Every community resident could be provided with curbside recycling (an environmental alteration antecedent), which has led to immediate participation in recycling (Jacobs, Bailey, & Crews, 1984). Communities could sponsor commitment drives to grass cycle (leave clippings on the lawn), thus saving tons of yard waste from entering landfills every year (Cobern et al., 1995) Such commitment could result in proenvironmental behavior being perceived as an important characteristic for good neighbors. Each of these ideas, along with many others, could make preserving the environment an immediate concern above and beyond vague feelings about global warming, damage to the ozone layer, and the future of spaceship Earth.

It should be pointed out, again, that research by social psychologists in social movements is also relevant in this arena. To the extent that our understanding is advanced regarding the context variables that promote social movements, community involvement, and the internalization of behavior controls, such knowledge can be invaluable for increasing the scope of contingencies that can be brought to bear on environmentally relevant behavior. It will also be important for addressing the behavior-maintenance issues facing applied behavior analysis (see Kazdin, 1994, for discussion of the problem of behavior maintenance).

Potential Combination of Behavioral Interventions and "Behavioral Marketing"

Porter et al. (1995) noted that research on environmental attitudes, personality, and other individual differences could help psychologists interested in promoting recycling behavior. Such variables, including those Borden (1986; recall Box 12–1) discussed, could be used to tailor behavioral interventions to reach specific, identified targets. Segmenting the potential "market" of "consumers" for behavior change is likely to increase the effectiveness of interventions promoted by environmental researchers (Geller, 1989). It is also possible that tailored interventions may increase the long-term behavior change, thereby alleviating the problem of limited behavior maintenance when employing behavior-change technology. However, as Porter et al. noted, to date little empirical research has been conducted to verify this claim.

Assuming that designing interventions to reach particular market segments is important, and there is no compelling reason to disbelieve the potential value of social marketing, then researchers and policy analysts must take into account individual differences in designing programs to encourage proenvironmental behavior. It may no longer be prudent to assume a whole community or city will increase recycling, for example, in response to one particular type of public service announcement or reward system. Perhaps one segment of the population will change as a result of a commercial, whereas another segment will be resistant to change unless its members are personally contacted by someone promoting the intervention. The main issue to remember is that human behavior is a product of genetics and reinforcement history. There are wide individual differences in our propensity to act in different contexts, and it is unwise and naive to expect that behavioral interventions to increase environmental preservation will affect everyone in the same way.

The early studies reviewed by Geller et al. (1982) and the later investigations reviewed by Dwyer et al. (1993) and Porter et al. (1995) all represent relatively straightforward attempts by experimenters to apply antecedents and/or consequences to alter environmentally relevant behavior, usually to relatively restricted samples. As Geller (1990) pointed out, most researchers have been reticent to take on the challenge of working with larger systems. As interesting as these "stand-alone" research efforts were, it is even more intriguing to work through larger systems and apply a wider foundation of applied social and organizational psychological knowledge to the task of effecting behavior change in larger populations. The public housing fire-prevention study (McConnell et al., in press) mentioned previously and the E-Team project described in the opening vignette are both examples of such efforts. Of course, such work requires a content knowledge of behavior-change technologies. But it also requires sophistication in several other areas, such as team and group processes, evaluation research, social facilitation, and organizational dynamics and political systems. Thus, it is, in many respects, an applied social psychologist's dream.

SUMMARY

The environment will continue to face increased threats and rapid ecosystem changes in the years to come (Stokols, 1995), making it imperative that behavior-change technology be applied today to motivate lifestyles that will be more ecocentric. Even though psychologists have been successful in promoting proenvironmental behavior changes in individuals and organizations, the short-term future of fruitful and recognized environmental study is uncertain. The reinforcers mitigating environmental research about which Geller (1990) wrote are largely still in place. Nevertheless, work toward preserving the environment still continues and is likely to progress.

In closing, then, four promising directions for research are proposed for the next generation of applied social psychologists interested in saving the environment. First, maintaining the course of studying *behavior* is all-important. Within this research program, interventions that have shown promise for promoting long-term change need further exploration (e.g., commitment, recruiting intervention agents, consequence strategies). Second, researchers need to consider the market for which they target behavior-change interventions. The concept of social marketing is promising, but has not yet received adequate experimental attention. Third, social scientists must begin to expand their scope of inquiry to include larger systems, perhaps despite the lack of systemic support. The time has passed when meaningful benefit to the environment results from studying only relatively small-group settings. To make a true impact, psychologists must climb down from the ivory tower and work with whole communities to change community behavior. In this regard, the further study of social movements could be extremely important. Finally, moving to the community and interacting with political systems requires an interdisciplinary focus. Psychologists cannot be content to work alone while in the community. Political scientists, cultural anthropologists, sociologists, human ecologists, and civil engineers, as well as elected and appointed officials, should all be considered potential collaborators in behavior-change projects. Social science, especially the social science involving applied research, could benefit immensely by pooling resources and knowledge to save the earth.

Since the first Earth Day celebration, society is now a quarter century wiser in our understanding of environmental behavior. Yet, the environment's future lies before us. What will be the focus of the next environmental psychology book? We only hope that it will reflect the trend of increased environmental consciousness.

SUGGESTED READINGS

Dwyer, W. O., & Leeming, F. C. (Eds.). (1995). *Earth's eleventh hour: Environmental readings from the Washington Post Writers' Group*. Boston: Allyn and Bacon.

The editors of this book address the trends in environmentally relevant behavior that could eventually cause ecological disaster for the planet. They compiled *Washington Post* articles from the past 5 years into 15 chapters detailing various environmental problems and the responses of communities and governments to confronting these issues.

Dwyer, W. O., Leeming, F. C., Cobern, M. K., Porter, B. E., & Jackson, J. M. (1993). Critical review of behavioral interventions to preserve the environment: Research since 1990. *Environment and Behavior, 25,* 275–321.

The authors review 54 studies with various antecedent- and consequence-intervention strategies for changing behavior. The review focuses on finding the most effective interventions for encouraging proenvironmental behaviors. Their taxonomy of behavior-change techniques is presented in Table 12–1.

Stokols, D. (1995). The paradox of environmental psychology. *American Psychologist, 50,* 821–837.

This author presents a broad overview of environmental psychology, including the approach discussed in this chapter. The article is well worth reading to appeciate the diversity of issues inherent in the discipline.

Thomashow, M. (1995). *Ecological identity: Becoming a reflective environmentalist.* Cambridge, MA: MIT Press.

In this book, which is written for the general public, Thomashow discusses how people develop an "ecological identity" and the relationship between personal experience and the tendency to become an environmental activist. He discusses the role environmental studies can play in facilitating this transition. This book will provide an alternative perspective from the ones in the other suggested readings.

13 Conflict and Conflict Management

Loraleigh Keashly

University of Guelph

James, the leader of a multiprofessional gerontology team at Mercy General Hospital, has been frustrated by ongoing hostilities and arguments between two team members: Jan, a psychologist, and Michael, a social worker. Whenever one of them presents a case, the other will make snide remarks and roll his or her eyes. The person presenting will then ask what the problem is and an argument about the validity of the patient assessment will ensue. James has had to intervene to ensure everyone has a chance to give input. Throughout the rest of the meeting, Jan and Michael will glare at each other, whisper offside to other members, and eventually stomp out of the room. James is surprised at the behaviors because both of them are knowledgeable, capable, and respectful professionals. James has spoken to each of them separately to find out what is going on. Jan believes Michael is disrespectful, does not acknowledge her experience, and thinks that he knows more than she does. Michael, on the other hand, thinks that Jan is on a power trip and likes to think she is the best diagnostician on the staff. In addition, Michael wonders if Jan is prejudiced because he is black. James has told each of them to try to "get along" and "be more professional" by staying focused on the patients. The arguments and hostile remarks continue and the team environment is deteriorating, with other team members taking sides.

Before reading any further, please write down your response to the following questions: What do you think is at the heart of this conflict? What would you suggest to resolve it?

This is a tough situation that may be familiar to many of us. The damage of this conflict has already spread from the two individuals to the team and may affect the quality of patient care. Although the extent of the impact of this workplace dispute is small relative to the human, social, and economic devastation of disputing on the global stage (e.g., the Palestinian-Israeli conflict, the Serb-Croat-Muslim conflict in Bosnia, and the Hutu-Tutsi conflict in Rwanda), these diverse situations reflect the tremendous challenges of confronting and dealing with differences in skills, values, resources, power, and autonomy. No matter where we live and who we know, conflict is part of our lives. And for many of us, it has had, and may continue to have, devastating effects. Thus, understanding conflict and developing ways to ameliorate its destructive consequences have important implications for the quality of human life and make conflict a critical area for applied social psychology. The purpose of this chapter is to discuss current conflict research and practice that have been informed by social psychological approaches to human behavior. This chapter begins with a brief discussion of some of what social psychologists have learned about the sources and processes of conflict. Based on this discussion, interventions or means of facilitating constructive processes for this workplace dispute and for disputing at the international level are then examined.

SOME PROPOSITIONS ABOUT CONFLICT

What Is Conflict?

"What is conflict?" is a deceptively simple question without a simple answer. It has been observed from the scholarly literature that there are over 160 definitions available (see Peterson, 1983). The two most common elements in these definitions are (a) actual or perceived incompatibility of one's own goals or activities with those of another, and (b) actual or perceived interference (or potential for interference) by another person or group in the achievement of one's goals or activities. Based on both the conflict literature and practical experience with disputants, there are at least three additional issues that need to be considered: (a) awareness, (b) expression, and (c) affect. The *awareness* aspect of defining conflict takes the two common elements mentioned earlier and poses the following question: Does a conflict exist between two parties if neither party perceives incompatibilities (even if they objectively exist) or if neither party thinks there is potential for interference? In the team vignette, what if unbeknownst to each other, Jan and Michael have applied for the leadership of a new hospital team? Their goals for promotion are incompatible because only one of them can have the job. Yet neither one of them is aware of the other's application. Is this a conflict?

The issue of *expression* concerns public display of the conflict. That is, even if people are aware of incompatibilities or interference, does a conflict exist if they do not act on this awareness? What if no one says or does anything differently? Are Jan and Michael in a conflict if they know they want the same job yet both decide to let the selection process take its course?

The third and final issue or challenge to defining conflict is the role of *affect*. Conflict is often preceded or accompanied by some negative emotion such as anger or anxiety. Another question, then, is does a conflict exist if both parties feel happy and excited by their interaction? It is likely that if these are the predominant emotions, the people themselves would not label it as a conflict even though the elements of incompatibility and interference are present.

Consideration of these issues shows that developing a definition of conflict that scholars, practitioners, and disputants alike would agree upon is difficult (now, is *this* a conflict?). It is important, however, to have one as a framework for further discussion. Thomas's (1992) definition from his review of conflict and negotiation in organizations will be used because it addresses all of these issues. Conflict is "the process that begins when one party perceives that the other has negatively affected, or is about to negatively affect, something that he or she cares about" (p. 653). This definition combines in a simple statement the elements of incompatibility and interference (negatively affect something one cares about), the need for awareness on the part of at least one person (perceives that the other . . .), negative emotion is present, and overt expression or public display is not required. This definition helps to distinguish conflict from other social interactions such as discussions and decision making, which may often involve differences of opinion and values.

Conflict Is a Mixture of Objective and Subjective Elements (Keashly & Fisher, 1990). The objective elements of conflict are goal or activity incompatibilities such as scarce resources (e.g., money) or questions of expertise (e.g., as seen with Jan and Michael). The subjective elements are the more social psychological processes of perception, communication, and attribution. Subjective conflicts are those that arise and exist primarily in the "minds" (perceptions and cognitions) of those involved. Thus, conflict can occur when no substantive or basic incompatibilities exist (Deutsch, 1973). It is not unusual as an observer to others' conflicts to see no basis for the fight yet the disputants are certain that incompatibilities or interference are present. In terms of Jan and Michael, the subjective elements can be seen in their perceptions of each other as disrespectful, power tripping, and prejudiced. What a social psychological perspective offers to the analysis and management of conflicts is a recognition that even when objective incompatibilities exist or interference occurs, the significance and intensity of the conflict will depend upon how the individuals or groups perceive and interpret the situation (i.e., the subjective elements).

Conflict Is Natural and Inevitable. In a world characterized by diversity on a number of levels, there will always be opportunities for disputes. To illustrate the "naturalness" of conflict, disputing occurs even among very young children. For example, toddlers fight on an average of nine times an hour (Lollis & Ross, 1988). What is not inevitable about conflict is that it will be destructive or productive. The destructive aspects of conflict such as mistrust, deliberate deception, harsh and often violent attacks, and destroyed relationships and lives are all too familiar to most people. The productive aspects are usually less clear. Worchel, Coutant-Sassic, and Wong (1993), in their review of the social psychological literature on conflict, noted that it can foster creative and innovative solutions to problems, act as a warning signal that something in the relationship needs to be attended to, facilitate personal and social change, and define personal and social identities and boundaries. Building on these productive aspects, there may be times when stimulating a conflict would be a good idea! The challenge, then, in dealing with conflict is to prevent or reduce the destructive aspects while realizing its potential benefits. The social psychological perspective on this challenge is that the pattern of interaction between disputants (i.e., competitive or cooperative) will determine whether the conflict becomes destructive or constructive, respectively (Deutsch, 1973). That is, competitive interactions may lead to destructive conflict whereas cooperative interactions may lead to productive conflict.

Given that we engage in conflict so early in our lives and continue to do so throughout our lives, it is clear that understanding the development of conflicts, the functions that conflicts serve in relationships and human growth, and the ways to manage them so that they are constructive become important priorities. A social psychological approach to gathering this knowledge involves focusing on conflict as an interactive process that is heavily influenced by subjective factors and that occurs within a broader social context. As noted earlier, the subjective factors concern the role of the individual's perceptions and cognitions in interpreting what is happening and using that interpretation as the basis for action or reaction to the other person. The interactive process highlights the importance of this action and reaction between people in moving the conflict in one direction or another. The social context draws attention to group and intergroup dynamics generally, and the role of culture and subculture in terms of sources, subjective interpretation, and the interactive process.

The Interactive Nature of Conflict

An understanding of conflict escalation processes is important for assessment and management decisions. It is also within escalation that the significance of social psychological (i.e., subjective) factors of conflict are emphasized. The work of Deutsch, Pruitt, and Rubin will be highlighted here because their focus on identifying basic social psychological processes, linking them to conditions for constructive and destructive conflict, and applying their knowledge and analysis to real-world conflict through practice interventions is truly *applied* social psychology.

Deutsch, a social psychologist at Teacher's College, Columbia University, has dedicated over 40 years of his career to the study of the conditions that would give rise to constructive or destructive processes of conflict management. Based on his earlier work on the effects of cooperation and competition upon group process, Deutsch (1973) argued that the features of cooperative social processes and competitive social processes characterized the constructive and destructive processes of conflict resolution, respectively. A reading of the characteristic features of these processes in Table 13–1 makes obvious the conceptual and practical link to productive and destructive conflict.

Based on observations of people's behavior in experimental gaming situations such as the Prisoner's Dilemma and the Acme-Bolt Trucking Game, Deutsch (1973) identified what is perhaps the main reason for the intransigence and persistence found in conflictual situations. "Deutsch's crude law of social relations" states that the use of a particular action will tend to elicit the same action. Essentially, cooperation breeds cooperation whereas competition breeds competition. Relating this law to the conflict process, cooperative relations continue to build in the direction of constructive resolution whereas competitive relations move quickly into destructive conflict.

Pruitt and Rubin (1986) drew on their own and other social psychological research to provide a detailed picture of the effects these negative attitudes and perceptions have on encouraging escalation and discouraging settlement of the conflict. In reading through this section, keep in mind that both sides in an escalated conflict hold the same or mirror images of each other and the resultant effects on behavior are dramatic.

Briefly, parties' hostile and suspicious attitudes toward one another and per-

TABLE 13–1 Features of Cooperative and Competitive Social Processes

Feature	Nature of Process	
	Cooperative	Competitive
Perceptions	Sensitive to similarities and minimizes differences in beliefs and values	Sensitive to differences and minimizes similarities in beliefs and values
Attitudes	Trusting, friendly, helpful	Suspicious, hostile, exploitive
Communication	Open, accurate, respectful	Indirect, misleading, threatening
Task orientation	Problem to be mutually solved	Contest to be won Unilateral solution

ceptions of differences rather than similarities lead to a number of destructive cognitions and behaviors. First, there is an increasing tendency to blame the other for
what is happening. The more disliked and distrusted the other person is, the more
likely he or she is to be blamed. For example, in the vignette, Jan and Michael each
blame the other for the tension experienced at team meetings. Second, the other's
actions are more likely to be seen as threatening because of the distrust and dislike
that has evolved in the competitive interaction. For example, Michael's suggestion
of a different diagnosis for a patient's problem is perceived by Jan as a threat to her
expertise. Third, the more disliked the other is, the greater the willingness to aggress
(either physically or verbally) against that person. The derogatory comments made
by both Jan and Michael are examples of aggressive behavior. These three effects
provide the "justification" for retaliatory action as a person needs to "defend" himself or herself. To the extent that both parties are experiencing the situation similarly, this sets up a downward spiral of revenge-counterrevenge as each new "defensive" action requires a "defensive" response (see Kim & Smith, 1993). This can be
seen in Jan's and Michael's dispute as they trade increasingly hostile remarks, emphasized by nonverbal behaviors such as rolling of the eyes.

These effects, in turn, lead to communication problems as one avoids the other
person who is so disliked and distrusted. At a time when Jan and Michael desperately need to be able to get accurate and clear information about each other's intentions and motivations, their hostility and suspiciousness drive them apart. A further
complication to communication is the developing inability to empathize with the
other. As noted earlier, in a competitive social process, the other person is perceived
to be so different on important values and beliefs that it becomes difficult to understand how and why he or she is behaving in a particular way. A costly result of this
lack of empathy is the inability to recognize how the other's behavior is a reaction to
one's own hostile behavior. As can be seen in Jan's and Michael's mutual accusations
of disrespect, each is unable to understand the other's perspective nor how their own
behaviors contribute to the situation.

With reduced information flow and reliance on one's own views comes what is
called *zero-sum thinking* (i.e., in order for one to gain the other has to lose). Such
thinking reduces the opportunity for perceiving the integrative or joint possibilities
in the situation. Thus, people feel forced into one of two choices: give up or fight it
out. Jan and Michael are choosing to fight it out as indicated by their increasingly
hostile behaviors and the involvement of other team members in their dispute. The
downward spiral continues as Jan and Michael reciprocate actions, reconfirming
their already negative views of one another. In effect, their original perceptions and
images of each other become real in a destructive form of self-fulfilling prophecy.

Thus, a conflict may start from more objective sources such as, in the case of
Jan and Michael, incompatibilities in how to achieve a shared goal such as quality
patient care. However, its movement into constructive or destructive patterns will
depend upon the perceptions, attitudes, orientations, and subsequent behaviors of
both parties. Jan's and Michael's dispute will continue to escalate unless something
is done to change these dynamics.

The Social Context of Conflict:
Group and Intergroup Influences

> Any conflict takes place within a context and is influenced by that context. . . . Social and political structures as well as cultural beliefs and values affect individual perception, thought, feeling, and interactions . . . conflicts can neither be understood nor resolved without consideration of their contexts, both small and large, contemporary and historical. (Taylor & Beinstein Miller, 1994, p. 2)

When we look at Jan and Michael, we see two *individuals* fighting. Yet their dispute is not occurring in a vacuum. They are part of a team, which, in turn, is part of an organization, which, in turn, is nested within a broader social, political, and cultural system. These various contexts and the dynamics inherent in them will influence Jan's and Michael's thoughts, feelings, perceptions, and behaviors. Thus, the context of their dispute must be taken into consideration in analyzing this conflict.

An important feature of social context is the notion of group affiliation and identity. In addition to their unique personalities, Jan and Michael are members of different groups or social categories to which they may have varying emotional attachment and which vary in their salience in any particular setting (Tajfel & Turner, 1986). Profession becomes an important and salient group identity because of the multiprofessional nature of the team and the specific challenges around validity of, and expertise for, the patient assessment. Race is also noteworthy and particularly salient to Michael as indicated by his comments about Jan (Alderfer, 1983). Finally, gender may also be a relevant identity here. (See Taylor & Beinstein Miller, 1994, for a review.)

Useful theoretical perspectives for understanding the influence of group membership on individual and interpersonal behavior come from intergroup theory (see Taylor & Moghaddam, 1994). Sherif (1966) and Tajfel (1982), two prominent social psychologists of somewhat different theoretical traditions (realistic conflict theory and social identity theory, respectively), have argued that group identification will be influential, to some degree, in interpersonal interaction. That is, the interaction between Jan and Michael may reflect their respective group memberships (gender, race, and professional) and the relations that exist among the groups within those social categories in the broader organizational or social context. In such an analysis, Jan's and Michael's dispute would be viewed more as an intergroup conflict than strictly as an interpersonal one. This has implications for the subsequent management or amelioration of the situation (Donnellon & Kolb, 1994).

Group Influences on Behavior. This aspect of the intergroup perspective focuses on questions concerning whether, in the vignette with Jan and Michael, men and women, Caucasians and people of color, and different professional groups define or perceive conflicts differently and whether they respond to and manage conflict differently.

The most prolific research and writing has been with regard to gender and conflict (see Taylor & Beinstein Miller, 1994, for multidisciplinary perspectives on this relationship). Evidence of gender-related differences is heavily influenced by what is focused on: subjective interpretation or actual behavior. Referring to subjective interpretation or perception of a conflict situation, there is evidence that men and women differ in what they initially perceive to be at the heart of a conflict. For example, in a study by Pinkley and Northcraft (1990), participants were given a written description of the negotiation they were about to engage in over buying a product. They were then asked to describe what was at issue in the upcoming negotiation. Women assessed the conflict as more rooted in the relationship between the buyer and the seller (i.e., the problem lay in their style of interacting and their concern for each other's interests). Men, however, focused on the structure of the task as more important (i.e., the problem involved determining costs and benefits of the particular item and alternative sources for the item).

When research attention shifts to differences in observable conflict behavior, there is little evidence of consistent differences between men and women. First, very few studies are based on observations of women and men in actual disputes. More often than not, women and men are asked to report on their use of different strategies such as confrontation and avoidance in vaguely defined situations such as "at work" or "at home" (Keashly, 1994). In one of the few studies of actual conflict behavior in a work setting, Korabik, Baril, and Watson (1990) found no gender differences in behavior. Briefly, MBA students completed a self-report instrument on preferred conflict styles (e.g., competing, accommodating, avoiding) and then role-played a supervisor working with three subordinates while being videotaped. Although men and women differed in their self-reported preferences, they did not differ in role-play performance nor in the outcomes they achieved. Of particular interest is the finding that women and men who used similar styles were evaluated differently by subordinates. A woman's effectiveness as a supervisor was rated lower when she used a confrontational style and higher when she used an accommodative style. This was not the case for men. So even though men and women may have similar skills and abilities in managing conflict, their actual behavior may be perceived and interpreted differently and, thus, reacted to on this basis. Clearly, gender is influential in conflict behavior but primarily through the subjective interpretations of those involved (i.e, social psychological factors tend to predominate in this relationship).

The literature on racial and ethnically related behaviors in interpersonal conflict is far less voluminous in the social psychology literature. A notable exception is research conducted by Leung (e.g., Leung, 1987, 1988; Leung & Bond, 1984), which takes a cross-cultural perspective on factors related to people's preferences for different approaches to conflict resolution. His particular focus is the role of individual differences in disputants' conflict behavior as reflected in cultural norms of collectivism and individualism. Briefly, collectivism refers to the tendency to be more concerned about the impact of one's own needs, interests, and goals on one's own group members; it includes a willingness to sacrifice personal interests for the collective interests. Thus, interpersonal harmony is highly valued in cultures that are collectivistic. Individualism, on the other hand, reflects the tendency to be concerned with how one's behavior affects the achievement of one's own needs and goals.

In his 1988 study of determinants of conflict avoidance, Leung argued that collectivists would show a stronger tendency to avoid a conflict with a member of one's own group (i.e., the ingroup) and a stronger tendency to pursue a conflict with members from another group (i.e., the outgroup) than would individualists. Both students and nonstudents from Hong Kong and the United States participated in this study. Briefly, participants were asked to read a dispute situation involving a buyer and a seller over a faulty appliance. The two students were described as either good friends (i.e., ingroup members) or complete strangers (i.e., outgroup members). The value of the appliance also varied from low ($40) to high ($640). Participants were asked to indicate their likelihood to sue the seller (pursuance of conflict) as well as complete measures of collectivism. Cultural collectivism was found to be related to increased likelihood to sue only for strangers and not for friends. Regarding the specific cultural groups, Chinese participants showed more conflict avoidance with friends and less avoidance with strangers than did American participants. These results are indicative of an important cultural dimension that relates to interpretation and subsequent behavior in a conflict situation. These results are particularly relevant to disputes in which parties are of different social groups. In most instances, conflict pursuance may be more likely if the other party is a member of a different group than if the person is a member of one's own group.

As to professional identity, the specific empirical literature is sparse. The most relevant work comes from the literature on intervention in conflicts. Roth and Sheppard (1989) conducted a study to examine how professional identity would affect what people identified as being at the heart of a dispute. Briefly, they provided students of clinical psychology, law, and industrial relations with a description of a conflict and asked them to make an assessment of the situation prior to acting as a third person who would intervene. Law students interpreted the conflict as one in which only one party could win. Industrial relations students viewed the same conflict as involving the need for tradeoffs on issues of differing importance. The clinical psychology students provided yet another perspective on the same dispute, viewing it as a reflection of underlying issues in the parties' interaction and relationship. The students' interpretations clearly reflected the professional roles for which they were being trained. Unfortunately, the study did not involve actually having the students intervene. Thus, it is unclear whether the student-professionals' initial orientation to the conflict affected their subsequent behavior in dealing with the dispute. This research does suggest, however, that different interpretations of a "shared" conflict could contribute to increased misunderstanding and escalation.

Regarding Jan and Michael, their respective group memberships suggest different subcultures with different expectations, practices, norms, and values that may lead to different interpretations of each other's behaviors and subsequently influence their responses to one another (Deutsch, 1994). Thus, management of this situation would require an opportunity for Jan and Michael to clarify and appreciate these differing interpretations and to understand how these interpretations affect their behavior toward one another. Such a management approach focuses on developing open, accurate communication and building trusting and helpful attitudes that are characteristic of cooperative interactions that lead to productive conflict resolution.

Intergroup Influences on Behavior. This aspect of the social context is not as well understood nor studied in social psychology as is the group influences perspective (see Taylor & Moghaddam, 1994). The essence of the intergroup influence perspective is that individuals in a dispute are playing out intergroup problems rather than some problem caused by their different individual interpretations. This perspective focuses on how issues (e.g., inequity, scarce resources) or processes (competitive, independent, adversarial) that occur between two groups in the broader organizational and social context (e.g., men-women, blacks-whites, psychology-social work) may affect Jan's and Michael's behaviors toward one another.

Regarding gender relations, a feminist perspective would argue that society is patriarchal and that women are in a disadvantaged position relative to men. Thus, Jan's interpretation may be, and, indeed, Michael's behavior may reflect, that a dominant group member is questioning or dismissing the experience and information of a subordinate group member. The notions of white privilege and Eurocentric bias focus on the inequitable power relations between white Europeans and people of color. Again using a dominant-subordinate analysis, Michael may perceive, and, indeed, Jan's behaviors may reflect, a denial or discounting of subordinate group members' perspectives. Thus, for both gender and race, conflict may generate from overt or subtle discriminatory behaviors based in these broader unequal power relationships.

Regarding interprofession relations, economic slow-downs and recessions can have a dramatic impact on employment opportunities, creating a situation of scarce resources between occupational groups claiming similar expertise or turf. In Canada, for example, cutbacks in health care dollars in the early to mid-1990s have resulted in downsizing of hospital staff. To ensure their survival within the hospital, both social workers and psychologists need to justify why they are worth the money. This may involve claiming of territory by one or the other and arguing that one group does it less expensively than the other. Thus, some of the hostilities between Jan and Michael may reflect the feelings of threat and tension that exist at the broader hospital level and the health care/governmental level for both professions.

The intergroup perspective suggests that any intervention or management strategy for Jan's and Michael's dispute will need to address the feelings of threat related to scarce resources in terms of both economics and expertise. As well, a recognition by the parties of the ways in which unequal and inequitable intergroup relations in the broader organizational and social context may affect their own interpersonal relationships and fuel the conflict is also necessary.

CONFLICT MANAGEMENT

To this point, we have talked about the processes of destructive and constructive conflict and the roles of group membership and intergroup relations in the development and maintenance of conflicts. This knowledge, although useful for understanding a conflict, is not sufficient for constructively managing that conflict. The challenge is to put this knowledge into practice. In this section, two approaches to effect change in people's behavior will be discussed: (a) interpersonal skills training and (b) third-party intervention.

Interpersonal Skills Training

> The factor of abilities and skills is not sufficiently emphasized in theoretical discussions . . . many destructive conflicts between nations, groups and individuals result from their lack of skills related to the procedures involved in constructive conflict resolution . . . training in these skills should be more widespread. (Deutsch, 1994, pp. 24–25)

Skills Overview. Deutsch (1994) identifies three broad sets of skills people need in order to develop constructive solutions to their own conflicts. They are those skills involved in: (a) establishing a cooperative, problem-solving relationship with the other person; (b) developing a creative process for expanding the options available for resolving the conflict; and (c) taking an "outsider" or analytic perspective to the conflict and preventing the parties from getting caught in the various destructive traps identified in the discussion of escalation. The specific skills that permit the achievement of these three objectives include the following (Deutsch, 1993; Katz & Lawyer, 1983):

1. Active or reflective listening—focusing on what the other person has said and communicating back what has been understood
2. Perspective-taking or empathy—an important feature of active listening—listening to the meaning and feeling in order to understand what the other is experiencing
3. Assertion—clearly articulating one's own thoughts and feelings about specific incidents or behaviors of concern; involves using "I" vs. "you" messages and focusing on specific behaviors rather than making attributions to the other's intent or personality; tone is one of respect, not derogation
4. Giving, receiving, and utilizing constructive feedback—using assertion and listening skills to identify positive and negative behaviors and the impact that they have on self, the other person, or both (this often means being prepared for own or the other's defensive response if feedback is negative)
5. Problem solving—once the issues have been defined using the previously listed skills, the focus is on generating creative and novel alternatives that produce joint satisfaction; involves distinguishing underlying needs from positions (i.e., proposed solutions); if mutual satisfaction is not possible, a fair procedure must be created and defined to determine who gets what

These skills, in combination with knowledge of the errors in perception and thought that occur in escalated conflict, one's own preferences for responding in different conflict situations, and an awareness of group and intergroup differences, set the stage for constructive conflict management.

Significant changes in behavior as a result of training will most likely occur when (a) there is an emphasis on skills and not just knowledge, and (b) there are opportunities to practice and receive specific feedback on the use of these skills within the session. Transfer to real-life situations is a bit more challenging and requires discipline, practice, and feedback within a social context in which use of these skills is encouraged (Deutsch, 1994).

With respect to Jan and Michael, training in these constructive conflict skills could be of some benefit for the immediate conflict and should be of even greater benefit for future conflictual interactions. What is positive about each of them is that, given their professional backgrounds, they likely have these skills fairly well developed. The challenge for them is dealing with the realization they are not using what they know. This experience alone is difficult for helping professionals because they think they should "know better." Although there may be truth to this, their misuse or nonuse of these skills is an example of the powerful effects of conflict escalation processes on disputants' perceptions and behaviors. It also may contribute to each of them feeling even more defensive, which may lead them to blame one another and then justify their behaviors as a necessary response. In such an escalated and heated dispute, a third party intervenor may be needed.

Teaching Children: An Example of Skills Training. To the extent that conflict is natural and inevitable, skills are required for constructively managing such interactions. Thus, it is important to introduce these social skills as early in life as possible. Schools have become a primary setting for this training because of the significant role they play in children's intellectual, social, and emotional development. In addition, there are positive aspects of conflict for the educational experience generally (e.g., controversy and creative problem solving). As a result, research evaluating the effectiveness of skills training is more prolific and extensive in school settings than other settings. Although there are an enormous number of programs available (Deutsch, 1993), this section focuses on the work of Johnson and Johnson, two psychologists (social and educational) who have dedicated much of their careers to facilitating creative conflict skills in children and whose work reflects an integration of social psychological theory, research, and practice that is a hallmark of a truly applied social psychological approach to conflict management.

It is clear from Deutsch's (1973) work that constructive conflict management requires that a cooperative context be established. However, school education in North America has traditionally followed a competitive model of learning in which children compete with each other for grades and for the teacher's attention. The emphasis has been on activities that require individual achievement as opposed to interdependent learning.

An extensive amount of research has been conducted over the past 100 years comparing the effects of competitive, individualistic, and cooperative learning on various instructional and personal outcomes (see Johnson & Johnson, 1989, for a review). Very briefly, cooperative learning tends to result in enhanced achievement effort, more positive relationships among students, and greater psychological and emotional adjustment.

Once a cooperative context has been established, the work of developing constructive conflict management skills and procedures can occur. To help children develop an analytic perspective to their conflicts and a creative process for dealing with these conflicts, Johnson and Johnson (1994) focused on two mechanisms: (a) academic controversy and (b) negotiation and peer mediation.

Academic controversy refers to a situation in which one student's information, ideas, theories, and opinions are incompatible with those of another and the two of them must seek an agreement. The resolution of these controversies is to involve deliberate discussion of the advantages and disadvantages of different actions within the context of creative problem solving to develop novel solutions to these dilemmas. Thus, academic controversies require both interdependence (i.e., reliance on each other for achievement of goals and the gathering of resources) and conflict (i.e., incompatibilities and differences) to ensure maximum productivity.

The controversy process consists of five steps (Johnson & Johnson, 1992):

1. Information is organized and conclusions are derived.
2. Conclusions or positions are presented and advocated. A process of argument and counterargument occurs.
3. Uncertainty and conceptual conflict are created. This is a result of hearing other alternatives and receiving information that is different and perhaps incompatible with one's own conclusions. (This process occurs in an open-discussion format.)
4. There is a search for additional information and an attempt to view issues from both perspectives. This involves perspective reversal, in which one is required to argue persuasively for the other side.
5. Based on this new reconceptualization, a synthesis of both perspectives is created.

The creation of structured academic controversy in the classroom mirrors this five-step process with a class period assigned for each step. Briefly, students are assigned to groups of four and then divided into two pairs. Each pair is to research and present to the other pair their assigned position on the topic. The group must then reach a consensus on the issue and develop and present a group report on which all group members are evaluated. Students are instructed to follow discussion rules during the controversy. These include: (a) be critical of ideas—not people; (b) focus on the best possible solution and not on winning; (c) encourage everyone to participate; (d) listen to everyone's ideas even if you do not agree; (e) bring out all facts and ideas from both sides and put them together to make sense; (f) try to understand both sides of the issue; and (g) change your mind if the evidence is convincing. Once the controversy is completed, there is group processing of the experience with emphasis on the special skills involved in this constructive conflict.

Johnson and Johnson (1994) provide evidence based on the past 20 years of their own research into the effects of academic controversy. As with cooperative learning, the findings indicate that students educated in this kind of environment display greater academic and cognitive skills and behaviors such as creativity, retention, recall, transfer of learning, and greater involvement in required tasks. In addition, these students were found to utilize the skills they developed in other situations with other intellectual topics. Structured controversy was also found to have positive social and personal outcomes including increased liking, social support, and self-esteem among group members. These positive results, however, were found only when the controversy occurred within a cooperative learning context. In a competitive context, controversy can result in a hostile and escalated conflict (Johnson & Johnson, 1994).

These latter results seem particularly relevant to Jan's and Michael's dispute. Part of their conflict involves disagreement over the assessment and evaluation of a patient's condition, which could be an example of intellectual conflict. If so, it is possible that it could be addressed using structured controversy. However, it is clear from their current behaviors and the analysis of other potential influences on their disputing—particularly interprofession relations—that this cognitive conflict is occurring in a competitive context. While structuring the controversy has not occurred here, the research on academic controversy suggests that the current intellectual conflict only fuels an already escalating dispute rather than containing it. Somehow, a cooperative context needs to be established in the Jan and Michael scenario.

Returning to Johnson and Johnson's program, once the ability to deal with intellectual conflict is established, students are ready to learn how to manage their differences with others constructively. The next step in Johnson and Johnson's (1994) approach is development of a *peer mediation program*. This includes both the interpersonal skills training discussed earlier (i.e., negotiation) and training in helping others handle their conflicts (i.e., mediation). Mediation will be discussed in more detail in the later section on third-party intervention; this discussion focuses on the specific interpersonal skills training used with children. Essentially, students are taught how to develop integrative agreements to their conflicts with each other that meet both parties' needs. This is accomplished by the following procedure (Johnson & Johnson, 1994, p. 128):

1. State what you want (e.g., "I want to use the book now").
2. State how you feel (e.g., "I feel frustrated").
3. State the reasons for your wants and feelings (e.g., "You have been using the book for the past hour. If I don't get to use the book soon my report will not be done on time. It's frustrating to have to wait so long").
4. Summarize your understanding of what the other person wants, how the other person feels, and the reasons underlying both (e.g., "My understanding of you is . . .").
5. Invent three optional plans to resolve the conflict.
6. Choose one and shake hands.

Note how the fundamental skills of assertion (I want, I feel), active listening (show understanding), and problem solving (optional plans) are incorporated into this relatively structured format.

The preliminary evidence of the impact of their programs on children's conflict resolution behavior is promising. Johnson, Johnson, Dudley, and Acikgoz (1994) evaluated their program using a pre-post procedure. Students whose classrooms had been randomly selected from an elementary school were given a number of measures before training began, immediately after the training ended, and 4 months following the end of training. The training involved negotiation and mediation skills and was delivered in each classroom for 30 minutes per day for 6 weeks. Use of negotiation skills was assessed prior to and immediately after training, using a total recall test and videotaping students negotiating a resolution to two conflicts. Transfer of these skills to natural settings was assessed by systematic observations of spontaneous student conflicts in the school, 4 months after the training.

Prior to the training, the majority of student conflicts were referred to teachers with students showing little evidence of negotiation skills in spontaneous and role-played conflicts. In fact, many conflicts were handled by physical (pushing, hitting) and verbal (insults, putdowns) aggression. After training, students demonstrated extensive knowledge of skills on the recall test and used these skills appropriately in simulated situations. Observations of spontaneous conflicts revealed that even in emotionally intense conflicts, students used negotiation skills and sought mediation from other students when they could not resolve the problem themselves. There was a noticeable decrease in conflict referrals to teachers, as well as a reduction in discipline problems after training, as students managed their own disputes constructively. In addition, students and parents reported the use of these skills outside the school setting. Those parents whose children had not been involved in the study requested that their children be trained. This evidence of transfer of skills to other situations supports Deutsch's (1993) contention that receiving such training has implications for the constructive management of conflicts more generally.

In sum, based on an understanding of the social psychological processes involved in constructive and destructive conflict, skills and procedures for constructive conflict management have been identified and implemented in a variety of formats. Preliminary evidence, particularly from school training programs, indicates that such training has an impact not only on the handling of a specific dispute but also on the quality of relationships and personal achievements.

Third-Party Intervention

When people, groups, or states are having difficulty or are unable to manage the conflict between them, a frequently sought after or offered alternative is to involve a third party to help resolve the situation. In the dispute between Jan and Michael, James acted in a third-party capacity when he spoke with each of them and then told them to end the hostilities by "being professional" and focusing on the patients' care. Some other approaches James could have taken are to (a) facilitate a face-to-face constructive dialogue between the two of them; (b) tell them if they do not work it out themselves, he will remove them from the team; (c) transfer only one of them to another team; (d) accept one person's interpretation and join that person in the dispute against the other; or (e) simply ignore their behaviors and encourage the team to focus on its caseload. Although these strategies are quite different in terms of the nature of James's involvement as well as the possible impact on the disputants, they are illustrative of the variety of ways that a third party can intervene informally in a dispute involving others. More formal intervention strategies include:

1. *Adjudication*—involves a judge or jury in a court setting
2. *Arbitration*—involves an independent third party who hears both sides of the problem and decides what the solution should be

3. *Conciliation*—involves an independent third party who brings disputants together so they can talk; may persuade them to meet face-to-face or may "shuttle" information back and forth; is not active in the actual discussion or agreement; is a communication link
4. *Mediation*—involves an independent third party who works with the disputants to identify the problems and to reach an agreement that satisfies both of them
5. *Fact finding*—involves an independent third party who gathers information to arrive at an independent judgment of the dispute, which is often only advisory; usually has little contact with the disputants

More social psychological research attention has been directed toward mediation than any other intervention approach; this is most likely a reflection of its ever-expanding use across a variety of settings (Wall & Lynn, 1993). Thus, discussion of third-party intervention will focus on mediation.

Mediation. To provide a clearer idea of what mediation can be, consider the following detailed definition provided by Lewicki, Weiss, and Lewin (1992) in their review of conflict, negotiation, and third-party interventions in organizations:

> By definition, mediators employ a variety of strategies and tactics to initiate and facilitate interactions between disputants, but leave the final resolution or terms of settlement in the hands of the disputants. Thus, mediation primarily relies on facilitating negotiation (problem-solving) among disputants. (p. 233)

A brief overview of the mediation process is presented to provide a better idea of what goes on there. Then the question of effectiveness is addressed by drawing heavily on Kressel and associates' (1989) review of mediation research.

There have been a variety of models proposed (particularly stage models) to characterize the mediation process (see Lewicki et al., 1992, for a review). Since the intention here is to convey a flavor of the mediation experience, a brief anecdotal description rather than a detailed identification of the stages, issues, and tactics that may occur or be utilized is provided. Mediation is characterized by face-to-face interaction between the disputants (or their representatives in the case of intergroup or international conflicts) in the presence of the mediator. The mediator may be a single person or a number of people. Prior to this interaction, there is often preliminary contact between the mediator and each disputant to get some sense of the issues and the disputants' willingness and commitment to proceed. Once this has been established, the interactive session begins with the mediator explaining the procedure and his or her role as a neutral third party in that process. At this point, ground rules for constructive dialogue are identified (e.g., no interrupting, no name-calling, confidentiality). Disputants are then given the uninterrupted time to tell their stories in turn with the mediator ensuring that the process stays constructive. Based on all this information, the mediator will often summarize and clarify the main issues. Disputants will further clarify or add in more issues if missed by the mediator. Then the disputants and the mediator enter into a problem-solving phase in which they review the concerns and interests and develop alternatives that will address these issues to disputants' mutual satisfaction. During this phase and the early phase on identifying issues, the mediator may "caucus" (i.e., meet with each disputant separately) if the discussion bogs down and the mediator wants to explore any reluctance or resistance he or she perceives in the disputants. Assuming that a variety of acceptable alternatives are generated, the disputants will reach an agreement, which is often written down in concrete and specific language and signed by both parties as an indication of their support. Although this discussion portrays the mediation process as linear, often there is cycling back to earlier phases. As a result, a mediation can take a lot of time and occur over a number of sessions.

The definition of success for mediation, as in any endeavor, seems to depend on the perspective from which the question is asked (disputant, third party, interested others, the courts) and what aspect of the conflict is addressed (settlement/agreement, disputants' relationship, costs). Regarding the settlement and agreement, Kressel and Pruitt (1989) report median settlement rates of 60% across all settings examined in their review, with a range between 20% to 80%. The nature or substance of these agreements is characterized by a more joint emphasis with individuals compromising from their previously held positions, particularly in contrast to adjudicated agreements. Kressel and Pruitt (1989) note that this compromising may have occurred in some mediation contexts as a result of mediator pressure or bias rather than disputants' desire to reach a mutually satisfying agreement.

In terms of compliance with agreements once they are reached, the evidence suggests that people maintain the commitments to which they have agreed (e.g., rates of 67% to 87% in neighborhood mediation centers). Given the typical voluntary nature of mediation programs, these agreement indicators may also reflect the nature of the disputants themselves, in that they have chosen to enter mediation rather than resorting to the more legalistic methods. That is, the reason settlement may be so much higher in mediation is that the disputants are already open to a joint agreement.

The efficiency and cost effectiveness of mediation relative to other procedures, particularly adjudication, are also used as indicators of mediation success. Kressel and Pruitt (1989) report that cases that reach mediation settle more quickly than those sent through adjudication. The specific financial costs has been a much more difficult indicator to develop and, hence, requires further work. What evidence there is suggests that, at the very least, mediation is less expensive than adjudication. Another indicator of cost effectiveness is more social psychological in nature; it involves perceptions of satisfaction and fairness. User satisfaction with, and perceived fairness of, the mediation process are reported to be quite high—75% even for those who fail to reach agreement. In contrast to adjudication, mediation is viewed as more satisfying and fairer.

With respect to the disputants' relationship, mediation tends to improve the interaction between disputants both within and outside the mediation setting. As evidence, Kressel and Pruitt (1989) refer to Pearson and Thoennes's (1989) review of 10 years of research on divorce mediation programs. Pearson and Thoennes found that many divorcing couples who did not reach agreement reported that they still found the process valuable as it facilitated their communication and, in a few cases, led to reconciliation. The argument is that the focus on constructive dialogue and problem solving between the disputants, with the mediator modeling these behaviors, creates a more hospitable and cooperative environment, making it easier for the disputants to try new behaviors with each other. A number of factors can influence just how effective mediation will be. The nature of the issue under mediation is particularly critical. Issues of "principle" or of values are extremely difficult to resolve. These are issues that are deeply felt and not easily amenable to compromise or either/or types of solutions. Other intervention approaches, such as interactive conflict resolution, may be more effective in these more deeply rooted, intractable disputes. (See Box 13–1 and Fisher, 1994, for examples.)

The disputants' relationship also moderates just how effective the mediation will be. The closer the relationship (family, friends, neighbors), the more likely an agreement will be reached. However, as Roehl and Cook (1985) report in their review of neighborhood mediation centers, many of these agreements do not hold. Mediation is also less effective if the relationship is one of unequal power. For example, in divorce mediation, women who are economically disadvantaged relative to their partner report less improvement in their relationship (Pearson & Thoennes, 1989). Another example of an unequal power relationship is one in which there is, or has been, violence—for example, spousal abuse. A great controversy rages over whether these cases should even be mediated (Wall & Lynn, 1993). Finally, the more motivated *both* disputants are to reach an agreement, and the greater their commitment to the mediation process, the more effective the mediation will be.

A clear majority of studies of mediation have focused on formal or contractual mediation in which it is the third party's recognized job to conduct conflict intervention (e.g., judges, labor mediators, divorce mediators). Far less attention has been paid to the more informal or emergent mediation and intervention work that occurs on a daily basis with parents and their children, friends with friends, coworkers with coworkers, and managers with employees (e.g., Keashly, 1994; Kolb, 1989; Sheppard, Blumenfeld-Jones, & Roth, 1989). Sheppard's (1983) work on managers as conflict intervenors is valuable here, particularly with reference to James's role in Jan and Michael's dispute. Briefly, a common finding in the organizational conflict literature is that managers use procedures that are quite different from those recommended by organizational behavior experts (i.e., conciliatory or mediational strategies). Based on interviews with managers about how they intervene in disputes, Sheppard (1983) identified three styles, none of which looked at all like mediation. The most frequently occurring procedure (inquisitorial style) involved managers actively controlling the discussion and determining what disputants could say and then making and enforcing decisions. The next most frequently described procedure (providing impetus style) involved managers calling the disputants together, asking what was going on, and then telling them to settle it or else. The third procedure (adversarial style) involved the manager passively listening to the disputants, often at their request, and then making the decision, rather like what a judge would do.

Based on these distinctions, James's style seems to be a combination of pro-

Box
13–1 *Addressing Intergroup and International Conflict:*
The Problem-Solving Workshop

Bosnia-Herzegovina. Rwanda. Cyprus. Israel. Somalia. Northern Ireland. Iraq. These are but a few examples of the deeply rooted, seemingly intractable conflicts between identity groups with histories of violence and destruction that exist in the world today. These conflicts are the epitome of the escalatory and self-perpetuating destructive spiral described in Deutsch's (1973) work on competitive processes. Because of this, effective conflict resolution efforts will require a focus on changing the patterns of these interactions to ones more conducive to integrative work. Traditional approaches such as mediation and peacekeeping have relied more on coercive methods (e.g., use of threats, denial of access to desired resources, forced separation) that treat the conflict as a win-lose contest. The conflict needs to be reframed as a problem to be solved, thus engendering integrative solutions.

One type of informal third-party approach that has been utilized in a variety of protracted international and interethnic conflict situations is *interactive conflict resolution* (Fisher, 1993; also see Burton, 1969; Kelman, 1972). This approach involves bringing together representatives from the warring sides, on an equal basis, for informal, analytical, noncommitting discussions of the current conflict. The discussions occur within a multiday problem-solving workshop format. These discussions are convened and facilitated by a third party composed of social scientist–practitioners (in many cases, political scientists and social psychologists) who have expertise in communication, group process, conflict analysis, and international relations. The focus is on dealing with the conflict analytically rather than through argument and debate. This is accomplished by encouraging parties to explore the ways in which the interaction between them at different levels creates the conditions for conflict and helps to exacerbate and perpetuate it (Kelman, 1979). Based on an understanding of the dynamics of their own conflict, the parties can begin developing ways to address concerns and create integrative solutions. The social psychological literature on attitude change, social influence, small group dynamics, and intergroup relations provides an important model for structuring the workshop. For example, the contact hypothesis and the conditions to facilitate positive and constructive intergroup contact are reflected in the structure of the problem-solving workshop (see Fisher, 1990; Kelman, 1993).

In addition to changing attitudes and increasing interaction among the workshop participants, the main hope of this third-party approach is that the new ideas and insights gained during this process will be transferred back to the communities involved and that they will eventually have some influence on the constructive resolution of the conflict. Discussion of concerns, fears, and constraints on possible joint activities and solutions reflects a recognition of the need for realistic elements in any solution. Selection of the workshop participants is particularly important. The closer they are to decision makers, the greater the opportunity for influence yet the less likely the individual is to show change as a result of the discussions. Thus, the participants typically are individuals who are part of the mainstream of their community and are viewed as credible across the political spectrum within the community. They can identify and articulate the key concerns and should be people who are politically influential yet not directly involved in public decision making (Kelman, 1993).

Although there have been a number of problem-solving efforts (see Fisher, 1993, for review), the focus here is on two projects conducted by social psychologists Herbert Kelman, from Harvard University, and Ronald Fisher, from the University of Saskatchewan. Kelman's (1992) work on the Palestinian-Israeli conflict has spanned over 20 years and involved over 3 dozen workshops. His approach has focused on bringing together Palestinian and Israeli influentials to analyze jointly and problem-solve on a number of initiatives. Although much of their work has involved self-contained workshops, Kelman and Rouhana have moved to a continuing workshop design in which the same participants met four times between 1990 and 1992 (see Rouhana & Kelman, 1994, for a fuller discussion). Participants continue to encourage further workshops; this, in itself, is a strong indicator of the utility of this forum for constructive dialogue and problem solving.

Kelman (1995) has suggested that the informal conflict resolution work he has done with his colleagues over the years has contributed to the current peace talks in three ways. First, a "cadre" of members from both communities have been involved in the problem-solving workshop over the years, many of whom are now in positions of influence relative to the negotiations. Second, the shared perceptions, mutual sensitivity, and new ideas for outcomes developed through these workshops have been fed into their communities and utilized in political debate and negotiations. Finally, Kelman argues that the workshops have helped create a political environment favorable to such negotiations that includes more differentiated images of each other, deescalatory language, a belief in a mutual desire for settlement, and a sense of hope.

Fisher's work in Cyprus has occurred over the past 6 years and has involved numerous visits and consultations there. It has also entailed four problem-solving workshops to date (Fisher, 1994). The conflict between the Greek Cypriot and Turkish Cypriot communities on Cyprus may seem quieter than the Palestinian-Israeli conflict yet it is as deeply rooted and as seemingly intractable. Fisher's first workshop occurred in Ottawa in December 1990 and involved Greek Cypriots and Turkish Cypriots living in Canada. His second workshop was convened in London, England, in June 1991 and involved Cypriots from the island. Based on this latter workshop, Fisher conducted two more in Cyprus during May and June 1993, focusing on education and involving Turkish Cypriot and Greek Cypriot educators. In these workshops on Cyprus, the participants focused on identifying potential areas of activities that would contribute to peacebuilding between the communities. Within the sessions, small groups were formed to develop ideas for specific projects. Subsequent bicommunal meetings with the participants were held to continue efforts to foster cooperation and communication between the two groups. At present, three teams have formed to develop proposals for a common reading book of collected literature, a program of student excursions, and a center for bicommunal teacher interaction. These concrete planning efforts highlight the utility of interactive conflict resolution as a means of creating cooperative activities between communities that are in conflict.

The problem-solving workshop is not seen as a substitute for more traditional negotiation and mediation approaches (Fisher, 1993; Kelman, 1993). Rather, it is viewed as a complementary approach to negotiations on substantive issues such as use of land, resources, and power. With its focus on interparty relationships and interactions, interactive conflict resolution efforts can be useful in the prenegotiation phase as they help develop a more positive and constructive relationship within which these discussions can occur. They can be useful during negotiations to deal with issues that arise as a result of deteriorating interactions. Finally, interactive conflict resolution can be useful in the postnegotiation phase as the communities build relationships that will enable the negotiated agreement to be implemented successfully.

viding impetus and adversarial procedures. Given the vignette, it is clear that this intervention was ineffective. A more mediational style may provide the opportunity for both Jan and Michael to tell her and his own story and hear each other's perspectives in the presence of a third party who will then facilitate a constructive discussion. This may be useful in breaking down the barriers to both communication and understanding that characterizes escalated disputes like this one. The question is, who would be the intervenor? James would likely need some mediation skills training. Someone outside the team but internal to the organization (another manager, coworker, human resources) might be helpful (see Kolb & Bartunek, 1992, for informal options and Ury, Brett, & Goldberg, 1989, for formal options).

METHODOLOGICAL CONCERNS

Although the general issues raised in the earlier chapter on methodology also apply to the study of conflict and conflict management (e.g., using students as subjects, lab versus field), there are at least two additional challenges that conflict researchers face. The first has to do with ethical considerations in the study of "experimentally created" conflict and actual conflict. The second challenge concerns the "levels of analysis" to which researchers direct their attention (i.e., at the individual, interpersonal, group, or intergroup level).

Regarding experimentally created conflict, the consideration is twofold: (a) the ethicality of involving people in a conflict; and (b) when people do become involved, how intense a conflict should it be. This is a classic dilemma. To examine responses in conflict, study participants need to be sufficiently involved to behave as they actually would in a dispute. Yet, to the extent they are involved, it may affect them beyond the moment of the study.

The issue of intensity is a particularly challenging one because from a theoretical perspective, intensity is an important factor in disputant behavior and third-party intervention. Thus, limiting or restricting the intensity of the conflict for ethical reasons may limit the generalizations that can come from the study. Typically, these concerns have been addressed by ensuring voluntary participation, informed consent, and detailed debriefing. Another argument proposes that a created conflict be no more "stressful" than what people are exposed to in their daily lives. Given the level of destructive conflict in some people's lives here and around the world, this criterion may not be strict enough. Rigorous ethical review often requires the researcher to justify his or her proposed methodology relative to other methods that may be less stressful for the participants. In the case of conflict, a less "stressful" method would be providing participants with a written description of a conflict situation and having them imagine themselves as disputants. This is a scenario study.

The study of actual conflict may address these concerns because these are "naturally occurring" conflicts. Indeed, the study of actual conflicts has value in terms of quality and detail of available information, relevance to the conflict parties, and opportunities to examine the complexities and dynamics of conflict. The challenges lie in terms of the effect of the researcher's presence on the conflict and the ethicality of being an observer to destructive conflicts, particularly. Regarding the effect of researcher presence, a study by Belliveau and Stolte (1977) found that the mere presence of a third person in the room affected the dynamics between the disputants. The effect of simply being a researcher-observer on disputants' behavior can be positive (encouraging cooperative behavior), neutral, or negative (causing disputants to act tough to impress the third party). Thus, researcher presence can bias the information gathered and, in some cases, intensify the conflict itself.

Regarding the ethicality of being an observer, a key element of a positivist approach to scientific study is that the researcher must be objective. Yet, how is the researcher to remain aloof if violence is occurring or if the researcher becomes aware of information that is critical to the conflict's direction (e.g., one party is planning a violent attack or hidden financial resources exist that could ease a situation of scarcity)? This often involves an inner battle for the researcher between the demands of morality and those of objective science. Does the researcher remain as the observer, leave the situation, or enter it as an intervenor or an advocate? What are the effects of any of these options on the research, the disputants, the conflict, and the broader context in which the conflict occurs?

The second challenge for conflict researchers focuses on levels of analysis and affects where attention is focused in studies and how the results of these studies are interpreted. The earlier discussion of the importance of social context in the analysis and intervention in a conflict situation such as Jan's and Michael's emphasizes the variety of factors and the different levels at which these factors operate and have their influence. Reflect for a moment on how your own (and, indeed, Jan's and Michael's) understanding of their dispute may have changed as a result of the discussion of group and intergroup influences. Recognizing that these may be influences has an impact on your own theorizing and interpretation. The same applies in research.

Focusing at the individual or interpersonal level and generalizing results to group and intergroup phenomena are problematic, potentially leading to limited theorizing on these behaviors. Much of social psychological research [a] into the processes and resolution of conflict has focused at the individual and interpersonal level (e.g., Carnevale & Pruitt, 1992; Deutsch, 1973). This is appropriate to the extent that generalizations stay focused at that level. However, important factors may be overlooked if researchers assume that how conflict operates at those levels is how it operates at these more macro levels. For example, explanations of prejudice and discrimination based on individual-level traits (e.g., authoritarianism, dogmatism) when used to explain group and intergroup discriminatory behavior essentially argue that it is just a few distorted people who do these things. This perspective may blind people to more systemic factors such as power and structural inequities between groups that affect even "normal" individuals. Thus, it is a challenge to and a responsibility of researchers to be clear in the focus of research and to recognize what can be interpreted and the limitations on what can be said. A particular challenge for social psychologists is to recognize the centrality of culture by incorporating the more macro-level variables (e.g., ethnicity, gender) and processes (e.g., power, justice) in research on conflict and conflict management.

IMPLICATIONS FOR FUTURE RESEARCH AND POLICY

Even though third-party intervention has been discussed as the major area of conflict management research, it is important to discuss briefly some challenges that point to areas of continuing and future research and practice.

Research

The first challenge concerns the acknowledgment of conflict stimulation as consistent with the notion of the potential of conflict for positive change (Worchel, Coutant-Sassic, & Wong, 1993). Despite this acknowledgment, the focus of much research and writing on conflict intervention is on ending conflicts. Recent research has begun to address this gap. For example, Evert Van de Vliert (1985) has examined intervention strategies in work teams to stimulate creative yet constructive conflict to enhance the quality and quantity of productivity. Johnson and Johnson's (1994) program and research on structured academic controversies is concerned with stimulating conflict. Worchel's (see Worchel, Coutant-Sassic, & Wong, 1993) work on group development highlights the role of intragroup and intergroup conflict in the establishment and development of group identity. This research suggests that at times group members may avoid conflict and at other times may invite it. In addition, to the extent that conflict involves an attempt to reestablish equity in unequal power relations, stimulating the conflict (e.g., staging a protest march or sit-in) may be a prime way of moving for social change. Theory and research on conflict intervention need to be broadened to explore the conditions under which conflict stimulation occurs and when it is effective.

Although conflict stimulation is a relatively unexplored aspect of conflict intervention, conflict suppression is an unexpected outcome of conflict resolution efforts. A recent critique by Donnellon and Kolb (1994) suggests that current conflict resolution approaches used in organizations to handle disputes may, in fact, *suppress* rather than openly deal with disputes that arise out of, or are complicated by, social diversity (e.g., race, ethnicity, class, gender). By managing the conflict through either organizational structures such as joint union-management committees or taskforces, training individuals in more interpersonal dispute skills, or sending disputants through formal resolution mechanisms such as grievance procedures, the organization and its members may fail to realize that the problem may be more systemic and widespread. The authors propose a number of ways in which organizations can manage diversity disputes constructively without suppression. These approaches involve broadening thinking beyond the individual and interpersonal level to include institutional and group concerns. The discussion in this chapter of group and intergroup influences in conflict should encourage you as the reader to think more broadly. More specific organizational actions include addressing power inequities between groups and supporting collective activities of each group. These approaches are useful for the work of researchers, as well, by encouraging the recognition and consideration of groups, the political/social context in which they operate, and how that may affect not only what is learned about conflict but what it suggests about the management of that conflict.

As the conceptualization and investigation of conflict intervention approaches broadens, it becomes clear that no single intervention or management effort is best and, indeed, over time, a variety of interventions may be necessary in order to fully address a specific conflict (Keashly & Fisher, 1990). Social psychological research needs to investigate a variety of intervention approaches in order to determine the conditions under which they are effective. Once these results are established, the impact of sequencing and coordinating these different approaches on the constructive management of disputes needs to be determined. The value of a contingency model of coordinated conflict intervention has been demonstrated by examining the history of intervention efforts in a number of international and interethnic disputes (see Keashly & Fisher, 1996, for a recent review). Given the intractable nature of many conflicts, coordination of intervention efforts represents a hopeful step.

Policy

The social psychological focus on conflict as an interactive process that occurs within a broader social context and is heavily influenced by subjective factors has important implications for social policy. Policies related to constructive conflict management need to address the development of personal and organizational knowledge of and skills in conflict analysis and conflict management. Regarding skills training, support (political and financial) for school- and community-based training programs is, and should continue to be, a major step in this direction. The results of comparative studies of mediation and adjudication suggest the need for making available an expanded range of third-party methods (Kressel et al., 1989). This "alternative dispute resolution" (ADR) movement is already underway in a variety of countries and has support from communities and governments. In addition, any policies must focus on the recognition and development of culturally relevant models of constructive conflict management that require the acknowledgment and explicit valuing of diversity in its many forms (see Boardman & Horowitz, 1994). Finally, in terms of the broader social and political context, social policy needs to address intergroup inequities (e.g., employment, housing, political involvement) that contribute in obvious and not-so-obvious ways to destructive conflict management. As with any change effort, it is important to evaluate the implementation and impact of these policies and their related procedures.

SUMMARY

Returning to Jan and Michael, without looking back at your earlier response, answer the following questions: (a) What is at the heart of their dispute, and (b) what would you suggest for managing it? Now compare your two sets of responses. How are they the same or different? How is your approach to analysis the same or different? Were your ideas affirmed? Were they challenged? Unless you have the marvelous ability to see all perspectives at all levels and are somewhat psychic to boot, this chapter and the social psychological work (both research and practice) that it reflects should have challenged and, perhaps, changed how you see conflict. It is this challenge that is one of the unexpected yet amazing outcomes of being an applied social psychologist working in conflict management. For not only does this work have the potential for facilitating the understanding and constructive management of conflict, it also has the potential, and indeed does, challenge the researcher in his or her own thinking and approach to research, practice, and life. As a result, the social psychologist is transformed in the process. And that is truly applied social psychology in action.

SUGGESTED READINGS

Deutsch, M. (1973). *The resolution of conflict*. New Haven, CT: Yale University Press.

This is a classic text in conflict resolution. Deutsch lays out the theoretical and research bases for constructive and destructive conflict processes. The discussion then moves to ways to facilitate the development of more cooperative and constructive means of managing conflict.

Fisher, R. J. (1990). *The social psychology of intergroup and international conflict resolution*. New York: Springer-Verlag.

This text provides a comprehensive review of the social psychological factors that fuel conflicts between groups, communities, and nations. Fisher develops an eclectic model for analyzing intergroup conflict that captures factors at the individual, group, and intergroup levels. Based on this analysis, he focuses on social psychological approaches to resolving such conflicts with a particular emphasis on the problem-solving approach of third-party consultation.

Kolb, D. M., & Bartunek, J. (1992). *Hidden conflict in organizations*. Beverly Hills, CA: Sage.

This edited volume focuses on conflicts that are embedded in the life and functioning of organizations and that are handled by means not typically identified or studied in scholarly writings on conflict management. The articles in this volume are diverse in their research methodologies, which are primarily qualitative in nature. These studies provide the basis for discussion of the private, informal, and nonrational dimensions of organizational conflict.

Kressel, K., Pruitt, D. G., & Associates (1989). *Mediation research*. San Francisco: Jossey-Bass.

This edited volume is considered the most extensive effort to date to review mediation efforts across a variety of settings including divorce, community, and international. Based on these broad-ranging studies, Kressel and Pruitt summarize what is known and not known about mediation processes and their effects and point to future directions for both research and practice in mediation.

Taylor, A., & Beinstein Miller, J. (1994). *Gender and conflict.* Cresskill, NJ: Hampton Press, Inc.

This edited volume is based on the Gender and Conflict Symposium that was held at George Mason University in Fairfax, Virginia, in January 1991. It is the first systematic collection and synthesis of research and writings from a variety of disciplines on issues of gender in conflict and conflict management.

14 Organizational Leadership

Roya Ayman
Illinois Institute of Technology

Industrial and organizational psychologists are often confronted with issues surrounding the selection, training, and development of leaders. On any given day, it is not unusual for an industrial/organizational psychologist to get telephone calls like the following: (a) "We are developing a program to help us identify leadership capabilities in our workers. Can you help us set this up? What qualities do we look for in a leader?" or (b) "We are in the process of putting together a management development program for our firm. Do you know of any training programs that build leadership skills and that are sensitive to a culturally diverse workforce?" or (c) "I am a consultant to real estate corporations. One of the things I am called upon to do is to help companies hire their chief executive officer. I have noticed that little is known or written about CEOs in the real estate industry. Can you help me in identifying the characteristics and attributes of these leaders and whether they might be different from leaders in other areas?" To address these issues, experts rely upon theories that have been validated by empirical research in order to provide the most accurate recommendations possible.

LEADERSHIP AND THE PSYCHOLOGICAL DISCIPLINES

The interest in understanding leadership is neither surprising nor new (Ayman, 1993; Bass, 1990). Lately, however, this interest appears to have increased. For example, in the period between 1990 and 1995, it is estimated that 2,624 books were published with the word "leader" or "manager" in the title. In addition, the number of autobiographies or biographies of business or political figures published between 1990 and 1995 has been estimated to be approximately 592,340 titles. Many of these books contain descriptions of key corporate leaders and managers and several titles have achieved best-seller status. Our society's preoccupation with leaders also can be seen by the number of articles in popular newspapers and magazines that address concerns about leadership and leaders—whether in politics or industry. Academics are also interested in studying leadership. This is evidenced by the publication of the journal *Leadership Quarterly,* which is devoted primarily to issues regarding leadership. Added to these are the proliferation of leadership and management training programs, many of which have been quite successful.

Several academic disciplines have studied the issue of leadership (e.g., sociology, philosophy, anthropology, history). The focus of this chapter is on the psychological approaches to leadership. More specifically, this chapter shows how researchers in both social psychology and industrial/organizational psychology share their ideas and research on leadership, to the benefit of both disciplines. To establish the distinction and similarities between these two areas of psychology, brief descriptions of each are provided. *Social psychology* has been defined as "A discipline that employs scientific methods to understand and explain how the thought, feeling, and behavior of individuals are influenced by the actual, imagined, or implied presence of others" (Allport, 1985, p. 3). *Industrial and organizational (I/O) psychology* is, in part, a special case, or subset, of social psychology. I/O psychology has been described as "an emerging blend of research, theory, and practice [that] offers great promise ... for further developing and extending our knowledge of those behavioral processes ... [that are] critical to an understanding of interactions between persons and the institutions and organizations of society" (Dunnette, 1990, p. 23).

I/O psychology, however, does not rely solely on psychology for its theories of how people act in these organizational contexts. I/O psychology has a multidisciplinary focus, and it is also highly dependent on the fields of business, communication, sociology, anthropology, clinical psychology, and education. However broadly focused I/O psychology is, there remains a strong historical and theoretical overlap between it and social psychology. This is particularly evident in the study of leadership. Many of the key researchers and theorists in leadership are strongly associated with social psychology, either by their training or by their academic position. Moreover, research published on the topic of leadership can be found in both social psychological and management journals. Therefore, the distinction between social psychology and I/O psychology is almost impossible to determine when examining the literature on leadership. One could say that social psychologists develop the theories of leadership whereas I/O psychologists conduct the field research and applied research to validate them, although this statement is by no means inclusive.

This chapter begins by providing the reader with an overview of the most re-searched theories or models of leadership. Finally, recent research on social cognition in leadership is discussed, as are the issues of diversity, gender, and power.

APPROACHES TO THE STUDY OF LEADERSHIP

In a recent review of psychology's contribution to the study of leadership, Hogan, Curphy, and Hogan (1994) note that "Leadership is persuasion . . . [that] only occurs when others willingly adopt, for a period of time, the goals of a group as their own" (p. 493). However, from *where* does leadership come? Some argue that leadership is a universal process that comes from *within* the individual (e.g., possession of certain personality traits or behavioral skills that make people more skillful leaders). If this is the case, then those with leadership abilities should be able to lead successfully in all situations. It is often the case, however, that even though a person may possess certain qualities, he or she will be a successful leader only in situations that call for the traits or abilities that he or she possesses (i.e., a *person-by-situation interaction*). For example, someone who is very task-oriented may be much more successful in situations in which the goals are objective and clear. This same person may be less successful in more ambiguous contexts or in situations that require coordinating diverse input from team members.

The focus, therefore, is on whether people's leadership abilities are transsituational or whether people with certain leadership skills are more effective in some situations than others. An interesting split has occurred between those who focus on the universal aspect of leadership and those who focus on the belief that being a successful leader depends on a combination of the person's abilities and the demands of the context. Most practitioners who deal with the selection and training of managers and CEOs have focused on leadership as a personal quality or a set of traits and skills that an effective manager possesses. Among academics, however, there is a stronger belief in the person-by-situation interaction. In other words, people in the field tend to be looking for universals that apply to *all* leaders, whereas academics tend to believe less strongly in universal leadership qualities because successful leaders will be successful only in certain situations. This distinction has important implications for the way an applied social psychologist specializing in leadership might be expected to answer some of the requests made to him or her by those in industry (such as those in the opening vignette) and are discussed later in the chapter.

Research on leadership can be grouped into three categories: the trait, behavioral, and contingency or situational approaches (Bass, 1990; Yukle & Van Fleet, 1992). Each approach builds on the belief that leadership can be found either within the person or by an interaction between the person and the situation. The trait approach assumes that leadership is a result of underlying characteristics that are part of an individual's psychological makeup. The behavioral approaches stress that leadership is a result of behaviors that are perceived to be exerted by the leader (i.e., leaders act in a way that demonstrates their role as a leader). In the various contingency approaches, however, leadership is thought to be an interaction between what the leader brings to the situation and the condition he or she faces. In other words, the contingency approach stresses that a leader is not *always* an effective leader; whether someone is an effective leader depends on the situation and whether he or she has the skills or traits necessary to cope successfully with the situation.

The Trait Approach

Historically, the trait approach was more popular in the earlier part of the twentieth century but received less attention until the 1980s, when there was a resurgence of interest in the traits that leaders possess (Hogan et al., 1994). Since then, numerous studies have examined the personality traits that distinguish leaders from non-leaders.

As early as 1948, Stogdill concluded that there is no universal trait, or set of traits, for leaders. However, he stated that, in most studies, *some* characteristics (i.e, self-confidence, other-directedness, intelligence, being task-focused, exhibiting a willingness to lead) are more strongly correlated with leadership than others. Lord, DeVader, and Alliger (1986) used a meta-analytical procedure to reanalyze previous reviews of the trait approach to leadership. They demonstrated that traits such as masculinity, intelligence, and flexibility differentiated those who became leaders from those who did not. More recently, Van Fleet and Yukle (1992) identified a list of traits that they have found to be related to effective leadership (e.g., high energy level, stress tolerance, integrity, emotional maturity, and self-confidence) across several studies.

As these examples demonstrate, most research on the trait approach has focused on the contribution of *one* trait at a time (i.e., individual correlations) to one's leadership abilities. But some researchers have argued that the combination of traits over time (often referred to as *personality*) is a better method for predicting leadership. Hogan et al. (1994) suggest that certain fundamental personality dimensions bear a substantial relationship to both leadership effectiveness and the emergence of leadership. Their review indicates that leaders tend to be high in surgency (e.g., dominance, activity level, sociability); emotional stability (e.g., adjustment, independence, self-confidence); conscientiousness (e.g., responsibility, initiative, ethical conduct); and agreeableness (e.g., friendliness, support for others).

In many instances, research using the trait approach has yielded inconclusive results, with some studies showing that certain traits are related to leadership and other studies failing to find this relationship. There are several possible reasons for this. First, traits are often correlated with leadership effectiveness; however, leadership effectiveness has been measured in several different ways across studies (e.g., as leadership emergence, evaluation of the leader's performance, the company's profit). Thus, the inconsistency in the findings may be a result of the lack of a single definition of leadership effectiveness.

A second problem is that researchers and practitioners have been using methods of analysis that address the unique contribution of single traits rather than developing a *profile* of those traits. Profile analyses may be a more useful way of showing how effective leaders capitalize on their strengths to overcome a weakness (Van Fleet & Yukle, 1992). Leaders may balance traits within themselves, or by sharing leadership with others (e.g., where, in a team, the leader and group members pool their different strengths to offset the team's weaknesses). If leaders do balance their leadership traits, then traditional sorts of studies that correlate ratings of a leader's effectiveness with ratings of their personality traits would be unable to detect this process.

The trait approach is especially attractive to human resource specialists (such as those requesting help from the leadership specialist in the opening vignette) for selection purposes. Although academic researchers and theorists remain skeptical with regard to the possibility of personality dimensions or traits predicting leadership success, practitioners are using a wide variety of personality measures (e.g., the MMPI, 16PF and Meyers Briggs) to identify leaders in corporations. The validation studies for this kind of personality testing, however, are not available and further research is needed to determine whether they actually *are* able to identify leaders. Thus, those seeking to identify leaders based on personality traits or dimensions need to know that science has not yet provided evidence to support the assumption that there are universal traits for leadership.

The Behavioral Approaches

Since Lewin, Lippitt, and White's (1939) classic experiment, which studied the effects of autocratic and democratic leadership in boys' clubs, researchers have investigated the behaviors and communication styles that are related to leadership. Some models have studied these leader behaviors or styles as an exchange between the leader and the follower (Hollander, 1993). This is known as the *transactional paradigm* of leader behavior. Others have identified behaviors that encourage change and evolution in a team of workers or individual subordinates (Bass & Avolio, 1985). This is known as a *transformational paradigm*.

In the transactional paradigm, two main categories of leadership behavior have prevailed after more than 40 years of research: (a) technical, task-focused, or goal-focused activities and (b) interpersonal or people-oriented activities (Yukle & Van Fleet, 1992). This research began in the late 1950s, when three independent research centers (Ohio State University, University of Michigan, and Harvard University) examined the behaviors of work groups and their leaders and concluded that leadership behaviors can be subsumed under the task- and interpersonally oriented categories.

The measures of leadership behavior most often used in research by both academics and practitioners are derivatives of the original Leader Behavior Description Questionnaire developed by researchers at Ohio State University. This single survey has been the basis for the development of a wide variety of other leadership measures, such as the Leader Behavior Description Questionnaire Form XII, the Supervisory Description Questionnaire, and the Leader Opinion Questionnaire

(Bass, 1990). These measures ask for people's perceptions of a leader's behavior. Each has 10 to 20 items that assess the leaders' task-related activities and 10 to 20 items that assess their interpersonal activities (Cook, Hepworth, Wall, & Warr, 1985). An example of *interpersonally oriented* leadership behavior is being open to new ideas; an example of *task-oriented* leadership behavior is assigning specific duties to individual group members.

Several studies have examined the effectiveness of task-oriented and interpersonal leadership behaviors. A review of this research (Fisher & Edwards, 1988) has found that interpersonally focused behaviors had a consistently positive correlation with leadership effectiveness. This finding emerged regardless of the way leadership effectiveness was measured or whether the leader or a subordinate made the ratings. However, for task-oriented leadership behaviors, the findings were less conclusive (Fisher & Edwards, 1988). On the one hand, task-oriented behaviors were positively correlated with measures of worker productivity; on the other hand, they were also positively related to turnover rates in the work group and negatively related with both the group's satisfaction with their leader and with the group's cohesion. Researchers have argued that the impact task-oriented leadership behaviors can have on the group may vary depending on the situation (Bass, 1990; Korman, 1966; Schriesheim & DeNisi, 1981). For example, when group members are new or have a lack of knowledge regarding the task, a leader who is focused on the task at hand can have a positive impact on the group.

Another behavioral approach is the transformational paradigm, also known as *charismatic leadership*. In the last decade, the transformational paradigm has attracted the attention of researchers and practitioners alike. This approach, although conceptually different from the transactional paradigm, is also based on the leader's behavior. It assumes that a good leader is a mentor to his or her followers, empowering subordinates (House & Shamir, 1993) and encouraging them to change and grow in their position (Conger & Kanungo, 1987).

To accomplish this change in their followers, transformational leaders tend to engage in four kinds of behaviors (Bass & Avolio, 1993). By using *inspirational motivation,* transformational leaders set an example for others to follow; they are optimistic and promote attainable goals for the future. *Individual consideration* is a second type of transformation behavior. Here, leaders show an interest in the well-being of their subordinates; they focus on individual strengths and weaknesses, and they assign projects based on those abilities. Leaders who address crises in a head-on manner, appeal to their subordinates on an emotional level, and are dedicated to their followers are using *charismatic* leadership behaviors. The fourth type of transformational leadership behavior is *intellectual stimulation*. When leaders use this kind of behavior, they encourage their subordinates to reexamine their assumptions and revisit old problems. They also encourage changes in thinking and listening to ideas that may, at first, seem foolish.

During the last decade, several studies have compared the effectiveness of transformational and transactional leaders (e.g., Avolio & Bass, 1993). In most of these studies, the subordinates have been the primary source of information about the leader's behaviors and leadership effectiveness. The majority of this research shows that transformational leaders were evaluated more favorably than transactional leaders.

The behavioral approaches to leadership are valued by practitioners who wish to identify the skills that are essential in leadership. However, as with the trait approach, researchers have concluded that there is no single set of behaviors that are effective for *all* leaders in *all* situations. There is some evidence that interpersonally focused behaviors may be superior to task-oriented behaviors because they appear not to have any negative consequences on leadership effectiveness. That is, an interpersonal orientation either increases leadership effectiveness or has no appreciable effect. The task-focused style of leader behavior may be effective in some contexts but has negative consequences in others. These two kinds of behaviors need to be chosen wisely by the leader and fitted to specific situations.

The behavioral approaches also provide practitioners with valuable information for building leadership skills. For example, there are existing training programs designed to build both transformational and transactional leadership abilities (Avolio & Bass, 1993; Blake & Mouton, 1982). However, the practitioner needs to be aware of the fact that there is no evidence that the subordinates' perceptions of the leader's behaviors and what the leader thinks he or she is doing always match. In other words, training the leader to engage in either transactional or transformational kinds of behaviors may be useless if leaders use them inappropriately or if their subordinates are unable to identify them. To this end, there are also training programs designed to build leaders' self-perception skills (Avolio & Bass, 1993).

The Contingency Approaches

In the late 1960s, a paradigm shift occurred in social psychology. Building on previous work by Lewin, Heider, and their peers, researchers developed a greater awareness of the role that the social context plays in determining the way people act. At about the same time, the first contingency model of leadership was introduced by Fiedler (1964, 1978), and the contingency paradigm has dominated leadership research ever since. The models making up the contingency paradigm assume that different leadership characteristics or behaviors are effective in different situations. The three most dominant contingency approaches are the *contingency model of effective leadership,* the *path-goal theory* and the *normative model of leadership decision making.* A brief description of each model follows.

Contingency Model of Effective Leadership. Historically, this is the first model in the contingency paradigm (Fiedler, 1964, 1978). It hypothesizes that leadership effectiveness is based on the interplay of two factors: the leader's *personality* traits (i.e., his or her orientation toward task accomplishment or interpersonal relationships in the workplace) and the amount of influence the leader has over the group, referred to as *situational control* (Ayman, Chemers, & Fiedler, 1995). The leadership trait measured here uses a standard questionnaire known as the Least Preferred Coworker Scale (Fiedler & Chemers, 1984). This scale measures the respondent's preferences for task-oriented versus interpersonally oriented personality dimensions in a leader. The leader's situational control is assessed by three elements: the favorability of the *relationship* between the leader and the group members, the *clarity* of the leader's task structure, and his or her *position of authority* (Fiedler & Chemers, 1984).

This model was based on early empirical research that showed how task-oriented leaders do best in both predictable settings and chaotic conditions, whereas interpersonally oriented leaders do best in situations when there is conflict among the team members or the task is unclear. The rationale for these assumptions is that, in predictable settings, the task-oriented leader's goal-oriented focus is already met so he or she can relax and become friendly. But, in chaotic situations, task-oriented leaders pursue their primary interest and this helps them get the group moving. For interpersonally focused leaders, the first priority is establishing a good relationship among members of the work group. This becomes an asset, helping either to work out any conflict or to capitalize on the group's strengths in order to find a solution for an unstructured task.

Fiedler (1993) expanded the Contingency Model of Effective Leadership to include the influence of a leader's intelligence and experience. Fiedler (1993) believes that, in some situations, intelligence is a leader's best asset but, in other situations, experience is more essential. According to Fiedler, in situations of uncertainty and stress, leaders who have the most experience are most effective. On the other hand, under situations of low stress and uncertainty, leaders with high intelligence outperform those with less intelligence (Fiedler, 1995; Fiedler & Garcia, 1987).

The contingency model of effective leadership can be useful in helping practitioners select and train leaders. First, it can help individual leaders assess their strengths and weaknesses. That is, by determining whether their strengths lie in being more task-oriented or interpersonally focused, leaders can select situations that are best suited to them. The practitioner can also use this kind of information to select potential leaders for specific leadership contexts or to train a leader with the necessary skills and resources to manage his or her situation better.

Path-Goal Theory. This contingency model focuses on the leader as a motivator of subordinates (House & Mitchell, 1975). It hypothesizes that because subordinates have different personalities, job tasks, and job structures (e.g., some work independently whereas others work as part of a team), what one person needs from a leader will vary from what another person needs. As a result, different subordinates will benefit from different kinds of leader behaviors in order to achieve their goals (House, 1971). The path-goal model has focused on four different kinds of behaviors leaders can use in order to motivate their followers: *consultative* (e.g., friendly and approachable), *participative* (e.g., consults with subordinates), *achievement oriented* (e.g., emphasizes goal to be achieved), and *directive* (e.g., makes the decisions and makes sure everyone knows what is expected of him or her).

Research has provided support for the model's contention that there are individual differences in the kinds of motivational behaviors subordinates need from their leaders and that meeting these different motivational needs enhances worker motivation and satisfaction (Indvik, 1986). For example, Abdel-Halim (1981) found that subordinates with an internal locus of control prefer leaders who use participative behaviors; those with an external locus of control prefer leaders who are more directive.

Practitioners have used this model's premise for training purposes. For example, Hersey and Blanchard (1974, 1993) have developed a training program known as *Situational Leadership,* which provides skill building for leaders. In this program, the leader evaluates his or her behavior in relation to situations with different levels of a subordinate's ability and willingness (what Hersey and Blanchard call "maturity"). The training program prescribes four different types of supervisory behaviors based on the leader's work group maturity. It recommends that leaders use a *selling style* (i.e., be very motivating) when supervising those who lack both the ability and the willingness to achieve the desired goal. Because the leader works with the subordinates to develop both motivation and skill, this style is both person- and task-oriented. When subordinates lack the ability to achieve the task but are highly motivated, Hersey and Blanchard (1993) believe that the leader should use a *telling style* (i.e., be very directive). This style is task-oriented and minimizes the interpersonal domain of leader behaviors. The third style is *participation,* which is used when the subordinates have the necessary skills to achieve the goal but lack willingness. The participation style is also highly task-oriented. Finally, Hersey and Blanchard's program teaches leaders to use *delegation of responsibility* to subordinates who are both highly skilled and motivated. Because the leader is delegating his or her responsibility, this leader behavior style is neither task-oriented nor interpersonally focused.

Normative Model of Leadership Decision Making. The normative model focuses on the leader's role in the decision-making process (Vroom & Yetton, 1973). The model identifies five styles of leadership decision making, ranging from an autocratic process to a more democratic process. Its premise is that in different situations, different levels of group participation in decision making are more effective. In the *Autocratic I* style, the leader makes the decision alone, without consultation with any of his or her subordinates. When the leader collects information relevant to the decision-making process from subordinates and then makes the decision alone, he or she is acting according to the *Autocratic II* style. The *Consultative I* style is used when leaders share the problem with their subordinates individually, getting recommendations from each before making the decision alone. In the *Consultative II* style, the leader would call a group meeting, share the problem with the group, and ask for analysis and recommendations. However, even at this stage the leader still makes the decision alone. Finally, the *Group* style of decision making is employed when the leader and the team discuss the issue together and jointly come to a decision.

The amount of group participation in decision making depends on the knowledge and skills of the group members and the leader regarding the issue, the level of support the leader feels from the group, and the amount of time available. As an instruction tool, the model provides the leader with a decision-making tree of elements that can guide him or her in estimating the factors in the situation and choosing the best strategy (Vroom & Jago, 1988). For example, when the leader has the relevant skills and is knowledgeable about the issue and there is little need for the support of the followers, the model recommends using a highly autocratic style whereby the leader makes the decision by himself or herself. However, as the nature of the task becomes more obscure to the leader, he or she is advised to get the members of the group involved. This may occur by simply asking for specific information without informing group members of the problem, or by individually approaching them for input about the problem, or by having the group provide recommendations by discussing the problem. The ultimate level of participation occurs when the leader feels comfortable with the knowledge and support of the group members and allows the group collectively to arrive at a decision that is subsequently implemented. Furthermore, the element of time spent to arrive at a decision cannot be ignored. The more the group members are involved in the decision-making process, the more time it may require. Therefore, depending on the time frame in which the decision needs to be made, the leader may have to sacrifice group input (Vroom & Jago, 1988).

The normative model has received some support (Vroom & Jago, 1988). Although the model recommends autocratic styles in certain situations, researchers have found that this does not necessarily yield the best result. Research by Heilman, Hornstein, Cage, and Herschlag (1984) found that even in situations where Hersey and Blanchard (1993) expect an autocratic style of decision making to be most effective, engaging in this style did not produce higher ratings of leadership effectiveness than the more consultative or group participative styles. Also, gender appears to have a moderating effect for this model. Women leaders using autocratic styles, regardless of the situation, received more negative evaluations, whereas men received modest to positive evaluations (Eagly, Makhijani, & Klonsky, 1992; Jago & Vroom, 1982).

SOCIAL COGNITIVE APPROACH TO LEADERSHIP

Most leadership studies have depended on social cognitive processes for measuring perceptions of a leader's behavior and effectiveness. The application of social cognition to the study of leadership began in the late 1970s and has not only sharpened the focus of leadership research but also has helped researchers and practitioners alike to develop a better understanding of the diversity of leadership. There are two main lines of research in this approach. One focuses on the presence of *implicit leadership theory* and its effect on perceiving and evaluating leaders. The other is focused on the leader's *attributional processes* regarding the subordinates' behaviors and the leader's choice of reactive behavior. Both of these approaches acknowledge that leadership is a social interaction influenced by social cognitive processes (Calder, 1977; Chemers, 1993), and each is discussed next.

Implicit Leadership Theory. Implicit leadership theory is based on the similarly ti-
tled *implicit personality theory* (Bruner & Tagiuri, 1954). Implicit personality theory
suggests that people have beliefs about specific types of people. The assumption is
that certain personality traits are more strongly associated with some types of people than they are for other types of people. Thus, people who perceive a noticeable
characteristic in others will also assume the presence of traits that are believed to be
associated with that characteristic. For example, Rosenberg and Sedlak (1972) observed that people tend to think that intelligent men and women are also friendly
and not very self-centered; on the other hand, they also believe that less intelligent
people are not very friendly and very selfish.

Implicit leadership theory extends this concept by suggesting that people associate certain personality traits with different kinds of leaders. Through careful laboratory experimentation, Lord and his colleagues have demonstrated that when people are presented with a particular schema of a leader (e.g., an effective leader), they
report the presence of behaviors that are consistent with their definition of a successful leader (Cronshaw & Lord, 1987; Lord, Binnings, Rush, & Thomas, 1978;
Phillips & Lord, 1981). For example, when subjects were led to believe that a leader
was successful, regardless of whether he or she used task behaviors often or infre-
quently, this belief influenced their perceptions of the leader's interpersonally oriented behaviors, as well as the frequency of task behaviors (i.e., they described behaviors that the leader did not actually display, but which were presumably
consistent with their schema of an effective leader).

Implicit leadership theory also states that people's recall of a leader's behavior
is affected significantly by the type of leader they expect either to see or interact
with. When people expect to see either a highly task-oriented leader or a leader who
is not task-oriented, they tend to focus on the task-oriented nature of the leader's
behavior and are more likely to remember that kind of behavior (Lord et al., 1978).

Some of Lord's research also presents the possibility that people hold a hierarchy of leadership schemata (Lord, Foti, & DeVader, 1984). That is, the more particular the label (e.g., military leader, political leader), the more descriptive and discriminating the information contained in the schema becomes. Thus, people will use
their various leadership schemata to differentiate between a military leader's behavior and that of a political leader. They will use their implicit expectations of these
leaders to judge the effectiveness of their actions. In this way, even though a military
and political leader may act in exactly the same way, people may perceive their behaviors differently.

Attribution Processes. The leadership attributional model (Green & Mitchell,
1979) is based on Weiner's (1974) theory of achievement attributions. According to
Weiner, people judge their own and others' successes and failures by attributing
them either to *internal* or *dispositional* factors (e.g., ability, effort, mood) or to *external* or *contextual* factors (e.g., luck, task difficulty, influence from another person).
Green and Mitchell (1979) adopted this model in an attempt to explain how a
leader's attributions of his or her subordinates' success, failure, or general performance (e.g., why they are late, why they have low levels of productivity, or why they

miss deadlines) can influence the future interactions between that leader and subordinate. Research has shown that when a subordinate has a history of poor performance and the effect of the poor performance is severe, the leader attributes the cause of poor performance to the subordinate (i.e., a dispositional attribution; Mitchell & Wood, 1980). In these situations the leader's subsequent behaviors will be focused on changing the subordinate, even if the situation had contributed to the poor performance.

These two social cognitive approaches to leadership help to provide a better understanding of the leadership process. Research conducted using the implicit leadership theory (Lord & Maher, 1991) illustrates the existence of several leadership schemata and their impact on leadership perception and evaluation. The attributional research demonstrates the impact that causal attribution has on leaders' behaviors. Both schema use and attributions are strongly affected by salient cues emanating from the social context. For example, the gender and cultural background of the leader and his or her subordinates are important factors that can have an impact on both of these cognitive processes. In the next section, these characteristics and their effect on leadership are discussed.

Diversity and Leadership

Since the passage of the Civil Rights Act and the establishment of affirmative action in the 1970s, the U.S. labor force has included an increasing number of women and minorities (Morrison & Von Glinow, 1990). With the rapid move of industry toward globalization, the workforce of international companies is also becoming more diverse. However, the models of leadership described here have primarily been developed and validated for the American male manager (Ayman, Kreiker, & Masztal, 1994).

In response to this limitation, American researchers have shown an increased interest in demonstrating the impact that a leader's gender can have on his or her leadership behaviors and effectiveness. Reviews of gender research in leadership (e.g., Eagly & Johnson, 1990; Eagly, Makhijani, & Klonsky, 1992; Korabik, 1990; Powell, 1993) have demonstrated that, in work settings, female and male leaders are not perceived to behave differently, even though female managers are evaluated slightly less positively. In other words, the same behavior tends to be judged differently depending on whether the actor (i.e., the leader) is a man or a woman. Research has shown that when subordinates interact with male or female leaders (who behave according to the *same* script), they display more negative nonverbal reactions (e.g., furrowed brow, tightening of the mouth, nods of disagreement) toward the female leader than toward the male leader (Butler & Geis, 1990).

Research has looked at the gender composition of the subordinate group and how that might affect their perceptions of the leader's behavior and their evaluation of the leader's effectiveness (Eagly, Makhijani, & Klonsky, 1992). Overall, the findings show that these perceptions vary as a function of the group's focus. When the group's goal is focused more on task accomplishment, women tend to take a subservient role to men in mixed-sex groups. This hesitancy to lead is not found in all female groups. However, women who do become leaders tend to be evaluated more negatively when they are in mixed-sex groups, as opposed to all-female groups.

Why are female leaders evaluated more negatively? One line of research has looked toward the implicit leadership theory, which examines the expectations or schemata that the public have regarding leaders and managers. In the past 20 years, researchers have found that Americans, regardless of their work experience and gender, hold a masculine image of a leader (Heilman, Block, Martell, & Simon 1989; Schien, 1973, 1975; Schien, Mueller, & Jacobson, 1989). More recent research with children has shown that boys also hold the schema of a leader being a man. However, among girls, there were more equal numbers of male and female images of a leader (Ayman, Bast, Ayman-Nolley, Friedman, & Runkle, 1994; Ayman-Nolley, Ayman, & Becker, 1993).

Across cultures these findings become more subtle. For example, Fagenson (1990) found that Japanese respondents also described a *manager* as masculine. But the attributes they associated with a *leader* were different. For example, in Japan, nurturance (a stereotypically feminine trait) is seen as a leadership quality and co-exists with masculine attributes when describing a leader. This attribute is not included in descriptions of masculinity in the United States.

Research using an attributional approach to leadership has focused on gender differences in the choice of subsequent behavior when the leader is faced with a poor performer. Male leaders who interact with poorly performing male and female subordinates more often attribute the cause of the poor performance to effort (i.e., an internal attribution) for the female poor performers than for the male poor performers. Male and female leaders also treated their poor performers differently. Men more often used equity (i.e., you get what you earn) as their base for distribution of rewards whereas women more often used equality (i.e., everyone gets the same) when rewarding subordinates (Dobbins, 1985).

As mentioned earlier in this chapter, research has shown that leaders' self-reported perceptions of their leadership behaviors have low correlations with those described by others (e.g., subordinates, superiors, and observers; Baril, Ayman, & Palmiter, 1994; Bass, 1990; Karlins & Hargis, 1988; Mitchell, 1970; Webber, 1980). Some researchers have provided evidence that when leaders' self-perceptions are similar to how their subordinates see them, their leadership effectiveness ratings are significantly higher (Atwater & Yammarino, 1992; Bass & Yammarino, 1991). More recently, research by Becker, Ayman, and Korabik (1994) has hinted that female leaders may experience more discrepancy with their subordinates' perceptions than men, especially in organizations that have been traditionally male-dominated (see Box 14–1 for the summary of a study on this topic).

Researchers have shown less of an interest in the influence of a leader's or subordinate's ethnic background (e.g., African American, Hispanic, or Native American). Ayman (1993), however, has argued that observers are cued by other salient physical characteristics of the actor, such as gender, skin color, facial features, and body structure. Each of these can provide information that might activate a strong schema that may be in contradiction with the more traditional (i.e., Caucasian,

Box
14–1 **Discrepancy of Perception Between Leaders
and Subordinates: Some Contributing Factors**

The issue of congruence in perception between leaders and their subordinates has a long history. Since the 1970s, various studies have shown the inconsistency between the leader's self-perception of his or her behavior and others' perceptions of these same kinds of behaviors. Despite various efforts made to increase the accuracy of evaluation procedures, this interest has developed because managers have to respond to diverse groups of people (their superiors, subordinates, and peers). These different constituencies may all have valid, but differing, views of the manager's performance. Awareness of these differences can assist an organization in developing more accurate evaluation procedures (these are ultimately used for personnel decisions such as a pay raise or a promotion). Knowledge of the areas in which a manager's self-perceptions differ from those of his or her subordinates can also assist in identifying areas that need improvement for the manager himself or herself. Several lines of research have evolved to address this issue. Some researchers studying performance appraisal and leadership have pursued an investigation of the *impact* of the congruence, or the lack of it, between a leader and his or her subordinates; others have examined the *contributing factors* to this discrepancy (Atwater & Yammarino, 1993; Landy & Farr, 1980).

Because research has provided evidence that a lack of congruence between a leader and his or her subordinates has negative effects on evaluated performance (Atwater & Yammarino, 1992), understanding the contributing factors seems ever more critical. For example, it is possible that the experience of the glass ceiling for women and members of minorities who are managers (i.e., members of these groups tend to go only so far in the management hierarchy and only very rarely do they get beyond that point) may be due, in part, to a discrepancy of perception. It may also be that women and minorities might experience a glass ceiling only in certain management situations or contexts (e.g., companies that are considered "masculine," such as those devoted to high technology). The following study was designed to test the role of gender and context on leaders' and subordinates' perceptual congruence.

Becker, Ayman, and Korabik (1994) examined the contributing influence of leaders' gender, the gender-congruent nature of their work context, and the leaders' degree of self-monitoring with regard to the disagreement (difference scores) between perceptions of their own task-oriented and interpersonal leadership behavior and their subordinates' perceptions of the leader's behavior in these same areas. The study's sample included 98 men and women in management positions, equally divided among traditionally masculine organizations (e.g., banks, insurance, and financial consulting) and a gender-neutral organization (e.g., a large suburban public school board with an equal ratio of men to women). The position of the female and male leaders was kept constant. For a leader to be included in this study, he or she had to have at least two male and two female subordinates. For each leader, Becker et al. sent questionnaires to four of their subordinates: two men and two women. The leaders and subordinates both described the leader's behavior using the LBDQ XII subscales of *consideration* (an interpersonal orientation) and *structuring* (a task-orientation). The responses of the subordinates of each leader were averaged.

The results of the study showed that on both consideration and structuring behaviors, there was a significantly greater discrepancy between women leaders in male-dominated organizations and their subordinates. Also, it was found that women leaders who described themselves as high self-monitors (i.e., they were more aware of how others saw them and sought to change their behavior to please others) had significantly more disagreements with their subordinates when the behavior described was the leader's structuring behavior. These results mean that in male-dominated organizations, women managers' perceptions of their own behavior is not in sync with those of their subordinates. For high self-monitoring women managers, this discrepancy seemed higher. This may indicate that high self-monitoring women leaders who are in unfamiliar environments are more attentive to the general norms than to the immediate social cues (a finding traditionally associated with high self-monitors). (See also Tunnell, 1980.)

The implication of this study in organizations is that women managers in male-dominated organizations seem not to have the same perceptions of themselves as their subordinates. Training them to increase their awareness of others' perception of them may help in reducing this discrepancy. The variance between self- and other ratings has a direct impact with regard to the promotion performance appraisal process, referred to as *360-degree feedback*. In this performance evaluation system, the leaders, their subordinates, and their superiors rate the leader's behavior. Subsequently, leaders are provided with feedback on the performance ratings and the discrepancy of ratings. This procedure is used to assist leaders to identify their shortcomings and look for means to improve themselves as leaders. Programs such as 360-degree feedback seem to have great value in providing assistance to leaders who are women. In addition, in male-dominated organizations, men can receive training to become aware of their own biases and to overcome these as they interact and evaluate women more effectively.

male) schema of a leader. For example, in a recent study in the United States, white and African American students from three universities were asked to describe a typical white person, a typical person of African American heritage, and a typical manager. The results showed that the white students' schemata of a white person and a manager was more similar than their schemata of an African American and a manager. The reverse, however, was true for the African American respondents (Runkle & Ayman, 1995). This perceptual bias may be due mostly to the observers' lack of experience with seeing a more diverse set of physical characteristics associated with people who occupy positions of power. As the number of people in powerful leadership positions with unique physical characteristics (e.g., gender and ethnicity) become more common, these characteristics should lose their saliency and strong differences in expectations will be lessened as a result.

The area of leadership diversity has provided important information for practitioners, particularly in the training and selection arenas. With regard to training leaders, it is not enough to train leaders to behave in a certain style. Leaders need to develop a *metaperception* (i.e., an awareness of others' perceptions of them). These metaperceptions will help leaders develop an appreciation for how perceptual processes influence their interactions with their subordinates. For example, a woman working with both male and female subordinates should learn that unfavorable ratings of her leadership behavior may not be an indication of her ability to lead but may reflect a perceptual bias based on social schemata of traditionally masculine leadership.

From a selection perspective, this line of research lends support to the need for policies on the inclusion of more nontraditional leaders in management, such as affirmative action and equal employment policies. As research has demonstrated, the more representation a minority group has in industry and management, the less salient its gender or racial cues become. In addition, the research on social cognition and diversity has provided insights and guidelines for selection interviews and performance evaluation systems to enhance the fairness of the personnel decision making and its process.

Leadership and Power

Power is a social phenomenon. When one person has a need to influence the behavior or thoughts of another, and is able to do so, then that is referred to as power. Power is caused most often by the presence of a conflict over an important issue. Limited resources, interdependency, and disagreements on goals, or processes for achieving them, all contribute to the presence of conflict (Pfeffer, 1981). Power and conflict, though found in several other social situations, are more prevalent in the leadership situations.

Although power is a fairly old topic in leadership, it has not consistently been integrated into the main models of leadership described. Only the *contingency model of effective leadership* (Fiedler, 1964, 1978) has incorporated the concept of power into the way it conceives of leadership. In this model, the three components of the leader's situational control combine with what French and Raven (1959) refer to as *sources of power* (Ayman, Chemers, & Fiedler, 1995). Therefore, it is necessary to examine the leader's sources of power.

French and Raven (1959), two social psychologists, identified five sources of power: *referent* (i.e., you exert power because people like you or want to be like you); *expert* (i.e., you exert power through your knowledge and expertise); *coercive* (i.e., you exert power because of your ability to punish others for failing to comply); *reward* (i.e., you exert power because you can reward others for their compliance); and *legitimate* (e.g., you exert power because of your position of authority, such as a police officer). People do not necessarily rely solely on one of these sources of power; rather, the same individual can use one or more types of power in order to achieve his or her goals. Podsakoff and Schreischeim (1985), however, have found that, although most people rely on the legitimate, coercive, and reward sources of power, the most *effective* sources of power (i.e., those with the longest lasting impact) are expertise and referent power.

The practitioner interested in selection of managers may be able to assess the tendency of the individual based on his or her reliance on using one source of power more than another. McClelland (1975) has provided a measure for testing both the person's need for social power and personal power. He defined *social power* as the need to gain control over the situation to assist the group in achieving its goal. *Personal power* was defined as the need for control in order to attain personal gain and advancement.

For practitioners, power has been primarily a topic considered when training leaders. Making individuals aware of the sources of their power, as well as the ways their power can be communicated to others, provides valuable information both for those who are leaders and those aspiring to leadership positions. For example, leaders can assess which sources of power are available to them and strategically manage those resources.

Practitioners also need to consider the important role power has in the *empowerment* and *mentoring* of men and women in organizations. Designing organizational policies and systems to encourage these behaviors is critical as our society moves toward the next century. Empowerment can be viewed as enhancing the number or influence of power sources available to employees. Usually the manager or some other leader in the work setting provides the mechanism for empowerment to occur (Conger & Kanungo, 1988); one example would be through the use of a transformational style of leadership that encourages the development of expertise. Mentoring, on the other hand, is essential in succession planning within organizations (Ragins, 1995). *Mentoring* is the process whereby those in positions of power (i.e., the ones who have access to different sources of power) show the junior members of the organization how to access and use those sources of power in a functional and effective manner. There are many companies that have both empowerment and mentoring programs formally in place (e.g., Motorola). They train their leaders in these activities and reward those who actively participate in the program.

SUMMARY

In summary, this overview of leadership research has focused on demonstrating the close relationship between social psychological theory development and industrial-organizational research and application of those theories. The evolution of the leadership models described here has benefited immensely from both laboratory research and field studies conducted with actual managers and leaders.

SUGGESTED READINGS

Bass, B. M. (1990). *Bass and Stogdill's handbook of leadership: Theory, research, and managerial applications* (3rd. ed.). New York: Free Press.

A comprehensive review of leadership research and application is contained in this handbook.

Chemers, M. M., & Ayman, R. (Eds.). (1993). *Leadership theory and research: Perspectives and directions.* New York: Academic Press.

This is a review of theories and issues in leadership research by key authors in the field. Their work reflects the research and application concerns of the various theories and topics such as diversity, group development, and decision making.

Chemers, M. M., Oskamp, S., & Costanzo, M.A. (Eds.). (1995). *Diversity in organizations: New perspectives for a changing workplace.* Thousand Oaks, CA: Sage.

Several of the chapters in this book are related to leadership and diversity, and the book covers key issues pertinent to leadership and diversity authored by experts in the field.

Dansereau, F. (Ed.). (1995). The special issue of *Leadership Quarterly:* Multi-level analysis and leadership.

This two-volume issue is of great value for readers who are interested in a state-of-the-art understanding of the leadership models and research.

Yukle, G., & Van Fleet, D. D. (1992). Theory and research on leadership in organizations. In M. D. Dunnette & L. M. Hough (Eds.), *Handbook of industrial and organizational psychology* (2nd ed., Vol. 3, pp. 147–198). Palo Alto, CA: Consulting Psychologists Press.

This handbook provides a good review of leadership research and recommendations for future research.

15 Applied Gender Issues

Karen Korabik

University of Guelph

In 1982, Ann Hopkins was denied a partnership at Price Waterhouse, a prestigious accounting firm, despite the fact that she was one of the company's top performers. She was told that her promotion was refused because she was too aggressive and that she should wear more makeup and jewelry and take a "charm school" course (Fiske, Bersoff, Borgida, Deaux, & Heilman, 1991). She filed a sex discrimination lawsuit against the firm. When the case eventually came before the Supreme Court of the United States (*Price Waterhouse v. Hopkins*, 1989), the American Psychological Association submitted an *amicus curiae* brief. The psychologists who drafted the brief utilized findings from social psychological research to show that sex-based stereotyping can lead to discriminatory decision making in environments where women are in the minority (Fiske et al., 1991). The majority of those on the Supreme Court agreed with this position and the case was remanded to a lower court, which found in favor of Ann Hopkins.

Every day of their lives, people's gender exerts a major impact on their relationships with others. As a large body of social psychological research has established, people's gender can, and often does, influence the manner in which they are expected to behave, the way that they are perceived and evaluated by others, the kinds of roles that they take on, and the opportunities that are available to them. The lives of individuals can be dramatically altered as a result of this, as can been seen in the case of Ann Hopkins in the opening vignette.

Throughout this chapter, the situation that Ann Hopkins encountered at Price Waterhouse is used to illustrate the manner in which social psychology can be applied to gender-related issues and processes. The focus of this example, and of much of the material covered in this chapter, is on what occurs in the workplace. However, the principles and dynamics that are discussed also pertain to other contexts in which men and women establish ongoing relationships with one another, for example, those of teacher and student or doctor and patient.

WHAT IS GENDER?

Over the past several decades, psychologists have struggled with the meaning of the term *gender*. At first glance, it seems that distinguishing between *sex* (i.e., whether someone is biologically a male or a female) and *gender* (i.e., the psychological and sociocultural ramifications of being a male or a female) should not be too difficult. However, separating what is biologically determined from what is psychologically determined is not always easy (Unger & Crawford, 1993). In their attempts to do so, individuals often rely on social inference processes. Consequently, they frequently make assumptions about gender based on information about biological sex and vice versa.

Gender is usually thought of as involving only an individual's personal identity or the traits, attitudes, beliefs, preferences, and behaviors that individuals internalize as a function of their socialization toward masculine or feminine roles. However, gender is enacted through a complex process of social interactions in which individuals "are simultaneously perceivers of others, targets of others' perceptions, and perceivers of themselves" (Deaux & Major, 1987, p. 370). Thus, gender also involves the expectations that individuals convey to others, as well as those that they have about others, and those that others have about them (Deaux & Major, 1987).

Individuals' perceptions of themselves often differ from others' perceptions of them because of the actor-observer bias. The nature of this bias is such that actors are more likely to perceive their own behavior as being due to situational causes, whereas those observing the actor are more likely to attribute the actor's behavior to dispositional causes (Jones & Nisbett, 1971). Because of the actor-observer bias, different aspects of gender are salient to actors and observers. When individuals focus on themselves as actors, it is the gender-role norms and expectations of the context they are in that is most salient to them and that exerts the most influence on their behavior. Observers, by contrast, have less information about the gender-role norms and constraints present in various situations. They, therefore, tend to base their perceptions, stereotypes, attributions, and attitudes about the actor primarily on salient dispositional cues. In this instance, it is often the noticeable external characteristics of others (things such as their biological sex, physical appearance, and demeanor) that are most likely to influence observers' judgments. When actors interact with observers, therefore, the actors' biological sex serves as a stimulus variable that influences the observers' tendency to make gender-related attributions about them.

So, for example, Ann Hopkins may have perceived the situation at Price Waterhouse to require that she act in a tough and aggressive manner. The impact of the situation on her behavior, however, was not what was salient to those who were observing and evaluating her. Instead, their perceptions of her were based on her sex, her appearance, and her grooming. Discrepancies between self- and others' perceptions are increased when, as was true for Ann Hopkins, gender is salient to either the actors or the observers. Because of this, individuals working in occupations where sex ratios are skewed rather than balanced may experience a variety of difficulties due to actor-observer dynamics.

SEPARATE GENDER ROLES

Historically, we have lived in a society that has prescribed separate social roles for men and women. Traditionally, labor force participation has been the domain of men, whereas women have taken care of the household (Betz & Fitzgerald, 1987; Powell, 1993). Although women are still the ones who are primarily responsible for childcare and domestic duties (Hoschild, 1989), recent societal changes have served to redefine their roles. Women have entered the workforce in large numbers. But, their labor force participation has been primarily in jobs such as nursing, teaching, and clerical work that are consistent with the feminine stereotype (Betz & Fitzgerald, 1987). And, even though record numbers of women are now entering formerly male-dominated occupations (such as law, medicine, and business management), they are still concentrated in certain specialties (e.g., family law, family medicine, and human resource management) that are seen to be more suitable for them (Betz & Fitzgerald, 1987).

In their attempt to contend with these separate roles, men and women face a number of choices. One choice is to accept the roles that society has traditionally prescribed for them. Men and women may find such roles to be comfortable and familiar. Moreover, these roles may be structured so as to facilitate women's ability to attend to the needs of their families (Betz & Fitzgerald, 1987). However, choosing such occupations creates problems for women that it does not create for men. This is because women's roles typically have lower status, power, prestige, and pay associated with them than men's roles do (Haslett, Geis, & Carter, 1993; Ridgeway, 1992). For example, study after study shows that even when they have comparable qualifications, women are paid considerably less than men for the work that they do (Betz & Fitzgerald, 1987; Powell, 1993).

A second option available to both men and women is to take on those roles that have traditionally been associated with the other sex. This involves becoming a member of a group that is in the numerical minority (e.g., male nurses or female police officers). As will be seen, minority group status can be associated with a variety of negative consequences (e.g., McCreary, 1994).

This was certainly true where Ann Hopkins was concerned. Out of 88 candidates who were considered for partnership at Price Waterhouse in 1982, she was the only woman (Fiske et al., 1991). Moreover, at that time only 2% of the firm's partners were women (Fiske et al., 1991). Why was it so detrimental for Ann Hopkins to be one of the only women in a male-dominated setting? One reason is that when most of those in a particular environment are similar to one another, those in the numerical minority are likely to be judged based on stereotypes (Fiske et al., 1991).

STEREOTYPES AND SCHEMAS

Stereotypes are generalizations about the kinds of characteristics that those in certain groups possess. In North American society, stereotypes about gender are grounded in the assumption of biopsychological equivalence (i.e., gender is congruent with biological sex). Because of this, masculine attributes (such as dominance and self-reliance) are associated with men and feminine attributes (such as nurturance and warmth) are associated with women (Powell, 1993). Some individuals are more likely to internalize these gender-role stereotypes than others. Consequently, people differ in the extent to which they apply these stereotypes to themselves and in the extent to which they utilize them when making judgments about others (Deaux & Major, 1987).

Sex-typed individuals have been socialized to accept society's traditional prescriptions regarding gender roles. As a consequence, sex-typed men incorporate many masculine (or instrumental) and few feminine (or expressive) traits into their personalities, whereas sex-typed women have personalities characterized by high expressivity and low instrumentality (Cook, 1985). Androgynous men and women, by contrast, have not been rigidly sex-typed. They have high levels of both instrumentality (or masculinity) and expressivity (or femininity) in their personalities (Cook, 1985). Sex-typed individuals are more likely than androgynous individuals to rely on gender schemas. That is, when processing information both about themselves and about others, they are more likely to use gender as a guide, to pay attention to gender-linked connotations, and to be concerned with gender-appropriateness (Cook, 1985). By shaping perceptions, interpretations, and memories, gender schemas can create self-fulfilling prophecies that serve to confirm individuals' stereotypical expectations about themselves and others (Haslett et al., 1993).

Individuals also hold stereotypes about various occupations. Perry, Davis-Blake, and Kulik (1994) call these stereotypes *jobholder schemas.* They consist of the attributes that are associated with those who occupy different kinds of jobs. Because of the different proportions of men and women in different occupations, jobholder schemas often have gender-linked connotations (Betz & Fitzgerald, 1987; Perry et al., 1994). For example, since nurses are usually women, the stereotypical nurse is seen both as a woman and as someone with feminine attributes such as sensitivity and compassion. By contrast, because managers have usually been men, the stereotypical manager is thought to be a man who has masculine attributes such as competitiveness and decisiveness (Powell, 1993).

Individuals' jobholder schemas can guide their career choices (Betz & Fitzgerald, 1987; Perry et al., 1994). By the time they are 3 years old, children know which occupations are considered to be appropriate for men and which are considered to be appropriate for women (Betz & Fitzgerald, 1987). These gender-linked occupational schemas are reinforced by parents, teachers, guidance counselors, and the media (Betz & Fitzgerald, 1987). They are resistant to change and tend to result in gender-linked career choices by individuals (Betz & Fitzgerald, 1987; Perry et al., 1994). This creates a vicious cycle that perpetuates the separation of men and women into different occupational categories (Perry et al., 1994).

When making decisions about career choice, however, individuals do not rely solely on information about the distribution of men and women into different social roles. They also take their own self-perceived gender-role characteristics into account (Betz & Fitzgerald, 1987). So, those who see themselves as feminine (e.g., as being sensitive and compassionate) may be more likely to choose nursing as a profession, whereas those who see themselves as masculine (e.g., as competitive and decisive) may be more likely to become managers (Powell, 1993). Given this, it is understandable that Ann Hopkins, like the majority of women who choose careers in male-dominated fields (Betz & Fitzgerald, 1987; Powell, 1993), had many qualities that were consistent with the masculine stereotype.

Individuals also use their jobholder schemas to make judgments about others, particularly in regard to their suitability for different types of work (Perry et al., 1994). Problems can occur when people's stereotypes about occupations and their stereotypes about individuals are inconsistent with one another. For example, the stereotypically masculine attributes that are considered to be ideal for managers are quite different from the stereotypically feminine attributes that are considered to be ideal for women (Powell, 1993).

This can put managerial women in a double bind. If a woman manager behaves in a manner that is consistent with the feminine stereotype or if others make the assumption that she has feminine qualities just because she is a woman, she may be seen as not having what it takes to be a good manager. Thus, research shows that women are perceived to be less suited to high level positions than men (Ridgeway, 1992). And, related to this, women in such positions are more likely than comparable men to have their authority questioned by their subordinates (Ridgeway, 1992).

One way that women may react to this situation is by getting tough and expressing their authority in a direct and overt manner. But, like Ann Hopkins, those women who ignore the stereotyped expectations that others have of women often find themselves confronting resistance that undercuts their attempts to be influential (Ridgeway, 1992). Much research shows that women managers who behave in a manner consistent with the masculine stereotype are appraised more negatively than men who behave in exactly the same way (Butler & Geis, 1990; Eagly, Makhijani, & Klonsky, 1992; Korabik, Baril, & Watson, 1993; Powell, 1993; Ridgeway, 1992).

Such stereotyped judgments are based on the selective perception and interpretation of information. The assets of individuals are downplayed and their faults are exaggerated. This is what happened to Ann Hopkins. The fact that she had generated more business for her company than any of her counterparts who were men was ignored (Fiske et al., 1991). She was seen as pushy instead of dynamic and overly aggressive instead of hard working and conscientious (Fiske et al., 1991).

Judgments of behaviors that violate stereotypes also tend to be polarized and unrealistic. So, for example, those at Price Waterhouse claimed that Ann Hopkins's problem was a lack of interpersonal skills. Yet, their suggested solutions that she "wear make-up, have her hair styled, and wear jewelry" (*Hopkins v. Price Water-house*, 1985, p. 1117, as cited in Fiske et al., 1991) were not aimed at overcoming this supposed deficit, but rather at bringing her appearance closer to the feminine ideal.

It should be noted that these dynamics also apply to men who evidence be-haviors or traits that violate gender-role stereotypes (Nieva & Gutek, 1982). For example, feminine men are equally as disliked by others as are masculine women (Korabik, 1982). And, when men use accommodating or obliging styles to manage conflicts, they are judged just as harshly by others as women who use a dominating approach (Korabik, Baril, & Watson, 1993).

PREJUDICE AND DISCRIMINATION

Negative stereotypes about members of certain groups can result in prejudiced atti-tudes and discriminatory actions toward the individuals in those groups. When the members of one group are more numerous or more powerful than the members of another group, a variety of ingroup/outgroup dynamics can occur. These involve the ingroup members showing favoritism toward those in their own group and include their holding less positive attitudes toward outgroup members, being less likely to attribute their successes to internal causes, and evaluating them not on their merit, but on category membership.

Gender is a salient stimulus characteristic that affects group identification. And, gender cues are even more salient for those with minority group status (Deaux & Major, 1987). This can result in biased judgments such that men and women in mi-nority group situations are evaluated differently from their majority group counter-parts even when their performance is similar.

Attributions

Attribution theory has been put forth in an attempt to explain how people make de-cisions about the underlying causes of behavior. Weiner (1972) has suggested that when trying to determine the reasons behind success or failure on a task, individuals make judgments about locus (internal or external) and stability. Performances that are seen as stable and internal (due to something within the person) are most likely to be viewed as predictable and consistently repeatable in the future, whereas those viewed as unstable and external (due to something outside the person) are most likely to be seen as unpredictable and accidental (Weiner, 1972).

Social psychological research shows that even when men and women behave identically, different attributions are made about their behavior. Men's successes are more likely to be attributed to ability (an internal/stable cause), whereas women's successes are more likely to be attributed to luck or effort (external causes). Conversely, men's failures are more likely to be attributed to external or unstable causes (such as bad luck or being confronted with a particularly difficult situation), whereas women's failures are more likely to be attributed to a lack of ability (an internal/stable cause) (Haslett et al., 1993). This means that men's failures are often discounted because they are viewed as transitory. However, for women, it is their competence that is often discounted due to the expectation that they will be unable to repeat their successful performance (Haslett et al., 1993).

Both men and women make these types of attributions and they use them not only to evaluate the behavior of others, but to evaluate their own behavior as well (Haslett et al., 1993). Such attributions may motivate women to lack confidence in their ability to succeed and may subsequently decrease their self-efficacy and achievement motivation (Nieva & Gutek, 1982). These types of attributions also may result in a perceptual bias that has detrimental effects on how women in professional occupations are evaluated by others (Heilman, Simon, & Repper, 1987).

Perceptual Biases

Much research has also demonstrated that when no objective standard is available, men's performance is judged to be better than women's. So, for example, Paludi and Strayer (1985) found that identical articles were evaluated more favorably when attributed to a male rather than to a female author. Similarly, women job applicants were rated less favorably than men on an identical work sample (Heilman, Martell, & Simon, 1988).

It should be noted that although most research has indicated an evaluation bias in favor of men, some studies have found no differences in the evaluations given to men and women, and still others have found that women are rated more favorably than men (Heilman et al., 1988; Nieva & Gutek, 1982). Evaluation biases that favor men over women are most likely when the evaluators are of higher status than those they are evaluating or when they are experts in the area being judged (Haslett et al., 1993). Evaluation biases that favor women over men are most likely when a woman succeeds despite expectations to the contrary and the excellence of her performance is confirmed by an external authority so it cannot be misattributed (Taynor & Deaux, 1973).

In addition, a large number of different cognitive and contextual factors interact to produce gender bias. These include (a) the beliefs and expectations of those who are doing the evaluating; (b) whether gender schema have been primed by recent incidents, the norms or culture in the setting, the sex composition of the group being evaluated, the nature of the task, or the characteristics of the individuals being evaluated; (c) whether the evaluator conveys differential expectations to males than to females; and (d) whether these cause those being evaluated to change their self-presentations (Deaux & Major, 1987; Perry et al., 1994). So, for example, tasks with gender-linked connotations are more prone to result in gender bias (Heilman et al., 1988; Nieva & Gutek, 1982). Thus, whereas women are often evaluated more negatively than men on masculine stereotyped tasks, men are often evaluated more harshly than women on feminine stereotyped tasks (Nieva & Gutek, 1982).

Moreover, gender bias depends on level of competence such that "competent males are rated more positively than equally competent females, while incompetent males are rated lower than equally incompetent females" (Nieva & Gutek, 1982, p. 80). Deaux and Taynor (1973) found that men who did poorly on a scholarship interview were judged to be more incompetent than women who did equally poorly. In addition, Feather and Simon (1975) found that when they failed, men were rated more harshly than women.

There is also a greater chance of gender bias when the criteria used to evaluate someone are subjective, unclear, or ambiguous (Haslett et al., 1993). Under such circumstances stereotyped judgments are more likely to occur. Thus, women and men may be judged according to different criteria and evaluated along dimensions that are narrowly related to their group's stereotype (Fiske et al., 1991). This was the case at Price Waterhouse where, because heresay evidence was allowed to play a part in the decision-making process, Ann Hopkins was judged on the basis of her interpersonal skills, rather than her talent and competence at getting business for the firm (Fiske et al., 1991).

Double Standards

The presence of an objective criterion, however, is no protection against gender bias. Even when a woman's performance can conclusively be demonstrated to be as good as, or better than, that of a man's, a devaluation of the woman's competence may occur because of gender-based double standards of evaluation (Foschi, 1992). Because gender acts as a diffuse status characteristic, it sets up an expectation among both men and women that men will do better than women at masculine tasks. This means that the same level of success will be interpreted differently for men and women. Thus, "women either have to perform better than men, or they have to exhibit additional qualities over and above those required of men, before both sexes exert comparable levels of influence" (Foschi, 1992, p. 198).

Double standards have been shown to affect evaluations about suitability for jobs. In one study, undergraduate students were asked to evaluate men and women job candidates. Men students were more likely to choose the man over the woman, even when the woman was the better performer. Moreover, they were more likely to recommend that no one be hired when the better performer was a woman than when the better performer was a man (Foschi, Lai, & Sigerson, 1991). These results may help to explain why Ann Hopkins was denied a partnership at Price Waterhouse despite the fact that she had brought more money into the firm than had her counterparts who were men.

Although the study cited earlier (Foschi et al., 1991) did not find evidence that women used different standards to evaluate men and women job candidates, other research has demonstrated that women are not immune to using double standards to evaluate the competence of others (Foschi, 1992). Women may also apply double standards of evaluation to themselves. Foddy and Graham (1987) found that when working on a masculine task, women held themselves to stricter standards than the ones their men partners used to evaluate themselves. These findings might shed some light on why women managers often report feeling that they must work harder than their male colleagues to get ahead (Rosin & Korabik, 1991).

Consequences of Gender Bias

The results of the social psychological research on gender bias support the claim that "the biggest barrier to advancement for white women and women and men of color continues to be prejudice" (Powell, 1993, p. viii). A study by Stroh, Brett, and Reilly (1992) illustrates this. They studied a select group of top-level managerial women whose qualifications were identical to men's. Even though these women had "all the right stuff," they still earned lower incomes and had slower career progression than their counterparts who were men. This study was particularly powerful because it was designed to rule out other factors (e.g., human capital variables, family circumstances, and self-selection) that have been postulated to account for why women have failed to advance through the ranks at the same rate as men.

It should be noted that although sex discrimination did exert a statistically significant effect in Stroh et al.'s (1992) study, the percentage of the variance it accounted for was small (less than 2%). Other research done in field settings has produced similar findings. This does not mean, however, that sex discrimination is not an important problem nor that some individuals are not severly disadvantaged as a result of it.

Although the effects of gender bias can be quite small at any one point in time, discrimination can occur repeatedly over someone's career (e.g., during resume screenings, selection interviewing, and performance appraisals) (Fenlason, 1991). As a result, women's access to jobs and training programs may be limited; they may be treated differently than men once they are on the job; and they may receive fewer pay increases and promotions than comparable men (Haslett et al., 1993). Consequently, the total amount of bias that can accumulate over time can be quite large (Martell, Lane, & Willis, 1992). And, because most organizations are pyramidal, those who are selected out early do not progress to the next level. This results in a smaller and smaller pool of women at each tier and illustrates why very few women have the necessary qualifications to make it to the top (Fenlason, 1991; Martell et al., 1992).

As has been illustrated thus far, gender stereotyping and gender bias are more likely to occur in roles or situations in which those of one sex are more numerous than those of the other sex. As is demonstrated in the next two sections, the ratio of men to women in various settings also influences the culture that develops in those settings and the degree to which those in the numerical minority experience problems with maintaining a positive sense of identity and with feelings of increased conspicuousness and social isolation.

CULTURE AND IDENTITY

Because in the past nearly all of those in business and the professions have been men, the norms and culture in the world of work have developed so as to reflect men's needs, attitudes, and values (Mills & Tancred, 1992). When any minority group of newcomers joins an already established majority group, they must fit into the way things are done by that group (i.e., into the majority group's culture) if they wish to belong. So, women are often pressured through organizational socialization to conform to the current business culture (Buono & Kamm, 1983).

Much evidence suggests that the culture of today's corporations is such that masculinity is valued and femininity is devalued. There is an emphasis on task-orientation and productivity and masculine qualities are associated with success (Powell, 1993). By contrast, person-oriented qualities and interpersonal skills are given low weight and the feminine traits that women generally acquire during their socialization are believed to be barriers to their effectiveness (Korabik, 1990). Adapting to such a culture may involve having to accept this negative view of femininity, which can create problems for women in maintaining a positive sense of identity (Korabik, 1993).

Research indicates that a devaluation of identity can occur when outgroup members internalize the negative views that those in the ingroup hold about them. So, for example, women who internalize the expectancy that their performance will be inferior to men's may come to devalue their own competence. Moreover, women who accept the message that what they do is not as important as the work done by men may come to devalue their own worth. This can affect their self-confidence so that they fail to perceive the discrimination that they encounter and instead blame themselves for the negative treatment and outcomes that they experience (Ruggerio & Taylor, 1995). One way that this is manifested is in women's belief that they deserve to be paid less than men for identical work (Jackson & Grabski, 1988).

The problems that result from being an outgroup member in a majority culture also mean that women in male-dominated occupations report being under increased psychological strain due to their sense of marginalization and lack of belongingness (Buono & Kamm, 1983; Rosin & Korabik, 1991). Additionally, they must deal with a larger number of work stressors than their male counterparts. Despite this, however, they do not report experiencing more stress than men. This could be because the multiple roles they hold act as protective buffers or because they have greater access to social support due to their gender-role expressivity (Korabik, McDonald, & Rosin, 1993).

Another problem with the masculine culture prevalent in today's corporations is that few concessions are made to women's social and reproductive roles (Nieva & Gutek, 1982). Many professional jobs are structured so as to make demands (e.g., 60-hour work weeks, frequent travel) that are difficult to fulfill unless someone else (usually a female spouse, parent, or housekeeper) assumes the primary responsibility for domestic obligations. And, women who wish to have families are asked to pay a price in terms of career success. So, for example, Felice Schwartz (1989) has proposed the establishment of what has since become known as the "mommy track," whereby career advancement would be truncated for managerial women if they had children.

SALIENCE AND SOCIAL ISOLATION

Other problems arise because the behavior of those who are in the numerical minority (i.e., tokens) is more noticeable and salient than that of those who are in the majority group (Fiske et al., 1991). This was certainly true of Ann Hopkins at Price Waterhouse. Research shows that situations in which one sex predominates are more likely to activate gender schema. As has been illustrated, this can affect others' behavior toward those who are in token positions, leading them to rely upon stereotyped judgments (Deaux & Major, 1987). And, because those in token positions may be more aware of how their gender influences their interactions with others, it can also affect the behavior of the tokens themselves (Deaux & Major, 1987).

Studies of male nurses, for example, have shown that their behavior tends to be noticed more than that of female nurses (Heikes, 1991). This can result in performance pressures to which they may respond by overachieving (Crocker & McGraw, 1984). However, some research indicates that male nurses may actually benefit from the higher visibility that they enjoy as tokens. They report that they are accorded higher status than female nurses by their patients (Powell, 1993) and even though they may not meet all of the performance requirements of nursing, they are assigned to leadership and administrative positions at a rate disproportionately higher than their female counterparts (Crocker & McGraw, 1984). This may be due to the process called *role encapsulation,* in which pressure is exerted upon tokens to conform to gender stereotyped roles (Powell, 1993).

Role encapsulation, however, works against women who are in token positions by forcing them into roles that are more limited and lower in status than those that are available to men (Powell, 1993). So, for example, a professional woman may be asked to play the role of secretary by being made responsible for taking notes at meetings. Because women's roles are generally lower in status and prestige than men's, research suggests that token women suffer many more negative effects than do token men (Cohen & Swim, 1995). So, for example, being a token is related to decreased self-esteem and increased gender stereotyping and discrimination for women, but not for men (Cohen & Swim, 1995).

Token women also have difficulty with social isolation (Powell, 1993). Because people's professional networks are more likely to be composed of those who are similar to themselves, women's networks have fewer, less powerful ties than men's (Ibarra, 1993; Powell, 1993). Women are often excluded from "old boys networks" and it is harder for them to find successful female role models (Powell, 1993).

Women's career progression can also be hampered because they are less likely than men to have mentors (Powell, 1993). Mentors provide support, coaching, and feedback. Those with mentors have more influence, self-confidence, self-efficacy, and job satisfaction and less job stress than those without mentors. Women have more difficulty than men in finding mentors because there are few women at high levels available to mentor them (Ragins & Cotton, 1991) and high-status men are often reluctant to do so (Powell, 1993). Men's reluctance may stem from the fact that cross-sex mentoring relationships are fraught with difficulties. The mentor and protégée may be dissimilar to one another, they may find it harder to trust one another, and they may have to contend with expectations or inferences about intimacy and sexuality (Powell, 1993; Ragins & Cotton, 1991).

The latter problem may be due to sex role spillover or the inappropriate carry over of societal gender role expectations into the workplace (Gutek & Cohen, 1987). Another way that sex role spillover manifests itself is through sexual harassment. Sexual harassment consists of persistent, unsolicited, and nonreciprocal behavior of a sexual nature (Betz & Fitzgerald, 1987). It is more prevalent when sex ratios are skewed than when there are equal numbers of men and women in a work setting (Gutek & Cohen, 1987). When the number of men and women in a setting is skewed, there is an expectation that men will be privileged and that women will be powerless and compliant. When there are many women in low-status positions and a few men are in power, harassment most often takes the form of a male superior making sexual advances (often accompanied by threats of sanctions) toward a female subordinate (Cleveland, 1994). Although the harassment of women by their male bosses is common, men in minority status positions are rarely harassed by their female bosses (Ridgeway, 1992).

In settings where there are a small number of women in high-status positions, a different type of harassment occurs. As was the case with Ann Hopkins, the women in such situations are likely to be subjected to a hostile work environment in the form of denigrating comments by their male coworkers, supervisors, subordinates, or clients (Cleveland, 1994). This serves both to devalue the women's contributions and to accentuate their status as outgroup members (Cleveland, 1994). Sexual harassment has been demonstrated to have many negative physical, psychological, emotional, and work-related consequences for women, and it is a significant factor in maintaining their disadvantaged position in organizations (Cleveland, 1994).

METHODOLOGICAL CONCERNS

As should be apparent from the preceding discussion, the social psychological processes that pertain to gender are complicated. This complexity is reflected in the current research on gender, which is characterized by a bewildering assortment of concepts, theories, and research paradigms. There appears to be little consensus about what terminology or methodology is most appropriate. Moreover, it is unlikely that the existing controversies will be resolved in the near future (Deaux, 1993; Gentile, 1993; Unger & Crawford, 1993).

Meanwhile, several prevalent methodological practices are problematic because they result in unnecessary inconsistency and imprecision. Researchers would do well to avoid them if they wish to foster theoretical and analytical progress. One problem is that researchers frequently use the terms *sex* and *gender* synonymously. Providing clear definitions for all sex- and gender-related terms that are used would help to alleviate the confusion that this causes.

A second major problem has been that most research on sex and gender has not been grounded in theory (Wallston, 1987). This has led to a multitude of studies in which men and women are simply compared to one another on a wide variety of variables. However, because a clear theoretical rationale has never been articulated, when differences between the two sexes are found, it is difficult to know *why* they have occurred. For example, there is often confusion about whether such differences are attributable to biological (sex), sociocultural (gender), or situational (e.g., status differences) causes. Moreover, because researchers have not been guided by theory, they have often focused on studying sex differences (i.e., comparing men and women to one another) when they should be examining gender-related processes (e.g., comparing individuals with masculine, feminine, and androgynous gender-role characteristics to one another or comparing individuals with traditional versus egalitarian gender-role attitudes to one another). To help alleviate this problem, researchers should be careful to make their underlying causal assumptions and theoretical rationale explicit, and they should strive to make their assumptions, their vocabulary, and the methodology that they employ consistent.

A related problem is that gender has been inappropriately operationalized in many studies. Partly, this has resulted from the failure of researchers to realize that many different types of gender-related processes occur and that the aspect of gender that is most relevant often depends upon the research question at hand. Gender is multidimensional in nature and its different components (e.g., traits, attitudes, and behaviors) do not always correspond to one another. So, choosing to focus on and measure the right component is important.

It is also necessary to recognize that the kinds of gender-related processes that occur within a person may be quite different from those that are involved in the perception of others. This is apparent from the voluminous literature demonstrating that there are few differences between men and women in their self-reports about their personalities, attitudes, or motivations once any differences due to their status and gender-role socialization have been controlled. Yet, men and women who behave identically are often evaluated differently by others due to the influence of gender-role sterotypes on the perceivers. Therefore, in order for researchers to make a proper interpretation of their findings, it is important for them to consider the source of their information (i.e., whether it comes from self-reports or others' reports).

Moreover, studies of gender-related processes that are physiological in nature (e.g., menopause) may require different operationalizations from those (such as personality or cognition) that are thought to rely on intrapsychic mechanisms or from those that are interpersonal in nature. For example, when investigating issues that concern a person's own perceptions, motivation, personality, attitudes, or behaviors, a researcher would most likely want to focus on the appropriate aspect of gender (e.g., self-reports about gender-role traits, gender-role attitudes). By contrast, a focus on biological sex (or a comparison of men and women) would probably be more appropriate in most research that concerns others' perceptions, stereotypes, attributions, attitudes, or behaviors toward a target person (e.g., in studies of sexism, sexual harassment, tokenism, or mentoring). Two things should be noted here, however. First, although in such studies the emphasis is on the target person's sex, it should not be on the sex of the perceiver, but rather on that person's gender (e.g., gender-role traits, attitudes, or behaviors). Second, although the target person's sex is the simplest and most likely explanation for any effects that might occur when dependent variables such as these are examined, there might also be complex interactions between the sex and gender of the target person and the sex and gender of the perceiver. For example, perhaps only some men (e.g., those who are highly masculine) are prone to sexually harass women or only some women (e.g., those who are very feminine) are prone to suffer harassment. Therefore, complex research designs that examine interactions between the sex and gender of perceivers, the sex and gender of targets, and the situational context in which interactions occur are often necessary if we are to fully understand how gender influences human behavior (Deaux & Major, 1987).

SUMMARY

The literature on applied social psychology can help us to understand and alleviate the problems that individuals encounter in the workforce due to the interaction of their gender with their minority group status. It should be clear from the research reviewed in this chapter that our perceptions about suitable job characteristics are based on stereotypes that do not necessarily relate to ability. Furthermore, there is abundant evidence that gender stereotypes can develop based solely on the different distribution of individuals into social roles without any factual basis. That is, they need not contain even a "kernel of truth" (Hoffman & Hurst, 1990). Supporting this is much research demonstrating that men and women in similar positions do not differ from one another in their goals, motives, personalities, or behaviors and that when sex differences are found they are usually attributable to differences in selection, socialization, or status (Powell, 1993).

The dynamics outlined in this chapter are particularly prevalent in situations in which status and power differentials exist between men and women. Because women are more likely to hold positions that are lower in status and power, they are more likely than men to be negatively affected by these processes. So, whereas women in male-dominated professions have more difficulty getting ahead than men, the reverse is not true for men in female-dominated fields (Crocker & McGraw, 1984).

This does not mean, however, that men do not also suffer as a consequence of their gender roles. Men's social roles tend to be more restricted than women's. There is pressure on them to be breadwinners and they are evaluated negatively when they are not. They may be hesitant to take advantage of parental-leave policies or to voice their family-related concerns to their employers out of fear that it will hamper their corporate advancement (Powell, 1993). Furthermore, research indicates that the masculine, task-oriented culture that currently pervades the workplace is detrimental to men as well as to women and that androgyny (i.e., a combination of masculine or instrumental qualities and expressive or feminine ones) is associated with increased effectiveness for both men and women (Korabik, 1990).

Social psychological research shows, however, that it is very difficult to change a culture that is dominated by a majority group and that prejudice and discrimination against those with minority group status will not be alleviated as long as power and status differentials remain. This has led to interventions, such as affirmative action programs, that are aimed at making the sex ratios in different occupations more balanced and to pay equity and comparable worth policies, which are aimed at eliminating the sex bias in compensation. Those hired or promoted as a result of affirmative action programs, however, may be viewed as unqualified (Heilman, Block, & Lucas, 1992; Heilman & Herlihy, 1984). Moreover, their success is often attributed to external causes, and their performance evaluations and job satisfaction may suffer as a result (Chacko, 1982).

Affirmative action programs and policies to ensure pay equity do help to establish a norm of fairness. However, in order for such programs and policies to be more than merely symbolic, they must be accompanied by an underlying change in the culture of organizations such that equity and diversity are truly valued and prejudice and discrimination are discouraged. An example of an organization that is working to bring about such change can be found in the accompanying research applications box (see Box 15–1). As illustrated in this example, fairness will be facilitated if there are motivational incentives for behaving in a bias-free manner and for fostering equitable conditions (Fiske et al., 1991).

Organizational norms, programs, and policies that promote gender equity can help to eliminate biased decision making by constraining the extent to which decision makers can rely on their stereotypes (Fiske et al., 1991; Perry et al., 1994). Other factors that may reduce dependence on gender stereotypes include (a) providing adequate and job-relevant information; (b) using competency-based selection and performance appraisal systems, unambiguous criteria, and standardized policies and procedures; and (c) making decision makers accountable for their decisions (Fenlason, 1991; Fiske et al., 1991; Perry et al., 1994). Organizations can also help to change the nature of decision makers' gender schemas by creating new gender-neutral job titles and job descriptions and by encouraging less stereotyped task assignments in order to bring about greater exposure to instances that are incongruent with existing schemas (Perry et al., 1994).

The distribution of men and women into different social roles creates stereotyped beliefs that can result in self-fulfilling prophecies. Thus, judgments about men's and women's suitability for certain roles can generate expectancies that may cause decision makers to engage in biased information processing. This can impact on vocational choice as well as on decisions about hiring, training, salary increases, and promotions that perpetuate the status quo. The manner in which gender bias operates as well as the negative consequences of such bias in terms of experiencing problems with cultural adaptation, maintaining a positive sense of identity, being

**Box
15–1** **Increasing Gender Equality and Diversity in the Workplace**

The Bank of Montreal has applied the findings from social psychological research to develop a program aimed at increasing gender equality and diversity. This was deemed necessary because 75% of employees at the bank were women, yet women comprised only 9% of the executives and 13% of senior managers (Totta & Burke, 1994). It was believed that bringing about gender equality would help to "develop a workforce that truly reflects the communities the bank serves, along with the commitment to become the workplace of choice for the best and brightest from all groups" (Totta & Burke, 1994, p. 14). Achieving this goal necessitated a massive transformation in the bank's culture and policies in which five components, drawn from the social psychological literature, were deemed essential (Totta & Burke, 1994).

Executive sponsorship. The first prerequisite was executive sponsorship. The literature on transformational leadership shows that to modify existing conditions, leaders must propose a clearly articulated vision that motivates their followers because it is tied to a purpose that they wish to attain (Bass, 1985). In organizations, this means that those in power must have a shared vision about the conditions that will result in a competitive advantage. At the bank, this vision was based on attaining such an advantage by creating a climate where equity and diversity were valued (Totta & Burke, 1994). From this came the commitment to change the company's culture. For this mission to be implemented successfully, high-level leadership was crucial. This was obtained by establishing task forces sponsored and led by senior bank executives (Totta & Burke, 1994).

Employee participation. If long-term systemic change is to occur, everyone in the organization must be involved in creating it. Therefore, the second essential ingredient is grassroots participation. To achieve this, input was sought from all the bank's employees through a survey of their stereotypes, needs, perceptions about barriers to advancement, and proposed remedies (Totta & Burke, 1994). Employees also served on the task forces and were involved in the formulation of action plans. This helped to ensure their commitment to the change process.

Communication. Another integral step is the communication of both the facts and the vision to everyone in the organization. In terms of the facts, the data from the bank clearly showed that women were underrepresented among management. Moreover, the employee survey revealed several commonly held stereotypes. These included the beliefs that women were less likely to be promoted than men because of their age, lack of education, lesser job commitment, and lower job performance. However, the data revealed that all of these assumptions were false (Bank of Montreal, 1991). In fact, the women at the bank were just as educated and dedicated to their careers as the men. Furthermore, men and women had been in their jobs for equivalent amounts of time and they performed their jobs equally well (Bank of Montreal, 1991). There was also a belief that women's advancement into higher ranks was just a matter of time. But the data showed that "at their current rate of progress, women would still make up only 18% of executives and 22% of senior managers by the year 2000" (Totta & Burke, 1994, p. 8). One important aspect of bringing about change at the bank was to make sure that all of the employees were aware of these facts. This was done by sending a personally addressed copy of a report dispelling these myths to every employee (Totta & Burke, 1994). It was also necessary to communicate the mission, the rationale for it, and the action plans to all of the employees. This was done through handbooks, newsletters, and an orientation guide for new employees, all of which made it clear that the company's norms were to respect equality and that discrimination would not be tolerated (Totta & Burke, 1994).

Inclusionary approach. Another aspect of the approach to change that was instituted at the bank was that it was inclusionary. Thus, it was "not acceptable to remove barriers to advancement for women by erecting barriers to advancement for men" (Totta & Burke, 1994, p. 9), but rather the aim was to remove barriers and increase opportunities for everyone. In this spirit, of the 26 action plans formulated to bring about gender equality, only 3 were aimed specifically at women.

These action plans led to dozens of new policies and programs, including a computer listing of all new job openings, a mentoring program, eldercare and childcare referral services, paid leave days for personal concerns, and opportunities for extended leaves and more flexible work arrangements (such as flextime, flexplace, and job sharing) (Totta & Burke, 1994). It was emphasized that career advancement would not be hampered for those who sought increased job flexibility or more leave time. The options that increased workers' flexibility have already paid off. They have not only resulted in greater worker productivity and customer satisfaction, but they have been beneficial to men as well as women. Totta and Burke (1994) report that although men comprise only 25% of the bank's employees, they make up 40% of those taking advantage of more flexible work schedules.

Accountability. Finally, true change is unlikely to be sustained over the long term without accountability. Wilhelm (1992) claims that to change corporate culture, desired behaviors must be recognized and rewarded for up to 10 years. At the bank, goals were set for the hiring, retention, and advancement of those in underrepresented groups, and managers were held accountable for meeting these goals (Totta & Burke, 1994). In order to assure that the focus was not just on increasing numbers by selecting unqualified tokens, a competency-based selection system was implemented so as to remove subjectivity and bias, and managers were made accountable for the performance levels of those that they hired or promoted. Managers were also rewarded for being good role models and mentors and for creating a climate that supported equality (Totta & Burke, 1994).

By utilizing social psychological principles, the Bank of Montreal was able to increase gender equality in a manner that was sustainable over the long term and that did not result in resistance or backlash. Moreover, the change in the bank's culture has benefited not only all of its employees (male and female alike), but its customers as well.

faced with sexual harassment and other work stressors, and having feelings of marginalization and isolation should also be clear from the proceeding discussion. All of these factors serve to create a "chilly climate" that increases women's discomfort in organizations and hampers their advancement in their careers (Korabik, 1993). Although these factors are extremely resistant to change, through the application of social psychological principles such change is possible and it will result in a better situation for both men and women.

SUGGESTED READINGS

Betz, N. E., & Fitzgerald, L. E. (1987). *The career psychology of women.* New York: Academic Press.

This is an excellent source of information about how individuals choose careers. It includes information about the career patterns that women and men follow, dual careers, work/family interface, and sexual harassment.

Haslett, B. J., Geis, F. L., & Carter, M. R. (1993). *The organizational woman: Power and paradox.* Norwood, NJ: Ablex.

An outstanding explanation of the dynamics of gender bias in the workplace, as well as plenty of practical advice about strategies that can be used to combat sexism, is contained in this book.

Lowe, R. H., & Wittig, M. A. (Eds.). (1989). Approaching pay equity through comparable worth [Special Issue]. *Journal of Social Issues, 45* (4).

The focus of these 14 articles is on gender bias in job evaluation and compensation and the alleviation of wage discrimination through pay equity.

Powell, G. N. (1993). *Women and men in management* (2nd ed.). Newbury Park, CA: Sage.

A critical examination of the effects of stereotypes on male/female work relationships, how individuals and organizations make employment-related decisions, the career patterns chosen by men and women, and workplace sexuality is featured in this book.

Ridgeway, C. L. (Ed.). (1992). *Gender, interaction, and inequality.* New York: Springer-Verlag.

This book includes nine chapters on topics related to how gender influences the enactment of inequality in social interactions; types of communication, leadership and power, and double standards of evaluation are discussed.

16 Applied Social Psychology Today and Tomorrow

Stuart Oskamp
Claremont Graduate School

> There are both crying social needs and, fortunately, paying professional positions for psychologists who have been trained to work on important current social issues. Much of their work can be both theoretically fruitful and empirically helpful to policymakers. It is vital to the future of psychology as well as the future of our society for us to fill those needs and positions with the best-trained and most highly motivated applied social psychologists that we can produce. (Oskamp, 1986, p. 19)

A 1996 report indicates that psychology is one of the two most popular major fields for college and university students, and that the number of bachelor's degrees awarded in psychology grew by almost 50% over a 5-year period (Murray, 1996). Many of these students hope to work in applied aspects of psychology when they graduate, and it appears that applied social psychology is one of the job areas that is still growing. Another recent article gives examples of a variety of such applied psychology jobs—in research on drug and alcohol abuse, personnel selection for companies and government agencies, evaluations of the ways new computer and communication technology is being used and how people should be trained to use it, advertising and marketing of products, analysis of the effectiveness of work groups and organizations, and clinical trials of the effectiveness of newly developed drugs (Kent, 1995).

In this text you have read about many other areas of applied research and practice that social psychologists take part in, from surveying attitudes and public opinion to assisting law enforcement; from helping groups and organizations manage and resolve conflicts to reducing problems of pollution and environmental destruction. Applied social psychology deals with many aspects of the everyday world around us, and it aims to help understand and solve social problems.

A LOOK BACK AND AHEAD

Paradoxically, although applied psychology aims to contribute to human welfare, it has received its greatest impetus in times of war. It got its first widespread use over 50 years ago, in World War II, when all the resources of the allied nations were funneled into the war effort. In those years of national emergency, the knowledge and methods of psychologists were in great demand for such tasks as selecting and training military personnel, analyzing enemy propaganda, and dealing with the problems of physical and emotional casualties (e.g., Hunter, 1946; Stouffer et al., 1949). On the home front, psychologists helped to increase factory production, dispel destructive rumors, maintain civilian morale (in Britain, even under repeated air raids), and plan for postwar reconstruction both at home and in enemy countries (e.g., Allport & Veltfort, 1943; Cartwright, 1948).

When the war was over, some military research programs continued (e.g., Flanagan, 1984), but most psychologists went back to teaching college students or to clinical and counseling positions. The social psychologists in academia then turned to theory-driven research using laboratory experiments, and this period lasted 2 decades or more, until sharp criticisms began to be leveled at the limited social relevance of such research (e.g., Ring, 1967). At that point, in the 1970s, serious doubts were even stated about the way many findings of social science research were actually being applied (cf. Meltzer, 1972; Oskamp, 1984). As you have seen from the chapters in this book, however, that issue is no longer raised, for a great deal of social science research is being successfully applied in a wide variety of social problem areas. Despite their utility, however, applied research studies often generate as many additional questions as they answer, and consequently, just as in past years, many current summaries of applied social research, such as the chapters in this book, conclude with calls for more research that will be focused on particular questions that have still not been resolved.

A *Reprise*. In 1986 I wrote an article that made predictions regarding important substantive areas of work for applied social psychologists up to the year 2000 (Oskamp, 1986). Later in this chapter, I look at those same areas and a few others to review progress there in the light of the developments summarized in this volume.[1]

In 1986, applied social psychology was experiencing steady growth, and its growth has continued, though at a slower pace in recent years that have been

---

[1] In instances where the same trends are continuing, some passages in this chapter are quoted or paraphrased from my 1986 article.

marked by economic recessions and the "downsizing" of many industries through employee layoffs. Its growth can be seen in the many new books in the field, including this one, and the increasing number of journals, including the *Journal of Applied Social Psychology, Basic and Applied Social Psychology, The Journal of Community and Applied Social Psychology,* and other more specialized periodicals in such areas as health psychology, consumer psychology and marketing, gender issues, law and behavior, educational evaluation, and interpersonal relationships. Even more than in 1986, another increasingly frequent occurrence is for social psychological researchers to combine both laboratory and field research approaches to the same general topic; a combination that was rare in the earlier heyday of theoretically based experimental social psychology. Influential early examples of this sort were Aronson's work on stimulating cooperative learning in desegregated schools; Zimbardo's research on deindividuation, which led to his simulation of prison conditions; and Milgram's studies of ways that people adapt to living in cities.

Graduate Training

Yet, as in 1986, it is still true that most graduate training programs in social psychology remain quite traditional in their emphasis on experimental methods, laboratory research settings, and use of undergraduates as research participants (Sears, 1986). As a result, many psychology graduates who go into applied work find it necessary to retool and learn many aspects of the field that they didn't get exposed to in college or graduate school. Two graduate programs that are particularly known for breaking this traditional mold and focusing on applied social psychology are Claremont Graduate School in California, where I teach, and Loyola University of Chicago. Examples of their applied emphases can be seen in recent volumes published by their faculty members (e.g., Chemers, Oskamp, & Costanzo, 1995; Heath et al., 1994). In Canada, similar applied programs exist at the University of Saskatchewan and the University of Guelph.

Some graduates of such applied programs may specialize in the area of *public affairs psychology,* which focuses particularly on public policy issues. As conceptualized by Brayfield and Lipsey (1976), public affairs psychologists would perform three major functions: creating new knowledge about various public issues and proposed policies (e.g., the effects of stricter criminal sentences), applying existing psychological knowledge to public issues (e.g., care of nursing home patients), and using and improving techniques for studying public policy issues (e.g., evaluation research methods). In all these activities, their goals would be to lessen social problems and improve the quality of people's lives.

The next section briefly considers various ways in which the research findings of such public affairs psychologists might be used in influencing policy decisions, presenting U.S. examples as illustrations.

USE OF SOCIAL RESEARCH IN PUBLIC POLICY

Direct Use for Problem Solving. Many applied social scientists would like to have their research findings used directly by policymakers—a role that has sometimes been referred to as "speaking truth to power." Though this is not the most common form of use, there are numerous instances in which research has been used in this way. Two examples are a major study of maternal and child health, sponsored by the U.S. Department of Health, Education and Welfare, which resulted in decreased infant mortality, and the Manhattan bail bond experiment, which led to reforms that saved about $50 million per year in prisoner detention costs (Abt, 1980). Similarly, many specially appointed commissions to investigate urgent national problems have based their recommendations on social science research that they have sponsored and/or summarized. Examples include the *Report of the National Advisory Commission on Civil Disorders* (1968) and the Surgeon General's Report on *Smoking and Health* (U.S. DHEW, 1979). On a local level, some of the research cited in Alcock's chapter in this volume on mental health issues has been used directly to aid individuals troubled by shyness or by panic attacks.

However, such direct use of research is the exception rather than the norm. Carol Weiss (1978) has identified several other forms of research use, including the following.

Use for Political Ammunition. This use of research findings is common, though it is undesirable or even illegitimate in its lack of objectivity. Proponents of one side of a policy issue may search for, cite, or even commission partisan research to support their viewpoint, without regard for the contrary evidence. This is frequently seen in the "stacking" of legislative committee hearings with witnesses on one side of an issue, or in presenting selective arguments for an election issue. For example, advocates of California's recent "three strikes and you're out" law, which requires lifetime imprisonment for individuals convicted of a third felony, ignored opposing findings about the financial and social costs of widespread and long-term incarceration and the demonstrated successes of lenient punishment and rehabilitation approaches. Policymakers may also call for more research in order to avoid taking action on a difficult social issue. A current example is seen in claims that "more evidence is needed" to verify the "greenhouse effect," despite a consensus in the scientific community that warming of the earth's atmosphere is beginning to change worldwide climate patterns and produce extreme floods, droughts, and agricultural losses (Begley, 1996; Flavin, 1996; Stevens, 1995).

Use for Conceptualization or Enlightenment. This category describes a more diffuse process, in which social research concepts and findings are used in thinking about policy issues, helping to determine the policy agenda, sensitizing officials to new issues, or redefining the nature of specific problems. This process is usually gradual and cumulative, rather than based on a single piece of research, and it may have ramifications for many issues and policies rather than just influencing one policy decision. A good example was seen in Moston's chapter on law enforcement issues, which described how findings from many different studies of children's memory have gradually led to changes in methods of legal interviewing and greater acceptance of children's testimony in legal cases.

Use as a Language of Discourse. This process is an even more diluted utilization of scientific ideas than the conceptualization process. It involves the widespread use of certain terms, concepts, and principles from the social sciences in the discourse and thinking of public officials. For instance, concepts such as parent-child attachment, self-esteem, social support from family members, authoritarianism, conformity, stereotypes, or learned helplessness may provide an intellectual background and help to influence the actions of policymakers.

IMPORTANT DOMAINS OF APPLIED ACTIVITIES

In 1986 I suggested six content domains as particularly important future areas for applied social psychological work. They were international affairs, environmental issues, mass media of communication, legal issues, educational issues, and family relationships. Certainly all of them remain important today, but they have had differing degrees of research and policy attention in the intervening years. In the following sections I briefly summarize some of the recent work in these areas and then add discussion of three other major areas that have emerged: health psychology, organizational behavior, and consumer psychology.

International Affairs

In 1986 I listed international affairs first, because avoiding nuclear war between the superpowers was fundamental to whether there would be any psychology or any inhabitable world in the future. In the 1980s there was a great upsurge of public fear that actions by the leaders of the great powers might set off a major nuclear exchange, and that the resulting worldwide radiation, fires, and destruction could produce a "nuclear winter," wiping out human life over much or all of the earth. Many psychologists were galvanized into action by these concerns and produced relevant volumes such as *Psychology and the Prevention of Nuclear War* (White, 1986). One of the key figures was Morton Deutsch, whose entire research career had focused on processes of cooperation and competition between individuals, groups, and nations. For instance, he had described the *malignant spiral of hostile interaction* as follows:

> Otherwise sane, intelligent leaders of the superpowers have allowed their nations to become involved in a malignant process which is driving them to engage in actions and reactions that are steadily increasing the chances of nuclear war—an outcome no one wants. (Deutsch, 1983, p. 5)

In the 1980s that process was illustrated by the U.S. air attack on Libya—apparently intended to kill its president, Mu'ammar Gadhafi—and in the USSR's massive attempt to wipe out rebel forces in Afghanistan.

Since the fall of the "iron curtain" in 1989 and the subsequent breakup of the USSR into separate republics, the danger of worldwide nuclear war has seemed much diminished. However, the likelihood of *smaller wars* appears even greater, as illustrated by the U.S. involvement in the 1991 Persian Gulf War, the continuing Russian military action against its seceding province of Chechnya, the terrible civil war in Bosnia and Croatia, and the tribal genocide in Rwanda. In many of these conflicts, the malignant spiral of hostile interaction can be plainly seen. In addition to the spread of such small wars, there is also an increasing risk of more disastrous destruction resulting from terrorism by subnational groups and/or from nuclear proliferation, for dozens of smaller nations will soon be able to produce their own nuclear weapons. The bombings of the World Trade Center in New York and the federal building in Oklahoma City give only a tiny illustration of the potential damage a single nuclear weapon could wreak in a modern city. Such bombs don't have to be dropped from airplanes; a "city-snuffing" bomb can be placed in a panel truck parked on a city street and can decapitate a nation's government or its commercial system at a single stroke. So the danger of international conflict still remains intense, though its most likely forms have changed.

What can social psychologists do to decrease the risks in this area? Keashly's chapter on conflict management in this volume presents many research findings that are applicable to international conflicts as well as interpersonal ones. In the international arena, a crucial contribution would be to work toward reversing the malignant spiral of hostile interaction, and Ralph White (1985) has suggested several useful approaches. One principle, which dates back some 35 years, is Osgood's (1962, 1986) *GRIT program*—an acronym standing for the features of the program: Graduated Reciprocal Initiatives in Tension-Reduction. This method for defusing tensions has shown success both in laboratory disputes (Lindskold, 1978) and in the real world. After the Cuban missile crisis, President Kennedy adopted a strategy similar to GRIT, which led to reduced international tensions and fostered a period of major-power cooperation (Etzioni, 1970). Similarly, in 1995, Israel and the Palestine Liberation Organization (PLO) appear to have followed some of the same tension-reducing steps, though more hesitantly than might be desired.

Another principle that often holds in international disputes is the idea of a perceptual *mirror image,* in which each party sees much the same failings and villainy in each other (Bronfenbrenner, 1961; Oskamp, 1965). Perceptual distortions of this sort can be greatly diminished by the kind of contact between contending parties that is created in international problem-solving workshops, as described in the chapter on conflict management. Such workshops have been developed and employed successfully for over 20 years in the Israeli-Palestinian dispute by Kelman and his colleagues (Kelman, 1995), and also more recently in the Northern Ireland conflict and the Greek-Turkish dispute on Cyprus (Fisher, 1993). These approaches have built on a large body of social psychological research on negotiation and especially on work concerning third-party mediation in both organizational and international settings (e.g., Bercovitch & Rubin, 1992; Kressel & Pruitt, 1989).

Other relevant research on international conflicts includes Janis's (1982) demonstration that a conformity-inducing process of *groupthink* has often prevented careful and reasoned decision making by national officials during dangerous crisis situations. More recently, a journal issue has summarized social psychological research findings stemming from the Persian Gulf War (Lehman, 1993). Many of the lessons from such research have been put to work in actual conflict situations, such as by UN peacekeeping forces in various nations and by relief officials trying to reduce the human misery in the Bosnian civil war (Sleek, 1996).

Finally, another psychological concept in the area of international affairs is the need for *organized group action* at the national level, to get the attention of governments and influence them to modify their policies. Though this is difficult, massive group organization can affect government policies, as shown in the American civil rights movement and the Vietnam War protests. To aid in accomplishing the goal of organized group action, some psychologists have focused on methods that can be used to create and sustain a pattern of *peace activism*—that is, getting people involved in activism and keeping them involved (e.g., Nevin, 1985).

Environmental Issues

Sustainability of Environmental Resources. Since the end of the cold war between the United States and the USSR, it has become increasingly clear that now the most dangerous threat to human life and well-being on the earth is human-caused damage to the earth's life-sustaining environmental resources. This threat includes warming of the earth's atmosphere caused by the greenhouse effect, the hole in the ozone layer that increases damage to life from cosmic rays; acid rain that kills lakes and rivers; genetic damage and cancer from dioxin and other deadly toxic chemicals; dangerous pesticides on our foodstuffs; toxic pollution of our air and drinking water; and so on. *All of these environmental problems are caused by human behavior, and they are all growing more serious each year* (cf. Oskamp, 1995). The United Nations Conference on Environment and Development, held in Rio de Janeiro in 1992, focused the world's attention on these problems and agreed on a plan of action for addressing them, called *Agenda 21,* which is being monitored by the UN Commission on Sustainable Development and by national agencies and citizen watchdog groups in many nations (Bartelmus, 1994; Walker, 1995).

As you have read in Dwyer et al.'s chapter on environmental issues, most of these environmental problems are rooted in the vastly increasing size of the earth's population, which in 1996 reached 5.8 billion, compared to only 2.0 billion in 1930. The earth's resources are finite, and there is a fast-approaching limit to the amount of food and shelter that it can provide to humanity and the amount of waste products that the oceans and the atmosphere can absorb. In fact, some social and environmental scientists have concluded that we have already overshot the earth's carrying capacity for human life over the long haul, so that we are, in effect, stealing vital resources from our descendants (Catton, 1980; Hardin, 1993; Meadows, Meadows, & Randers, 1992). To correct these abuses of our earth, we need to work on many fronts toward transforming current patterns of human behavior into ones that are sustainable over the centuries ahead—for example, by not using up more of the earth's resources of land, forests, food, and water than can be replaced (Cohen, 1995; Ludwig, Hilborn, & Walters, 1993). The following discussion illustrates some of the areas in which social scientists can help in this effort, as highlighted in recent volumes that have appeared on this complex but crucial topic (e.g., McKenzie-Mohr & Oskamp, 1995; Stern, Young, & Druckman, 1992).

Population Control. Social science efforts are essential to persuade people all over the globe to reduce their desires concerning family size and begin effective programs of family planning. If population stabilization and/or reduction are not accomplished by these voluntary measures, they will eventually be enforced coercively by the death rate catching up with the birth rate—through starvation and famines, diseases (e.g., AIDS, which is already ravaging Africa), or wars and genocide (Hardin, 1993).

There have been some major successes in family planning programs around the world. However, much more must be done, because the earth's population is still increasing at a record rate of 90 million per year *despite a dramatic decrease* in average lifetime fertility in developing countries (United Nations Population Fund, 1993). Family planning accessibility and contraceptive use have increased markedly in developing countries in the last 30 years (Segal, 1993), but there is still a huge unmet demand for family planning services that could bring average fertility rates down further and faster (Sinding, cited in Brown et al., 1993, p. 125). Many research reports have demonstrated the success of scientifically based family planning programs in various countries (e.g., David, 1994; Severy, 1993). One of the key ingredients in many of these programs is increasing the economic opportunities and potential earnings for women, which makes them more economically independent and provides an incentive for both women and men to limit their family size (Abernethy, 1993).

In the United States, a central problem is that the rate of teenage pregnancy is the highest of any nation in the developed world—it is six times as high as Denmark's—in spite of the fact that the rate of teenage abortion is also much higher than that of most nations (David, 1994). Thus it is just as important for applied social scientists to work toward better family planning in the United States as in more exotic foreign countries.

Use of Fossil Fuel. The gasoline that we use for transportation and the fuel oil, natural gas, and coal that we use for heating and for producing electricity are not simply diminishing resources. Their heavy use is also responsible for nearly half of the gradual heating of the earth's atmosphere, which is known as the greenhouse effect. In this process, the carbon dioxide produced when these fuels are burned rises and forms a layer in the upper atmosphere that reduces the amount of the earth's heat that can be radiated into space, just as the glass panes in a greenhouse let in warming sunlight but prevent warm air from escaping.

In 1990, the United States and the other industrialized countries of the Western world used 50% of the world's commercial energy, and the Eastern bloc of socialist industrialized countries used another 23% (Lenssen, 1993, pp. 102–104). These facts indicate that the industrialized countries are the prime villains; they need to become more efficient in their fuel usage and thus reduce the total amount of carbon dioxide that is added to the atmosphere.

There are many steps that can be taken to make our fuel use more efficient. For instance, the efficiency of energy use in the United States increased 25% between 1973 and 1985 (Stern et al., 1992, p. 120). Despite this substantial progress, much more is needed and is possible, as shown by the fact that Japan's energy efficiency is nearly double that of the United States (Brown, Kane, & Roodman, 1994, p. 127).

Though the use of energy is often thought of as a technical, engineering question, it has many behavioral aspects. Consequently, psychologists have been involved in research on energy conservation (cf. Gardner & Stern, 1996; Katzev & Johnson, 1987) and in studying effective ways to spread the use of new technology, which can help to reduce our use of fossil fuels. One major step in this direction would be wider adoption of small-scale, local sources of energy, particularly renewable ones (relying on solar cells, wind machines, ocean currents, etc.; Flavin, 1995; Flavin & Lenssen, 1994). A useful guide to the many possibilities for adopting renewable energy in diverse situations is the recent book *Renewables Are Ready* (Cole & Skerrett, 1995). Another major step would be persuading individuals and organizations to invest in energy-efficient technology such as more efficient lights, motors, and automobiles. Cars that get as much as 50 mpg are commercially available, and so are battery-powered electric cars that emit no CO_2 or pollution. Research has shown that one-time investments, such as more efficient cars or home insulation, can save dramatically more energy than repeated minor actions such as turning down thermostats or turning off lights (Gardner & Stern, 1996, pp. 258–261).

Avoiding Pollution. Another serious environmental problem is environmental pollution—of air, drinking water, pesticides on crops, carcinogenic materials endangering public health, and the unsolved, critically important problem of nuclear waste disposal. Again these are technical problems, but applied social psychologists have a role to play in publicizing them, studying and trying to influence public opinion about them, and providing research and policy advice on behavioral approaches to preventing or overcoming them. The chapter on environmental issues by Dwyer et al. earlier in this book gives an excellent example of this; the E-Team, which is a carefully planned and coordinated program, uses psychological knowledge to help preserve environmental quality in a broad metropolitan area.

To reduce environmental pollution frequently requires the kind of organized group activity that was described earlier in this chapter, for the polluters are very often governments or powerful corporations that are impervious to individual complaints. For instance, the Russian government has never admitted the widespread and disastrous results of the atomic reactor explosion at Chernobyl (Chernousenko, 1995–1996). Similarly, U.S. corporations have been silent about the approximately 50% loss of sperm count that has been observed in men worldwide during the last 40 years, apparently due to the widespread use of chlorinated chemicals all over the world in those years (Wright, 1996). One of the most deadly ingredients in modern chemicals is dioxin, which was involved in the poisoning of homeowners at Love Canal in Niagara Falls, New York, and of military personnel exposed to Agent Orange in the Vietnam War. Dioxin is a component or byproduct of many plastics and pesticides. Because of pesticide residues on foods, dioxin is now building up to alarming levels in the body tissues of most Americans (Institute of Medicine, 1994; Schecter, 1994). In potentially dangerous situations like these, we need to enlist the power of the mass media (see next section) to publicize the problems and keep attention on them until solutions are proposed and implemented. A recent volume that describes techniques of group action that can be used to influence large corporations to reduce their polluting activities is *Dying from Dioxin* (Gibbs, 1995).

Mass Media of Communication

The mass media are a two-edged sword. They have both enormous potential for improving our society and equally great potential for damaging crucial social values. Historically, this tension between media benefits and dangers to society has been a major concern accompanying the advent of each new form of mass communication. This was true when early newspapers and magazines began to expand beyond their original local areas; when "movies" were used for propaganda purposes; and after the start of radio broadcasting in 1920, when demagogues in many nations tried to achieve public support and political power through appeals to its mass audience. During each of these eras, applied social scientists studied and often tried to counteract the propagandists' emotional and biased appeals.

When television became a mass medium in the late 1940s, the same kinds of concerns were expressed about its potential influence on a trusting, or even gullible, public; and social scientists rushed to study all aspects of its use, contents, and effects. Since then, as McCreary's chapter on mass media pointed out, television has far surpassed all other media in its pervasiveness in our lives. In the United States, the average household has one or more TV sets turned on for *7 hours every day,* and the average person watches TV for *3 hours every day*. The ubiquitous presence of TV in people's lives might logically suggest that it has an equally great amount of influence, but on that point we find a paradox. Most studies of TV programs—whether educational, entertaining, or persuasive, and including political and advertising appeals—have shown only weak and short-lived effects on audiences' knowledge, attitudes, or behavior. TV executives have made fervent and frequent use of these research findings to oppose all proposals for limitations or regulations on their program content or operations, as in the 1993 U.S. congressional hearings about the amount of violence on TV. Yet, at the same time, these TV executives continually extol television to advertisers as the ideal way to influence the attitudes and behaviors of millions of viewers, and the advertisers pay billions of dollars every year for that privilege!

Because any single program or ad will generally have at most a small and brief effect and may soon be counteracted or offset by another one, it seems that the more important research question—and the far more difficult one to study—concerns the *cumulative* effect of media exposure. For example, what is the cumulative effect of an average child viewer being exposed to 20,000 commercials in a year, or of viewing 200,000 violent acts on TV before reaching age 18? Despite the difficulties in this area of research, a number of research groups have made important contributions, such as the NOTEL study of the longitudinal effects of the introduction of television into a community and George Gerbner's long series of studies on violence in television, both of which were described by McCreary in his earlier chapter on mass media.

An even broader problem is that U.S. television and movies do not just exert their influence on Americans; they are in great demand and are being shown all over the world, even in communist countries such as China. What norms of material possessions, daily activities, and relationships are people in other lands learning, and what values of individualism versus collectivism or materialism versus spiritualism do they find in our TV shows and movies? These questions are closely tied to the issues of human impact on the environment that were discussed earlier. If the rest of the world begins to aspire to, and achieve, a North American level of material possessions and natural resource consumption, that would enormously increase the human impact on the earth's resources and the environment.

Following from these points, it is clear that the content and effects of the mass media are crucial topics of controversy and concern. Controversial topics that have been extensively studied include role portrayals of women, ethnic minorities, and other special groups; the effects of violence and of sexuality on TV; effects of advertising, especially on children; the possibilities for desirable "prosocial" media effects; and the desirability of public regulation and what kind of regulations are needed. Applied psychologists, as well as many other social scientists, have been heavily involved in research and policy advocacy on these issues, and they will undoubtedly continue to be (e.g., Bryant & Zillman, 1994; Durkin, 1985; Oskamp, 1988; Wilson & Gutierrez, 1995). McCreary's chapter in this volume on the influence of mass media clearly spelled out TV's effects on people's use of time and some of the effects of its portrayal of violence and gender stereotypes. A recent volume entitled *The Commercialization of American Culture* has exhaustively detailed the ever-increasing invasiveness of advertising in American mass media (McAllister, 1996).

In addition to these negative aspects of the media, applied social psychologists have been especially interested in the possible prosocial and educational effects of mass media. Psychologists were major contributors to the planning of such educational TV programs as *Sesame Street* (e.g., Ball & Bogatz, 1970), and they have helped to pioneer formal television education programs such as Great Britain's Open University. Some psychologists have served as consultants for network TV entertainment shows, giving advice to the producers on how to present controversial topics such as divorce, drugs, and sexuality in a prosocial way. Many others have done continuing research on the educational and prosocial effects of specific programs or formats of presentation. It seems certain that psychologists in the future will continue their past deep involvement in offering advice to TV producers and to legislators, courts, and other policymakers regarding desirable procedures or regulations to ensure that broadcasting for children serves their educational needs and that TV in general more actively serves the public interest (e.g., deGroot, 1994).

A final challenge to social scientists working on media issues is the proliferation of "new media," which was described briefly earlier in this book. It was much easier to study and to advise on media problems and procedures when almost all television consisted of the major networks and a few local stations that largely showed reruns of former network shows. The 1980s, however, brought VCRs and video stores, satellite receivers, and multiple cable TV channels, none of which adhered to the networks' production guidelines, which had restrained offensive presentations of sexuality, violence, language, and stereotypic roles. These developments led to the vastly increased availability of pornographic and sexually violent material (e.g., "slasher" films) to children and unwitting viewers. Considerable research has shown the harmful effects of these kinds of materials (cf. Donnerstein & Linz, 1994).

Still more recently, the huge popularity of interactive video games has raised fresh concerns over the extreme levels of violence they portray, as well as their monopolization of children's time. For adults, individualized worldwide electronic communication systems, such as the Internet, have raised new issues about privacy rights, offensive speech, and distribution of pornographic and obscene materials. The great variety of these new media has made it almost impossible to regulate them adequately or to study them thoroughly (cf. Mayer, 1994). By the same token, there is an even greater need for social scientists to study all aspects of these new media: public attitudes, needs, and viewing patterns; media content; social effects; and evaluation of regulations and practices. There will be plenty of important tasks for media researchers as far ahead as we can imagine.

Legal Issues

The field of law and psychology has grown tremendously since 1986. It offers a host of different areas for applied research and practice and all of them have the attraction that crucial real-life consequences for plaintiffs, defendants, and practitioners may ride on the procedures and/or the findings. As you have seen in the chapters by Pfeifer and Moston in this volume, a great deal of the social science research and practice in this area concerns procedures in the courtroom. This includes many years of research on jury decision making and much social science consultation with lawyers on procedures for selecting a favorable jury. In addition, the topics of eyewitness testimony and the interviewing techniques by which testimony is elicited have received much research attention.

Social psychological knowledge is also called on in courts for expert testimony on a variety of topics. Emerging issues include the accuracy of children's testimony, signs of battered woman's syndrome, consequences of rape or sexual abuse, child custody concerns, adequacy of product warning labels, fraudulent advertising, and public viewpoints regarding libel or obscenity. Reviews of these and other related topics can be found in Monahan and Walker (1994) and Wrightsman, Kassin, and Willis (1987).

Unfortunately, social science research knowledge is often ignored in many judicial decisions, including rulings by appellate and supreme courts that establish legal precedents for a whole category of cases. One example, which was explored in this book, was the U.S. Supreme Court's ruling that 6-member juries were acceptable even though research had shown that they are inferior to 12-member juries in their amount of deliberation, reliability of verdicts, sensitivity to majority pressure, and representation of various community groups (*Williams v. Florida,* 1970; Saks, 1977). More recently, this type of situation occurred in a U.S. Supreme Court ruling that states could require the use of "death-qualified" jurors (those who have no objection to the death penalty) even though the research evidence showed that such jurors are especially likely to vote for conviction and thus are, in effect, biased against a defendant (*Lockhart v. McCree,* 1986; Costanzo & Costanzo, 1994). These unfortunate cases show that in order to get social science information used appropriately in judicial rulings, it is important to have research evidence well established before appellate court rulings are made, and to have the findings bear directly on the issues that will be central to the court's future decision. This is a tall order and will provide tasks for many future legal researchers.

For those who wish to contribute to legal psychology, however, it is important to realize that the courtroom plays only a small part in the broad sweep of the legal system. In the U.S. civil justice system, only about 2% of cases that are filed end with a court decision, and even in the criminal justice system, the figure is only about 10%. Nearly 90% of criminal convictions result from confessions of guilt and plea bargains rather than court verdicts (Saks & Hastie, 1978).

Apart from courtroom trials, psychologists have a major role to play in research on how other parts of the justice system operate and how they could be improved. Such areas include private lawyers, district attorneys, public defenders, police, probation and parole departments, prisons, judges and magistrates, and juvenile authorities. Another little-studied area is white-collar and corporate crime, which is far more widespread than is usually recognized. A corporate decision to dump toxic waste illegally, for instance, can be much more lethal to a community than a single murder; this kind of crime merits much more attention than it has received from the justice system or from researchers (cf. Geis & Stotland, 1980).

Educational Issues

In comparison with social pressure or coercion, education is a highly desirable way to change people's attitudes and behavior—"the leading of human souls to what is best," according to John Ruskin (1853). Consequently, education has long been one of the main fields of study and application for psychologists. Their efforts have taken into account a wide range of concerns. These include infant care and training programs, preschool socialization and instruction, all the levels of the formal education system, and many areas of adult education and job training. A large proportion of social psychologists, like the authors in this volume, work as educators. Many of them also study and give policy advice about educational topics. Though theories, methods, and findings have varied over the decades (e.g., from the "three Rs" to "progressive education" to "education for change"), the whole area of education remains a major focus in applied social psychology.

One of the topics that has caught researchers' interest is the effect that teachers' expectations (often unstated, or even out of the teacher's awareness) can have on students' performance. This topic was pioneered by Rosenthal and Jacobson's (1968) provocative volume, *Pygmalion in the Classroom,* and masses of later research were summarized by Harris and Rosenthal (1985). Though some of the individual findings and research methods have been critically reviewed, it has been clearly established that teachers can convey their expectations to students nonverbally, by their intonation, words, and indications of their emotions. The four main ways in which this is done are the degree of warmth they display, their feedback of praise or criticism, the level of challenge they present, and their frequency of direct interaction. Students, in turn, raise or lower their self-esteem, their level of effort, and their degree of success partly on the basis of teachers' behavior toward them. The implications of these findings may be either good or bad, ranging from failure and high dropout rates for many minority group students to the astounding achievement in calculus displayed by ghetto-area high school students spurred on by their teacher, Jaime Escalante, whose methods were popularized in the 1988 movie *Stand and Deliver.*

Social science research was cited in the 1954 Supreme Court decision that banned racially segregated education in the United States. Since that time, many social psychologists have been working to achieve the "American dream" of equality in the field of education. Unfortunately, the effects of school desegregation have rarely been as positive as desired, largely due to absence of the necessary conditions specified by Allport (1954): equal status contact, cooperative relationships, and support by authorities. However, many demonstration projects have shown better ways to create these conditions and have found that much more beneficial effects resulted for both majority and minority students. One of the best-known examples is the system of *cooperative learning* implemented in Aronson et al.'s (1978) "jigsaw classroom," and many other social psychologists are working on similar schemes for building social science knowledge into improved educational practices.

A closely related topic, stemming from the dramatic increase in immigration to North America, is multicultural education, which has many aspects but is most often debated in terms of bilingual education. Children from other language backgrounds obviously need systematic help in learning their new host country's language, but finding the best way to deliver that help is the subject of much controversy. Proposed answers range from schools requiring complete immersion in the new language ("mainstreaming"), through various methods and schedules for combining the two languages ("bilingualism"), to offering instruction for many years solely in the student's first language. These questions, unfortunately, have become highly politicized, but there are research data that show that an initial period of instruction in a bilingual classroom facilitates learning the new language and improves performance in other subjects (e.g., DeVillar, Faltis, & Cummins, 1994). After that, mainstreaming is usually more accepted and more successful.

Years of research on Head Start, a key program for culturally disadvantaged preschool children, have shown that it is helpful in aiding children's educational progress, as well as highly cost effective in saving later government expenditures on other social services (Barnett, 1985; Zigler & Muenchow, 1992). In higher education, affirmative action programs to open access to formerly underrepresented minority groups have been clearly successful in that goal in many areas. However, in the middle 1990s they have become more controversial due to charges of "reverse discrimination" and consequently have been abandoned by some groups, such as the prestigious University of California Board of Regents. In the midst of this emotional dispute, it is helpful to realize that a strong body of social science research gives a foundation for affirmative action programs and suggests important safeguards in their operation (e.g., Turner & Pratkanis, 1994).

Returning to the topic of second languages, the computer is becoming a second communication system for many people in our rapidly changing society. To aid their future success, children need to be taught "computer literacy" (which definitely does not mean just playing video games). Therefore, an important challenge to education is to incorporate the computer revolution effectively into instruction, a topic to which psychologists and evaluation researchers can contribute substantially (e.g., Schofield, 1995).

Two current educational controversies are the issues of setting higher and more objective standards for students (for instance, statewide tests to graduate from high school) and, similarly, standards for the competency of teachers. Both of these proposals rely on the use of objective tests to assess competency, and this fact raises many psychological questions of test reliability and validity for researchers to investigate. On the related issues of using standardized tests with minority pupils or job applicants, there is a large body of psychological theory and research and a number of conflicting court rulings that need to be integrated through future work (Dana, 1993; Sackett & Wilk, 1994).

Family Relationships

The family is one of our society's fundamental institutions, and in recent years politicians from both major parties have competed to see who could stress "family values" most strongly. However, the idealized "nuclear family" (breadwinner father, homemaker mother, and children) never was the preeminent form, as it is typically portrayed in the media. Other family types, such as single-parent families and extended families with many possible combinations of relatives living together or close at hand, have become increasingly common in recent decades. Even for U.S. children below the age or 6, only about 30% lived in two-parent families with one breadwinner as of 1993, whereas 38% were in dual-earner families, 28% were in single-parent families, and a small percentage were in no-parent situations (Hernandez, 1993). As of 1989, only about 26% of U.S. children were in families with a breadwinner father and a homemaker mother, whereas nearly 70% were in dual-earner or one-parent families. Though the decrease in two-parent nuclear families is often lamented, in today's labor market in which a majority of married women are employed outside the home, even two-parent families typically need help from friends and relatives in their parenting duties.

Social psychologists have recognized the fundamental importance of knowledge about the family and have carried out relevant research of several different types. One major area of research, called *close relationships,* includes study of friendships, dating, courtship, marriage, and divorce, as well as various types of family patterns (cf. Kelley et al., 1983). In this area, Harold Kelley (1979) was one of the main pioneers with his analysis of the structure and processes of personal relationships. There are now multiple national and international professional organizations that bring together researchers and practitioners on aspects of close interpersonal relationships. Another overlapping area of work is more therapeutically oriented, aiming to strengthen families and help resolve interpersonal conflicts, and drawing on knowledge from clinical and counseling psychology as well as social psychology (e.g., Barker, 1992). You read about some of its methods and accomplishments in Alcock's chapter on mental health in this volume.

One of the positive aspects of family networks is the provision of social support, which can range from emotional concern and empathy, to useful advice, to material and functional help with everyday activities. Research has shown that the availability of social support can enhance individuals' well-being and adjustment, and also buffer them against stressful events and situations (e.g., Perlman & Rook, 1986). Another important issue is the integration of family life with work roles and activities (e.g., Crosby, 1991). This issue is often most central for women, but as gender roles in our society have changed toward greater equality, it has become a more crucial issue for many men as well (cf. Winstead & Derlega, 1993).

More specific potential problem areas in the family that are getting needed attention from social psychologists include the strengths and liabilities of single-parent families, effects of divorce on children (e.g., Walsh, 1993), problems of step-parenting (e.g., Pasley & Ihinger-Tallman, 1987), the causes and consequences of wife assault (e.g., Dutton, 1995) and child assault, and problems in the aging family (e.g., Spacapan & Oskamp, 1989). All of these social trends are expected to continue or increase as we enter the next century.

Health Psychology

Probably the fastest growing area of applied social psychology is health psychology, which in the last 20 years has become a major field by itself (cf. Taylor, 1995). Part of this explosive growth has been due to the tremendous increase in economic resources devoted to health care. In the United States, the costs of health care were $820 billion in 1992 (well over $3,000 per man, woman, and child), and health care expenditures have grown from 6% of the gross national product in 1966 to an estimated 16% for 1998 (O'Donnell & Harris, 1994). Consequently, strenuous efforts have been made to reduce health care costs and people's need for health care; psychologists have many relevant skills, methods, and findings to offer in this area.

The central fact that makes psychology so relevant is that most of today's most threatening diseases and leading causes of death are chronic conditions that are largely caused not by infectious organisms but by patterns of behavior, such as one's general lifestyle, diet, exercise, exposure to stress, smoking, alcohol and drug use, and so on. This is true of the top two killers, heart disease and cancer, as well as of others high on the list such as strokes, bronchitis, emphysema, and AIDS (National Center for Health Statistics, 1993). Since these deaths and diseases are largely caused by human behavior, psychology is the logical field to help in improving these patterns of behavior, so that people can live longer and healthier lives.

There are many ways in which applied social psychologists can contribute to these goals. One is to investigate the connections between various psychosocial causal factors (e.g., emotional stress) and particular health conditions (e.g., high blood pressure). A second is to study people with illnesses and try to understand which behaviors and experiences help them to improve and which are counterproductive. Another contribution is to implement and study the effectiveness of behaviorally oriented treatment programs for people who have high health risks—for example, smoking-cessation or weight-loss programs. A fourth approach is to develop and disseminate health promotion programs that are designed to help people avoid becoming ill, such as wellness and fitness programs in work settings, or prenatal health care for expectant mothers.

Psychologists have made valuable contributions in all of these areas, as evidenced in several earlier chapters. Sadava's chapter on health care emphasized the importance of the doctor-patient relationship in encouraging optimal health self-care and faster recovery for patients. Alcock's chapter on mental health described social psychologically based treatment programs for conditions such as depression, panic attacks, aggressive and violent behavior, and chronic pain. And Ziegler's chapter on gerontology illustrated how social stereotypes and negative self-attributions can discourage healthy behaviors among aging individuals, whereas lifestyle and behavioral training programs can dramatically improve their physical functioning and emotional adjustment.

In addition to conducting research with patients suffering from specific diseases such as heart disease, cancer, and AIDS, health psychologists have produced much valuable knowledge on more general health conditions, such as ways to control chronic pain; reactions to, and antidotes for, stressful life situations; origins and treatment of alcoholism; and factors involved in obesity (e.g., Maes et al., 1988). They have also been heavily involved in research on smoking, which is "the largest preventable cause of death in America" (U.S. Department of Health, Education and Welfare, 1979, p. ii). For instance, they have studied many techniques for breaking the smoking habit, programs to prevent smoking in young children before they get started, the effects of warning labels on cigarettes and advertising, and aspects of public policies regarding smoking, such as citywide bans on smoking in workplaces (e.g., U.S. Department of Health and Human Services, 1987, 1994).

Finally, health psychologists can contribute to health care policy. Because health care in the United States has become prohibitively expensive to individuals and to the nation, it is widely agreed that U.S. health care policy must be reformed, but there is great disagreement about the desirable direction of reform. Here the contrast between Canada and the United States is instructive. Canada has an excellent level of health care, organized through a national, single-payer system, in which every citizen has health coverage and the government pays health care providers on a uniform scale for the services they provide (Daschle, Cohen, & Rice, 1993; U.S. General Accounting Office, 1991). The United States also has an excellent level of care, paid for either through individual fee-for-service charges or through "managed care," in which health maintenance organizations (HMOs) contract with health care providers to treat their members at set fees; however, about 40 million residents cannot afford or obtain insurance coverage and so do not have access to routine medical care. The Canadian system is much less costly than the U.S. system (nearly 30% less per person in 1989) and 91% of citizens and most health care providers view it as better than the U.S. system (Hugick, 1991). In the United States, many citizens and health care providers are dissatisfied with the fractionated and inefficient system, and only 26% of citizens see it as better than the Canadian system (Hugick, 1991). However, it is avidly supported by the large insurance companies and health care organizations and physicians who profit from it most strongly.

Despite nearly 2 years of extensive hearings and political debate after the 1992 U.S. election, no clearcut plan for reforming the U.S. health care "nonsystem" emerged, and the nation seems destined to stagger along with this increasingly expensive patchwork approach in the immediate future. In this situation, applied social psychologists can perform an important public service by gathering and interpreting data about the failures and inefficiencies of the current system and showing how alternative approaches could be fairer and more effective.

Organizational Behavior

The impact of organizations is pervasive in people's lives because most of us work in organizations, and in our leisure time we often join together in organizations for recreation or to achieve worthwhile social goals. Consequently, psychologists have found it important to study organizational structures and procedures and the way that people in organizations respond to them. The field of organizational behavior is another offshoot of social psychology that has grown tremendously and achieved independent status as a field of psychology in its own right (cf. Dunnette & Hough, 1990–1994).

One of the oldest applications of psychology in organizations is personnel selection and job placement based on psychometric tests, interviews, and/or work samples. After employees are chosen, training and development of their skills comprise another major area of applied work. Another key topic is evaluation of employees' job performance and providing appropriate feedback about their successes and failures. As you read in Ayman's chapter on organizational leadership in this volume, one of the most popular and heavily studied areas of organizational psychology is leadership—what characteristics and behaviors make a good leader, and how people can be trained to lead more effectively.

In studying these general areas, the focus is often placed on *small group processes,* a topic of research pioneered by applied social psychologists, starting with Kurt Lewin (e.g., 1948). This area is particularly relevant because much of the world's work is accomplished in small groups, teams, or committees. Another major area of research is the twin topic of the quality of working life and the job satisfaction of employees—what factors raise or lower it, and how it is related to productivity on the job, as well as to activities and attitudes off the job. As mentioned in the section on family relationships, the balance between work and family roles and satisfactions is an important aspect of people's feelings about their overall quality of life.

Because most people spend half of their waking hours in work settings for 40 years or more of their life, all of these aspects of organizations are crucial topics for study and for improvements in practice.

Consumer Psychology

Just as we are all workers, we are also all consumers, and consumer psychology studies that important aspect of our lives. There are several subgroups of consumer psychologists who approach the field from different perspectives. One group might be called academics; they mainly do research on basic processes of persuasion and attitude change, as you have read in Rhodes's chapter on consumer behavior. They study topics such as perception, memory, cognition, emotion, learning, and motivation—all as applied to information about products or services that consumers might want (cf. Mullen & Johnson, 1990).

A second group of consumer psychologists focuses more directly on the applied questions of selling—for instance, how to design attractive products, how to market them, and what kind of advertising will get the maximum response from consumers. Their interest is less in the basic processes of persuasion, and more in the outcome—the sale of a particular kind of product or service. However, they often study the same specific steps as the basic researchers: the audience's exposure to advertising, attention to it, comprehension of it, persuasion by it, consideration of alternatives, decision making, and, finally, the purchase and use of the product. They primarily work for advertising agencies, manufacturers who design and produce the merchandise, or the media companies that plan slick advertising campaigns. Some consumer psychologists also work for market research companies that evaluate the success or failure of the sales campaigns.

A third, smaller group of consumer psychologists adopts the perspective of the consumer rather than the producer or the advertiser. They are more varied in their employment positions and their specific focus of concern; they may do research on issues of consumer protection (e.g., Friedman, 1991); work for regulatory agencies that oversee advertising claims or product safety (cf. Richards, 1990); or assist non-profit and public service organizations, such as churches, homeless shelters, or community medical clinics, to get their message across to people who need their help. Some of them are among the media researchers mentioned in an earlier section who study media effects from the standpoint of protecting children and families from unfair or exploitive marketing or who analyze advertising practices with the goal of protecting the public interest (e.g., Hill, 1995).

SUMMARY

You have seen that there are important jobs to be done in each of the areas previously described that require the skills and knowledge of applied social psychologists. I can report that graduates from our psychology program at Claremont Graduate School are working productively in each of the areas discussed here and are creatively using the skills developed in their doctoral study. Some have continued in jobs at agencies or companies where they worked while in graduate school, taking on increased responsibilities and pay. Some have followed the academic route, taking postdoctoral fellowships and/or faculty positions. A few particularly enterprising or enthusiastic graduates have developed or created new positions that are structured around their own expertise and interests, such as running a consulting business on computer information systems or managing a public policy research firm.

Most of our graduates, however, have found established jobs that use their applied, public-affairs interests and skills in any of a wide variety of organizational settings. Such settings include mental health research, traffic research, social policy research institutes, research administration, multinational corporations, university computer centers, hospitals, and local governments. I think they are making valuable contributions to the work of these organizations and to their own and their colleagues' quality of life. I hope that many readers of this volume will also choose to become applied social psychologists and will find equally worthwhile and satisfying jobs in which to apply their skills.

References

Abdel-Halim, A. A. (1981). Personality and task moderators of subordinate responses to perceived leader behavior. *Human Relations, 34,* 73–88.

Abernethy, V. D. (1993). *Population politics: The choices that shape our future.* New York: Plenum.

Abramson, L. Y. (Ed.). (1988). *Social cognition and clinical psychology: A synthesis.* New York: Guilford.

Abt, C. C. (1980). Social science in the contract research firm. In R. F. Kidd & M. J. Saks (Eds.), *Advances in applied social psychology* (Vol. 1). Hillsdale, NJ: Erlbaum.

Adler, N. E., Boyce, T., Chesney, M. A., Cohen, S., Folkman, S., Kahn, R. L., & Syme, S. L. (1994). Socioeconomic status and health: The challenge of the gradient. *American Psychologist, 49,* 15–24.

Aguinis, H. (1993). Action research and scientific research. *Journal of Applied Behavioral Science, 29,* 416–431.

Ajzen, I., & Fishbein, M. (1972). Attitudes and normative beliefs as factors influencing behavioral intentions. *Journal of Personality and Social Psychology, 21,* 1–9.

Ajzen, I., & Fishbein, M. (1973). Attitudinal and normative variables as predictors of specific behaviors. *Journal of Personality and Social Psychology, 27,* 41–57.

Ajzen, I., & Fishbein, M. (1977). Attitude-behavior relations: A theoretical analysis and review of empirical research. *Psychological Bulletin, 84,* 888–918.

Alcock, J. E. (1986). Chronic pain and the injured worker. *Canadian Psychology, 7,* 196–203.

Alcock, J. E., Carment, D. W., & Sadava, S. W. (1994). *A textbook of social psychology* (3rd. ed). Scarborough, Ontario: Prentice Hall.

Alderfer, C. P. (1983). An intergroup perspective on group dynamics. In J. Lorsch (Ed.), *Handbook of organizational behavior.* Englewood Cliffs, NJ: Prentice Hall.

Alker, H. R., Hosticka, C., & Mitchell, M. (1976). Social process. *Law and Society, 11,* 9–41.

Allen, P. R. (1986). The relation of control to health in old age. *Science, 233,* 1271–1276.

Alloy, L. B., Albright, J. S., Abramson, L. Y., & Dykman, B. M. (1990). Depressive realism and nondepressive illusions: The role of self. In R. E. Ingram (Ed.), *Contemporary psychological approaches to depression: Treatment, research and theory.* New York: Plenum.

Allport, G. W. (1935). Attitudes. In C. A. Murchison (Ed.), *Handbook of social psychology* (pp. 798–844). Worcester, MA: Clark University Press.

331

Allport, G. W. (1954). *The nature of prejudice*. Reading, MA: Addison-Wesley.

Allport, G. W. (1985). The historical background of social psychology. In G. Lindzey & E. Aronson (Eds.), *Handbook of social psychology* (3rd ed., Vol. 1, pp. 1–46). New York: Random House.

Allport, G. W., & Veltfort, H. R. (1943). Social psychology and the civilian war effort. *Journal of Social Psychology, SPSSI Bulletin, 18,* 165–233.

Alwitt, L. F., & Mitchell, A. A. (1985). Concluding remarks. In L. F. Alwitt & A. A. Mitchell (Eds.), *Psychological processes and advertising effects: Theory, research and application*. Hillsdale, NJ: Lawrence Erlbaum Associates.

American Association of Advertising Agencies and the Association of National Advertisers. (1991). *1990 Television Commercial Monitoring Report*. New York: AAAA and ANA.

American Psychological Association. (1992). Ethical principles of psychologists and code of conduct. *American Psychologist, 47,* 1597–1628.

Andersen, A. E., & DiDomenico, L. (1992). Diet vs. shape content of popular male and female magazines: A dose-response relationship to the incidence of eating disorders? *International Journal of Eating Disorders, 11,* 282–287.

Anderson, C. A., & Ford, C. M. (1986). Affect of the game player: Short-term effects of highly and mildly aggressive video games. *Personality and Social Psychology Bulletin, 12,* 390–402.

Andreasen, A. R. (1990). A public policy research agenda for the 1990's. In P. E. Murphy & W. L. Wilkie (Eds.), *Marketing and advertising regulation: The Federal Trade Commission in the 1990's*. Notre Dame: University of Notre Dame Press.

Andrews, J. C., Akhter, S. H., Durvasula, S., & Muehling, D. D. (1992). The effects of advertising distinctiveness and message content involvement on cognitive and affective responses to advertising. *Journal of Current Issues and Research in Advertising, 14*(1), 45–58.

Andrews, J. C., & Shimp, T. A. (1990). Effects of involvement, argument strength, and source characteristics on central and peripheral processing of advertising. *Psychology and Marketing, 7,* 195–214.

Applebaum, C. (1990, Nov. 5). Targeting the wrong demographic. *Adweek's Marketing Week, 20.*

Arabie, P., Carroll, J. D., DeSarbo, W., & Wind, Y. (1981). Overlapping clustering: A new method for product positioning. *Journal of Marketing Research, 18,* 310–317.

Argyle, M. (1988). Social relationships: Interpersonal communication. In M. Hewstone, W. Stroebe, J-P. Codol, & G. M. Stephenson (Eds.), *Introduction to social psychology. A European perspective*. Oxford: Basil Blackwell Ltd.

Argyle, M. (1992). *The social psychology of everyday life*. London: Routledge.

Argyle, M., Furnham, A., & Graham, J. A. (1981). *Social situations*. Cambridge: Cambridge University Press.

Arms, R. L., Russell, G. W., & Sandilands, M. L. (1979). Effects on the hostility of spectators of viewing aggressive sports. *Social Psychology Quarterly, 42,* 275–279.

Arndt, J. (1967). Perceived risk, sociometric integration, and word of mouth in the adoption of a new product. In D. F. Cox (Ed.), *Risk taking and information handling in consumer behavior* (pp. 289–316). Cambridge, MA: Harvard University Press.

Aronson, E., Blaney, N., Stephan, C., Sikes, J., & Snapp, M. (1978). *The jigsaw classroom*. Beverly Hills, CA: Sage.

Aronson, E., Wilson, T. D., & Akert, R. M. (1994). *Social psychology: The heart and the mind*. New York: HarperCollins.

Asch, S. E. (1951). Effects of group pressure upon the modification and distortion of judgments. In H. Guetzkow (Ed.), *Groups, leadership, and men*. Pittsburgh: Carnegie Press.

Asher, H. B. (1976). *Causal modeling*. Beverly Hills: Sage.

Atkinson, P., & Hammersley, M. (1994). Ethnography and participant observation. In N. K. Denzin & Y. S. Lincoln (Eds.), *Handbook of qualitative research*. Thousand Oaks, CA: Sage.

Atwater, L. E., & Yammarino, F. J. (1992). Does self-other agreement on leadership perceptions moderate the validity of leadership and performance predictions? *Personnel Psychology, 45,* 141–164.

Ayman, R. (1993). Leadership perception: The role of gender and culture. In M. M. Chemers and R. Ayman (Eds.), *Leadership theory and research: Perspectives and directions*. New York: Academic Press.

Ayman, R., Bast, J., Ayman-Nolley, S., Friedman, N., & Runkle, J. (1994, August). *Influence of children's gender on ideal leader schema*. Paper presented at annual meeting of American Psychological Association, San Francisco.

Ayman, R., & Chemers, M. M. (1991). The effect of leadership match on subordinate satisfaction in Mexican organizations: Some moderating influences of self-monitoring. *International Review of Applied Psychology, 40,* 299–314.

Ayman, R., Chemers, M. M., & Fiedler, F. (1995). The contingency model of leadership effectiveness: Its levels of analysis. *The Leadership Quarterly, 6,* 147–168.

Ayman, R., Kreiker, N., & Masztal, J. J. (1994). Defining global leadership in business environments. *Consulting Psychology Journal, 46,* 64–77.

Ayman-Nolley, S., Ayman, R., & Becker, J. (1993, June). *Gender affects children's drawings of a leader.* Paper presented at the annual convention of the American Psychological Society, Chicago.

Bagnall, P. (1994). Hypnotherapy: Who is abusing whom? *New Scientist, 143,* No. 1936, 30 July, 46–47.

Bagozzi, R. P. (1981). Attitudes, intentions, and behavior: A test of some key hypotheses. *Journal of Personality and Social Psychology, 41,* 607–627.

Bagozzi, R. P., Baumgartner, H., & Yi, Y. (1992). State versus action orientation and the theory of reasoned action: An application to coupon usage. *Journal of Consumer Research, 18,* 505–518.

Baldus, D. C., Woodworth, G., & Pulaski, C. A. (1991). Law and statistics in conflict: Reflections on *McCleskey v. Kemp.* In D. K. Kagehiro & W. S. Laufer (Eds.), *Handbook of psychology and law* (pp. 251–271). New York: Springer-Verlag.

Baldus, D. C., Woodworth, G., & Pulaski, C. A. (1985). Monitoring and evaluating contemporary death sentence systems: Lessons from Georgia. *University of California-Davis Law Review, 18,* 1375–1407.

Baldwin, J. (1992). *Video taping police interviews with suspects: A national evaluation.* London: HMSO.

Ball, S., & Bogatz, G. A. (1970). *The first year of Sesame Street: An evaluation.* Princeton, NJ: Educational Testing Service.

Ballew v. Georgia, 435 U.S. 223, 98 S.Ct. 1029, 55 L.Ed. 2d 234 (1978).

Bandura, A. (1973). *Aggression: A social learning analysis.* Englewood Cliffs, NJ: Prentice Hall.

Bandura, A. (1977). *Social learning theory.* Englewood Cliffs, NJ: Prentice Hall.

Bandura, A. (1994). Social cognitive theory of mass communication. In J. Bryant & D. Zillmann (Eds.), *Media effects: Advances in theory and research.* Hillsdale, NJ: Lawrence Erlbaum.

Bandura, A., Ross, D., & Ross, S. A. (1961). Transmission of aggression through imitation of aggressive models. *Journal of Abnormal and Social Psychology, 63,* 575–582.

Bank of Montreal. (1991, November). *The task force on the advancement of women in the bank: Report to employees.* Toronto: Author.

Banziger, G., & Roush, S. (1983). *Gerontologist, 23,* 527–531.

Bargal, D., Gold, M., & Lewin, M. (1992). Introduction: The heritage of Kurt Lewin. *Journal of Social Issues, 48*(2), 3–14.

Baril, G. L., Ayman, R., & Palmiter, D. J., Jr. (1994). Measuring leader behavior: Moderators of discrepant self and subordinate descriptions. *Journal of Applied Social Psychology, 24,* 82–94.

Barker, P. (1992). *Basic family therapy* (3rd ed.). New York: Oxford University Press.

Barnett, W. S. (1985). The Perry Preschool Program and its longterm effects: A benefit-cost analysis. *High/Scope Early Childhood Policy Papers.* Ypsilanti, MI: High/Scope.

Baron, R. A. (1983). The control of human aggression: An optimistic perspective. *Journal of Social and Clinical Psychology, 1,* 97–119.

Bartelmus, P. (1994). *Environment, growth and development: The concepts and strategies of sustainability.* London: Routledge.

Bass, B. M. (1985). *Leadership and performance beyond expectations.* New York: Free Press.

Bass, B. M. (1990). *Bass & Stogdill's handbook of leadership: Theory, research, and managerial applications* (3rd ed.). New York: Free Press.

Bass, B. M., & Avolio, B. J. (1993). Transformational leadership: a response to critiques. In M. M. Chemers and R. Ayman (Eds.), *Leadership theory and research: Perspectives and directions.* New York: Academic Press.

Bass, B. M., & Yammarino, F. J. (1991). Congruence of self and others' leadership ratings of naval officers for understanding successful performance. *Applied Psychology: An International Review, 40,* 437–454.

Bast, J. D., Ayman, R., and Korabik, K. (1996, April). *The relationship between gender, transformational leadership and leader effectiveness.* Paper presented at Society of Industrial and Organizational Psychology, San Diego, CA.

Baum, W. M. (1994). *Understanding behaviorism: Science, behavior, and culture.* New York: HarperCollins College Publishers.

Beatty, S. E., & Kahle, L. R. (1988). Alternative hierarchies of the attitude-behavior relationship: The impact of brand commitment and habit. *Journal of the Academy of Marketing Science, 16*(2), 1–10.

Beck, A. T. (1976). *Cognitive therapy and emotional disorders.* New York: International Universities Press.

Beck, A. T., Sokol, L., Clark, D. A., & Berchick, R. (1992). A crossover study of focused cognitive therapy for panic disorder. *American Journal of Psychiatry, 149,* 778–783.

Becker, J. T., Ayman, R., & Korabik, K. (1994). *Discrepant perceptions of the leader's behavior: The role of gender, self-monitoring, and context.* Unpublished manuscript.

Becker, M. H. (1985). Patient adherence to prescribed therapies. *Medical Care, 23,* 539–555.

Beentjes, J. W. J., & Van der Voort, T. H. A. (1988). Television's impact on children's reading skills: A review of research. *Reading Research Quarterly, 23,* 389–413.

Begley, S. (1996, January 22). He's not full of hot air. *Newsweek,* pp. 24–29.

Bell, P. A., Fisher, J. D., Baum, A., & Greene, T. E. (1990). *Environmental psychology* (3rd ed.). Fort Worth, TX: Holt, Rinehart and Winston, Inc.

Belliveau, L. M., & Stolte, J. B. (1977). The structure of third party intervention. *The Journal of Social Psychology, 103,* 244–250.

Bentler, P. M., & Speckart, G. (1979). Models of attitude-behavior relations. *Psychological Review, 86,* 452–464.

Bercovitch, J., & Rubin, J. Z. (Eds.). (1992). *Mediation in international relations: Multiple approaches to conflict management.* New York: St. Martin's Press.

Berkowitz, L. (1993). *Aggression: Its causes, consequences, and control.* New York: McGraw-Hill.

Berkowitz, L., & LePage, A. (1967). Weapons as aggression-eliciting stimuli. *Journal of Personality and Social Psychology, 7,* 202–207.

Bermant, G., & Coppock, R. (1973). Outcomes of six- and twelve-member jury trials: An analysis of 128 civil cases in the state of Washington. *Washington Law Review, 48,* 593–596.

Bermant, G., McGuire, M., McKinley, W., & Salo, C. (1974). The logic of simulation in jury research. *Criminal Justice and Behavior, 1,* 224–233.

Bernard, J. L. (1979). Interaction between the race of the defendant and that of the jurors in determining verdicts. *Law and Psychology Review, 5,* 103–111.

Berscheid, E., & Walster, E. (1974). A little bit about love. In T. L. Houston (Ed.), *Foundations of interpersonal attraction.* New York: Academic Press.

Bersoff, D. N., & Ogden, D. W. (1987). In the Supreme Court of the United States: *Lockhart v. McCree. American Psychologist, 42,* 59–68.

Bessey, B. L., & Ananda, S. M. (1991). Age discrimination in employment. *Research on Aging, 13,* 413–457.

Bettman, J. R. (1979). *An information processing theory of consumer choice.* Reading, MA: Addison-Wesley.

Bettman, J. R. (1986). Consumer psychology. *Annual Review of Psychology, 37,* 257–289.

Betz, N. E., & Fitzgerald, L. F. (1987). *The career psychology of women.* New York: Academic Press.

Bickman, L. (1987). The functions of program theory. In L. Bickman (Ed.), *Using program theory in evaluation.* San Francisco: Jossey-Bass.

Binstock, R., & George, L. (Eds.). (1990). *Handbook of aging and the social sciences* (3rd. ed.). San Diego, CA: Academic Press.

Birren, J. E., & Schaie, K. W. (Eds.). (1990). *Handbook of the psychology of aging* (3rd. ed.). San Diego, CA: Academic Press.

Blair, M. H., & Rosenberg, K. E. (1994). Convergent findings increase our understanding of how advertising works. *Journal of Advertising Research, 34*(3), 35–45.

Blake, R. R., & Mouton, J. S. (1982). Management by grid principle or situationalism: Which? *Group and Organizational Studies, 7,* 207–210.

Blauner, R. (1972). *Racial oppression in America.* New York: Harper and Row.

Blazer, D. G. (1982). Social support and mortality in an elderly community population. *American Journal of Epidemiology, 115,* 684–694.

Blinder, M. (1978). Picking juries. *Trial Diplomacy Journal, 1,* 8–13.

Boardman, S. K., & Horowitz, S. V. (1994). Constructive conflict management and social problems: An introduction. *Journal of Social Issues, 50*(1), 1–12.

Bogner, M. S. (Ed.). (1994). *Human error in medicine.* Hillsdale, NJ: Lawrence Erlbaum Associates.

Bolger, N., Foster, M., Vinokur, A. D., & Ng, R. (1996). Close relationships and adjustment to a life crisis: The case of breast cancer. *Journal of Personality and Social Psychology, 70,* 283–294.

Borden, R. J. (1985). Personality and ecological concern. In D. B. Gray, R. J. Borden, & R. H. Weigel (Eds.), *Ecological beliefs and behaviours: Assessment and change.* Westport, CT: Greenwood.

Borden, R. J. (1986). Ecology and identity. In *Proceedings of the First International Ecosystems Colloquy.* Munich: Man and Space.

Borgida, E., & Park, R. (1988). The entrapment defense: Juror comprehension and decision making. *Law and Human Behavior, 12,* 19–40.

Bourhis, R. Y., Roth, S., & MacQueen, G. (1989). Communication in the hospital setting: A survey of medical and everyday language use among patients, nurses and doctors. *Social Science and Medicine, 28,* 339–346.

Bradbury, T. N., & Fincham, F. D. (1990). Attributions in marriage: Review and critique. *Psychological Bulletin, 107,* 3–33.

Braithwaite, V., Lynd-Stevenson, R., & Pigram, D. (1993). An empirical study of ageism: From polemics to scientific utility. *Australian Psychologist, 28,* 9–15.

Brayfield, A. H., & Lipsey, M. W. (1976). Public affairs psychology. In P. J. Woods (Ed.), *Career opportunities for psychologists: Expanding and emerging areas.* Washington, DC: American Psychological Association.

Brekke, N. J., Enko, P. J., Clavet, G., & Seelau, E. (1991). Of juries and court-appointed experts: The impact of non-adversarial versus adversarial expert testimony. *Law and Human Behavior, 15,* 451–475.

Brennan, M., & Brennan, R. E. (1988). *Strange language: Child victims under cross examination* (3rd ed.). Wagga Wagga, New South Wales, Australia: Riverina Institute of Higher Education.

Bridges, J. S. (1993). Pink or blue: Gender stereotypic perceptions of infants as conveyed by birth congratulations cards. *Psychology of Women Quarterly, 17,* 193–205.

Brigham, J. C., Van Verts, M., & Bothwell, R. K. (1986). Accuracy of children's eyewitness identifications in a field setting. *Basic and Applied Social Psychology, 7,* 295–306.

Brinberg, D., & Cummings, V. (1983). Purchasing generic prescription drugs: An analysis using two behavioral intention models. *Advances in Consumer Research, 11,* 229–234.

British Psychological Society (1995). *Code of conduct, ethical principles, and guidelines.* Leicester, England: British Psychological Society.

Brodt, S. E., & Zimbardo, P. G. (1983). Modifying shyness-related social behavior through symptom misattribution. *Journal of Personality and Social Psychology, 41,* 437–449.

Brody, J. (1994, August 11). Why weights are going strong. *The Globe and Mail,* A14.

Bronfenbrenner, U. (1961). The mirror image in Soviet-American relations: A social psychologist's report. *Journal of Social Issues, 17*(3), 45–56.

Brown, L. R., Kane, H., & Ayres, E. (1993). *Vital signs 1993.* New York: Norton.

Brown, L. R., Kane, H., & Roodman, D. M. (1994). *Vital signs 1994.* New York: Norton.

Bruner, J. S., & Tagiuri, R. (1954). The perception of people. In G. Lindzey (Ed.), *Handbook of social psychology* (pp. 634–654). Reading, MA: Addison-Wesley.

Bryant, F. B., Edwards, J., Tindale, R. S., Posavac, E. J., Heath, L., Henderson, E., & Suarez-Balcazar, Y. (Eds.). (1992). *Methodological issues in applied social psychology.* New York: Plenum.

Bryant, J., & Zillmann, D. (Eds.). (1994). *Media effects: Advances in theory and research.* Hillsdale, NJ: Erlbaum.

Bulman, R. J., & Wortman, C. B. (1977). Attributions of blame and coping in the "real world": Severe accident victims react to their lot. *Journal of Personality and Social Psychology, 35,* 351–363.

Buono, A. F., & Kamm, J. B. (1983). Marginality and the organizational socialization of female managers. *Human Relations, 36,* 1125–1140.

Burgess, R. G. (1984). *In the field: An introduction to field research.* London: Unwin Hyman.

Burish, T., Carey, M., Wallson, K., Stein, M., Jamison, P., & Lyles, J. (1984). Health locus of control and chronic disease: An external orientation may be advantageous. *Journal of Social and Clinical Psychology, 2,* 326–332.

Burke, R. R., & Srull, T. K. (1988). Competitive interference and consumer memory for advertising. *Journal of Consumer Research, 15*(2), 55–68.

Burman, B., & Margolin, G. (1992). Analysis of the association between marital relationships and health problems: An interactional perspective. *Psychological Bulletin, 112,* 39–63.

Burn, S. M. (1991). Social psychology and the stimulation of recycling behaviors: The block leader approach. *Journal of Applied Social Psychology, 21,* 611–629.

Burnkrandt, R. E., & Unnava, H. R. (1989). Self-referencing: A strategy for increasing processing of message content. *Personality and Social Psychology Bulletin, 15,* 628–638.

Burton, J. W. (1969). *Conflict and communication: The use of controlled communication in international relations.* London: Macmillan.

Bushman, B. J. (1988). The effects of apparel on compliance: A field experiment with a female authority figure. *Personality and Social Psychology Bulletin, 14,* 459–467.

Butler, D., & Geis, F. L. (1990). Nonverbal affect responses to male and female leaders: Implications for leadership evaluations. *Journal of Personality and Social Psychology, 58,* 48–59.

Butler, R. N. (1978). Thoughts on aging. *American Journal of Psychiatry, 135,* 14–16.

Butler, R. N. (1980). Ageism: A foreword. *Journal of Social Issues, 36,* 8–11.

Cairns, H. (1935). *Law and the social sciences.* New York: Harcourt Brace.

Calder, B. J. (1977). An attribution theory of leadership. In B. M. Staw and G. R. Salancik (Eds.), *New directions in organizational behavior.* Chicago: St. Clair.

Campbell, A. (1981). *The sense of well being in America: Recent patterns and trends.* New York: McGraw-Hill.

Campbell, A., Converse, P., Miller, W., & Stokes, D. (1960). *The American voter.* New York: Wiley.

Campbell, D. T. (1969). Reforms as experiments. *American Psychologist, 24,* 409–429.

Campbell, D. T., & Fiske, D. W. (1959). Convergent and discriminant validation by the multitrait-multimethod matrix. *Psychological Bulletin, 56,* 81–105.

Campbell, D. T., & Stanley, J. C. (1966). *Experimental and quasi-experimental designs for research.* Chicago: Rand McNally.

Canadian Psychological Association. (1986). *A Canadian code of ethics for psychologists.* Old Chelsea, Quebec: Author.

Canadian Psychological Association. (1991). *Canadian code of ethics for psychologists: Companion manual.* Old Chelsea, Quebec: Author.

Carnevale, P. J., & Pruitt, D. G. (1992). Negotiation and mediation. *Annual Review of Psychology, 43,* 531–582.

Carroll, J. S., Kerr, N. L., Alfinin, J. J., Weaver, F. M., MacCoun, R. J., & Feldman, V. (1986). Free press and fair trial: The role of behavioral research. *Law and Human Behavior, 10,* 187–201.

Cartwright, D. (1948). Social psychology in the United States during the Second World War. *Human Relations, 1,* 333–352.

Carver, C. S., Pozo, C., Harris, S. D., Noriega, V., Scheier, M. F., Robinson, D. S., Ketcham, A. S., Moffat, F. L., & Clark, K. C. (1993). How coping mediates the effects of optimism on distress: A study of women with early stage breast cancer. *Journal of Personality and Social Psychology, 65,* 375–390.

Catton, W. R., Jr. (1980). *Overshoot: The ecological basis of revolutionary change.* Urbana: University of Illinois Press.

Ceci, S. J., & Bruck, M. (1993a). The suggestibility of the child witness: A historical review and synthesis. *Psychological Bulletin, 113,* 403–443.

Ceci, S. J., & Bruck, M. (1993b). Child witnesses: Translating research into policy. *Social Policy Report. Society for Research in Child Development,* Vol. 7, No. 3. Ann Arbor: University of Michigan Press.

Ceci, S. J., Leichtman, M., & White, T. (in press). Interviewing preschoolers: Remembrance of things planted. In D. P. Peters (Ed.), *The child witness: Cognitive, social and legal issues.* Netherlands: Kluwer.

Ceci, S. J., & Loftus, E. F. (1994). Memory work: A royal road to false memories. *Applied Cognitive Psychology, 8,* 351–364.

Ceci, S. J., Ross, D. F., & Toglia, M. P. (1987). Suggestibility of children's memory: Psycholegal implications. *Journal of Experimental Psychology: General, 116,* 38–49.

Centerwall, B. S. (1989). Exposure to television as a risk factor for violence. *American Journal of Epidemiology, 129,* 643–652.

Chacko, T. I. (1982). Women and equal employment opportunity: Some unintended effects. *Journal of Applied Psychology, 57,* 119–123.

Chaiken, S. (1980). Heuristic versus systematic information-processing and the use of source versus message cues in persuasion. *Journal of Personality and Social Psychology, 39,* 752–766.

Chaiken, S. (1987). The heuristic model of persuasion. In M. P. Zanna, J. M. Olson, & C. P. Herman (Eds.), *Social Influence: The Ontario Symposium* (Vol. 5, pp. 3–39). Hillsdale, NJ: Erlbaum.

Chattopadhyay, A., & Alba, J. W. (1988). The situational importance of recall and inference in consumer decision making. *Journal of Consumer Research, 15,* 1–12.

Check, J. V. P., Perlman, D., & Malamuth, N. M. (1985). Loneliness and aggressive behavior. *Journal of Social and Personal Relationships, 2,* 243–252.

Chemers, M. M. (1993). An integrative theory of leadership. In M. M. Chemers & R. Ayman (Eds.), *Leadership theory and research: Perspectives and directions.* New York: Academic Press.

Chemers, M. M., Oskamp, S., & Costanzo, M. A. (Eds.). (1995). *Diversity in organizations: New perspectives for a changing workplace.* Thousand Oaks, CA: Sage.

Chernousenko, V. (1995–1996, Winter). We shall be killed in silent ways. *Earth Island Journal,* p. 33.

Christakis, N. A., & Asch, D. A. (1995). Physician characteristics associated with decisions to withdraw life support. *American Journal of Public Health, 85,* 367–372.

Christensen, A. J., Wiebe, J. S., Smith, T. W., & Turner, C. W. (1995). Predictors of survival among hemodialysis patients: Effects of perceived family support. *Health Psychology, 13*, 521–525.

Christie, R. (1976). Probability v. precedence: The social psychology of jury selection. In G. Bermant, C. Nemeth, & N. Vidmar (Eds.), *Psychology and the law: Research frontiers* (pp. 265–281). Lexington, MA: Lexington Books.

Cialdini, R. B. (1993). *Influence: Science and practice* (3rd ed.). New York: HarperCollins.

Cialdini, R. B., Reno, R. R., & Kallgren, C. A. (1990). A focus theory of normative conduct: Recycling the concept of norms to reduce littering in public places. *Journal of Personality and Social Psychology, 58*, 1015–1026.

Clarke, D. B. (1986). Helping patients make health care decisions. *Euthanasia Review, 1*, 85–95.

Cleveland, J. N. (1994). Women and sexual harassment: Work and well-being in U.S. organizations. In M. Davidson & R. Burke (Eds.), *Women in management*. London: Paul Chapman.

Cobb, C. (1985). Television clutter and advertising effectiveness. *Proceedings of the 1985 Educator's Conference*. Chicago, IL: American Marketing Association.

Cobern, M. K., Porter, B. E., Leeming, F. C., & Dwyer, W. O. (1995). The effect of commitment on adoption and diffusion of grass cycling. *Environment and Behavior, 27*, 213–232.

Coch, L., & French, J. (1948). Overcoming resistance to change. *Human Relations, 1*, 512–532.

Cogswell, B. E., & Weir, D. D. (1964). A role in process: The development of medical professionals' role in long-term care of chronically diseased patients. *Journal of Health and Social Behavior, 5*, 95–103.

Cohen, J. E. (1995). *How many people can the earth support?* New York: Norton.

Cohen, L. L., & Swim, J. K. (1995). The differential impact of gender ratios on women and men: Tokenism, self-confidence, and expectations. *Personality and Social Psychology Bulletin, 21*, 876–884.

Cohen, S., & Syme, S. L. (1985). *Social support and health*. New York: Academic Press.

Cohen, S., & Wills, T. A. (1985). Stress, social support and the buffering hypothesis. *Psychological Bulletin, 98*, 310–357.

Cohn, E. S., & Swift, M. B. (1992). Physical distance and AIDS: Too close for comfort? *Journal of Applied Social Psychology, 22*, 1442–1452.

Cole, N., & Skerrett, P. J. (1995). *Renewables are ready: People creating renewable energy solutions*. Post Mills, VT: Chelsea Green.

Colgrave v. Battin, 413 U.S. 149, 93 S.Ct. 2448, 37 L.Ed.2d 522 (1973).

Colman, A. M. (1991). Crowd psychology in South African murder trials. *American Psychologist, 46*, 1071–1079.

Colpin, H. (1994). Parents and children of reproductive technology: Chances and risks for their well-being. *Community Alternatives: International Journal of Family Care, 6*, 49–71.

Colvin, C. R., & Block, J. (1994). Do positive illusions foster mental health? An examination of the Taylor and Brown formulation. *Psychological Bulletin, 116*, 3–20.

Committee on Ethical Guidelines for Forensic Psychologists. (1991). Speciality guidelines for forensic psychologists. *Law and Human Behavior, 15*, 655–665.

Cone, J. D., & Hayes, S. C. (1980). *Environmental problems: Behavioral solutions*. Monterey, CA: Brooks/Cole Publishing Company.

Conger, J. A., & Kanungo, R. A. (1987). Towards a behavioral theory of charismatic leadership in organizational settings. *Academy of Management Review, 12*, 637–647.

Conger, J. A., & Kanungo, R. (1988). The empowerment process: Integrating theory and practice. *Academy of Management Review, 12*, 637–647.

Conley, J., O'Barr, W., & Lind, A. (1978). The power of language: Presentation style in the courtroom. *Duke Law Journal*, 1375–1399.

Conlon, G. (1990). *Proved innocent*. London: Penguin.

Conrad, P. (1986). The social meaning of AIDS. *Social Policy, 17*, 51–56.

Converse, J. M., & Presser, S. (1986). *Survey questions: Handcrafting the standardized questionnaire*. Beverly Hills: Sage.

Cook, D. J., Guyett, G. H., Jueschke, R., Reeve, J., Spanier, A., King, D., Malloy, D. W., Wilan, A., & Streiner, D. L. (1995). Determinants in Canadian health care workers of decision to withdraw life support from the critically ill. *Journal of the American Medical Association, 273*, 703–708.

Cook, E. P. (1985). *Psychological androgyny*. New York: Pergamon.

Cook, J. D., Hepworth, S. J., Wall, T. D., & Warr, P. B. (1985). *The experience of work: A compendium and review of 249 measures and their use*. New York: Academic Press.

Cook, T. D., & Campbell, D. T. (1979). *Quasi-experimentation: Design and analysis issues for field settings.* Boston: Houghton-Mifflin.

Cook, T. D., & Flay, B. R. (1978). The persistence of experimentally induced attitude change. In L. Berkowitz (Ed.), *Advances in experimental social psychology* (Vol. 2, pp. 1–57). San Diego, CA: Academic Press.

Cooper, A. M. (1994). The ABCs of challenge for cause in jury trials: To challenge or not to challenge and what to ask if you get it. *Criminal Law Quarterly, 37,* 62–69.

Cooper, J., & Mackie, D. (1986). Video games and aggression in children. *Journal of Applied Social Psychology, 16,* 726–744.

Corteen, R. S., & Williams, T. M. (1986). Television and reading skills. In T. M. Williams (Ed.), *The impact of television: A natural experiment in three communities.* New York: Academic Press.

Costanzo, M., & Costanzo, S. (1994). The death penalty: Public opinions, legal decisions, and juror perspectives. In M. Costanzo & S. Oskamp (Eds.), *Violence and the law* (pp. 246–272). Thousand Oaks, CA: Sage.

Costley, C. L. (1988). Meta analysis of involvement research. *Advances in Consumer Research, 15,* 554–562.

Cousins, N. (1979). *Anatomy of an illness.* Toronto: Bantam Books.

Crocker, J., Alloy, L. B., & Kayne, N. T. (1988). Attributional style, depression, and perception of consensus for events. *Journal of Personality and Social Psychology, 54,* 840–846.

Crocker, J., & McGraw, K. (1984). What's good for the goose is not good for the gander. *American Behavioral Scientist, 27,* 357–369.

Cronshaw, S. F., & Lord, R. G. (1987). Effects of categorization, attribution, and encoding processes on leadership perceptions. *Journal of Applied Psychology, 72,* 97–106.

Crosby, F. J. (1991). *Juggling: The unexpected advantages of balancing career and home for women and their families.* New York: Free Press.

Cruse, D., & Brown, B. A. (1987). Reasoning in a jury trial: The influence of instructions. *Journal of General Psychology, 114,* 129–133.

Cutrona, C. E. (1982). Transition to college: Loneliness and the process of social adjustment. In L. A. Peplau & D. Perlman (Eds.), *Loneliness: A sourcebook of current theory, research, and therapy.* New York: Wiley Interscience.

Dakof, G. A., & Taylor, S. E. (1990). Victims' perception of social support: What is helpful from whom? *Journal of Personality and Social Psychology, 58,* 80–89.

Dale, P. S., Loftus, E. F., & Rathbun, L. (1978). The influence of the form of the question on the eyewitness testimony of preschool children. *Journal of Psycholinguistic Research, 7,* 269–277.

Dana, R. H. (1993). *Multicultural assessment perspectives for professional psychology.* Boston: Allyn & Bacon.

Dane, F. C. (1992) Applying social psychology in the courtroom: Understanding stereotypes in jury decision making. *Contemporary Social Psychology, 16,* 33–36.

Daschle, T. A., Cohen, R. J., & Rice, C. L. (1993). Health care reform: Single-payer models. *American Psychologist, 48,* 265–269.

David, H. P. (1994). Reproductive rights and reproductive behavior: Clash or convergence of private values and public policies? *American Psychologist, 49,* 343–349.

Davidson, W., Molloy, W., & Bédard, M. (1995). Physician characteristics and prescribing for elderly people in New Brunswick: Relation to patient outcomes. *Canadian Medical Association Journal, 152,* 1227–1234.

Davis, J. A., & Smith, T. W. (1993). *General Social Surveys: 1972–1993 cumulative codebook.* Chicago: National Opinion Research Center.

Deaux, K. (1993). Sorry wrong number: A reply to Gentile's call. *Psychological Science, 4,* 125–126.

Deaux, K., & Major, B. (1987). Putting gender into context: An interactive model of gender-related behavior. *Psychological Review, 94,* 369–389.

Deaux, K., & Taynor, J. (1973). Evaluation of male and female ability: Bias works two ways. *Psychological Reports, 32,* 261–262.

deGroot, G. (1994). Psychologists examine what makes TV "good." *APA Monitor, 25*(6), 5.

Denzin, N. K., & Lincoln, Y. S. (Eds.). (1994a). *Handbook of qualitative research.* Thousand Oaks, CA: Sage.

Denzin, N. K., & Lincoln, Y. S. (1994b). Introduction: Entering the field of qualitative research. In N. K. Denzin & Y. S. Lincoln (Eds.), *Handbook of qualitative research.* Thousand Oaks, CA: Sage.

Derlega, V. J., Hendrick, S. S., Winstead, B. A., & Berg, J. H. (1992). Psychotherapy as a personal relationship: A social psychological perspective. *Psychotherapy, 29,* 331–335.

DesRoches, G. (1994). An adman's struggle with Joe Camel and free speech. *Advertising Age, 65*(40), 23.

Deutsch, M. (1969). Conflicts: Productive and destructive. *Journal of Social Issues, 25*(2), 7–41.

Deutsch, M. (1973). *The resolution of conflict.* New Haven, CT: Yale University Press.

Deutsch, M. (1983). The prevention of World War III: A psychological perspective. *Political Psychology, 4,* 3–31.

Deutsch, M. (1993). Educating for a peaceful world. *American Psychologist, 48,* 510–517.

Deutsch, M. (1994). Constructive conflict resolution: Principles, training, and research. *Journal of Social Issues, 50*(1), 13–32.

Deutsch, M., & Gerard, H. B. (1955). A study of normative and informational social influences upon individual judgment. *Journal of Abnormal and Social Psychology, 51,* 629–636.

DeVillar, R., Faltis, C., & Cummins, J. (Eds.). (1994). *Cultural diversity in schools: From rhetoric to practice.* Albany: State University of New York Press.

Devine, P. G. (1989). Stereotypes and prejudice: Their automatic and controlled components. *Journal of Personality and Social Psychology, 56,* 5–18.

Diamond, W. D., & Loewy, B. Z. (1991). Effects of probabilistic rewards on recycling attitudes and behavior. *Journal of Applied Social Psychology, 21,* 1590–1607.

DiFranza, J. R., Richards, J. W., Jr., Paulman, P. M., Wolf-Gilespie, N., Fletcher, C., Jaffe, R. D., & Murray, D. (1991). RJR Nabisco's cartoon camel promotes camel cigarettes to children. *Journal of the American Medical Association, 266,* 3149–3153.

Dillman, D. A. (1978). *Mail and telephone surveys: The total design method.* New York: Wiley.

DiMatteo, M. R., & DiNicola, D. D. (1982). *Achieving patient compliance.* New York: Pergamon.

DiMatteo, M. R., Hays, R. D., & Prince, L. M. (1986). Relationship of physicians' nonverbal communication skills to patient satisfaction, appointment noncompliance and physician workload. *Health Psychology, 5,* 581–594.

DiMatteo, M. R., Sherbourne, C. D., Hays, R. D., Ordway, L., Kravitz, R. L., McGlynn, E. A., Kaplan, S., & Rogers, W. H. (1993). Physicians' characteristics influence patients' adherence to medical treatment: Results from the Medical Outcomes Study. *Health Psychology, 12,* 93–102.

Doan, B., & Gray, R. E. (1992). The heroic patient: A critical analysis of the relationship between illusion and mental health. *Canadian Journal of Behavioural Science, 24,* 253–266.

Dobbins, G. H. (1985). Effects of gender on leaders' responses to poor performers: An attributional interpretation. *Academy of Management Journal, 28,* 587–598.

Donnellon, A., & Kolb, D. M. (1994). Constructive for whom? The fate of diversity disputes in organizations. *Journal of Social Issues, 50*(1), 139–156.

Donnerstein, E., & Linz, D. (1994). Sexual violence in the mass media. In M. Costanzo & S. Oskamp (Eds.), *Violence and the law* (pp. 9–36). Thousand Oaks, CA: Sage.

Donovan, J. L., & Blake, D. R. (1992). Patient noncompliance: Deviance or reasoned decision-making? *Social Science and Medicine, 34,* 507–532.

Duncan v. Louisiana, 391 U.S. 145, 88 S.Ct. 1444, 20 L.Ed.2d 491 (1968).

Dunkel-Schetter, C., Feinstein, L. G., Taylor, S. E., & Falke, R. L. (1992). Patterns of coping with cancer. *Health Psychology, 11,* 79–87.

Dunnette, M. D. (1990). Blending the science and practice of industrial and organizational psychology: Where are we and where are we going? In M. D. Dunnette & L. M. Hough (Eds.), *Handbook of industrial and organizational psychology* (2nd ed., Vol. 1, pp. 1–28). Palo Alto, CA: Consulting Psychologists Press, Inc.

Dunnette, M. D., & Hough, L. (Eds.). (1990–1994). *Handbook of industrial and organizational psychology* (4 Vol.). Palo Alto, CA: Consulting Psychologists Press.

Durkheim, E. (1951). *Suicide: A study in sociology.* (J. A. Spaulding, G. Simpson, Trans.). Glencoe, IL: Free Press. (Original work published 1897)

Durkin, K. (1985a). Television and sex-role acquisition: Content. *British Journal of Social Psychology, 24,* 101–113.

Durkin, K. (1985b). *Television, sex roles, and children.* Milton Keynes: Open University Press.

Durkin, K. (1985c). Television and sex-role acquisition: Effects. *British Journal of Social Psychology, 24,* 191–210.

Durkin, K. (1986). Sex roles and the mass media. In D. J. Hargreaves & A. M. Colley (Eds.), *The psychology of sex roles.* London: Harper and Row.

Dutton, D. G. (1995). *The domestic assault of women: Psychological and criminal justice perspectives* (rev. ed.). Vancouver: University of British Columbia Press.

Dwyer, W. O., Leeming, F. C., Cobern, M. K., Porter, B. E., & Jackson, J. M. (1993). Critical review of behavioral interventions to preserve the environment: Research since 1980. *Environment and Behavior, 25,* 275–321.

Dyas v. United States, D.C. App. 376 A.2d 827 (1977).

Eagly, A. H., & Chaiken, S. (1993). *The psychology of attitudes.* Fort Worth: Harcourt Brace Jovanovich.

Eagly, A. H., & Johnson, B. T. (1990). Gender and leadership style: A meta-analysis. *Psychological Bulletin, 108,* 233–256.

Eagly, A. H., Makhijani, M. G., & Klonsky, B. G. (1992). Gender and the evaluation of leaders: A meta-analysis. *Psychological Bulletin, 111,* 3–22.

Ebbesen, E. B., Duncan, B., & Konecni, V. J. (1975). Effects of content of verbal aggression on future verbal aggression: A field experiment. *Journal of Experimental Social Psychology, 11,* 192–204.

Edney, J. J. (1980). The commons problem: Alternative perspectives. *American Psychologist, 35,* 131–150.

Eggerton, S. C., & Berg, A. O. (1984). Is it good practice to treat patients with uncomplicated myocardial infarction at home? *Journal of the American Medical Association, 251,* 349–350.

Ehrlich, P. R., & Ehrlich, A. H. (1990). *The population explosion.* New York: Simon & Schuster.

Ekman, P., & O'Sullivan, M. (1989). Hazards in detecting deceit. In D. C. Raskin (Ed.), *Psychological methods in criminal investigation and evidence.* New York: Springer-Verlag.

Elder, R. G. (1973). Social class and lay explanations of the etiology of arthritis. *Journal of Health and Social Behavior, 14,* 28–38.

Elliot, R. (1991). Social science data and the APA: The Lockhart brief as a case in point. *Law and Human Behavior, 15,* 59–76.

Elliot, S. (1991, April 30). Critics claim multiple deals risk saturation. *USA Today, 9,* 1D–2D.

Ellsworth, P. C. (1991). To tell what we know or wait for Godot? *Law and Human Behavior, 15,* 77–90.

Elms, A. C. (1975). The crisis of confidence in social psychology. *American Psychologist, 30,* 967–976.

Elwork, A., Sales, B. D., & Alfini, J. J. (1977). Juridic decisions: In ignorance of the law or in light of it? *Law and Human Behavior, 1,* 163–189.

Ende, J., Kazis, L., Ash, A., & Moskowitz, M. A. (1989). Measuring patients' desire for autonomy: Decision making and information-seeking preferences among medical patients. *Journal of General Internal Medicine, 5,* 23–30.

Engel, J. F., Blackwell, R. D., & Miniard, P. W. (1986). *Consumer behavior* (5th ed.). Chicago: Dryden.

Eron, L. D., & Peterson, R. A. (1982). Abnormal behavior: Social approaches. In M. R. Rosenzweig & L. W. Porter (Eds.), *Annual Review of Psychology, 33,* 231–264.

Etzioni, A. (1970). The Kennedy experiment. In E. I. Megargee & J. E. Hokanson (Eds.), *The dynamics of aggression: Individual, group and international analysis.* New York: Harper & Row.

Evans, R. (1993). The conduct of police interviews with juveniles. *Royal Commission on Criminal Justice Research Study, No. 8.* London: HMSO.

Fagenson, E. A. (1990). Perceived masculine and feminine attributes examined as a function of individual's sex and level in the organizational power hierarchy: A test of four theoretical perspectives. *Journal of Applied Psychology, 75,* 204–221.

Fay, R. E., Turner, C. F., Klassen, A. D., & Gagnon, J. H. (1989). Prevalence and patterns of same-gender sexual contact among men. *Science, 243,* 338–348.

Fazio, R. H. (1986). How do attitudes guide behavior? In R. M. Sorrentino & E. T. Higgins (Eds.), *Handbook of motivation and cognition: Foundation of social behavior* (pp. 204–243). New York: Guilford Press.

Fazio, R. H., Powell, M. C., & Williams, C. J. (1989). The role of attitude accessibility in the attitude-to-behavior process. *Journal of Consumer Research, 16,* 280–288.

Feather, N. T., & Simon, J. G. (1975). Reactions to male and female success and failure in sex-linked occupations: Impressions of personality, causal attributions, and perceived likelihood of different consequences. *Journal of Personality and Social Psychology, 31,* 20–31.

Fenlason, K. J. (1991). Sex bias in the evaluation of women in management: A systems perspective. *Equal Opportunities International, 3/4,* 10–18.

Ferber, R., Sheatsley, P., Turner, A., & Waksburg, J. (1980). *What is a survey?* Washington, DC: American Statistical Association.

Festinger, L., Riecken, H., & Schachter, S. (1956). *When prophecy fails.* Minneapolis: University of Minnesota Press.

Fiedler, F. E. (1964). A contingency model for the prediction of leadership effectiveness. In L. Berkowitz (Ed.), *Advances in experimental social psychology* (Vol. 1). New York: Academic Press.

Fiedler, F. E. (1967). *A theory of leadership effectiveness.* New York: McGraw-Hill.

Fiedler, F. E. (1978). The contingency model and the dynamics of the leadership process. In L. Berkowitz (Ed.), *Advances in experimental social psychology* (Vol. 11). New York: Academic Press.

Fiedler, F. E. (1993). The leadership situation and the black box in contingency theories. In M. M. Chemers & R. Ayman (Eds.), *Leadership theory and research: Perspectives and directions.* New York: Academic Press.

Fiedler, F. E. (1995). Cognitive resource and leadership. *Applied Psychology: An International Review, 44,* 5–28.

Fiedler, F. E., & Chemers, M. M. (1984). *Improving leadership effectiveness: The leader match concept* (2nd ed.). New York: Wiley.

Fiedler, F. E., & Garcia, J. E. (1987). *New approaches to effective leadership: Cognitive resources and organizational performance.* New York: Wiley.

Field, H. S. (1979). Rape trials and jurors' decisions: A psycholegal analysis of victim, defendant, and case characteristics. *Law and Human Behavior, 3,* 261–284.

Fincham, F. D., & Bradbury, T. N. (1993). Marital satisfaction, depression, and attributions: A longitudinal analysis. *Journal of Personality and Social Psychology, 64,* 442–452.

Fishbein, M., & Ajzen, I. (1975). *Belief, attitude, intention and behavior: An introduction to theory and research.* Reading, MA: Addison-Wesley.

Fishbein, M., & Ajzen, I. (1981). Acceptance, yielding and impact: Cognitive processes in persuasion. In R. E. Petty, T. M. Ostrom, & T. C. Brock (Eds.), *Cognitive responses in persuasion* (pp. 339–359). Hillsdale, NJ: Erlbaum.

Fisher, B. M., & Edwards, J. E. (1988). Consideration and initiating structure and their relationships with leader effectiveness: A meta analysis. *Best Papers proceedings, Academy of Management,* Anaheim, CA, 201–205.

Fisher, R. J. (1972). Third party consultation: A method for the study and resolution of conflict. *Journal of Conflict Resolution, 16,* 67–94.

Fisher, R. J. (1982). *Social psychology: An applied approach.* New York: St. Martin's Press.

Fisher, R. J. (1990). *The social psychology of intergroup and international conflict resolution.* New York: Springer-Verlag.

Fisher, R. J. (1993). Developing the field of interactive conflict resolution: Issues in training, funding, and institutionalization. *Political Psychology, 14*(1), 123–138.

Fisher, R. J. (1994, July). *Conflict analysis workshops on the potential role of education in peacebuilding in Cyprus.* Paper presented at the Annual Scientific Meeting of the International Society of Political Psychology, Barcelona, Spain.

Fiske, S., Bersoff, D. N., Borgida, E., Deaux, K., & Heilman, M. (1991). Social science research on trial: Use of sex stereotyping research in *Price Waterhouse v. Hopkins. American Psychologist, 46,* 1049–1060.

Fitness, J., & Fletcher, G. J. O. (1993). Love, hate, anger, and jealousy in close relationships: A prototype and cognitive appraisal analysis. *Journal of Personality and Social Psychology, 65,* 942–958.

Flanagan, J. C. (1984). The American Institutes for Research. *American Psychologist, 39,* 1272–1276.

Flavin, C. (1995). Harnessing the sun and the wind. In L. R. Brown et al., *State of the world 1995.* New York: Norton.

Flavin, C. (1996). Facing up to the risks of climate change. In L. R. Brown et al., *State of the world 1996.* New York: Norton.

Flavin, C., & Lenssen, N. (1994). Reshaping the power industry. In L. R. Brown et al., *State of the world 1994.* New York: Norton.

Fletcher, J. E., & King, M. (1993). Use of voter surveys to plan bond campaigns for parks and recreation. *Journal of Park and Recreation Administration, 11,* 17–27.

Florida v. Zamora, Trial Transcript (Case No. 77-2566), Circuit Court, Dade County, FL (1977).

Foddy, M., & Graham, H. (1987, June). *Sex and double standards in the inference of ability.* Paper presented at the annual meeting of the Canadian Psychological Association, Vancouver, BC.

Foley, L. A., & Chamblin, M. H. (1982). The effect of race and personality on mock jurors' decisions. *Journal of Psychology, 112,* 47–51.

Foltz, K. (1985, August 12). Ads popping up all over. *Newsweek, 2,* 50

Fontana, A. F., Kerns, R. D., Rosenberg, R. L., & Colonese, K. L. (1989). Support, stress and recovery from coronary heart disease: A longitudinal causal model. *Health Psychology, 8,* 175–193.

Foschi, M. (1992). Gender and double standards for competence. In C. L. Ridgeway (Ed.), *Gender, interaction, and inequality* (pp. 181–207). New York: Springer-Verlag.

Foschi, M., Lai, L., & Sigerson, K. (1991). *Double standards in the assessment of male and female job candidates.* Paper presented at the West Coast Conference on Small Group Research, San Jose, CA.

Fraboni, M., Saltstone, R., & Hughes, S. (1990). The Fraboni Scale of Ageism (FSA): An attempt at a more precise measure of ageism. *Canadian Journal of Aging, 9,* 56–66.

Frankel, M., & Sinclair, C. (1982). Quality assurance: An approach to accountability in a mental health center. *Professional Psychology, 13,* 79–84.

Frederick, J. T. (1984). Social science involvement in voir dire: Preliminary data on the effectiveness of "scientific jury selection." *Behavioral Sciences and the Law, 2,* 375–394.

Frederick, J. T. (1987). *The psychology of the American jury.* Charlottesville, VA: Michie.

Freedman, J. L., & Fraser, S. C. (1966). Compliance without pressure: The foot-in-the-door technique. *Journal of Personality and Social Psychology, 4,* 195–203.

Freeman, H. E., & Giovannoni, J. M. (1969). Social psychology of mental health. In G. Lindzey & E. Aronson (Eds.), *The handbook of social psychology* (2nd ed., pp. 660–701). Reading, MA: Addison-Wesley.

French, J. R. P., & Raven, B. (1959). The bases of social power. In D. Cartwright (Ed.), *Studies in social power.* Ann Arbor: University of Michigan, Institute for Social Research.

Frey, D., & Rogner, O. (1987). The relevance of psychological factors in the convalescence of accident patients. In G. R. Semin & B. Krahé (Eds.), *Issues in contemporary German social psychology: History, theories and application* (pp. 241–257). London: Sage Publications.

Frey, J. H. (1989). *Survey research by telephone.* Newbury Park, CA: Sage.

Frieze, I. H., Bar-Tal, D., & Carroll, J. S. (Eds.). (1979). *New approaches to social problems.* San Francisco: Jossey-Bass.

Frye v. United States, 293 F. 1013, 34 A.L.R. 145 (D.C.Cir. 1923).

Fulero, S. M., & Penrod, S. D. (1990). Attorney jury selection folklore: What do they think and how can psychologists help? *Forensic Reports, 3,* 233–259.

Furnham, A., & Bitar, N. (1993). The stereotyped portrayal of men and women in British television advertisements. *Sex Roles, 29,* 297–310.

Furu, T. (1962). *Television and children's life: A before-after study.* Tokyo: Japan Broadcasting Association.

Gabora, N. J., Spanos, N. P., & Joab, A. (1993). The effects of complainant age and expert psychological testimony in a simulated child sexual abuse trial. *Law and Human Behavior, 17,* 103–119.

Gadberry, S. (1980). Effects of restricting first graders' TV-viewing on leisure time use, IQ change, and cognitive style. *Journal of Applied Developmental Psychology, 1,* 45–57.

Gardner, D. M. (1975). Deception in advertising: A conceptual approach. *Journal of Marketing, 39*(1), 40–46.

Gardner, G. T., & Stern, P. C. (1996). *Environmental problems and human behavior.* Boston: Allyn & Bacon.

Gardner, M. P. (1985). Mood states and consumer research. *Journal of Consumer Research, 12*(3), 281–300.

Gardner, M. P. (1994). Responses to emotional and informational appeals: The moderating role of context-induced mood states. In E. M. Clark, T. C. Brock, & D. W. Stewart (Eds.), *Attention, attitude, and affect in response to advertising.* Hillsdale, NJ: Lawrence Erlbaum Associates.

Garfield, B. (1995). Joe Camel lights fire under Clinton, constitution. *Advertising Age, 66*(32), 3.

Geis, G., & Stotland, E. (Eds.). (1980). *White-collar crime: Theory and research.* Beverly Hills, CA: Sage.

Geller, E. S. (1989). Applied behavior analysis and social marketing: An integration for environmental preservation. *Journal of Social Issues, 45,* 17–36.

Geller, E. S. (1990). Behavior analysis and environmental preservation: Where have all the flowers gone? *Journal of Applied Behavior Analysis, 23,* 269–273.

Geller, E. S., Berry, T. D., Ludwig, T. D., Evans, R. E., Gilmore, M. R., & Clarke, S. W. (1990). A conceptual framework for developing and evaluating behavior change interventions for injury control. *Health Education Research: Theory & Practice, 5,* 125–137.

Geller, E. S., Chaffee, J. L., & Ingram, R. E. (1975). Promoting paper recycling on a university campus. *Journal of Environmental Systems, 5,* 39–57.

Geller, E. S., Winett, R. A., & Everett, P. B. (1982). *Preserving the environment: New strategies for behavior change.* New York: Pergamon Press.

Gentile, D. A. (1993). Just what are sex and gender anyway?: A call for a new terminological standard. *Psychological Science, 4,* 120–122.

Gerbner, G., Gross, L., Morgan, M., & Signorielli, N. (1994). Growing up with television: The cultivation perspective. In J. Bryant & D. Zillmann (Eds.), *Media effects: Advances in theory and research.* Hillsdale, NJ: Lawrence Erlbaum.

Gergen, K. J. (1973). Social psychology as history. *Journal of Personality and Social Psychology, 26,* 373–383.

Gheorghiu, V. A., Netter, P., Eysenck, H. J., & Rosenthal, R. (Eds). (1989). *Suggestion and suggestibility: Theory and research.* Berlin: Springer-Verlag.

Gibbs, L. (1995). *Dying from dioxin.* Boston: South End Press.

Gifford, R. (1987). *Environmental psychology: Principles and practice.* Boston: Allyn & Bacon.

Giles, H., Bourhis, R. Y., & Taylor, D. (1977). Towards a theory of language in ethnic group relations. In M. L. McLaughlin (Ed.), *Language, ethnicity and interpersonal relations* (pp. 307–348). London: Academic Press.

Gilmore, R. F., & Secunda, E. (1993). Zipped TV commercials boost prior learning. *Journal of Advertising Research, 33*(6), 28–38.

Glasgow, R. E., McCaul, K. D., & Schafer, L. C. (1987). Self-care behaviors and glycemic control in Type 1 diabetes. *Journal of Chronic Diseases, 40,* 399–412.

Glass, D. C., & Singer, J. E. (1972). *Urban stress: Experiments on noise and social stressors.* New York: Academic Press.

Gleason, J. M., & Harris, V. A. (1975). Race, socio-economic status, and perceived similarity as determinants of judgements by simulated jurors. *Social Behavior and Personality, 3,* 175–180.

Goldberg, M. E., & Gorn, G. J. (1987). Happy and sad TV programs: How they affect reactions to commercials. *Journal of Consumer Research, 14,* 387–403.

Goldman, A. H. (1986). Cognitive psychologists as expert witnesses: A problem of professional ethics. *Law and Human Behavior, 10,* 29–45.

Goodman, G. S (1984). Children's testimony in historical perspective. *Journal of Social Issues, 40*(2), 9–31.

Goodman, G. S., Hirschman, J. E., Hepps, D., & Rudy, L. (1991). Children's memory for stressful events. *Merrill-Palmer Quarterly, 37,* 109–158.

Goodman, G. S., Jones, D. P. H., Pyle, E. A., Prado-Estrada, L., Port, L. K., England, P., Mason, R., & Rudy, L. (1988). The emotional effects of criminal court testimony on child sexual assault victims: A preliminary report. In G. M. Davies & J. Drinkwater (Eds.), *The child witness: Do courts abuse children? Issues in criminological and legal psychology, 13.* Leicester: British Psychological Society, Division of Criminological and Legal Psychology.

Gordon, C. (1985). Justice ignored: The discriminatory use of peremptory challenges. *University of Missouri, Kansas City Law Review, 53,* 446–467.

Grant, L., & Evans, A. (1994). *Principles of behavior analysis.* New York: HarperCollins.

Gray, D. B., & Ashmore, R. D. (1976). Biasing influence on defendants' characteristics on simulated sentencing. *Psychological Review, 38,* 727–738.

Graziano, S. J., Panter, A. T., & Tanaka, J. S. (1990). Individual differences in information processing strategies and their role in juror decision making and selection. *Forensic Reports, 3,* 279–301.

Green, S. G., & Mitchell, T. R. (1979). Attributional processes of leaders in leader-member interactions. *Organizational Behavior and Human Performance, 23,* 429–458.

Greenberg, J., & Baron, R. A. (1993). *Behavior in organizations* (4th ed.). Boston: Allyn & Bacon.

Greene, E. (1990). Media effects of jurors. *Law and Human Behavior, 14,* 439–450.

Greene, E., & Wade, R. (1987). Of private talk and public print: General pretrial publicity and juror decision making. *Applied Cognitive Psychology, 2,* 123–135.

Groves, R. M. (1987). Research on survey data quality. *Public Opinion Quarterly, 51,* 168–178.

Grunert, K. G., & Dedler, K. (1985). Misleading advertising: In search of a measurement methodology. *Journal of Public Policy and Marketing, 4,* 153–165.

Guba, E. G., & Lincoln, Y. S. (1989). *Fourth generation evaluation.* Thousand Oaks, CA: Sage.

Gudjonsson, G. H. (1992). *The psychology of interrogations, confessions and testimony.* Chichester: John Wiley.

Gudjonsson, G. H., & Gunn, J. (1982). The competence and reliability of a witness in a criminal court. *British Journal of Psychiatry, 141,* 624–627.

Gudjonsson, G. H., & Le Begue, B. (1989). Psychological and psychiatric aspects of a coerced-internalized false confession. *Journal of the Forensic Science Society, 29,* 261–269.

Gudjonsson, G. H., & MacKeith, J. (1988). Retracted confessions: Legal, psychological and psychiatric aspects. *Medicine, Science and the Law, 28,* 187–194.

Gudjonsson, G. H., & Sigurdsson, J. F. (1994). How frequently do false confessions occur?: An empirical study of personality variables. *Psychology, Crime and Law, 1,* 21–26.

Gunter, B. (1994). The question of media violence. In J. Bryant & D. Zillmann (Eds.), *Media effects: Advances in theory and research.* Hillsdale, NJ: Lawrence Erlbaum.

Gutek, B. A., & Cohen, A. G. (1987). Sex ratios, sex role spillover, and sex at work: A comparison of men's and women's experiences. *Human Relations, 40,* 97–115.

Hagan, J. (1974). Extra-legal attributes and criminal sentencing: An assessment of a sociological viewpoint. *Law and Society Review, 8,* 357–383.

Hall, J. A., Epstein, A. M., DeCiantis, M. L., & McNeil, B. J. (1993). Physicians' liking for their patients: More evidence for the role of affect in medical care. *Health Psychology, 12,* 140–146.

Hall, J. A., Epstein, A. M., & McNeil, B. J. (1989). Multidimensionality of health status in an elderly population: Construct validity of a measurement battery. *Medical Care, 27*(3, Supplement), S168–S177.

Hall, J. A., Irish, J. T., Roter, D. L., Ehrlich, C. M., & Miller, L. H. (1994). Gender in medical encounters: An analysis of physician and patient communication in a primary care setting. *Health Psychology, 13,* 384–392.

Hall, J. A., Roter, D. L., & Katz, N. R. (1986). Meta-analysis of correlates of provider behavior in medical encounters. *Medical Care, 26,* 657–675.

Hamad, C. D., Bettinger, R., Cooper, D., & Semb, G. (1980–1981). Using behavioral procedures to establish an elementary school paper recycling program. *Journal of Environmental Systems, 10,* 149–156.

Hans, V. P., & Vidmar, N. (1986). *Judging the jury.* New York: Plenum Press.

Hardin, G. (1968). The tragedy of the commons. *Science, 162,* 1243–1248.

Hardin, G. (1993). *Living within limits: Ecology, economics, and population taboos.* New York: Oxford University Press.

Hardy, K. R. (1957). Determinants of conformity and attitude change. *Journal of Abnormal and Social Psychology, 54,* 289–294.

Harms, T., & Clifford, R. (1980). *The Early Childhood Environmental Rating Scale.* New York: Teachers College Press.

Harootyan, R. (1988). Improving environmental design technologies for the elderly. *American Behavioral Scientist, 31,* 607–613.

Harris, M., & Rosenthal, R. (1985). Mediation of the interpersonal expectancy effect: 31 meta-analyses. *Psychological Bulletin, 97,* 363–386.

Harrison, J. (1978). Warning: The male sex role may be dangerous to your health. *Journal of Social Issues, 34*(1), 65–86.

Harrison, L. F., & Williams, T. M. (1986). Television and cognitive development. In T. M. Williams (Ed.), *The impact of television: A natural experiment in three communities.* New York: Academic Press.

Harvey, M. G., & Rothe, J. T. (1985). Video cassette recorders: Their impact on viewers and advertisers. *Journal of Advertising Research, 25*(10), 19.

Haslett, B. J., Geis, F. L., & Carter, M. R. (1993). *The organizational woman: Power and paradox.* Norwood, NJ: Ablex.

Haugtvedt, C., Petty, R. E., Cacioppo, J. T., & Steidley, T. (1988). Personality and ad effectiveness: Exploring the utility of need for cognition. *Advances in Consumer Research, 15,* 209–212.

Hawkins, J. W., & Aber, C. S. (1993). Women in advertisements in medical journals. *Sex Roles, 28,* 233–242.

Haynes, S. G., & Feinleib, M. (1980). Women, work and coronary heart disease: Prospective findings from the Framington Study. *American Journal of Public Health, 70,* 133–141.

Hays, R. D., & DiMatteo, M. R. (1987). Key issue and suggestions for patient compliance assessment: Sources of information, focus of measures and nature of response options. *Journal of Compliance in Health Care, 2,* 37–53.

Heath, L., Tindale, R. S., Edwards, J., Posavac, E. J., Bryant, F. B., Henderson-King, E., Suarez-Balcazar, Y., & Myers, J. (Eds.). (1994). *Applications of heuristics and biases to social issues.* New York: Plenum.

Heath, T. B., McCarthy, M. S., & Mothersbaugh, D. L. (1994). Spokesperson fame and vividness effects in the context of issue-relevant thinking: The moderating role of competitive setting. *Journal of Consumer Research, 20,* 520–534.

Heikes, E. J. (1991). When men are in the minority: The case of men in nursing. *Sociological Quarterly, 32,* 389–401.

Heilman, M. E., Block, C. J., & Lucas, J. A. (1992). Presumed incompetent? Stigmatization and affirmative action efforts. *Journal of Applied Psychology, 77,* 536–544.

Heilman, M. E., Block, C. J., Martell, R. F., & Simon, M. C. (1989). Has anything changed? Current characterizations of men, women and managers. *Journal of Applied of Psychology, 74,* 935–942.

Heilman, M. E., & Herlihy, J. M. (1984). Affirmative action, negative reaction? Some moderating conditions. *Organizational Behavior and Human Performance, 33,* 204–213.

Heilman, M. E., Hornstein, H. A., Cage, J. H., & Herschlag, J. K. (1984). Reactions to prescribed leader behavior as a function of role perspective: The case of the Vroom-Yetton model. *Journal of Applied Psychology, 69,* 50–60.

Heilman, M. E., Martell, R. F., & Simon, M. C. (1988). The vagaries of sex bias: Conditions regulating the undervaluation, equivaluation, and overvaluation of female job applicants. *Organizational Behavior and Human Decision Porcesses, 41,* 98–110.

Heilman, M. E., Simon, M. C., & Repper, D. P. (1987). Intentionally favored, intentionally harmed? Impact of sex-based preferential selection on self-perceptions and self-evaluations. *Journal of Applied Psychology, 72,* 62–68.

Hernandez, D. J. (1993). *America's children: Resources from government, family, and the economy.* New York: Russell Sage Foundation.

Hersey, P., & Blanchard, K. H. (1974). So you want to know your leadership style? *Training and Development Journal, 28,* 22–37.

Hersey, P., & Blanchard, K. H. (1993). *Management of organizational behavior* (6th ed.). Englewood Cliffs, NJ: Prentice Hall.

Hester, R. K., & Smith, R. E. (1973). Effects of a mandatory death penalty on the decisions of simulated jurors as a function of heinousness of the crime. *Journal of Criminal Justice, 1,* 319–326.

Hickey, T., Hickey, L., & Kalish, R. A. (1968). Children's perceptions of the elderly. *Journal of Genetic Psychology, 112,* 227–235.

Hill, E., & Pfeifer, J. E. (1992). Nullification instructions and juror guilt ratings: An examination of modern racism. *Contemporary Social Psychology, 16,* 6–10.

Hill, R. P. (Ed.). (1995). *Marketing and consumer behavior research in the public interest.* Thousand Oaks, CA: Sage.

Hilsman, R., & Garber, J. (1995). A test of the cognitive diathesis-stress model of depression in children: Academic stressors, attributional style, perceived competence, and control. *Journal of Personality and Social Psychology, 69,* 370–380.

Himmelweit, H. T., Oppenheim, A. N., & Vince, P. (1958). *Television and the child: An empirical study of the effect of television on the young.* London: Oxford University Press.

Hirshman, E. C. (1986). Humanistic inquiry in marketing research: Philosophy, method and criteria. *Journal of Marketing Research, 23,* 237–249.

Hite, S. (1976). *The Hite report: A nationwide study of female sexuality.* New York: Macmillan.

Hoffman, C., & Hurst, N. (1990). Gender stereotypes: Perception or rationalization? *Journal of Personality and Social Psychology, 58,* 197–208.

Hogan, R., Curphy, G. J., & Hogan, J. (1994). What we know about leadership: Effectiveness and personality. *American Psychologist, 49,* 493–504.

Holahan, C. J. (1982). *Environmental psychology.* New York: Random House.

Holbrook, M. B., & O'Shaughnessy, J. (1988). On the scientific status of consumer research and the need for an interpretive approach to studying consumption behavior. *Journal of Consumer Research, 15,* 389–402.

Hollander, E. P. (1993). Legitimacy, power, and influence: A perspective on relational features of leadership. In M. M. Chemers & R. Ayman (Eds.), *Leadership theory and research: Perspectives and directions.* New York: Academic Press.

Hollien, H. (1990). The expert witness: Ethics and responsibilities. *Journal of Forensic Sciences, 35,* 1414–1423.

Holmes, T. H., & Rahe, R. H. (1967). The social readjustment rating scale. *Journal of Psychosomatic Research, 11,* 213–218.

Hopper, J. R., & Nielson, J. M. (1991). Recycling as altruistic behavior: Normative and behavioral strategies to expand participation in a community recycling program. *Environment and Behavior, 23,* 195–220.

Horowitz, I. A. (1988). Jury nullification: The impact of judicial instructions, arguments, and challenges on jury decision making. *Law and Human Behavior, 12,* 439–453.

Hoschild, A. (1989). *The second shift.* New York: Avon.

House, R. J. (1971). A path goal theory of leader effectiveness. *Administrative Science Quarterly, 16,* 321–338.

House, R. J., & Mitchell, T. R. (1974). Path-goal theory of leadership. *Journal of Contemporary Business, 3,* 81–97.

House, R. J., & Shamir, B. (1993). Toward the integration of transformational, charismatic, and visionary theories. In M. M. Chemers & R. Ayman (Eds.), *Leadership theory and research: Perspectives and directions.* New York: Academic Press.

Hovland, C. I., Janis, I. L., & Kelley, H. H. (1953). *Communication and persuasion*. New Haven, CT: Yale University Press.

Hugick, L. (1991, August). American unhappiness with health care contrasts with Canadian contentment. *Gallup Poll Monthly*, No. 311, pp. 2–3.

Hunter, W. S. (1946). Psychology in the war. *American Psychologist, 1*, 479–492.

Ibarra, H. (1993). Personal networks of women and minorities in management: A conceptual framework. *Academy of Management Review, 18*, 56–87.

Idler, E. L., & Kasl, S. V. (1991). Health perceptions and survival: Do global evaluations of health status really predict mortality? *Journal of Gerontology, 46*, S55–S65.

Inbau, F. E., Reid, J. E., & Buckley, J. P. (1986). *Criminal interrogation and confessions* (3rd ed.). London: Williams and Wilkins.

Indvik, J. (1986). Path-goal theory of leadership: A meta-analysis. *Proceedings, Academy of Management*, Chicago, 189–192.

Institute of Judicial Administration. (1972). *A comparison of six- and twelve-member juries in New Jersey Superior and County courts*. New York: Author.

Institute of Medicine. (1994). *Veterans and Agent Orange: Health effects of herbicides used in Vietnam*. Washington, DC: National Academy Press.

Inui, T. S., Yourtee, E. L., & Williamson, J. W. (1976). Improved outcomes in hypertension after physician tutorials: A controlled trial. *Annals of Internal Medicine, 84*, 646–651.

Irving, B., & Hilgendorf, L. (1980). Police interrogation: The psychological approach. *Royal Commission on Criminal Procedure Research, Study No. 1*. London: HMSO.

Isaacs, L. W., & Bearison, D. J. (1986). The development of children's prejudice against the aged. *International Journal of Aging and Human Development, 23*, 175–194.

Jackson, L. A., & Grabski, S. V. (1988). Perceptions of fair play and the gender wage gap. *Journal of Applied Social Psychology, 18*, 606–625.

Jacobs, H. E., & Bailey, J. S. (1982–1983). Evaluating participation in a residential recycling program. *Journal of Environmental Systems, 12*, 141–152.

Jacobs, H. E., Bailey, J. S., & Crews, J. I. (1984). Development and analysis of a community-based resource recovery program. *Journal of Applied Behavior Analysis, 17*, 127–145.

Jacobson, N. S., McDonald, D. W., & Follette, W. C. (1982). Reactivity to positive and negative behavior in distressed and non-distressed married couples. *Journal of Consulting and Clinical Psychology, 50*, 706–714.

Jacoby, J., & Hoyer, W. D. (1982). Viewer miscomprehension of televised communication: Selected findings. *Journal of Marketing, 46*(Fall), 12–26.

Jacoby, J., & Hoyer, W. D. (1987). *The comprehension and miscomprehension of print communications: An investigation of mass media magazines*. Hillsdale, NJ: Erlbaum.

Jago, A. G., & Vroom, V. H. (1982). Sex differences in the incidence and evaluation of participative leader behavior. *Journal of Applied Psychology, 67*, 776–783.

Janis, I. L. (1958). *Psychological stress*. New York: Wiley.

Janis, I. L. (1982). *Groupthink: Psychological studies of policy decisions and fiascoes* (2nd ed.). Boston: Houghton Mifflin.

Janis, I. L., Hovland, C. I., Field, P. B., Linton, H., Graham, E., Cohen, A. R., Rife, D., Abelson, R. P., Lesser, G. S., & King, B. T. (1959). *Personality and persuasibility*. New Haven, CT: Yale University Press.

Jenkins, J. H., & Karno, M. (1992). The meaning of repressed emotion: Theoretical issues raised by cross-cultural research. *American Journal of Psychiatry, 149*, 184–188.

Johnson, G. B. (1941, Sept.). The Negro and crime. *Annals of the American Academy of Political and Social Science*, pp. 93–106.

Johnson, D. W., & Johnson, R. T. (1989). *Cooperation and competition: Theory and research*. Edina, MN: Interaction Book Company.

Johnson, D. W., & Johnson, R. T. (1992). *Creative controversy: Intellectual challenge in the classroom*. Edina, MN: Interaction Book Company.

Johnson, D. W., & Johnson, R. T. (1994). Constructive conflict in the schools. *Journal of Social Issues, 50*(1), 117–138.

Johnson, D. W., Johnson, R., Dudley, B., & Acikgoz, K. (1994). Effects of conflict resolution training on elementary school students. *Journal of Social Psychology, 134*, 803–817.

Jones, D. P. H., & Krugman, R. D. (1986). Can a three-year-old bear witness to her sexual assault and attempted murder? *Child Abuse and Neglect, 10*, 253–258.

Jones, E. E., & Nisbett, R. E. (1971). The actor and the observer: Divergent perceptions of the causes of behavior. In E. E. Jones, D. E. Kanouse, H. H. Kelley, R. E. Nisbett, S. Valins, & B. Weiner (Eds.), *Attribution: Perceiving the causes of behavior.* Morristown, NJ: General Learning Press.

Josephson, W. L. (1987). Television violence and children's aggression: Testing the priming, social script, and disinhibition predictions. *Journal of Personality and Social Psychology, 53,* 882–890.

Jowett, B. (1943). *Aristotle's politics* (translation). New York: Random House.

Kagitcibasi, C., & Berry, J. W. (1989). Cross-cultural psychology: Current research and trends. *Annual Review of Psychology, 40,* 493–531.

Kalton, G. (1983). *Introduction to survey sampling.* Beverly Hills: Sage.

Kalven, H., & Zeisel, H. (1966). *The American jury.* Chicago: University of Chicago Press.

Kandrack, M., Grant, K. R., & Segall, A. (1991). Gender differences in health related behaviour: Some unanswered questions. *Social Science and Medicine, 32,* 579–590.

Kaplan, B. M. (1985). Zapping . . . The real issue is communication. *Journal of Advertising Research, 25*(2), 9–12.

Kaplan, R. M. (1991). Health-related quality of life in patient decision-making. *Journal of Social Issues, 47*(4), 69–90.

Kaplan, R. M., & Simon, H. J. (1990). Compliance in medical care: Reconsiderations of self-predictions. *Annals of Behavioral Medicine, 12*(2), 66–71.

Kaplan, R. M., & Toshima, M. T. (1990). Social relationships in chronic disease and disability. In I. G. Sarason, B. R. Sarason, & G. R. Pierce (Eds.), *Social support. An interactionist perspective* (pp. 267–295). New York: Wiley.

Kapp, M. B. (1993). Life-sustaining technologies: Value issues. *Journal of Social Issues, 49*(2), 151–167.

Karlins, M., & Hargis, E. (1988). Inaccurate self-perception as a limiting factor in managerial effectiveness. *Perceptual and Motor Skills, 66,* 665–666.

Kassin, S. M., & McNall, K. (1991). Police interrogations and confessions: Communicating promises and threats by pragmatic implication. *Law and Human Behavior, 15,* 233–251.

Kassin, S. M., & Wrightsman, L. S. (1979). On the requirements of proof: The timing of judicial instructions and mock juror verdicts. *Journal of Personality and Social Psychology, 37,* 1877–1887.

Kassin, S. M., & Wrightsman, L. S. (1985). Confession evidence. In S. M. Kassin & L. S. Wrightsman (Eds.), *The psychology of evidence and trial procedure.* London: Sage.

Kassin, S. M., & Wrightsman, L. S. (1988). *The American jury on trial: Psychological perspectives.* New York: Hemisphere Publishing.

Katz, N. H., & Lawyer, J. W. (1983). Communication and conflict management skills strategies for individual and systems change. *National Forum: The Phi Kappa Phi Journal, 63*(4), 31–35.

Katzev, R. D., & Johnson, T. R. (1987). *Promoting energy conservation: An analysis of behavioral research.* Boulder, CO: Westview.

Katzev, R. D., & Mishima, H. R. (1992). The use of posted feedback to promote recycling. *Psychological Reports, 71,* 259–264.

Kazdin, A. E. (1994). *Behavior modification in applied settings* (5th ed.). Pacific Grove, CA: Brooks/Cole Publishing Company.

Keashly, L. (1994). Gender and conflict: What can psychology tell us? In A. Taylor & J. B. Miller (Eds.), *Gender and conflict* (pp. 167–190). Cresskill, NJ: Hampton Press.

Keashly, L., & Fisher, R. J. (1990). Towards a contingency approach to third party intervention in regional conflict: A Cyprus illustration. *International Journal, 45,* 424–453.

Keashly, L., & Fisher, R. J. (1996). A contingency perspective on conflict intervention: Theoretical and practical considerations. In J. Bercovitch (Ed.), *Resolving international conflict.* Boulder, CO: Lynne Rienner Publishers.

Keith, T. Z., Reimers, T. M., Fehrmann, P. G., Pottebaum, S. M., & Aubey, L. W. (1986). Parental involvement, homework, and TV time: Direct and indirect effects on high school achievement. *Journal of Educational Psychology, 78,* 373–380.

Keller, K. L. (1991). Memory and evaluation effects in competitive advertising environments. *Journal of Consumer Research, 17*(1), 463–476.

Kelley, H. H. (1979). *Personal relationships: Their structures and processes.* Hillsdale, NJ: Erlbaum.

Kelley, H. H., Berscheid, E., Christensen, A., Harvey, J., Huston, T. L., Levinger, G., McClintock, E., Peplau, A., & Peterson, D. R. (1983). *Close relationships.* San Francisco: Freeman.

Kelman, H. C. (1972). The problem-solving workshop in conflict resolution. In R. L. Merritt (Ed.), *Communication in international politics* (pp. 168–204). Urbana: University of Illinois Press.

Kelman, H. C. (1979). An interactional approach to conflict resolution and its application to Israeli-Palestinian relations. *International Interactions, 6,* 99–122.

Kelman, H. C. (1992). Informal mediation by the scholar/practitioner. In J. Bercovitch & J. Rubin (Eds.), *Mediation in international relations: Multiple approaches to conflict management* (pp. 64–96). New York: St. Martin's Press.

Kelman, H. C. (1993). Coalitions across conflict lines: The interplay of conflicts within and between Israeli and Palestinian communities. In S. Worchel & J. A. Simpson (Eds.), *Conflict between people and groups: Causes, processes, and resolutions* (pp. 236–232). Chicago: Nelson-Hall Publishers.

Kelman, H. C. (1995). Contributions of an unofficial conflict resolution effort to the Israeli-Palestinian breakthrough. *Negotiation Journal, 11,* 33–41.

Kent, D. (1995). Psychology careers outside the academic realm. *APS Observer, 8*(6), 11, 22–23.

Kent, R. J. (1993). Competitive versus noncompetitive clutter in television advertising. *Journal of Advertising Research, 33*(2), 40–46.

Kenyon, G. M. (1992). Why is ageism a serious social problem and what can be done about it? *Canadian Journal on Aging, 11,* 2–5.

Kessler, J. B. (1973). An empirical study of six-member and twelve-member jury decision-making processes. *University of Michigan Journal of Law Reform, 6,* 712–734.

Kidd, R. F., & Saks, M. J. (1980). What is applied social psychology? An introduction. In R. F. Kidd & M. J. Saks (Eds.), *Advances in applied social psychology* (Vol. 1, pp. 1–24). Hillsdale, NJ: Lawrence Erlbaum Associates.

Kiecolt-Glaser, J. K., & Glaser, R. (1990). Behavioral influences on immune function: Evidence for the interplay between stress and health. In T. Field, P. McCade, & A. Schneiderman (Eds.), *Stress and coping* (Vol. 2, pp. 189–206). Hillsdale, NJ: Lawrence Erlbaum Associates.

Kiecolt-Glaser, J. K., & Glaser, R. (1991). Psychosocial factors, stress, disease and immunity. In R. Ader, D. L. Felton, & N. Cohen (Eds.), *Psychoimmunology* (pp. 231–254). San Diego, CA: Academic Press.

Kiesler, S., Siegel, J., & McGuire, T. W. (1984). Social psychological aspects of computer-mediated communication. *American Psychologist, 39,* 1123–1134.

Kim, S. H., & Smith, R. H. (1993). Revenge and conflict escalation. *Negotiation Journal, 9,* 37–43.

Kimball, M. M. (1986). Television and sex-role attitudes. In T. M. Williams (Ed.), *The impact of television: A natural experiment in three communities.* New York: Academic Press.

Kimmel, D. C. (1988). Ageism, psychology, and public policy. *American Psychologist, 43,* 175–178.

King, K. B., Reis, H. T., Porter, L. A., & Norsen, L. H. (1993). Social support and long-term recovery from coronary artery surgery: Effects on patients and spouses. *Health Psychology, 12,* 56–63.

King, M. (1987). When you can't experiment. [Review of *Principles and methods of social research.*] *Contemporary Psychology, 32,* 565–566.

King, M., Atkinson, T., & Murray, M. (1982). Background, personality, job characteristics and satisfaction with work in a national sample. *Human Relations, 35,* 119–247.

King, M., & Sobel, D. (1975). Sex on the college campus: Current attitudes and behavior. *Journal of College Student Personnel, 16,* 205–209.

King, M. A., & Yuille, J. C. (1987). Suggestibility and the child witness. In S. J. Ceci, M. P. Toglia, & D. F. Ross (Eds.), *Children's eyewitness testimony.* New York: Springer-Verlag.

Kinsey, A. C. and staff of the Institute for Sex Research, Indiana University (1953). *Sexual behavior in the human female.* Philadelphia: W. B. Saunders.

Kinsey, A. C., Pomeroy, W. B., & Martin, C. E. (1948). *Sexual behavior in the human male.* Philadelphia: W. B. Saunders.

Kipnis, D. (1994). Accounting for the use of behavior technologies in social psychology. *American Psychologist, 49,* 165–172.

Kite, M., & Johnson, B. (1988). Attitudes toward older and younger adults: A meta-analysis. *Psychology and Aging, 3,* 233–244.

Klein, K., & Creech, B. (1982). Race, rape, and bias: Distortion of prior odds and meaning changes. *Basic and Applied Social Psychology, 3,* 21–33.

Kolb, D. M. (1989). Labor mediators, managers, and ombudsmen: Roles mediators play in different contexts. In K. Kressel, D. G. Pruitt, & associates, *Mediation research* (pp. 91–114). San Francisco: Jossey-Bass.

Kolb, D. M., & Bartunek, J. (1992). *Hidden conflict in organizations.* Beverly Hills, CA: Sage.

Konecni, V. J., & Ebbesen, E. B. (1986). Courtroom testimony by psychologists on eyewitness identification issues. *Law and Human Behavior, 10,* 117–126.

Konner, M. (1987). *Becoming a doctor: A journey of initiation in medical school.* New York: Penguin Books.

Korabik, K. (1982). Sex-role orientation and impressions: A comparison of differing genders and sex roles. *Personality and Social Psychology Bulletin, 8,* 25–30.

Korabik, K. (1990). Androgyny and leadership style. *Journal of Business Ethics, 9,* 9–18.

Korabik, K. (1993, May). Strangers in a strange land: Women managers and the legitimization of authority. *SWAP Newsletter, 17,* 26–34.

Korabik, K., Baril, G. L., & Watson, C. (1993). Managers' conflict management style and leadership effectiveness: The moderating effects of gender. *Sex Roles, 29,* 407–422.

Korabik, K., McDonald, L. M., & Rosin, H. M. (1993). Stress, coping, and social support among women managers. In B. C. Long & S. Kahn (Eds.), *Women, work, and coping: A multidisciplinary approach to workplace stress* (pp. 133–153). Montreal: McGill-Queens University Press.

Korman, A. K. (1966). "Consideration," "initiating structure," and organizational criteria. *Personnel Administration, 18,* 349–360.

Kortenhaus, C. M., & Demarest, J. (1993). Gender role stereotyping in children's literature: An update. *Sex Roles, 28,* 219–232.

Krantz, M. J., & Johnson, L. (1978). Family members' perceptions of communications in late-stage cancer. *International Journal of Psychiatry in Medicine, 8,* 203–216.

Kraut, R. E. (1980). Humans as lie detectors: Some second thoughts. *Journal of Communication, 30,* 209–216.

Kressel, K., & Pruitt, D. G. (Eds.). (1989). *Mediation research: The process and effectiveness of third-party intervention.* San Francisco: Jossey-Bass.

Kressel, K., Pruitt, D. G., & Associates (1989). *Mediation research.* San Francisco: Jossey-Bass.

Kulik, J. A., & Mahler, H. I. M. (1989). Social support and recovery from surgery. *Health Psychology, 8,* 221–238.

Kwock, M. S., & Winer, G. A. (1986). Overcoming leading questions: Effects of psychosocial task variables. *Journal of Educational Psychology, 78,* 289–293.

Landy, F., & Farr, J. (1980). Performance rating. *Psychological Bulletin, 87,* 72–107.

Langer, E. J., & Rodin, J. (1976). The effects of choice and enhanced personal responsibility for the aged: A field experiment in an institutional setting. *Journal of Personality and Social Psychology, 34,* 191–198.

Lasswell, H. D. (1948). The structure and function of communication in society. In L. Bryson (Ed.), *The communication of ideas: Religion and civilization series* (pp. 37–51). New York: Harper & Row.

Laudan, L. (1983). The demise of the demarcation problem. In R. Laudan (Ed.), *The demarcation between science and pseudo-science* (Vol. 2.). Blacksburg, VA: Center for the Study of Science in Society, Virginia Polytechnic Institute.

Laumann, E. O., Gagnon, J. H., Michael, R. T., & Michaels, S. (1994). *The social organization of sexuality: Sexual practices in the United States.* Chicago: University of Chicago Press.

Lawton, M. P. (1980). *Environment and aging.* Monterey, CA: Brooks/Cole.

Lawton, M. P. (1990). Residential environment and self-directedness among older people. *American Psychologist, 45,* 638–640.

Leape, L. L. (1994). Errors in medicine. *Journal of the American Medical Association, 272,* 1851–1857.

Lee, G. R., Seccombe, K., & Shehan, C. L. (1991). Marital status and personal happiness: An analysis of trend data. *Journal of Personality and Social Psychology, 53,* 839–844.

Lefkowitz, M. M., Eron, L. D., Walder, L. O., & Huesmann, L. R. (1972). Television violence and child aggression: A follow-up study. In G. A. Comstock & E. A. Rubenstein (Eds.), *Television and social behavior* (Vol. 3: *Television and adolescent aggressiveness*). Washington, DC: United States Government Printing Press.

Lehman, D. R. (Ed.). (1993). Psychological research on the Persian Gulf War [Special issue]. *Journal of Social Issues, 49*(4).

Leigh, B. C., Temple, M. T., & Trocki, K. F. (1993). The sexual behavior of U.S. adults: Results from a national survey. *American Journal of Public Health, 83,* 1400–1408.

Lenssen, N. (1993). Providing energy in developing countries. In L. R. Brown et al., *State of the world 1993* (pp. 101–119). New York: Norton.

Leung, K. (1987). Some determinants of reactions to procedural models of conflict resolution: A cross-national study. *Journal of Personality and Social Psychology, 53,* 898–908.

Leung, K. (1988). Some determinants of conflict avoidance. *Journal of Cross-Cultural Psychology, 19*(1), 125–136.

Leung, K., & Bond, M. H. (1984). The impact of cultural collectivism on reward allocation. *Journal of Personality and Social Psychology, 43,* 793–804.

Levin, H. M. (1975). Cost-effectiveness analysis in evaluation research. In M. Guttentag & E. L. Struening (Eds.), *Handbook of evaluation research* (Vol. 2, pp. 89–122). Beverly Hills, CA: Sage.

Levin, J., & Levin, W. C. (1980). *Ageism: Prejudice and discrimination against the elderly.* Belmont, CA: Wadsworth.

Levitt, L., & Leventhal, G. (1986). Litter reduction: How effective is the New York State bottle bill? *Environment and Behavior, 18,* 467–479.

Levy, B., & Langer, E. (1994). Aging free from negative stereotypes: Successful memory in China and among the American Deaf. *Journal of Personality and Social Psychology, 66,* 989–997.

Lewicki, R. J., Weiss, S. E., & Lewin, D. (1992). Models of conflict, negotiation, and third party intervention: A review and synthesis. *Journal of Organizational Behavior, 13,* 209–252.

Lewin, K. (1944). *Field theory in social science.* New York: Harper.

Lewin, K. (1946). Action research and minority problems. *Journal of Social Issues, 2,* 34–46.

Lewin, K. (1948). *Resolving social conflicts.* New York: Harper.

Lewin, K. (1958). Group decision and social change. In E. Maccoby, T. Newcomb, & E. Hartley (Eds.), *Readings in social psychology* (3rd ed., pp. 197–211). New York: Holt, Rinehart and Winston.

Lewin, K., Lippitt, R., & White, R. K. (1939). Patterns of aggressive behavior in experimentally created social climates. *Journal of Social Psychology, 10,* 271–301.

Lewis, C. E., Lewis, M. A., Lorimer, A., & Palmer, B. B. (1977). Child-initiated care: The use of school nursing services in an "adult-free"system. *Pediatrics, 60,* 499–507.

Ley, R. (1991). The efficacy of breathing retraining and the centrality of hyperventilation in panic disorder: A reinterpretation of experimental findings. *Behavior Research and Therapy, 29,* 301–304.

Liang, M. I. (1989). Compliance and quality of life: Confessions of a difficult patient. *Arthritis Care and Research, 2,* 571–574.

Lief, A. (1930). *The social and economic views of Mr. Justice Brandeis.* New York: Vanguard Press.

Lincoln, Y. S., & Guba, E. G. (1985). *Naturalistic inquiry.* Newbury Park, CA: Sage.

Lind, A., Eriksen, B., & O'Barr, W. (1978). Social attribution and conversation style in trial testimony. *Journal of Personality and Social Psychology, 36,* 1558–1567.

Lindskold, S. (1978). Trust development, the GRIT proposal, and the effects of conciliatory acts on conflict and cooperation. *Psychological Bulletin, 85,* 772–793.

Lindsley, O. R. (1964). Geriatric behavioral prosthetics. In R. Kastenbaum (Ed.), *New thoughts on old age* (pp. 41–60). New York: Springer.

Lipton, J. A., & Marbach, J. J. (1984). Ethnicity and the pain experience. *Social Science and Medicine, 19,* 1279–1298.

Lippitt, R., & White, R. K. (1943). The social climate of children's groups. In R. G. Barker, J. Kounin, & H. Wright (Eds.), *Child behavior and development* (pp. 485–508). New York: McGraw-Hill.

Lockhart v. McCree, 476 U.S. 162, 106 S.Ct. 1758, 90 L.Ed.2d 137 (1986).

Loftus, E. F. (1993). The reality of repressed memories. *American Psychologist, 48,* 518–537.

Loftus, E. F., & Palmer, J. C. (1974). Reconstruction of automobile destruction. *Journal of Verbal Learning and Verbal Behavior, 13,* 585–589.

Lollis, S., & Ross, H. (1988, May). *Rules for sibling interaction: Parents' beliefs and practices.* Paper presented at the University of Waterloo Conference on Child Development, Waterloo, Ontario.

Loomis, J., & King, M. (1994) Comparison of mail and telephone-mail contingent valuation surveys. *Journal of Environmental Management, 41,* 309–324.

Lord, R. G., Binnings, J. F., Rush, M. C., & Thomas, J. C. (1978). The effect of performance cues and leader behavior on questionnaire rating of leadership behavior. *Organizational Behavior and Human Performance, 21,* 27–39.

Lord, R. G., DeVader, C. L., & Alliger, G. M. (1986). A meta-analysis of the relation between personality traits and leadership perceptions: An application of validity generalization procedures. *Journal of Applied Psychology, 71,* 402–410.

Lord, R. G., Foti, R. J., & DeVader, C. L. (1984). A test of leadership categorization theory: Internal structure, information processing, and leadership perceptions. *Organizational Behavior and Human Performance, 34,* 343–378.

Lord, R. G., & Maher, K. J. (1991). *Leadership and information processing: Linking perceptions and performance.* New York: HarperCollins.

Ludwig, D., Hilborn, R., & Walters, C. (1993, April 2). Uncertainty, resource exploitation, and conservation: Lessons from history. *Science, 260,* 17, 36.

Lutsky, N. S. (1980). Attitudes toward old age and elderly persons. In C. Eisdorfer (Ed.), *Annual Review of Gerontology and Geriatrics* (pp. 287–336). New York: Springer.

Luyben, P. D., & Bailey, J. S. (1979). Newspaper recycling: The effects of rewards and proximity of containers. *Environment and Behavior, 11,* 539–557.

Lynch, J., & Schuler, D. (1994). The matchup effect of spokesperson and product congruency: A schema theory interpretation. *Psychology and Marketing, 11,* 417–445.

Macer, D. R. J. (1994). Perception of risks and benefits of in vitro fertilization, genetic engineering and biotechnology. *Social Science and Medicine, 38,* 23–33.

MacLeish, A., & Prichard, E. F. (1939). *Law and politics: Occasional papers of Felix Frankfurter.* New York: Harcourt Brace.

Madden, M. E., & Janoff-Bulman, R. (1981). Blame, control and marital satisfaction: Wives' attributions for conflict in marriage. *Journal of Marriage and the Family, 43,* 663–674.

Maddox, G. (1990). *Inventing the future of aging.* Keynote address presented at the Canadian Association on Gerontology Conference, Victoria, British Columbia.

Maes, S., Spielberger, C. D., Defares, P. B., & Sarason, I. G. (Eds.). (1988). *Topics in health psychology.* New York: Wiley.

Males, M. (1992). Tobacco: promotion and smoking. *Journal of the American Medical Association, 267,* 3282.

Maloney, J. C. (1994). The first 90 years of advertising research. In E. M. Clark, T. C. Brock, & D. W. Stewart (Eds.), *Attention, attitude, and affect in response to advertising* (pp. 13–54). Hillsdale, NJ: Lawrence Erlbaum Associates.

Mandese, J. (1993, November 22). Glut of rival brands worsens ad clutter. *Advertising Age, 64*(49), 28.

Marin, B. V., Holmes, D. L., Guth, M., & Kovac, P. (1979). The potential of children as witnesses. *Law and Human Behavior, 3,* 295–306.

Marrow, A. S. (1969). *The practical theorist.* New York: Basic Books.

Marsella, A. J. (1980). Depressive experience across cultures. In H. C. Triandis, & J. C. Draguns (Eds.), *Handbook of cross-cultural psychology* (Vol. 6, pp. 237–289). Boston: Allyn & Bacon.

Martell, R. F., Lane, D. M., & Willis, C. E. (1992, August). *Demonstrating the danger of using "variance explained" to assess the practical significance of research findings: A little sex bias can hurt women a lot.* Paper presented at the annual meeting of the American Psychological Association, Washington, DC.

Martin, R., Davis, G. M., Baron, R. S., Suls, J., & Blanchard, E. B. (1994). Specificity in social support: Perceptions of helpful and unhelpful provider behaviors among irritable bowel syndrome, headache and cancer patients. *Health Psychology, 13,* 432–439.

Martín-Baro, I. (1990). Religion as an instrument of psychological warfare. *Journal of Social Issues, 46,* 93–107.

Matarazzo, J. D. (1980). Behavioral health and behavioral medicine: Frontiers for a new health psychology. *American Psychologist, 35,* 807–817.

Mayer, W. G. (1994). The polls-poll trends: The rise of the new media. *Public Opinion Quarterly, 58,* 124–146.

Mayo, C., & LaFrance, M. (1980). Towards an applicable social psychology. In R. F. Kidd & M. J. Saks (Eds.), *Advances in applied social psychology* (Vol. 1, pp. 81–96). Hillsdale, NJ: Lawrence Erlbaum Associates.

Mazzella, C., Durkin, K., Cerini, E., Buralli, P. (1992). Sex role stereotyping in Australian television advertisements. *Sex Roles, 26,* 243–259.

Mazzella, R., & Feingold, A. (1994). The effects of physical attractiveness, race, socioeconomic status, and gender of defendants and victims on judgments of mock jurors: A meta-analysis. *Journal of Applied Social Psychology, 24,* 1315–1344.

McAllister, M. P. (1996). *The commercialization of American culture: New advertising, control and democracy.* Thousand Oaks, CA: Sage.

McAndrew, F. T. (1993). *Environmental psychology.* Pacific Grove, CA: Brooks/Cole Publishing Company.

McCaul, K. D., & Kopp, J. T. (1982). Effects of goal-setting and commitment on increasing metal recycling. *Journal of Applied Psychology, 67,* 377–379.

McCauley, C., Thangavelu, K., & Rozin, P. (1988). Sex stereotyping of occupations in relation to television representations and census facts. *Basic and Applied Social Psychology, 9,* 197–212.

McClelland, D. C. (1975). *Power: The inner experience.* New York: Irvington Publishers.

McClelland, L., & Cooke, W. S. (1979–1980). Energy conservation effects of continuous in-home feedback in all-electric homes. *Journal of Environmental Systems, 9,* 169–173.

McCleskey v. Kemp, 481 U.S. 279, 107 S.Ct. 1756, 95 L.Ed.2d 262 (1987).

McConahay, J. B., Mullin, C. J., & Frederick, J. (1977). The uses of social science in trials with political and racial overtones: The trial of Joan Little. *Law and Contemporary Problems, 41,* 205–229.

McConkey, K. M. (1995). Hypnosis, memory and the ethics of uncertainty. *Australian Psychologist, 30,* 1–10.

McConnell, C. F., Dwyer, W. O., & Leeming, F. C. (in press). A behavioral approach to reducing fires in public housing. *Journal of Community Psychology.*

McConville, M., Sanders, A., & Leng, R. (1991). *The case for the prosecution: Police suspects and the construction of criminality.* London: Routledge.

McCracken, G. (1986). Culture and consumption: A theoretical account of the structure and movement of the cultural meaning of consumer goods. *Journal of Consumer Research, 13,* 71–84.

McCreary, D. R. (1994). The male role and avoiding femininity. *Sex Roles, 31,* 517–531.

McDevitt, T. M., & Carroll, M. (1988). Are you trying to trick me? Some social influences on children's responses to problematic messages. *Merrill-Palmer Quarterly, 34,* 131–145.

McGinniss, J. (1969). *The selling of the president.* New York: Trident Press.

McGuire, W. J. (1968). Personality and attitude change: An information processing theory. In A. G. Greenwald, T. C. Brock, & T. M. Ostrom (Eds.), *Psychological foundations of attitudes* (pp. 171–196). San Diego, CA: Academic Press.

McGuire, W. J. (1985). Attitudes and attitude change. In G. Lindzey & E. Aronson (Eds.), *Handbook of Social Psychology* (3rd ed., Vol. 2, pp. 233–346). New York: Random House.

McKenzie-Mohr, D., & Oskamp, S. (Eds.). (1995). Psychology and the promotion of a sustainable future [Special issue]. *Journal of Social Issues, 51*(4).

McKibbon, B. (1989). *The end of nature.* New York: Random House.

Meadows, D. H., Meadows, D. L., & Randers, J. (1992). *Beyond the limits.* Post Mills, VT: Chelsea Green.

Meltzer, L. (1972). *Applied, applicable, appealing, and appalling social psychology.* Unpublished manuscript, Cornell University.

Mercer, S., & Kane, R.A. (1979). Helplessness and hopelessness among the institutionalized aged: An experiment. *Health and Social Work, 4,* 91–116.

Merskey, H. (1978). Pain and personality. In R. A. Sternbach (Ed.), *The psychology of pain* (pp. 111–128). New York: Raven Press.

Metalsky, G., & Joiner, T. E., Jr. (1992). Vulnerability to depressive symptomatology: A prospective test of the diathesis-stress and causal mediation components of the hopelessness theory of depression. *Journal of Personality and Social Psychology, 63,* 667–675.

Michela, J. (1986). Interpersonal and individual impacts of a husband's heart attack. In A. Bauym & J. E. Singer (Eds.), *Handbook of psychology and health* (Vol. 5, pp. 255–301). Hillsdale, NJ: Lawrence Erlbaum Associates.

Midden, C. J., Meter, J. E., Weening, M. H., & Zieverink, H. J. (1983). Using feedback, reinforcement and information to reduce energy consumption in households: A field experiment. *Journal of Economic Psychology, 3,* 65–86.

Miller, G. A. (1969). Psychology as a means of promoting human welfare. *American Psychologist, 24,* 1063–1075.

Miller, G. T., Jr. (1993). *Environmental science: Sustaining the earth* (4th ed.). Belmont, CA: Wadsworth Publishing Company.

Miller, P. V. (1995). They said it couldn't be done: The national health and social life survey. *Public Opinion Quarterly, 59,* 404–419.

Mills, A., & Tancred, P. (Eds.) (1992). *Gendering organizational analysis.* Newbury Park, CA: Sage.

Mills, L. R. (1973). Six-member and twelve-member juries: An empirical study of trial results. *University of Michigan Journal of Law Reform, 6,* 671–711.

Milord, J. T. (1976). Human service needs assessment: Three non-epidemiological approaches. *Canadian Psychologist, 17,* 260–269.

Mishkind, M. E., Rodin, J., Silberstein, L. R., & Striegel-Moore, R. H. (1986). The embodiment of masculinity: Cultural, psychological, and behavioral dimensions. *American Behavioral Scientist, 29,* 545–562.

Mitchell, T. R. (1970). The construct validity of three dimensions of leadership research. *The Journal of Social Psychology, 80,* 89–94.

Mitchell, T. R., & Wood, R. E. (1980). Supervisor's responses to subordinate poor performance: A test of an attributional model. *Organizational Behavior and Human Performance, 25,* 123–138.

Mittal, B. (1994). Public assessment of TV advertising: Faint praise and harsh criticism. *Journal of Advertising Research, 34*(1), 35–53.

Mizerski, R. W. (1982). An attribution exploration of the disproportionate influence of unfavorable information. *Journal of Consumer Research, 9,* 301–310.

Monahan, J., & Walker, L. (1994). *Social science in law: Cases and materials* (3rd ed.). NY: Westbury, Foundation Press.

Monroe, S. M., & Steiner, S. C. (1986). Social support and psychopathology: Interactions with preexisting disorder, stress and personality. *Journal of Abnormal Psychology, 95,* 29–39.

Montepare, J. M., & Vega, C. (1988). Women's vocal reactions to intimate and casual male friends. *Personality and Social Psychology Bulletin, 14,* 103–113.

Moran, G., Cutler, B. L., & Loftus, E. F. (1990). Jury selection in major controlled substance trials: The need for extended voir dire. *Forensic Reports, 3,* 331–348.

Mord, M. S., & Gilson, E. (1985). Shorter units: Risk-responsibility-reward. *Journal of Advertising Research, 25*(4), 9–19.

Morgan, J., & Williams, J. (1993). A role for a support person for child witnesses in criminal proceedings. *British Journal of Social Work, 23,* 113–121.

Morgan, M. (1982). Television and children's sex role stereotypes: A longitudinal study. *Journal of Personality and Social Psychology, 43,* 947–955.

Morrison, A. M., & Von Glinow, M.A. (1990). Women and minorities in management. *American Psychologist, 45,* 200–208.

Morse, S. J. (1990). The misbegotten marriage of soft psychology and bad law: Psychological self-defense as a justification for homicide. *Law and Human Behavior, 14,* 595–618.

Moss, R. A. (1986). The role of learning history in current sick role behavior and assertion. *Behavior Research and Therapy, 24,* 681–683.

Moston, S. (1987). The suggestibility of children in interview studies. *First Language, 7,* 67–78.

Moston, S. (1992). Social support and children's eyewitness testimony. In R. Flin & H. Dent (Eds.), *Children as eyewitnesses.* Chichester, England: John Wiley.

Moston, S., & Engelberg, T. (1992). The effects of social support on children's eyewitness testimony. *Applied Cognitive Psychology, 6,* 61–75.

Moston, S., & Engelberg, T. (1993). Police questioning techniques in tape recorded interviews with criminal suspects. *Policing and Society, 3,* 223–237.

Moston, S., & Stephenson, G. M. (1993). The changing face of police interrogation. *Community and Applied Social Psychology, 3,* 101–115.

Moston, S., Stephenson, G. M., & Williamson, T. M. (1992). The effects of case characteristics on suspect behavior during police questioning. *British Journal of Criminology, 32,* 23–40.

Mullen, B., & Johnson, C. (1990). *The psychology of consumer behavior.* Hillsdale, NJ: Lawrence Erlbaum Associates.

Munsterberg, H. (1908). *On the witness stand: Essays on psychology and crime.* New York: Doubleday Page.

Murray, B. (1996). Psychology remains top college major. *APA Monitor, 27*(2), 1, 42.

Murray, J. P., & Kippax, S. (1978). Children's social behavior in three towns with differing television experience. *Journal of Communication, 28,* 19–29.

Mutz, D. C., Roberts, D. F., & van Vuuren, D. P. (1993). Reconsidering the displacement hypothesis. *Communication Research, 20,* 51–75.

National Center for Health Statistics. (1993). *Health United States 1992.* Hyattsville, MD: U.S. Public Health Service.

Nelson, C., & McLemore, T. (1988). *National Center for Health Statistics. The National Ambulatory Medical Care Survey: U.S. 1975–81 and 1985 trends. Vital and Health Statistics, series 13, no. 93, DHHS pub. no. (PHS) 88–1754.* Washington, DC: U.S. Government Printing Office.

Netemeyer, R. G., & Bearden, W. O. (1992). A comparative analysis of two models of behavioral intention. *Journal of the Academy of Marketing Science, 20*(1), 49–59.

Neuman, S. B. (1988). The displacement effect: Assessing the relation between television viewing and reading performance. *Reading Research Quarterly, 23,* 414–440.

Nevid, J. S., Rathus, S. A., & Greene, B. (1994). *Abnormal psychology in a changing world.* Englewood Cliffs, NJ: Prentice Hall.

Nevin, J. A. (1985). Behavior analysis, the nuclear arms race, and the peace movement. In S. Oskamp (Ed.), *International conflict and national public policy issues: Applied social psychology annual* (Vol. 6). Beverly Hills, CA: Sage.

New Jersey v. Cavallo, 88 N.J. 508, 443 A.2d 1020 (1982).

New York Times (1994, August 9). Educating elderly on AIDS, p. A8.

Nicassio, P. M., Wallston, K. A., Callahan, L. F., Herbert, M., & Pincus, T. (1985). The measurement of helplessness in rheumatoid arthritis: The development of the Arthritis Helplessness Index. *Journal of Rheumatology, 12,* 462–467.

Nieva, V. F., & Gutek, B. A. (1982). *Women and work: A psychological perspective.* New York: Praeger.

Norell, S. E. (1981). Accuracy of patient interviews and estimates by clinical staff determining medication compliance. *Social Science and Medicine, 15,* 57–61.

Norman, P., Collins, S., Conner, M., Martin, R., & Rance, J. (1995). Attributions, cognitions, and coping styles: Teleworkers' reactions to work-related problems. *Journal of Applied Social Psychology, 25,* 117–128.

O'Donnell, M. P., & Harris, J. S. (Eds.). (1994). *Health promotion in the workplace* (2nd ed.). Albany, NY: Delmar.

Ofshe, R. J. (1992). Inadvertent hypnosis during interrogation: False confession due to dissociative state: Mis-identified multiple personality and the satanic cult hypothesis. *International Journal of Clinical and Experimental Hypnosis, 40,* 125–156.

Ofshe, R. J., & Watters, E. (1993). Making monsters. *Society,* March/April, 4–16

Ogloff, J. R. P., & Vidmar, N. (1994). The impact of pretrial publicity on jurors: A study to compare the relative effects of television and print media in a child sex abuse case. *Law and Human Behavior, 18,* 507–525.

Oliver, R. L., & Bearden, W. O. (1985). Crossover effects in the theory of reasoned action: A moderating influence attempt. *Journal of Consumer Research, 12,* 324–340.

Olson, M. H., & Primps, S. B. (1984). Working at home with computers: Work and nonwork issues. *Journal of Social Issues, 40*(3), 97–112.

Olweus, D. (1991). Bully/victim problems among school children: Basic facts and effects of a school based intervention program. In D. Pepler & K. Rubin (Eds.), *The development and treatment of childhood aggression* (pp. 411–448). Oxford: Heinemann.

Orvis, B. R., Kelley, H. H., & Butler, D. (1976). Attributional conflict in young couples. In J. H. Harvey, W. J. Ickes, & R. E. Kidd (Eds.), *New directions in attribution research* (Vol. 1). Hillsdale, NJ: Lawrence Erlbaum Associates.

Osgood, C. E. (1962). *An alternative to war or surrender.* Urbana: University of Illinois Press.

Osgood, C. E. (1986). Graduated and reciprocated initiatives in tension-reduction: GRIT. In R. K. White (Ed.), *Psychology and the prevention of nuclear war* (pp. 194–207). New York: New York University Press.

Oskamp, S. (1965). Attitudes toward U.S. and Russian actions: A double standard. *Psychological Reports, 16,* 43–46.

Oskamp, S. (1984). *Applied social psychology.* Englewood Cliffs, NJ: Prentice Hall.

Oskamp, S. (1986). Applied social psychology to the year 2000 and beyond. *Contemporary Social Psychology, 12*(1), 14–20.

Oskamp, S. (Ed.). (1988). *Television as a social issue: Applied social psychology annual* (Vol. 8). Newbury Park, CA: Sage.

Oskamp, S. (1995). Applying social psychology to avoid ecological disaster. *Journal of Social Issues, 51*(4), 217–239.

Ouellette, J., & Wood, W. (1995). *Attitude and habit predict behavior: A theoretical analysis and meta-analytic synthesis.* Unpublished manuscript, Texas A&M University.

Palmore, E. B. (1977). Facts on aging: A short quiz. *Gerontologist, 17,* 315–320.

Palmore, E. B. (1981). The facts on aging quiz: Part two. *Gerontologist, 21,* 431–437.

Paludi, M. A., & Strayer, L. A. (1985). What's in an author's name: Differential evaluations of performance as a function of author's name. *Sex Roles, 12,* 353–361.

Pancer, S. M. (1989). "Up-front" evaluation. *Children's Mental Health, 2,* 9–11.

Pancer, S. M., & Cameron, G. (1995). Resident participation in the Better Beginnings, Better Futures Prevention Project: Part I—The impacts of involvement. *Canadian Journal of Community Mental Health, 13,* 197–211.

Pancer, S. M., McKenzie-Mohr, S., & Orr, S. (1995). *Evaluation of the Men's Treatment Program of the John Howard Society of Waterloo-Wellington.* Kitchener, Ontario: John Howard Society of Waterloo-Wellington.

Pancer, S. M., & Westhues, A. (1989). A developmental stage approach to program planning and evaluation. *Evaluation Review, 13,* 56–77.

Pardini, A. U., & Katzev, R. D. (1983–1984). The effect of strength of commitment on newspaper recycling. *Journal of Environmental Systems, 13,* 245–254.

Parker, E. B. (1963). The effects of television on public library circulation. *Public Opinion Quarterly, 27,* 578–589.

Parsons, T. (1951). *The social system.* Glencoe, IL: Free Press.

Pasley, K., & Ihinger-Tallman, M. (Eds.). (1987). *Remarriage and stepparenting: Current research and theory.* New York: Guilford.

Patton, M. Q. (1986). *Utilization-focused evaluation (*2nd ed.). Newbury Park, CA: Sage.

Patton, M. Q. (1990). *Qualitative evaluation and research methods.* Newbury Park, CA: Sage.

Pearlin, L. I., Meaghan, E. G., Lieberman, M. A., & Mullen, J. T. (1981). The stress process. *Journal of Health and Social Behavior, 22,* 337–356.

Pearson, J., & Thoennes, N. (1989). Divorce mediation: Reflections on a decade of research. In K. Kressel et al., *Mediation research.* San Francisco: Jossey-Bass.

Pendergrast, M. (1993). *For God, country, and Coca-Cola: The unauthorized history of the great American soft drink and the company that makes it.* New York: Charles Scribner's Sons.

Pennington, N., & Hastie, R. (1988). Explanation-based decision making: Effects of memory structure on judgment. *Journal of Experimental Psychology: Learning, Memory and Cognition, 14,* 521–533.

Pennsylvania v. Cohen, 489 Pa. 167, 413 a.2d 1066 (1980).

Penrod, S. D. (1990). Predictors of jury decision making in criminal and civil cases: A field experiment. *Forensic Reports, 3,* 261–277.

Peplau, L. A., Russell, D., & Heim, M. (1979). The experience of loneliness. In I. H. Frieze, D. Bar-Tal, & J. S. Carroll (Eds.), *New approaches to social problems: Applications of attribution theory.* San Francisco: Jossey-Bass.

Perdue, C. W., & Gurtman, M. B. (1990). Evidence for the automaticity of ageism. *Journal of Experimental Social Psychology, 26,* 199–216.

Perlman, D., & Rook, K. S. (1986). Social support, social deficits, and the family: Toward the enhancement of well-being. In S. Oskamp (Ed.), *Family processes and problems: Social psychological aspects: Applied social psychology annual* (Vol. 7). Beverly Hills, CA: Sage.

Perry, E. L., Davis-Blake, A., & Kulik, C. T. (1994). Explaining gender-based selection decisions: A synthesis of contextual and cognitive approaches. *Academy of Management Review, 19,* 786–820.

Peter, J. P. (1991). Philosophical tensions in consumer inquiry. In T. S. Robertson & H. H. Kassarjian (Eds.), *Handbook of consumer behavior.* Englewood Cliffs, NJ: Prentice Hall.

Peterson, D. A. (1987). *Career paths in the field of aging: Professional gerontology.* Lexington, MA: Lexington Books.

Peterson, D. R. (1983). Conflict. In H. H. Kelley et al. (Eds.), *Close relationships.* New York: W. H. Freeman.

Petty, R. E., & Cacioppo, J. T. (1984). Source factors and the elaboration likelihood model of persuasion. In T. Kinnear (Ed.), *Advances in consumer research* (Vol. 11, pp. 668–672). Ann Arbor, MI: Association for Consumer Research.

Petty, R. E., & Cacioppo, J. T. (1986). *Communication and persuasion: Central and peripheral routes to attitude change.* New York: Springer-Verlag.

Petty, R. E., Unnava, R. H., & Strathman, A. J. (1991). Theories of attitude change. In T. S. Robertson & H. H. Kassarjian (Eds.), *Handbook of consumer behavior.* Englewood Cliffs, NJ: Prentice Hall.

Pfeffer, J. (1981). *Power in organizations.* Boston: Pitman.

Pfeifer, J. E. (1990). Reviewing the empirical evidence on jury racism: Findings of discrimination or discriminatory findings? *Nebraska Law Review, 69*(1), 230–250.

Pfeifer, J. E. (1991). *Mock juror decision-making and modern racism: An examination of the role of task and target specificity on judgmental evaluations.* Dissertation: University of Nebraska, Lincoln.

Pfeifer, J. E., & Brigham, J. C. (1993). Psychologists and the law: Experiences of non-clinical forensic witnesses and consultants. *Ethics and Behavior, 3,* 329–343.

Pfeifer, J. E., Brigham, J. C., & Robinson, T. (in press). Euthanasia: Attitudes toward non-physician assisted death. *Journal of Social Issues, 52*(2).

Pfeifer, J. E., & Ogloff, J. R. P. (1988, June). *Prejudicial sentencing trends of simulated jurors in Canada.* Paper presented at the annual meeting of the Canadian Psychological Association, Montreal, Quebec.

Pfeifer, J. E., & Ogloff, J. R. P. (1991). Ambiguity and guilt determinations: A modern racism perspective. *Journal of Applied Social Psychology, 21,* 1713–1725.

Phillips, J. S., & Lord, R. G. (1981). Causal attributions and perceptions of leadership. *Organizational Behavior and Human Performance, 28,* 143–163.

Piaget, J. (1962). *Play, dreams and imitation in childhood.* New York: Norton.

Pierce, J. P., Gilpin, E., Burns, D. M., Whalen, E., Rosbrook, B., Shopland, D., & Johnson, M. (1991). Does tobacco advertising target young people to start smoking? *Journal of the American Medical Association, 266,* 3154–3158.

Pinkley, R. L., & Northcraft, G. B. (1990). *Cognitive interpretations of conflict: Implications for dispute processes and outcomes.* Unpublished manuscript, Southern Methodist University.

Platt, J. (1973). Social traps. *American Psychologist, 28,* 641–651.

Podsakoff, P. M., & Schreischeim, C. A. (1985). Field studies of French and Raven's bases of power: Critique, reanalysis and suggestions for future research. *Psychological Bulletin, 97,* 387–411.

Poole, D. A., & White, L. T. (1991). Effects of question repetition on the eyewitness testimony of children and adults. *Developmental Psychology, 27,* 975–986.

Poole, D. A., & White, L. T. (1993). Two years later: Effects of question repetition and retention interval on the eyewitness testimony of children and adults. *Developmental Psychology, 29,* 844–853.

Porter, B. E., Leeming, F. C., & Dwyer, W. O. (1995). Solid waste recovery: A review of behavioral programs to increase recycling. *Environment and Behavior, 27,* 122–152.

Porter, B. E., Leeming, F. C., Dwyer, W. O., & LeBaron, L. (1995, November). *The environmental team (E-Team): Evaluation changes the face of code enforcement.* Paper presented at the Evaluation '95 Conference, Vancouver, British Columbia, Canada.

Posavac, E. J., & Carey, R. G. (1992). *Program evaluation: Methods and case studies (*4th ed.). Englewood Cliffs, NJ: Prentice Hall.

Potter, W .J. (1987). Does television viewing hinder academic achievement among adolescents? *Human Communication Research, 14,* 27–46.

Potter, W. J. (1991). The linearity assumption in cultivation research. *Human Communication Research, 17,* 562–583.

Powell, G. N. (1993). *Women and men in management* (2nd ed.). Newbury Park, CA: Sage.

Price Waterhouse v. Hopkins, 109 S. Ct. 1775 (1989).

Pruitt, D. G., & Rubin, J. Z. (1986). *Social conflict.* New York: Random House.

Pryor, J. B., Reeder, G. D., & Vinacco, R. (1989). The instrumental and symbolic functions of attitudes towards persons with AIDS. *Journal of Applied Social Psychology 19,* 377–404.

Pyszczynski, T. A., & Greenberg, J. (1985). Depression and preference for self-focusing stimuli after success and failure. *Journal of Personality and Social Psychology, 49,* 1066–1075.

Pyszczynski, T. A., & Greenberg, J. (1987). Self-regulatory preservation and the depressive self-focusing style: A self-awareness theory of reactive depression. *Psychological Bulletin, 102,* 122–138.

Quanty, M. B. (1976). Aggression catharsis: Experimental investigations and implications. In R. C. Geen & E. C. O'Neal (Eds.), *Perspectives on aggression.* New York: Academic Press.

Rachlis, M., & Kushner, C. (1989). *Second opinion: What's wrong with Canada's health care system and how to fix it.* Toronto: Harper and Collins.

Ragins, B. R. (1995). Diversity, power, and mentorship in organizations: A cultural, structural, and behavioral perspective. In M. M. Chemers, S. Oskamp, & M. A. Costanzo (Eds.), *Diversity in organizations: New perspectives for a changing workplace.* Thousand Oaks, CA: Sage.

Ragins, B. R., & Cotton, J. L. (1991). Easier said than done: Gender differences in perceived barriers to gaining a mentor. *Academy of Management Journal, 34,* 939–951.

Ray, M. L., & Webb, P. H. (1986). Three prescriptions for clutter. *Journal of Advertising Research, 26*(1), 69–77.

Reed, J. (1965). Jury deliberations, voting and verdict trends. *Southwest Social Science Quarterly, 45,* 361–370.

Regnier, V., & Pynoos, J. (1992). Environmental intervention for cognitively impaired older persons. In J. E. Birren, R. B. Sloane, & G. D. Cohen (Eds.), *Handbook of mental health and aging (*2nd ed.). San Diego, CA: Academic Press.

Reid, D. W., & Ziegler, M. (1981). The Desired Control measure and adjustment among the elderly. In H. Lefcourt (Ed.), *Advances and innovations in locus of control research (*Vol. 2). London: Academic Press.

Reid, L. N., & Soley, L. C. (1983). Decorative models and the readership of magazine ads. *Journal of Advertising Research, 23*(2), 27–32.

Reiss, C. (1986, October 27). Fast-forward ads deliver. *Advertising Age, 2,* 3.

Renaud, M., Beauchemin, J., Lalonde, C., Poirer, H., & Berthiaume, S. (1980). Practice settings and prescribing profiles: The simulation of tension headaches to general practitioners working in different practice settings in the Montreal area. *American Journal of Public Health, 70,* 1068–1073.

Report of the National Advisory Commission on Civil Disorders. (1968). New York: Bantam.

Rhodes, N. (1995). *Social influence in the evaluation of women's fashions.* Unpublished manuscript, Texas A&M University.

Rhodes, N., & Wood, W. (1991). Self-esteem and intelligence affect influenceability: The mediating role of message reception. *Psychological Bulletin, 111,* 156–171.

Rice, R. E. (1984). *The new media: Communication, research, and technology.* Beverly Hills: Sage.

Rice, R. E., & Love, G. (1987). Electronic emotion: Socioemotional content in a computer-mediated communication network. *Communication Research, 14,* 85–108.

Richards, J. I. (1990). *Deceptive advertising: Behavioral study of a legal concept.* Hillsdale, NJ: Lawrence Erlbaum Associates.

Richins, M. L. (1983). Negative word-of-mouth by dissatisfied consumers: A pilot study. *Journal of Marketing, 47,* 68–78.

Ridgeway, C. L. (Ed.). (1992). *Gender, interaction, and inequality.* New York: Springer-Verlag.

Riley, J. W., Jr. & Riley, M. W. (1991). Social science and the ADEA. *Research on Aging, 13,* 458–462.

Rime, B. (1983). Nonverbal communication or nonverbal behavior? In W. Doise & S. Moscovici (Eds.), *Current issues in European social psychology* (Vol. 1, pp. 85–141). Cambridge: Cambridge University Press.

Ring, K. (1967). Experimental social psychology: Some sober questions about frivolous values. *Journal of Experimental Social Psychology, 3,* 113–123.

Ritchie, D., Price, V., & Roberts, D. F. (1987). Television, reading and reading achievement: A reappraisal. *Communication Research, 14,* 292–315.

Roberson, M. H. B. (1992). The meaning of compliance: Patient perspectives. *Qualitative Health Research, 2,* 7–26.

Robinson, J. P., Shaver, P. R., & Wrightsman, L. S. (1991). *Measures of personality and social psychology attitudes.* San Diego: Academic Press.

Rodin, J., & Ickovics, J. R. (1990). Women's health. Review and research agenda as we approach the 21st century. *American Psychologist, 45,* 1018–1034.

Rodin, J., & Langer, E. (1977). Long-term effects of a control-relevant intervention with the institutionalized aged. *Journal of Personality and Social Psychology, 35,* 897–902.

Rodin, J. & Langer, E. (1980). Aging labels: The decline of control and the fall of self-esteem. *Journal of Social Issues, 36,* 12–29.

Roehl, J. A., & Cook, R. F. (1985). Issues in mediation: Rhetoric and reality revisited. *Journal of Social Issues, 41,* 161–178.

Rollins, B. (1978). *First you cry.* Philadelphia: Lippincott.

Rook, D. W., & Gardner, M. P. (1993). In the mood: Impulse buying's affective antecedents. *Research in Consumer Behavior, 6,* 1–28.

Rosenbaum, E. E. (1988). *A taste of my own medicine: When the doctor is the patient.* New York: Random House.

Rosenberg, K. E., & Blair, M. H. (1994). Observations: The long and short of persuasive advertising. *Journal of Advertising Research, 34* (4), 63–69.

Rosenberg, S., & Sedlak, A. (1972). Structural representations of implicit personality theory. In L. Berkowitz (Ed.), *Advances in experimental social psychology* (Vol. 6, pp. 235–297). New York: Academic.

Rosenthal, R., & Jacobson, D. (1968). *Pygmalion in the classroom.* New York: Holt, Rinehart and Winston.

Rosin, H. M., & Korabik, K. (1991). Executive women: A closeup view of the corporate experience. *Equal Opportunities International, 10,* 37–44.

Rossi, P. H., & Freeman, H. E. (1993). *Evaluation: A systematic approach* (5th ed.). Newbury Park, CA: Sage.

Rossi, P. H., & Lyall, K. C. (1976). *Reforming public welfare: A critique of the negative income tax experiment.* New York: Russell Sage Foundation.

Rossi, P. H. (1978). Issues in the evaluation of human services delivery. *Evaluation Quarterly, 2,* 573–599.

Rossiter, J. R., & Percy, L. (1987). *Advertising and promotion management.* New York: McGraw-Hill.

Roter, D., Lipkin, M., & Korsgaard, A. (1991). Sex difference in patients' and physicians' communication during primary care medical visits. *Medical Care, 29,* 1083–1093.

Roter, D. L., & Hall, J. A. (1992). *Doctors talking with patients/Patients talking with doctors.* Westport, CT: Auburn House.

Rotfield, H. (1994). Don't blame cigarette ads, enforce law on minors. *Advertising Age, 65*(51), 29.

Roth, J., & Sheppard, B. H. (1989). *The framing of disputes: An empirical test.* Paper presented at the European Congress of Psychology, Amsterdam, Holland.

Rouhana, N. N., & Kelman, H. C. (1994). Promoting joint thinking in international conflicts: An Israeli-Palestinian continuing workshop. *Journal of Social Issues, 50*(1), 157–178.

Ruberman, W., Weinblatt, E., Goldberg, J. D., & Chaudhary, B. S. (1984). Psychosocial influences on mortality after myocardial infarction. *New England Journal of Medicine, 134,* 6441–645.

Rudy, L., & Goodman, G. S. (1991). Effects of participation on children's reports: Implications for children's testimony. *Developmental Psychology, 27,* 527–538.

Ruggiero, K. M., & Taylor, D. M. (1995). Coping with discrimination: How disadvantaged group members perceive the discrimination that confronts them. *Journal of Personality and Social Psychology, 68,* 826–838.

Rule, B. G., Milke, D. L., & Dobbs, A. R. (1992). Design of institutions: Cognitive functioning and social interactions of the aged resident. *Journal of Applied Gerontology, 11,* 475–488.

Runkle, J., & Ayman, R. (1995). *Relationship between racial and ethnic stereotypes and managerial characteristics.* Unpublished manuscript, Illinois Institute of Technology.

Rush, B., & Ogborne, A. (1991). Program logic models: Expanding their role and structure for program planning and evaluation. *Canadian Journal of Program Evaluation, 6,* 95–106.

Rutman, L. (1977). Planning an evaluation study. In L. Rutman (Ed.), *Evaluation research methods: A basic guide.* Beverly Hills, CA: Sage.

Rutman, L. (1980). *Planning useful evaluations: Evaluability assessment.* Beverly Hills, CA: Sage.

Sabini, J. (1992). *Social psychology.* New York: W. W. Norton.

Sackett, P. R., & Wilk, S. L. (1994). Within-group norming and other forms of score adjustment in preemployment testing. *American Psychologist, 49,* 929–954.

Sadava, S. W., & Matejcic, C. (1987). Generalized and specific loneliness in early marriage. *Canadian Journal of Behavioural Science, 19,* 56–66.

Sadava, S. W., & Pak, A. W. (1991, June). *Loneliness, social support and personal vulnerability: Longitudinal evidence.* Paper presented at the Canadian Psychological Association, Calgary, Alberta.

Sadava, S. W., & Thompson, M. M. (1986). Loneliness, social drinking, and vulnerability to alcohol problems. *Canadian Journal of Behavioural Science, 18,* 133–139.

Saks, M. J. (1974). Ignorance of science is no excuse. *Trial, 10,* 18–20.

Saks, M. J. (1977). *Jury verdicts: The role of group size and social decision rule.* Lexington, MA: Lexington Books.

Saks, M. J. (1990). Expert witnesses, nonexpert witnesses, and nonwitness experts. *Law and Human Behavior, 14,* 291–313.

Saks, M. J., & Hastie, R. (1978). *Social psychology in court.* New York: Van Nostrand Reinhold.

Sampson, E. E. (1977). Psychology and the American ideal. *Journal of Personality and Social Psychology 35,* 767–782.

Sapp, S. G., & Harrod, W. J. (1989). Social acceptability and intentions to eat beef: An extension of the Fishbein-Ajzen model using reference group theory. *Rural Sociology, 54,* 138–144.

Sarason, B., Sarason, I. G., Hacker, T. A., & Basham, R. B. (1985). Concomitants of social support: Social skills, physical attractiveness and gender. *Journal of Personality and Social Psychology, 49,* 469–480.

Sarason, I. G., Levine, H. M., Basham, R. B., & Sarason, B. R. (1983). Assessing social support: The social support questionnaire. *Journal of Personality and Social Psychology, 44,* 127–139.

Sarason, S. B. (1978). The nature of problem solving in social action. *American Psychologist, 33,* 370–380.

Saywitz, K. J., Goodman, G. S., Nicholas, E., & Moan, S. F. (1991). Children's memories of a physical examination involving genital touch: Implications for reports of child sexual abuse. *Journal of Consulting and Clinical Psychology, 59,* 682–691.

Schachter, S. (1959). *The psychology of affiliation.* Stanford: Stanford University Press.

Schaie, K. W. (1965). A general model for the study of developmental problems. *Psychological Bulletin, 64,* 92–107.

Schaie, K. W. (1988). Ageism in psychological research. *American Psychologist, 43,* 179–183.

Schaie, K. W. (1993). Ageist language in psychological research. *American Psychologist, 48,* 49–51.

Schecter, A. (Ed.). (1994). *Dioxins and health.* New York: Plenum.

Scheier, M. E., & Carver, C. S. (1993). On the power of positive thinking: The benefits of being optimistic. *Current Directions in Psychological Science, 2,* 26–30.

Scheonbach, V. J., Kaplan, B. H., Fredman, L., & Kleinbaum, D. G. (1986). Social ties and mortality in Evans County. *American Journal of Epidemiology, 123,* 577–591.

Schien, V. E. (1973). The relationship between sex role stereotypes and requisite management characteristic. *Journal of Applied Psychology, 57,* 95–100.

Schien, V. E. (1975). The relationship between sex role stereotypes and requisite characteristics among female managers. *Journal of Applied Psychology, 60,* 340–344.

Schien, V. E., Mueller, R., & Jacobson, C. (1989). The relationship between sex-role stereotypes and requisite management characteristics among college students. *Sex Roles, 20,* 103–110.

Schmidt, D. F. & Boland, S. M. (1986). Structure of perceptions of older adults: Evidence for multiple stereotypes. *Psychology and Aging, 1,* 255–260.

Schofield, J. W. (1995). *Computers and classroom culture.* New York: Cambridge University Press.

Schonfield, D. (1982). Who is stereotyping who and why? *Gerontologist, 22,* 267–272.

Schramm, W., Lyle, J., & Parker, E. B. (1961). *Television in the lives of our children.* Stanford: Stanford University Press.

Schriesheim, C. A., & DeNisi, A. S. (1981). Task dimensions as moderators of the effects of instrumental leadership: A two sample replicated test of Path-Goal Leadership Theory. *Journal of Applied Psychology, 66,* 589–597.

Schuller, R. A. (1992). The impact of battered woman syndrome evidence on jury decision processes. *Law and Human Behavior, 16,* 597–620.

Schulman, J., Shaver, P., Colman, R., Emrich, B., & Christie, R. (1973, May). Recipe for a jury. *Psychology Today,* 37–44, 77–84.

Schulz, R. (1976). Effects of control and predictability on the physical and psychological well-being of the institutionalized aged. *Journal of Personality and Social Psychology, 33,* 563–573.

Schulz, R., & Hanusa, B. H. (1978). Long-term effects of control and predictability-enhancing interventions: Findings and ethical issues. *Journal of Personality and Social Psychology, 36,* 1194–1201.

Schumaker J. F. (Ed.). (1991). *Human suggestibility: Advances in theory, research and application.* London: Routledge.

Schumann, D. W., Petty, R. E., & Clemons, C. S. (1990). Predicting the effectiveness of different strategies of advertising variation: A test of the repetition variation hypothesis. *Journal of Consumer Research, 17,* 192–202.

Schwartz, F. N. (1989, January–February). Management women and the new facts of life. *Harvard Business Review,* 65–76.

Schwarz, N., Bless, H., & Bohner, G. (1991). Mood and persuasion: Affective states influence the processing of persuasive communications. *Advances in Experimental Social Psychology, 24,* 161–199.

Schweinhart, L. J., & Weikart, D. B. (1988). The High/Scope Perry Preschool Program. In R. H. Price, E. L. Cowen, R. P. Lorion, & J. Ramos-McKay (Eds.), *Fourteen ounces of prevention: A casebook for prevention* (pp. 53–65). Washington, DC: American Psychological Association.

Schwitzgebel, R. L., & Schwitzgebel, R. K. (1980). *Law and psychological practice.* New York: Wiley.

Scriven, M. (1967). The methodology of evaluation. In R. W. Tyler, R. M. Gagne, & M. Scriven (Eds.), *Perspectives of curriculum evaluation* (pp. 39–83). Chicago: Rand McNally.

Sears, D. O. (1986). College sophomores in the laboratory: Influences of a narrow data base on social psychology's view of human nature. *Journal of Personality and Social Psychology, 51,* 515–530.

Sechrest, L., & Sidani, S. (1995). Quantitative and qualitative methods: Is there an alternative? *Evaluation and Program Planning, 18,* 77–87.

Segal, S. J. (1993). Trends in population and contraception. *Annals of Medicine, 25,* 51–56.

Seligman, M. E., Peterson, C., Kaslow, N. J., Tanenbaum, R. L., Alloy, L. B., & Abramson, L. Y. (1984). Attributional style and depressive symptoms among children. *Journal of Abnormal Psychology, 93,* 235–238.

Severence, L. J., & Loftus, E. F. (1982). Improving the ability of jurors to comprehend and apply criminal jury instructions. *Law and Society Review, 17,* 153–197.

Severy, L. J. (Ed.). (1993). *Advances in population: Psychosocial perspectives* (Vol. 1). London: Kingsley.

Shadish, W. R., Jr., Cook, T. D., & Leviton, L. C. (1991). *Foundations of program evaluation.* Newbury Park, CA: Sage.

Shanas, E. (1979). The family as a social support system in old age. *Gerontologist, 19,* 169–174.

Shanas, E. (1980). Older people and their families: The new pioneers. *Journal of Marriage and the Family, 42,* 9–18.

Shapiro, A. K., & Morris, L. A. (1978). Placebo effects in medical and psychological therapies. In A. E. Bergin, & S. L. Garfield (Eds.), *Handbook of psychotherapy and behavior change: An empirical analysis* (2nd ed., pp. 312–356). New York: Wiley.

Shapiro, R. S., Simpson, D. E., & Lawrence, S. L. (1989). A survey of sued and nonsued physicians and suing patients. *Archives of Internal Medicine, 149,* 2190–2196.

Sheatsley, P. B., & Mitofsky, W. J. (1992). *A meeting place: The history of the Amerian Association for Public Opinion Research.* Ann Arbor, MI: AAPOR.

Sheppard, B. B., Hartwick, J., & Warshaw, P. R. (1983). The theory of reasoned action: A meta-analysis of past research with recommendations for modifications and future research. *Journal of Consumer Research, 53,* 325–343.

Sheppard, B. H. (1983). Managers as inquisitors: Some lessons from the law. In M. Bazerman & R. J. Lewicki (Eds.), *Negotiation in organizational settings.* Beverly Hills, CA: Sage.

Sheppard, B. H., Blumenfeld-Jones, K., & Roth, J. (1989). Informal thirdpartyship: Studies of everyday conflict intervention. In K. Kressel & D. G. Pruitt (Eds.), *Mediation research* (pp. 166–189). San Francisco: Jossey-Bass.

Sherbourne, C. D., Hays, R. D., Ordway, L., DiMatteo, M. R., & Kravitz, R. L. (1992). Antecedents of adherence to medical recommendations: Results from the Medical Outcomes Study. *Journal of Behavioral Medicine, 15,* 447–468.

Sherif, M. (1966). *In common predicament: Social psychology of intergroup conflict and cooperation.* Boston: Houghton Mifflin.

Shure, M. B., & Spivack, G. (1988). Interpersonal cognitive problem solving. In R. H. Price, E. L. Cowen, R. P. Lorion, & J. Ramos-McKay (Eds.), *Fourteen ounces of prevention* (pp. 69–82). Washington, DC: American Psychological Association.

Siegel, L. M., Attkisson, C. C., & Carson, L. G. (1978). Need identification and program planning in the community context. In C. C. Attkisson, W. A. Hargreaves, M. J. Horwitz, & J. E. Sorensen (Eds.), *Evaluation of human service programs* (pp. 215–252). New York: Academic Press.

Sigelman, L., & Sigelman, C. K. (1982). Sexism, racism, and ageism in voting behavior: An experimental analysis. *Social Psychology Quarterly, 45,* 263–269.

Signorielli, N., & Lears, M. (1992). Children, television, and conceptions about chores: Attitudes and behaviors. *Sex Roles, 27,* 157–170.

Silver, R. L., Boon, C., & Stones, M. H. (1983). Searching for meaning in misfortune: Making sense of incest. *Journal of Social Issues, 17,* 171–178.

Silvern, S. B., & Williamson, P. A. (1987). The effects of video game play on young children's aggression, fantasy, and prosocial behavior. *Journal of Applied Developmental Psychology, 8,* 453–462.

Silverstein, B., Perdue, L., Peterson, B., & Kelly, E. (1986). The role of the mass media in promoting a thin standard of bodily attractiveness for women. *Sex Roles, 14,* 519–532.

Sinclair, C., & Frankel, M. (1984). The effect of quality assurance activities on the quality of mental health services. *Journal of Quality Assurance, 8,* 7–15.

Singer, J. L., Singer, D. G., Desmond, R., Hirsch, B., & Nicol, A. (1988). Family mediation and children's cognition, aggression, and comprehension of television: A longitudinal study. *Journal of Applied Developmental Psychology, 9,* 329–347.

Singh, K., Leong, S. M., Tan, C. T., & Wong, K. C. (1995). A theory of reasoned action perspective of voting behavior: Model and empirical test. *Psychology and Marketing, 12,* 37–51.

Skinner, B. F. (1953). *Science and human behavior.* New York: The Free Press.

Skinner, B. F. (1983). Intellectual self-management in old age. *American Psychologist, 38,* 239–244.

Sleek, S. (1996). Psychologists build a culture of peace. *APA Monitor, 27*(1), 1, 33.

Slesinger, D., & Pilpel, E. M. (1929). Legal psychology: A bibliography and a suggestion. *Psychological Bulletin, 26,* 677–692.

Slivinske, L. R., & Fitch, V. L. (1987). The effects of control enhancing intervention on the well-being of elderly individuals living in retirement communities. *Gerontologist, 27,* 176–181.

Slobogin, C. (1989). The "ultimate issue" issue. *Behavioral Sciences and the Law, 7,* 259–266.

Slovenko, R. (1993). The "revival of memory" of childhood sexual abuse: Is the tolling of the statute of limitations justified? *The Journal of Psychiatry and Law,* Spring, 7–34.

Smith, L., & Malandro, L. (1986). *Courtroom communication strategies.* New York: Kluwer.

Smith, R. A., Hingson, R. W., Morelock, S., Heeren, T., Mucatel, M., Mangione, T., & Scotch, N. (1984). Legislation raising the legal drinking age in Massachusetts from 18 to 20: Effect on 16 and 17 year-olds. *Journal of Studies on Alcohol, 45,* 534–539.

Smith, R. E., & Swinyard, W. R. (1983). Attitude-behavior consistency: The impact of product trial versus advertising. *Journal of Marketing Research, 20,* 257–267.

Smith, V. L., & Ellsworth, P. C. (1987). The social psychology of eyewitness accuracy: Misleading questions and communicator expertise. *Journal of Applied Psychology, 72,* 294–300.

Solomon, M. R. (1992). *Consumer behavior.* Boston: Allyn & Bacon.

Sommer, R., & Ross, H. (1958). Social interaction in a geriatrics ward. *International Journal of Social Psychiatry, 4,* 128–133.

Spacapan, S., & Oskamp, S. (Eds.). (1989). *The social psychology of aging.* Newbury Park, CA: Sage.

Spencer, J. R., & Flin, R. (1990). *The evidence of children: The law and the psychology.* Exeter: Blackstone Press Limited.

Stake, R. E. (1994). Case studies. In N. K. Denzin & Y. S. Lincoln (Eds.), *Handbook of qualitative research.* Thousand Oaks, CA: Sage.

Statistics Canada. (1995). *Summary report of Statistics Canada's telework pilot* (Report No. 75F0008XPE). Ottawa: Ministry of Industry, Science, and Technology.

Stein, J. A., Newcomb, M. D., & Bentler, P. M. (1996). Initiation and maintenance of tobacco smoking:

Changing personality correlates in adolescence and young adulthood. *Journal of Applied Social Psychology, 26,* 160–187.

Stephan, C. W., & Stephan, W. G. (1986). Habla ingles? The effects of language translation on simulated juror decisions. *Journal of Applied Social Psychology, 16,* 577–589.

Stephan, C. W., & Stephan, W. G. (1990). *Two social psychologies* (2nd ed.). Belmont, CA: Wadsworth.

Stephenson, G. M., & Moston, S. (1993). Attitudes and assumptions of police officers when questioning criminal suspects. *Issues in Criminological and Legal Psychology, 18,* 30–36.

Stern, P. C., Young, O. R., & Druckman, D. (Eds.). (1992). *Global environmental change: Understanding the human dimensions.* Washington, DC: National Academy Press.

Stevens, W. K. (1995, September 10). Experts confirm human role in global warming. *New York Times,* pp. 1, 8.

Stewart, C., Smith, C., & Denton, R. E., Jr. (1984). *Persuasion and social movements.* Prospect Heights, IL: Waveland Press, Inc.

Stewart, D. W., & Shamdasani, P. N. (1990). *Focus groups.* Newbury Park, CA: Sage.

Stewart, M. (1983). Patient characteristics which are related to the doctor-patient interaction. *Family Practice, 1,* 30–35.

Stogdill, R. M. (1948). Personal factors associated with leadership: A survey of the literature. *Journal of Psychology, 25,* 35–71.

Stokols, D. (1995). The paradox of environmental psychology. *American Psychologist, 50,* 821–837.

Stouffer, S. A., Suchman, E. A., DeVinney, L. C., Starr, S. A., & Williams, R. M., Jr. (1949). *The American soldier: Adjustment during army life* (Vol. 1). Princeton, NJ: Princeton University Press.

Strawn, D. U., & Buchanan, R. W. (1976). Jury confusion: A threat to justice. *Judicature, 59,* 478–483.

Strickland, B. R. (1988). Sex-related differences in health and illness. *Psychology of Women Quarterly, 12,* 381–399.

Stroh, L. K., Brett, J. M., & Reilly, A. H. (1992). All the right stuff: A comparison of female and male managers' career progression. *Journal of Applied Psychology, 77,* 251–260.

Strong, S. R. (1987). Social-psychological approach to counseling and psychotherapy: "A false hope"? *Journal of Social and Clinical Psychology, 5,* 185–194.

Suchman, E. A. (1973). Action for what? A critique of evaluation research. In C. H. Weiss (Ed.), *Evaluating action programs* (pp. 52–84). Boston: Allyn & Bacon.

Sudman, S. (1976). Sample surveys. In *Annual Review of Sociology* (Vol. 2, pp. 107–120). Palo Alto: Annual Reviews.

Sudman, S., & Bradburn, N. M. (1982). *Asking questions: A practical guide to questionnaire design.* San Francisco: Jossey-Bass.

Summit, R. C. (1983). The child sexual abuse accommodation syndrome. *Child Abuse and Neglect, 7,* 177–193.

Sweeney, P. D., Anderson, K., & Bailey, S. (1986). Attribution style in depression: A meta-analytic review. *Journal of Personality and Social Psychology, 50,* 974–991.

Szasz, T. S. (1961). *The myth of mental illness.* New York: Harper & Row.

Tabachnick, B. G., & Fidell, L. S. (1989). *Using multivariate statistics (*2nd ed.). New York: HarperCollins.

Tajfel, H. (1982). *Social identity and intergroup relations.* Cambridge: Cambridge University Press.

Tajfel, H., & Turner, J. C. (1986). The social identity theory of intergroup behavior. In S. Worchel & G. Austin (Eds.), *Psychology of intergroup relations* (pp. 7–24). Chicago: Nelson-Hall.

Tan, A. S. (1986). Social learning of aggression from television. In J. Bryant & D. Zillmann (Eds.), *Perspectives on Media Effects.* Hillsdale, NJ: Lawrence Erlbaum Associates.

Tanford, J. A. (1990). The law and psychology of jury instructions. *Nebraska Law Review, 69*(1), 71–111.

Tannen, D. (1990). *You just don't understand: Women and men in conversation.* New York: Morrow.

Tavris, C., & Sadd, S. (1977). *The Redbook report on female sexuality: 100,000 married women disclose the good news about sex.* New York: Delacorte.

Taylor, A., & Bernstein-Miller, J. (1994). *Gender and conflict.* Cresskill, NJ: Hampton Press, Inc.

Taylor, D. M., & Moghaddam, F. M. (1994). *Theories of intergroup relations* (2nd ed.). Westport, CT: Praeger.

Taylor, S., & Todd, P. (1995). Decomposition and crossover effects in the theory of planned behavior: A study of consumer adoption intentions. *International Journal of Research in Marketing, 12*(2), 137–155.

Taylor, S. E. (1979). Hospital patient behavior: Reactance, helplessness or control. *Journal of Social Issues, 35,* 156–184.

Taylor, S. E. (1989). *Positive illusions: Creative self-deception and the healthy mind.* New York: Basic Books.

Taylor, S. E. (1995). *Health psychology* (3rd ed.). New York: McGraw-Hill.

Taylor, S. E., & Brown, J. D. (1988). Illusions and well-being: A social psychological perspective on mental health. *Psychological Bulletin, 103,* 193–210.

Taylor, S. E., Helgeson, V. S., Reed, G. M., & Skokan, L. A. (1991). Self-generated feelings of control and adjustment to physical illness. *Journal of Social Issues, 47*(4), 91–109.

Taylor, S. E., Lichtman, R. R., & Wood, J. V. (1984). Attributions, beliefs about control and adjustment to breast cancer. *Journal of Personality and Social Psychology, 96,* 489–502.

Taynor, J., & Deaux, K. (1973). When women are more deserving than men: Equity, attribution, and perceived sex differences. *Journal of Personality and Social Psychology, 28,* 360–367.

Telch, C. F., & Telch, M. J. (1986). Group coping skills instruction and supportive group therapy for cancer patients: A comparison of strategies. *Journal of Consulting and Clinical Psychology 54,* 802–808.

Thibaut, J. W., & Kelley, H. H. (1959). *The social psychology of groups.* New York: Wiley.

Thoits, P. A. (1986). Social support as coping assistance. *Journal of Consulting and Clinical Psychology, 54,* 416–423.

Thomas, K. W. (1992). Conflict and negotiation processes in organizations. In M. D. Dunnette & L. M. Hough (Eds.), *Handbook of industrial and organizational psychology* (2nd ed., Vol. 3, pp. 651–718). Palo Alto, CA: Consulting Psychologists Press.

Thompson, K. E., Haziris, N., & Alekos, P. J. (1994). Attitudes and food choice behavior. *British Food Journal, 96*(11), 9–13.

Thompson, L. W., Gallagher, D., & Breckenridge, J. S. (1987). Comparative effectiveness of psychotherapies for depressed elders. *Journal of Consulting and Clinical Psychology, 55,* 385–390.

Thompson, S. C., & Sobolew-Shubin, A. (1993). Perceptions of overprotection in ill adults. *Journal of Applied Social Psychology, 23,* 85–97.

Thompson, S. C., Sobolew-Shubin, A., Graham, M. A., & Janagian, A. S. (1989). Psychosocial adjustment following a stroke. *Social Science and Medicine, 28,* 239–247.

Tobey, A. E., & Goodman, G. S. (1992). Children's eyewitness memory: Effects of participation and forensic context. *Child Abuse and Neglect, 16,* 779–796.

Totta, J., & Burke, R. (1995). Integrating diversity and equality into the fabric of the organization. *Women in Management Review, 10*(7), 46–53.

Tourila, H. (1987). Selection of milks with varying fat contents and related overall liking, attitudes, norms and intentions. *Appetite, 18,* 1–14.

Triandis, H.C. (1977). *Interpersonal behavior.* Monterey, CA: Brooks/Cole.

Trice, A. D., & Price-Greathouse, J. (1986). Joking under the drill: A validity study of the coping humor scale. *Journal of Social Behavior and Personality, 1,* 265–266.

Triplet, R. G., & Sugarman, D. B. (1987). Reactions to AIDS victims: Ambiguity breeds contempt. *Personality and Social Psychology Bulletin, 13,* 265–274.

Tripp, C., Jensen, T. D., & Carlson, L. (1994). The effects of multiple product endorsements by celebrities on consumers' attitudes and intentions. *Journal of Consumer Research, 20,* 535–547.

Trower, P., Bryant, B., Argyle, M., & Marziller, J. (1978). *Social skills and mental health.* London: Metheun and Co.

Tucker, L. A. (1986). The relationship of television viewing to physical fitness and obesity. *Adolescence, 21,* 797–806.

Tunnell, G. (1980). Individual consistency in personality assessment: The effect of self-monitoring. *Journal of Personality, 48,* 220–232.

Turk, J. & Turk, A. (1988). *Environmental science* (4th ed.). New York: W. B. Saunders.

Turner, M. E., & Pratkanis, A. R. (Eds.). (1994). Social psychological perspectives on affirmative action [Special issue]. *Basic and Applied Social Psychology, 15*(1, 2), 1–220.

Uchino, B. N., Kiecolt-Glaser, J. K., & Cacioppo, J. T. (1992). Age-related changes in cardiovascular response as a function of a chronic stressor and social support. *Journal of Personality and Social Psychology, 63,* 839–846.

Ugwuegbu, D. C. (1979). Racial and evidential factors in juror attributions of legal responsibility. *Journal of Experimental Social Psychology, 15,* 133–146.

Ullmann, L. P., & Krasner, L. (1975). *Psychological approach to abnormal behavior* (2nd ed.). Englewood Cliffs, NJ: Prentice Hall.

Unger, R. K., & Crawford, M. (1993). Commentary: Sex and gender—the troubled relationship between terms and concepts. *Psychological Science, 4,* 122–124.

United Nations Population Fund. (1993). *Population issues: Briefing kit, 1993.* New York: Author.

United States Jury Selection and Service Act, 28 U.S.C. Sec. 1861–69 (1968).

United States v. Dougherty, 473 F2d. 113 (1972).

Unnava, H. R., Burnkrant, R. E., & Erevelles, S. (1994). Effects of presentation order and communication modality on recall and attitude. *Journal of Consumer Research, 21*(3), 481–490.

Ury, W., Brett, J. M., & Goldberg, S. B. (1989). *Getting disputes resolved.* San Francisco: Jossey-Bass.

U.S. Bureau of Census. (1991, September). Global aging: Comparative indicator and future trends. Washington, DC: U.S. Department of Commerce Economics and Statistical Division.

U.S. Department of Health, Education and Welfare, Public Health Service. (1979). *Smoking and health: A report of the Surgeon General* (DHEW Publication No. PHS 79–50066). Washington, DC: Author.

U.S. Department of Health and Human Services. (1987). *A review of the research literature on the effects of health warning labels: A report to the U.S. Congress* (Publication No. ADM 281–86–0003). Washington, DC: Author.

U.S. Department of Health and Human Services. (1994). *Preventing tobacco use among young people: A report of the Surgeon General.* Washington, DC: U.S. Government Printing Office.

U.S. General Accounting Office. (1991). *Canadian health insurance: Lessons for the United States* (GAO/HRD–91–90). Washington, DC: U.S. Government Printing Office.

Valkenburg, P. M., & Van der Voort, T. H. A. (1994). Influence of TV on daydreaming and creative imagination: A review of research. *Psychological Bulletin, 116,* 316–339.

Van de Vliert, E. (1985). Escalative intervention in small-group conflicts. *Journal of Applied Behavioral Science, 21*(1), 19–36.

Van Dyke, J. (1970). The jury as a political institution. *Catholic Law Review, 16,* 224–270.

Varela, J. A. (1971). *Psychological solutions to social problems: An introduction to social technology.* New York: Academic Press.

Veitch, R., & Arkkelin, D. (1995). *Environmental psychology: An interdisciplinary perspective.* Englewood Cliffs, NJ: Prentice Hall.

Verbrugge, L. M. (1989). The twain meet: Empirical explanations of sex differences in health and mortality. *Journal of Health and Social Behavior, 30,* 282–304.

Veroff, J., Kulka, R. A., & Douvan, E. (1981). *Mental health in America: Patterns of help-seeking from 1957–1976.* New York: Basic Books.

Vidmar, N., & Judson, J. W. (1981). The use of social science data in a change of venue application: A case study. *Canadian Bar Review, 59,* 76–102.

Vidmar, N., & Melnitzer, J. (1984). Juror prejudice: An empirical study of challenge for cause. *Osgoode Hall Law Journal, 22,* 487–505.

Vroom, V. H., & Jago, A. G. (1988). *The new leadership: Managing participation in organizations.* Englewood Cliffs, NJ: Prentice Hall.

Vroom, V. H., & Yetton, P. W. (1973). *Leadership and decision-making.* Pittsburgh: University of Pittsburgh Press.

Waite, B. M., Hillbrand, M., & Foster, H. G. (1992). Reduction of aggressive behavior after removal of Music Television. *Hospital and Community Psychiatry, 43,* 173–175.

Waitzkin, H. (1985). Information giving in medical care. *Journal of Health and Social Behavior, 26,* 81–101.

Waldron, I. (1983). Sex differences in human mortality: The role of genetic factors. *Social Science and Medicine, 17,* 321–333.

Walker, M., Langmeyer, L., & Langmeyer, D. (1993). Commentary: Celebrity endorsers—do you get what you pay for? *Journal of Product and Brand Management, 2*(3), 36–43.

Walker, P. R. (1995). United Nations' Commission on Sustainable Development, 1994: Work in progress. *Population & Environmental Psychology Bulletin, 21*(2), 8–13.

Wall, J. A., & Lynn, A. (1993). Mediation: A current review. *Journal of Conflict Resolution, 37*(1), 160–194.

Wallston, B. S. (1987). Social psychology of women and gender. *Journal of Applied Psychology, 17,* 1025–1050.

Walsh, F. (Ed.). (1993). *Normal family processes* (2nd ed.). New York: Guilford.

Wang, T. H., & Katzev, R. D. (1990). Group commitment and resource conservation: Two field experiments on promoting recycling. *Journal of Applied Social Psychology, 20,* 265–275.

Ward, S., Leventhal, H., Easterling, D., Luchterhand, C., & Love, R. (1991). Social support, self-esteem and communication in patients receiving chemotherapy. *Journal of Psychosocial Oncology, 9,* 95–116.

Ward, S., Reale, G., & Levinson, D. (1972). Children's perceptions, explanations and judgments of television advertising: A further explanation. In E. A. Rubinstein, G. A. Comstock, & J. P. Murray

(Eds.), *Television and social behavior* (pp. 468–490). Washington, DC: U.S. Government Printing Office.

Warshaw, P. R. (1980). A new model for prediction behavioral intentions: An alternative to Fishbein. *Journal of Marketing Research, 17,* 153–172.

Wartella, E., & Reeves, B. (1985). Historical trends in research on children and the media: 1900–1960. *Journal of Communication, 35,* 118–133.

Watson, D., & Pennebaker, D. (1989). Health complaints, stress and distress: Exploring the central role of negative affectivity. *Psychological Review, 96,* 234–254.

Webb, P. H., & Ray, M. L. (1979). Effects of TV clutter. *Journal of Advertising Research, 19*(3), 7–12.

Webber, R. A. (1970). Perceptions of interactions between superiors and subordinates. *Human Relations, 23,* 235–248.

Weigel, R. H., & Newman, L. S. (1976). Increasing attitude-behavior correspondence by broadening the scope of the behavioral measure. *Journal of Personality and Social Psychology, 33,* 793–802.

Weiner, B. (1972). *Theories of motivation.* Chicago: Rand-McNally.

Weiner, B. (1974). *Achievement motivation and attribution theory.* Morristown, NJ: General Learning Press.

Weisman, C. S., & Nathanson, C. A. (1985). Professional satisfaction and client outcomes: A comparative organizational analysis. *Medical Care, 23,* 1179–1192.

Weiss, C. (1983). The stakeholder approach to evaluation: Origins and promise. In A. S. Bryk (Ed.), *Stakeholder-based evaluation* (pp. 3–14). San Francisco: Jossey-Bass.

Weiss, C. H. (Ed.). (1977). *Using social research in public policy making.* Lexington, MA: Heath.

Weiss, C. H. (1978). Improving the linkage between social research and public policy. In L. E. Lynn Jr. (Ed.), *Knowledge and policy: The uncertain connection* (Study Project on Social Research and Development, Vol. 5). Washington, DC: National Academy of Sciences.

Weiten, W., & Diamond, S. S. (1979). A critical review of the jury simulation paradigm. *Law and Human Behavior, 3,* 71–93.

Whipple, G. M. (1913). Review of "Les temoignes d'enfants dans un proces retentissant" by J. Varendock. *Journal of Criminal Law and Criminology, 4,* 150–154.

Whitbourne, S. K., & Hulicka, I. M. (1990). Ageism in undergraduate psychology texts. *American Psychologist, 45,* 1127–1136.

White, R. K. (1985). Ten psychological contributions to the prevention of nuclear war. In S. Oskamp (Ed.), *International conflict and national public policy issues: Applied social psychology annual* (Vol. 6). Beverly Hills, CA: Sage.

White, R. K. (Ed.). (1986). *Psychology and the prevention of nuclear war.* New York: New York University Press.

Whitehead, P. C., Craig, J., Langford, N., MacArthur, C., Stanton, B., & Ferrence, R. G. (1975). Collision behavior of young drivers: Impact of the change in the age of majority. *Journal of Studies on Alcohol, 36,* 1208–1223.

Wholey, J. S. (1987). Evaluability assessment: Developing program theory. In L. Bickman (Ed.), *Using program theory in evaluation.* San Francisco: Jossey-Bass.

Wicker, A. W. (1969). Attitude versus actions: The relationship of verbal and overt behavioral responses to attitude objects. *Journal of Social Issues, 25*(4), 41–78.

Wiegman, O., Kuttschreuter, M., & Baarda, B. (1992). A longitudinal study of the effects of television viewing on aggressive and prosocial behaviors. *British Journal of Social Psychology, 31,* 147–164.

Wiemann, J. M., & Giles, H. (1988). Interpersonal communication. In M. Hewstone, W. Stroebe, J-P Codol, & G. M. Stephenson (Eds.), *Introduction to social psychology: A European perspective.* Oxford: Basil Blackwell.

Wilhelm, W. (1992). Changing corporate culture—or corporate behavior? How to change your company. *Academy of Management Executive, 6,* 72–77.

Wilkinson, R. (1986). Income and mortality. In R. Wilkinson (Ed.), *Class and health: Research and longitudinal data* (pp. 88–114). London: Tavistock.

Willcox, S. M., Himmelstein, D. U., & Woodhandler, S. (1994). Inappropriate drug prescribing for the community dwelling elderly. *Journal of the American Medical Association, 272,* 292–296.

Williams v. Florida, 399 U.S. 78, 90 S.Ct. 1893, 26 L.Ed.2d 446 (1970).

Williams, F., Rice, R. E., & Rogers, E. M. (1988). *Research methods and the new media.* New York: The Free Press.

Williams, T. M. (1986a). Background and overview. In T. M. Williams (Ed.), *The impact of television: A natural experiment in three communities.* New York: Academic Press.

Williams, T. M. (1986b). *The impact of television: A natural experiment in three communities.* New York: Academic Press.

Willson, P., & McNamara, J. R. (1982). How perceptions of a simulated physician-patient interaction influence intended satisfaction and compliance. *Social Science and Medicine, 16,* 1699–1703.

Wilson, C. C., II, & Gutierrez, F. (1995). *Race, multiculturalism, and the media: From mass to class communication* (2nd ed.). Thousand Oaks, CA: Sage.

Wilson, D. W., & Donnerstein, E. (1977). Guilty or not guilty? A look at the "simulated" jury paradigm. *Journal of Applied Social Psychology, 7,* 175–190.

Wind, J., Rao, V. R., & Green, P. E. (1991). Behavioral methods. In T. S. Robertson & H. H. Kassarjian (Eds.), *Handbook of consumer behavior.* Englewood Cliffs, NJ: Prentice Hall.

Winett, R. A., Leckliter, I. N., Chinn, D. E., & Stahl, B. (1984). Reducing energy consumption: The long-term effects of a single TV program. *Journal of Communication, 34,* 37–51.

Winett, R. A., Leckliter, I. N., Chinn, D. E., Stahl, B., & Love, S. Q. (1985). Effects of television modeling on residential energy conservation. *Journal of Applied Behavior Analysis, 18,* 33–44.

Wingard, D. L. (1984). The sex differential in morbidity, mortality and lifestyle. *Annual Review of Public Health, 5,* 433–458.

Wingard, D. L., & Cohn, B. A. (1990). Variations in disease-specific sex-morbidity and mortality ratios: United States vital statistics data and prospective data from the Alameda County Study. In M. G. Ory & H. R. Warner (Eds.), *Gender, health and longevity: Multidisciplinary perspectives* (pp. 247–275). New York: Springer.

Winslow, R. W., Rumbault, R. G., & Hwang, J. (1989). AIDS, FRAIDS and quarantine: Students' responses to pro-quarantine initiative in California. *Journal of Applied Social Psychology, 19,* 1453–1478.

Winstead, B. A., & Derlega, V. J. (Eds.). (1993). Gender and close relationships [Special issue]. *Journal of Social Issues, 49*(3).

Wiseman, C. V., Gray, J. J., Mosimann, J. E., & Ahrens, A. H. (1992). Cultural expectations of thinness in women: An update. *International Journal of Eating Disorders, 11,* 85–89.

Witherspoon v. Illinois, 391 U.S. 510, 88 S.Ct. 1770, 20 L.Ed.2d 776 (1968).

Witmer, J. F., & Geller, E. S. (1976). Facilitating paper recycling: Effects of prompts, raffles, and contests. *Journal of Applied Behavior Analysis, 9,* 315–322.

Wood, W., Wong, F. Y., & Chachere, J. G. (1991). Effects of media violence on viewers' aggression in unconstrained social interaction. *Psychological Bulletin, 109,* 371–383.

Worchel, S., Cooper, J., & Goethals, G. R. (1991). *Understanding social psychology* (5th ed.). Pacific Grove, CA: Brooks/Cole.

Worchel, S., Coutant-Sassic, D., & Wong, F. (1993). Toward a more balanced view of conflict: There is a positive side. In S. Worchel & J. A. Simpson (Eds.), *Conflict between people and groups: Causes, processes, and resolutions* (pp. 76–89). Chicago: Nelson-Hall Publishers.

Worth, L., & Mackie, D. M. (1987). Cognitive mediation of positive affect in persuasion. *Social Cognition, 5,* 76–94.

Wortman, C. B., & Dunkel-Schetter, C. (1979). Interpersonal relationships and cancer: A theoretical analysis. *Journal of Social Issues, 35*(1), 120–155.

Wright, L. (1996, January 15). Silent sperm. *New Yorker,* pp. 42–55.

Wright, J. S., & Bostio, J. R. (1983). The advertising message. In S. H. Britt & N. F. Guess (Eds.), *The Dartnell marketing manager's handbook* (pp. 1039–1052). Chicago: Dartnell

Wrightsman, L., Kassin, S., & Willis, C. (Eds.). (1987). *In the jury box: Controversies in the courtroom.* Newbury Park, CA: Sage.

Wrightsman, L. S. (1987). *The trial process.* Belmont, CA: Wadsworth.

Wrightsman, L. S., Nietzel, M. T., & Fortune, W. H. (1994). *Psychology and the legal system.* Pacific Grove, CA: Brooks/Cole.

Yammarino, F. J., & Atwater, L. E. (1993). Understanding self-perception accuracy: Implications for human resource management. *Human Resource Management, 32,* 231–247.

Yesenosky, J. M., & Dowd, E. T. (1990). The social psychology of counseling and psychotherapy: A base for integration. *British Journal of Guidance and Counselling, 18,* 170–185.

Yuille, J. C. (1986). Meaningful research in the police context. In J. C. Yuille (Ed.), *Police training and selection.* Dordrecht, Netherlands: Martinus Nijoff.

Yuille, J. C. (1993). We must study forensic eyewitnesses to know about them. *American Psychologist, 48,* 572–573.

Yuille, J. C., & Cutshall, J. L. (1986). A case study of eyewitness memory of a crime. *Journal of Applied Psychology, 71,* 291–301.

Yukle, G., & Van Fleet, D. D. (1992). Theory and research on leadership in organizations. In M. D. Dunnette and L. M. Hough (Eds.), *Handbook of industrial and organizational psychology* (2nd ed., Vol. 3). Palo Alto, CA: Consulting Psychologists Press.

Zamora v. State, 361 So.2d 776 (1978).

Zemore, R., & Shepel, L. F. (1989). Effects of breast cancer and mastectomy on emotional support and adjustment. *Social Science and Medicine, 28,* 19–27.

Ziegler, M., & Reid, D. W. (1983). Correlates of changes in desired control scores and in life satisfaction scores among elderly persons. *International Journal of Aging and Human Development, 16,* 135–146.

Ziegler, S., & Rosenstein-Manner, M. (1991). *Bullying in school.* Toronto: Toronto Board of Education.

Zigler, E., & Muenchow, S. (1992). *Head Start: The inside story of America's most successful educational experiment.* New York: Basic Books.

Zillman, D. (1971). Excitation transfer in communication-mediated aggressive behavior. *Journal of Experimental Social Psychology, 7,* 419–434.

Zillman, D. (1984). Transfer of excitation in emotional behavior. In. J. T. Cacioppo & R. E. Petty (Eds.), *Social psychophysiology: A sourcebook* (pp. 215–240). New York: Guilford Press.

Zimbardo, P. G. (1977). *Shyness: What it is and what to do about it.* Reading, MA: Addison-Wesley.

Zimbardo, P. G., & Leippe, M. R. (1991). *The psychology of attitude change and social influence.* New York: McGraw-Hill.

Zimberg, S. (1974). The elderly alcoholic. *The Gerontologist, 14,* 221–224.

Zufryden, F. S., Pedrick, J. H., & Sankaralingam, A. (1993). Zapping and its impact on brand purchase behavior. *Journal of Advertising Research, 33*(1), 58.

Author Index

Subject Index